*Also in the Variorum Collected Studies Series:*

**DAVID ABULAFIA**
Mediterranean Encounters, Economic, Religious, Political, 1100–1550

**DAVID ABULAFIA**
Commerce and Conquest in the Mediterranean, 1100–1500

**DAVID ABULAFIA**
Italy, Sicily and the Mediterranean, 1100–1400

**KENT EMERY, JR.**
Monastic, Scholastic and Mystical Theologies in the Later Middle Ages and Beyond

**ELENA LOURIE**
Crusade and Colonisation: Muslims, Christians and Jews under the Crown of Aragon

**WILLIAM CHESTER JORDAN**
Ideology and Royal Power in Medieval France: Kingship, Crusades and the Jews

**GILES CONSTABLE**
Culture and Spirituality in Medieval Europe

**MARIE-THÉRÈSE D'ALVERNY**
La connaissance de l'Islam dans l'Occident médiéval

**RICHARD E. SULLIVAN**
Christian Missionary Activity in the Early Middle Ages

**BERNARD HAMILTON**
Monastic Reform, Catharism and the Crusades (900–1300)

**CH. -E. DUFOURCQ (Ed. Jacques Heers & Georges Jehel)**
L'Ibérie Chrétienne et le Maghreb (XIIe–XVe siècles)

**HENRI BRESC**
Politique et société en Sicile, XIIe–XVe siècles

**ANNA SAPIR ABULAFIA**
Christians and Jews in Dispute: Disputational Literature and the Rise of Anti-Judaism in the West (c. 1000–1150)

VARIORUM COLLECTED STUDIES SERIES

# The Making of Christian Malta

Anthony Luttrell

# The Making of Christian Malta

## From the Early Middle Ages to 1530

Routledge
Taylor & Francis Group
LONDON AND NEW YORK
VARIORUM
Aldershot · Burlington USA · Singapore · Sydney

First published 2002 by Ashgate Publishing

Reissued 2018 by Routledge
2 Park Square, Milton Park, Abingdon, Oxon, OX14 4RN
711 Third Avenue, New York, NY 10017

*Routledge is an imprint of the Taylor & Francis Group, an informa business*



A Library of Congress record exists under LC control number: 2001053594

ISBN 13: 978-1-138-70482-4 (hbk)
ISBN 13: 978-1-138-70475-6 (pbk)
ISBN 13: 978-1-315-20256-3 (ebk)

VARIORUM COLLECTED STUDIES SERIES CS722

## CONTENTS

This volume contains viii + 342 pages

# PREFACE

With the coming of national independence to the Maltese islands in 1964 it became particularly desirable to revise the interpretations of their history which had long been current. That was true of historical attitudes to the period of British occupation, to the three centuries of rule by the Knights of Saint John and to the preceding millennium. The Department of History in the University of Malta had only recently been founded, and general perceptions of the medieval period still followed the clerical tradition derived essentially from Gian Francesco Abela's influential work of 1647, *Della Descrittione di Malta*, which presented a picture of a supposed continuity of Christianity on Malta somehow surviving from Roman and Byzantine times through several centuries of Muslim domination. A response to this situation was the presentation in 1975 of a collection of articles by nine scholars which were published or republished in a single volume entitled *Medieval Malta: Studies on Malta before the Knights*, edited by the author of the present volume. The lengthy introductory essay, republished below, served as an historiographical guide to the state of the question and its bibliography in 1975, as a summary of the volume's contents, and as a set of suggestions for future research. The opening item below briefly assesses progress during the subsequent quarter century. It considers various omissions and failures of *Medieval Malta* while pointing to a theme which inspired many of the present author's subsequent researches, that is an emphasis on the emergence of a Christian community on Malta.

*Medieval Malta* contained an article on Byzantine Malta which included some discussion of the Muslim period; the volume provided no overall treatment of that topic but some supplementary considerations on the Muslim centuries are represented below (items IV–X). For the Christianization of Malta in the thirteenth century, Giliberto Abbate's report of about 1241, now republished and reinterpreted (IX), is fundamental. For the following period, the poverty of the thirteenth- and fourteenth-century documentation surviving on Malta itself (XII) made it essential to exploit archives in Palermo, Barcelona, Siracusa, Catania and the Vatican, all utilized in various articles republished below. One group of studies (XV–XVIII) concentrates on the development of Christian life, on the emergence of a parish system and on the arrival of various religious orders. The history of Gozo, given scant attention in the 1975 volume, is covered in two items (XIV, XIX). From about 1400 to 1530 a mass of written material is available, but for earlier periods it seemed necessary to turn to non-written sources such as coins (VI). One particular multi-disciplinary initiative was the intensive study of a small country settlement through the archives, through a limited topographical survey, through the restoration of its unique fresco cycle and through the excavation of the twin churches at Hal Millieri (XX–XXI). Certain of the author's writings on Malta, including a number which were concerned with Malta's place in the late-medieval Aragonese–Catalan 'empire' and which were summarized in the 1975 introduction, are not included. A few pieces contain references to plates and figures which could not be reproduced below. This volume could not contain any comprehensive survey or listing of the numerous publications which have appeared since 1975. The process of reprinting unavoidably leads to an element of repetition, but it is hoped that this volume may draw the attention of non-Maltese readers to an island whose history provides an interest out of all proportion to its size, and that it may assist them by presenting some materials which can be extremely difficult to consult outside the Maltese islands.

The original publishers of these studies deserve the greatest gratitude for permitting their reproduction; so do Godfrey Wettinger, Mario Buhagiar and Stanley Fiorini who kindly helped with the first item below. The resulting volume is dedicated in grateful thanks to all the many Maltese and other friends and colleagues who have participated in various ways in the creation of its contents, and especially to the memory of a great friend Tom Blagg, excavator at Hal Millieri, who died in 2000.

ANTHONY LUTTRELL

*Bath*
*May, 2001*

# I

## Medieval Malta: Approaches and Reproaches

The nine studies published in 1975 were intended to provide within a single volume a coherent point of departure for the study of Malta's medieval past. A selection of articles by Maltese and other scholars established the state of the question, while the editorial introduction, entitled 'Approaches to Medieval Malta', included a survey of the historiographical background and the archival sources.[1] Inevitably there were gaps, errors, omissions and other points which, more than twenty-five years later, invite reproaches and impose revisions.

Since 1975 research and publication have accelerated in an extraordinary fashion, far outstripping any possibility of brief condensation. The leading scholars have been Godfrey Wettinger, Malta's foremost medievalist,[2] Mario Buhagiar and, more recently, Stanley Fiorini, while many others have made serious contributions, especially through a number of fine and well-illustrated collaborative volumes; medieval Malta has been revolutionized.[3] The early researches of Godfrey Wettinger and Mario Buhagiar marked a heroic stage in Maltese historiography, as they worked as school teachers, travelled the island by bus and on foot, and copied documents by hand; they lacked photocopiers, word processors, reference works, proper library facilities and travel grants. More recent research has been extensive but has lacked overall synthesis, though the Buhagiar – Fiorini volumes devoted to Mdina go some way towards a general survey applicable to the whole island.[4] The most recent scholarly treatment of the whole medieval period is still Andrew Vella's *Storija* published as long ago as 1974.[5] Its author, the university's first

[1] *Medieval Malta: Studies on Malta before the Knights*, ed. A. Luttrell (London, 1975): introduction reprinted *infra* II.

[2] C. Dalli, 'Enlightening the Middle Ages', in *Karissime Gotifride: Historical Essays presented to Professor Godfrey Wettinger on his Seventieth Birthday*, ed. P. Xuereb (Malta, 1999), surveys Wettinger's numerous achievements but certain comments seem somewhat hagiographic; Wettinger's publications are listed *ibid.*, 185–7.

[3] No comprehensive bibliography can be given here; in addition to works cited throughout this volume, the collaborative volumes cited in notes 4, 54, 56, 68, contain important recent lists.

[4] M. Buhagiar – S. Fiorini, *Mdina: The Cathedral City of Malta*, 2 vols. (Malta, 1996).

[5] A. Vella, *Storja ta' Malta*, i (Malta, 1974), 55–181; this work was not available to those writing for *Medieval Malta*. The undocumented medieval section of C. Cassar, *A Concise*

Professor of History, made important contributions to the island's historical process, for example by encouraging undergraduate thesis work and by fostering foreign contacts, but his training was that of a theologian whose book, published in Maltese, constituted a cautious partial advance which was useful for school teaching and for a general public; it remains a standard work. Its medieval section marked only limited progress and is seldom cited. On the Norman incursions for example, Vella stuck doggedly to the outdated interpretations advanced in Gian Francesco Abela's seventeenth-century history.[6] Abela's classic does however contain much material still of value and it has meanwhile been reprinted.[7]

New materials and fresh insights have come from the island's medieval archives, the contents of which were outlined in a publication of 1974.[8] The notarial registers, the acts of the *università* or council at Mdina and parts of the holdings of the cathedral archives were already well known. The cathedral documents include building accounts, court cases concerning Jews and a variety of other materials, some quite recently discovered, which have been extensively exploited by Wettinger and Fiorini. The fundamental problem, however, is that so little of this material dates before circa 1400. The very small number of fourteenth-century documents surviving on Malta, almost all of them in copy, have been studied with comments on their background and diplomatic problems.[9] For other pre-1400 texts concerning Malta, research outside the island became imperative. Fortunately, more than 100 late-thirteenth century documents and *notamenti* from Naples were published before the Angevin archive there was destroyed in 1943, and others are available in the well-indexed reconstructions of the lost registers.[10] Archives containing further sources include those in Venice, Dubrovnik, Marseille, Barcelona, Siracusa, Catania and, above all, Palermo.[11] Contributions based on various Sicilian archives have come from the French scholar Henri Bresc, who alone has used

---

*History of Malta* (Malta, 2000), 58–81, is too brief and too debatable to replace Vella's work; it is much concerned with legends.

[6] Compare A. Vella, 'I Normanni a Malta', and A. Luttrell, 'Malta nel Periodo Normanno', both in *Atti del Congresso Internazionale di Studi sulla Sicilia Normanna* (Palermo, 1973).

[7] G. Abela, *Della Descrittione di Malta* ... (Malta, 1647: reprinted Malta, 1984).

[8] G. Wettinger, 'Our Medieval Historical Archives and their Care' and other contributions in *Maltese History: What Future?*, ed. A. Williams – R. Vella Bonavita (Malta, 1974).

[9] *Infra* XII.

[10] Publications discussed *infra* II, 5.

[11] Documents from these archives are utilized in various items below and in A. Luttrell, 'Venetians at Medieval Malta', *Melita Historica*, iii, no. 1 (1960), and *idem*, 'Malta and Dubrovnik towards the year 1380', *ibid.*, v, no. 2 (1969); the Dubrovnik archives contain materials relevant to Malta which await study.

notarial documents from Sicily to illuminate Maltese topics;[12] a variety of Sicilian possibilities were taken up by Luttrell and Wettinger,[13] and a selection of Palermitan texts has been edited by Fiorini.[14]

For much of the seven centuries before the accession of the Angevins in 1268 the written evidence is so minimal that recourse to non-written materials, and occasionally to inscriptions and coins, is essential.[15] The Roman and late-Roman centuries have been covered thoroughly by Anthony Bonanno.[16] For the post-Roman or Byzantine period, arguably commencing with the visit to Malta of the Byzantine general Belisarius in 533, the written evidence, presented by T.S. Brown in 1975,[17] must be supplemented by the extensive and meticulous topographical work and record taking, especially of catacombs and other rock-cut features, conducted over many years by Mario Buhagiar, whose rescue achievement is particularly precious in view of the widespread destruction wrought by modern upheavals across the Maltese countryside.[18] The obscurity of this early-medieval period is compounded by the practical difficulties inherent in excavation. The Maltese islands are notably small and rocky, the soil cover is very shallow and much earth has been moved around or seriously disturbed. Archeologically useful stratifications are, therefore, extremely rare. There is no local tradition of medieval archaeology, and since 1970 even the brief annual reports issued by the Museum Department, which had usefully summarized finds and activities, have been discontinued.

---

[12] Most notably H. Bresc, 'Documents on Frederick IV of Sicily's Intervention in Malta: 1372', *Papers of the British School at Rome*, xviii (1973); *idem*, 'The "Secrezia" and the Royal Patrimony in Malta: 1240–1450', in *Medieval Malta* (1975); *idem*, 'Sicile, Malte et Monde Musulman', in *Malta: A Case-Study in International Cross-Currents*, ed. S. Fiorini – V. Mallia-Milanes (Malta, 1991). Bresc's *Un Monde Méditerranéen: Économie et Société en Sicile 1300–1450*, 2 vols. (Rome, 1986), is fundamental to any understanding of late-medieval Malta.

[13] *Infra* II 5–6, and A. Luttrell, 'A Maltese Casale: 1430', *Melita Historica*, vi, no. 3 (1974); G. Wettinger, 'The Archives of Palermo and Maltese Medieval History: A First Report', in *Proceedings of History Week 1982* (Malta, 1983).

[14] *Documents in the State Archives, Palermo*, i: *Cancelleria Regia: 1259–1400*, ed. S. Fiorini (Malta, 1999).

[15] Problems discussed in A. Luttrell, 'L'Abitato Medievale a Malta: un Approccio Archeologico', in *Atti del Colloquio Internazionale di Archeologia Medievale*, i (Palermo, 1976); *idem*, 'Medieval Malta: The Non-Written and the Written Sources', in *Malta: A Case-Study* (1991).

[16] E.g. A. Bonanno, 'Malta in the Third Century', in *The Roman West in the Third Century: Contributions from Archaeology and History*, ed. A. King – M. Henig (Oxford, 1981); see also Buhagiar – Fiorini, i, 2–42.

[17] T.S. Brown, 'Byzantine Malta: A Discussion of the Sources', in *Medieval Malta* (1975).

[18] M. Buhagiar, *Late Roman and Byzantine Catacombs and Related Burial Places in the Maltese Islands* (Oxford, 1986); *idem*, 'Early Christian and Byzantine Malta: Some Archaeological and Textual Considerations', *Library of Mediterranean History*, i (1994).

The obstacles to excavation, which offers perhaps the most likely chance of filling some of the enormous gaps in medieval Maltese history, are most unfortunate. In 1963 excavations were begun by a mission financed by the Italian Ministry of Foreign Affairs, an institution whose own archives have been used by an outspoken Italian historian to demonstrate how scientifically disastrous a blatantly political approach to Mediterranean archaeology has often been.[19] Two of Malta's very potentially productive medieval sites, at Tas-Silg and San Pawl Milqi, were partially ruined. Eight volumes of preliminary reports contained just one stratigraphical section and no final report appeared. In 1975 it seemed useful to include a summary of these activities as an archaeological item in *Medieval Malta* but its conclusions have been dismantled. The search for Saint Paul largely distorted both the direction of the investigations and the interpretation of some of the results, as a leading Italian scholar Margherita Guarducci promptly pointed out,[20] while the presentation of the medieval findings at San Pawl Milqi was simply indefensible.[21] The excavation process in Malta was seriously compromised.

The injection of an archaeological approach into Malta's medieval historiography, and especially into the study of its countryside, was renewed from a different angle through a project on the late-medieval *casale* with its four churches at Hal Millieri. The excavations were preceded by archival research, the detailed planning of the buildings, the restoration and study of the important fifteenth-century fresco cycle and a small-scale topographical survey which was supplemented by details from the late-medieval notarial registers and from a list of field names compiled for wartime purposes in 1944.[22] These researches were integrated into an historical account which defined a number of problems worth archaeological investigation, and these essential preliminaries were published in 1976 before any digging was

[19] M. Petricoli, *Archeologia e Mare Nostrum: le Missioni archeologiche nella Politica mediterranea dell'Italia 1898–1943* (Rome, 1990).

[20] Summary in M. Cagiano de Azevedo, 'Medieval Buildings Excavated at Tas-Silg and San Pawl Milqi in Malta', in *Medieval Malta* (1975), discussed, with references to Guarducci, *infra* II, 20–23, and in detail in M. Buhagiar, 'The Early Christian Remains at Tas-Silg and San Pawl Milqi, Malta: A Reconsideration of the Archaeological Evidence', *Melita Historica*, xii, no. 1 (1996), 3–5, but without considering the argument (*infra* IV, 128–9) that Cagiano's proposed late-fourth or early-fifth century date for the rectangular baptistery at Tas-Silg is too early.

[21] Detailed discussion in Buhagiar (1996), 15–30; add the precise considerations in T. Blagg – A. Luttrell, 'Notes on San Pawl Milqi', in T. Blagg – A. Bonnano – A. Luttrell, *Excavations at Hal Millieri, Malta* (Malta, 1990).

[22] *Infra* XX, 26; the preservation of this pencil-written list, if it still survives, would be extremely important.

undertaken.[23] The excavations proved valuable in some ways but disappointing in others, since no useful pottery sequence was established and almost nothing was discovered for the period before the fourteenth century.[24] Elsewhere there are places where a stratigraphy which might throw light on medieval Maltese developments still exists, but such sites await investigation, as for example in the citadel on Gozo where reasonable opportunities have not been exploited;[25] medieval information, for example that uncovered at the Marsa in 1993, remains unpublished.[26] This situation is damaging not only to the historical process but also to the development and protection of the heritage, with economic losses arguably resulting, for example, from the failure to encourage a more sophisticated foreign tourism. For decades the responsibility for this blockage has lain in ministeries, in parliament and, in the last resort, with public opinion.

With regard to the pottery, Carmel Cassar's recent concise history proposes that the importation of seventh- and eight-century Byzantine wares was at a remarkably high level, that Malta was 'fully integrated within the cultural and economic systems enjoyed in the Maghreb and Sicily', and that after about 1268 a period of lively commercial activity was overtaken by 'an apparently rigid autarchic economy and the abrupt end of importation of ceramics from Sicily, Italy and the Magreb' with only 'local poor quality pottery' being found. He deduces that 'under the Aragonese Crown Malta was transformed into an economically impoverished and inward-looking community'.[27] The last point conflicts, at least partially, with firm documentary information on shipping routes and artistic importations,[28] while it is doubtful how far so few pottery finds can safely indicate broad economic developments or the state of Maltese mentalities. There was apparently no glazed pottery produced on Malta. The possibilities, and the difficulties, of using ceramic

---

[23] *Hal Millieri: A Maltese Casale, its Churches and Paintings*, ed. A. Luttrell (Malta, 1976): introduction *infra* XX.

[24] Blagg – Bonanno – Luttrell: postscript *infra* XXI.

[25] Compare developments on Gozo since 1981 with proposals in A. Luttrell, *Gozo Citadel, Malta: Report Submitted to the Division of Cultural Heritage, UNESCO* (typescript: Malta, 1981); this report, though technically reserved, has occasionally been been cited and may be consulted in the Malta University Library.

[26] Despite offical assurances: see curious exchanges in *Sunday Times of Malta* (3 Oct.), 18,(10 Oct.), 18, (17 Oct.), 18, (24 Oct.), 18 (31 Oct. 1993), 18. D. Cutajar, *The Medieval Chapel of Sancir Malta: The Story of its Rehabilitation* (Malta, n.d.), provides an exception, but its interpretation as an estate chapel for royal *villani* seems debatable.

[27] Cassar, 58–60, 66–7.

[28] S. Fiorini, 'The Shipment of Works of Art to Medieval Mdina, Malta', *Journal of Mediterranean Studies*, ix, no. 1 (1999).

evidence to explore medieval Maltese history have long been noted.[29] In 1969, when late-medieval Mediterranean pottery was still largely unstudied, Franco D'Andria published short notes on fewer than thirty unstratified medieval sherds from Tas-Silg, classing them roughly in five groups.[30] The Hal Millieri excavations produced some 154 medieval sherds, 22 per cent of them stratified; these were described in detail with the identification of two late-medieval types of burnished and painted Maltese coarse ware.[31]

More recently a short preliminary study by Alessandra Molinari and Nathaniel Cutajar divided the fine ceramic materials available in 1999 by find spots, proposed datings, pottery types and places of origin. They note that archaeological and archival sources are apparently in conflict, while they repeatedly, and correctly, warn of the numerous limitations of their exercize which nevertheless draws attention to potentially important lines of study; however, they also announce a number of broad general deductions.[32] These are the generalizations repeated by Carmel Cassar, who at times copies them verbatim but without the reservations of the original. The suggestion made by Molinari and Cutajar that a heavy trade in 'transiting amphorae' was passing through Malta in the late-tenth and eleventh centuries is certainly revolutionary and might eventually lead to important revisions, but the interpretations seem premature. It is scarcely justifiable to draw such conclusions from extremely small and very possibly unrepresentative samples in which many sherds lack reliable stratigraphy or detailed expert analysis presented in published form. Furthermore, the study takes no real account of the local coarse wares.

T.S. Brown's article in *Medieval Malta* included some pages on the Muslim period but, partly because of the poverty of the sources, there was no separate treatment of Muslim Malta, though the topic was covered in the contribution on Norman legends by Joseph Cassar Pullicino and in the introductory essay.[33] The volume's consensus, that any continuity of a Christian presence or tradition on Malta was highly unlikely and that Muslim predominance on the island was scarcely disturbed by the Normans in 1091 has, with a few somewhat bizarre exceptions, been accepted. There were some who suggested that what

---

[29] E.g. *infra* II, 12–13, 22; XXI, 103.

[30] F. D'Andria, 'Note sulla Ceramica Invetriata: Catalogo', in *Missione Archeologica Italiana a Malta: Rapporto Preliminare della Campagna 1968* (Rome, 1969), with plates.

[31] T. Blagg, 'The Finds, i: The Pottery', in Blagg – Bonnano – Luttrell, 68–80.

[32] A. Molinari – N. Cutajar, 'Of Greeks and Arabs and of Feudal Knights', *Malta Archaeological Review*, iii (1999); the authors' methodological assumptions that 'archaeology' can provide a separate 'objective' acccount of medieval Malta, its 'feudal knights', its 'voiceless' Maltese population and so forth demands serious debate.

[33] J. Cassar Pullicino, 'Norman Legends in Malta', in *Medieval Malta* (1975), and *infra* II, 21–32.

could not be proved from written texts was none the less justified by ancient tradition; that objection was overcome by the demonstration that such supposed traditions were in reality deliberately invented in early-modern times first by Girolamo Manduca and then by none other than Gian Francesco Abela.[34] The 'Arabs' in Malta were briefly but authoritatively treated by Godfrey Wettinger, to whose views only marginal additions have been made:[35] Joseph Brincat reinvigorated the subject by introducing hitherto unused evidence from the writer al-Himyarî;[36] the comments of Ibn Hauqal received notice;[37] a hoard of Muslim coins has been studied;[38] and the Arabic inscriptions excavated at Rabat have been republished.[39]

The gradual reintroduction of Christianity, apparently initiated in 1127, largely took place during the thirteenth century. In 1135 a Greek from Sicily in exile on Malta described himself as surrounded by Muslims.[40] On the conversion and replacement of the Muslims, there is some risk that Mario Buhagiar's unpublished doctoral thesis may replace a discredited myth, that of a Christian continuity from Roman times, with a new one, involving Basilian monks of the Greek rite, which has gained considerable acceptance. It is true that Henri Bresc pointed to the presence on the Maltese islands of a very small number of persons with Greek names; he also suggested that there may have been a Greek monastery on the island before 1300 and he cursorily identified Malta as a 'point of resistance by Greek culture'.[41] Buhagiar has concluded that the initial conversion and Christianization of the inhabitants was the work of Greek monks from Sicily who possibly fabricated a Pauline cult and who introduced a Byzantine iconography traceable in rock-cut

---

[34] A. Luttrell, 'Girolamo Manduca and Gian Francesco Abela: Tradition and Invention in Maltese Historiography', *Melita Historica*, vii, no. 2 (1977); the proposed study of Byzantine coins (*ibid.*, 113, n. 39) was abandoned because the coins available lack a secure Maltese provenance.

[35] G. Wettinger, 'The Arabs in Malta', in *Malta: Studies of its Heritage and History* (2nd edn.: Malta, 1986), with further thoughts in *Sunday Times of Malta* (19 Nov. 1989), 24, (18 Feb.), 16, (8 Apr.), 28, (26 Aug.), 23, (30 Nov. 1990), 16. Wettinger has shown that the Norman *razzia* occurred in 1091, not 1090 as stated throughout *Medieval Malta* and elsewhere.

[36] J. Brincat, *Malta 870–1054: Al-Himyarî's Account* (revised edn.: Malta, 1995).

[37] A. Luttrell, 'Ibn Hauqal and Tenth-Century Malta', *Hyphen* [Malta], v, no. 4 (1987).

[38] H. Brown, 'The Coins of Muslim Malta', *Melita Historica*, ix, no. 1 (1992), and *infra* VI.

[39] V. Grassi, 'Materiali per lo Studio della Presenza Araba nella Regione Italiana, i: l'Epigrafia Araba nelle Isole Maltesi', *Studi Magrebini* xxi (1989). The provenance of the Maimuna tomb slab of 1174 now on Gozo (text *infra* II, 29) is now highly dubious: *infra* V, 97, n. 3; XIX, 52–3; G. Bonello, *Histories of Malta: Deceptions and Perceptions*, i (Malta, 2000), 9–12.

[40] A. Pertusi, 'Le Isole Maltesi dall'Epoca bizantina al Periodo normanno e svevo (secc. VI–XIII)', *Byzantinische Forschungen* v (1977), 289.

[41] Bresc (1986), ii, 589, 593; cf. Luttrell (1991), 37–9, and *infra* IX, 18–19.

churches and their paintings.[42] Conceivably Malta's inhabitants did prefer the Greek rite to that of their Latin conquerors; very possibly some immigrants from Sicily or Southern Italy were Greek speaking and the presence of Basilian monks cannot be excluded. However, there was no known monastic foundation, royal or otherwise, on Malta and the explicit evidence for a Basilian presence is lacking. The theory would eventually demand a demonstration that various rock-cut features discovered by Buhagiar really were churches or monasteries; that they can reasonably be dated to the relevant period; that they coincided fairly precisely with place-names in *dejr* studied by Wettinger but seldom located; and that *dejr* did mean monastery or convent, as Buhagiar maintains, rather than simply sheepfold, as Wettinger holds was normally the case.[43] The Sicilian background, itself unclear, provides only limited direct evidence concerning any Basilian activities in the conversion of Arabic-speaking Muslim *villani* on Sicily, where Greek monasteries were already in decline during the thirteenth century. Furthermore, the new hypothesis overlooks the point that in Sicily some indigenous Muslims whose Greek-speaking families had originally been Greek Christians were likely to be reconverted to a Greek form of religion, whereas on Malta and Gozo there can scarcely have been any significant group of former Greek Christians waiting to revert to earlier practices; instead there was a community some part of which remained on Malta and Gozo and continued to speak Arabic after being converted to Christianity.[44]

The major piece of evidence for the composition of the islands' population is the report made to the Emperor Frederick II in about 1241 by his own governor, Giliberto Abbate. This awkward text, in which evident corruptions ensure that all interpretations remain debatable, has been re-edited; in consequence of the recognition that the reading *cusia* should be corrected to *gisia*, a term denoting a tax imposed on Muslims rather than on tailors, the

---

[42] M. Buhagiar, *Christian Catacombs, Cult Centres and Churches in Malta to 1530* (unpublished Ph.D. thesis: London, 1993), 315–59; broad conclusions in e.g. *idem*, 'The First Christian Churches in Malta', *Treasures of Malta*, v, no. 2 (1999), and Buhagiar – Fiorini, i, 279.

[43] Cf. G. Wettinger, *Place-Names of the Maltese Islands: ca. 1300–1800* (Malta, 2000), 1, 107–10.

[44] J. Johns, 'The Greek Church and the Conversion of Muslims in Norman Sicily?' *Byzantinische Forschungen*, xxi (1995), 144–57; cf. Bresc (1986), 587–94; *infra* IX, 18–19; and, more generally, M. Scaduto, *Il Monachesimo Basiliano nella Sicilia Medievale: Rinascita e Decadenza Sec. XI–XIV* (expanded edn.: Rome, 1982). Given the absence of clear evidence,it might equally be proposed, on linguistic grounds, that – as was reportedley the case in Sicily from about 1340 – an Arabic rite was in use on Malta: cf. H. Bresc, 'Arab Christians in the Western Mediterranean (XIth–XIIIth Centuries)', *Library of Mediterranean History*, i (1994).

information on the dues paid provides a new indicator for the size of the islands' different groups. The most likely conclusion is that while there were indeed expulsions, conceivably, though without specific documentation, in about 1224 and probably again in about 1245, and immigrations and transportations, the latter at least partly from Italy rather than from Greek-speaking parts of Sicily, the bulk of the population changed its religion but retained an Arabic speech.[45] Malta and Gozo were not like Sicily. After about 1270 no Muslim community retained any political or legal rights or position in the islands, and to what extent any older traditions remained alive in underground ways cannot be estimated. No one has taken up Henri Bresc's suggestion that following the conversion of Malta its defeated 'notables' turned defensively to the 'ecclesiastical institution', that is that the leaders among those who had once been Muslims preserved their status by taking control of the Maltese church, with the result that the cathedral chapter became the 'seed-bed' or nursery of the 'families of notaries and intellectuals who ensured the survival of the cultural and linguistic Arabism'.[46]

The period from about 1240 to 1400 also suffers from a scarcity of documentation, though the published Angevin texts once at Naples have yet to be exploited fully. A little has been added, mainly from Sicilian sources which, for example, provide new details concerning the Genoese Counts of Malta.[47] After 1282 Malta became an outpost of an extended Catalan-Aragonese confederation.[48] Surprises are always possible, as in the case of

---

[45] New edition and discussion *infra* IX; Ibn Khaldun's date of 1249 for expulsions is, against the evidence, still commonly accepted. It seems unlikely that the original of Giliberto's report gave, as sometimes accepted, the figure of 47 for the Christian families on Malta, since the surviving text is a copy, with evident corruptions, of a recapitulation or summary of the original text. The ethnic composition of the apparently mainly Muslim inhabitants is altogether unknown and it seems confusing to continue to describe them as 'Arabs.' H. Bresc, 'Esclaves auliques et Main d'Oeuvre servile agricole dans la Sicile des XIIe et XIIIe Siècles', in *Figures de l'Esclave au Moyen-Age et dans le Monde Moderne*, ed. H. Bresc (Paris, 1996), 113, speaks of the royal estates in about 1241 as a 'vaste entreprise esclavagiste' but, while there were 84 slaves from Djerba, the *villani curie*, technically not slaves, appparently constituted a limited proportion of the rural population: *infra* IX, 13–14, 20–24.

[46] H. Bresc, 'De l'État de Minorité à l'État de Resistance: le Cas de la Sicile normande', in *État et Colonisation au Moyen Age*, ed. M. Balard (Paris, 1989), 342; cf. *idem* (1986), ii, 626–7.

[47] E.g. *infra* VIII, X, XII–XVI, and A. Luttrell, 'Malta e Gozo: 1268–1282', in *XI Congresso della Storia della Corona d'Aragona*, iii (Palermo, 1984). Cf. S. Fiorini, 'The De Malta Genoese Counts of Malta: c. 1192–c. 1320', *Melita Historica*, xii, no. 4 (1999), resolving a confusion (*infra* II, 44, n. 240; X, 599, n. 31) between Andriolo de Mari of Genoa and the Genoese Andriolo Count of Malta.

[48] A. Luttrell, 'Malta and the Aragonese Crown: 1282–1530', *Journal of the Faculty of Arts: Royal Malta University*, iii, no. 1 (1965); *idem*, 'The House of Aragon and Malta: 1282–1412', *ibid.*, iv, no. 2 (1970). Cf. J. Pryor, 'The Naval Battles of Roger of Lauria', *Journal of Medieval*

the customs records from Sardinia which unxpectedly revealed a fourteenth-century Maltese cotton trade to Catalunya.[49] Stanley Fiorini has published 293 texts from Palermo, many of them previously unknown, which are especially important as they date before 1400; but only three of them are earlier than 1360 and those three were already known.[50] A concentration on archives outside Malta would further understanding of the relatively unknown thirteenth and fourteenth centuries, while the fifteenth-century materials are extraordinarily rich. Godfrey Wettinger's publication of 977 acts of the Mdina council, the well-known but hitherto scarcely used text of Università Ms. 11 running from 1434 to 1499, is an immense, complex and enormously valuable scholarly monument.[51] Other publications include 766 acts of notary Giacomo Zabbara drawn up between 1468 and 1497, recently edited by Stanley Fiorini.[52] Much other material, published or cited during the last 25 years, covers the history of towns and countryside, commerce and agriculture,[53] demography, religion and culture, social life and customs. Summaries of the results appear in recent collaborative works on Birgu,[54] Mdina[55] and Gozo,[56] in *Melita Historica*, in the publications of the Malta Historical Society's History Weeks, and in a wide variety of other studies and articles. Topics relating to the period following the arrival of the Hospitallers in 1530 may also be relevant, since much of the fabric of medieval Malta arguably survived until the great Ottoman siege of 1565 and even thereafter.[57]

---

*History*, ix (1983); L. Mott, 'The Battle of Malta, 1283: Prelude to Disaster', in *The Circle of War in the Middle Ages: Essays on Medieval Military and Naval History*, ed. D. Kagay – L. Wilson (Bury St. Edmunds, 1999). H. Bresc, 'Malta dopo il Vespro Siciliano', *Melita Historica*, vi, no. 3 (1974), publishes a text of 1299 from Barcelona, where many other relevant texts exist.

49 L. Galoppini, 'Notizie su Maltesi e il Cotone di Malta a Cagliari nella Seconda Metà del Trecento', *ibid.*, x, no. 1 (1988).

50 *Supra*, 3 n. 14.

51 G. Wettinger, *Acta Iuratorum et Consilii Civitatis et Insulae Maltae* (Palermo, 1993).

52 *Notary Giacomo Zabbara R494/1(1): 1486–1488*, and *R494/1(II–IV): 1494–1497*, ed. S. Fiorini, 2 vols. (Malta, 1996–1999).

53 Especially important is G. Wettinger, 'Agriculture in Malta in the Late Middle Ages', in *Proceedings of History Week 1981* (Malta, 1982).

54 *Birgu: A Maltese Maritime City*, ed. L. Bugeja – M. Buhagiar – S. Fiorini, 2 vols. (Malta, 1993).

55 *Supra*, 1 n. 4.

56 G. Wettinger, 'The History of Gozo from the Early Middle Ages to Modern Time', in *Gozo: The Roots of an Island*, ed. C. Cini (Malta, 1990); this volume is discussed *infra* XIX. Cf. *Gozo and its Culture*, ed. L. Briguglio – J. Bezzina (Malta, 1995).

57 E.g. S. Fiorini, 'Malta in 1530', and A. Luttrell, 'Malta and Rhodes: Hospitallers and Islanders', both in *Hospitaller Malta 1530–1798: Studies on Early Modern Malta and the Order of St John of Jerusalem*, ed. V. Mallia-Milanes (Malta, 1993).

A major theme in later-medieval Maltese and Gozitan history is the creation, on two small and isolated islands, of a community that was not merely Christian but very strongly so. Post-Roman Malta was at least partly Christian but after 870 circa Christianity was apparently eliminated. There were some Christians of uncertain origin, probably all or mostly captives or slaves, on eleventh-century Malta, and a few could perhaps have survived the reported removal of many Christian captives by the Normans in 1091. A few decades later a small Christian group, probably mostly Italian merchants, was established on the island. At some time after about 1220 expulsions of Muslims from Malta and forced immigrations from Italy led to the formation of a Christian population, so that it seems likely that by about 1270 the only Muslims on Malta and Gozo were slaves; there remained, especially in Mdina, an important closed community of Jews whose expulsion in 1492 was a further step in the Christianization of Malta.[58] Very little is known of the actual process of conversion which presumably centred on the Sicilian outpost in the castle by the sea at Birgu and on the main town at Mdina. Apparently there was no parochial system but only a group of clergy or *capillani* who were attached to the cathedral at Mdina and perhaps also to a church on Gozo; the first known mention of a separate parish was that at Birkirkara in 1402.[59] The *biduini* or country people may have been 'old Muslims' who harboured a hostility to the foreign Latin religion. A bequest of 1363 intended to establish on Malta a Benedictine house whose members could have functioned as proselytizers was frustrated by the monks in Sicily who clearly did not want to settle on Malta.[60] Only in the fifteenth century did Franciscans, Augustinians, Carmelites, Dominicans and female Benedictines establish themselves permanently on Malta, mainly in and around Mdina.[61]

The gradual emergence of a common identity, of a feeling that there was a group of people belonging on Malta who were Christians but used an Arabic language, must have been cemented by their common speech. The study of this virtually unwritten dialect was long conducted by philologists who interpreted lists of words for which they had no early date; in effect they were

---

[58] Pioneering, richly documented treatment in G. Wettinger, *The Jews of Malta in the Late Middle Ages* (Malta, 1985).

[59] *Infra* XVII–XVIII.

[60] *Infra* XV.

[61] *Infra* II, 63–4, and XVI, considerably amended in G. Aquilina – S. Fiorini, 'New Documents relating to the Origins of Religious Orders in Malta', in *Proceedings of History Week 1994* (Malta, 1996), in their *The Origin of Franciscanism in Late Medieval Malta* (Malta, 1995), and in Buhagiar – Fiorini, i, 277–349; summary in S. Fiorini, 'Origins of Religious Orders in the Maltese Islands', *Treasures of Malta*, ii, no. 2 (1996).

theorizing about medieval matters on the basis of modern Maltese.[62] A partial remedy is provided by the many place and personal names in the late-medieval documents. Godfrey Wettinger has studied lists of persons and compiled an enormous and meticulously documented study of toponyms and microtoponyms. Inescapably, many places cannot be located precisely and the interpretation of some place and personal names remains debatable, while the application of fifteenth- or sixteenth-century names to discussions of thirteenth-century or earlier developments invariably results in debatable hypotheses. Wettinger and Michael Fsadni discovered the notary Pietru Caxaro's brief poem, the *Cantilena*, which is the sole surviving example of late-medieval Maltese literature and has attracted much discussion.[63]

Human nature abhors a vacuum and peoples tend to invent 'traditions' derived from words belonging to their own language with scant regard for logic. A few Maltese words may be of Punic origin but their provenance is uncertain and they can neither prove nor indicate a continuous occupation of the islands by any ethnic group unchanged from late-Roman times onwards. The Christians on Malta in 1091 may have chanted *Kyrie Eleison* but they were captives rather than indigenous islanders, and they were not necessarily Greek-speaking since the phrase formed part of the Latin liturgy. *Milqi* is a classical Arabic term but is not recorded on Malta before 1673 when it was evidently introduced specifically to name the church at San Pawl Milqi.[64] Modern Maltese masons apparently use more Romance than Arabic technical terms, but it scarcely follows that 'Arab' masons were expelled in the mid-twelfth century and that for a long time the 'Maltese' were not competent to take their place.[65] The problem is that the Maltese language was seldom written down before the eighteenth century while only a handful of the surviving personal and place names are datable before 1400. A few comparatively early personal names suggest a division by about 1275 between a wealthier Romance ruling class and an inferior group with Arabic names,[66] but they provide no more than a glimpse of the ways in which a Christian population was formed.

---

62 Exceptionally, J. Brincat, 'Language and Demography in Malta: The Social Foundations of the Symbiosis between Semitic and Romance in Standard Maltese', in *Malta: A Case Study*, does attempt to explain medieval linguistic changes against an historical background.

63 Text and English translation *infra* II, 67.

64 *Infra* II, 24–5; III, 419–20; V, 101–103; Luttrell (1997), 125, n. 97, correcting 1616 to 1673.

65 As proposed in L. Mahoney, *A History of Maltese Architecture from Ancient Times up to 1800* (Malta, 1988), 52–9, 337–40.

66 Bresc (1986), ii, 625–6, and (1991), 51–3; these ideas are elaborated in G. Wettinger, 'The Origin of the "Maltese" Surnames', *Melita Historica*, xii, no. 4 (1999).

The islanders' art and architecture embodied a visual expression of their Christian devotion. Both topics have benefitted from Mario Buhagiar's painstaking accumulation of discoveries. His *Iconography* provides a brief but broad introductory survey of the painting[67] and is supplemented by much other publication which largely supercedes his own article of 1975 in *Medieval Malta*. The Saint Paul altar-piece for the cathedral, to be studied anew following its cleaning, was an important painting with a Siculo-Catalan background.[68] At Hal Millieri there was an early, perhaps thirteenth- or fourteenth-century, frescoed church which was rebuilt in about 1480 with a new fresco cycle.[69] Such works reflected Malta's Sicilian cultural context, as did paintings by several members of the Maltese family of Saliba who were associated with the school of Giovanni Saliba's brother-in-law, Antonello da Messina.[70] The detailed expenditures made for the cathedral recorded medical, educational, musical, building and many other activities.[71]

Much more is now known about late-medieval Maltese architecture. Rock-cut features were always important, and there may have been cave settlements such as the later dwellings at Ghar il-Kbir.[72] There were also many smaller stone-built rural buildings, often using diaphragm arches; these constructions are excellently studied and illustrated by Carol Jaccarini, though examples can seldom be dated before 1530.[73] The diaphragm arch was necessitated by the shortage of wood and was made possible by the strength of Maltese stone, but the technique was not unique to the Maltese islands.[74] Late-fifteenth

67 M. Buhagiar, *Iconography of the Maltese Islands 1400–1900: Painting* (Malta, 1988), 10–31.

68 Buhagiar (1988), 15, and Buhagiar – Fiorini, i, 142–9, 156–60, attributing it to the Catalan 'circle of Luis Borassa'; on the Pauline cult, *St. Paul's Grotto, Church and Museum at Rabat, Malta*, ed. J. Azzopardi (Malta, 1990), and T. Freller, *St Paul's Grotto and its Visitors: Pilgrims, Knights, Scholars and Sceptics* (2nd edn.: Malta, 1996).

69 *Infra* XXI, 126–8; M. Buhagiar, 'The Fresco Cycle in the Church of the Annunciation at Hal Millieri: Some Iconographical and Historical Considerations', *Melita Historica*, xi, no. 2 (1993); see also Mahoney (1988), 51–75. Din L-Art Helwa did not publish any detailed report on the fresco restorations at Bir Miftuh.

70 Buhagiar (1988), 26–9, and Buhagiar – Fiorini, i, 287–94, correcting and greatly expanding various details given *infra* II, 64–5, and in A. Luttrell, 'The Madonnna del Soccorso at Mdina', *Heritage*, 47 (1983).

71 E.g. S. Fiorini, *The 'Mandati' Documents at the Archives of the Mdina Cathedral, Malta: 1473–1539* (Malta 1992).

72 In addition to Buhagiar's many publications, see *infra* III, 129–30; A. Luttrell, 'Malta Trogloditica: Ghar il-Kbir', *Heritage* 24 (1979); A. Messina, 'Trogloditismo Medievale a Malta', *Melita Historica*, x, no. 2 (1989).

73 C. Jaccarini, *Ir-Razzett: The Maltese Farmhouse* (Malta, 1998).

74 *Infra* XXI, 115–25; J. Fuguet i Sans – A. Luttrell, 'Diaphram Arches and Stone Slab Roofs', *Melita Historica*, xi, no. 4 (1995), noting medieval buildings in Catalunya.

century texts naturally employed Arabic terms for the rooms of town houses, for the *siqifah* or covered passageways and for other features,[75] but twisting village streets and courtyard houses with zig-zag entrances should surely be considered as Mediterranean or even worldwide rather than necessarily 'Arabic' in origin.[76] The Hal Millieri excavations allowed the foundations and structure of two late-medieval churches to be investigated.[77] The graves excavated there, when studied in the light of notarial documents, demonstrate how a concern with burial influenced the arrangement of side chapels and other aspects of some ecclesiastical buildings and led to the construction of many small churches and chapels.[78] The late-medieval Castellan's palace at Birgu[79] has recently been restored. There is much new detail concerning grand houses in the Sicilian style at Mdina, where the Palazzo Santa Sofia conceivably dates to 1233, and on the churches of the religious orders and the cathedral, within which significant Roman substructures have recently been discovered.[80] These ecclesiastical buildings constituted another manifestation of Christian tradition; in 1575 there were some 430 churches and chapels on the two islands.

With so much prosopographical and other information available,[81] the structure of fifteenth-century Maltese politics and the interaction of group and personal interests, which were both 'Maltese' and foreign, can now be analysed. Race, language, religion, ethnic grouping and nationality are mutually confusing categories. Henri Bresc may have gone too far in seeking to fit Maltese developments into a Sicilian model. His suggestion of a process in

---

[75] Wettinger (1986), 95–6; the placing of this late-fifteenth century data in a section concerning a much earlier period might be confusing, especially as it assumes that Arabic nomenclature indicates 'Moorish styles'.

[76] *Infra* XX, 27–31, 34–5, and discussion in Buhagiar – Fiorini, i, 51–68. Mahoney (1988), 77–88, and *idem*, *5000 Years of Architecture in Malta* (Malta, 1996), 79–82, combines sharp architectural insights with historical fantasy and inaccuracy.

[77] Blagg *et al.*, summarized *infra* XXI.

[78] *Infra* XXI, 107–14; G. Wettinger, 'Burials in Maltese Churches: 1419–1530/40', in Blagg *et al.* An early-fourteenth century foundation is now the earliest known: S. Fiorini, 'Sibilla d'Aragona and the Foundation of the Saqqajja Benefice on Gozo', *Melita Historica*, xii, no. 4 (1999), amending *infra* XXI, 109.

[79] A. Luttrell, 'The House of the Castellan at Malta', *Heritage*, 9 (1978).

[80] The tentative suggestions of 1975 (*infra* II, 64–5) are revised in considerable detail in Buhagiar – Fiorini, i, 74–211; cf. D. De Lucca, *Mdina: A History of its Urban Space and Architecture* (Malta, 1995), 38–47, with important suggestions and Sicilian parallels, and with certain debatable points. G. Spatrisano, *Lo Steri di Palermo e l'Architettura siciliana del Trecento* (Palermo, 1972), should be consulted.

[81] G. Wettinger – M. Fsadni, *Il-Ghanja ta' Pietru Caxaru: Poezija bil-Malti Medjevali* (Malta, 1983), demonstrated how much data can be assembled for a particular early-sixteenth century family.

which notaries and other intellectuals sought to maintain an Arabic heritage and language has tacitly been ignored in the literature, yet an understanding of Sicilian institutions is clearly fundamental to any interpretation of late-medieval Malta. It remains debatable how far the island's politics became a matter of an 'old Muslim' resistance to Christian outsiders as such or whether it was rather that local notables and their kinsmen were simply trying to control the town council in opposition to a royalist foreign regime installed in the castle at Birgu. Equally uncertain is the extent to which some cathedral canons were, as members of an island establishment, merely defending their monopolies in seeking to exclude foreign clergy on the grounds that they could not conduct pastoral work in Maltese. Local members of oligarchic groupings sought profit from marriage, from municipal or royal office, from piracy or from church benefices, in competition with foreign captains and placemen who were Sicilians, Catalans, Aragonese, even Castilians.[82] A restricted élite could utilize the *capitoli* or petitions from the *universitas* to the crown to establish its own privileges. On at least one occasion another group, the *universitas* of a rural *casale* at Tarxien, made its own petition to the crown against the landholders.[83] The part played by Jews, businessmen, artisans and the rural *biduini* requires study, as does the way in which foreigners, nobles and others, acquired fluency in Maltese as well as in Latin and Sicilian, sometimes marrying local women and having children who became Maltese in speech and mentality. Society was mobile as well as clannish. Recent work has approached such basic questions, but no more than partially.[84]

The mass of documentary sources for the century before 1530 and the speed with which they are emerging have created problems of digestion; the publication of texts and surveys is essential to progress. Certain themes have, understandably, been preferred to others and the temptation to study purely

[82] Bresc as *supra*, 3 n. 12, especially Bresc (1986), ii, 622–8; cf. *infra* II, 49–50, 67–9.

[83] Luttrell, 'A Maltese Casale' (1974).

[84] E.g. G. Wettinger, 'The Nature of Maltese Politics: c. 870–1964', in *The British Colonial Experience, 1800–1964: The Impact on Maltese Society*, ed. V. Mallia-Milanes (Malta 1988); C. Dalli, 'Medieval Communal Organization in an Insular Context: Approaching the Maltese *Universitas*', in *The Making and Unmaking of the Maltese Universitas* (Malta, 1993), and *idem*, 'Capitoli: The Voice of an Elite', in *Malta Historical Society: Proceedings of History Week 1992* (Malta, 1994); P. Corrao, 'Assemblee Municipali nella Sicilia tardomedievale: Note sul Caso maltese', in *Karissime Gotifride*. Buhagiar – Fiorini, i, 99–115, 141–51, constitutes the most developed treatment. G. Wettinger, 'The Pawning of Malta to Monroy (in 1421)', *Melita Historica*, vii, no. 3 (1978), reinterprets an important incident; amend *infra* II, 49–50. The medieval section of J. Montalto, *The Nobles of Malta: 1530–1800* (Malta, 1979), requires revision, though certain medieval documents in private possession are not available for study.

Maltese matters while partly ignoring wider factors is compounded by problems of travel and the limitations of libraries. Equally, non-Maltese scholars who do not speak the language, who have never lived in a Maltese village and who cannot easily appreciate local conditions, naturally tend to adopt more broadly-based interpretations of the islands' affairs. Only Henri Bresc has treated Malta and Gozo in any detail as an integral part of the Sicilan economy and society.[85] Fernand Braudel's seminal study considered Malta as of major Mediterranean importance but at a time long after the Hospitallers' arival in 1530. The geohistorical realities sketched out in the 1975 volume naturally remain unchanged, and it still seems true that before 1530 the Maltese islands were not at a 'strategic cross-roads'.[86] More nuanced analyses have discerned a diversity of overlapping or 'fuzzily' defined Mediterranean worlds or sub-regions of which Malta and Gozo might form a minor but unique example.[87] They were not part of an extended archipelago nor were they offshore islands integrated into a mainland economy or sub-region but, as their inhabitants well knew, they were little isolated rocks 'in the middle of the sea', dependent on Sicilian grain and on their own cotton monoculture, and endlessly in danger while defending a distant frontier of Christendom.[88] This isolation may have contributed to the strength of Malta's post-medieval Christian sentiment. The determination behind this religiosity may have reflected a need to reconcile a consciousness of a Muslim past and a continuing Arabic speech with a dedication to Latin Christianity. It remains difficult to gauge the extent of the late-medieval origins of what has been called 'the hardening and fossilizing ... of the xenophobic brand of Christianity which has characterized the islands in the last few hundred years ... .'[89]

Medieval Malta: What Future? The post-1400 materials are astonishingly rich and the volume of publication impressive, while public interest, stimulated by the very influential editorial initiatives of Paul Mizzi and by excellent semi-popular periodicals such as his *Heritage* and its various imitators, remains strong. Malta possesses a weekly, *The Sunday Times of Malta*, which actually

---

[85] *Supra*, 3 n. 12; for the Catalan-Aragonese connection, *infra* II, 41–52.

[86] *Infra* II, 17–19.

[87] P. Horden – N. Purcell, *The Corrupting Sea: A Study of Mediterranean History* (Oxford, 2000); this detailed book's only significant references to Malta are to its Roman weaving industry and to contemporary bird trapping (*ibid.*, 196, 358).

[88] *Infra* II, 51; C. Dalli, '*In Fronteria Barbarorum*: Waiting for the Turks on Late Medieval Malta', in *Proceedings of History Week 1994* (Malta, 1996).

[89] The judgement in Wettinger (1985), 150; earlier observations *infra* IV, 416–18. The significant synthesis in H. Bresc, 'Genèse de l'Identité maltaise', in *Mutations de l'Identités en Méditerranée: Moyen Age et Epoque Contemporaine*, ed. H. Bresc – C. Veauvy (Paris, 2000), which was not available at the time of writing, demands further reflection and discussion.

carries learned contributions with footnotes, and the Malta Historical Society listed 445 members in 1999.[90] Other considerations are less favourable. No extended general history of Malta has appeared since 1974 and that is in Maltese. The easy-going village ambiente of saints and fireworks in which talented priests, doctors, lawyers and others made truly valuable scholarly contributions on themes of their choice, has been replaced by a more complex world of narrower, more technical expertise. Academic study on medieval Malta is essentially in the hands of one university professor in retirement, his recently-appointed medievalist successor, an art historian-cum-archaeologist in the Faculty of Architecture and Engineering, and a professor of Mathematics. Research on medieval Malta is therefore much stronger than its teaching; in fact, the university provides no formal instruction in palaeography. Maltese talents and enthusiasms will doubtless overcome these difficulties, but the drastic absence of written sources for almost nine-tenths of the medieval millennium profoundly unbalances the whole subject. A nation's history, and the archaeology which is an indispensable component of it, are vital both to its political health and to its heritage and its economy. Malta's failure to address the question of its medieval archaeological infrastructure is not merely frustrating but threatens to damage the future of its past.

[90] *Melita Historica*, xii, no. 4 (1999), 445–52.

# II

## APPROACHES TO MEDIEVAL MALTA[1]

MEDIEVAL Malta had no chronicler of its own, and it is unlikely that any contemporary attempt was made to write its history; certainly no such work has survived. There are references to Malta and Gozo in a number of Latin, Greek, Arabic and Hebrew writings, but most of these are extremely brief and general, or they deal with particular incidents. The most important account is contained in the letter sent by the Emperor Frederick II in reply to Gilibertus, his agent at Malta, in about 1241.[2] The earliest real descriptions of Malta and Gozo result from their connection with the Knights of St. John; the report made by the Knights' commissioners in 1524 before the Order accepted the islands in 1530 is now lost, but details from it are preserved.[3] The earliest description available, running to some 4,000 words, is that of the Hospitaller Jean Quintin, written in Malta in 1533 and first published at Lyons three years later.[4] In the classicizing style then in vogue, Quintin concentrated on the island's ancient history and remains, so that his utility to the medieval historian is limited. Interest in the struggle with the Turks, which culminated in the dramatic siege of Malta in 1565, ran high during the sixteenth century and led to much writing and publication, though this literature has yet to be systematically exploited as a source of information about Malta's medieval past.[5]

The first and in some ways still the most coherent attempt to cover the whole history of medieval Malta appeared in the *Descrittione di Malta*, published in 1647 by a notable scholar, antiquarian and collector, the Maltese Gian Francesco Abela, Vice-Chancellor of the Order of St. John. Abela, who was interested in language,

[1] No attempt can be made in this introductory, and inevitably somewhat dense and indigestible, article to do more than outline achievements, problems and possibilities, and that in an uneven fashion designed partially to compensate for gaps not filled below. A comprehensive bibliography of works on medieval Malta remains a *desideratum*. J. Mizzi, 'A Bibliography of the Order of St. John of Jerusalem: 1925–1969', in *The Order of St. John in Malta* [ed. Council of Europe] (Malta, 1970), is useful, especially because it lists the other bibliographies; see also the lists of printed books and mss. in *Archivio Storico di Malta* [= *ASM*], 13 vols. (1929–1942), *passim*, especially T. Guarnaschelli—E. Valenziani, 'Saggio di una Bibliografia di Malta . . .', *ASM*, ix (1937/8).

[2] C. Dessoulavy, 'Malta in the Middle Ages', *Journal of the Malta University Literary Society*, ii nos. 10–12 (1937), discusses a number of texts, including that of Ludolph von Sudheim (ca. 1340); for those of ca.1241 and of Niccolò de Martoni (1394), *infra*, 36 n. 208, 46 n. 248.

[3] The Latin original, now lost, was summarized *in ristretto, et in sostanza* in G. Bosio, *Dell'Istoria della Sacra Religione et Illustrissima Militia di San Giovanni Gierosolimitano*, iii (1st ed: Rome, 1602), 30–31; Bosio had access to the Hospitallers' archives. The purported summary in L. de Boisgelin, *Ancient and Modern Malta*, ii (London, 1804), 15–17, does not altogether concord with Bosio's version.

[4] Quintin's *Insulae Melitae Descriptio* was completed *Melitae xx die Ianuarij, . . . M.D.XXXIII* [possibly 1534]. E. Leopardi, 'The First Printed Description of Malta, Lyons 1536', *Scientia* [Malta], xv (1949), provides a useful study, reproducing the frontispiece and the map of Malta; there is a copy of the rare first edition in the Gozo Public Library and the British Museum has another, but it was several times reprinted, notably in J. Graevius, *Thesaurus Antiquitatum et Historiarum Siciliae*, xv (Leyden, 1725) [owing to its brevity, references below are not annotated].

[5] To the references and bibliographies in Mizzi, add J. Galea, *Bibliography of the Great Siege of Malta: 1565–1965* (Malta, [1965]). For some details on Maltese customs, see C. Dessoulavy, 'Visitors to Malta from the 15th to the 18th Century', *The Sundial: The Journal of the Royal University of Malta Literary Society*, iii nos. 4–8 (1940). Bosio's own description of Malta (iii. 90–96) includes information not drawn from Quintin or from the 1524 report.

place-names, archaeology, folk-lore and natural history, has justifiably been called the 'Father of Maltese Historiography' and the 'Founder of the Malta Museum'. His history, one of the very first books printed in Malta, was reprinted in Latin in 1725 in the fifteenth volume of Johannes Graevius' *Thesaurus Antiquitatum et Historiarum Siciliae*, and it was re-edited at Malta, in two volumes entitled *Malta Illustrata*, by Giovannantonio Ciantar. Ciantar went blind before the publication of the first volume in 1771 and died before that of the second in 1780, so that the revised edition probably contained more errors than the first.[6] Born in 1582, Abela was very much a man of his times, educated in the university at Bologna and much interested in classical remains and pseudo-philological speculation. His work was written in Italian and conceived in the encyclopaedic manner, being subdivided into *libri* and *notitie*. For the earlier medieval period Abela used published chronicles and histories such as those of the historians of Sicily Rocco Pirri and Tommaso Fazello, often copying their errors uncritically and without always naming his source. For the post-1350 period he employed documents found on the island and transcripts from Palermo already available in Malta, publishing lists of place-names, churches, convents, bishops, officials and notable families.

Abela utilized unreliable materials and he introduced into his work an extensive mythology, a good deal of which survives both as popular folk-lore and, unfortunately, in learned works whose authors still tend to regard him as quasi-infallible.[7] The most recent treatment reflects the unavoidable ambivalence of the scholar torn between admiration for Abela's very considerable achievements, for the accuracy and elegance of some of his observation, for his lively intelligence and his deep knowledge of Malta, and frustration at Abela's readiness to repeat all manner of legends and to misinterpret documents in order to sustain those beliefs, natural to a patrician Maltese cleric, according to which Malta was essentially European and Christian rather than African and Muslim. Abela is, to some extent, to blame if 'a litter of discarded theories trails over the whole island like a mad paper-chase,'[8] but it is a tribute to his powers and talents that so many of the errors he perpetuated still survive. Probably he has suffered just because he was the first major historian of Malta to appear in print, and only a detailed investigation of the unpublished writings of the predecessors and contemporaries on whom Abela must have relied can establish to what extent they misled him, and how far what he called 'ancestral traditions' were of his own invention. Some of these traditions appeared in the *Descrizione dell'Isola di Malta*, written in about 1610 by a doctor from the Knights' galleys, which awaits study.[9] In fact, there is room for a comprehensive analysis of all the varied sources used in the medieval sections of Abela's work.

[6] G.-F. Abela, *Della Descrittione di Malta Isola nel Mare Siciliano* (Malta, 1647) [the edition cited throughout]; cf. C. Clair, *The Spread of Printing—Eastern Hemisphere: Malta* (Amsterdam, 1969), 8–12. For Abela, and for many details concerning subsequent antiquarian and scholarly activity in Malta, see *Gian Francesco Abela: Essays in his Honour by Members of the 'Malta Historical Society'* ... (Malta, 1961); see also E. Sipione, in *Dizionario biografico degli Italiani*, i (Rome, 1960), 45–46.

[7] For some examples, see the analyses of Abela's treatment of the Norman period (*infra*, 29–34, 96–100) and of his uncritical use of Pirri (B. Fiorini, in *Abela Essays*, 82–87).

[8] N. Dennis, *An Essay on Malta* (London, 1972), 6 *et passim*, containing a perceptive if somewhat debatable appreciation of Abela's work. On his *ambiente* and contemporaries, G. Mangion, 'La letteratura barocca a Malta (con testi inediti)', *Journal of the Faculty of Arts: Royal University of Malta*, iv no. 4 (1971).

[9] Royal Malta Library, Biblioteca Ms. 631. For other 'traditions', see the *Relazione sopra lo stato, dazij ed altre notizie Curiose dell'Isola di Malta* of ca. 1630 (Biblioteca Ms. 5, f. 563–584); an edition by G. Wettinger is forthcoming.

For two centuries or more Abela's history continued to hold the field, and a third edition, never published, was initiated in 1842.[10] A considerable volume of work did appear, but most of it repeated extant errors without adding much of value to medieval Maltese history. The Gozitan scholar Agius de Soldanis wrote a history of Gozo in 1746.[11] G. Vassallo's *Storia di Malta*, published in 1854, was probably the most successful new work. Meanwhile the eighteenth-century Maltese priest Giuseppe Vella had produced his notorious Arabic forgeries which, though soon exploded, continued to influence the historiography of Muslim Malta even after the publication of Michele Amari's great work on Muslim Sicily and of his Italian translation of the Arabic texts upon which it was based.[12] A. A. Caruana who wrote widely on Maltese antiquities and history, especially in his 496-page 'Fragment', accepted that Vella was a forger but unfortunately maintained that some of his materials were, none the less, reliable.[13] Ecclesiastical and legal histories by A. Ferris and P. De Bono, though full of errors, constituted useful collections of references.[14] A Society of Archaeology, History and Natural Sciences was founded in 1866 and planned a collective history of Malta, only to collapse a few years later.[15] A more critical spirit was making itself felt. The German scholar Albert Mayr wrote well on the Roman and Byzantine period,[16] and a new Historical and Scientific Society was founded which in 1910 began to publish the *Archivum Melitense.* This review contained an important series of knowledgeable, though amazingly jumbled, medieval contributions derived from the Maltese archives by Alfredo Mifsud.[17]

The emergence of a more scientific approach coincided with an era of political passion in which the 'imperialists' argued for a Punic origin of Maltese and imposed English in the schools, while the 'nationalists' sought to demonstrate the Italian origin of Maltese institutions. The Italian Fascist government initiated a cultural campaign which claimed that Malta was a *terra irridenta* belonging by ancient right to Italy; its chief historical weapon was the Regia Deputazione di Storia di Malta.[18] The *Archivio Storico di Malta*, launched in 1929, was managed in Rome by competent professional historians torn by the demands of the regime and their own better scientific feelings, which sometimes triumphed.[19] It collected scattered references, listed sources and published documents, particularly from Naples and from Malta

[10] E. Leopardi, in *Abela Essays*, 27.

[11] Eventually published in translation: G. Agius de Soldanis, *Għawdex bil-ġrajja tiegħu*, 2 vols. (Malta, 1936–1953), but best consulted in the Italian original (Royal Malta Library, Biblioteca Ms. 145).

[12] M. Amari, *Storia dei Musulmani di Sicilia*, revised by C. Nallino, 3 vols. (Catania, 1933–1939), i. 6–11, has an interesting account of the Vella affair; texts in M. Amari, *Biblioteca arabo-sicula: versione italiana*, 2 vols. (Turin—Rome, 1880–1881).

[13] A. A. Caruana, *Frammento Critico della Storia Fenicio-Cartaginese, Greco-Romana e Bisantina, Musulmana e Normanna-Aragonese delle Isole di Malta* (Malta, 1899).

[14] A. Ferris, *Descrizione storica delle chiese di Malta e Gozo* (Malta, 1866); P. De Bono, *Sommario della storia della legislazione in Malta* (Malta, 1897).

[15] Cf. J. Cassar Pullicino, in *Melita Historica*, i no. 2 (1953), 122–124.

[16] *Infra*, 20 n. 123, 27 n. 162.

[17] These are frequently cited below; see also *infra*, 16 n. 331.

[18] See *Giornale di politica e di letteratura*, x fasc. 11–12 [Fascicolo dedicato a Malta] (1934), 513–514, 688–695.

[19] Eg. F. Borlandi's deservedly savage review of L. Viviani, *Storia di Malta*, 2 vols. in 3 (Turin, [1934]), in *ASM*, vii (1935/6), 100–104.

itself.[20] A history of Malta by A. Savelli, though Fascist in inspiration, undocumented and sometimes inaccurate, was based on the *Archivio* and did provide a not unreasonable outline of events.[21] The Italians were scarcely interested in the non-Italian pre-Norman period.[22] Their outstanding contributor was Roberto Valentini, whose many articles still constitute the standard point of departure for Maltese history from about 1200 onwards.[23] Valentini returned to the documents, a number of which he published; he placed Maltese history in its Sicilian context; and he made many valuable points. But he never escaped the Italian bias, the full ideological implications of which were clearly presented in a most unfortunate propaganda piece issued in collaboration with Pietro Fedele. This spoke of Mussolini and the *mare nostrum.* It exaggerated the use of the Sicilian dialect in medieval Malta. It attacked the Knights of St. John for suppressing the Italian-style *comune* and allegedly preventing Abela from giving a proper account of the ancient and natural links with Sicily, and it castigated the Spaniards both for ruining the Maltese islands and for repeatedly granting them out in an un-Italianate manner which, supposedly, was strongly resisted by the Maltese in the best traditions of *italianità.*[24]

Subsequently, activity was encouraged by several new journals, notably *Melita Historica* published by the new Malta Historical Society set up in 1950,[25] and there has been progress in the margins of the subject, in folk-lore, in art and architecture, and in archaeology, with the Italians returning as archaeologists whose medieval interests have stimulated a variety of studies.[26] Yet the difficulties of forming a class of linguistically and paleographically prepared Maltese medievalists remain, while distinguished Maltese medieval scholars, such as Daniel Callus and Mauro Inguanez, have tended to be clerical in training and interests, and to abandon the island and its historical problems. In 1962 Professor Lionel Butler gave a series of lectures which excited great interest in Malta but were not published. The geographer Brian Blouet produced an original *The Story of Malta* in 1967 though, in the absence of materials, it inevitably had little new to say on the medieval period. The *Maltese History: What Future?* symposium of 1971 and the Arab-Berber congress held in Malta in 1972, and the prompt publication of their acts, represent notable advances.[27] Improved accessibility to the Maltese archives has recently and significantly extended research possibilities, as demonstrated by the publications of the Maltese medievalist Godfrey Wettinger, while a fundamental obstacle, the absence of much essential

[20] There also appeared *The Institute of Historical Research Malta: Bulletin,* 7 vols. (1931–1950), very little of which concerns the medieval period. This institute was set up by the Malta Government in 1931 as a branch of the Comité International des Sciences Historiques, following reports by M. Coville, E. Rossi and F. Ryan, in *Bulletin du Comité International des Sciences Historiques,* xv (1932).

[21] A. Savelli, *Storia di Malta dai primordi ai giorni nostri* (Milan, 1943).

[22] For E. Rossi as an exception, *infra,* 26 n. 159.

[23] *ASM,* v-xiii (1934-1942), and *Archivum Melitense,* ix no. 4 (1935); see Valentini's obituary in *Bullettino dell'Istituto Storico Italiano per il medio evo,* lxv (1953), 161–162.

[24] P. Fedele—R. Valentini, *Per la storia dell'italianità di Malta nel Medio Evo* (Rome, 1940).

[25] *Scientia* [Malta], i (1935) onwards; *Melita Historica,* i no. 1 (1952) onwards; *Journal of the Faculty of Arts: Royal University of Malta,* i no. 1 (1957) onwards; *Journal of Maltese Studies,* i (1961) onwards. Useful information is also contained in numerous other reviews, newspapers and pamphlets published in Malta.

[26] *Missione Archeologica Italiana a Malta: Rapporto preliminare della Campagna 1963* [etc.], 8 vols. (Rome, 1964–1973) [cited as *Missione 1963* etc.].

[27] *Maltese History: What Future?* (Malta, 1974); *Actes du Premier Congrès d'Études des Cultures méditerranéenes d'influence arabo-berbère* (Algiers, 1973) [cited as *Congrès arabo-berbère*]. The general history of Malta being prepared in Maltese by Professor Andrew Vella will shortly appear.

printed literature, is gradually being overcome with the expansion of the Royal University of Malta library, by xeroxes and microfilms, and through opportunities for foreign study.[28]

Turning from past problems to future possibilities, the limiting factor is that of the sources. Down to the end of the Norman period in 1194 the written sources are strictly limited, and there is no evident probability of adding significantly to them; further information may become available on the Arabic side and the existing evidence certainly requires further study, but only archaeological techniques promise any considerable increase in knowledge. From 1194 to about 1270, materials are still meagre. For the years of Frederick II's minority, the age of the Genoese Counts of Malta, there is a mélange of royal charters, chronicle references, notarial documents from Genoa and elsewhere, and even a Provençal troubadour. For Frederick II and his Hohenstaufen successors there survive a few imperial letters and privileges, and in particular Gilibertus' report of about 1241; together with certain Latin and Arab chronicles and a few other references, these permit the construction of an outline of the Sicilian administration in Malta.[29] For Angevin rule from 1268 until 1282, and to a lesser extent for the decades following, the destruction in 1943 of the Angevin archives at Naples is a major disaster, relieved only by the previous publication of many documents concerning Malta[30] and by the systematic collection of these and other Angevin sources in the reconstructed registers.[31] For the period from 1282 to 1530 the archive sources are those for the history of Sicily plus, from about 1350, the originals and copies preserved in Malta itself. These sources must always be supplemented by many kinds of notices and texts, published and unpublished, in a variety of chronicles and collections. The Vatican archives undoubtedly contain much relevant information;[32] so do other major archives such as those of Barcelona,[33] Genoa[34] and Venice,[35] while a host of lesser sources from many parts of the Mediterranean world require patient collection.[36]

Malta and Gozo formed part of the Kingdom of Sicily, and materials concerning them are to be found throughout the whole body of Sicilian documentation.[37] The

[28] Outside Malta, and apart from the major scholarly libraries, there are useful collections of 'Melitensia' in the Scicluna Collection at Rhodes House, Oxford, and at Rome in the libraries at Palazzo Malta and the British School at Rome.

[29] *Infra*, 29–40, 104–125, 130–134.

[30] V. Laurenza, 'Malta nei documenti angioini del R. Archivio di Napoli', *ASM*, v (1934), publishes 66 documents (1270–1300); R. Moscati, 'Fonti per la Storia di Malta nel R. Archivio di Stato di Napoli' *ASM*, vii (1935/6), publishes 9 *notamenti* of lost documents (1271–1283) and 30 texts (1270–1287).

[31] *I Registri della Cancelleria Angioina ricostruiti*, ed. R. Filangieri *et al.*, i- (Naples, 1950– ) [cited as *Cancelleria Angioina*]; 30 vols. reaching 1290 by 1971.

[32] The standard guide to the materials and literature is now L. Boyle, *A Survey of the Vatican Archives and of its Medieval Holdings* (Toronto, 1972).

[33] Eg. A. Rubió i Lluch, *Diplomatari de l'Orient català: 1301–1409* (Barcelona, 1947); see also *infra*, 42 n. 232.

[34] The Genoese material is difficult to manage and has scarcely been touched. F. Perroni, 'Malta nei documenti del R. Archivio di Stato di Genova', *ASM*, xii (1941), 190–191, lists only 5 documents, all in print, for the medieval period, but see D. Abulafia *infra*.

[35] Eg. A. Luttrell, 'Venetians at Medieval Malta', *Melita Historica*, iii no. 1 (1960).

[36] Eg. A. Luttrell, 'Malta and Dubrovnik towards the year 1380', *ibid.*, v no. 2 (1969) [a number of misprints in the Latin texts require correction].

[37] F. Natale, *Avviamento allo studio del Medio Evo siciliano* (Florence, 1959), which surveys the bibliography, the printed sources and the historiographical problems, is an indispensable handbook.

main sources are the largely unexplored royal documents at Palermo, including the chancery registers, the *Lettere Viceregie*, the *Protonotaro del Regno*, the *Conservatorio di Registro* and other series;[38] the *capitoli* or petitions granted by the Crown to individual cities, which for Malta and Gozo survive from about 1409 onwards;[39] and a series of largely unpublished notarial and private acts from Palermo and other Sicilian towns, notably Trapani and Syracuse, which throw vital statistical light on such matters as Maltese trade and shipping.[40] The archives of Sicilian monasteries on which Maltese religious houses and properties depended may contain relevant information.[41] The *Capibrevi* and the *Liber de Secretiis* compiled by Gian Luca Barberi from the royal archives at Palermo in the early sixteenth century recorded many details of Maltese gabelles and fiefs reaching back to 1316.[42] Transcriptions from Barberi's works and of a few dozen documents known to him were made at Palermo by the notary Leonardo Biasini in 1644 and sent to Malta.[43] Extensively used in Abela's work of 1647 and, more recently, by Mifsud, Valentini and others, they constitute the bulk of the pre-1400 documentation now available in Maltese archives. The texts in the Palermo registers should in theory be preferred,[44] but some of these may have been lost in the destructions there in 1848.

In Malta itself, many more documents are available for study than in 1914 when Mifsud published his notes on the archives.[45] The main repositories of pre-1530 documents are the Università and Biblioteca sections of the Royal Malta Library at Valletta, the Cathedral Museum at Mdina, and the Notarial Archives deposited in Valletta.[46] In the Royal Malta Library, Università Mss. 3, 4, and 10 consist of original documents on parchment and paper, mostly dating after 1421. Università Ms. 7, formerly Biblioteca Ms. 858, contains royal and viceregal grants from 1397 onwards which were confirmed by the Hospitallers in 1530; the few copies made from original privileges then presented in Malta may provide a better text than careless entries in the royal registers at Palermo. Biblioteca Ms. 670 contains some pre-1530 materials once in the archives of the *universitas*, while post-1530 transcripts of medieval ecclesiastical documents are scattered through a number of inadequately-indexed manuscript miscellanies. Some of these texts were published by Mifsud and Valentini. Most important of all is Università Ms. 11, a 600-folio collection containing

[38] An important group of *cancelleria* texts is published in H. Bresc, 'Documents on Frederick IV of Sicily's Intervention in Malta: 1372', *Papers of the British School at Rome*, xli (1973); documents from the other series are utilized by H. Bresc *infra*.

[39] *Capitoli* are published in *Capitoli inediti delle città demaniali di Sicilia*, i, ed. S. Giambruno—L. Genuardi, (Palermo, 1918), 323–338 (Gozo), 375–444 (Malta), and by R. Valentini, in *ASM*, viii–x (1936–1939). G. la Mantia, 'Capitoli e statuti amministrativi dell'Isola di Malta approvati dal Re o Vicerè di Sicilia: 1130–1530', *ASM*, viii (1936/7), publishes no texts. The systematic publication of the *capitoli* for the period 1466 to 1530 is desirable.

[40] Eg. *infra*, 58 n. 306, 149 n. 150; cf. Natale, 131–138.

[41] Eg. *infra*, 63 n. 348.

[42] *I Capibrevi di Giovanni Luca Barberi*, ed. G. Silvestri, iii (Palermo, 1888), 415–455; J. Luca de Barberiis, *Liber de Secretiis*, ed. E. Mazzarese Fardella (Milan, 1966), 72–89. Barberi is discussed *infra*, 126–127.

[43] See especially Royal Malta Library, Università Ms. 206 (*olim* Biblioteca Ms. 870).

[44] Except where the originals or early copies from the originals survive.

[45] A. Mifsud, 'Appunti sugli archivi di Malta', *Archivum Melitense*, ii nos. 13–16 (1912/13); this article is still useful despite its confusing presentation. Extracts and summaries of *universitas* documents dating back to 1351 and preserved 'in a leaden chest' at Mdina were published in W. Eton, *Authentic Materials for a History of the People of Malta*, 3 parts (2nd ed: London, 1803–1807), part 3, 108–129.

[46] Details in G. Wettinger, 'Our Medieval Historical Archives and their Care', and other contributions in *Maltese History: What Future?*

records of the *consiglio* and various other municipal documents for 1450, 1460–1464, 1468–1483 and 1498–1499; in addition, Ms. 13 includes 38 misplaced folios for 1467–1468 and Ms. 12 covers 1512–1531. These documents are written in a difficult mélange of Latin and Sicilian, they are often scarcely legible, and their interior organization and binding is chronologically confused; only brief and scattered extracts have so far been published.[47]

The archives now in the Cathedral Museum at Mdina have recently been reorganized and made more readily available. For some reason they include a section of the *universitas* documentation. Ms. 33 contains some 130 early originals of *capitoli* and of royal or viceregal acts, a few of which have been published. Ms. 34, rich in *capitoli* and other texts, is an immensely thick manuscript, unsystematically arranged and unindexed. Ms. 36 contains numerous orders of payment on the incomes of the *universitas* between 1473 and 1530, with details about hospitals, doctors and plagues, wall-building and guards, schoolmasters, sermons, bell-ringers and so forth, while Ms. 37 includes a few other relatively unimportant pre-1530 documents. A section of *Quaderni diversi* comprises 16 administrative items of major importance, including *angara* or corvée lists, militia rolls, lists of families at Rabat around 1483, payments of fines for absence from services due, and the accounts for Birgu castle running from about 1502 to 1525 and for the Hospital of Santo Spirito at Rabat for 1494 and 1518.[48] Pre-1530 materials in the cathedral archives proper include a few bulls and prebendary records, various *Mandati diversi*, and sundry entries, some in later copies, in a register of *Acta Capitularia*. There is also a large collection of transcripts and summaries of public and ecclesiastical documents, a few as early as the fourteenth century. Many of these require careful use, since dates are often lacking and the copying may be erroneous; the source is seldom apparent; and the numbering, pagination and indexing of volumes is sometimes confusing. The equivalent of nine volumes of pre-1530 material consisting of the acts of the court of the bishop or of his vicar-general has recently been discovered in great confusion and sorted under the title *Curia Episcopalis Melitae*. These documents should vastly increase knowledge of fifteenth-century social developments, particularly on Gozo where all records surviving were destroyed in 1551.[49] The later medieval history of Gozo will have to be reconstructed above all from Sicilian archives.

Though no register earlier than 1467 remains in the Notarial Archives, the pre-1530 notarial deeds, in some 25 volumes, constitute a tremendously valuable fund of information about many aspects of Maltese life.[50] No more than a few fragments of

[47] Notably by E. Leopardi, in *Melita Historica*, ii nos. 2–4 (1957–1959); a number of other documents are scattered through the literature. The publication of the transcript of these *consiglio* records prepared by Dr. Godfrey Wettinger is a major *desideratum* in late medieval Maltese studies. Ms. 11 contains a list of royal privileges and other writings which in 1471 were *intra la caxa di la Universitati:* text in Leopardi, ii. 259–261. For a reference of 1488 to the *Archiuium Dni. Capitanei Ciuitatis Melite*, see Royal Malta Library, Biblioteca Ms. 737, f. 203 (modern copy).

[48] For use of these lists by G. Wettinger, see *infra*, 53 n. 270, 68 n. 374, 184-187.

[49] M. Inguanez, 'The Archives of the *Università del Gozo:* a Classified List', *Melita Historica*, ii no. 1 (1956). E. Leopardi, 'The Island of Gozo: 1432–1453', *ibid.*, iii no. 3 (1962); iv no. 1 (1964), depended entirely on the *capitoli* in Giambruno—Genuardi, i. 323–338. See also the pamphlet by B. Blouet, *Gozo* (Malta, 1965).

[50] This point is admirably made by the detailed use of notarial records in G. Wettinger—M. Fsadni, *Peter Caxaro's Cantilena: a Poem in Medieval Maltese* (Malta, 1968); the poem itself was found, in copy, in the Notarial Archives. Pre-1467 references may be gleaned indirectly, eg. *infra*, 62.

the records of the civil courts and tribunals survive, but there could be original materials or transcripts still in the Archiepiscopal Curia at Valletta. There are some pre-1530 notarial deeds, in original and copy, at the Dominican house at Rabat. A number of medieval documents certainly remain in family hands;[51] these should be saved from damage or dispersal since some of them, particularly the wills, contain interesting details concerning properties in Mdina, in the country or even in Sicily, or illustrate family relationships, children, servants and slaves, and so forth. The post-1530 archives both of the *universitas* and of the Order of St. John[52] contain copies of medieval documents as well as other materials which throw considerable light on medieval conditions. The parish registers begin in the mid sixteenth century, and Pietro Dusina's Apostolic Visitation of 1575, already much used by historians of art and architecture, as well as by ecclesiastical historians and others, is particularly important.[53] Some of this Maltese material is in a seriously deteriorated condition, and proposals for the care of public records and for their improved accessibility to the public naturally deserve careful attention, as does the production of a detailed guide to Malta's archives.[54] It should be emphasized that, apart from the copies or copies of copies derived from Palermo, almost all the documentation preserved in Malta is post-1397.

In addition to the conventional written sources of the archives, there are other approaches to Maltese history. With one brief exception, no medieval literature survives, but Malta's rich folklore has been extensively studied and recorded, especially through J. Cassar Pullicino and his *Maltese Folklore Review* first published in 1962.[55] The medievalist's difficulty with folklore material is that while stories of pirates and Turkish raiders provide vivid detail and a picturesque insight into local conditions, it is difficult to show that they refer to the medieval period, and often they contain traditional motifs found on islands and coastlines around much of the Mediterranean.[56] The miraculous appearance of St. Paul at the defence of Mdina in 1429, represented in the seventeenth-century painting by Mattia Preti in the cathedral there, is an example of a different kind of tradition. The myth-making process is also conditioned by historical novels on medieval themes, such as *A*

[51] A few are published in Anon., *Memoirs of the Family of Inguanez* (Malta, 1888).

[52] See A. Zammit Gabarretta, J. Mizzi *et al.*, *Catalogue of the Records of the Order of St. John of Jerusalem in the Royal Malta Library*, i- (1964- ).

[53] V. Borg, 'The Ecclesiastical Archives of the Maltese Islands', in *Maltese History: What Future?* Visitation documents are published in G. Marchi, 'Ricerche storiche negli archivi di Malta , in *Missione 1964*. J. Cassar Pullicino, 'Malta in 1575: Social Aspects of an Apostolic Visit', *Melita Historica*, ii no. 1 (1956), makes excellent use of Dusina's acts, providing information of interest to the medievalist; see also M. Buhagiar *infra*. The call for an edition (*ibid.*, i no. 2 [1953], 67) has unfortunately remained unheeded. It should be based on the original in Archivio Vaticano, S. Congregatio Concilii, Visite Apostoliche, 39: Malta 1575 (ff. 477, some blank; unbound but clearly legible). The various copies available in Malta, some of them relatively late ones, are apparently not altogether reliable. Dusina's *Discorso di Malta*, with useful statistics, is published in A. Vella, 'La missione di Pietro Dusina a Malta nel 1574', *Melita Historica*, v no. 2 (1969).

[54] The inventories drawn up following the reports of Professor I. Evans in 1951/2 were never published: cf. [S. Zarb], 'The Archives of Malta', *Scientia* [Malta], xxii (1956), 107–110.

[55] For a complete bibliography and an invaluable theme-index of Cassar Pullicino's work, see G. Mifsud-Chircop, *Gużè Cassar Pullicino: Folklorista* (unpublished B.A. thesis: Royal University of Malta, 1972).

[56] Eg. J. Cassar Pullicino, 'Pirates and Turks in Maltese Tradition', *Scientia* [Malta], xiv (1948). That traces of Punic folklore could well have reached Malta *after* 1530 is effectively demonstrated in *idem*, 'Some Considerations in Determining the Semitic Element in Maltese Folklore', in *Congrès arabo-berbère*.

*Baroness of Malta* by S. Frendo de' Mannarino, published in Maltese in 1893 and in English in 1953, or a play such as A. Cremona's *The Ransom of the Peasants*, which is set around the crisis of 1427 to 1429 and was produced in Malta in 1970.[57] Folklore merges into cultural anthropology, and the sociological analysis of modern Maltese society may also throw indirect light on village conditions and popular mentalities,[58] though the medievalist has to treat such material with great care.

When traditional folk memories concentrate around a particular incident, such as Roger the Norman's Maltese expedition of 1090, they have usually become legend, and while the techniques of the folklore specialist can demonstrate how such stories acquire popularity and how they may be evaluated, it is difficult to be sure that the popular traditions are not the results of a 'feed-back' from antiquarian myth-makers. Most of the legends concerning Count Roger can be traced back no further than Abela's publication of 1647. Certain of these myths were taken from other historians, some of whom wrote only slightly earlier than Abela himself. He and his fellow-Maltese Domenico Magri referred to the ancient 'traditions' of their forefathers, but it is often impossible to establish an earlier origin for tales which are in some cases either demonstrably false or inherently improbable.[59] Such legends deserve to be recorded and studied in their own right, while it is important to clarify their origins and to distinguish clearly between fact and tradition, tradition and myth, especially when some historians, faced with the demolition of the evidence for certain assertions, simply maintain them as 'strong traditions', much as Abela did. Except possibly in the case of the Pauline memories, there is little or no evidence to suggest that these traditions were continuous.

Paintings and buildings are to some extent datable stylistically, and the study of military, domestic and ecclesiastical architecture is especially important.[60] Certain types of material object are of interest to the medievalist. The collection, recording and study of mills and presses, agricultural instruments, domestic utensils, saddles, costumes[61] and so on, may repay unexpected dividends, especially if excavation or the uncovering of unknown frescoes should suddenly produce similar items, or pictures of them, in a datable context. The projected national collection of cultural anthropology or traditional arts along the lines of the Pitrè Museum at Palermo should be formed rapidly before the bulk of such materials is lost for ever.[62] The Gozo Museum does already display a small selection of implements. Particularly useful, because datable, are coins, which survive in some quantity in museums and private hands. Only the classical coinage has received study.[63] Byzantine coins

[57] English version in *Journal of the Faculty of Arts: Royal University of Malta*, i no. 4 (1960); ii no. 2 (1962); iv no. 1 (1969); iv nos. 3–4 (1971). Roger the Norman legends reappear in N. Monsarrat's novel *The Kappillan of Malta* (London, 1973), 213–222.

[58] See J. Boissevain, *Saints and Fireworks: Religion and Politics in Rural Malta* (London 1965); *idem, Hal-Farrug: a Village in Malta* (New York, 1969).

[59] *Infra*, 29–34, 96–103.

[60] Discussion and references *infra*, 55, 58–59, 64–66.

[61] J. Cassar Pullicino, 'Notes for a History of Maltese Costume', *Maltese Folklore Review*, i no. 3 (1966), with medieval and early modern texts.

[62] Cf. *idem*, 'Ethnographic Exhibition', in *Congrès arabo-berbère*, with plates, and 'Background Material for the Study of Folk Arts and Crafts', *Maltese Folklore Review*, i no. 4 (1973), and notes *ibid.*, 348–354.

[63] E. Coleiro, 'Ricerche numismatiche', in *Missione 1964; idem*, 'Maltese Coins of the Roman Period' *The Numismatic Chronicle*, 7 ser., xi (1971).

were being discovered in the fifteenth and early sixteenth century,[64] and Byzantine and Arab coins have subsequently been found, particularly at Mdina where a notable hoard of gold and copper monies came to light in 1698.[65] Unfortunately, it is impossible to make more than limited scientific use of the coins in the Cathedral Museum at Mdina and in other collections, since they mostly lack any properly recorded archaeological provenance.[66]

There is much still to discover about the islands' medieval topography. The lists elaborated by Wettinger, which make an excellent start in the precisely dated recording of place-names in their exact contemporary form, will reinvigorate the subject.[67] They constitute a useful starting point for the further investigation of settlements, properties and fiefs, though few toponyms can be documented before 1372. In the absence of other materials, controversy concerning the Maltese language has turned above all on the interpretation and antiquity of the toponymic evidence.[68] There may be philological reasons for considering certain place-names to be much older than the dates at which they are first securely documented, but the historian should take great care. The misinterpretation of toponyms may lead to the invention and perpetuation of legends.[69] Names indicating ruins, marshes or wastelands sometimes suggest the site of abandoned villages or settlements on marginal land,[70] but other evidence can be ambiguous; a name such as 'the spring of the olives' may mean not that the island was covered with olives, but that olives were so rare that the presence of one or two of them distinguished the spring. Abela published lists of Maltese trees and plants in 1647, but he also said that most of the trees had gone.[71]

Early charts and portolans, such as Idrīsī's map completed in Sicily in 1154, show that the rest of the world had some idea where Malta and Gozo were and of their distances from major Mediterranean ports, but they give little or no information about the islands themselves.[72] The most interesting old portolan, *Lo Compasso de Navegare*, contained a description of distances from Malta to other ports accompanied by a seaman's view of the islands and their harbours, with special reference to the prevailing winds and other nautical conditions; it was probably Pisan in origin and

[64] *Infra*, 11, 136.

[65] Abela, 248–249; G.-F. Abela—G. Ciantar, *Malta Illustrata*, 2 vols. (Malta, 1772–1780), i. 692–693.

[66] *Infra*, 21–23. Mifsud, in *Archivum Melitense*, iii no. 5 (1918), 207–208, argues that there was a Maltese coinage in the Byzantine and Muslim periods; this seems unlikely and no such coins are known. Sicilian money was current in later medieval Malta, yet Mifsud produces a number of references to *pecunia e moneta Malte*, to *pecunia e moneta gaudisii*, etc.; he documents both a shortage of small coin in Malta and attempts to prevent its exportation. There was some sort of *moneta Malte que computatur ad racionem de septem pro una de moneta Sicilie* (*infra*, 127 n. 4). Possibly this was a money of account; perhaps the Maltese used a Muslim coinage, or made their own small coin. This puzzle is discussed, but not solved, in M. Sant, *Coinage Problems Facing the Order of St. John in Malta* (unpublished M.A. thesis; Royal University of Malta, 1967), 23 28. Meanwhile it is impossible to make use of much available 15th-century statistical information given in *moneta Malte*.

[67] *Infra*, 205–216 *et passim*.

[68] J. Aquilina, 'A Brief Survey of Maltese Place-Names', in his *Papers in Maltese Linguistics* (2nd ed: Malta, 1970); P. Saydon, 'Die Ortsnamen der maltesischen Inseln', *Annali dell'Istituto Universitario Orientale di Napoli*, ns. xvi–xvii (1966–1967); and references *infra*, 24 n. 143, 25 n. 150.

[69] As demonstrated *infra*, 97–99.

[70] Eg. *infra*, 54, 181–204.

[71] G. Lanfranco, 'The Natural History of Malta as presented by Abela in 1647', in *Abela Essays*.

[72] M. Amari—C. Schiaparelli, 'L'Italia descritta nel *Libro del Re Ruggero* compilato da Edrisi', *Atti della Reale Accademia dei Lincei*, cclxxiv = 2 ser., viii (1876/7), 21–22 and frontispiece.

was first composed in the mid-thirteenth century.[73] The wealth of accurate detail it provides, compared with the information given a century earlier by Idrīsī, suggests that the invention of the compass had almost literally put Malta on the map for long-distance shipping. The Turkish sea-atlas of Piri Reis, completed by 1527, gave the outline of Malta but almost no useful internal information.[74] Quintin published a map in 1536 which bore little relation to his text but did show Mdina as a fortified town though without its church, and the Gozo citadel as lacking walls; it also showed the *Marsa Hortus* and a number of crude houses. Thenceforth, and particularly after 1565, there was a stream of pictures, prints, maps, and similar materials; many of them show houses, churches, *casali* and other features, but most of these seem to be mere conventional drawings of dubious value as a guide to real building positions and types. A published corpus of seven maps from that of Quintin in 1536 to that of Abela in 1647 suggests that few of the details are of much utility to the medieval historian; Lafreri's map of circa 1551 is the most interesting, particularly as it shows roads linking the villages.[75] Invaluable in this respect, though unfortunately limited in scope, is the intensive building-by-building inventory and photography of selected villages being carried out at the National Museum under the auspices of the Council of Europe.[76] It is vitally important, in a period of expansion, development and road building, to record all available topographical information as rapidly and accurately as possible. It should eventually be feasible by combining archival and topographical data, to produce a detailed, documented map of fifteenth-century Malta and its road-system, an invaluable preliminary to the study of abandoned sites, population shifts and other problems. Much of the urban topography of Mdina, Rabat and Birgu could also be reconstructed.

Malta has been an archaeological hunting-ground for many centuries. People have always sought hidden treasure and sometimes it has been discovered by accident, as in the case of the little *pichulilli* who found a hoard of 248 Byzantine gold pieces in 1458/9.[77] There was a lawsuit *de inventione thesauri* in 1461, and in 1526 a case was brought against a goldsmith named Giovanni Scarpa who had purchased part of a hoard of late Roman coins—*di la monita di S. Elena;* in 1530 Luca d'Armenia and Antonio Callus even received a licence to seek ancient treasure of gold and silver.[78]

[73] Text in B. Motzo, *Il Compasso da Navigare: opera italiana della metà del secolo XIII* (Cagliari, 1947), 79–80, 111–113; a later version reproduced in *ASM*, vii (1935/6), 389–390, was mistakenly supposed to be earlier than that published by Motzo. For later texts and a now outdated list of appearances of the Maltese isles and place-names in the portolans, K. Kretschmer, *Die italienischen Portolane des Mittelalters* (Berlin, 1909), 308, 476–478, 617; the Greek portolan texts reproduced in *Missione 1968*, 24–25, require some revision.

[74] Istanbul, Topkapi Palace Museum, Inv. No. H 642, in *Order of St. John in Malta*, 312 and end-cover; cf. maps and texts in M. Agius-Vadala, *Piri Reis Map of the Maltese Islands* (Malta, 1966).

[75] R. Almagià, *Monumenta Italiae Cartographica* (Florence, 1929), 23–24, 32–33, 63, 74–75; tavole xxv 2–5, xxxvi 3–4, lxiii 2. A further census is desirable; preliminary survey in E. Hutten Czapski, 'Les cartes géographiques de Malte du XVI siècle', *Annales de l'Ordre Souverain Militaire de Malte*, xxiv (1966), based on R. Tooley, 'Maps in Italian Atlases of the Sixteenth Century', *Imago Mundi*, iii (1939), 36–37. A selection of early maps is displayed in the Valletta Armoury; and there are others in the Royal Malta Library. See also Matteo Perez d'Aleccio, *The True Depiction of the Investment . . . of Malta*, ed. D. Calnan (Malta, 1965), and Q. Hughes, *Fortress: Architecture and Military History in Malta* (London, 1969).

[76] Details in *Museum Report 1970*, 8–9; [the annual reports of the National Museum at Valletta, which have appeared under a number of varying titles since 1904, are cited in this form throughout.]

[77] *Infra*, 136.

[78] References given by Valentini, in *Archivum Melitense*, ix. 175.

Interest however has been fixed mainly on the prehistoric and classical. The Muslim tombs uncovered in 1881 and between 1920 and 1925 during the excavations of the Roman house just outside Mdina were not published.[79] The major exception to the general absence of medieval archaeological activity has been the sustained campaigns of the Italian Mission at Tas-Silġ and San Pawl Milqi. The final reports have yet to be published, but the lavish and prompt preliminary accounts make it clear that large-scale excavation, in what may be called the traditional style, can produce valuable information concerning the period before 1200 for which the sources are otherwise so meagre; they also suggest that it is futile to demand first-class stratigraphy from thin soil disturbed by generations of Maltese farmers. These excavations point to a comparatively flourishing Byzantine period, a violent Muslim conquest followed by Muslim occupation, and a subsequent period of Latin reconstruction.[80] Few other zones offer such rewarding opportunities since the islands are small and the modern urban sprawl severely limits the possibilities, but well-placed excavations, for example within the walls of Mdina or of the citadel on Gozo (plate 4a), should repay even limited digging with the emphasis on stratification and the study of the pottery and small finds; the results might well be spectacular.[81] Both the documents, and the wells, walls and lanes which are marked on the 1 : 2,500 maps of ca. 1909 and which frequently remain visible, should permit the identification of certain abandoned settlements where excavation might also be profitable.[82] It may prove possible to date the styles and types of the round and square well-heads, and of the numerous surviving wells and cisterns, rock-cut or stone-built, arched or pillared, plastered or unlined.[83] Underwater archaeology may also produce medieval information, especially where used in conjunction with aerial photography.[84]

The problems of medieval archaeology are considerable. In such small islands with a largely artificial landscape and a very thin soil covering, traces of settlement have often been largely or totally eliminated by intensive land use or erosion, by carting, quarrying, terracing, manuring and the dumping of inorganic town refuse; in Gozo the soil lies deeper but the destructions of the sixteenth century were much more widespread.[85] Such obstacles greatly increase the difficulties of interpreting aerial photographs and they impede surface surveying. The soft and easily-worked

[79] *Infra*, 21–22.

[80] The medieval results are summarized by M. Cagiano de Azevedo *infra;* see also the *Missione, passim,* and general interpretations by S. Moscati and M. Cagiano de Azevedo, in *Atti della Pontificia Accademia Romana di Archeologia: Rendiconti,* xxxvi–xxxix (1963/4–1966/7). Professoressa Antonia Ciasca most kindly showed the author the site and materials at Tas-Silġ. It should be emphasized that more definitive judgements concerning these excavations must await the publication of final reports.

[81] It cannot be too strongly emphasized, however, that unless such excavations are properly conducted on a reasonably large scale, and then satisfactorily published, they are likely to do more harm than good; finance, experience and preliminary study designed to elucidate the problems and possibilities are essential to this sort of medieval excavation.

[82] See G. Wettinger's appeal for excavations and, in particular, his list of place-names mentioning ruins, *infra,* 195–199, 213–216; the modern maps are listed *infra,* 189 n. 25, 205.

[83] For a well dated to 1541, see *Missione 1968,* 89.

[84] See the under-water archaeological map of Malta (containing a reference to medieval pottery found) in *Missione 1964,* fig. 1. Add a 'mediaeval Arab pot': H. Frost, *The Mortar Wreck in Mellieha Bay* (London, 1969), 22. Cf. G. Schmiedt, *Contributo della foto-interpretazione alla ricostruzione della situazione geografico-topografica dei porti antichi in Italia* (Florence, 1964). Collections of aerial photographs of Malta and Gozo are held in the Royal University of Malta Library and by the Royal Air Force.

[85] D. Lang, *Soils of Malta and Gozo* (London, 1960), 16–21, discusses soil disturbance, provides chemical analyses and a detailed soil-map, and rejects the idea that soil was imported from Sicily.

Maltese stone is also almost undatable. The chief datable element should be the pottery, collections of which are in the Valletta, Rabat and Gozo Museums. These include considerable quantities of Islamic pottery painted in red and white with 'narrow-line' decoration.[86] Much material from the excavations at Tas-Silġ and San Pawl Milqi also awaits study; a preliminary catalogue of the glazed wares has already appeared.[87] Though the cruder wares were doubtless produced on the islands, there is as yet no evidence for pottery kilns. In 1647 *vasi delicati* were still being made at Zurrieq without a wheel.[88] If all glazed wares had to be imported that would account for their apparent rarity, and the pottery found in Malta must be studied in terms of that produced in Sicily, in North Africa, in Byzantium and in Spain. The most important source was probably Sicily, where medieval archaeology is now established[89] and where the pottery has received considerable preliminary study.[90] However, even if pottery and glass found in properly stratified excavations can be dated, and there are now scientific methods of effecting this with some degree of accuracy,[91] such precision is only relative. Old styles and techniques may remain in use long after new wares have been introduced, and pots may survive for generations before being broken; their presence would not, in any case, necessarily imply the political domination in Malta of the rulers of the area where the pots were made.[92] Where dated pottery is more useful is when significant quantities of it can be plotted over reasonably wide areas, for then it may well indicate patterns of settlement; glazed and datable medieval sherds are, however, only rarely to be found on the surface,[93] partly perhaps because sherds were systematically collected to be ground down for the *deffun* used to waterproof roofs. In any case the constant shifting of soil would frequently invalidate deductions from such sporadic finds.

Even when such marginal or auxiliary evidence has been considered, enormous gaps will remain in the islands' medieval history. The temptation is to try to fill

[86] D. Whitehouse, 'Medieval Painted Pottery in South and Central Italy', *Medieval Archaeology*, x (1966), 43. The difficulty with the red and white painted 'Arab tradition' wares is that they apparently continued to be made at least into early modern times.

[87] F. d'Andria, 'Nota sulla ceramica invetriata: Catalogo', in *Missione 1968*, with tavole 16–17; other materials are recorded in *Missione, passim*.

[88] Abela, 102.

[89] See *GRAM: Notiziario del Gruppo Richerche Archeologia Medievale—Palermo* (1971 onwards), with discussions of rock-cut, thatched and wood-built dwellings, pottery and kilns, and so on. Particularly important is the excavation of the abandoned medieval settlement at Brucato; preliminary notices in F. d'Angelo, 'Brucato', *Sicilia Archeologica*, no. 9 (1970). Professor Jean-Marie Pesez and his associates kindly showed the writer the site they are excavating.

[90] For recent work, see F. d'Angelo, 'La ceramica nell'archeologia medievale siciliana', *GRAM: Notiziario* . . . (Aug. 1971); *idem*, 'Recenti ritrovamenti di ceramiche a Palermo', *Faenza*, lviii (1972); *idem*, 'La ceramica normanna in Sicilia', *Atti del Congresso Internazionale di Studi sulla Sicilia Normanna* (Palermo, 1973); see in addition A. Ragona, 'Echi del *Vespro* nella ceramica siciliana del sec. XIV', *Faenza*, lviii (1972).

[91] R. Berger *et al.*, *Scientific Methods in Medieval Archaeology* (Berkeley, Cal., 1970).

[92] Cf. A. Luttrell, 'La datazione della ceramica medioevale', *Atti: V Convegno Internazionale della Ceramica* (Albisola, 1973).

[93] Preliminary surface surveying has produced disappointingly few recognizably medieval sherds. A trial investigation of the general area of *Raħal* or *Casale Spital* (Ħas Saptan), documented at ca. 560662 by Wettinger (*infra*, 188–189, 191, 211) as containing a late medieval settlement, revealed a hitherto unknown prehistoric promontory site [560660] with remains of ancient walls and a variety of prehistoric sherds (kindly identified by Dr. David Trump), but no surface sign of medieval occupation whatsoever. Yet considerable quantities of painted 'Arab tradition' pottery lie just below ground nearby [562666] with the *casale* itself probably at 562664.

these lacunae by adducing analogies, particularly from Sicily. It is essential that the historian of Malta should be well grounded in Sicilian and Italian history; ideally, he should be equally expert in North African studies; and he would have much to learn from the overlapping of Christians, Muslims and Jews in the Iberian peninsula. The comparative study of such Mediterranean islands as Pantelleria, Menorca, Rhodes or Chios, isolated, precarious and restricted, can throw light on developments on Malta and Gozo, as indeed can the 'geohistorical' realities of the entire Mediterranean world. Unfortunately the notion of Malta as a Mediterranean microcosm is not always helpful, and the procedure by analogy is most likely to be applied precisely where it is least reliable, that is where there is little or no evidence. A striking example of this occurred when Alberto Stilon repeatedly attempted to show, on the basis of an exposition of developments in Sicily, that Malta had an Italian-style *comune* in the Norman and Hohenstaufen periods. Quite apart from the debatable nature of the argument about Sicily, there is no real evidence with regard to Malta and, as Alfredo Mifsud intervened to point out after Stilon had read his second paper, the only truly relevant document actually stated that in about 1241 the Maltese and Gozitans had their own customs—*uiuunt alijs moribus et constitucionibus quam alij homines Regni nostri Sicilie*, and furthermore that the Emperor Frederick II accepted this fact.[94] Malta was attached to Sicily for many centuries, but it was also a small and barren island off the African coast, situated further south than Tunis. Malta was influenced by Spain and Byzantium as well as from Sicily and Italy, and the persistence of its fundamentally non-European language is only the most striking pointer to the unreality of many Sicilian parallels. One prehistorian has, in fact, become so suspicious of alleged internal Mediterranean 'influences' and 'diffusions' as to seek illumination of Maltese problems from Pacific islands rather than 'continental' Sicily or Aegean Greece.[95] Maltese institutions changed slowly, often lagging well behind the developments of those who ruled them from afar. Parallels and analogies with other lands or with other epochs of Maltese history may be extremely illuminating, but where there is no evidence they tend to be arbitrary and unsound; where they are useful is in the interpretation of such firm evidence as can be found.[96]

The tendency to view Malta's history in terms of foreign developments has largely determined approaches to the problem of chronological divisions. Periods have no historical reality of their own, and periodization is in the last resort a historians' tool, a matter of convenience. Though control of the archipelago has occasionally changed rather suddenly, institutional and social changes have tended to drag slowly behind dramatic political changes. Island life is notoriously archaic, and in Malta even the towns have been isolated from the main stream of continental progress, while the predominantly agrarian character of North-west Malta and above all of Gozo, which is cut off even from Malta, has left the peasants working their lands in time-worn ways, to some extent immune from change. This time-lag runs right through

[94] A. Stilon, 'Della Esistenza dei Comuni durante la Dominazione Normanna', *Archivum Melitense*, i nos. 8–10 (1911/2), and 'L'Imperatore Federico II di Svevia ed i Comuni del Regno di Sicilia', *ibid.*, iii no. 1 (1917); cf. A. Mifsud, *ibid.*, iii. 20, and *infra*, 60.

[95] Cf. C. Renfrew, *Before Civilization: The Radiocarbon Revolution and Prehistoric Europe* (London, 1973), 147–166 *et passim*.

[96] This fundamental belief lies behind the construction of this book. Non-Maltese evidence has not been altogether neglected but the primary task is, as far as possible, to establish the facts concerning the islands; these facts can receive interpretation in successive stages of study.

Maltese history. The Romans ended Carthaginian control of the islands in the third century BC, yet traces of Punic survival are found centuries later. Throughout the Roman period Malta was a marginally flourishing minor provincial outpost, frequented by those who were wrecked or exiled there and by pirates. Christianity came and at a certain stage the ultimate dominion was transferred to Constantinople, but life on the villas continued; of barbarians and Vandals there is no direct evidence. It is hard to see any real turning-point in Roman Malta until the Muslim conquest in 870, and any attempt to fix a precise starting date for the middle ages in Malta is even more arbitrary than elsewhere. Roger the Norman conquered the islands temporarily in 1090, but Arab culture was possibly at its strongest there in the twelfth century and the Muslims were not 'expelled' until 1224 or later. When the Norman dynasty came to an end in 1194, Malta was scarcely Latin in any real sense at all, but thereafter it was firmly within a Northern and Western Mediterranean framework, and in strictly political terms it was dominated by the nordic Franco-German dynasties, Hohenstaufen and Angevin, which secured control of the Sicilian Crown. The Sicilian Vespers did mark an important change, because while Malta continued after 1282 to depend on Sicily it was a Sicily which, together with Malta, formed part of a West Mediterranean and North African community dominated politically, economically and culturally from the Iberian heartlands of the Aragonese Crown.

In theory some non-political or non-religious criteria could be utilized, but in practice so little is known about significant economic or social changes that any periodization based on them would tend to be imprecise and unhelpful. The introduction of the compass in the thirteenth century may have opened up Malta to shipping in an altogether new way. There was a moment in the fourteenth century when Malta ceased to export grain, and its economy came to depend on the exportation of cotton and the importation of wine and, above all, grain; serfs and *latifundia* disappeared, and Malta became more than ever dependent on Sicily for its food. In the end, however, medieval Maltese history can most conveniently be divided into three main periods: a late Roman or Byzantine era which was in effect a continuation of the classical period; a Muslim period running from 870 to about 1200; and three centuries of Western European predominance resulting from Latin control of the seas. In all these periods Malta and Gozo depended in the last resort upon Sicily. From 1282 until the coming of the Knights of St. John in 1530 what mattered was not whether the King of Sicily was Aragonese or whether he was half-Castilian, but whether Malta was being ruled by a king, a viceroy or a count, whether the centre of power and decision was in Palermo, Barcelona, Naples, Valladolid or Brussels, or in Malta itself.[97] After 1530 the situation changed rapidly. Malta's rulers were in Malta itself; they had non-Sicilian sources of income and they converted the island into a fortress defended by its own fleet, while the centre of affairs shifted from Mdina to Birgu and the *universitas* and other institutions went into eclipse. Naturally, there were elements of continuity. As the Turks showed in 1565, Malta was scarcely defensible and desperately reliant on Sicilian assistance. Only thereafter were the Knights fully committed to a permanent presence on the

[97] The generally accepted notion of a 'Castilian' period leads to absurd errors; eg. that the 'souverains de Castille' governed Malta after 1410: J. Godechot, *Histoire de Malte* (2nd ed: Paris, 1970), 26. The abandonment of the 'Castilian' period of the text-books is advocated *infra*, 49.

islands. It was then that Valletta was built, that Malta really emerged from its medieval poverty and backwardness; and it was then that it became retrospectively clear that 1530 had, in fact, been a decisive moment in Malta's history.[98]

In addition to the inconveniences resulting from an over-rigid periodization, other ambiguities have been created by those who have read their history backwards, who have assumed, often unconsciously, that Malta was destined to be Latin and Christian. For some writers, both Maltese and foreign, there had to be Maltese Christians waiting to be liberated by Roger the Norman, and if they had not been Christian they would not have been 'Maltese'. This is a familiar historiographical phenomenon; perhaps the nearest parallel is the *homo hispanicus* of certain Spanish historians, the archetypal Castilian who retained his identity through centuries of invasion and occupation by Romans, Visigoths and Africans.[99] The argument for continuity was sustained, for example, by Sir Themistocles Zammit who held that modern Maltese have skulls like prehistoric ones, that there was no sign of colonization by the Romans, and that the population remained Punic: 'The Maltese continued to till their fields, as they had quietly done during the Phoenician, the Roman and the Moorish governments . . . No ethnographic changes are expected in the people who received laws, rules and corn from Sicily but no colonists'.[100] It has, indeed, often been argued that there is a 'Maltese race' which survived above all in the backward and isolated agricultural areas, but it seems hard to reconcile such theories with the known facts of medieval Malta. The only serious ethnological investigation so far attempted involved the measurement of bones and bodies classed as: Bronze Age; Romano-Maltese; 'Late Medieval'; and modern, the modern measurements being taken in Valletta, in the Maltese countryside and in Gozo. Unfortunately, the 'Late Medieval' bones were actually seventeenth- and eighteenth-century ones.[101] It should yet be possible to obtain enough truly medieval bodies to fit into the picture. Meanwhile the fact that, for instance, 'the head breadth is remarkably consistent from Romano-Maltese times onwards'[102] might be explained by a series of immigrations from the same place or by similar peoples; such statistics do not prove the existence of a 'Maltese race', while philological arguments from surnames and place-names illustrate rather than demonstrate ethnological theory.[103]

In the later medieval period at least, it must have been reasonably clear who was Maltese; wherever his immediate ancestors came from, if a man had been born in

[98] That 1565 was a turning-point is evident architecturally, for example: *infra*, 217–223. The elements of continuity are well emphasized in L. Butler, 'The Maltese People and the Order of St. John in the Sixteenth Century', *Annales de l'Ordre Souverain Militaire de Malte*, xxiii–xxiv (1965–1966).

[99] See J. Vicens Vives, *Aproximación a la Historia de España* (2nd ed: Barcelona, 1960) [English translation: *Approaches to the History of Spain* (Berkeley, Cal., 1970)], who deals lucidly with such theories of 'race' and 'nation'.

[100] T. Zammit, 'The Inhabitants of the Maltese Islands', *Archivum Melitense*, i nos. 11–12 (1911/2), 242 *et passim*, but historical inaccuracies weaken his case.

[101] L. Dudley Buxton, 'The Ethnology of Malta and Gozo', *Journal of the Royal Anthropological Institute*, lii (1922). *Idem*, 'Malta: an Anthropogeographical Study', *Geographical Review*, xiv (1924), adds little, but emphasizes (pp. 81–83) the continuation from the Bronze Age into modern times of Eastern 'Armenoid' as opposed to 'Mediterranean' characteristics.

[102] Dudley Buxton (1922), 178.

[103] R. Bradley, *Malta and the Mediterranean Race* (London, 1912), contains some curious theories. The most recent approach, in R. Gayre of Gayre, 'The Ethnology of the Maltese Islands', *Scientia* [Malta], xxxiii (1970), advances hypotheses which many medievalists would be unlikely to accept.

Malta, if he felt he was Maltese and was accepted as such, and above all if he spoke Maltese, then he was Maltese. Despite the immigrations of rulers, garrisons, merchants, sailors, slaves and captives, despite consecutive expulsions of Christians, Muslims and Jews, and despite repeated razzias, plagues and other forms of depopulation which for long kept the total population probably well under 10,000,[104] there was presumably continuity of a sort. Even in the depths of the countryside, where foreign serfs and slaves were used to farm the land and where the population was so exposed to corsair raids that part of the country was deserted in the later medieval period, this continuity can scarcely have been a predominantly racial one. Those who lived in the archipelago were not unlike their Mediterranean neighbours, whether they were Muslim, Christian or Jewish, or had changed from one of these religions to another. Whatever it was, apart from language, which distinguished those who were accepted as Maltese, those qualities must surely have been acquired by assimilation and influence, by environment rather than heredity.[105]

No historian is now likely to write a major work on Malta without being influenced by the notions concerning the geohistorical unities of the whole Mediterranean region advanced in Fernand Braudel's classic book. Braudel says little about Malta, and that in a post-medieval context, though he has stimulating ideas about islands in general.[106] Basic studies concerning the geology, relief, water-supply, soil, climate, crops, land-use and so on are now available, and the modern statistics supplied open up stimulating lines of speculation for the medievalist;[107] a chapter on Malta and other islands in an excellent and historically-minded geographical study of the Western Mediterranean places these data in their wider context.[108] The difficulty is to integrate such knowledge with the limited medieval information available.[109] British Admiralty marine charts could be compared with the medieval *Lo Compasso de Navegare* [110] and with information about shipping-routes and shipwrecks, to produce a nautical history of medieval Malta, bearing in mind probable constants, such as winds and currents, and the considerable changes in the sea-level, which may have significant effects on small islands and deserve further study.[111] Roughly at the

[104] Statistics *infra*, 53.

[105] Cf. J. Aquilina, 'Race and Language in Malta', in his *Papers*; though the medievalist would wish to revise certain details, this sensible paper separates the issues of 'race' and language, pointing to the prejudices which have bedevilled many issues involved.

[106] F. Braudel, *La Méditerranée et le monde méditerranéen à l'époque de Philippe II* (2nd ed: Paris, 1966) [English translation, 2 vols. (London, 1972–1973)].

[107] H. Bowen-Jones, J. Dewdney, W. Fisher, *Malta: Background for Development* (Durham, 1961), with numerous maps, plans, tables and photos; unfortunately, the oft-repeated medieval population figures at pp. 133, 135 are either fictitious or unreliable. See also H. Hyde, *The Geology of the Maltese Islands with special reference to Water Supply . . .* (Malta, 1955); B. Nehring, *Die Maltesischen Inseln* (Tübingen, 1966). The best approach is through the carefully explained plans, models, photographs and specimens in the geology section of the Museum of Natural History at Mdina.

[108] J. Houston, *The Western Mediterranean World: an Introduction to its Regional Landscapes* (London, 1964), 639–643 *et passim*.

[109] B. Blouet, *The Story of Malta* (London, 1967), which provides an excellent introduction to the historical geography by a geographer, manages only 9 pages (pp. 40–48) on the medieval period.

[110] Cf. *supra*, 10–11.

[111] A. Gunther, 'Re-Drawing the Coast Line of Southern Italy: a Survey of Shifting Sea-Levels from Gaeta to Malta, with reference to Paestum', *Illustrated London News*, 244 (1964), 86–89; his chart is reproduced in *Missione 1963*, fig. 1 (2).

centre of the long east-west axis of the Mediterranean, Malta lies to one side of the narrow channel between Sicily and Tunisia which divides the Eastern and Western Mediterranean, and only if fortified does it effectively control Mediterranean shipping. Gozo is 80 kilometres south of the nearest landfall in Sicily, and Malta is some 380 kilometres from Tunis, so that the islands are close to both Sicilian and African harbours; but they were not an essential port-of-call on any major route,[112] and in fact, despite Malta's excellent deep-water harbours and the shelter they could offer, much medieval shipping probably sought to avoid shipwreck or pirates there.[113] The compass presumably made Malta not only easier to find but also easier to avoid. Through most of the middle ages Malta was controlled from Sicily, and what the rulers of Sicily ultimately feared was that it would fall into enemy hands; the textbook repetition of assertions concerning its role as a 'strategic cross-roads' do not really apply to the medieval period.

Set in one of the great 'liquid plains' of the inland sea, at approximately 36° North and 14° East, Malta and Gozo cover 243 and 69 square kilometres respectively. The islets of Comino, Cominotto and Filfla were normally uninhabited. Containing roughly 30 inhabitants per square kilometre, assuming a population of 10,000, the islands were formed of various types of soft limestone rock which is easy to quarry and build with; it also decays into fertile natural soil. A layer of impermeable blue clay regulates the water supply; the mineral resources are negligible. Malta is 37 kilometres in length and slopes down from the high cliffs which face south-west to the coastlines facing east, where the cracks and ridges that run across the island form inlets which often make good harbours but are hard to defend. There, to the east, lay the Grand Harbour with its medieval port at Birgu. Malta is far from being flat, and the ancient town of Mdina, with its suburb known as Rabat, is set on a ridge to the west overlooking much of the island; the highest point is 258 metres above sea-level. In the south and south-east is a plateau with soft undulating hills crossed by *wieds* or water-courses, while the much hillier north-western part of the island, isolated by a cliff known as the Great Fault, tended to be thinly populated.[114] Gozo, separated from Malta by some five kilometres of sea, lacks good harbours but its clay is deeper and therefore more fertile; it has a number of strangely flat-topped hills and, unlike Malta, the modern villages tend to be built along ridges. The summer can be extremely hot and enervatingly humid, especially when the *xlokk* or *scirocco* blows in from the Sahara. Really cold weather and frosts are rare. The winter is variable, bringing most of the rain at an average annual precipitation of 58 centimetres which can, however, fall catastrophically low. In 1473 the population was threatening to flee as the crops would not grow for lack of rain: *ex quo non pluit et tucti li seminati su suchj.*[115] Much of the island was always bare, rocky and windswept, and deforestation had undoubtedly encouraged the erosion of precious earth and affected the water-supply. There were a number of springs, and at Mdina water was stored in cisterns.[116] Quintin stated in 1533 that the water was brackish, that the springs

[112] Cf. Luttrell, in *Melita Historica*, iii. 74–78.

[113] St. Paul and many others would have disagreed with Godechot, 7: 'pendant des siècles, tout navigateur a eu la certitude de trouver dans l'île un refuge assuré contre la tempête ou contre le pirate, . . .'

[114] Cf. *infra*, 181 and n. 3.

[115] Text of 1473 in Leopardi, in *Melita Historica*, ii. 255.

[116] Bosio, iii. 30.

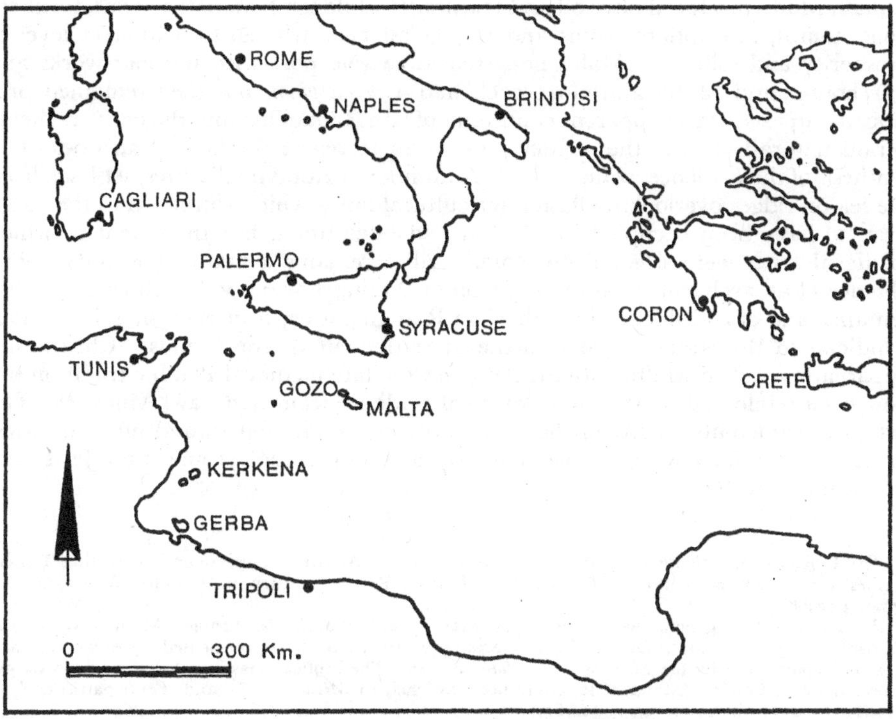


FIG. I. MALTA IN THE CENTRAL MEDITERRANEAN

often dried up in summer, and that drinking water came from tanks and ditches; he also remarked that the summer dust had a bad effect on the eyes.

The evidence of prehistoric occupation in the form of giant temples and strange 'cart-tracks' in the bare rock must have been visible in various parts of the islands, and many medieval place-names referred to ancient ruins and Roman towers,[117] but otherwise its lively prehistoric and ancient past can have impinged little on Malta's medieval inhabitants.[118] By about 1000 BC the vegetation was already much as it is today, with grass, weeds, some shrubs and a very little pine and olive; Malta had few trees.[119] The scrub was important since, in the absence of wood, twigs and thistles were collected for fuel.[120] The Phoenicians arrived in about the ninth century BC and used Malta's harbours as part of a network of Mediterranean trade. Malta subsequently became a colony of Carthage and, in the third century, of Rome. For hundreds of years the islands were a base for pirates, who often wintered there.[121]

[117] Examples *infra*, 195–199; on Roman towers, see also M. Cagiano de Azevedo, in *Missione 1963*, 20–22.

[118] The prehistory has attracted extensive attention; the standard work is J. Evans, *The Prehistoric Antiquities of the Maltese Islands: a Survey* (London, 1971). D. Trump, *Malta: An Archaeological Guide* (London, 1972), provides an excellent, well-illustrated introduction to pre-medieval Malta.

[119] Pollen analysis from an excavation in water-logged clay: *Museum Report 1961*, 8.

[120] Texts in Valentini, in *ASM*, viii. 495–496 (1450); Bosio, iii. 30 (1524).

[121] J. Busuttil, 'Maltese Harbours in Antiquity', and 'Pirates in Malta', both in *Melita Historica*, v no. 4 (1971).

Roman Malta produced olive oil and textiles,[122] while temples, baths, villas, fortifications, tombs, inscriptions, coins and wrecks all bear witness to a discreet level of prosperity and culture. Malta possessed an active port with harbour-works and warehouses, and Malta and Gozo each had a *municipium*, but they remained provincial outposts. The apparent continuity of late Roman life into the early medieval period naturally causes the medieval historian to regret the lack of an up-to-date synthesis of the evidence available.[123] A number of Roman villa sites, set back from the sea on ridges overlooking flatter agricultural lands which run down to the coast, seem to have been occupied in Muslim and later times, but the extent to which medieval *casali* were situated on Roman villas remains a matter for study. The absence of an archaeological map of Roman Malta showing villas, roads and other remains, and of collections of datable late Roman pottery from such sites, is a serious handicap to the study of early medieval settlement in the islands. Christianity apparently reached Malta with St. Paul and the late medieval Pauline tradition has now been reinforced by the archaeological evidence from San Pawl Milqi.[124] The extensive catacombs, many of them probably of the late fourth and fifth centuries, provide Christian, Jewish and pagan inscriptions and symbols; some of the Jews were Greek-speaking.[125]

[122] M. Rossignani, 'Note sui pressoi', in *Missione 1965*. Analysis of specimens shows that Roman textiles were of flax, not cotton: J. Busuttil, 'The Maltese Textile Industry in Antiquity', *Melita Historica*, iv no. 3 (1966).

[123] The standard general works are still A. Mayr, *Die Insel Malta im Altertum* (Munich, 1909), and T. Ashby, 'Roman Malta', *Journal of Roman Studies*, v (1915), to be supplemented by excavation and museum reports, and by the *Missione . . . a Malta, passim*. The Biblical, classical and patristic texts are collected by E. Coleiro, 'Malta nelle letterature classiche', in *Missione 1963*, and 'Fonti patristiche', in *Missione 1966*; on the coins, *supra*, 9 n. 63.

[124] M. Cagiano de Azevedo, *Testimonianze archeologiche della tradizione paolina a Malta* (Rome, 1966). The medieval commentators on the biblical text recording Paul's Maltese visit (*Acts*, xxvii–xxviii) apparently showed little interest in Malta, but detailed researches in the commentaries might conceivably throw light on the cult's establishment. The excavation of the buildings and rebuildings at S. Pawl provides rather strong evidence (summarized *infra*, 93–95) for an early-medieval tradition, broken ca. 870 but revived after ca. 1200. The reading and interpretation of the S. Pawl graffiti and their iconography is highly controversial; see M. Guarducci and M. Cagiano de Azevedo, in *Archeologia classica*, xviii (1966), 144–151, 305–306; xix (1967), 177–183; and in *Aevum*, xl (1966), 565–566. Written evidence for the tradition, possibly fostered by the religious orders which mostly reached Malta in the 15th century (*infra*, 63–64), is late: correct the erroneous details in *Missione 1963*, 141. *Beniarrad* is first found as *Benerandu* in 1400: Palermo, Archivio di Stato, Cancelleria 38, f. 64v–65v. The church is first documented, and that in a late copy, as *in contrata sancti Pauli tal Bincichi* in 1448 (later as *Bindichi*), and as *ad Milchi* (Maltese *Milghqi*) only in 1616: texts in Marchi, in *Missione 1964*, 29–32. The Pauline dedication of the cathedral is documented in 1299: text in course of publication by H. Bresc. An image of St. Paul was reported to be stamped on a bell at Mdina cathedral made in Venice in 1370: text of 1645 in A. Mifsud, in *La Diocesi*, ii (1917/8), 76–77. A cemetery at Rabat had been dedicated to St. Paul by 1372: text in H. Bresc, in *Papers of the British School at Rome*, xli, doc. 36. Only 58 out of some 1600 Maltese Christians in the 1419/20 militia list were named Paulu; none was named Publius: G. Wettinger, in *Melita Historica*, v. 86. Only 11 of the island's 411 churches were dedicated to St. Paul in 1575: M. Buhagiar, in *Scientia* [Malta], xxxv (1972), 27.

[125] E. Becker, *Malta Sotterranea: Studien zur altchristlichen und jüdischen Sepulkralkunst* (Strassburg, 1913); see also A. Ferrua, 'Antichità cristiane: le catacombe di Malta,' *Civiltà Cattolica*, iii quaderno 2381 (3 Sept. 1949); G. Agnello, 'Le catacombe di Sicilia e di Malta e le loro caratteristiche strutturali', *Atti del XV Congresso di Storia dell'Architettura* (Rome, 1970); see also Trump, 77–78, 87–89, 114–117, 132. The problems of the catacombs, and their design, decoration and iconography, are bedevilled by the loss of various inscriptions and uncertainty as to the provenance of others. Further study of the catacombs, their typology, inscriptions and lamps, seems essential for early medieval Maltese history.

Even the outline of Malta's post-Roman history remains extremely hypothetical. Sixty-five bronze coins found in a hoard at Rabat in 1961 date, with one marginal exception, to the years 352–360. Some were struck at Rome, but the rest all seem to come from Eastern mints; this may suggest administrative as opposed to economic connections with the East, since bronze coins were used locally for small change rather than in international commerce.[126] Malta may have been conquered from Africa by the Vandals who invaded Sicily and held it for a while in the mid-fifth century. There is only one piece of written evidence indicating a possible Vandal presence but it does not explicitly mention Malta,[127] and the excavations so far conducted suggest no abrupt changes; five Vandal and eleven Ostrogothic coins in the National Museum date to the fifth and sixth centuries, but their provenance is uncertain.[128] It seems probable that towards the end of the fifth century, as Roman dominion itself evaporated, Malta came under the distant control of the Ostrogothic rulers who succeeded the Vandals in Italy, and that it then passed into the Byzantine sphere of influence. The Byzantine general Belisarius possibly 'touched' the island in 533 on his way to campaign against the Vandals in Africa, and the Byzantines conquered Sicily in 535. A number of North African Christians, fleeing before the Berbers, possibly reached Malta in 544; probably by 553 and certainly by 592 Malta had a bishop. Ecclesiastical organization was connected with Sicily and controlled from Rome; there may have been monasteries on Malta and a papal estate on Gozo. The Sicilian connection is clear, and both Sicily and much of Italy belonged to a world which was being extensively Hellenized under Byzantine control. Early in the seventh century Malta and Gozo figured in a list of Sicilian towns; by 637 Malta had a *dux*; and a seventh- or eighth-century seal shows that there was also a *droungarios* and *archon*, perhaps some sort of military or naval commander. Byzantine Malta was a place of exile, and possibly a minor naval base; it was strong enough to hold out against the Muslims until 870. Its bishops were attached to the province of Sicily which itself passed under the ecclesiastical jurisdiction of Constantinople, probably in 756 or soon after.[129]

The written sources give no picture of life in Byzantine Malta. There was a system of heavy round towers, built in Roman times, which seem to have been both defensive and, since they were inter-visible, to have acted as look-out and signalling stations, but they are difficult to date. That at Ta' Gawhar was probably destroyed in an accidental fire around the year 300, while the site of another, at Ta' Cieda, was later used for numerous Muslim burials.[130] Some of the Muslim graves uncovered at Rabat rested directly on Roman floors and pavements (fig. 2; plate 6b), and the excavations at Tas-Silġ and San Pawl Milqi also suggest a continuity of occupation on late Roman sites which remained largely undisturbed until the Arab incursions of the ninth century; the stratification at San Pawl gives a picture of gradual decline

[126] *Museum Report 1961*, 8–10; Mr. Terence Volk kindly advised on the situation of the major Roman mints in this period.

[127] *Infra*, 71–72.

[128] Details in *Museum Report 1956/57*, 8–10.

[129] The best treatment of the Byzantine period was that in Mayr, while J. Busuttil, 'Fonti greche per la storia delle Isole Maltesi', in *Missione 1968*, collects, without comment, many of the written sources; see now T. Brown *infra*.

[130] Details in *Museum Report 1960*, 6–7 and plates I–IV; *Missione 1963*, 21–22; Trump, *Malta*, 87, 89–91, 121, 128; *infra*, 183–184.

interrupted finally by the Muslim catastrophe, at which point a layer of ash and burnt materials covered the Byzantine pottery.[131] There was apparently a basilica, possibly with baptistery, at Tas-Silġ, and presumably there were other Byzantine churches elsewhere, including some of the rock-cut churches associated with early Christian catacombs.[132] A great deal of Byzantine pottery was scattered across the sites at San Pawl Milqi and Tas-Silġ;[133] this material awaits detailed study, in which recent advances in the dating of late Roman pottery and lamps should make greater precision possible.[134] Other materials include the Byzantine coins in the islands'

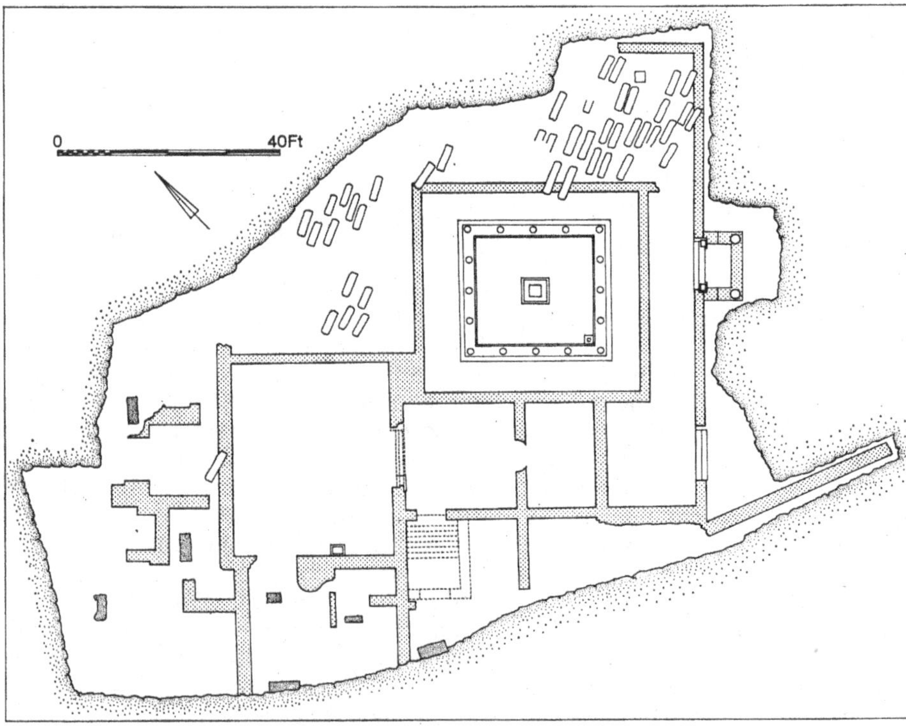


FIG. 2. THE MUSLIM CEMETERY OUTSIDE MDINA SHOWING MUSLIM GRAVES RESTING DIRECTLY ON THE FOUNDATIONS OF A ROMAN HOUSE
(Redrawn from E. L. Galizia's excavation plan of 1881; compare with plate 6b)

[131] In addition to M. Cagiano de Azevedo, *infra*, 88–95, see *Missione 1964*, 133–134; on the Rabat graves, see *Museum Report 1921/22*, 5; and for coin evidence of similar continuity at the Marsa, see Ashby, 28–29.

[132] *Infra*, 89–93, 163–170; for details of a possible Byzantine church at Tad-Dejr, see also *Museum Report 1926/27*, p. ix; *1933/34*, p. ix; and *infra* plate 5a.

[133] On S. Pawl, *Missione 1964*, 134, 150–154; *1966*, 72, 75; on Tas-Silġ, T. Martinelli Coco, 'Ceramica romana e bizantina . . .', *Missione 1969*, and *Missione, passim*. On a fragment apparently comparable with Roman 'Forum Ware' and possibly datable to the 7th–9th centuries, see *Missione 1968*, 83; fig. 6 (3); tavola 17 (3). On such wares and their Mediterranean distribution, which includes Syracuse, see O. Mazzucato, *La Ceramica a vetrina pesante* (Rome, 1972), 47, 69 *et passim*.

[134] Cf. J. Hayes, *Late Roman Pottery* (London, 1972), studying African 'Red Slip Ware' until ca. 700; the Maltese material is discussed and placed in context.

museums.[135] The San Pawl villa was presumably occupied until the late ninth century, and it was fortified. There was no church there, but the very controversial graffiti which were found may point to Christian occupation, though they can only be dated on hypothetical iconographic grounds. One seems to show a ship, possibly meant to be that of St. Paul, attributable from the style of its rigging to the sixth century onwards. Another may represent St. Paul holding a stick which, iconographically, suggests an origin in an Egyptian monastery at some point in or after the fifth century; this motif could have reached Malta as the result of one of a succession of emigrations from Africa.[136]

To the archaeological evidence and the graffiti are to be added a number of hypotheses. It has been suggested that the 'Siculo-Byzantine' church of San Ciro, allegedly datable to the immediate post-Muslim period, was built on pre-Muslim foundations;[137] that certain paintings can be dated to before 870;[138] that the name of the Gozitan fishing port of Xlendi derives from the Byzantine *xelandion* or long-ship;[139] that Maltese building techniques were influenced from Syria and Anatolia;[140] that certain Maltese churches were dedicated to Egyptian or Oriental saints such as Ciro and Catherine;[141] and that the survival of six Greek liturgical terms in modern Maltese shows that the Greek rite was used in Maltese churches from the fourth century onwards.[142] Some of these suggestions are not inherently improbable. The difficulty is that while many of them have been used to support each other, none of them can actually be proved. There is one notice of Africans fleeing 'to the islands', which probably included Malta, and it seems plausible that there were contacts with Cirenaica or Tunisia, but there is no decisive evidence to support theories concerning the immigration of colonists from Egypt or Syria. Very few dedications of Maltese churches can be documented before the fifteenth century, while Maltese rural building styles could have come from Tunisia rather than the Levant, and in any case they were determined by the materials locally available. San Ciro could have been built on top of an earlier, Byzantine, church; the style of Maltese rock-cut churches could indirectly have been influenced from Anatolia by way of Southern Italy; Xlendi could derive from *xelandion*, though it might have come from the Italian *scialando* which also

[135] The provisional classification at the Cathedral Museum in Mdina should now be revised in the light of P. Grierson, *Catalogue of the Byzantine Coins in the Dumbarton Oaks Collection and in the Whittemore Collection*, ii part 1 (Washington, 1968); the provenance of these coins is uncertain and they await proper study. The Byzantine coins in the Gozo Museum do not come from Gozo. The Byzantine lead seal found in Gozo (*Museum Report 1960*, 13) is edited *infra*, 87 and in plate 5b and c.

[136] In addition to references *supra*, 20 n. 124, see *Missione 1965*, 120–121; *1968*, 112–113. Events at S. Pawl may seem less obscure when the pottery has been studied in detail.

[137] V. Bonello, 'La chiesa bizantina di S. Ciro a Malta', *Brutium*, xvii no. 1 (1938) [and, as 'La chiesa siculo-bizantina . . .', in *Malta*, no. 15, 225 (18 Dec. 1937)].

[138] R. Bonnici Calì, 'Saint Luke's Madonnas in Malta', *Scientia* [Malta], xv (1949); his unconvincing hypotheses are based on 'traditions' such as that of the African Augustinians who fled from the Vandals and inscribed Greek letters on an ikon at Mellieha in Malta.

[139] Aquilina, *Papers*, 234.

[140] See *infra*, 55 n. 290.

[141] Eg. Bonello, in *Brutium*, xvii no. 1, 6; M. Buhagiar, 'The Cult of St. Catherine of Alexandria in Malta', *Scientia* [Malta], xxxv (1972), 25–26.

[142] P. Saydon, 'Traces of the Byzantine Rite in the Church of Mal ta', *Melita Theologica*, vii (1954), 47–48. G. Lupi, 'Il rito greco a Malta', in *La chiesa greca in Italiadall' VIII al XVI secolo* (Padua, 1973), summarizes usefully much of the varied evidence for Oriental influences.

means ship; and the six Greek liturgical terms could have been in the language before 870. But even if these hypotheses were correct they would only indicate a Byzantine presence, not Oriental colonization; they involve assumptions concerning the uncertain continuity of Christian life during several hundred years of Muslim predominance; and, in fact, they remain unproved.

Behind many of these assumptions and hypotheses lies a lengthy and inconclusive philological debate. The general absence of pre-Arabic place-names suggests a decisive break in and after 870. The theory, advanced by P. Saydon, that a corrupt form of Latin was used in Malta before 870 is based largely on the names *Malta* and *Għawdex*, or Gozo, and only four other toponyms, including Skala and Pwales allegedly derived from *scala* a harbour and *palus* a swamp;[143] this argument has found little acceptance. As against Saydon's six Maltese liturgical or ecclesiastical terms of Greek origin, which include *Lapsi* for Ascension, and *miru* for chrism or confirmation, Aquilina presented other Maltese liturgical words, such as *knisja* for church and *qassis* for priest, which he held must be of 'Christian Arabic', possibly Maronite, derivation.[144] This might be correct, but none of the liturgical terms under discussion is documented for the early period and such words could have arrived in a number of ways; variations of *knisja*, for example, could have come directly from Berber Arabic.[145] Abela noted traces of Greek in the Maltese language in 1647,[146] but all these words are really known in modern or early modern rather than medieval Maltese, and their earliest appearance is not documented. Much the same is true of the place-name evidence. Greek influences might have come in various ways, from Sicily after 1090 or from the numerous Greeks in Malta from 1530 onwards; in 1575 there was a Greek priest in Malta who had been ordained in Cairo.[147] One place-name, Wied-ir-Rum meaning the Valley of the Christians, is documented in 1467 as *guedirrum*,[148] and references of both 1472 and 1476 to *la porta di li grechi* or *porta grecorum*, through which rubbish was being conveyed at Mdina, might also suggest a Greek presence, but they neither prove nor date it.[149]

The absence of contemporary texts on which to base philological hypotheses concerning what language was spoken on pre-Muslim Malta inevitably makes this discussion a most unsatisfactory one. It is important, therefore, to publish all the 500 or more surnames and nicknames and the more than 3,200 place-names, practically all of which have been drawn from notarial and other documents dating before 1545. These names reflect a strong Arab, and particularly Berber or Tunisian, influence surviving well into the fifteenth century. They include *qā'id*, *sharīf* and other words

[143] P. Saydon, 'The Pre-Arabic Latin Element in Maltese Toponymy', *Orbis*, v (1956). J. Busuttil, 'Marsa', *Orbis*, xxi (1972), argues that four names composed of *Marsa* (Arabic: harbour) plus an earlier toponym (eg. Marsamxett) are basically pre-Arabic. Its intrinsic merits apart, this argument is based on texts of 1442, 1465, 1551 etc., whereas earlier forms are available from the immediately post-Muslim period, eg. *Marza Mosecto* in 1296 (*Compasso da Navigare*, 112).

[144] J. Aquilina, 'Maltese Christian Words of Arabic Origin', in *Congrès arabo-berbère*.

[145] W. Vycichl, 'Les études chamito-sémitiques', in *Congrès arabo-berbère*, 132–133.

[146] J. Cassar Pullicino, 'G. F. Abela and the Maltese Language', in *Abela Essays*, 33.

[147] See Dusina's examinations of Greek priests and their rites: Visitation (discussed *supra*, 8 n. 53) at f. 251–256.

[148] *Infra*, 99 n. 14; whether *Rum* referred specifically to Greeks or more generally to Christians is debatable.

[149] Texts in Leopardi, in *Melita Historica*, ii. 191–192 (1472), 194 (1476).

for governing officials; the name for new Muslims of non-Arabic extraction; and so forth.[150] With such material, each word documented and dated, the philological discussions could be renewed on ground much closer to the subject of debate. Meanwhile, to the historian, the most probable explanation for the various terms derived from Islamic religious practice—such as *Randan*, from the Arabic *Ramaḍān*, used in Christian Maltese for 'Lent'—which are now found in the religious parlance of the modern Maltese, is simply that such phrases remained in the language when the islands' inhabitants abandoned Islam, but not their Semitic tongue, in the thirteenth century. Greek, Hebrew or Punic elements may have infiltrated the language in comparatively modern times; alternatively they may already have been established in the islanders' speech or have been preserved among minority groups of Christians or Jews, though positive evidence for the survival of such groups during the Muslim period is almost completely lacking. It has been argued that in 870 there was still a strong sub-foundation of Punic,[151] which might account for the ease with which Arabic was, presumably, assimilated and for the strength which Maltese has shown by its subsequent survival as a fundamentally Semitic language; there were Greek-speaking elements, at least in ecclesiastical and in administrative circles; and there is no reason why Latin and Hebrew[152] should not have been current as well. Malta has almost always been a place where several languages were spoken.

The rise of Islam and the consequent shifts in the balance of Mediterranean power naturally affected Malta and Gozo which, with Sicily, moved into an African sphere of influence. The Maltese evidence must be interpreted against events in Africa, where Christian Roman provinces were overrun by Arab conquerors whose empires were, however, far from monolithic; Berbers resisted Arabs, and dynasty fought dynasty. Islam took to the sea in the seventh century, but Greek fire and superior naval techniques enabled the Byzantines to defend their vital sea-lanes and to control Sicily and the Central Mediterranean. The Muslims were raiding Sicily before 700, in which year they took Pantelleria and built a naval base at Tunis, but then they were diverted by conquests in the Mahgrib and in Spain.[153] Later, when the Aghlabid rulers of Tunisia began their overseas conquests, Malta presumably came increasingly under pressure; yet it held out. The Muslims captured Palermo in 831, and there is a reference to a raid on 'the islands near Sicily' in 836 by Abu

[150] G. Wettinger, 'Arabo-Berber Influences in Malta: Onomastic Evidence', in *Congrès arabo-berbère*; cf. his other articles *infra* and elsewhere (*infra*, 53 n. 270, 68 n. 374).

[151] Punic and neo-Punic finds, especially those from Tas-Silġ, still await study. It is doubtful if any inscription can yet be dated later than ca. 100 AD at the latest: cf. V. Borg – B. Rocco, 'L'ipogeo di Tac-Caghki a Malta', *Sicilia Archeologica*, v (1972). Other proposed evidence for later Punic survivals is debatable; see Cassar Pullicino, in *Congrès arabo-berbère*, and P. Grech, 'Are there any Traces of Punic in Maltese?' *Journal of the Faculty of Arts: Royal University of Malta*, i (1961).

[152] In addition to Jewish inscriptions (*supra*, 20), the toponyms *Malta, Goder* and *Ghuxa* might be Hebrew in derivation, according to Aquilina, *Papers*, 195-197; but only *Malta* is documented in the early period.

[153] The African background to medieval Malta requires expert study not provided in this volume, but see especially M. Talbi, *L'Émirat aghlabide 184–296/800–909: Histoire politique* (Paris, 1966); H. Idris, *La Berbérie orientale sous les Zīrīdes: Xe–XIIe siècles*, 2 vols. (Paris, 1959); H. Brunschvig, *La Berbérie orientale sous les Hafsides des origines à la fin du XVe siècle*, 2 vols. (Paris, 1940–1947); see also E. Rossi, *Storia di Tripoli e della Tripolitania dalla conquista araba al 1911* (Rome, 1968). For recent summaries, consult *Cambridge History of Islam*, 2 vols. (Cambridge, 1970); for general Mediterranean developments, including the important works of A. Lewis, H. Arhweiler and E. Eickhoff, see T. Brown *infra*.

al-Aghlab, who took 'great booty'. Almost certainly the conquest of Malta did not take place until 870, and then it came from Sicily and met notable resistance. The sources are somewhat confused, but they suggest a Muslim occupation or siege in 869 which may have failed to take a citadel, perhaps at Mdina; a Byzantine attempt at relief or reconquest, which received the support of the Christian population; and a definitive Muslim conquest in 870 by the Aghlabid governor of Muslim Sicily, with subsequent retaliations against the inhabitants. The tenth century is an almost complete blank. In 1038 the Byzantine general George Maniaces attempted to recapture Sicily and, probably soon afterwards, there was a Byzantine attack on Malta which, according to the Arabic writer al-Qazwīnī, the Muslims beat back with the help of the servile population.[154] Forty years later, however, resistance to the Norman Count Roger was very feeble, and Muslim Malta and Gozo entered a period of subjection to the Christian rulers of Sicily which lasted until the Latin colonization of the islands and the expulsion or conversion of many Muslims in the thirteenth century.

Muslim rule is almost as sparsely documented as that of the Byzantine dominion it replaced. A few Arabic texts provide a little information;[155] there is no useful evidence in Greek;[156] and the Hebrew sources have so far proved disappointing.[157] Further researches in Arab archives and libraries may produce more information, as in the case of the text concerning the marble columns exported to Tunisia from Malta after 870.[158] The known Maltese inscriptions, some in Kufic script, provide little more than a few names, dates and Koranic quotations, and they cannot profitably be studied philologically, though the style of the lettering and the decoration would repay investigation.[159] Furthermore, a good part of this material relates to the period after the Norman 'conquest' of 1090. The archaeological evidence, which could be increased considerably, must be used to confirm and expand the picture derived from the written sources. The excavations at Tas-Silġ and San Pawl Milqi both testify, in a somewhat uncertain way, to destructions and rebuildings which fit

[154] T. Brown, *infra*, 84–85, with translation and discussion of al-Qazwīnī; Amari's version (*Biblioteca*, . 240–241) falsified the issue by giving 'Maltese' where the text has 'slaves'. The Byzantine attack, dated to 1049/50 by al-Qazwīnī, probably took place a decade earlier.

[155] Texts scattered through Amari, *Biblioteca*; many are reproduced, at least in part, with the original Arabic text in P. Minganti, 'Fonti storiche arabe', in *Missione 1964*. Another collection, based on other editions and mss., appears in French translation only in M. Redjala, 'L'archipel maltais dans la littérature historico-géographique d'expression arabe à l'époque médiévale', in *Congrès arabo-berbère*. A group of texts describing Malta as inhabited only by sheep and donkeys apparently results from a confusion, and should be ignored. A new *corpus*, based on the mss. and accompanied by accurate literal translations, is a *desideratum*.

[156] T. Brown, *infra*, 81–82, 86.

[157] Malta is not mentioned in S. Goitein, *A Mediterranean Society: the Jewish Communities of the Arab World as portrayed in the Documents of the Cairo Geniza*, 2 vols. (Berkeley, Cal., 1967–1971); these documents provide plentiful evidence for Mediterranean contacts from the 10th to 13th centuries.

[158] *Infra*, 83–84.

[159] 18 inscriptions mostly from Rabat, published with photographs and translations in E. Rossi, 'Le lapidi sepocrali arabo-musulmane di Malta', *Rivista degli studi orientali*, xii (1929/30). Rossi, 431 n. 1, denies the existence of the inscription, cited by Caruana, *Frammento*, 458, concerning a *hakim* or Muslim governor supposedly found at Saqqajja (Rabat) in 1881 which allegedly read: 'piange l'infedeltà della popolazione di Malta'. Yet this supposition is still being repeated, eg. in A. Bonnici, *History of the Church in Malta*, i (Malta, 1967), 59, as a proof for the assertion that 'the greater part of the Maltese remained loyal to their old Faith'.

with a period of several decades of Arab raids previous to a definite conquest in 870. A mosque may have been constructed in the Byzantine baptistery at Tas-Silġ, while the Arabs destroyed the villa at San Pawl Milqi and installed themselves in the ruins where they constructed crude fortifications, leaving fragments of glazed pottery and amphora.[160] The older excavations were never scientifically published. The investigations of Roman buildings just outside Mdina were begun in 1881 and continued in and after 1920. They revealed a Muslim cemetery with numerous graves, many of them built directly on top of Roman floors (fig. 2; plate 6b). The tombs were usually made of small roughly-squared stones and were covered by sawn stone slabs. The sawing technique was never Maltese and suggests foreign workmanship, while the contrast between the grander and poorer graves points to considerable social divisions. There were apparently some wooden coffins held together by iron clamps, and fragments of pottery; the bodies were buried east-west lying on their side with the head at the west, facing south. Apart from the inscriptions, the only other object found was a solid silver ring inscribed *Rabbī Allāh wāḥid*—'My Lord is one God'; the fifty skulls preserved for anthropological investigations seem not to have survived World War II. A number of other Muslim tombs have subsequently been uncovered at Rabat, the suburb of Mdina, and elsewhere.[161]

The question of Christian survival during the Muslim period is as tricky as it is important. Christians are not mentioned in the surviving evidence, and no Bishop of Malta is known between 878 and 1156. Mayr argued long ago that the slaves who resisted the Byzantines in or around 1049/50 were presumably not Christians; that the Christians described by the chronicler Malaterra as being at Malta in 1090 were certainly not indigenous Maltese; and that the island remained Muslim during the twelfth and early thirteenth centuries.[162] The general rule of Muslim tolerance, as exercized in Sicily for example, may not have been followed in Malta. The island seems to have resisted invasion for a long period, and a Christian revolt in 869/70 could well have provoked a harsh Muslim reaction; the Bishop of Malta was in chains at Palermo in 878, and there is the archaeological evidence for destructions at Tas-Silġ and San Pawl Milqi. The curious story according to which the numerous slaves of the Muslim regime joined with their rulers to resist the Byzantines in about 1050 and were given a measure of freedom as a result, suggests that they may not have been predominantly Christian, but it does seem likely that some at least were

[160] *Infra*, 88–95; Cagiano de Azevedo, *Testimonianze*, 54–56; *Missione 1964*, 151, 183; *1965*, 162; *1966*, 120; *1968*, 84–85, 113; *1969*, 134; *1970*, 99–100; *et passim.*

[161] T. Zammit, 'Excavations at Rabat, Malta', *Antiquaries Journal*, iii (1923), 219, and *idem*, 'Saracenic Remains in Malta', *Melita*, v (1925), 1–2, contain only the most summary accounts; see also *Museum Report 1921/22*, 5; *1924/25*, p. iv; *1925/26*, p. v; *1956/57*, 7; *1957/58*, 9 (seven tombs: plates V, VI, VII); *1959/60*, 6 (near Marsaxlokk); *1960*, 6 (Ta'Cieda). A very similar grave is illustrated in J. Lacam, *Les sarrazins dans le haut moyen-âge français: histoire et archéologie* (Paris, 1965), 76–77. Fig. 2 is based on the map of 1881 in A. A. Caruana, *Recent Discoveries at Notabile* (Malta, 1881); it does not record T. Zammit's discoveries of 1920–1925, but these are now being partially reconstructed from Zammit's notebooks and photographs preserved in the National Museum at Valletta, where the Director, Mr. Francis Mallia, and the Curator, Mr. Tancred Gouder, generously provided every assistance. A study of the pottery, now in the Roman Villa Museum at Rabat, is also planned. The Arabic coins in the National Museum at Valletta lack secure provenance (Sant, 17–20), though a group is known to have been found at Mdina in 1698 (details in Abela – Ciantar, i. 692–693; ii. 96–97).

[162] A. Mayr, 'Zur Geschichte der älteren christlichen Kirche von Malta', *Historisches Jahrbuch*, xvii (1896), 486–496.

captive Christians from other lands, just as there were many Christian captives at Malta in 1090. There is no hint that Roger the Norman found any indigenous Christians to welcome or collaborate with him in 1090; Malta was described as being inhabited by Saracens in 1175, and the report of about 1241, probably made after the 'expulsion' of the Muslims, showed that there were still at least 836 Muslim families on the two islands.[163] It seems, therefore, most unlikely that any significant community of Christians survived through some three centuries or more of Muslim predominance, which is not however to deny the possibility of an underground and undocumented persistence of a Christian element which cherished its traditions in the way the Pauline cult, or some memory of it, was apparently kept alive at San Pawl Milqi. In North Africa, the indigenous Christians were much reduced in numbers, more by isolation than by persecution, but they did survive into the eleventh and twelfth centuries as tributaries paying the *jizya* or capitation tax.[164] In Malta such Christians would presumably have followed the Byzantine rite, as in Sicily, but what language they would have spoken it is impossible to say; speech, religion and 'race' did not necessarily coincide. Malta was very much smaller than Sicily, so that sweeping changes are more likely on Malta; and, in the absence of real evidence, the Sicilian analogy may be misleading. Other island patterns are possible, such as those on Crete, where a Greek population was ruled by independent Muslim emirs; or Cyprus, which was neutralized and demilitarized; or Mallorca, which remained strongly Muslim and Jewish into the thirteenth century.

At Malta there was a governor, the *qā'id* or *kaid*, and a group of leading Muslim citizens; in about 1050 the servile class apparently outnumbered the free men.[165] Agriculture is likely to have flourished, and it is possible that the Muslims introduced irrigation techniques, cotton and citrus fruits.[166] Malta lay on trade-routes between Sicily and Africa, and there was a Muslim community at Mdina with its cemetery just outside the town. Arab writers dedicated little space to Malta. Their comments are laconic, and some were clearly describing the wrong island; others mention its prosperity, its single town, its harbours, pastures, fruits and honey.[167] Two Arabic poets of Malta, Abū-al-Qāsim-ibn-Ramaḍān and As-Samītī, and the Maltese artisan whom they jointly celebrated for having built a marvellous mechanical clock, probably lived in the mid-eleventh century in the time of *kaid* Yaḥyā, Lord of Malta. Abū-al-Qāsim was apparently the Maltese poet who moved to Palermo and was there refused permission by Count Roger to return to Malta. Another Arabic poet, 'Abd-ar-Raḥmān-ibn-Ramaḍān known as Ibn-as-Sūsī, was born and raised in Malta, possibly in the twelfth century. This small class of educated Maltese evidently moved in a cosmopolitan world. Thus the Maltese Ibn-as-Sūsī, who also

[163] *Infra*, 30–34, 38–40, 82–85.

[164] Brunschvig, i. 430; W. Seston, 'Sur les derniers temps du Christianisme en Afrique', *Mélanges d'archéologie et d'histoire*, liii (1936); C.-E. Dufourcq, *L'Espagne catalane et le Maghrib aux XIIIe et XIVe siècles* (Paris, 1966), 105–106.

[165] *Infra*, 30, 84–85.

[166] According to Blouet, *Malta*, 41, but without evidence. Roman Malta had flax (*supra*, 20 n. 122); cotton is first mentioned in 1164 and then ca. 1320 (*infra*, 53). J. Galea – E. Bonnici, 'Leprosy in Malta', *Leprosy Review*, xxviii (1957), 140, suggest that the Arabs introduced leprosy; the Maltese word for the disease derives from the Arabic.

[167] Cf. texts and comment in Redjala, 203–207.

emigrated from Malta to Palermo, belonged to a family which may have originated from Susa in Africa, and which was also mentioned on an inscription found at Sannat in Gozo.[168] This was carved on a piece of re-used Roman marble which became the beautiful tomb-stone of Maimūna, who died on Thursday 21 March 1174 (plate 6a):

In the name of God the Compassionate and Merciful. God look kindly upon the Prophet Muhammad and his family, and grant them eternal well-being. To God belongs power and everlasting life, and his creatures are destined for death: *And you have a fine example in the Prophet of God.*[169]

This is the tomb of Maimūna, daughter of Hassān, son of Ali 'al-Hudali called Ibn as-Sūsī; she died, may the mercy of God be with her, on the fifth day, the sixteenth of the month of Sha'ban of the year 569, witnessing that there is no God but the only God, who has no equal.

Look around with your eyes. Is there anything in the world which can stay or repel death, or cast a spell upon it? Death took me away from my palace and, alas, neither doors nor bars could save me from it. I have become a pledge, carrying my past deeds with me for my redemption, and that which I have achieved remains.

You who look upon this grave. I am already decayed within it; the dust has covered the lids and sockets of my eyes. In my resting place and in my position in death there is a warning, and at my resurrection when I shall come before my Creator. Oh brother, be excellent and repent.[170]

Muslim predominance at Malta was interrupted by the Norman attack of 1090. The difficulty with the historiography of Malta in the Norman period is, once again, the lack of information. The standard account, based on the traditional sources, is still the article published in 1939 by Roberto Valentini, who considered the post-1090 period as one of Latinization.[171] There is little new material, but notice should be taken of subsequent developments in the whole field of Central Mediterranean history which have altered the general context within which particular events at Malta must be interpreted.[172] The first task is the dismantling of myth and legend, much of it grounded in the prestigious work of Abela who contributed only errors to the history of 'Norman' Malta. Abela turned the Christian slaves present in Malta in 1090 into indigenous Maltese; he provided a bogus list of Norman bishops of Malta lifted uncritically from the Sicilian historian Rocco Pirri; he repeated the story given by Tommaso Fazello that Count Roger built a castle at Mdina; he wrote that Roger fortified a castle by the sea built by the Arabs, and that he restored the 'cathedral' in Malta; he stated that Count Roger personally appointed a bishop, who was then consecrated by the pope; and he produced erroneous evidence for the establishment of a Benedictine community in Malta around 1130. Furthermore Abela alleged that Roger's siege of Mdina lasted three days; that he was aided by indigenous

[168] Texts in Amari, *Biblioteca*, i. 241–242; ii. 433, 446–447; see also *Storia*, ii. 485 n. 1; iii. 218, 702–703, 773–774, 784–785. A certain confusion still surrounds these poets and their dates. On *kaid* Yaḥyā, see C. Seybold, 'Analecta arabo-italica, 4: Malta e Galita in Jāqūt', *Centenario della Nascita di Michele Amari*, ii (Palermo, 1910), 210.

[169] *Koran*, xxxiii. 21.

[170] This translation for which thanks are due to Dr. David Marshall, is based on the text in Rossi, 433; the last section is somewhat obscure.

[171] R. Valentini, 'Il comune demaniale di Malta dall'origine alla crisi sveva', *ASM*, x (1939).

[172] Useful syntheses in *Atti del Congresso Internazionale di Studi sulla Sicilia Normanna* (Palermo, 1973). Much of what is said here appears, in preliminary form here somewhat amended, in A. Luttrell, 'Malta nel periodo normanno', *ibid.* A. Vella, 'I Normanni a Malta', *ibid.*, published after the present work had gone to press, provides a more detailed, more traditional approach; Professor Vella's interpretation will be elaborated, in Maltese, in his forthcoming history of Malta.

Christians; that he expelled some of the Muslim inhabitants from the island; that he left a garrison in Malta and Gozo; and that he settled 'nuovi coloni' in the islands and distributed lands to them. Abela also repeated a 'traditione da' nostri Antenati' that Count Roger chased the Muslims out of Mdina to a place named *Kalaa tal Bahria*, and he mistakenly dated the expulsion of the Muslims from Malṭa to 1127, connecting it with a 'tradition' concerning a Muslim plot.[173] None of this can be proved and most of it is clearly wrong.

Many of these 'traditions' have acquired a place in Maltese folklore and legend. It is still maintained that the 'Christian' Maltese were liberated by Roger the Norman, who settled the archipelago and introduced various Latin institutions from Sicily. The Normans probably became popular precisely because they never attempted to settle the islands and became so remote as no longer to be resented. These fables derived from the misinterpretation of place-names, from politically-inspired fabrications, or from learned antiquarian myth-making. Unfortunately, the whole process of maintaining a Maltese 'national' consciousness in the face of centuries of foreign rulers has encouraged the development of the unspoken assump, tion that there was always a race of Maltese and Gozitans, indigenous and Christian-who differed in some fundamental way from all those who came to exploit or settle the islands. These beliefs largely turn on the Norman period.[174]

The Norman attack of 1090 followed a major change in the Mediterranean balance of power in which Western naval superiority was decisive; the Latins were to capture Jerusalem in 1099. The successful expedition to the great pirate base at Mahdia in Tunisia in 1087 must greatly have weakened the Muslim position on Malta and Gozo, and the Norman conquest of Sicily was completed in 1090. The Normans, already conquerors in France, England and Italy, were aware of Malta's strategic value both as a base from which the Muslims could threaten Sicily and as one from which the Latins themselves would be able to strike at North Africa. A Norman assault on the islands was always likely, and as early as 1071, when the Normans were attacking Catania, they were able to pretend that their real objective was Malta: *fingens se Maltam debellatum ire*. Knowledge of the Norman raid of 1090 depends almost exclusively on the evidently partisan account given by Count Roger's own scribe and chronicler, the French monk Geoffroi or Goffredo Malaterra. Roger made preparations to assemble a fleet, and in July he landed on Malta. His small force overcame the feeble resistance of the inhabitants, the *incolarum multitudo;* he then plundered the island, and advanced on the town at Mdina. The *kaid* and the *cives*, who were unpractised in arms, submitted. They surrendered horses, mules, arms and *infinita peccunia*, and swore according to their own religion to become *confoederati* and pay an annual tribute. The Latins were welcomed by a great multitude of *captivi christiani* whom they actually transported away from Malta towards their homes in various kingdoms. There must have been many fewer Christians in Malta after Roger's invasion than before it. Roger seems to have left Malta almost at once, devastating the island of Gozo, which he also reduced to tributary status, on his way back. Malaterra provided no evidence that there were

[173] Abela, 67, 80–81, 260–269, 302, 388.
[174] Cf. J. Cassar Pullicino *infra*.

indigenous Christians in the islands, that a Latin garrison was left or that any kind of colonization was attempted.[175] It seems likely that Roger never intended to conquer Malta; he was making a reconnaissance in force, a razzia designed to demonstrate his strength, to secure booty and to prevent Malta being used as a Muslim base, a frontier operation which reduced the Muslims of Malta to tributary status.

After 1090 Malta disappears from the documents; presumably it relapsed into the African sphere of influence during the troubles resulting from the minority which followed Count Roger's death in 1101 and the consequent resurgence of Muslim power. Malta had to be conquered again by Roger II in 1127,[176] and the Arab writers Ibn-al-Athīr and an-Nuwayrī both ascribe the conquest of Malta to Roger II.[177] This more definitive conquest of 1127 must be understood in terms of the general revival of commerce in the twelfth century, and of Latin expansion across the whole Mediterranean. After the Sicilians had destroyed the Muslim pirate base on the Tunisian island of Gerba in 1135, Malta acquired, or maintained, a commercial importance of its own as a staging point between Africa and Sicily, as the Siculo-Muslim geographer Idrīsī recognized. The Pisans and, in particular, the Genoese played a leading role in this maritime expansion. Documents on a Genoese presence at Malta are lacking, perhaps because it was too small to be cited explicitly in notarial contracts; however, there was a quantity of Maltese cotton at Genoa in 1164.[178] Piracy doubtless flourished. In about 1184 a Pisan captain seized a Tunisian ship at Malta with the goods aboard it, and threw the crew into the sea.[179] The Sicilian Crown presumably sought fiscal advantages from this general situation, but the evidence is entirely wanting; nothing is known of fortifications, enfeoffments, taxation or a royal *demanium*. Probably there was some sort of local council based on

[175] Gaufredus Malaterra, *De rebus gestis Rogerii* . . . , ed. E. Pontieri, in *Rerum Italicarum Scriptores*, ns. v part 1 (Bologna, 1927), 94–96. The translation of this passage made by Simone da Lentini in 1358 is more or less faithful, but it omits the conquest of Gozo, stating that the Gozitans *si arrinderu a lu Conti pachificamenti, senza dapnu:* text in *La Conquesta di Sichilia fatta per li Normandi translatata per frati Simuni da Lentini*, ed. G. Rossi-Taibbi (Palermo, 1954), 134–140. Capitulations similar to that at Malta were made in Sicily, at Rametta for example: see Malaterra, 33, and *Storia de' Normanni di Amato di Montecassino*, ed. V. de Bartholomaeis (Rome, 1935), 238. The first to confuse the *captivi christiani* of Malaterra with indigenous Maltese seems to have been Abela, 262. Valentini, in *ASM*, x. 191–192, maintains unconvincingly: 'Se tanta gente conservò nella captività la propria fede, trovò certamente assistenza spirituale e conforti in quella parte del popolo maltese che, in attesa di un liberatore, non aveva abiurato.' The conquest of Malta followed that of Noto, which took place in Feb. 1090 according to Malaterra, 93. Other writers date the two conquests to 1091, as suggested by certain Arab sources (Amari, *Storia*, iii. 133 n. 1, 180 n. 1); this date is not impossible. On the incident of 1071, see Malaterra, 52; Simone da Lentini deformed this passage thus: *Lu Conti volia andari a Malta a conquistarila et munstrava di non si curari nenti di Palermu* (ed. Rossi-Taibbi, 72).

[176] *Invaserat enim ac alias Insulas, quarum una Malta vocabatur, cumque ad alias iterum occupandas Insulas, terrasque attonitus persisteret, repente audivit praefatum Ducem Guilielmum ab hac luce Salerni discedisse, qui doluit valde, quod se ignorante defunctus sit, quodque se, ut sibi vivens statuerat, si filium non haberet, haeredem non fecisset. Unde moram non patitur, sed praeparato navali itinere, quantocyus Salernum tetendit.* This text, in Alessandro Telesino, *De rebus gestis Rogerii Siciliae Regis*, ed. L. Muratori, in *Rerum Italicarum Scriptores*, v (Milan, 1724), 617, has been slightly corrected on the basis of the Barcelona ms. (information kindly supplied by Miss Dione Clementi). Duke Guglielmo died on 26 June 1127. The passage in the anonymous *Chronicon Siciliae*, in *ibid.*, x (1727), 813, which says that Count Roger conquered Malta but had to leave the island on account of his brothers' deaths, makes no sense and must be a conflation of Malaterra and Telesino.

[177] Texts in Amari, *Biblioteca*, i. 450; ii. 146; Minganti, 19, fails to make it clear that it was Roger II who was involved.

[178] D. Abulafia, *infra*, 106–108.

[179] Text in M. Amari, *I diplomi arabi del R. Archivio fiorentino* (Florence, 1863), 271–272.

Muslim practice, perhaps similar to that for Pantelleria where, in 1221, the Sicilian Crown accepted an arrangement by which half the tribute was to go to Tunis and all jurisdiction over Muslims was to be in the hands of a Muslim.[180] African coinage, and the Sicilian coins which were based upon it, probably circulated in Malta at least until the mid thirteenth century, when the Latin florin and ducat emerged.[181]

There is no explicit evidence that Latins of any sort were established in Malta before the close of the Norman period in 1194. The Norman rulers repeatedly encouraged the Benedictines to settle the islands of Lipari and Patti as part of a general policy of increasing the productivity of their domains, but the Aeolian islands were uninhabited and uncultivated, and they were not on the African frontier; in any case, the settlement of Lipari was not restricted to *homines lingue latine.*[182] It was not Norman policy to demand the conversion of Muslims in Sicily,[183] and there is no evidence that they did so in Malta which was far from being a desert island. The chief contemporary account is that of Roger II's Muslim geographer Idrīsī: *Malta, a large island with a safe harbour which opens to the east. Malta has a city. It abounds in pasture, flocks, fruit and, above all, honey.* Idrīsī also reported that shipping reached Sicily from Malta and, inaccurately perhaps, that Gozo had a safe harbour.[184] Apart from the Norman expeditions of 1090 and 1127, the first clear reference to a Latin presence in Malta comes with the Pisan visit of about 1184, while the earliest mention of a particular Bishop of Malta, even outside Malta, dates to 1168.[185] Burchard Bishop of Strassburg, who probably touched at the island on his way to Egypt in 1175, recorded Malta as *a Sarracenis inhabitata, et est sub dominio regis Sicilie.*[186] Latin sailors and merchants presumably visited the islands, and there may have been a garrison and perhaps some clergy, but there is no evidence of Latin colonization. The situation changed rapidly after 1194, but at that date the bulk of the population probably remained non-Latin in speech, religion and culture. Malta was never really Norman at all.

Many myths concerning the church in 'Norman' Malta are still repeated as 'traditions'. The story that Count Roger restored the cathedral and bishopric, and that he endowed the episcopal see and elected a bishop who was consecrated by the pope apparently began with the Sicilian Rocco Pirri.[187] The idea that Roger founded canonries and 'benefices', and dictated ecclesiastical legislation is a modern

[180] Text (with incorrect date) in *Monumenta Germaniae Historica: Leges*, sectio IV, ii (Hanover, 1896), 187–189. H. Bresc, 'Pantelleria entre l'Islam et la Chrétienté', *Cahiers de Tunisie*, xix (1971), contains important comparisons with Malta.

[181] The few Norman coins in the Cathedral Museum at Mdina lack provenance.

[182] C. Garufi, 'Per la storia dei secoli XI e XII', *Archivio Storico per la Sicilia Orientale*, ix (1912); L. White, *Latin Monasticism in Norman Sicily* (Cambridge, Mass., 1938), 84–86.

[183] Texts in Amari, *Biblioteca*, i. 450; ii. 146.

[184] Text *ibid.*, i. 53, 75. Idrīsī said that ships reached Scicli in Sicily 'from Calabria, Africa, Malta and many other places'. Valentini, in *ASM*, x. 195, claimed, without justification: 'apprendiamo da Edrisi che le navi di Malta frequentavano quella costa meridionale della Sicilia . . .'

[185] *Infra*, 33 n. 189.

[186] Text in *Monumenta Germaniae Historica: Scriptores*, xxi (Hanover, 1869), 236.

[187] R. Pirri, *Notitiae siciliensium ecclesiarum*, ii part 2 (1st ed.: Palermo, [1641]), 592–593, citing a document then already lost! Pirri's pretences were repeated by Abela, 261–262, 266, 302.

invention.[188] The alleged Norman Bishops of Malta from 1089 onwards who appear in the often-repeated list of Pirri were apparently Bishops of Mileto or *Militensis* in Calabria; in any case, none of them is documented as being in Malta. The post-Muslim Bishopric of Malta is first reliably mentioned in 1156, when it was a suffragan of Palermo, and a certain Johannes Bishop of Malta was active in Sicily from 1168 to 1212.[189] Once again, therefore, Malta had a bishop; he may have visited the island, but there is no evidence that he did so. It is possible that in post-Muslim times a number of pre-Muslim churches were brought back into use;[190] clear evidence is lacking while the archaeological materials provide no precise date for the construction or reconstruction of churches.[191]

More could be done to follow up available clues. For example, in 1647 Abela wrote that a Benedictine named Costantino Gaetano had provided him with an extract from the Benedictine martyrology of Pulsano recording a notice which suggested a monastic foundation in Malta around 1130 at a place associated by Abela with the place known as *Abbatija tad-Dejr;* this story is still accepted. The text given by Abela reads:

> Pridie Kal. Martii, Sancti Iordani Abbatis, discipuli Sancti Ioannis Pulsanensis Abbatis, qui ipsum suscitauit a mortuis in Monasterio Pulsanensi, postea misit ipsum in Melitam Insulam Abbatem, illic vitam haeremiticam duxit, et virtutibus coruscauit.[192]

It was not implausible that at the moment of conquest in 1127 Roger II should have turned to a vigorous new Benedictine congregation to establish a Christian presence in Malta. However, it is known that in 1139 Giordano succeeded San Giovanni de Matera, the founder of the congregation of Pulsano, as Abbot of Pulsano. The passage from the martyrology, which had in fact been transcribed by Giovanni Francesco de Blasiis in 1609, actually opened: *Pridie Kal. Martii. Eodem die Joannis abbatis, discipuli s. Joannis . . .*[193] The remainder of Abela's quotation is correct. The substitution of Giordano for the other Giovanni, also a saint, was not however so fundamental a matter as the near certainty that the *Melita Insula* was the Dalmatian island of Melida which lies across the Adriatic from Pulsano. The *ecclesia sancti*

[188] De Bono, 112–127, provides a crude account of Norman legislation in Sicily without giving the slightest evidence for its application in Malta; he states that Roger introduced feudalism to Malta in 1090 and even claims that Malaterra, 94–96, distinguished between feudal service (*servilis exactio*) and tribute (*data*)!

[189] As convincingly shown in 1896 by Mayr, in *Historisches Jahrbuch*, xvii. 488–492, with documentation and discussion. Bishop *Johannes* was mentioned in 1168 in the chronicle of Ugo Falcando and in a Greek diploma of June 1186 (text in Busuttil, in *Missione 1968*, 23). He subscribed a Greek charter in Latin in 1177: text in P. Collura, *Le più antiche carte dell'archivio capitolare di Agrigento: 1092–1282* (Palermo, 1961), 72. The pretended bishop of 1113 appears as *Johannes Militensis episcopus* in a 14th-century ms.: Madrid, Archivo Histórico Nacional: Ordenes militares, cod. 649B, f. 78 (kindly communicated by Dr. Rudolf Hiestand). Many of the alleged Bishops of Mileto were, in any case, found in false or dubious diplomas; the best list is in L.-R. Ménager, 'L'abbaye bénédictine de la Trinité de Mileto, en Calabre, à l'époque normande', *Bullettino dell'Archivio Paleografico Italiano*, ns. iv–v (1958/9), 65/66 n. 4.

[190] Detailed claims in A. A. Caruana, *Monografia critica della Cattedrale Apostolica di Malta restaurata dal Conte Ruggero il Normanno l'anno 1090* (2nd ed.: Malta, 1899).

[191] *Infra*, 89–95, 163–169.

[192] Abela, 388–389.

[193] Text and ms. tradition in *Vita S. Joannis a Mathera Abbatis Pulsanensis Congregationis Fundatoris*, ed. [A. Pecci] (Putignano, 1938), 76–77; further references in *Bibliotheca Sanctorum*, vi (Rome, 1965), 633–634, 825–828.

*Michaelis in Meleta* was confirmed to the Benedictines of Pulsano in 1177;[194] the monks had already been granted the whole island, on which they had founded a monastery, in 1151.[195]

Trial trenches in selected churches or excavations elsewhere offer the best chances of discovering more about twelfth-century Malta. Evidence or memories of an earlier Christian presence presumably survived at Tas-Silġ. The probable Byzantine basilica there having apparently been occupied and profaned by the Muslims, the Latins seem to have built a crude apsed church, and possibly even a monastic foundation, close by the earlier basilica; a number of tombs and a scattering of glazed and other pottery were found. At San Pawl Milqi a tradition associating the ancient cistern with the Apostle Paul seemingly survived into post-Muslim times, when a church was built there. However, there are no archaeological grounds for dating the tombs, the pottery or the two churches themselves to the twelfth rather than the thirteenth century, and the general absence of a Latin or Christian presence in twelfth-century Malta makes a later date more probable.[196] In fact, no building in Malta can be dated securely to the Norman period; nor can the few surviving 'Romanesque' capitals.[197] The Latins may have maintained defences at Mdina,[198] but there is no evidence that the castle in the Grand Harbour was built by the Muslims[199] or that the Normans had a stronghold there, though the port was perhaps fortified in some crude way.[200] Naturally enough there is no sign of grandiose Norman palaces or mosaic-covered churches, and the cultural flowering of Norman Sicily can scarcely have reached Malta.

If Malta was never really Norman, then parallels drawn from Norman Sicily are largely irrelevant; developments on the other islands, Lampedusa or Pantelleria, are more likely to illuminate twelfth-century Malta. If Norman institutions, settlers, building styles or loan-words[201] did reach Malta it is unlikely to have been before about 1200. Even in Sicily the Normans had difficulty in imposing their rule and customs; to what extent the Normans introduced 'feudalism' into Sicily is still hotly debated, but there was much strife and the Muslim, Greek and Jewish sections of the population were by no means eliminated. Malta's integration into the Sicilian realm most likely began with Frederick II's reorganization of the kingdom after about 1220, but before that there was an interlude during which Malta was largely

[194] G. Mittarelli - A. Costadoni, *Annales Camaldulenses*, iv (Venice, 1759), appendices, 64–66.

[195] References in V. Novak, 'La paleografia latina e i rapporti dell'Italia meridionale con la Dalmazia', *Archivio storico pugliese*, xiv (1961), 152.

[196] M. Cagiano de Azevedo *infra*; see also *Missione 1968*, 89; *1969*, 134; *et passim*. On the pottery, *supra*, 13; but even if the pottery could be dated to the Norman period, that would still not constitute proof of Latin settlement in Malta.

[197] *Infra*, 164 n. 6.

[198] T. Fazello, *De rebus siculis* (Palermo, 1558), 438, wrote *Capta Melita, et arce munita . . .*, but without documentation; a detailed survey of the earliest remaining portions of the walls of Mdina might throw light on this question.

[199] As claimed in Abela, 263, followed in *Missione 1963*, 30.

[200] There was a *castrum maris* by ca. 1241 (*infra*, 36).

[201] A. Bliss, 'A Possible Norman Loanword in Maltese', *Scientia* [Malta], xxii (1956), admits that Maltese *kwejru* (razor-strop) from Norman *queir* and Siculo-Norman *queiru* (leather), may—like the razor-strop itself—have reached Malta long after the 12th century.

controlled by a succession of foreign Counts. Norman rule in Sicily formally ended in 1194, after a brief period of struggles between the descendants of the Normans and the German pretenders. It was during this period, some time between 1192 and 1194, that the renowned pirate Margarito of Brindisi, who became a Sicilian royal Admiral, acquired the title of Count of Malta.[202] This title probably derived from an attempt by King Tancred to secure himself reliable political support. What rights Margarito had on the island and whether he even went there is not clear, but the alienation of Malta from the royal *demanium* by granting it out to non-Maltese Counts was, though initiated by the last Norman ruler of Sicily, essentially a post-Norman phenomenon.

Margarito's successors were all Genoese, a fact which reflected both the importance of the Genoese establishment in Sicily and the significance of Malta as a base on the flanks of the Genoese sea-routes to their African and Levantine colonies and markets. These Counts were typically Genoese in their blend of patriotism with private initiative, of official service with piracy; their close naval, financial and diplomatic links with Genoa meant that their unofficial activities verged on official policy. Margarito was imprisoned by the Emperor Henry VI, who had by marriage become ruler of Sicily, and he was succeeded by the corsair Guglielmo Grasso of Genoa. Guglielmo Grasso may well have gone to Malta and provoked resentments there, for in 1198 Henry's Norman wife, Costanza of Sicily, granted the Maltese a charter incorporating the islands perpetually to the royal *demanium*, which meant direct dependence on the Crown. However, by 1203 Guglielmo Grasso had been followed as Count of Malta by his son-in-law Henry known as 'Pescatore'. A powerful figure in Mediterranean waters, Henry was able in 1205 to produce four galleys and considerable funds for attacks on the Pisans in Sicily. Using Malta as his principal base, Henry then pirateered in the Levant and, reaching Tripoli in Syria with 300 *iuvenes Maltenses* whose exact identity remains obscure, he fought successfully against the Muslims on land; on his return to Malta from this crusading venture he was acclaimed by the islanders and by a Provençal troubadour. He next attempted to set up a kingdom in Crete, where he was able to maintain some sort of hold until 1212. In 1218 Henry went to Germany on an embassy to the Emperor Frederick II, who was also King of Sicily and who in 1221 appointed him as Admiral of Sicily. After arriving at Damietta with the imperial fleet too late to save from the Egyptians the crusaders besieged within the city, Henry was imprisoned and deprived of the County of Malta, probably in 1222. He was soon back in imperial favour, though he seems to have lost real power at Malta; by May 1232 his son Nicoloso held the title of Count, and Henry was presumably dead.[203]

The years during which Henry controlled Malta and used it as an independent naval base and source of income must have seen a degree of settlement and Latinization, but detailed evidence is lacking. Once Frederick II had come of age and asserted his power in his Italian and Sicilian kingdom he ensured that the island could not be used as a centre of resistance against his royal power. Frederick went

[202] Little is known about Margarito; references and discussion in L.-R. Ménager, *Amiratus-'Αμηράς: l'Émirat et les origines de l'Amirauté (XIe–XIIIe siècles)* (Paris, 1960), 96–103.

[203] Details in D. Abulafia *infra*, using Genoese notarial documents as well as Genoese and Venetian chronicles, but they provide no direct information on Henry's rule in Malta or the island's internal history.

to Sicily in 1220 and the Genoese lost their favoured position there.[204] After about 1222 Henry retained the title of *comes* of Malta, presumably with certain accompanying incomes, but the *castrum* passed under royal command, while Frederick probably renewed Costanza's privilege of 1198 to the inhabitants of Malta.[205] Henry's son Nicoloso never exercized power there. In 1224 Frederick apparently expelled many Muslims and colonized the islands from Italy. In 1239 and 1240 Frederick's proctor in the islands, Paolino de Malta, was sending the incomes of the royal *curia* to Naples, provisioning the castles and their garrisons, and guarding prisoners exiled in Malta. Paolino was also concerned with the imperial menagerie. He had to send eight camels and two leopards to Frederick; to keep camels in Malta for breeding; to buy leopards and young horses in Africa; and to pay the expenses and transport of no less than nineteen falconers Frederick was sending to Malta.[206] The emperor was extremely interested in his animals, and above all in the falcons which gave Malta a real importance in the eyes of Sicilian monarchs.[207]

By this time the Sicilian administration was in full control. The *dohana* with its gabelles and taxes functioned in Malta and Gozo; there were two castles in Malta, that at Mdina and the *castrum maris;* the garrison numbered some 150 men plus 70 wives, and this included 25 seamen. The emperor was concerned that his agent Gilibertus should institute a proper inquest to recover any lands or rights lost from the royal *demanium.* The customs and constitutions of Malta and Gozo were reported to be different from those of Sicily, and the emperor was prepared to accept this as long as it did not harm the *curia* financially.[208] The Maltese, and probably the Gozitans as well, must have had some sort of representative council, possibly Muslim in origin, through which they had twice protested to earlier monarchs in order to secure their direct attachment to the Sicilian Crown; royal agents probably had to deal with it over taxation matters concerning the *curia.*[209] Gilibertus' report to

[204] Cf. T. van Cleve, *The Emperor Frederick II of Hohenstaufen: Immutator Mundi* (Oxford, 1972).

[205] The text of 1283 referred to *privilegia Imperatricis Constancie et Imperatoris Frederici,* probably two separate privileges, as presumed *infra,* 109, but possibly a joint charter issued very late in 1197 or before 28 Nov. 1198: R. Ries, 'Regesten der Kaiserin Constanze . . .', *Quellen und Forschungen aus italienischen Archiven und Bibliotheken,* xviii (1926), 73, 99–100. The *castrum* mentioned here may have been either that at Mdina, or the *castrum maris,* first mentioned in ca. 1241 (*infra,* 58), but probably existing earlier.

[206] Three documents in J. Huillard-Bréholles, *Historia diplomatica Friderici Secundi,* v parts 1–2 (Paris, 1857–1859), 525, 931–932, 969–971. During 1235 Frederick II granted Paolino the *Casalem Stafende situm in pertinentiis Spaccafurni* in Sicily: the present author will publish this text shortly. The generic sense of *malta* to mean 'prison', as in Dante, Jacopone and others might conceivably have resulted from Malta's use as a place of exile: further references and examples in Huillard-Bréholles, vi part 2 (1861), 917–919; Valentini, in *ASM,* vii. 423–424 (with references muddled); P. Toynbee, *Dante Dictionary* (rev. ed.: Oxford, 1968), 416; *Enciclopedia Dantesca,* iii (Rome, 1971), 796.

[207] Many editions, eg. Fridericus II, *De Arte Venandi cum Avibus,* ed. C. Willemsen (Graz, 1969).

[208] Details from a document of fundamental importance in Maltese history, Frederick II's reply to Gilibertus' report of ca. 1241: text in E. Winkelmann, *Acta Imperii Inedita seculi XIII.* (Innsbruck, 1880), 713–715. The document survives in a copy of ca. 1300, and discrepancies in the statistics indicate corrupt ons. The date is also uncertain, while Winkelmann's text requires a number of corrections; the present author will publish a revised text. The financial aspect is discussed in detail *infra,* 129–136, and by Valentini, in *ASM,* xiii. 4–6.

[209] Valentini, in *ASM,* x, certainly demonstrated the existence of some sort of local government, but in seeking to prove that it was an Italian-type *comune* he undervalued (p. 221 n. 90) the statement, accepted by Frederick II in ca. 1241, that Malta's *constituciones* were not like those of Sicily (*supra,* 14); see also *infra,* 60 n. 328.

Frederick indicated an economy based on the royal estates, cereal-producing *latifundia* worked by slaves and servile labourers, the *villani*. There were also 60 *servi* and *ancille*, male and female slaves used by the *curia* for building and other work in the three royal castles; 84 *servi* from Gerba, presumably Muslims captured on a raid, who worked on lands of the *curia*; 55 cowherds, 10 shepherds, and sundry others listed along with numerous animals.[210] Part of the population was apparently exported; a Florentine sold a ten-year-old white Maltese girl named Maimuna, presumably a Muslim, as a slave at Genoa in 1248,[211] and there were others.[212] The *homines insularum* who had their own constitutions and whose *consilium* Gilibertus was instructed to take, may have been Christian Latin immigrants or indigenous Muslims who had converted to Christianity to escape expulsion. Expulsion of some sort certainly occurred; a text of 1271 referred to the possessions of *quondam Sarraceni* who had been expelled from the islands, their lands devolving to the *curia*.[213]

A possible date for the expulsion of the Muslims is provided by Riccardo de San Germano whose chronicle stated that in May 1224 the population of Celano in the Abruzzi was sent to Malta:

> Henricus de Morra iussu imperiali Celanenses reuocat ubique dispersos, ut ad propria redeant, et redeuntes capit et in Siciliam mittit, quos apud Maltam dirigit Imperator.[214]

Whether the population of Celano was large and whether it remained in Malta is doubtful. This transfer of Latins to Malta may have accompanied a diminution in the number of Muslims there. Henry Count of Malta lost effective control of the island in about 1222; he was, however, involved in repressing the Muslim revolt in Sicily in 1223; 1223 was also the year in which the emperor's fleet attacked Gerba and other islands, taking numerous slaves; Frederick II's arrangement concerning Pantelleria had come in 1221; and Count Henry was himself at Celano in April 1223.[215] All this points to 1224 for the expulsion of the Muslims from Malta. The fourteenth-century historian Ibn Khaldūn reported:

> The tyrant of Sicily besieged the Muslims in their fortress on the hill, surrounded them, forced them to come down from their castle and sent them beyond the straits establishing them at Lucera, a populous part of that province. Then he passed to Malta and chased out the Muslims who lived there, sending them to keep company with their brethren. This tyrant ruled over Sicily and the adjacent isles, and abolished there the law of Islam, substituting that of his own infidelity.[216]

Ibn Khaldūn placed these events after 1249 but, as far as is known, Frederick II never went to Malta, and in 1250 he died. Presumably Ibn Khaldūn was actually giving a

[210] Text in Winkelmann, 713–715; cf. H. Bresc, *infra*, 131.

[211] Text in R. Lopez, 'La vendita d'una schiava di Malta a Genova nel 1248', *ASM*, vii (1935/6), 391; somewhat unusually, the girl gave her consent to her own sale.

[212] R. Balard, 'Remarques sur les esclaves à Gênes dans la seconde moitié du XIIIe siècle', *Mélanges d'archéologie et d'histoire*, lxxx (1968), 668–669.

[213] Text in *Cancelleria Angioina*, vi. 213.

[214] *Ryccardi de Sancto Germano notarii Chronica*, ed. C. Garufi, in *Rerum Italicarum Scriptores*, ns. vii part 2 (Bologna, 1938), 112–113; that the final phrase mentioning Malta appears only in the second version of the chronicle need not cast doubt on its veracity. Note the *sarracenus* named *Dallesium Maltesium* at Altamura in 1301: text in P. Egidi, *Codice Diplomatico dei Saraceni di Lucera* (Naples, 1917), 222–224.

[215] Details in Amari, *Storia*, iii. 613–619; *supra*, 32; *infra*, 121–122.

[216] Text in Amari, *Biblioteca*, ii. 212–213; Minganti, 20.

partially accurate description of the events of 1224 when Frederick was in Sicily and crushed the Sicilian Muslims, many of whom were then sent to Lucera.[217] It is reasonable to suppose that some at least of the Muslims of Malta were expelled and Christian rule installed there.

The available population statistics, derived from the report of about 1241, have normally been accepted.[218] The number of families in the islands is given as follows:

| *Families* | *Christians* | *Muslims* | *Jews* | *Total* |
|---|---|---|---|---|
| Malta | 47 | 681 | 25 | 753 |
| Gozo | 203 | 155 | 8 | 366 |
| Total | 250 | 836 | 33 | 1,119 |

The apparent precision of these figures suggests a genuine count, presumably for fiscal purposes, and points to an almost exclusively Muslim island affected by a minimal Christian immigration which had only just begun around 1241; these statistics provide no evidence for large-scale immigration, except perhaps in Gozo, and they would demonstrate the persistence of a Muslim majority of almost exactly three in four, 836 families out of a total of 1,119. The figures for the Jews are acceptable, but it would seem odd that the Christians should be concentrated in Gozo where they outnumber the Muslims; it would also be strange that the population of Gozo should be given as almost exactly half that of Malta which is over three times its size, a phenomenon never known to recur in later times. One possibility is that the document was exclusively administrative and concerned only with taxation, and that there were numerous Christians on Malta who were not included: bachelors in the garrison who did not constitute a family; other tax-exempt residents of the *castrum;* and the *fideles* and others whose counsel Abbot Gilibertus was instructed to receive and who may have paid other taxes for which Gilibertus did not account.

The report mentioned the incomes from the *villani curie* who paid 2,516 *tarini* in Malta, where they surely amounted to more than 47 families, and 584 *tarini* in Gozo. It also spoke of the *villani curie sarraceni* who owed a fourth part of their produce in kind. If the *villani curie* were really distinct from the *villani curie sarraceni* and were Latins,[219] it would be strange that while there were 47 Christian families in Malta and 203 in Gozo, the *villani curie* of Malta paid 2516 *tarini* as against 584 *tarini* from those of Gozo; and the origin and status of these Christian *villani* would still remain unexplained. This interpretation also assumes that these hypothetical Christian *villani*, who could conceivably have been converted Muslims, would have paid taxes in cash, while the *villani sarraceni* paid only in kind. If this were the case, there would have been many more than 47 Christian families on Malta. An alternative interpretation is that there were no Christian *villani*, but only Muslim *villani curie*, also called

[217] Amari, *Storia*, iii. 609–617; E. Kantorowicz, *Kaiser Friedrich der Zweite: Ergänzungsband* (Berlin, 1931), 46.

[218] Eg. in Wettinger—Fsadni, 33.

[219] As supposed by Valentini, in *ASM*, x. 224, who holds that the document makes the distinction clear. There were many Christian *villani* in twelfth-century Sicily, but this can scarcely have been the case in Malta; the Sicilian *villani* disappeared rapidly after ca. 1200: I. Peri, *Il villanaggio in Sicilia* (Palermo, 1965).

*villani curie sarraceni*, who paid taxes both in cash and kind. It is notable that the ratio of *tarini* paid by *villani curie* in Malta to *tarini* paid by *villani curie* in Gozo, that is 2,516 to 584 or 4·3, is almost precisely that of Muslim families in Malta to Muslim families in Gozo, that is 681 to 155 or 4·4.[220] This suggests that the figures for Muslim families are correct, and that all Muslims remaining on Malta, or alternatively all those counted by Gilibertus, were *villani curie.* It might follow that, at the moment of their 'expulsion', the Muslims had divided into various groups: those who actually left the islands and whose lands devolved to the *curia;* those who were converted and were counted as Christians, which again would bring the number of Christian families to more than 47; those who remained on Malta unconverted, becoming *villani curie* and paying taxes in both cash and kind; and a few who were sold as slaves. This, however, remains a hypothesis.

Furthermore, this hypothetical interpretation leaves unexplained the low figure of 47 Christian families. The text of Gilibertus' report as it survives is the result of successive copying and recopying, and at least some of the income figures do not add up correctly and must be incorrect.[221] The figures could be amended in various ways; perhaps 47 should read 147 or 547, or even 2,047. The most feasible suggestion is that an '*m*' or *mille* was lost between the contraction of *christianoru*[*m*] and the beginning of the number — *quadraginta septem* — which followed,[222] in which case the situation would have been:

| *Families* | *Christians* | *Muslims* | *Jews* | *Total* |
|---|---|---|---|---|
| Malta | 1,047 | 681 | 25 | 1,753 |
| Gozo | 203 | 155 | 8 | 366 |
| Total | 1,250 | 836 | 33 | 2,119 |

This emendation gives a similar proportion of Muslim to Christian families throughout the islands; produces a reasonable total population of some 10,000;[223] and reduces the proportion of Gozitan families, both Christian and Muslim, to less than a fourth. It suggests a situation in which the islands had been Christianized, leaving a minority of unconverted Muslims working the royal lands as *villani;* and it provides the Christians alluded to in Gilibertus' report. These new suggestions provide an arguable hypothesis, though they do involve numerous assumptions. If it is true

[220] A point never before noted, but evidently of some significance.

[221] Winkelmann, 713–715.

[222] This suggestion advanced, without the supporting arguments adduced here, in K. Beloch, *Bevölkerungsgeschichte Italiens*, i (Berlin, 1937), 164–165, and Valentini, in *ASM*, x. 222–225, has hitherto received almost no support. Those authors buttress the argument with the fact that in Jan. 1277 Malta was to pay 350 *uncie* out of a *generalis subventio* of 7500 for the whole kingdom (text in *ASM*, v. 142), but it is not clear what this might prove. In July 1277 a royal document stated: *cum proventus dicte insule Malte consueverint valere olim dominis regni Sicilie precessoribus nostris annuatim unc. auri M et plus* (text in *Cancelleria Angioina*, xvi. 104).

[223] Renfrew guesses, reasonably, that in prehistoric times the islands' physical resources could have supported a maximum of 11,000, which fits with medieval indications for the period before the population, and foodstuff imports, increased in the 15th century (*infra*, 53, 184–186). Renfrew's 'statistics' in *Before Civilization*, 153–155, 161, and in *World Archaeology*, ii (1970), 208, are based on multipliers derived from South Iran, Naxos and Easter Island (in 1722), and these produce a minimum population of 500 arbitrarily raised to a maximum of 11,000; a maximum of 18,000 reduced to 10,000 or less; and an estimate of ca. 7000!

that there was little or no Latin settlement in the twelfth century,[224] then either a considerable wave of Christian immigrants arrived in the years immediately prior to about 1241, conceivably from Celano; or, more probably, there were massive conversions. In the latter case, the actual population would have changed only marginally, so that Malta and Gozo counted 836 families of unconverted Muslims with another 1,250 families, all or most of them converted 'Christians', which would explain the persistence of the spoken Arabo-Berber language.

Frederick II died in 1250, and his Hohenstaufen successors Manfred and Conradin were eliminated in 1266 and 1268 by Charles of Anjou who won control of Sicily. The replacement of a German by a French dynasty in Southern Italy and Sicily was of major significance in Italian and European history, but it was not really a turning-point for Malta since the Angevins followed the old policies of the Normans, of Frederick II and Manfred; they too represented a northern thrust into the Mediterranean aimed at Sicily, North Africa and the islands between them, at Syria and at the Greek lands of *Romania*. The French king St. Louis sailed to Tunis and died there in 1270; Charles of Anjou failed to overthrow the Byzantine Emperor Michael VIII Palaeologus and was himself ousted from Sicily in 1282 by the Aragonese, who then followed many of the same policies, but with a different emphasis. Malta passed, with Sicily, to Aragon, but the whole period from 1250 to about 1300 was one of uncertainties which saw a renewed if sporadic interest in the islands, some of it plainly piratical, on the part of Genoese, Pisans and Venetians. After Frederick II's death, with Manfred in difficulties and the Maltese resentful of Hohenstaufen exploitation, there was some sort of rebellion on Malta fostered by a group of Genoese who were anxious to restore their position in Sicily, and who played on the old claims of Count Henry's son Nicoloso. Then in 1257 Manfred and the Genoese came to terms according to which Nicoloso was to have all his father's lands, privileges and incomes on Malta and Gozo, while Manfred was to retain control of the castles; Nicoloso could, if he wished, exchange these Maltese lands for others in Sicily, Calabria or Apulia. This agreement had to be renewed in 1259, and again in 1261. The Genoese fought the Venetians from a base in Malta, while in June 1267 Conradin agreed to give Malta to the Pisans in return for the support of their fleet.[225]

After Conradin's death in 1268, the Angevins restored firm government of a type that aroused dislike throughout the Sicilian kingdom; it also left its mark in the royal registers, and henceforth the documentation of Maltese history is, quantitatively speaking, of a very different order.[226] Once again an efficient Sicilian administration sought to control, cultivate and exploit the royal *demanium*. A Captain or Castellan commanded a garrison of 150 *ultramontani* or *servientes gallici boni*, that is

[224] As argued *supra*, 29–34.

[225] Details and references in Valentini, in *ASM*, x. 226–229, amended by Luttrell, in *Melita Historica*, iii. 74–75; this period in Maltese history deserves to be thoroughly reworked. Nicoloso was still alive in 1271: text in *Cancelleria Angioina*, vi. 174.

[226] The Angevin registers destroyed in 1943 provided a number of published documents (see *supra*, 5) on which this paragraph is based; brief preliminary use of some of these is made in J. Galea, 'Malta under the Angevins: 1266–83', *Scientia* [Malta], xvii (1951), but there is room for a much more detailed and lengthy study of these and other sources. It should be emphasized that whereas down to ca. 1260 almost every known document referring directly to Maltese history has been utilized either in this paper or in those below, thenceforth no more than suggestive outlines and an indication of the sources can be attempted.

trusty French troops; there was an armed *sagittia* for naval defence, and other shipping to provision the *castrum maris* from Gozo; the *castrum maris* had an interior and an exterior section, and detailed inventories were kept of its armaments, which included 100 *salme* of wood. Other officials collected taxes and managed the *servi* on the royal *massarie;* some land was *inculte* and had to be leased. In 1277 the king claimed that his predecessors had received more than 1000 gold *uncie* a year from Malta. The *curia* was also concerned with pigs, falcons and leopards, and in 1270 the king commanded 7,000 or 8,000 chickens to be sent to Syracuse.[227] Oaths of fealty were exacted; there were petitions to the king *ex parte universorum hominum insularum* against official misappropriations, and considerable resistance to royal taxation. A notary public served the two islands, and the Angevin officials, who included two *Judices civitatis Malte*, quarrelled over jurisdictions with the Maltese Church.[228] Much of this was doubtless merely the restoration of the Hohenstaufen administrative tradition, but for the first time a European, Latin, Christian style of government and society is clearly visible on Malta and Gozo, which were entering a more cosmopolitan context; in 1277 the royal officials were instructed to sell surplus victuals at Malta in Tunis, Acre, Greece, Venice or elsewhere. The islands suffered from the Angevins' quarrels. Two Genoese ships were seized at Malta in 1272; in revenge the Genoese sacked Gozo in 1274—*Gaudium depopulavit.*[229] Charles of Anjou's ambitions in Byzantium provoked the catastrophe of 1282, the revolt of the Vespers and the Aragonese conquest of Sicily which were naturally reflected in Malta, but it is possible that harsh Angevin government produced popular enthusiasm for the change in Malta and Gozo.

In 1282 Sicily, and Malta with it, passed into a new Western Mediterranean sphere of interest, that of the confederation of the Aragonese Crown, within which it remained until long after 1530.[230] From Abela onwards, Malta's historians have looked to Italy,[231] while Roberto Valentini, the leading modern writer on medieval Malta, was an Italian, preoccupied with anti-Aragonese notions of the *italianità* of the Maltese past; furthermore, Spanish books and languages scarcely penetrated to Malta, and medieval Malta has not been properly understood in the context of Sicily's Hispanic connections. The spectacular advances made since about 1950 in the study of the Aragonese Crown and its Mediterranean expansion have yet to be

[227] Texts in *Cancelleria Angioina*, v. 61–62 (1270); xvi. 104 (1277); *et passim.*

[228] For the Maltese Church, *infra*, 60–64.

[229] *Annali Genovesi*, ed. C. Imperiali di Sant'Angelo, iv (Rome, 1926), 168.

[230] One difficulty is that while Aragon proper covered only a small part of the Iberian peninsula, its kings ruled in Catalunya, Valencia, Mallorca, Sicily and elsewhere. The term 'Aragonese' scarcely conveys this fact; 'Catalano-Siculo-Aragonese' is clumsy and still insufficient. It seems best to refer to the 'Aragonese Crown' and its 'lands'—*los paises de la corona de Aragón.* The following two paragraphs partly repeat A. Luttrell, 'Malta and the Aragonese Crown: 1282–1530', *Journal of the Faculty of Arts: The Royal University of Malta*, iii no. 1 (1965). Details and references for *infra*, 42–48, are contained in *idem*, 'The House of Aragon and Malta: 1282–1412', *ibid.*, iv no. 2 (1970), here partly paraphrased; this article is a slightly revised translation from the Catalan of 'La casa de Catalunya-Aragó i Malta: 1282–1412', in *Estudis d'Història Medieval*, i = *Estudis Ferran Soldevila*, i (Barcelona, 1969). Further details are contained in the articles by Valentini but much of the story remains obscure; for the Sicilian background, see in particular V. d'Alessandro, *Politica e società nella Sicilia aragonese* (Palermo, 1963).

[231] P. de Jové y Hevia, *Indagaciones acerca de la dominación de España en Malta de 1285 a 1530* (Madrid, 1863), remained an exception, rare, outdated and ignored by Maltese historiography.

synthesized in satisfactory standard works. The extensive bibliography has far outrun the consensus of agreed opinions, but some understanding of this background is essential to an appreciation of Maltese history after 1282.[232]

The Kings of Catalunya-Aragon ruled in barren and mountainous Aragon, where the Christian conquerors lived alongside Muslim and Jewish communities, and in the Catalan coastlands whose prospering mercantile classes constituted the basis of a remarkable expansion which began with the reconquest and resettlement of Muslim Valencia and the Balearic islands. In 1282 Pedro III of Aragon could claim Sicily through his wife Costanza, daughter of Frederick II's son Manfred; in 1311 the Catalan Companies seized Thebes and Athens; Sardinia was conquered in 1324; and subsequently the Aragonese Crown repeatedly fought the Angevins and Genoese in defence of Sicily and Sardinia. Catalan, Valencian and Mallorquin traders, slavers and sailors were active in the Levant and North Africa, and many settled in Sardinia, Sicily and Greece. Malta and Gozo fitted into this Catalan-Aragonese community by virtue of their attachment to and dependence on Sicily. Their importance to the Aragonese Crown was strategic rather than commercial. Malta was a port-of-call for vessels trading to Tripoli, but it did not lie on any major sea-lane since shipping bound from the Western Mediterranean towards the markets of Egypt, Asia and Byzantium normally followed a more northerly route through the Straits of Messina, partly perhaps to avoid African pirates; the Venetians making for Spain, the Atlantic or North Africa also preferred to sail along the north coast of Sicily.[233] Of 109 vessels recorded as leaving Candia in Crete between July 1359 and June 1360 just one was bound for Malta.[234] Genoese and Venetian interest in Malta was never long sustained during this period; Venice was often allied to Aragon, and the Genoese presumably realized that it would be hard to retain Malta while the Aragonese controlled Sicily. Malta and Gozo were situated on the very fringe of the Aragonese common market for, while Catalan trade in the Maghrib was of paramount importance, the two islands lay south-east of the direct routes from Sicily to Tunis. In any case, the Aragonese Crown was only marginally interested in Levantine areas such as Cyprus or Athens where it had no vital interests but could make diplomatic and consular arrangements which ensured access to important markets without over-extending its limited administrative and military resources.[235]

[232] The standard political history is F. Soldevila, *Història de Catalunya*, i–ii (2nd ed: Barcelona, 1962). The more modern ideas outlined here largely derive from the many works of J. Vicens Vives, who was responsible for a historiographical revolution in Iberian and Mediterranean studies; see also F. Giunta, *Aragonesi e Catalani nel Mediterraneo*, 2 vols. (Palermo, 1953–1959), and M. del Treppo, *I mercanti catalani e l'espansione della Corona d'Aragona nel secolo XV* (Naples, 1972). Two books not in Castilian or Catalan which summarize much new work are P. Vilar, *La Catalogne dans l'Espagne moderne*, i (Paris, 1962), and J. Elliott, *Imperial Spain: 1469–1716* (London, 1963). The *Indice Histórico Español*, i– (Barcelona, 1953– ), provides a complete annual bibliography; for recent syntheses, see the numerous papers on 'La investigación de la historia hispánica del siglo XIV: problemas y cuestiones', *Anuario de estudios medievales*, vii (1970/1). The outline and bibliography given here are entirely incomplete and inevitably unsatisfactory; they can take no account of the varying interpretations of the *catalaniste* and other schools.

[233] In addition to Dufourcq, see details on trading-routes in Luttrell, in *Melita Historica*, iii. 74–76.

[234] K. Mertzios, 'É Nautiliake Kinesis tou Kandakos kata ta ete 1359–1360' [in Greek], *Acts of II International Congress of Cretological Studies*, iii (Athens, 1968), 174.

[235] This thesis is argued in A. Luttrell, 'La Corona de Aragón y la Grecia catalana: 1379–1394', *Anuario de estudios medievales*, vi (1969).

Soon after 1300 the visionary Mallorquin Ramon Lull suggested that Malta should be used as a crusading base from which Christian merchants could be prevented from trading illegally with the Muslims,[236] but the Aragonese rulers were realists for whom Malta was merely a frontier station on the eastern margin of their Western Mediterranean sphere of influence; their chief concern was that it should not fall into enemy hands.

Behind the Sicilian uprising of March 1282 lay some kind of collusion between Pedro III of Aragon, who had Sicilian and North African objectives, and the Byzantine emperor Michael VIII, whom the Angevins were planning to overthrow. A later fabrication, *Lu Rebellamentu di Sichilia*, described how Giovanni de Procida attempted to subvert certain Sicilians with Byzantine gold at Trapani in 1280, and stated that the talks were moved to Malta to escape Angevin control, a story which, though suspect, may have reflected a state of discontent on Malta.[237] Partly because of Angevin oppression and partly because Malta depended on Sicilian grain, the populace and the Angevin governor, Dionigi da Barba, had gone over to the new rulers of Sicily by December 1282. Pedro III nominated Manfredi Lancia as Captain of Malta; granted facilities for grain to be sent from Sicily; and confirmed the privileges by which Costanza and Frederick II had incorporated Malta and Gozo into the royal *demanium.* The *castrum maris,* considered impregnable, held out and in mid-1283 a large Angevin fleet from Marseilles arrived at Malta, threatening the whole Aragonese position in Sicily and its African supply-lines. The danger vanished a few days later when the Aragonese Admiral, Ruggiero Lauria, won a decisive battle in the Grand Harbour at Malta on 8 July 1283, his men fighting to the cry *Arago! Arago! via sus! via sus!* The inhabitants received Lauria with money, jewels and provisions, and he left behind 300 Catalan soldiers to hold the islands since, without siege-engines, he was unable to take the *castrum maris,* which was revictualled by sea and resisted at least until February 1284.[238]

The Aragonese certainly appreciated Malta's strategic significance, and the chronicler Ramon Muntaner described their joyful reception in 1283 of rumours that the *castrum maris* had fallen; he wrote 'the castle is most royal and fine, and the castle and the island stand well to the island of Sicily as the stone suits the ring'.[239] The conquest of Malta was completed by Manfredi Lancia; Lancia's kinsman, Ruggiero Lauria, captured and acquired titles to the islands of Gerba and Kerkena, thus establishing a semi-independent maritime principality between Sicily and Africa. In 1287 an Angevin fleet briefly recaptured the *castrum* at Malta, and then attacked Augusta in Sicily. On 16 June 1290 Charles of Anjou, King of Naples, hoping perhaps for support from Genoa, recognized the ancient claims to the County of Malta of

[236] Text in A. Gottron, *Ramon Lulls Kreuzzugsideen* (Berlin-Leipzig, 1912), 86.

[237] *Lu Rebellamentu di Sichilia*, ed. E. Sicardi, in *Rerum Italicarum Scriptores*, ns. xxxiv part 1 (Bologna, 1935), 14, 54, 70, 112. Giovanni de Procida and a Lombard knight named Accardo are said to have met Palmiere Abbate and other Sicilian barons. The whole question of Giovanni de Procida and the *Rebellamentu* has been endlessly debated; see, most recently, C. Tsirpanlis, 'The Involvement of Michael VIII Palaeologus in the Sicilian Vespers: 1279–1282', *Byzantina*, iv (1972).

[238] See especially *Chronik des edlen En Ramon Muntaner*, ed. K. Lanz (Stuttgart, 1884), 138–146.

[239] *Ibid.*, 180.

a Genoese named Andreolo, who declared himself ready to attack the island;[240] but Andreolo soon went over to Jaime of Aragon, King of Sicily, who by October 1292 had recognized his title as Count of Malta. In 1287 and again in 1290 Jaime insisted that, whatever peace conditions were agreed with the Angevins, he should retain not only Sicily but also Malta, Gozo, Pantelleria and the joint Siculo-Catalan fonduk at Tunis. In 1292, having also become King of Aragon, Jaime gave orders for the strengthening of the garrison and castle at Malta. In 1296 Jaime renounced the Sicilian Crown to his younger brother Frederick. There followed a period of antagonism between the two brothers, during which Malta was in some danger both from Jaime and from Ruggiero Lauria, who retained control of Gerba. On 25 March 1296 Frederick III appointed Lauria as Admiral of Sicily, but Lauria soon abandoned Frederick and on 2 April 1297 Jaime reappointed him Admiral of Aragon, after which Malta and Gozo were attacked and devastated by an Aragonese fleet in 1297. Lauria then passed into Angevin service, and in April 1300 Charles of Anjou invested him and his heirs with the County of Malta in perpetuity; on Ruggiero's death in January 1305 the claim passed to his son Rogeró, but his rule at Gerba was ineffective and short-lived. Malta remained in Sicilian hands.

The urban patriciates of Catalunya, with their ports and industries, were responsible for the emergence of a single economic and strategic unit, a Western Mediterranean common market in which the merchants of Valencia, Barcelona and Perpignan could buy and sell in the Balearics, Sardinia and Sicily, while at the same time controlling in those islands the safe harbours they needed along their routes to lucrative markets in North Africa and the Levant. The Catalans also needed imports, notably Sicilian grain, and this economic inter-dependence was reflected in the political structure of the union. Flexible institutions enabled the Crown to respond rapidly to pressures from its diverse subject peoples who retained their own laws and assemblies, while a network of royal governors-general and viceroys acted in the separate parts of the commonwealth, holding *cortes*, receiving homages and raising taxes. Between 1296 and 1377, the Sicilian kingdom was ruled by a cadet branch of the house of Aragon but, despite moments of tension, Sicily remained politically and economically within the orbit of the Aragonese confederation. Malta fitted conveniently into this pattern. In 1345, for example, the Sicilian king authorized the Catalan consul at Messina to nominate a vice-consul at Malta and Gozo.

In 1300 Frederick III of Sicily considered enfeoffing the *castrum* at Malta to the Genoese, but Malta was eventually acquired by Guglielmo Raimondo Moncada. The king recovered the island from Moncada in exchange for lands in Sicily in 1320, and later Frederick granted Malta and Gozo to his younger son Guglielmo who, by 1330, had ceded them to his half-brother Alfonso Federigo d'Aragona. On the latter's death, by 1349 at the latest, Malta passed to his eldest son Pietro Federigo d'Aragona, who was Lord of Salona in Greece where he resided; he had lost the County by 7 October 1350 when, at their inhabitants' request, Malta and Gozo were

[240] This seems to have been a sea-captain named Andreolo de Mari, who was apparently connected to Henry Pescatore's clan; the lands he claimed in Sicily, which were said to have been confirmed by Henry VI, by Costanza and by Frederick II, included a *domus Guillelmi Crassi quam habuit in Messana:* text of 1290 in Laurenza, in *ASM*, v. 168–169. Grasso was Pescatore's father-in-law (*infra*, 110–111).

returned to the royal *demanium* by King Ludovico of Sicily. A clear pattern was emerging: the Crown conceded the islands to royal cadets or Sicilian magnates; the population, anxious to escape exploitation by rapacious and presumably absentee Counts, petitioned for reincorporation into the *demanium;* the Crown conceded this request in perpetuity, but subsequently in a moment of weakness granted out the County once again. The Counts enjoyed certain rights, such as the nomination of Captains and Justiciars or the exercise of the *jurisdictio criminalis* and the *merum et mixtum imperium*, but it is not known what profits they may have derived from the islands. Malta and Gozo, however, remained part of the Kingdom of Sicily; the royal *curia* and the Admiral of Sicily imposed taxes and exercized certain powers; and, ecclesiastically, Malta continued to suffer from papal interdicts imposed on the Sicilian kingdom. In 1356 the troops of Jeanne of Anjou, Queen of Naples, captured Messina and Palermo. On 30 March 1357 Jeanne issued a diploma enfeoffing her powerful favourite and Grand Seneschal, the Florentine Niccolò Acciaiuoli, with the County of Malta and Gozo.[241] The Neapolitans were soon expelled from Sicily and the Acciaiuoli claim was never made good, yet the threat had been real enough; the Acciaiuoli were no friends to the Aragonese who suffered severely from their activities in Greece, where Niccolò's son Nerio became Lord of Corinth and the greatest enemy of the Catalans of Thebes and Athens. Meanwhile, on 29 December 1360, Frederick IV of Sicily granted the County of Malta and Gozo to Guido Ventimiglia, but in 1362 Guido died and the islands again reverted to the Crown.

In 1366 Frederick IV visited Malta to deal with certain problems the exact nature of which is now unknown. On his return the king fell into the power of Manfredi Chiaramonte, Admiral of Sicily, to whom on 4 May he enfeoffed Malta and Gozo in perpetuity; but Malta was apparently in revolt, since on the next day Chiaramonte was granted Terranova in Sicily *usque ad acquisitionem insularum Meliveti et Gauditii.* Royal power in Sicily had collapsed in the face of baronial intransigence; the enfeoffment of 1366 was a mere formality soon revoked, but Manfredi Chiaramonte had cotton interests in Malta which, some years later, he was exploiting in collaboration with a group of Genoese merchants and financiers.[242] Malta's subsequent rebellion remains obscure. The royal Captain of Malta, Giacomo de Pellegrino of Messina, was married to a royal kinswoman, Margherita d'Aragona. Pellegrino may, overambitiously, have hoped to establish an independent lordship of his own; perhaps he offended the Chiaramonte; probably he had made piratical attacks on the Genoese, to some of whom he owed large sums of money. In 1372 Frederick, supported by ten Genoese galleys, returned to restore order at Malta; local royalists recaptured the *castrum maris;* and Pellegrino was banished. The king appointed new officials and

[241] Every year Acciaiuoli was to provide 'the service of one black slave, dressed in crimson cloth and bathed the night before . . .' His son Angelo Acciaiuoli was still using the title in 1391. There is no evidence that the Acciaiuoli actually controlled Malta, as is often alleged. [Count] Zeininger de Borja, 'Counts of Malta in Greece', *Scientia* [Malta], xxxv (1959), is unreliable. The Acciaiuoli were bankers. Another Florentine banking house, the Bardi, had a *fondaco* at Malta in 1314, according to R. Davidsohn, *Storia di Firenze*, iv part 2 (Florence, 1965), 826, citing *Frammenti in possesso del principe Andrea Corsini*, f. 1, but this notice requires confirmation.

[242] In 1366 also Giovanni Chiaramonte was named Captain of Gerba and Kerkena, which he had conquered: F. Giunta, 'Sicilia e Tunisi nei secoli XIV e XV', in his *Medioevo Mediterraneo: saggi storici* (Palermo, 1954), 157.

rewarded faithful service with grants from royal lands and those of the rebels. Some grants were made in return for military service; others for a *census* paid in agricultural produce. The Crown was diminishing its patrimony in order to secure support, yet the appointment on 31 January 1376 of yet another royal kinsman, Giovanni Federigo d'Aragona, as Captain of Malta provoked a new revolt in which the faithful royalist of 1372, the notary Lancia Gatto, took a leading part.[243]

Frederick IV died on 27 July 1377, leaving his kingdom to his young daughter Maria. Some of the magnates recognized her as Queen of Sicily, but Pedro IV of Aragon also had claims and a protracted struggle ensued in Sicily, complicated after 1378 by the diplomatic repercussions of the interminable schism in the Roman church. It had already been suggested, in 1370, that Frederick might temporarily make over to the Aragonese Crown all the incomes and rights of Malta and Gozo. Frederick bequeathed the County of Malta to his natural son Guglielmo, but this provision had little or no effect and in September 1380 Pedro IV asserted his sovereignty over the County.[244] Meanwhile, Maria of Sicily had been carried off to Spain and married to Martín of Aragon whose father, Martín Duke of Montblanch, was Pedro IV's son. Pedro's claims to Sicily were transferred to the young couple, but the *quattro vicari*, Manfredi Chiaramonte, Artale Alagona, Francesco Ventimiglia and Guglielmo Peralta, divided the kingdom into spheres of influence and presided over a regulated anarchy. Manfredi Chiaramonte, the most powerful of these magnates, put into effect his old claims as Count of Malta. In 1388 he led an expedition which seized the Tunisian island of Gerba, possibly using Malta as a base; the response was a Hafsid attack on Gozo in 1389.[245] Chiaramonte also fostered Adriatic contacts. In 1380 Maltese Jews and Maltese shipping were trading at Dubrovnik, and a Dubrovnik ship carrying Dalmatian timber arrived in Malta; there was even a proposal for a trade agreement between Dubrovnik and Malta.[246] The Venetians showed less interest, and the wrecking of a Venetian *cocca* in the Grand Harbour in 1397 or 1398 doubtless discouraged them.[247] The economic effects of these years of trouble cannot be measured, but a visitor in 1394 found the islands in a reasonably prosperous state; he mentioned the production of cotton, cumin, wine and meat, and claimed that there were as many as 4,000 hearths in Malta and 400 on Gozo.[248]

Manfredi's will, drawn up in 1390, provided for the *comitatus* of Malta and the *insula* of Gozo to pass to his daughter Elisabetta Chiaramonte, wife of Niccolò Peralta, but in March 1392 Martín Duke of Montblanch arrived in Sicily and

[243] On this period, important aspects of which remain obscure, see texts and references in Valentini, in *ASM*, v. 10–13, 34–36; Bresc, in *Papers of the British School at Rome*, xli, *passim*. Abela, 421–422, misinterpreted Frederick's visit of 1372 as an attempt to restore the s tuation following a Genoese attack on Malta.

[244] In 1380 Pedro confirmed the claims of Ludovico Federigo d'Aragona, Count of Salona, whose support in Greece he was anxious to ensure. Ludovico Federigo, a nephew of the Pietro Federigo dispossessed of the County in 1350, remained in Greece where he died in 1382, his Greek claims and titles passing to his wife Helena Cantacuzena; he had no influence upon events in Malta, and neither his widow nor their daughter Maria claimed the islands.

[245] On the Hafsid attack, Brunschwig, i. 198.

[246] Texts in Luttrell, in *Melita Historica*, v. 159–164.

[247] Luttrell, in *Melita Historica*, iii. 77–80.

[248] L. le Grand, 'Relation du pèlerinage à Jérusalem de Nicolas de Martoni, notaire italien: 1394–1395', *Revue de l'Orient latin*, iii (1895), 578–579.

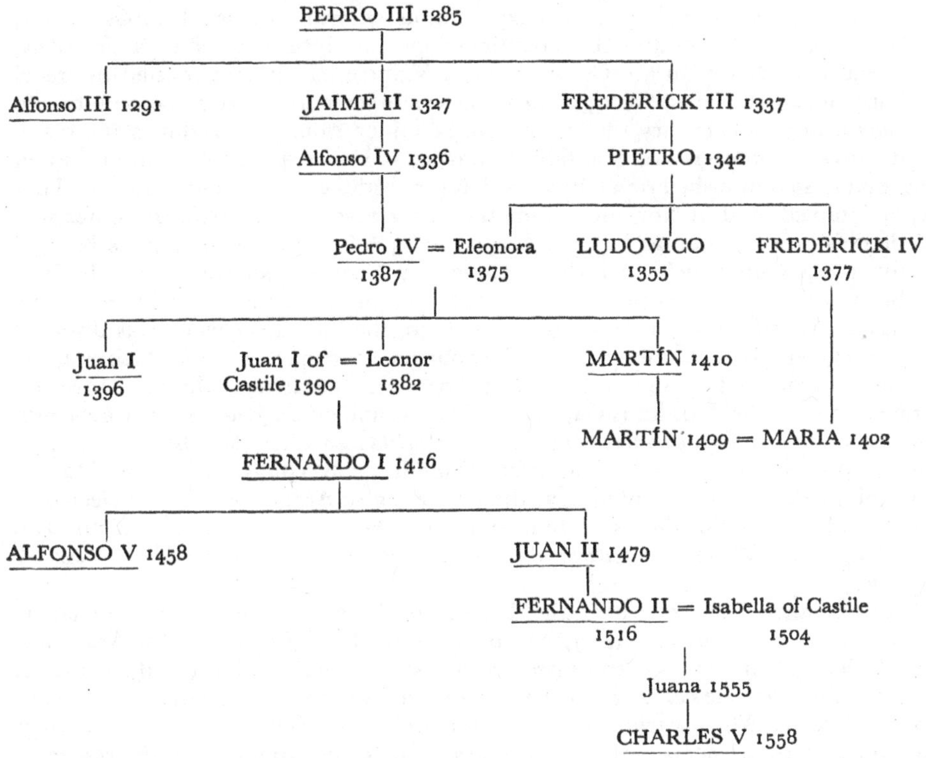


Simplified genealogy of the House of Aragon (rulers of Sicily in capitals; Kings of Aragon underlined; the dates given are those of death). Pedro III's wife, Costanza of Hohenstaufen, was the daughter of Frederick II's son Manfred. Jaime II became King of Sicily in 1285 and of Aragon in 1291, but relinquished Sicily to Frederick III in 1296. Pedro IV had claims to Sicily in and after 1377, but subsequently they were transferred to the younger Martín; the latter was succeeded by his father Martín in 1409, at which point Aragon and Sicily were reunited.

launched a five-year struggle to reverse the disintegration of royal power. Malta remained at the mercy of the Sicilian magnates, who used it as a base for resistance to the Aragonese Crown. Martín repeatedly sought to secure support in Sicily by granting out the County of Malta—to Giovanna Alagona in 1391, to Guglielmo Raimondo Moncada in 1392, to Artale Alagona in 1393. After 1393 Artale Alagona changed sides frequently, and in 1396 he attacked the Sicilian coast with two galleys apparently armed at Malta.[249] The islands were granted on 13 December 1396 as a marquisate to Guglielmo Raimondo Moncada; in April 1397 he was sending envoys to receive homages in Malta, by June he had received a delegation from the Maltese, but in November he, in turn, was formally deprived of the marquisate. Then,

[249] The Genoese were again involved, and at one point four Genoese galleys carried Alagona to Malta: text of 26 July 1398 in D. Girona Llagostera, 'Itinerari del Rey en Martí: 1396–1402', *Anuari del Institut d'Estudis Catalans*, iv (1911/2), 122. The events of 1377–1397 in Sicily and Malta are too confusing to be summarized adequately here.

following decades of oppression and exploitation by tyrannous or rebellious Counts, the *universitates* of Malta and Gozo petitioned for their return to the royal *demanium,* to direct dependence on the Crown. Some Maltese had in fact resisted the rebel Counts, and on 16 November 1397 the islands were reincorporated in perpetuity into the *demanium;* in February 1398 they were exempted from various duties and taxes, while royal supporters were suitably rewarded. However, these exemptions and concessions so diminished royal incomes that the castles at Malta and Gozo could not be maintained, and in November 1399 they were revoked. Martín the Elder succeeded his brother Juan as King of Aragon in 1396 and his son Martín as King of Sicily in 1409, in which year the Maltese and Gozitan *universitates* sent him an embassy which presented their complaints but emphasized their attachment to the dynasty. When the elder Martín died in 1410, the Sicilian regency was disputed between Queen Bianca, the widow of the younger Martín, and Bernat Cabrera, the Grand Justiciar, who secured control of Gozo and threatened Malta. However, Francesco Gatto held Malta as Captain for Bianca, and on 24 June 1411 she gave him permission to reduce Gozo to obedience *per la inclita casa di Aragona*; his chief opponent in Gozo, Antonio la Barba, was defeated and his lands confiscated. The Maltese recognized Fernando de Antequera, the new King of Aragon and Sicily elected in 1412, and the articles they sent him in 1416 looked back to the time of the two Martíns, when Malta was *reducta a la sou naturali signuri, zo esti a la sacra casa di Aragona.*

The balance of power within the domains of the Aragonese Crown did change. Barcelona faced serious decline when its banks crashed in 1381; in 1412 the Aragonese and Valencians imposed a semi-Castilian dynasty on the Catalans; and soon after, Alfonso V moved the centre of the confederation away from his peninsular domains towards Italy. The doctrine of *pactisme*, the notion of a contract between the ruler and the leading elements among his peoples, of allegiance to the king who respected his subjects' rights and customs, was particularly strong in Catalunya. When in 1410 there was no direct male heir to the throne, the Catalans insisted on a peaceful and strictly legal settlement of the crisis. The constitutional formulae followed in 1412, when representatives of the estates of Aragon, Valencia and Catalunya chose one of six candidates, helped to maintain the union by enabling the Catalans to accept Fernando de Antequera, to whom they were strongly opposed; he was also accepted by the Mallorquins and Sicilians who were not represented in the election. While recognizing the special problems of their various domains, the kings often thought of their peoples in a general way as their subjects or *naturales*, rather than as 'Aragonese', 'Catalans' or 'Sicilians'. Often it would have been difficult to do otherwise. Many Sicilian barons, for example, were Aragonese or Catalan by name and origin, with family ties and possessions in various lands; they understood a variety of languages, and lived in palaces in Palermo or Syracuse built in much the same style as those of Barcelona or Gerona. Politically, economically and culturally, this was a Western Mediterranean community to which the Maltese were conscious that, willingly or otherwise, they belonged.[250]

[250] Valentini, of course, saw Malta's 'integrationism' in a different light: 'la sua fedeltà alla corona aragonese e castigliana non è devozione ad un re straniero: è bisogno della Sicilia e niente altro' (*ASM*, vii. 69). But that was only a part of the truth.

Maltese protestations of attachment to Aragon had other, more practical meanings. The *universitas* and its council persistently resisted alienation from the royal *demanium*, while demanding tax-exemptions on imported Sicilian grain. From 1397 to 1530 Malta was not granted out as a County, though it was alienated in other ways;[251] in this respect, the fifteenth century differed from the fourteenth. Maltese historiography has traditionally regarded the election of Fernando de Antequera in 1412 as inaugurating a 'Castilian' period. Fernando's father, Juan of Trastámara, was King of Castile but his mother was an Aragonese princess and his grandmother a Sicilian princess, so that he had genuine claims to the Crowns of Aragon and Sicily. Under Fernando's son Alfonso V, who was born and bred in Castile, a number of Castilian administrators reached Malta, yet it was Alfonso who abandoned both Castile and Aragon for Sicily and Italy. There were few Spaniards in fourteenth-century Malta; it was in the fifteenth century that Malta was most truly Aragonese. Even the marriage in 1469 between Fernando, King of Sicily and heir to the Crown of Aragon, and Isabella, the heiress of Castile, did not bring Malta into direct dependence on the Crown of Castile, for the subsequent union of the Aragonese and Castilian Crowns in their Burgundian grandson, Charles V, was a personal one and only very gradually led to the unification of their kingdoms. Castilian and Aragonese policies in the Mediterranean did come under common direction, yet legally, administratively and economically Aragon and Castile, and their domains, remained clearly distinct long after 1530. The notion that there was a 'Castilian' period in Maltese history has no real justification, and is best abandoned. For the rest, historians have concentrated on the islanders' struggles and sacrifices to buy out the hated intruder Gonsalvo de Monroy in 1428, a much misunderstood episode long seen as a turning-point in a struggle for liberty; in and after 1524 the *universitas* was to rest its opposition to a new royal enfeoffment of the islands, by Charles V to the Knights Hospitallers, on the royal privilege of 1428.[252] The period between 1412 and 1458 is covered by the articles of Roberto Valentini, whose treatment is marred by his Italianate anxiety to prove that the Aragonese connection was ruinous in every way.[253] The period from 1458 to 1530, though the most heavily documented, has received no coherent modern treatment at all.

Fernando's viceroy in Sicily, his younger son Juan, made a number of sensible reforms in 1416, ending the disastrous practice by which the Castellan of the Birgu castle could sell exemptions from guard-duty. But Alfonso V, who succeeded in 1416 and spent only 12 out of 42 years of his reign in Spain, had ambitious policies in Italy, Africa and the Levant which outran the real resources of the Aragonese confederation and shifted its centre towards Sicily and Naples; and this altered the Crown's attitude towards the Maltese, who suffered in particular from the king's recurrent temptation to finance his costly wars at their expense. In 1420 Alfonso

[251] The Monroy grant was made by contract but was not—as often claimed—an enfeoffment; Alfonso V . . . *pignoraverit seu cum carta gracie alienaverit, vendiderit et concessit* (text in Valentini, in *ASM*, viii. 307).

[252] References and texts in Valentini, in *Archivum Melitense*, ix. 145–146, 168–171, 183–184, 224–226. The Maltese *Memorial* of 1801 to the British Government misleadingly interpreted the 1428 privilege, which it misdated to 1397, as Malta's *Magna Charta*; text of 1801 in Eton, part 1 (1802), 21–37.

[253] Eg. R. Valentini, 'Ribellione di Malta e spedizione alla Gerba come conseguenze dell'inefficienza della flotta aragonese nel Mediterraneo', *ASM*, viii (1936/7); 'L'espansionismo aragonese nel Mediterraneo come causa della decadenza di Malta', *ASM*, xii (1941).

pawned the royal incomes and jurisdictions in the archipelago to Viceroy Antonio Cardona for 30,000 florins of Aragon, a sum which Cardona was naturally anxious to extort from the islanders as rapidly as possible. In 1426 a renewed pawning, to Gonsalvo de Monroy, produced immediate protests. Viceroy Guglielmo Moncada went to Malta in person and was insulted; Monroy's goods were pillaged at Mdina, and his wife was besieged in Birgu castle. Threats from Sicily and lack of food supplies forced the Maltese to treat; on the other hand the next viceroy, Niccolò Speciale, realized that the Crown could not afford to lose Malta. The Maltese were allowed to buy out Monroy, and actually succeeded in raising 20,000 florins, rhetorically pledging themselves to sell their own persons and their sons and daughters. The *universitas* was to control the incomes of the *secrezia* or Crown finance office for ten years and a local notable, Antoni Desguanes, became Castellan. In 1428 the king promised an amnesty and perpetual incorporation into the Crown of Sicily, while the Maltese were to have the right to resist *manu forte* any further attempted alienation. Meanwhile Gonsalvo de Monroy died, pardoning the Maltese the 10,000 florins still owing.

Malta's wealth was strictly limited and Alfonso was, in a sense, consuming it in advance when he sold future tax incomes to foreign barons or to officials who would pay cash. The king knew that the profits of such investments would have to be squeezed from the islanders, who complained repeatedly of invasions, plagues, bad weather, depopulation, overtaxation, corrupt officials and the rest. No doubt the average Maltese disliked being detached from the Crown, partly for traditional sentimental reasons of political loyalty, partly because such action heralded baronial exploitation; and doubtless such feelings were voiced through the *universitas*, membership of which was broadly based. However, there was another class of Maltese or Siculo-Maltese who really dominated the *universitas;* these were the leading men of Malta such as Francesco Gatto and Antoni Desguanes, Pedro de Busco and Simone de Mazzara, men whose interests were threatened by the Cardonas and Monroys, men who aspired to control the *secrezia* and the *castellania* of the castle, to rent the gabelles, to occupy the fiefs, to manage the cotton trade, and in general to dominate Maltese incomes themselves. In fact, a few years after the uprising against Monroy, Pedro de Busco held both Castellanies and the two *secrezie* of Malta and Gozo, and a number of fiefs as well. Often these men were really Sicilians or Spaniards; many fought as naval captains for Alfonso V, and some were also corsairs or pirates, but though they served as galley-captains and held fiefs in return for military service, they did not really constitute a purely military aristocracy because their lands, their marriages and their position in the *universitas* all gradually assimilated them to the local notables. It suited those who held a semi-monopoly of public office to appeal in the name of liberty to ancient customs and to a certain local patriotism, and at all costs to resist the greater operators such as Monroy. Naturally, when such lesser oligarchs themselves secured royal support and grew over-powerful, as in the case of the Desguanes and their clan, the rest turned against them.[254]

Malta was exposed not only to the Crown's creditors but also to its enemies, to the Genoese and above all to the growing power of the Hafsids of Tunisia. Alfonso's

[254] Valentini, in *ASM*, xiii. 23–27; H. Bresc, *infra*, 141–151.

policies provoked raids on Malta and Gozo without providing adequate defence, for though there was a foreign garrison in Birgu castle the islands were guarded largely by the islanders themselves. The Tunisians attacked Malta, apparently capturing its bishop, in 1423; Alfonso's brother Pedro riposted with an expedition to Kerkena in 1424; the Hafsids then raided Sicily, and in 1429 a large fleet ravaged Malta for three days, all but capturing Mdina and carrying off 3,000 captives or more. Finally Guttierez de Nava arrived from Sicily with reinforcements and refortified the castle, and in 1432 Alfonso himself led a somewhat unsuccessful punitive raid on Gerba, possibly visiting Malta on his return;[255] the resultant truces at least produced an end to major Hafsid attacks. In 1435, however, Alfonso was defeated at sea off Ponza by the Genoese, and Calabrian ships devastated Gozo in 1439. There was a series of Genoese incursions, while ceaseless piratical activity, in which the Maltese themselves took part, centred on the islands. The king had no positive policy; he could not risk losing Malta and had to maintain its garrison, but he did not make it an outpost for maritime operations, as he did, for example, with the small island of Kastellorizzo between Rhodes and Cyprus. Alfonso can have had little profit from Malta, except perhaps briefly after 1420. In 1450 he was planning to alienate the islands to the Valencian military order of Montesa, a project soon abandoned in the face of Maltese threats to invoke the charter of 1428 and resist by force.[256] In 1458, just before his death, Alfonso finally acted both to restrain the profiteers to whom he had continued to pawn the islands' incomes, and to restore the *universitas* its rights. He reduced the powers of the Castellan of Birgu castle and introduced reforms concerning food supplies, military service, clerical absenteeism and elections to public office.[257]

There was relative peace after 1432. The effects on the population and economy of foreign razzias, administrative malpractices and continual fiscal exploitation are hard to gauge, particularly as the main sources are the *capitoli*, the eloquent but exaggerated complaints and requests sent to the king or viceroy. In 1439 the Gozitans spoke of 13 *uncie* paid out in taxes *li quali, teste Deo, extrahirimu quasi di intra li ossa nostri*,[258] while in 1466 the Maltese complained: *quista insola e quasi unu parvulu scoglectu situatu in mezu mari, remotu undique da omni succursu et rifrigeriu . . .*[259] The *capitoli* lamented the thousands of Maltese seized by Hafsid raiders but they also bemoaned the cost of ransoming them back again.[260] Wine and grain had to be imported from Sicily but this was not necessarily a sign of economic collapse. Piracy brought employment and profits, as well as losses. There was overtaxation, emigration to Sicily, plague, the collapse of viticulture which was said to sustain 1,000 souls, and depopulation at Mdina, but it is hard to treat such factors statistically, or to estimate the real effects on the Maltese; their sufferings were not measurable. The

[255] F. Cerone, 'A proposito di alcuni documenti sulla seconda spedizione di Alfonso V contro l'isola Gerba', *Anuari del Institut d'Estudis Catalans*, iii (1909/10); see also C. Trasselli, *Sicilia, Levante e Tunisia nei secoli XIV e XV* (Trapani, 1952). Alfonso's visit to Malta is, apparently, not documented.

[256] On the Montesa project, Valentini, in *Archivum Melitense*, ix. 145–146; explanation of this incident requires further study of Montesa's maritime interests.

[257] Text in Valentini, in *ASM*, ix. 110–123.

[258] Text in Giambruno—Genuardi, i. 330–331.

[259] Text in Valentini, in *ASM*, x. 70.

[260] *Infra*, 133, 191–193.

problems and paradoxes of economic decadence and cultural flowering throughout the Aragonese domains, as indeed in the whole of Western Europe in the fifteenth century, remain unresolved.[261] In Malta, evidence for a state of crisis has to be set against indications of immigration and population growth, of a certain wealth based on cotton and piracy, and of the construction of churches, convents and palaces in Mdina and Rabat. It is too simple merely to say that Alfonso's ill-founded Italian ambitions ruined his finances and prevented him from defending Malta, and that he sacrificed the island to his greedy officials. It seems, in fact, that equally serious crises came after Alfonso's death in 1458, with revolts and upheavals in Sicily and Catalunya, and several decades of depression in Malta itself. Then, after about 1480, came a dramatic and as yet unexplained rise in population.[262]

After 1458 Malta was still a minor shipping centre; at one point in 1479, for example, three Catalan vessels were in port.[263] The diffusion of Ottoman power into North Africa and the Western Mediterranean brought new dangers, and Turkish raiders attacked Birgu in 1488. Malta had become a serious objective for the Turks, and Fernando II of Aragon, his viceroys and captains did take measures to secure its defence.[264] In general Malta remained within its Siculo-Aragonese context. As King of Aragon, Fernando II renewed Alfonso V's interventions in the Italian wars, while the campaigns during which his forces, with valuable Maltese help, captured Tripoli in 1510 represented a fusion of Aragonese commercial interests with an extension into Africa of the old Castilian ideal of the *reconquista*. Turkish expansion into North Africa after 1516, and the events which led to the Hapsburg Charles V becoming not only King in Sicily, Aragon and Castile, but also emperor in Germany and ruler of a world-empire with lands in North Africa as well as in Europe and America, resulted in a widening of the struggle. On the southern margin of Mediterranean Christendom, Malta formed the central point of a defensive axis stretching from Tripoli to Sicily. It lay on the frontiers of a conflict between two universal powers, Ottoman Turkey and Hapsburg Spain, and it was dangerously exposed to Muslim attacks; Mosta was sacked in 1526.[265] Charles V opted for an inexpensive way of defending both Malta and Tripoli when he granted them to the Order of St. John in 1530, but he did so as King of Sicily. Malta and Gozo again became, technically at least, a fief held from the Sicilian Crown, and the islanders' resistance to this new enfeoffment showed how little some things had changed.[266]

From about 1270 onwards the surviving materials permit the construction of a reasonably detailed, if notably uneven, outline of events at Malta. Such *histoire événementielle* can no longer be regarded as constituting real history but none the less it remains essential for the further study of those social, economic and cultural

[261] Del Treppo, 582–605 *et passim*, discusses this paradox; his work provides an essential background to the 15th-century period.

[262] *Infra*, 53 n. 270.

[263] Text in Leopardi, in *Melita Historica*, ii. 132–133.

[264] L. Suárez Fernández, *Politica internacional de Isabel la Católica*, ii (Valladolid, 1966), 146–147.

[265] Abela, 432–434, 438, 442 *et passim*.

[266] According to the anonymous writer of ca. 1630, it was predicted after the coming of the Knights *che la Religione non starà più in Malta di anni cento in circa, mà che da Malta anderà in Sardegna, oue finalmente si risoluerà da se stessa in fumo . . .*: Royal Malta Library, Biblioteca Ms. 5, f. 569.

developments which now form the centre of historians' interests, and without which the course of events itself can scarcely be understood. The overwhelming bulk of the documentation dates only from about 1410 or even later. A detailed study of fifteenth-century Malta which will replace the articles of Mifsud and Valentini is now being written,[267] but it will always be difficult to trace the origins and development of fifteenth-century institutions in the partial obscurity of the preceding centuries; paradoxically, the period of direct Sicilian rule in the fourteenth century, which must be studied above all at Palermo, remains dimmer than the later thirteenth century, for which Angevin and Aragonese documents are available.[268]

The fundamental question of the islands' population is a difficult one. It can scarcely have been more than 10,000 in about 1241, and may have been considerably less; it was estimated, presumably with some exaggeration, at 4,400 hearths, perhaps 20,000 people, in 1394.[269] Early fifteenth-century figures suggest a total of some 10,000, which decreased slightly after 1420 but increased after 1480 to about 20,000 in 1530.[270] In such small islands razzias, plagues, emigrations or expulsions tended to provoke disproportionately severe demographic repercussions. More fundamentally, the economy apparently changed during the late fourteenth century. Cotton was being exported to Sicily in some quantity,[271] and the Catalans were importing raw and spun Maltese cotton, either directly from Malta or from Sicily, at least from 1404 onwards; they carried cloth, oil, sardines and dried fruits to Malta in exchange.[272] Grain and wine were seldom exported thereafter, but had to be imported, while the island's economy probably became dangerously dependent on piracy and a single crop, cotton. Though there were still household slaves—black and white, Christian and Muslim—in the fifteenth century, the disappearance of the *servi* and *villani* presumably reflected the end of the great royal estates, agriculturally unprofitable and increasingly alienated.[273] There is a good deal of evidence for the abandonment of settlements, but deserted sites do not necessarily imply a falling population; they may mean that the country people—the *biduini* or 'bedouins' as they were known[274]—moved from one set of caves and mud houses to another, that they were leaving exhausted fields for more fertile lands, that they had changed their crops

[267] The various articles of G. Wettinger prelude a forthcoming major publication.

[268] H. Bresc and G. Wettinger (*infra*) are severely handicapped by this lack of materials.

[269] *Supra*, 39.46.

[270] G. Wettinger, 'The Militia List of 1419–20: a New Starting Point for the Study of Malta's Population', *Melita Historica*, v no. 2 (1969), 83 and *infra*, 184–186. C. Trasselli, ('Richerche su la popolazione della Sicilia nel XV secolo', *Atti dell'Accademia di Scienze Lettere ed Arti di Palermo*, 4 ser., xv part 2 1954/5), 226–227, 244, 265, produces totals for both islands of ca. 5000 in 1464 and 1478; these seem too low, perhaps because they are derived from taxation records. Quintin calculated over 20,000 inhabitants in 1533. For what it is worth, Mifsud, in *Archivum Melitense*, iii. 182, mentions a copy of an affirmation of various old men, made in 1531, that the population had doubled in the previous 100 years. For later figures, Beloch, i. 165–168.

[271] H. Bresc, *infra*, 131–132, and *idem*, in *Papers of the British School at Rome*, xli, 186,188 n. 41 *et passim*. On Maltese cotton in 1164 *infra*, 106. Sugar from *Marta* was mentioned by Marino Sanuto, ca. 1306–1321: J. Bongars, *Gesta Dei per Francos*, ii (Hanover, 1611), 24. *Bambagio di Malta* and *cotone mapputo*, cotton and cotton wool, were apparently circulating ca. 1340: Francesco Balducci Pegolotti, *La Practica della Mercatura*, ed. A. Evans (Cambridge, Mass., 1936), 293, 367. See also Mifsud, in *Archivum Melitense*, iii. 191–192, 228–229; A. Vella, 'The Cotton Textile Industry in Malta', *Melita Historica*, iv no. 3 (1966), 210.

[272] Del Treppo, 159–161, 167–168, 174–176, 551 *et passim*.

[273] *Infra*, 131.

[274] Late-medieval reference to *lj persunj sunnu tenutj ad habitarj ala chitatj et dilj bidujnj*: Royal Malta Library, Biblioteca Ms. 670, f. 22v.

or were fleeing from raiders. Quintin in 1533 and Abela in 1647 were still remarking on the deserted lands, yet the fifteenth-century *capitoli* repeatedly complained that Mdina was small and partly uninhabited, that the town dwellers were moving out to the *casali*. The meaning of the word *casale* was itself obscure. It was interchangeable with *raħal* and may have signified a farmstead, estate or village;[275] it also defined an administrative district usually producing from 20 to 100 men for militia service.[276] Little is known about the typical Maltese *casale*; whether it was fortified, whether it had a tower or a church, whether it corresponded to an economic unit, how it was managed, what its social structure was. In what way agricultural labourers held land, whether the workers made contracts of the *mezzadria* type, or what size their holdings were are other unresolved problems. Excavation might provide some illumination, and the notarial and other documents can certainly help; the Sicilian models may also be relevant.[277]

The commissioners' report of 1524 and Quintin's *Descriptio* of 1533 emphasized the harshness of life, the lack of wood, the heat, wind and dust, the fevers, the brackish drinking water, the stoniness of the fields, the descents of corsairs. Gozo seems to have been more fertile. Malta had water in places; thistles and grasses provided fuel and fodder; there were fruits and olives, honey, cotton, flax, and herbs such as cumin. What kind of agricultural revolution cotton production may have provoked after about 1350 is not clear, but Quintin described cultivation methods:

> Since the sun dries it all up, I am surprised that although the earth is rather warm, the farmers mix dung in it to manure it. The ground is sown in springtime, but first it is watered; the ploughed field is then at once sown, for they hold that that makes the soil become more fertile, and then the ploughed land is covered by dragging a harrow or rake over it. At the proper time it is hoed and freed of weeds and useless grasses both by hand and by hoe; during the harvest, the rains are much feared. The inhabitants seek, if they are at all able, to sow grain more than anything else, since they draw the greatest profit from the grain, as the island is not excessively fruitful in it. . . . The trees bear fruit twice annually, and there are often two harvests a year, for when the barley has been cut, it is soon followed by the cotton, and indeed the cotton by the barley, so much so that the land never ceases to produce. Thus, where the soil is suitable, it is extremely fertile; one *modius* of seed may give sixteen *modii* or sometimes more. Over the whole island the fields normally yield a ten or twelvefold return . . .[278]

It may be possible to use medieval place-names to trace marshlands and marginal areas, as has been done for the early modern period.[279] Certain districts, notably in

[275] G. Wettinger (*infra*) provides discussion and bibliography on the problems of *casali* and abandoned sites.

[276] Text in Wettinger, in *Melita Historica*, v. 88–106; some *casali* produced considerably less than 20. A document of 1479 referred to *dicto casali et eius conturiu*: text in Leopardi, in *Melita Historica*, ii. 252.

[277] H. Bresc—F. d'Angelo, 'Structure et évolution de l'habitat dans la région de Termini Imerese: XIIe-XVe siècles', *Mélanges de l'École française de Rome: Moyen Age—Temps Modernes*, lxxxiv (1972). M. Aymard—H. Bresc, 'Problemi di storia dell'insediamento nella Sicilia medievale e moderno: 1100–1800', *Quaderni storici*, xxiv (1973), constitutes the essential background, while G. Wettinger and A. Luttrell cover Maltese aspects and plans for a topographical survey in *Les habitats médiévaux en Méditerranée Occidentale: les rapports de l'archéologie et de l'histoire* [forthcoming].

[278] 1524 report in Bosio, iii. 30–31; on Quintin, *supra*, 1. Quintin's crop yields seem exaggeratedly high.

[279] B. Blouet, 'The Distribution of Marshland in Malta during the Seventeenth Century', and 'Some Observations on the Distribution of Xagħra Place-Names in Malta', *Journal of Maltese Studies*, ii and iv (1964 and 1967); cf. *idem*, 'Rural Settlement in Malta', *Geography*, lvi (1971).

north-west Malta, were not settled but farmers may have walked or ridden considerable distances in order to work them. It is difficult to gauge how far marginal lands were exploited in the late middle ages, but uncultivated areas were used for grazing and hunting.[280] There were also gardens and closed orchards.[281] To what extent the countryside had been terraced or turned into small fields is also uncertain. Unmortared stone walls and two-faced rubble-filled walls were already being constructed, at least in buildings, in prehistoric times.[282] Such walls used up loose stones, broke the wind, contained valuable soil and marked boundaries.[283] They also shut in animals[284] or, elsewhere, excluded them.[285] Some at least of the peasants lived in natural or rock-cut caves, as described by Quintin: *Trogloditae in ea multi: specus excavant: hae illis domus.*[286] Quintin also said that even the Birgu houses were unmortared. Despite its scarcity, some wood may have been used in houses,[287] particularly in view of the frequent shifting or abandonment of sites. The *casale* itself may have had a central building or tower, rectangular and flat-roofed, built with squared stone slabs laid across internal arches and finished with a waterproof and strongly-resistant paste of lime, broken pottery and water, as described by Francesco Laparelli da Cortona in 1566/7.[288] Many sixteenth-century houses still had reed roofs, which were sometimes blown away.[289] Datable evidence is, however, scarce and domestic buildings can seldom be dated on stylistic grounds.[290]

Town life was largely limited to Mdina, though there were communities outside the castle at Birgu and in the Gozo *castello*. At Gozo, as at Mdina, the Muslim and post-Muslim urban area was so contracted that it occupied only the most defensible, fortified fraction of the Roman town.[291] Then in the later medieval period the suburbs spread out again within, and at Mdina beyond, the ancient Roman limits. Mdina itself was outgrown; in 1419/20 its suburb of Rabat produced 234 militiamen

[280] A. Mifsud, 'Sulla caccia in Malta nel passato', *Archivum Melitense*, iii nos. 3–4 (1918), 118–119.

[281] *Infra*, 129 n. 11.

[282] D. Trump, *Skorba* (London-Malta, 1966), with plates and excavation plans; note that mud-bricks and timber were used in prehistoric buildings.

[283] Text in Leopardi, in *Melita Historica*, ii. 133 (1479).

[284] Text of 1365 in Catania, Archivio di Stato, Fondo Benedettini Ms. 159 f, 121v–123v (late copy): *quedam pecciuncula terre muro circumdata deputata pro includendis animalibus sita in quodam spacio communi Casalis uocati Rachal kjber* . . . .

[285] Text *infra*, 57.

[286] Cf. *infra*, 188 n. 24. A. Kircher, *Mundus Subterraneus*, ii (3rd ed: Amsterdam, 1678), 119–120, fascinatingly described the troglodytic community at Għar il-Kbir, and another on Gozo, in 1637.

[287] Cf. H. Bresc, 'Case di Legno in Sicilia', *Gruppo Richerche Archeologica Medievale—Palermo* (20 Aug. 1971).

[288] Quoted, in translation, in Hughes, *Fortress*, 31–32; see also *idem*, *Building*, 196–198. This technique was also mentioned by Quintin in 1533.

[289] References in Dessoulavy, in *The Sundial*, iii nos. 4–8, 98–99.

[290] For the analogy with the present: A. Harrison—R. Hubbard, 'Maltese Vernacular', *Architectural Review*, cv (1949); cf. Q. Hughes *et al.*, 'Malta', *ibid.*, cxlvi (1969). For analogies with surrounding lands: G. Valussi, *La casa rurale nella Sicilia Occidentale* (Florence, 1968); cf. F. Bonasera, *Studi sulle isole minori pertinenti alla Sicilia: indagini sulla forma della casa rurale—Guida integrativa all'indagine diretta (sopraluogo)* (Faenza, 1967). M. King, *Housing in the Maltese Islands: an Analysis of Influences on Built Form* (unpublished M.Arch. thesis: Royal University of Malta, 1971), argues interestingly for Syrian and other Oriental influences, using philological evidence of the type discussed *supra*, 23–25, but Tunisian or Sicilian influences seem more probable. Though its historical assumptions are debatable, this thesis contains useful information on troglodytic settlements, construction techniques and building terminology. See also P. Cassar, 'The Corbelled Stone Huts of the Maltese Islands', *Man*, lxi (1961).

[291] Trump, *Malta*, 104–117 (with plan of Roman Rabat), 148–153.

as against 132 from Mdina.[292] The port at Birgu was an increasingly strong centre of foreign influence. The parallel peninsula on which Senglea was later built was scarcely occupied before 1530. The *universitas* records provide a detailed picture of life at Mdina in the fifteenth century with decisions concerning the fountains and water-supply, the sale of fish, gambling, education and all the petty affairs of a small town. The council regulated the price of many kinds of meat—mutton, pork and beef—and of beans, honey, milk, cheese and so forth.[293] The 'civic nobility' had their palaces in Mdina, and there lived the island's few judges and notaries, and its Jewish community. Perhaps 500 strong, the Jews were grouped in their *aljama* and dependent on the Jewry of Sicily; they had a synagogue and a cemetery, and their own notary. As well as being artisans and barbers, the Jews were active in commerce; they had to raise their own taxes, maintain men-at-arms and subsidize royal galleys. In the fifteenth century there were repressive measures against them, yet they owned so much property that it was difficult to sell it all when they were expelled in 1492.[294] Mdina and Rabat had a middling element of artisans who were organized in guilds and brotherhoods ,and who had to resist efforts, in 1475 for example, to exclude them from office in the *universitas*.[295] Malta's doctors were almost all Jewish. There was a hospital at Rabat by 1372, and other hospitals, one of them in Gozo, were founded during the fifteenth century. Rigorous quarantine measures were taken against recurrent epidemics, and when plague arrived from Africa in 1523 Birgu was cut off by a cordon of guards.[296]

In addition to the military command with its own officials and garrison under the Castellan at Birgu castle, and to the *secreto* and other representatives of the Sicilian *curia* who administered the taxes, gabelles and royal estates, a local government, the *universitas* at Mdina, was headed by its Captain, known in Maltese as the *hakem*. In 1372 the king nominated Guglielmo Murina as Captain, with Lancea Gatto and Paolo Maniavacca as judge and notary to his court; there were parallel arrangements in Gozo. These men were among the notables of the islands, but in the fifteenth century the terms 'noble' or 'baron' were used without any evident precision, as was 'fief'. Most Maltese must have been unsure of the technical difference between a *rahal*, a *casale*, a *feudum* or *fegho*, a *tenimentum terrarum* held at *census*, a *tenimentum burgensaticum* which was allodial land not held in feudal tenure, and so forth.[297] A text of about 1400 confusingly described one holding as:

> Tenuta altra di terrj uocata lu fegu di rachalniculosu in lu casalj di rachalbibir alu locu dictu haiar lym, diuisa in diuersi pezi cum spazij, cum casi et cum mandrj siti in lu dictu fegu . . .

[292] *Infra*, 186; these incomplete figures ignore the Mdina Jews and others.

[293] Eg. text of 1472 in Leopardi, in *Melita Historica*, ii. 125; *infra*, 135.

[294] C. Roth, 'The Jews of Malta', *Transactions of the Jewish Historical Society*, xii (1931), a work derived largely from Sicilian documents; Dr. Godfrey Wettinger plans to publish a more detailed study based on the Maltese archives. On Jews active in foreign commerce ca. 1380, see texts in Luttrell, in *Melita Historica*, v. 161–164.

[295] A. Mifsud, 'I nostri Consoli e le Arti ed i Mestieri', *Archivum Melitense*, iii no. 1 (1917), 37 n. 3 *et passim*.

[296] P. Cassar, *Medical History of Malta* (London, 1964), 11–17, 23–24, 153, 157, 164–165. There seems to be no clear evidence that the great plague, the Black Death, reached Malta in 1347/8.

[297] On officials, land-tenures and their confusions, see H. Bresc and G. Wettinger *infra*, and details and texts in Bresc, in *Papers of the British School at Rome*, xli. Bresc wrote without seeing C. Galea Scannura, 'The Office of the Secrezia of Malta . . .', *Melita Historica*, vi no. 2 (1973), which covers the period 1450–1530 not studied by Bresc; it is essential to consult Galea Scannura's addenda in *ibid*, vi no. 3 (1974), 324.

An item from the *capitoli* of 1475 illustrated similar uncertainties:

> Item suplica la Uniuersitati preditta alo prefato Ill. signuri che la pena la quali e solita per via di bandu publicu imponirisi de mandato alicuius magistratus a quilli che trasinu et mettinu apaxiri loru animali inferendu damnu in li possessioni di autrui non si poza Imponiri ultra di unczi quatru pecunie meliueti alu officiu di la capitania et unu agustali alu bagliu di malta et che tali pena haia locu solum quantu pertangi ali possessioni circumdati et Inclusi di mura et In li feghi et etiam tenimenti di terri burgensatichi appellati et nominati In lingua dicte Insule per casam quod in lingua latina Importat feghi et non in haltri terreni aperti In liquali solum si haya hauirj considerationi di li damnj ut s[upra] comu sempri ex antiquo si haui obseruato per tollirj tutti nouitati et noui extorsioni: *Placet dno. Viceregi.*[298]

Evidently the distinction between *feghi* and *tenimenti di terri burgensatichi* was blurred in the Maltese term *casam* or *qasam* which now means simply 'estate'. Fief-holders could be relatively humble men, and those who bought or sold fiefs, or had them confiscated, cannot have felt that their status ultimately depended on fief-holding. No doubt there was a semi-urban patriciate, a recognizable establishment which included clerical figures like the bullying archdeacon Lancea Desguanes. Fief-holders held lands or other properties in the Sicilian manner; some did owe military service, but the 'feudal' contract was really an economic one, the concession of an income by the Crown. Fiefs could be purchased, sold or otherwise alienated; they were all held direct from the Crown, which could if it wished replace them with a money-grant, and there were no feudal courts or jurisdictions. The case of Alvaro de Nava illustrates one aspect of the system. He was attached to the royal household and was captain of two galleys when, in 1465, the king granted him 200 gold florins annually out of the Crown's *rentas;* later the viceroy changed these, first into an income from the Maltese *secrezia*, and then into the incomes of the fief of Benwarrad. Subsequently in 1477 the king, having borrowed 3,000 florins from Alvaro de Nava without paying interest, granted him and his heirs the actual possession of the fief until such time as the whole sum had been repaid.[299] This was one way in which the royal patrimony was dissipated. In 1530 the Grand Master of the Hospitallers complained to Charles V that nothing, not even the castle, was left: *non ce un palmo di terra che non sia dato o Impegnato Infino al Castello medemo.*[300]

Sicilian expenditure on Malta's defence was minimal, though there was a garrison of mercenaries at Birgu which could be used against the population if need be.[301] Land tenure involved military service, and absentee holders of property—*tantu pheudali quantu burgensatici*—were supposed to provide men and horses.[302] A local militia numbered at least 1,667 in 1419,[303] and in 1499 King Fernando, exaggeratedly no doubt, claimed that eight parishes around Mdina could provide 4,000 armed fighting men—*hombres de pelea.*[304] The royal fleet was a distant comfort in

[298] Text of ca. 1400 in Catania, Archivio di Stato, Fondo Benedettini Ms. 153, f. 505; 1475 text in Mdina, Cathedral Archives Ms. 34, f. 392. A text of 1523 described the *cusaim di rahal birabar quod latine sonat feudulum casalis birabar* (*infra*, 206).

[299] Barberi, *Capibrevi*, iii. 453–455; Royal Malta Library, Università Ms. 7, f. 158–159.

[300] Text in Valentini, in *Archivum Melitense*, ix. 228–231.

[301] Details *infra*, 138–139; cf. A. Mifsud, 'La Milizia e le Torri antiche di Malta', *Archivum Melitense*, iv no. 2 (1920), an important article.

[302] Text of 1450 in Valentini, in *ASM*, viii. 495; other details in Mifsud, in *Archivum Melitense*, iii. 272–277, and Bresc, in *Papers of the British School at Rome*, xli, docs. 4, 28, 32 (1372).

[303] *Infra*, 186; there were also coastguard obligations.

[304] Royal Malta Library, Biblioteca Ms. 737, f. 225–228 (modern copy).

critical moments, so that naval defence depended largely on local shipping; Francesco Gatto, *miles* and *civis Meliveti*, was appointed by the king to command Malta's galley or galliot in 1398.[305] There was no exploitation of the harbour as a major base before 1530, but many of the leading families on Malta, such as the de Nava, were galley-captains or had their own galleys. There were also fishing vessels and shipping which brought provisions from Sicily. A Sicilian port-book for the year 1407/8 showed that 19 Maltese vessels carried almost all the grain exported to Malta; 295 *salme* from Vindicari, 58 from Syracuse, 48 from Agrigento and 81—of which 44 went to Gozo—from Terranova.[306] There must have been a minor ship-building or ship-repairing industry; some timber from Dalmatia, for example, was sold or seized at Malta as early as 1376.[307] Spectacular profits came from piracy and from the more official *guerra di corso* which occupied an important place in Malta's economy; piracy flourished during the endless warfare of the Sicilian Crown, and gave Malta a special importance. All classes could suffer as well as profit. In 1409 the Maltese complained that whereas their corsairs had once been completely free to attack Muslim shipping, they were then being made to give a fifth of their booty to the Sicilian Admiralty. Piracy, however, drew men away from the land, so that in 1440 foreign vessels were forbidden to recruit at Malta; in 1449 both Maltese and foreigners were forbidden to arm ships for the *corso* at Malta. In 1460 there were Maltese protests against 'friendly' corsairs and against the forcible recruitment of oarsmen by the Aragonese.[308] The island's most famous pirate, Michele de Malta, operated around Cyprus and Rhodes in the 1460's.[309] In 1525 and 1526 Maltese pirates based on Tripoli were active in the Aegean, provoking protests from the government of Crete.[310]

The coastal towers, primarily look-out and signal posts, were probably difficult to defend. One was to be built on Comino in 1418 while the tower in the port of Benwarrad, where shipping was accustomed to shelter, needed repair in 1494.[311] Even the Gozo *castello* was in ruins in 1442.[312] The defence of Malta depended essentially on the *castrum maris* at Birgu which existed by 1241 at the latest,[313] and in

[305] Text in *Memoirs of the Family of Inguanez*, 23–25 [with incorrect date]; on Pedro de Busco and the guard-galley in 1443, *infra*, 146.

[306] C. Trasselli, 'Sulla esportazione di cereali dalla Sicilia nel 1407–08', *Atti della Accademia di Scienze, Lettere e Arti di Palermo*, 4 ser., xv part 2 (1954/5), 336, 354, 365; tables I, IIIa. On Maltese shipping arrested in 1427, text in Valentini, in *ASM*, viii. 292.

[307] Text in Luttrell, in *Melita Historica*, v. 161–162.

[308] Texts in Valentini, in *ASM*, viii.75, 482, 492–493; x. 62–63.

[309] P. Cassar, 'The Maltese Corsairs and the Order of St. John of Jerusalem', *Scientia* [Malta], xxix (1963), 28–30 [also in *Catholic Historical Review*, xlvi (1960), 139–141]; the whole subject demands much further attention, but see H. Bresc, 'Course et piraterie en Sicile: 1250–1450', *I Congreso Internacional de Historia Mediterránea* [forthcoming]. A. Cremona, 'La Marina Maltese dal Medio Evo all'Epoca Moderna . . .', *Journal of Maltese Studies*, ii (1964), provides little medieval information.

[310] N. Iorga, *Notes et extraits pour servir à l'histoire des croisades au XVe siècle*, vi (Bucarest, 1916), 111–112, 117, 135–136; cf. F. B[orlandi], 'Corsari maltesi a Ragusa nel Quattro e nel Cinquecento', *ASM*, vii (1934/5), 243–245.

[311] Details in Mifsud, in *Archivum Melitense*, iv. 67–70; to what extent pre-medieval buildings were used and how far the surviving remains date before 1530 is yet to be established. A tower on the site of the later Fort Sant'Elmo was projected in 1488, but probably not built.

[312] *Infra*, 136 n. 62.

[313] Text in Winkelmann, 713–715.

Angevin times it was provided with effective munitions[314] which made it hard to take.[315] By 1274 there was an inner and an outer *castrum*,[316] and in 1533 Quintin described a fortress with the *borgo* at its foot. The development of artillery[317] and the appearance of the Turks must have accentuated the problems of its defence. The 1524 commissioners found the castle in a ruined state with few armaments, and they realized that in an age of gunpowder it not only failed to control the harbour, but was itself overlooked and dominated from across the water; furthermore, it could easily be mined. There were 40 houses within the castle, which was separated by a ditch from the Birgu, a considerable settlement which was not, however, defended by a wall across the landward end of the peninsula. In case of attack the *castrum maris* and its cannon did not even control the Grand Harbour;[318] and the villagers, those of Żeitun for example, were supposed to take shelter up at Mdina.[319] Mdina stood on the site of that part of the Roman town which evidently became the Byzantine *kastron* and then the Arab capital, and it must have undergone a succession of repairs and rebuildings.[320] In 1454 the *universitas* was petitioning to be allowed to rent out space within the ruined *castrum* at Mdina in the hope of attracting the population back from the *casali* to defend the town and to provide an income with which to repair the walls. The *universitas* claimed, falsely perhaps, that before 1377 the *castrum maris* had sufficed to defend the island, and that the castle and the internal wall at Mdina had been built by the tyrannous Chiaramonte merely to oppress the populace. The *torre mastra* above the gate was said to be in ruins, and permission was given to use the stone from the wall dividing the *castrum* from the town in order to repair the outer gate and walls.[321] In 1473 the *universitas* was considering the purchase of six bombards to defend the city.[322] Yet, despite constant repairs and expenses, Mdina's defences were in a hopeless state in 1524 when it was reported that only twenty of its houses could be put into reasonable repair.[323]

The *universitates* of both islands had numerous functions. They petitioned the king or viceroy for free grain or for exemptions from taxes on grain exported from Sicily,[324] and they nominated the consuls who protected Maltese and Gozitans in

[314] Inventories are published in Laurenza, in *ASM*, v. 132–136 (1274) and *infra*, 158–160 (April, 1429).

[315] Eg. from 1282 to 1284 (*supra*, 43).

[316] Text of 1274 in Laurenza, in ASM, v. 132–136.

[317] There were bombards at Birgu by 1429 (texts *infra*, 158–160). For an iron cannon or bombard some 65 cm. long, probably early 15th-century in date and found in Malta, G. Laking, *A Catalogue of the Armour and Arms in the Armoury of the Knights* . . . (London, n.d), 44 and plate XXXII.

[318] Bosio, iii. 30–31, 89; cf. J. McPartlin, 'The Defences of Malta', *Journal of the Faculty of Arts: Royal University of Malta*, iii no. 1 (1965), 11–12.

[319] Mdina, Cathedral Archives Ms. 34, f. 110 v (1494).

[320] *Supra*, 30,34,55.

[321] Texts, showing Mdina in almost perpetual ruin, in Valentini, in *ASM*, viii. 465 (1432), 476–477 (1438?), 495 (1450); ix. 102–103 (1454); see also Mifsud, in *Archivum Melitense*, iii. 404–405; iv. 68–70. Mdina's medieval topography awaits detailed study; the ambiguities of the term *castrum* require attention.

[322] Text in Leopardi, in *Melita Historica*, ii. 257.

[323] Bosio, iii. 30.

[324] A. Mifsud, 'L'approvigionamento e l'Università di Malta nelle passate Dominazioni', *Archivum Melitense*, iii no. 5 (1918).

Sicilian ports; the Sicilians had their consuls with jurisdiction in Malta.[325] The extensive documentation available has yet to be used to unravel the complex problems of who was eligible for membership and office in the *universitas*, how elections were made, how the constitution and finances functioned.[326] In moments of crisis representatives could be summoned from the clergy and from the countryside: in 1450 each *capella* or district was to produce at least four men; in 1462 six delegates from each *casale* were to intervene along with the clergy and with Gozitan representatives; and in 1474 the *capillani* were to bring their *parrochani* to a *parlamentu generali.*[327] The fifteenth-century *universitas* was broadly similar to many town councils throughout the Mediterranean regions of the Latin West, but its earlier development remains obscure. Roberto Valentini showed that there was some sort of local council by about 1198 when the Maltese demanded incorporation in the *demanium*, and Gilibertus' report of about 1241 referred to an advisory body, but Valentini exaggerated in his attempts to demonstrate that this was a *comune* in the Italian style.[328] The council of the *universitas* dealt with numerous items of local business. It was responsible for the walls, markets and hygiene of Mdina; it could elect its own officials, raise taxes and petition the Crown. Business was in the hands of the Captain of Mdina, four jurats, and other officials whose election was confirmed annually by the viceroy.[329] The *magnifici* and *nobiles* generally dominated proceedings and there were attempts to exclude the artisan element, yet when necessary the *universitas* effectively mobilized a wide degree of popular participation; it provided a platform for conflicting interests and gave scope for real debate. At a meeting of the *consiglio* in 1479 no less than 32 speakers, including judges and notaries, debated whether they should provide a grant for a Maltese Augustinian to study abroad.[330]

The other major institution of later medieval Malta was the Latin Church. Despite much sporadic writing, largely on the fifteenth century, there is no satisfactory

[325] Mifsud, in *Archivum Melitense*, iii. 57–60, 78–79. Maltese representatives do not seem to have attended assemblies in Sicily. Valentini's claim (*ASM*, vii. 45) that the Maltese had a right to send their bishop is based on the presence of Bishop Nicolaus, who may never have been to Malta, at a special *colloquium generale* held at Terranova in 1314 to deal with the question of a duel between the Kings of Sicily and Naples: text in H. Finke, *Acta Aragonensia*, iii (Berlin, 1922), 257–258.

[326] On the sporadic publication of the *universitas* records, *supra*, 6–7.

[327] A. Mifsud, in *La Diocesi: Bollettino ufficiale ecclesiastico di Malta*, ii (1917/8), 40–42, 305.

[328] See especially *ASM*, vii. 44–63; x. 199–200, 205–213, 217. Valentini had ideological motives for seeking to date the *universitas* as early as possible. His idea (*ASM*, viii. 126) that it was a Norman innovation is surely unjustified (cf. *supra*, 36) as is the notion that it was copied directly from Sicily (*supra*, 14). It can really only be traced clearly from 1409 (texts in *ASM*, viii. 74–79) onwards. Valentini used a phrase in a text of 1450—*la dicta universita ab annis tricentis et ultra* (*ASM*, viii. 496)—to take the *universitas* back to before 1150, but probably *tricentis* meant 'trecento', ie. 14th-century. Valentini argued for '*comune*' when the document of 1208 clearly meant '*comite*' (*infra*, 116). Again (*ASM*, vii. 44–63), he used a series of papal bulls from 1304 onwards to prove that the *universitas* existed and was recognized by the Church. But inspection of the papal registers shows that phrases such as *universis vassallis ecclesie Melivetane* or *Universitatem vestram* were simply common-form addresses regularly found in bulls addressed to dioceses, abbeys and other institutions throughout Latin Christendom; they prove nothing. Much remains to be said on this topic. The earliest explicit reference to the Maltese *Universitas* dates to 1375: Palermo, Archivio di Stato, Cancelleria 13, f. 150v.

[329] Viceregal text of 1478 in Leopardi, in *Melita Historica*, ii. 135–136. On taxes, corvées (*angharie*) and gabelles, see Leopardi, *passim*, and Mifsud, in *Archivum Melitense*, iii. 404–413, 429–430.

[330] Text in Wettinger—Fsadni, 48–49.

standard survey.[331] The earliest known post-Muslim bishop dates to 1168,[332] but bishops rarely resided in or even visited the islands. However, by about 1270 there was an organized Roman diocese with canons, an archdeacon and a cantor; it functioned as a suffragan of Palermo, paying its tenths and contesting jurisdictions with the civil courts.[333] There were disputes and confusions which derived in part from the ancient claims of the Sicilian Crown to rights in the presentation of candidates to episcopal sees, a position further complicated by papal quarrels with the Crown. In May 1267 the pope instructed his legate to provide a bishop;[334] when that bishop died, the legate replaced him with a *normandus* named Johannes, who by November 1268 had in turn resigned the see to the pope; the see then remained vacant, though in 1272/3 a Franciscan, Jacobus de Malta, was said to be bishop.[335] The new Angevin regime seems to have opposed these papal nominations; in 1270 the king instructed the Maltese clergy *ut non soluant in collectis*, and in 1272 he ordered the Castellan of Malta to protect the procurator of the allegedly vacant diocese.[336] Jacobus was eventually accepted as bishop, but died in about 1278.[337] For a century after 1282 the situation was further bedevilled by papal recognition of Angevin, as opposed to Aragonese, claims in Sicily.[338] From 1393 onwards the Aragonese were again attempting to install their own candidates, a process complicated by the schism in the Roman church; the Crown followed the pope of Avignon, Pedro de Luna, who was himself Aragonese, but the Romanist clergy in Sicily supported the anti-Aragonese baronial rebels. The king's nominees, often royal chaplains or confessors, were mainly Sicilians who were chiefly interested in the lands of the Maltese

[331] A. Mifsud scattered useful information and documents through *La Diocesi: Bollettino ufficiale ecclesiastico di Malta*, i-iv (1916–1920). Bonnici (*Church in Malta*) surveys the older work without attempting new research and, in general, much of what is derived from Ferris and Abela requires control or revision; on these works and the ecclesiastical archives, *supra*, 2–3, 7–8. Many topics await detailed attention.

[332] On the Maltese Church and its dubious bishops before 1168, *supra*, 33. The best episcopal list, from 1253 onwards, that of Fiorini, in *Abela Essays*, 94–96, provides important information and corrections, but still requires much amendment. A *Ioannes Zafarana* was a *Maltensis canonicus* in 1244: text in Collura, 129–130.

[333] Texts of 1275/80, 1308/10 and 1370 (with serious errors of transcription) in P. Sella, *Rationes Decimarum Italiae nei secoli XIII e XIV: Sicilia* (Vatican, 1944), 25–26, 136; cf. *Cancelleria Angioina*, iv. 168–169. See also J. Glénisson, 'Documenti dell'Archivio Vaticano relativi alla collectoria di Sicilia: 1372–1375', *Rivista di Storia della Chiesa in Italia*, ii (1948), 250, 256.

[334] K. Ganzer, *Papsttum und Bistumsbesetzungen in der Zeit von Gregor IX. bis Bonifaz VIII.* (Cologne, 1968), 276/7 n. 24.

[335] A text from Viterbo of 1272/3 listed Malta as a vacant see in the Archbishopric of Palermo: *Malten. hoc modo mortuo ipsius ecclesie episcopo per legatum proviso, idem legatus de quodam normando Iohanne nomine, providit eidem ecclesie, qui post exitum legati de regno renuntiavit in manu domni Clementis, in quo quidam frater minor nomine Iacobus de Malta et quidam alius hospitalarius de facto dicuntur ellecti. Valere dicitur ultra C uncias.* This text, published by F. Orioli, in *Giornale Arcadico di Scienze, Lettere ed Arti*, cxxviii (1852), 189–190, with corrections *ibid.*, cxxxvii (1854), 196, will be dated and republished in vol. iii of N. Kamp, *Kirche und Monarchie im Staufischen Königreich Sizilien*, i- (Munich, 1973- ).

[336] Texts in *Cancelleria Angioina*, iv. 169 (1270); Moscati, in *ASM*, vii. 480 (1272).

[337] Text in Sella, 25. M.-H. Laurent, 'Contributo alla storia dei Vescovi del Regno di Sicilia: 1274–1280', *Rivista di storia della Chiesa in Italia*, ii (1948), 377, wrongly identified *Jacobus* with Giacomo da Mileto, nominated Bishop of Mileto on 27 May 1259; he may have been mistaken in rejecting two subsequent Bishops of Malta: N. (from 1266 on) and Andreas Bancherini, OP (ca. 1270).

[338] This is not the occasion for the construction of a new list of bishops but, in addition to Fiorini, see details and references in Valentini in *ASM*, vii. 44–68.

diocese in Sicily, where they resided; when King Martín unsuccessfully proposed his confessor Giovanni de Pino in 1393, many canons of Malta were at Catania, where the election was due to take place. In 1410 the king appointed a royal confessor, the Franciscan Joan Eximeno of Mallorca, as administrator of the see of Malta, *veents que la esgl̨eya de Malta, per tal com era destituida de idoneu pastor, era mal servida.*[339] There may even have been an episcopal presence on the island, since in 1423 Bishop Mauro was actually carried off by Tunisian raiders, apparently from Malta itself.[340]

Despite external control by kings and bishops from Sicily or beyond, Christian life in Malta showed genuine vitality; possibly this was precisely because of the need to implant and sustain it on formerly Muslim islands. One sign of this was the repeated demand for Maltese-speaking clergy who could carry doctrine and sacraments directly to the people.[341] The number of churches in Malta documented before 1350 is minimal,[342] yet by 1575 there were about 430, if chapels and shrines are included; an astounding multiplicity of churches and chapels, often clustered in groups, stretched across the countryside, while some of the main 'parish' churches stood alone, as at Bir Miftuħ, in the centre of the district they served rather than in the midst of a built-up area.[343] The copies and calendars surviving in the Cathedral Archives may throw light on this process of Christian construction, as suggested by this early-modern summary of a lost notarial act:

> Testamento di Manfredo Xeberras est in actis Notarij Luce de Sillato 20 Januarij 1449 in quo fecit heredem uniuersalem Leonardum Xeberras eius filium, et fecit quoddam pium legatum in favorem ecclesie ss.me Annunciationis per eum constructe in Casale Bircacara.[344]

Little is known of the quality and organization of the clergy before 1436 when the bishop, from Sicily, ordered a *quinterniolus pro concordia taxarum* which listed the incomes of 144 benefices in the islands, including 79 *animagii*, 37 *benefitii*, various *prebende*, *cappelle* and so on, many of them endowments for the celebration of masses; in numerous cases the patronage, the *iuspatronatus*, remained in the hands of the founding family. In 1436 the cathedral had an archdeacon, deacon, cantor, treasurer and twelve others all given as *donnus* and presumably canons; another thirteen were each given as *presbiter;* and there was a *Frater Benedictus*, and a Henrico Fabiano Zamit who held the benefice of Santa Maria on the rock of Filfla. Many of their names were Maltese. The twelve *cappelle* or 'parishes', including one in Rabat and one in Birgu, each contained a church corresponding to the Italian rural *pieve*, where baptisms, marriages and other sacraments were administered, and on which

[339] Fiorini, 90–91, 95, 106–109; Luttrell, in *Journal of the Faculty of Arts*, iv. 167.

[340] Valentini in *ASM*, viii. 256–257.

[341] Text of 1481 in Mifsud, in *La Diocesi*, iii. 203–205; see also Wettinger-Fsadni, 25–26.

[342] Apart from Mdina cathedral and a group of churches stylistically or archaeologically datable from their material remains (*supra*, 32–34; *infra*, 89–85, 163–171), there are only the two churches in the *castrum maris*, S. Maria and S. Angelo, in 1274 (*infra*, 164) and S. Maria on Comino (*Compasso da Navigare*, 111); there must have been others, including at least one on Gozo.

[343] *Infra*, 179, 212 n. 73.

[344] Mdina, Cathedral Archives Ms. 280, f. 179.

the scattered chapels depended.[345] There were protests from the inhabitants of the *casali* against the exactions of the *cappellani* or rural archpriests, who had their tithes to collect,[346] and in 1481 against the extortions of the powerful Archdeacon of Mdina, Lancea Desguanes.[347]

There is no evidence concerning the actual process of conversion and Christianization in the islands; in fact, somewhat inexplicably, the religious orders came to Malta relatively late. In 1364, the Benedictines of San Nicolò d'Arena at Catania, who had been bequeathed lands in Malta, declined to found a house there, alleging the distance and dangers, and the difficulties of pastoral work in an unknown language. By 1371, however, they had secured control of these Maltese lands, and they continued to receive further donations in the island.[348] The Franciscans had reached Malta by 1372, when Nicola Papalla was nominated rector of their hospital at Rabat; a new apse to their church there was being paid for by Giovanni de Nava in 1480.[349] The Augustinians had a convent in Malta by 1413;[350] Carmelites and Benedictine nuns came as well.[351] By 1452 there were one Maltese and two Sicilian Dominicans at Rabat, where their order subsequently acquired the church of Santa Maria della Grotta. In 1473 the Maltese Dominicans were formally recognized as constituting a priory; they built a new church at Rabat in 1505, and in 1527 they were granted a house at Birgu.[352] The friars, who sometimes studied abroad,

[345] Cf. R. Brentano, *Two Churches: England and Italy in the Thirteenth Century* (Princeton, 1968), 67–76. The 1436 text, the so-called *rollo* of Bishop Senatore de Mello, survives in 16/17th-century copy in Royal Malta Library, Biblioteca Ms. 721, f. 2–4v; it was clumsily published, without the incomes, in Abela, 313–316. Abela, 360, assumed that the places mentioned as *cappelle* were 'parishes'; the identifications and dedications he gives for each 'parish' (*ibid.*, 360) do not appear in the text and cannot all be documented as early as 1436. There is no evidence for the generally-accepted idea that the bishop organized or reorganized a parish system, or established 10 new parishes in 1436; Ferris, 70, even states that Pope Eugenius IV instituted 10 parishes. The *cappelle* mentioned in 1436 had incomes varying from 25 *uncie* at Rabat (*S. Paulu di fora*) to only 2 *uncie* at Birgu, Mellieħa and S. Domenica (ie. Tartarni). In 1419 this last '*casale*' appeared as *Capella sancta dominica tartarni et dinkili* with 40 names on the militia list (*infra*, 186–212); later in the century came a reference to *totam parrochiam seu capellam de casali dragu* (cited *infra*, 187 n. 22). In 1450 an exceptional meeting of the *consilium universale* was supposed to include *quatuor ad minus de qualibet capella*, while in 1474 eight *cappillani* were to bring their *parrochani* to a *parlamentu generali* (text of 1474 and other details in Mifsud, in *La Diocesi*, ii. 42, 305.) In 1533 Quintin stated that there were eight parishes outside the city. In 1574 Dusina gave: *Cappelle, ò vogliamo dire Parrochie Regale no. 8* (text in Vella, in *Melita Historica*, v. 183). For the text of 1436 and lists of late medieval benefices, founders and holders, and on the papal indult of 1521 restricting benefices primarily to Maltese, see V. Borg, *Important Canonical Enactments on the Ecclesiastical Benefices of the Maltese Islands* (unpublished D. Theol. thesis: Royal University of Malta, 1960).

[346] Mdina, Cathedral Archives Ms. 28, f. 256–259 (ca. 1510: modern copy).

[347] Texts in Mifsud, in *La Diocesi*, ii. 20–21.

[348] D. la Ferlita, 'I possedimenti dei benedettini di Catania a Malta', *ASM*, vii (1935/6), using documents from Catania, Archivio di Stato: Fondo Benedettini; the present author will publish these important texts, with various corrections.

[349] B. Fiorini, 'Il Convento di S. Francesco in Rabat (Malta) dei frati minori conventuali', *Melita Historica*, iii no. 3 (1962), 3–5, 16–17; the text there published (p. 32) as of 1370 is actually that of 1372, republished in Bresc, *Papers of the British School at Rome*, xli, doc. 36. The myth that St. Francis visited Malta was invented in 1882.

[350] Palermo, Archivio di Stato, Cancelleria 48, f. 165; the previously accepted date was 1440.

[351] The best general survey, in Bonnici, i. 100–105, requires careful revision, especially with regard to the chronology. For texts illustrating early-modern traditions concerning late-medieval hermits, see Marchi, in *Missione 1964*, 26–29, 34–35.

[352] M. Fsadni, *Il-Miġja u l-Ħidma ta' l-Ewwel Dumnikani f'Malta: 1450–1512* (Malta, 1965), gives an excellent idea of the variety of sources available for this sort of study, and a continuation volume is forthcoming; see also S. Forte, in *Archivum Fratrum Praedicatorum*, xxxiv (1964), 277–279.

brought a new, educated element into Maltese society, and their churches and paintings bear witness to a certain prosperity among the orders.[353] The Maltese Church had numerous practical problems, such as its relations with the *universitas* and its obligations to help maintain the walls of Mdina.[354] The islands lay exposed on the frontiers of Christendom, and in 1533 Quintin paid tribute to the fervour of their Christian belief and their devotion to St. Paul. Other saints, such as St. Catherine[355] and St. George,[356] were also highly venerated.

The civil and religious architecture of medieval Malta has now received considerable attention,[357] but more could be done to study surviving buildings, notably the ruined but important, because unrestored, houses within the citadel at Gozo. The recent demonstration of the way in which the Chiaramonte family patronized a style of palace found in many parts of Sicily[358] might be extended to Mdina and elsewhere, for Chiaramonte influence was strong in late fourteenth-century Malta. Gothic window-frames and other decorative features were possibly pre-fabricated and imported directly from Catalunya or Valencia.[359] Individual architects such as Matteo Coglituri, who was *mastru marammeri* or prefect of building at Mdina by 1523[360] and who carried out important work for the Knights in Birgu after 1530,[361] deserve attention. Many churches were adapted caves or were cut out of the rock, while others were constructed with a system of arches which supported a roof of long stone slabs;[362] and by the fifteenth century churches were being built in very considerable numbers. Giovanni de Nava, Castellan of Birgu castle, ordered a marble tomb in 1487.[363] A font for the cathedral at Mdina came from the Sicilian workshop of Domenico Gagini around the end of the fifteenth century,[364] while the

[353] *Infra*, 65–66.

[354] Mifsud, in *La Diocesi*, i-iv *passim*.

[355] *Supra*, 23 n. 141.

[356] J. Bezzina, 'San Ġorġ Dejjem Ħarisna: Studju Storiku-Folkloristiku', in *Il-Hajja* (19 and 23 July 1971) [and apart (Malta, 1971)], relates St. George, patron of Catalunya, to guard-towers and watch-sites around the coast; the difficulty lies in dating towers and chapels, place-names and dedications.

[357] M. Buhagiar and J. Ward-Perkins *infra*, with bibliography. Hughes, *Building*, 41–50, 125–127 *et passim*, requires some revision, especially on points of medieval chronology; it provides further bibliography—see also *supra*, 55 n. 290.

[358] G. Spatrisano, *Lo Steri di Palermo e l'architettura siciliana del trecento* (Palermo, 1972).

[359] B. Gilman Proske, 'Spanish Details in the Gothic Architecture of Sicily', *Notes Hispanic*, iv (1944), 23, discusses Catalan exports, though without documenting them conclusively. The 'exposition throne', the *intarsia* choir panels, and other items at Mdina (*infra*, 178–179) deserve more detailed study. On the 'Romanesque' capitals from Mdina, *infra*, 164 n. 6, and plate 18c,d.

[360] Mdina, Cathedral Archives Ms. 36, f. 193 *et passim*; on the *marammeri* or *sopramarammeri*, see Valentini, in *ASM*, viii. 138–139.

[361] Hughes, *Building*, 208 (but the claim that Coglituri probably taught Tommaso Dingli, who was born in 1591, seems scarcely credible).

[362] Eg. in St. Cecilia, Gozo, illustrated in Hughes, *Fortress*, 168, remarkably well preserved, and apparently the oldest surviving church in Gozo. This system of arches and slabs is not found in Sicily where wood is available.

[363] Valentini, in *ASM*, v. 23 n. 74.

[364] H. Kruft, *Domenico Gagini und seine Werkstatt* (Munich, 1972), 55, 244; plates 221–233. The traditional date of 1495, which Kruft accepts, is merely the year of election of Bishop Valguarnera (1495–1501) whose arms are said to be those on the font, which could have been made even after the bishop's death. It is not known when the sculpture of a Madonna and Child by Antonello Gagini, signed and dated 1504 and now in Rabat, reached Malta; it was probably also a workshop piece: V. Bonello—J. Cauchi, *L'arte sacra a Malta* (Malta, 1960), 103–104. The base of this carving is in the National Museum of Fine Arts, Valletta.

cathedral's *intarsia* choir stalls were originally commissioned in 1482, for the Dominicans at Rabat, from Parisio and Pierantonio Calachura, *carpinterij* of Catania (plate 18a,b).[365] By this period the Maltese could afford to decorate some of their churches and monasteries with the products of competent artists, and they turned to Sicily when the need arose. Other work, such as stone-carving, was likely to be done in the islands. The Gozo Museum houses a carved tombstone with an unusual chalice design, and a stone relief of two saints which is difficult to date but might be thirteenth-century. There is room for a study of Maltese decorative motifs, comparing the Muslim tombstones at Rabat with the sculptures in St. Agatha at Rabat and the carved doors dated 1520 in Mdina cathedral.[366]

A tentative preliminary study of the wall-paintings in these medieval churches suggests the possibility of a local school of painters strongly influenced from Sicily and, to a lesser extent, from Catalunya; but much remains to be investigated. A Byzantinesque fresco of a Madonna, conceivably fourteenth-century, has recently been uncovered in a rock-cut sanctuary at Mellieħa. The painted apse in the Abbatija tad-Dejr (plate 14a) possibly dates between 1270 and about 1412; the frescoes now restored at Ħal Millieri, which include numerous frontal pictures of saints (plate 16a,b), were probably done *circa* 1450; while the murals in the rock-cut church of St. Agatha at Rabat (plate 15a,b) are datable around 1510.[367] The Sicilian and Spanish background of the surviving panel paintings also needs to be unravelled. It is important to document the presence of these panels in Malta before 1530, and to identify their patrons and artists. The Augustinian church at Rabat possesses a fine Sicilian Madonna flanked by saints painted in the 'International Gothic' manner during the early fifteenth century. The collection in the Cathedral Museum includes the extremely large and impressive St. Paul retable from the cathedral (plate 17), strongly Catalan in style; a Valencian panel with three iconographically interesting scenes and strange shields, which has no secure provenance; and a painting of St. John the Baptist most recently attributed to the circle of a Southern French painter working close to Tommaso de Vigilia in Palermo.[368] A Deposition at Rabat by Antonio de Saliba, a nephew of Antonello da Messina, is related to a crucifix in London attributed to the same artist.[369] On 20 February 1505 at Messina the Dominican Guglielmo de Chilia contracted on behalf of the nuns of San Pietro at Mdina for Giovanni Salvo di Antonio, another nephew of the great Antonello, to

[365] The contract survives in the archives of the Dominican house at Rabat (partial facsimile in Fsadni, 68; cf. *infra*, 179).

[366] Cf. *infra*, 178, and R. Bourouiba, 'L'influence de l'art sanhadjien du Maghrib sur l'art des Normands de Sicile', in *Congrès arabo-berbère;* A. Florensa, 'L'architettura di Spagna a Malta', *Atti del XI Congresso di Storia dell'Architettura* (Rome, 1970), figs. 1–4.

[367] M. Buhagiar *infra*, and G. Mathew, 'Schools of Painting in Medieval Malta', *Journal of the Faculty of Arts: Royal University of Malta*, vi no. 1 (1974); cf. E. Sammut, 'A Handlist of Writings on Art in Malta', *Melita Historica*, iv no. 1 (1964). Though written before the uncovering of the fresco and repeating innumerable 'traditions', R. Bonnici Calì, *Our Lady of Mellieha, Malta*, (Malta, 1952), contains useful references and information. There was a Byzantinesque fresco of a 'Blessing Christ' in the apse at S. Ciro: Bonello 5. Other works may yet be revealed elsewhere. Restorations at Ħal Millieri will be followed by publication of studies on the church and its paintings.

[368] S. Bottari, *La pittura del quattrocento in Sicilia* (Florence, 1954), 43 n. 3 (wrongly describing it as John the Evangelist).

[369] C. Kauffmann, 'Notes on Two Paintings', *Victoria and Albert Museum Yearbook*, i (1969), 49; cf. Bottari, fig. 163.

paint in oils a large polyptych, parts of which survived in the San Pietro convent.[370] Again, these works emphasize the predominance of the Sicilian connection.

The non-specialist interested in the problems of the late medieval Maltese language faces a confusion of controversies and theories, of proverbs, riddles, surnames, nicknames and place-names. Such evidence is important for, apart from Pietro Caxaro's *Cantilena*, no written medieval Maltese is known. Though written in Latin script, the *Cantilena*, only recently discovered in a copy made in or just after 1533, throws unique light on the still predominantly Arabic nature of the Maltese vocabulary, in its poetic form. Behind this poem lay a minor world of provincial culture. By 1471 there was a school at Mdina run by the *universitas* and the cathedral, usually with a Sicilian or Italian schoolmaster teaching at least Latin and music; further education for the friars and others meant travel to Sicily or the continent. There was much illiteracy, even among the clergy, and any Maltese who knew no other language had to rely on an interpreter for official or legal business.[371] There were some notably well-educated exceptions among the clergy and lawyers; the medical men were almost all Jews. The old legal tag *quod omnes tangit debet ab omnibus approbari* opened a clause in the *capitoli* of 1419; yet, curiously, it heralded not a theory of taxation by consent, but the demand that the Gozitans should contribute to the cost of a tower on Comino.[372] The humanist notary who dabbled in classical literature was a familiar figure in Italy, and Pietro Caxaro certainly knew his Latin. A member of a leading Mdina family, with his properties, slaves and numerous kinsmen, he was active as judge, envoy to Sicily, cathedral proctor and spokesman in the island's council; he died in 1485. Probably wifeless and childless, his private affairs seem to have provoked the following *Cantilena* or lament:[373]

> Aliquantulum exhilaratus memorans cantilenam diu compositam quondam mei maioris Petri de Caxaro philosophi poete et oratoris cui aliquando dictum fuit confla precor calamum Caxaro clara propago: te cupiant ninphe te tua musa . . . quam lingua melitea hic subicio.

[370] The contract was for a Madonna and Child or 'Scordia', flanked by Saints Peter and Benedict, surmounted by a Crucifixion with Mary and St. John, on either side of which were to be an Annunciation and an Archangel Gabriel; below was to be a predella of Christ and Apostles, flanked by Saints Blandano and Peter Martyr. Details in G. di Marzo, *Di Antonello da Messina e dei suoi congiunti: studi e documenti* (Palermo, 1903), 94 [where for 'Mileto in Calabria' read 'Malta'], from a document at Messina which was destroyed in 1943; Chilia (or Chumi) was clearly Maltese (Fsadni, 75, 78 and n. 200). Two panels from the Benedictine sisters of S. Pietro at Mdina, now in the Cathedral Museum there, presumably formed part of this polyptych. One is a predella of Christ and Disciples, signed *Magister Saluu de a*[ . . .]*i de messanensis me pinsit 510* (Bottari, figs. 183–188); and the other is a comparatively large fragment with St. Peter. A smaller group of panels in the same museum, said to have come from S. Maria del Soccorso at Cospicua, reproduces a scheme somewhat similar to that of the 1505 contract, except that St. James takes the place of St. Benedict (Bottari, fig. 182); this polyptych is attributed to Giovanni Salvo's workshop.

[371] In addition to the numerous details and documents, many drawn from the 15th-century notarial records, in Wettinger—Fsadni (*Peter Caxaro's Cantilena*), see on the schools, Valentini, in *ASM*, viii (1936/7), 18–20; on the philological problems, the works by Aquilina and others cited *supra*, 10–24; and for a notion of the language, A. Arberry, *A Maltese Anthology* (Oxford, 1960). Parallel survivals occurred; Palermo Jews spoke Arabic in 1479: H. Bresc—S. Goitein, 'Un inventaire dotale des juifs siciliens: 1479', *Mélanges d'archéologie et d'histoire*, lxxxii (1970).

[372] Text in Valentini, in *ASM*, viii. 82.

[373] Text and translation from Wettinger—Fsadni, 36–38; the authors most generously permitted reproduction. Previously, the earliest known passage in Maltese of more than a couple of lines was a late 17th-century poem.

Xideu il cada ye gireni tale nichadithicum
Mensab fil gueri uele nisab fo homorcom
Calb mehandihe chakim soltan ui le mule
Bir imgamic rimitine betiragin mucsule
fen hayran al garca nenzel fi tirag minzeli
Nitila vy nargia ninzil deyem fil bachar il hali.

Huakit hi mirammiti lili zimen nibni
Mectatilix mihallimin me chitali tafal morchi
fen timayt insib il gebel sib tafal morchi
vackit hi mirammiti.

Huakit hy mirammiti Nizlit hi li sisen
Mectatilix il mihallimin ma kitatili li gebel
fen tumayt insib il gebel sib tafal morchi
Huakit thi mirammiti lili zimen nibni
Huec ucakit hi mirammiti vargia ibnie
biddilihe inte il miken illi yeutihe
Min ibidill il miken ibidil il vintura
halex liradi 'al col xebir sura
hemme ard bayda v hemme ard seude et hamyra
Hactar min hedann heme tred minne tamara.

> Somewhat enlivened in recalling a song composed long ago by my late ancestor, Peter de Caxaro, philosopher, poet and orator, of whom it was once said: 'Manufacture a pen for Caxaro, I entreat you, O noble progeny: let the nymphs seek thee; let thy muse . . . invite thee', I write it down here in the Maltese language.

A recital of my misfortunes, O my neighbours, the following I shall tell you,
Such as has not been found either in the past or in your lifetime.
An ungoverned, kingless, and lordless heart
Has thrown me into a deep well without a way up
Into which, desiring death by drowning, I descend by the steps of my downfall,
Rising and falling always in the stormy sea.

My house, it has fallen down, the one I have long been a-building.
The workmen themselves were not to blame, but it was the loose clay that gave way.
I found loose clay where I had hoped to find rock;
My house! It has fallen down!

My house! It has pushed down its foundations.
The workmen were not to blame, but the rock gave way.
I found loose clay where I had hoped to find rock;
The house I had long been a-building has collapsed!
And that's how my house fell down! Build it up again!
Change for it the place that harms it.
He who changes his neighbourhood changes his fortune;
For there is a difference of kind in every span of land:
Some land there is which is white, some black, some red.
More than this. There should you . . .

Language must have been a significant matter by the fourteenth and fifteenth centuries, when Sicilian immigration was considerable and doubtless resented. If the place-names remained largely Semitic, nicknames and surnames suggest Sicilian influence on the language and population, but care should be taken in making deductions from them. Notaries tended to romancify or translate surnames, while slaves might take the name of their master.[374] The Sicilian connection was the most permanent and prominent one, though the Angevins kept a garrison of over 100 Frenchmen at Birgu and some of the 300 'Catalans' left in the islands in 1283 may have settled there. During the fourteenth century Iberian influences were limited. In 1356, however, a Catalan named Joan Marserio was travelling from Sicily to reside in Malta and to conduct business on the island of Lampedusa; and in 1362 Francesco Ros planned to travel from Sardinia to Malta to receive three pieces of cloth from Arnaldo Cicera, an inhabitant of Malta. Arnau Gerau of Barcelona was granted a fief in Malta in 1398, but he may not have resided there. The Gerau Desguanes whom King Martin sent to collect taxes in Malta in 1405, and who was appointed Castellan of Birgu castle, had possibly come directly from Catalunya to settle in Malta; the family did not appear in Malta before about 1400, but *Antonius de Isguanes* held a fief there in 1408. The Desguanes do not seem to have been settled in Sicily, but other Maltese notables with Catalan names belonged to families long established there.[375] Alfonso V brought in a number of Castilian captains, officials and favourites, such as Guttierez de Nava [376] and Diego de Guevara,[377] yet in 1452 Pedro Gonzalvo de la Rua, *regni Castelle oriundus et in regno illo degens,* was declared ineligible to inherit a fief in Malta on the grounds that he was not an *incola* nor a *fidelis aut subditus* of Alfonso V.[378]

The nature of everyday life on a Maltese *casale* or the way in which the *universitas* functioned are questions important not only in themselves but also because they are essential to an elucidation of one central problem of medieval Malta, that is the structure and mentality of the curious mixed society which developed there.[379] After 1397 Malta was never again granted out as a County, but the experiment of direct royal government collapsed in the face of the incompetence and corruption of the Sicilian bureaucracy; royal lands, offices and incomes were alienated, more or less in perpetuity, and public power fell back into private hands, as Gian Luca Barberi was to complain at the beginning of the sixteenth century.[380] Offices and their profits were disputed between the established notables and foreign captains and placemen. Some of these married into Maltese society and settled in palaces in Mdina, while others retained their Sicilian lands and connections; but all wished to insert themselves into the round of profits, to dominate and thus to exploit the

[374] G. Wettinger, 'The Distribution of Surnames in Malta in 1419 and the 1480's', and 'Late Medieval Maltese Nicknames', *Journal of Maltese Studies*, v (1968) and vi (1971).

[375] References in Luttrell, in *Journal of the Faculty of Arts*, iv. 166–167. Without much more detailed work, it is impossible to decide whether settlers with Spanish names came directly from the Iberian peninsula or belonged to families long established in Sicily. For example the *Jaymucio Catalano* who held lands in Gozo before 1372 may have been a Sicilian and not (as Valentini, in *ASM*, xiii. 13 n. 44, claims) a 'prova della espansione catalana in queste isole'.

[376] A Castilian, according to Soldevila, ii. 652; the de Nava were strongly established at Syracuse (Del Treppo, 499–500).

[377] A Castilian, according to Soldevila, ii. 671–672; for other Castilians, *infra*, 144–155.

[378] Text in Barberi, *Liber de Secretiis*, 81, 83. In 1481 Carlos de Guevara sought Maltese citizenship after marrying a Maltese: text in Mifsud, in *La Diocesi*, iv. 35.

[379] This central problem is defined and approached, at least in a preliminary way, by H. Bresc *infra*, 144–151; much, inevitably, remains to be done.

[380] The comments of Mazzarese Fardella, in *Liber de Secretiis*, 89 n. 78, on the disastrous manner in which the Crown allowed a corrupt bureaucracy to alienate royal incomes are expanded in detail by H. Bresc *infra*.

*universitas*, and to resist further royal nominees. Many became in effect Maltese, raised their sons as natives, and then supported demands that offices and ecclesiastical benefices be given only to indigenous Maltese; repeated demands of this type demonstrated, incidentally, that the local inhabitants held clear notions as to who was or was not Maltese. Out of this intermingling, out of joint resistance to royal exploitation, and out of the very isolation and apartness of the islands and their language, there developed a certain 'proto-national' sentiment. Quarrels and factions, particularly after about 1416, must be explained partly in terms of the conflicting interests within this hybrid group, and a detailed prosopographical study of the leading families, their origins, lands, connections and assimilation into Maltese society seems essential.[381] Such family history must be extended far beyond Malta, for that island's society mirrored the ambiguities of the broad and varied cosmopolitan world of Alfonso V and his followers, at once humanists and bureaucrats, nobles and merchants, tax-farmers, sea captains and condottieri, men with chivalric and crusading ideals who practised the licensed piracy of the *corso* but were also experts in government and business, capable of extortion and corruption both for personal gain and to further more grandiose political and commercial ambitions, such as those of the king himself.[382]

Post-Muslim Malta looked towards the Christian, Latin Europe of the Western Mediterranean, and it was bound to Sicily by reason of its exposed position and its foodstuff requirements. Its ruling class and government officials, its garrison and clergy, were often Sicilians. Yet in some special sense its inhabitants were conscious of being Maltese; and the Gozitans, with their own *universitas*, remained distinctively Gozitan.[383] In 1533 Jean Quintin evidently found that those who were raised in the islands and spoke the language had a character of their own; the women beautiful but so timid in their veiled seclusion that 'to have seen a woman was to have seduced her', and the men so religious in their Maltese way that they 'thought St. Paul was God'. These people kept their Semitic language, yet their Christian sentiment was so intense that by the sixteenth century there were more than 430 churches and chapels on Malta and Gozo. In 1530 the Knights were received at Mdina by bearded Maltese, some of them extremely old, who were mounted on donkeys, armed with swords, daggers and *azagaglie* or axes, and dressed in bullet-resistant, arrow-proof lengths of quilted cotton.[384] Malta inherited a measure of Muslim tastes and traditions; its architecture and customs were clearly influenced from Sicily, yet Sicilian fashions were themselves affected by Sicily's Iberian links and Muslim past, so that it is often almost impossible to judge the movement of trends and influences. When Charles V granted Malta to the Order of St. John in 1530 there was still, practically speaking, no such thing as 'Spain', and even Machiavelli did not define

[381] Wettinger – Fsadni, *Peter Caxaro's Cantilena*, shows how family interests can be reconstructed in minute detail.

[382] This *ambiente* is brilliantly portrayed in Del Treppo's book.

[383] Eg. in the reaction of Gozo's *universitas* to the Knights' arrival: Valentini, in *Archivum Melitense*, ix. 170 n. 4.

[384] Bosio, iii. 89.

the 'Italian state' in such a way as to include in it the Kingdom of Naples.[385] The contemporary inscription on the Castelnuovo at Naples described Alfonso V as *Rex Hispanus, Siculus, Italicus.* Malta and Gozo formed a distant and special part of the Sicilian kingdom, within which they preserved many of their own ways of life and speech and thought; they were neither Spanish nor Italian.

[385] F. Chabod, *Machiavelli and the Renaissance* (London, 1958), 71–76 *et passim*; see also D. Hay, 'The Italian View of Renaissance Italy', *Florilegium Historiale: Essays presented to Wallace K. Fergusson* (Toronto, 1971).

III

# MALTA BEFORE 870: SOME LIBYAN CONNECTIONS

In Roman times Malta was linked to Africa in various ways. The island lay on routes from Sicily to Libya, that is to Tripolitania and Cyrenaica, but it was too far to the east of the axis between Sicily and Carthage to have a major strategic importance. In fact Malta came into the Punic sphere only when Carthage became interested in Libya, and the Romans, like the Tunisian Muslims centuries later, were remarkably slow to conquer the island.[1] Even after the Roman conquest, many of Malta's contacts were with the Punic world of Carthage which lay to the west,[2] and following 870 Malta was again dominated from Tunisia, whose Aghlabid rulers had conquered the island; possibly there were Tunisian influences not only in speech and religion but also in matters such as water supplies and housing.[3] Even before the Muslim conquest of 870 there may have been contacts with Tunisia. The Byzantine general Belisarius touched or passed by Malta on his way from Kaukana in Southern Sicily to Carthage in 553.[4] During the fifth century Malta was probably incorporated into the African Church which apparently held properties on Malta as late as 592.[5] A passage in Procopius suggests that a number of Africans may

---

1. As emphasized in F. Rizzo, "Malta e Sicilia in Età romana: Aspetti di Storia politica e costituzionale," *Kokalos,* xxii-xxiii tomo I (1976-1977); similar points concerning the medieval period are made by A. Luttrell, "Approaches to Medieval Malta," in *Medieval Malta: Malta before the Knights,* ed. A. Luttrell (London, 1975), 17-18, 42. Rizzo's article constitutes a contribution to Maltese historiography which should provoke considerable debate. *Pace* Rizzo, 178, however, Pliny's *insulae ad Africam versae* seems to mean merely that Malta lay south rather than north of Sicily, as noted in A. Bonanno, "Malta in the Third Century," in *The Roman West in the Third Century: Contributions from Archeology and History,* ed. A. King - M. Henig, ii (Oxford, 1981), 505.
2. In addition to Rizzo, see Luttrell, 25, for references to a Punic inscription of ca. 100 AD and other evidence; in due course the pottery and other finds may provide a fuller picture.
3. *Hal Milleri: a Maltese Casale, its Churches and Paintings,* ed. A. Luttrell (Malta, 1976), 27-31, 34-35.
4. Procopius of Caesaria, *History of the Wars,* ed. H. Dewing, ii (London, 1953), 130; cf. T. Brown, "Byzantine Malta: a Discussion of the Sources," in *Medieval Malta,* 73.
5. Brown, 72-73, 75.

have fled to Malta in 544 as a result of Berber devastations at Susa; Procopius said that some "Libyans", who clearly came from Tunisia, "fled to Sicily and the other islands," but he did not actually mention Malta nor did he say whether the exile was permanent.[6] Subsequently, during the centuries before 870, Malta was certainly in Byzantine hands but its history in that period is very scantily documented. A traditional response to this difficulty has been to transfer to Malta various presumptions concerning the situation in Sicily, while there has also been a tendency to invoke Oriental or North African immigrations and influences in order to explain certain liturgical and linguistic features found, centuries later, on Malta.[7]

Given the scarcity of information about Malta, deductions from Libyan parallels must be very largely hypothetical. The only known major Maltese monument of the period is the basilica church excavated at Tas-Silġ and said to be datable only to the late-fourth or early-fifth century. Given the disturbances in the stratifications and pending the problematical publication of a final excavation report, it appears that this date turns on the rectangular baptistry basin built in the prehistoric temple outside the basilica church and on the altar of a type with a single leg or support. Other evidence of continued building activities - the presbitery or *schola cantorum*, the columns with crosses and the sixth-century tarsia work which was very probably imported – are all considered to point to a later period of splendour and perhaps to a fifth century or, more probably, a sixth or seventh century monastery, but they cannot provide an earlier date, especially in view of the fact that the plan of the basilica church was conditioned by that of the ancient temple into which it was built.[8] There is no apparent reason why the baptismal font should be assigned with any confidence to the late-fourth century.[9] Square basins cannot be dated so early in Sicily.[10] In Cyrenaica basilica churches have seldom been

---

6. Procopius, ii. 414; cf. Brown, 73 *et passim*.
7. Cf. Luttrell, 23-25. For the earlier period, Maltese historiography looked to the Greek world: A. Bonanno, "The tradition of an Ancient Greek Colony in Malta," *Hyphen* (Malta), iv no. 1 (1983).
8. *Missione Archeologica Italiana a Malta: Rapporto preliminare della Campagna 1963* (etc.), 8 vols. (Rome, 1964-1973), at *1965*, 160-161; *1966*, 118-119; *1967*, 100-101. Cf. M. Cagiano de Azevedo, "Medieval Buildings Excavated at Tas-Silġ and San Pawl Milqi in Malta," in *Medieval Malta*, 89.
9. M. Cagiano de Azevedo, in *Missione 1966*, 119, merely cites A.Khatchatrian,*Les Baptistères paléochrétiens: Plans, Notices et Bibliographie* (Paris, 1962), but this work gives very few, if any, square basins securely datable as early as the late-fourth century.
10. This results from the systematic control of the references given in A. Messina, "Battisteri rupestri e Vasche battesimali nella Sicilia bizantina," *Archivio Storico Siracusano*, n.s. i (1971).

dated by excavation and almost none is datable before ca. 400.[11] In Tripolitania there is one possible exception at Sabratha where the so-called Church III is dated, though only by the style of its mosaic, as probably being of the last quarter of the fourth century. To the south of this church is a room which formed part of an undated but earlier building and which contained a simple square baptismal basin set in a mosaic similar to and probably of the same date as that in the main church; this basin may be reasonably assigned to the same period presumed as the church.[12] It seems furthermore that there is no evidence for single-leg altars before the fifth century.[13]The Tas-Silġ plan with its presbitery is common in Libya and could date to the fifth century. At Siracusa and elsewhere in Sicily the transformation of pagan temples into churches such as occurred at Tas-Silġ is not normally dated before the sixth century.[14] The Tas-Silġ basilica church appears most likely therefore to date to the sixth or possibly to the late-fifth century.

There is no positive evidence for any contacts between Libya and Byzantine Malta, though both to some extent shared arid and rocky conditions which might have encouraged comparable developments in rural housing.[15] In late-Roman Libya there were extensive regions of frontier settlement with many small farm buildings and large central storehouses or estate centres known by the term *gasr;* the typical *gasr* was stone-built and defensible, but it was primarily agricultural rather than defensive in purpose.[16] The Maltese islands were not part of a continental *limes* or frontier settlement zone and apparently had

---

11. S. Stucchi, *Architettura Cirenaica* (Rome, 1975), 360-364. This work contains a wealth of detail but tends to derive chronologies from stylistic considerations rather than from more cautiously topographical and stratigraphical approaches: critical reviews by D. White, in *Art Bulletin,* lix (1977), 623-626, and J. Ward Perkins, in *American Journal of Archaeology,* lxxxiii(1979), 363-365.
12. P. Romanelli, "La Basilica cristiana nell'Africa Settentrionale Italiana," *Atti del IV Congresso Internazionale di Archeologia Cristiana,* i (Rome, 1940), 262; J. Ward Perkins – R. Goodchild, "The Christian Antiquities of Tripolitania," *Archaeologia,* xcv (1953), 15-17 and Plates VIIIb, XXVII.
13. *Reallexikon für Antike und Christentum,* i (Stuttgart, 1950), 336-338.
14. References collected in A. Guillou, "La Sicile byzantine: État de Recherches," *Byzantinische Forschungen,* v (1977), 135-138.
15. Stucchi, 502-503 *et passim.*
16. The pioneer work of R.G. Goodchild and the views of Stucchi must be revised: B. Jones – G. Barker, "Libyan Valleys Survey," *Libyan Studies,* xi (1979/80); G. Barker – G. Jones, "The UNESCO Libyan Valleys Survey 1980," *ibid.,* xii (1980/81); G. Barker – B. Jones, "UNESCO Libyan Valleys Survey 1979-1981: Palaeoecology and Environmental Archaeology in the Pre-Desert," *ibid.,* xiii (1982). For a Roman wall and its rectangular towers, see O. Brogan, "Hadd Hajar, a *clausura* in the Tripolitanian Gebal Garian south of Asabaa," *ibid.,* xi (1979/80).

no large farmhouses similar to the *gasr*. The round tower at Ta' Ġawhar was apparently being used as a farmstead when it was destroyed towards the end of the third century AD.[17] There were a number of these round towers on Malta which were probably built in the third century BC and may well have been used again for defensive purposes in the third century AD.[18] They could have formed part of a warning system built on high inland sites and designed to send signals around the Maltese islands;[19] there were small round towers in Southern Tunisia which were normally placed on high ground, probably as signal stations.[20] In Malta and Gozo many ordinary people outside the main towns may have lived in caves[21] or in rural houses of the non-military Byzantine type such as those excavated at Kaukana on the south coast of Sicily facing Malta.[22]

One general characteristic of the period may have been a slow but

---

17. (D. Trump), in *Report on the Working of the Museum Department for the Year 1960* (Malta, 1962), 6-7; Figs. 4-5· Plates I-IV.
18. *Missione 1963*, 21-22; Luttrell, in *Medieval Malta*, 21 n. 130; Bonanno (1981), 509. The towers at Tal-Baqqari and Ta' Ċieda present remarkable indications of continuity: M. Buhagiar – D. De Lucca – A. Luttrell, "The Tal-Baqqari Churches," in *Hal Millieri*, and A. Luttrell, "The *Cappella* of Birkirkara: 1402," *Melita Historica*, viii no. 2 (1981), 157 n. 6. D. Trump, *Malta: an Archaeological Guide* (London, 1972), 89, seems to contradict his own report of 1960 in dating the tower at Ta' Ġawhar to the third century AD.
19. Cf. P. Pattenden, "The Byzantine Early Warning System," *Byzantion*, liii (1983).
20. P. Trousset, *Recherches sur le Limes Tripolitanus du Chott el-Djerid à la Frontière tuniso-libyenne* (Paris, 1974), 65, 141-142; cf. D. Pringle, *The Defence of Byzantine Africa from Justinian to the Arab Conquest* (Oxford, 1981). See also E. Fentress, *Numidia and the Roman Army: Social, Military and Economic Aspects of the Frontier Zone* (Oxford, 1979), 90-91 *et passim*, for a few round towers and signalling with mirrors.
21. A. Luttrell, "Malta Troglodytica: Għar-il-Kbir," *Heritage* (Malta), no. 24 (1979); M. Buhagiar, "Medieval Cave-Dwellings and Rock-Cut Churches in Malta," *Atrium* (Malta), no. 3 ((1983?)). Possible North African influences in Maltese catacombs are discussed in M. Buhagiar, *Late Roman and Byzantine Catacombs and Related Burial Places in the Maltese Islands* (M. Phil. thesis: London, 1982), which awaits publication.
22. References in Guillou (1977), 112-115; plan of Kaukana in Pelagatti, "Scavi e Ricerche archeologiche nella Provincia di Ragusa: 1961-1966," *Archivio Storico Siracusano*, xii (1966), 26; colour photograph in V. von Falkenhausen, "I Bizantini in Italia," in G. Cavallo *et al.*, *I Bizantini in Italia* (Milan, 1982), plate 15. Cf. G. Tchalenko, *Villages antiques de la Syria du Nord: le Massif du Bélus à l'Époque romaine*, 3 vols. (Paris, 1953-1958); T. Kirilova Kirova, "Il Problema della Casa bizantina," *Felix Ravenna*, 4 ser., ii (1971); A Guillou, "L'Habitat nell'Italia bizantina: Esarcato, Sicilia, Catepanato (VI-XI secolo)," in *Atti del Colloquio Internazionale di Archeologia Medievale*, i (Palermo, 1976).

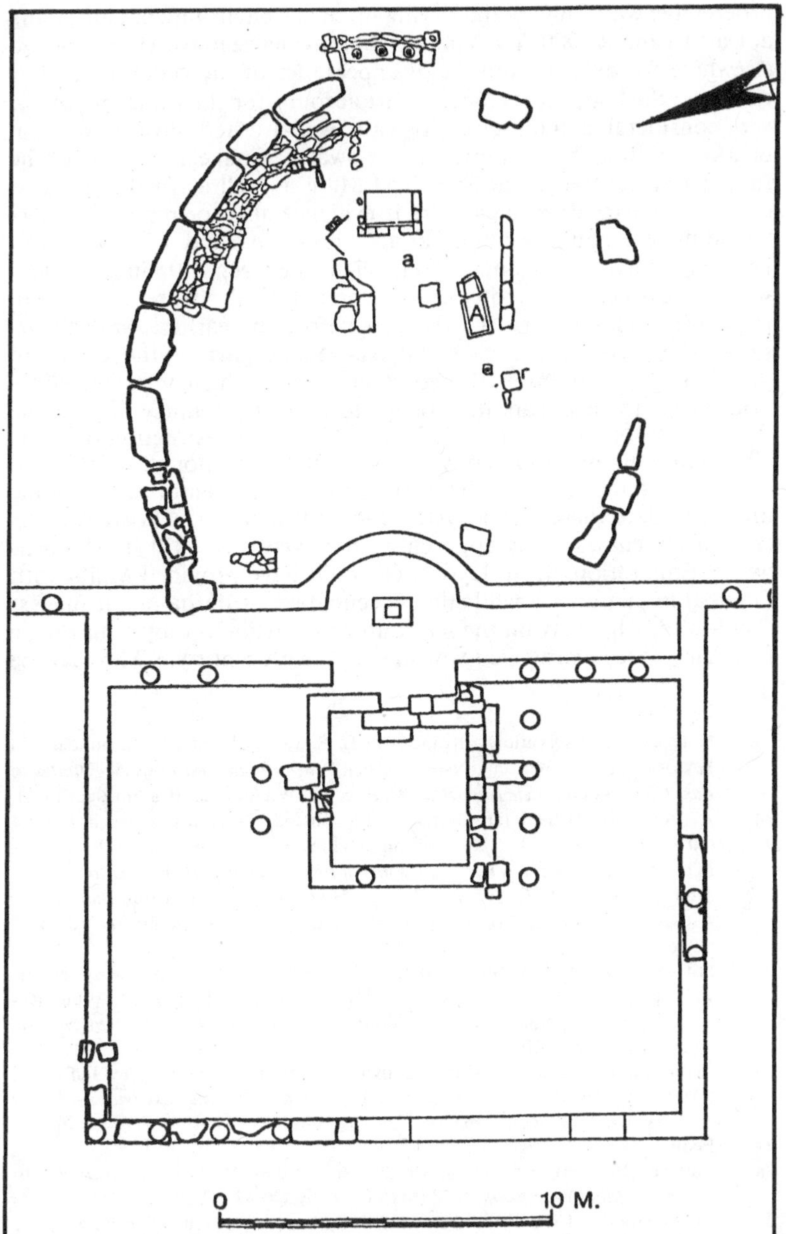


The Palaeochristian Basilica at Tas-Silġ with Square Baptistry at (a):
Sketch based on Plans in *Missione* Reports.

progressive warming up and drying up of the environment continuing at least to about 1000 AD. There is some evidence in North Africa and elsewhere for drought and the disappearance of the widespread olive culture.[23] Such a process may in part account for the ruination of the very considerable and archaeologically well-attested olive production on Malta,[24] though that subject really awaits a final elaboration of the finds from the "villa" at San Pawl Milqi as well as further excavations. In coastal Cyrenaica there is evidence also for major disasters including earthquakes, "barbarian" invasions and a catastrophic drought which is documented especially between 591 and 640 and which provoked an exodus of the comparatively dense Cyrenaican populace.[25] This flight occurred just before the earliest Arab incursions into Cyrenaica in 642 and 645. Some part of the Christian population remained on the coast at Barqa, which later served as bridgehead for a Byzantine attempt to hold the country against the Arabs with forces sent from Sicily in 688/9. The destruction of many Christian churches apparently came around 720, though Coptic and other Christians seem to have survived for many centuries;[26] at some uncertain date there was a systematic destruction of Christian churches in Cyrenaica, [27] as apparently there was after 870 in Malta as well.[28] Emigrations from Cyrenaica could have provided Malta with Oriental immigrants,[29] while the reoccupation of Barqa might suggest that Malta, which lay on the sea-route from Sicily to Libya, may have had some special strategic value in the seventh century.[30] The Maltese

23. Note various reservations advanced in B. Shaw, "Climate, Environment and History: the case of Roman North Africa," in *Climate and History: Studies in Past Climates and their Impact on Man,* ed. T. Wigley *et al.* (Cambridge, 1981).
24. A. Bonanno, "L'Habitat maltese in Età romana," *Kokalos,* xxii-xxiii tomo I (1976-1977), and *idem,* "Distribution of Villas and Some Aspects of the Maltese Economy in the Roman Period," *Journal of the Faculty of Arts: University of Malta,* vi, no. 4(1977). See also R. Virzi Hägglund, "Ghar ta' Iburdan: un Insediamento troglodito in Età romana," *Kokalos,* xxii-xxiii tomo I (1976-1977).
25. Stucchi, 357, 547-548. Stucchi presents numerous examples of the systematic walling-up of doorways (Figs. 570-573) as evidence of an exodus, but this seemingly inexplicable blocking of doorways seems more likely to have been the result of later squatting.
26. According to Stucchi, 553-555; see also the convenient summary by J. Pedley, "The History of the City," in *Apollonia, the Port of Cyrene: Excavations by the University of Michigan, 1965-1967,* ed. J. Humphrey (Tripoli, (1975)), 20-24.
27. Pedley, 24.
28. Luttrell, 26-27; Brown, 83-84; see also A. Luttrell, "The Christianization of Malta", *Malta Year Book 1977* (Malta, 1977), 420-421.
29. Cf. S. Hood, "Isles of Refuge in the Early Byzantine Period," *Annual of the British School at Athens,* lxv (1970), which documents refugees through datable pottery finds.
30. Cf. Brown, 73-78.

islands were firmly in Byzantine hands down to 870; immigrations and influences from Libya are possible, but they lack firm documentation and will probably continue to do so until scientific excavation and a further study of pottery are able to provide information which is more than that at present available.

IV

# THE CHRISTIANIZATION OF MALTA

Christianity first reached Malta through the accident of St. Paul's shipwreck in AD 60. Symbols and inscriptions in the catacombs and elsewhere attest a periodic if not a continuous Christian presence on the island during subsequent centuries. There were probably a number of churches of the Byzantine type, such as the basilica at Tas-Silġ, as well as certain centres of cult, notably the well on the Late Roman farm at San Pawl Milqi which was apparently connected with a tradition concerning the Apostle Paul. Indigenous Christianity may have been reinforced by North African, conceivably even by Egyptian or Syrian, Christians fleeing from Vandals, Berbers or Arabs in the fifth, sixth and seventh centuries, but ecclesiastically Malta and Gozo depended on the Pope in Rome. There was probably a Bishop of Malta by 553 and there was certainly one by 592, when Pope Gregory I was intervening in the affairs of the bishopric. Probably in or soon after 756 Sicily, and Malta with it, passed under the ecclesiastical jurisdiction of the Patriarchate of Constantinople, and by then the Maltese church had presumably adopted the Byzantine rite with Greek as the liturgical language. Malta was conquered by the Muslims in or close to 870; its bishop was imprisoned at Siracusa, columns which came from Malta and probably from a church there were exported to Africa, and in all likelihood the native Christianity of the island was more or less completely extinguished. Malta could still be described as "inhabited by Saracens" in 1175.

Count Roger the Norman conducted a three-day razzia on Malta in 1090, reducing it temporarily to a somewhat distant tributary status. He was met by a number of non-indigenous "Christian captives" who sailed away with him and finally returned to "their own kingdoms". Norman domination was indirect and discontinuous, but it must have brought occasional Christians to Malta, and from 1168 at the latest there was a Bishop of Malta who apparently held his office *in partibus* while residing in Sicily. Latin colonization probably began around 1200 and the Muslims were "expelled", most probably in 1224; some lost their lands and others perhaps even left the island, but many must have changed their religion while continuing to speak their Semitic language. These converts, together with the Latin colonists from Sicily, Italy and elsewhere, obviously required religious instruction and organization. The enduring Christianization of Malta and Gozo took place at this point: churches were built and endowed with lands and incomes, jurisdictions and tithes were established, and by about 1270 the Maltese diocese was operating as a suffragan of Palermo and had an archdeacon, a cantor and a group of canons. The Sicilian connection involved Malta in the political difficulties facing the church in Sicily during the fourteenth century, with some bishops being provided by the French popes at Avignon while others, often royal confessors, were nominated by the Aragonese rulers of Sicily.

A closer approximation to standard Latin practices came in the fifteenth century, as the Maltese church took on the aspect of a regular Italian diocese. There had been a cathedral church dedicated to St. Paul at Mdina since the thirteenth century. The cathedral had its complement of canons and other dignitaries, and sometime before 1436 Malta was divided into twelve *cappelle* or "arch-parishes", including one in Rabat and one in Birgu, while in Gozo there was a "major" church or *matrice*. The *cappelle*, each with its own endowments and incomes, had their own *cappellanus* or archpriest who administered baptisms, marriages and the other sacraments from a central church which corresponded roughly to the Italian rural *pieve*. This church was not necessarily situated inside one of the villages within the circumscription of the *cappella* but might, like that at Bir Miftuħ, be placed outside and between a number of the settlements it served. Other clergy and numerous scattered rural chapels were dependent on the central *cappella* and its *kappillan*, as he came to be known in Maltese.

The bulk of the clergy were indigenous and Maltese-speaking even if the best posts tended to go to representatives of the Siculo-Aragonese patriciate, such as the prominent fifteenth-century archdeacon Lancea Desguanes who was able to wield considerable power since the bishop was always an absentee. The appointment of non-Maltese clerics aroused strong and repeated local protests, but a foreign element did reach the island through the religious orders. The Benedictine monks never established themselves on Malta, though they held lands there, while the friars, who might have been expected to have been active in an area demanding missionary work, came surprisingly late. The Benedictines of Catania evaded the obligation to set up a house on Malta which had been attached in 1362 to a legacy of property there, partly on the grounds that they would not be able to provide brethren linguistically capable of pastoral work with the Maltese-speaking populace. A hospital and a church had been dedicated to St. Francis at Rabat by 1372 when the king nominated a Sicilian Franciscan to govern the hospital. By 1413 the Augustinians had a convent at Rabat; the Carmelites apparently reached Malta between 1418 and 1441, and the Dominicans, after rejecting an opportunity to found a convent on Malta in 1431, finally installed themselves there around 1450. The Benedictine sisters had two nunneries inside Mdina, while at the end of the fifteenth century the Observant Franciscans also founded a house at Rabat. Religious establishments and hospitals multiplied both on Malta and Gozo, and in the sixteenth century Capuchins, Jesuits and others joined the older orders. These regular clergy, with their foreign membership and connections and their willingness to educate Maltese brethren abroad, undoubtedly made a significant contribution to Malta's cultural and spiritual life.

Numerous fifteenth-century wills demonstrated the strength of the Maltese people's devotion to their church through bequests for the saying of masses, the establishment of family endowments in *juspatronatus*, the foundation of side-chapels and of small country churches, and the patronage of paintings and other embellishments for churches and religious houses; by 1575 there were some 430 churches and chapels in Malta and Gozo. The small *casale* at Ħal Millieri near Żurrieq, for example, consisted of only fifteen households yet in 1575 it had four churches standing in two groups of two abutting chapels. The Annunciation church there was covered in the mid-fifteenth century with a series of standing saints painted in fresco in the panels formed by the arches which sustained the stone roof-slabs. Such churches had no priest and mass was celebrated there only on special feast-days, but they had their own endowments, often in the shape of incomes secured on particular fields and administered by a procurator who was responsible for the maintenance of altar furnishings, sanctuary lamps and suchlike, and for the organization of the annual festivities. At Ħal Millieri the whole apparatus of masses, festas and field-rents continued under the supervision of a procurator long after the moment when the inhabitants of the *casale* had totally abandoned the settlement in about 1700. Intensely local institutions such as these helped to keep the bulk of the rural populace closely in touch with their Christian faith.

This insular Maltese church was naturally affected by universal developments. The Jews were expelled in 1492; the Knights of St. John took over the government of the islands in 1530, bringing with them a number of Greeks and a multitude of cosmopolitan connections; the infidel Turks invaded and were stubbornly, and triumphantly, resisted in 1565; and at the end of the sixteenth century there were even scares of Protestant plots. At the same time Malta participated in the main currents of the Counter-Reformation with the coming of the Jesuits, the foundation of schools and seminaries, the introduction of the Inquisition, and the arrival of Pietro Dusina to carry out the Apostolic Visitation of 1575 which revealed numerous irregularities, doctrinal and moral, in Maltese ecclesiastical life. The Maltese clergy, like those elsewhere, clearly needed reformation; some were ignorant and ill-prepared for their task while many kept concubines. After 1530 the bishop, though still not a Maltese, was normally resident on the island. The arrival of the Knights and their followers, military, naval and otherwise, was followed by a dramatic rise in the indigenous population and by the foundation of Valletta and the development of the larger villages, so that the bishop had to face many fresh problems. The establishment of new urban parishes, the foundation of religious confraternities, the building of new style baroque churches by Girolamo Cassar and others, and the introduction of more modern forms of devotion all contributed to the unending work of Christianization, to that pastoral process which continued to pose new difficulties and to evoke new solutions in each successive generation.

Maltese religion was strengthened by a propaganda campaign sustained by members of the religious orders who deliberately fostered a series of historical inventions many of which were reproduced, and thereby established almost ineradicably, in Gian Francesco Abela's authoritative *Descrittione di Malta* published in 1647. Notable among these myth-makers was the Maltese Jesuit Girolamo Manduca who died in 1643 having written and worked extensively to cultivate popular sympathy for St. Paul and other saints, fabricating a network of pious legends on which Abela leant heavily. Manduca could, however, cite earlier enthusiasms such as that of Matteo Surdo, Archpriest of Malta, who was attempting in 1549 to restore the Pauline cult at St. Paul's cemetery in Rabat which, he complained, had been neglected for over a hundred years. Saintly dedications, reverence for the Virgin Mary and for St. Agatha, the carved souls in purgatory, the ex-voto paintings in the shrines and other such manifestations of popular religiosity all bore witness to the success of such promotions. A *Legendario Melitense* produced in 1775 reported among the claims to sanctity for the Jesuit Giovanni Maria Vella of Lija, who died in 1689, that "he professed a singular devotion towards St. Paul and St. Publius whose cults he laboured to propagate to everyone in the whole island, and he was a great devotee of the Holy Souls of Purgatory."

The strong attachment of the Maltese to their Catholic Christian faith may, in some curiously indefinable way, have been conditioned by their position on the frontier of Latin Christendom as a dimly felt response to the threatening proximity of Islamic Africa, or even as an almost unconscious form of compensation for that non-Christian past of which their non-European language was a perpetual memorial. Following their conversion to Christianity, some sections of the indigenous population probably tried to maintain their language in order to preserve the old way of life, as rustic and artisan sought to protect themselves against colonial exploitation by Romance-speaking Latin settlers. Something similar happened among the Valencian Moors, but they were defending a religion as well as their group identity. In Malta there was no religious barrier. The settlers' sons grew up as Maltese-speaking Maltese, while many of those who spoke only Maltese may have learnt Sicilian in order to avoid exclusion from continental contacts and from public affairs in Malta itself. The protests of the Maltese clergy against non-Maltese appointments suggest a "protonationalistic" element in the church as early as the fifteenth century. With the coming of the Knights, who established themselves as a ruling caste of foreign individuals who could have no permanent family or territorial connections in the island, a section of the Maltese clergy emerged among the leaders of local resentment and resistance against foreigners, conducting interminable jurisdictional quarrels with the Knights, participating in the armed uprising against the French in 1798, and subsequently propagating the Italian language as a form of opposition to British rule and culture. In terms of education, welfare and politics, the church at the middle of the twentieth century was still so firmly embedded in the parochial and national life of the island that it provided the Maltese with one element of their identity as a separate people.

* * * *

The abundant evidence for the post-1436 period has been utilized in recent work by J. Boissevain, Alexander Bonnici, Arthur Bonnici, V. Borg, J. Cassar Pullicino, M. Fsadni, Q. Hughes, A. Vella, G. Wettinger and others, while their works cite further studies of individual parishes, confraternities, churches, and so forth. Even so, there is much scope for further research, especially on religious aspects of folklore and sociological aspects of Maltese religiosity. For the earlier period, of which all too little is known, see the references and materials in *Medieval Malta: Studies on Malta before the Knights*, ed. A. Luttrell (London, 1975). V. Borg's study of the Early Christian remains is in the press. The coming of the orders is documented in A. Luttrell, "The Augustinians at Malta: 1413," *Analecta Augustiniana*, xxxviii (1975); the text of 1441 given there shows, when taken with the evidence in S. Abela, *L-Ewwel Karmelitani f'Malta u l'Ewwel Knisja u Kunvent Tagħhom 'Il-Lunzjata l-Qadima'*: 1418-1659 (Malta, 1976), 6-8, that the Carmelites had a Maltese convent by 1441. On the secular clergy, see G. Wettinger, "Early Maltese Popular Attitudes to the Government of the Order of St. John," *Melita Historica*, vi no. 3 (1974), and "Concubinage among the Clergy of Malta and Gozo: 1420-1550" (forthcoming). The religious life and culture of a rural community are studied in *Ħal Millieri: A Maltese Casale, its Churches and Paintings*, ed. A. Luttrell (Malta, 1976). An article on Abela, Manduca and their contemporaries awaits publication; on Manduca, see J. Cassar Pullicino, "Il-Leġġenda tal-Maltin assedjati fl-Imdina," *Leħen il-Malti*, xlv (1976); the Matteo Surdo text is in G. Gatt Said, *Risposta ... sulla primitiva chiesa vescovile in Malta* (Malta, 1868), 52/3 note b; for Manduca's use of it, see Valletta, Royal Malta Library, Ms. 25, f. 184-185; on Giovanni Maria Vella, see Mdina, Cathedral Archives, Ms. 57, f. 166-166v.

For the period from 870 to 1194 the materials are meagre and the dissension great, though the myths which once obscured these centuries are slowly being dismantled (*Medieval Malta*, 23-25, 96-103). The issue has been much confused when particular texts, such as the puzzling passage in al-Qazwini, have been interpreted unsoundly in isolation from the main context. There is still no single clear and positive piece of evidence that indigenous forms of Christianity survived through this period, but that is not to assert that Christianity was definitely or totally extinguished on Muslim Malta; in one debatable instance, that of the possible continuity of a Pauline cult at San Pawl Milqi, there is in fact some evidence for its survival (*ibid.*, 20, 28, 93-95).

New information is most likely to be provided by archaeological methods. The "continuationists" have often sought philological proof in alleged "Christian Arabic" survivals in the Maltese language. This debate remains at a preliminary stage, since the linguists still concentrate on the language in its modern form. They employ techniques and terminologies which the historian can seldom understand; they persistently interpret their findings within a historical framework largely rejected by historians; and they usually ignore the earliest texts and word forms. New approaches are now necessary, as various linguists have themselves suggested; see the views and references assembled in G. Mangion, "A Bibliography of Maltese: 1953-1973," *Melita Historica*, vi no. 3 (1974). The primary task is the completion of the extensive work of Godfrey Wettinger, who is publishing and studying all available Maltese names, place-names and microtoponyms for the century or more following 1419. Then, instead of comparing modern Maltese to Koranic Arabic or to modern "classical" Arabic, the fifteenth-century Maltese form of Arabic should be compared both to modern Maltese and to medieval Arabic as spoken at Palermo, at Tunis and elsewhere: cf. W. Cowan, "Caxaro's Cantilena: a Checkpoint for Change in Maltese," *Journal of Maltese Studies*, 10(1975). Meanwhile, it has yet to be demonstrated that the "Christian Arabic" terms in Maltese actually are both "Christian" and "Arabic" in origin, and also that they were really, or even probably, in use on Malta before about 1200. Given the complete absence of pre-1200 Maltese texts and the numerous opportunities for such words to have been imported into the language at the moment of conversion in the thirteenth century or at various later stages, this would be difficult to prove.

L. Trimble, "Some Linguistic Comments on Religious Terms in Maltese," *ibid.*, 9(1973), assumes that Maltese Christianity continued from AD 60 right through the Muslim period; that a pre-Arabic layer of religious terms, some of them shared with Syriac, survived in Maltese Arabic; and that the "Arabs" were expelled in 1090. Trimble argues that certain Christian prayers received their modern form in the Muslim period and even contain pre-870 elements. His claim that "evidence from place names indicates an early Semitic structure, perhaps influenced by Punic," for the language spoken in Malta is a brave one, since no Maltese toponym can be documented before about 1250, by which time the island had been "converted" from Islam. Maltese was scarcely ever written before the eighteenth century. The modern Maltese forms of the *Credo* and *Paternoster* which Trimble analyses cannot be traced back further than Francesco Wzzino's *Dottrina Cristiana* of 1752, and when that was being compiled problems arose and the bishop was worried precisely because no standard form of these prayers was in existence: J. Cassar Pullicino, *Kitba w Kittieba tal-Malti,* i (Malta, 1962), 46-59. At the time of Dusina's visitation in 1575 a number of priests were teaching the catechism to children and others, and some of these priests could not read Latin but must have taught in Italian or, more probably, Maltese; again, however, there is no evidence for written texts: Valletta, Royal Malta Library, Ms. 643, f.488, 527 *et passim.*

Words such as *Ġesù Kristu* and *Marija* may in some sense be "etymologically non-Semitic", as Trimble holds, but it could fairly be asked what other forms could reasonably be expected for them; for example, the Arabic for *Marija* is *Maryam.* Furthermore, it is hard to accept suggestions that Greek, Latin, Punic or Syrian elements can be identified in the "pre-Arabic sub-strata" of the Maltese form of Arabic when there is no substantial Maltese text datable earlier than ca. 1485. J. Aquilina, "Maltese Toponymic Stratification," *Onoma,* xiii (1968), 276, suggests that it is philologically possible that the word *Milqi* found at San Pawl Milqi "continues a pre-Arabic Carthaginian residue," but the historian is bound to observe both that there is no proof that the philological process involved took place in Malta and also that the most extensive research on this key point has not been able to document that toponym before 1616 (*Medieval Malta,* 20 n.124); possibly it was imported or invented shortly before that date by someone anxious to propagate the Pauline cult. If there were any direct Syriac influences in the pre-870 language, they presumably disappeared in or shortly after 870. Post-870 Syriac importations could have come well after 1200, but they might also have come with the Muslims. In 827, for example, a thousand families of Egyptian Copts were sent from Egypt to Tunis to construct and man a fleet, and other Eastern Christians are known to have travelled to Tunisia and to have Orientalized its Christianity: references in H. Idris, in *Revue Africaine,* xcviii (1954), 271/2 n. 39, 275 *et passim.* According to al-Qazwini (text in *Medieval Malta,* 84-85), the servile population of Malta outnumbered the free Muslims in about 1040, so that Muslim Malta may well have had non-indigenous "Christian Arab" inhabitants.

Al-Qazwini's passage, with its description of the servile majority as *abid* which normally meant "slaves", is difficult to interpret. Al-Qazwini was a thirteenth-century Persian author some of whose information about Malta was altogether confused, and whose sources for this affair remain unknown. Most probably he did not intend to refer either to Muslim slaves, who were seldom at all numerous and who would have been unlikely to have constituted a majority, or to indigenous Christians who, had they survived, would normally have become not slaves but *dhimmis,* free citizens inferior in status: cf. R. Brunschvig, "Abd," Encylopaedia *of Islam,* i (revised ed: Leiden, 1960), 24-40. It could be argued that the inhabitants had been reduced to the status of slaves rather than *dhimmis* just because they resisted the Muslims in 870, but there is almost no other evidence to support such an interpretation. More likely al-Qazwini was reporting rather imprecisely some notice concerning non-indigenous non-Muslims many or most of whom could have been either Oriental Christians or Greeks and Latins such as the *captivi christiani,* presumably prisoners-of-war, who — as the chronicler Malaterra made clear — originated outside Malta in countries to which they returned after being freed by Count Roger in 1090. Quite possibly, the population of eleventh-century Malta included a mélange of some or all of such groups.

It has often been assumed that after 870 the indigenous Christians did survive with the subservient legal status of *dhimmis,* as occured in Sicily and many other places. This assumption is, on balance, contradicted by the available evidence for resistance and persecution on Malta, which includes the archaeological indications of destructions at the moment of conquest, the imprisonment of the Bishop of Malta (and there is no clear evidence that he was subsequently released), the probable removal of the columns of a Maltese church to Tunisia, and — *ex silentio* — the absence of any positive evidence to support such an interpretation; see *Medieval Malta,* 22, 83-84, 89 *et passim,* together with J. Barnard, "The Arab Conquest," *Journal of the Faculty of Arts*: *Royal University of Malta,* vi no.2(1975), and note that it is possible, though unlikely given the evidence for the destruction of a church at Tas-Silġ, that the columns did not come from a church. Byzantine Malta may well have been drastically crushed, conceivably by fierce nomadic tribesmen in Aghlabid service. There are many cases of departures from the strict theoretical letter of the Muslim laws of tolerance which, in any case, allowed scope for a diversity of interpretations and applications. There were numerous examples of slaughter and of the destruction of churches, while the rights of those who surrendered peaceably were distinguished clearly from the penalties incurred by those who resisted conquest: A. Tritton, *The Caliphs and their Non-Muslim Subjects* (London, 1930); A. Fattal, *Le Statut legal des non-Musulmans en pays d'Islam* (Beirut, 1958); C. Cahen, *"Dhimma," Encyclopaedia of Islam,* ii (revised ed: Leiden, 1965), 227-231. A relevant example of this distinction between capitulation and conquest was provided by the African judge Abu l'H'asan al-Qabisi, who died in 1012 when he ruled that Muslims could reuse the stones of a Christian church if the Christians had ceased to use the church at the moment of Muslim conquest, but not if the Christians had capitulated: cited by H. Idris, in *Mélanges d'histoire et d'archéologie de l'Occident Musulman*: *Hommage à Georges Marçais,* ii (Algiers, 1957), 105-106. The probable reuse in Tunisia of the columns of a Maltese church would, therefore, suggest that Byzantine Malta did not capitulate, in which case its Christian population may have been ruthlessly reduced or even eliminated. These puzzling problems certainly require further study.

# V

# SLAVES AND CAPTIVES ON MALTA: 1053/4 and 1091

Despite the desperate scarcity of sources, it is now generally agreed that between about 870 and about 1200 Malta was in Muslim hands and that any element of Christian continuity from before 870 can virtually be excluded. Where texts are lacking legend may flourish; but the notion of some Christian survival through the Muslim period, an idea long accepted as ancient unbroken tradition of the type described by Gian Francesco Abela in 1647 as the *approuate traditioni hauute da nostri Maggiori*, is demonstrably an early-modern invention.[1] Most of the sources available for the period were indicated and discussed, somewhat disjointedly, in 1975,[2] while others were supplied in Godfrey Wettinger's standard synthesis on Muslim Malta as revised in 1986.[3] Doubts remain however, especially since Joseph Brincat recently added an important new element to the discussion by noting a passage in the writing of al-Himyari who died in 1494 but used earlier sources.[4] Further such literary discoveries remain possible but excavation, which might well solve vital problems in this period, is unlikely to be able to

1. A. Luttrell, 'Girolamo Manduca and Gian Francesco Abela: Tradition and Invention in Maltese Historiography', *Melita Historica*, vii, no. 2 (1977).
2. T. Brown, J. Cassar Pullicino, A. Luttrell *et al.*, in *Medieval Malta: Studies on Malta before the Knights*, ed. A. Luttrell (London, 1975); note that the Norman invasion should be dated to 1091 and not to 1090.
3. G. Wettinger, 'The Arabs in Malta', revised edition in *Malta: Studies of its Heritage and History*, ed. Mid-Med Bank (Malta, 1986); a third edition is forthcoming. V. Grassi, 'Materiali per lo Studio Della Presenza araba nella Regione italiana: i. L'Epigrafia araba nelle Isole maltesi,' *Studi Magrebini*, xxi (1989). At least one other Arabic inscription on Malta deserves publication. The Maimuna stone, which Grassi, 25, 35 notes as in a class of its own and as coming from Gozo, is first documented in Valletta in 1772 and could have been imported from abroad: A. Luttrell, 'The Roots of Medieval Gozo,' *Al-Masaq*, iv (1991), 52-53; G. Bonello, 'New Light on Majmuna's Tombstone,' *Sunday Times* (Malta), 735 (8 November 1992), 41. The inscription's stone awaits analysis.
4. J. Brincat, *Malta 870-1054: Al-Himyari's Account* (Malta, 1991); G. Wettinger's reactions in *Sunday Times* (Malta), 620 (26 August 1990), 23; 625 (30 September 1990), 16.

do so for some time.[5] The Maltese language was scarcely written down until modern times and cannot throw convincing light on the period before 1200, though toponyms, and especially microtoponyms which clearly persisted for many centuries,[6] are documented in very considerable number for the fifteenth century and, occasionally, a little earlier. Whether such place names can safely be adduced as evidence for the period before 1091 is extremely doubtful, but since none of them indicates a probable pre-870 toponym they would, if anything, strengthen any theory of a break following the conquest of 870 circa.[7]

There are strong indications, and al-Himyari's text reinforces them, of a Christian opposition to the Muslim attack of 870 which resulted in the dismantling of one or more churches and the death or exile of the bishop and many of the Christian inhabitants on Malta.[8] Outright resistance on farms or in caves would scarcely have been possible on a small, flat island. It is possible that after 870 there were no Christians, but only Muslims, on Malta; or that a few hundred indigenous Christian inhabitants survived as *dhimmi*, that is as free citizens of inferior status; or that some inhabitants became *mawali* or converts to Islam and were accepted as equals; or that they became slaves precisely because they resisted the conquerors of 870. On a small and distant island the laws of Islam were not necessarily followed strictly and other situations are conceivable. Thus in the tenth century Ibn Hauqal described rural communities in Western Sicily in which Muslim men married Christian women as Islam permitted, their male children being brought up as Muslims and the females as Christians.[9] In the late-thirteenth century the Sicilian Bartolomeo de Neocastro reported a more fantastic but possibly significant story told by a Muslim on Gerba, according to which the inhabitants of the islands, explicitly including Malta, were the

5. Cf. A. Luttrell, 'Medieval Malta; the Non-Written and the Written Evidence,' in *Malta: A Case Study in International Cross-Currents*, ed. S. Fiorini and V. Mallia-Milanes (Malta, 1991).
6. E.g. M.A. and D. Aquilina *et al.*, in *Hal Millieri: a Maltese Casale, its Churches and Paintings*, ed. A. Luttrell (Malta, 1976), 26-27 and Fig. 2
7. Wettinger (1986), 90-91.
8. Brown, 81-84; Luttrell (1975), 21-28; Wettinger (1986), 90-91; Brincat, 2, 6-7. Wettinger, 91, says that Maltese Christians must 'undoubtedly' have fled from Sicily to the Italian mainland; but that is a hypothesis.
9. Ibn Hauqal, *Configuration de la Terre (Kitab Surat al-Ard)*, trans. and ed., J. Kramers and G. Wiet, i (Beirut - Paris, 1964), 198; cf. A. Luttrell, 'Ibn Hauqal and Tenth-Century Malta', *Hyphen* (Malta), v, no. 4 (1987),159.

out to the more numerous slaves that in the event of a Byzantine victory they would be subjected to a captivity and bondage worse than that which would face the free Muslims, who would have friends or allies or a community to redeem them, and the masters promised their slaves that if they joined in resistance to the Byzantines they would, if victorious, be granted their freedom and the daughters of the free minority in marriage. The slaves fought harder than the free Muslims and the majority of the Byzantines were killed, just one ship escaping.[15] Though some Byzantine prisoners, not necessarily Greeks, conceivably remained on Malta following this defeat, the fact is that no surviving source mentions any other Christians, indigenous or otherwise, on Malta between just after 870 and 1091, and the non-written evidence is similarly silent.[16]

Joseph Brincat seems to accept al-Himyari's account of an island uninhabited for some 180 years and of a deliberate attempt at recolonization. That would imply a complete ethnic break between Byzantine and Muslim Malta, yet he is reluctant to dismiss the implausible notion of Christian communities from before 870 surviving on tiny Malta for a long period in 'hills and valleys ... living or hiding in caves' but leaving no apparent trace of their existence. Despite the strong evidence for Christian opposition in 870 Brincat considers that 'any Maltese survivors from the 870 massacre must have increased, and unless they offered resistance (which would be unlikely) would have been integrated with the new settlers, probably among the slaves.' In that case, however, there would have been no total abandonment. Brincat claims that there are no clues as to the race, creed, or language of the immigrant slaves of 1048/9 but suggests that quite possibly they were neither Arab nor Berber but Christians from Sicily who were of three types: Sicilian Christians, ex-Christians, and Slavs.[17]

15. Text and translation in Brincat, 2-5. Al-Qazwini's less detailed version, which did not mention daughters or marriages, is given in translation by Brown, 84-85. Al-Qawzini dated the Byzantine attack to 440 (1048/9); Brown, 85, suggests 1038. Wettinger (1986), 91, interpreting Qazwini's slaves as 'a subject population, perhaps indeed partly of indigenous origin, already Islamicized and Arabized ...' implies that al-Qazwini wrote of the Muslims and slaves as 'Maltese'.
16. Wettinger (1986), 91-92; T. Blagg and A. Luttrell, 'Notes on San Pawl Milqi', in T. Blagg, A. Bonanno and A. Luttrell, *Excavations at Hal Millieri, Malta* (Malta, 1990).
17. Brincat, 7-9.

offspring of black African men and Byzantine women form Sicily.[10] Arabic-speaking or Coptic Christians might have reached Malta from the Levant or from Africa; in 827, for example, many Copts were sent from Egypt to Tunisia where they orientalized its Christianity.[11]

It was stated by Ibn Hauqal and a number of other Arabic writers that Malta was totally abandoned in the tenth century. Al-Himyari's account of the conquest strengthens the picture of destruction and abandonment in and after 870, and his claim that Muslims repeopled the island and built a city after 440, that is after 1048/9, implies a total depopulation of some 180 years and a complete break in ethnic, linguistic, and religious continuities. Al-Himyari repeats the story, known to al-Qazwini in the thirteenth century, of a Byzantine attack on Malta with many ships and a siege of the city, dating it to 445 or 1053/4 and adding new details.[12] It could have been that a Muslim settlement of 1048/9 circa provoked an almost immediate Byzantine riposte, and it would be unwise to dismiss entirely the idea of a complete abandonment since that would explain the general absence of evidence for continuing occupation; but the balance of probability seems to lie against a complete desertion. The various descriptions of an abandoned island have been explained, quite convincingly, as the result of textual confusion with another place with the similar name of Galita,[13] and it may be that al-Himyari, faced with evidence both for a total abandonment before 1053/4 and of a community on Malta in that year, sought to resolve the apparent contradiction by inventing a slightly earlier repopulation and the building, or perhaps a rebuilding, of the city. At present only a detailed and exhaustive investigation of al-Himyari's sources and of their manuscript traditions offers even an outside hope of settling that problem.[14]

According to al-Himyari, the 400 free Muslims on Malta and their more numerous *abid* or slaves were attacked in 1053/4 by the *Rum*, that is the Byzantines, 'and the Muslims asked them for clemency and they refused it, except for women and belongings.' The free Muslims then pointed

10. Bartholomaeus de Neocastro, *Historia Sicula*, ed. G. Paladino, in *Rerum Italicarum Scriptores*, n.s., xiii, part 3 (Bologna,1922), 63-65.
11. A. Luttrell, 'The Christianization of Malta', *Malta Year Book 1977* (Malta, 1977), 420.
12. Text and translation in Brincat, 2-5.
13. Most recently Wettinger (30 September 1990), 16.
14. Brincat, 9-20, discusses such investigations and announces future contributions; Wettinger (26 August 1990), 23, and (30 September 1990), 16, indicates various problems.

Had the slaves of 1053/4 been descendants of the pre-870 inhabitants they would probably have remained on the island with their women, unless the latter alone had been deported or absorbed by Muslim conquerors, and the men would have had no pressing need to marry the free Muslims' daughters. Had they been Christians, the threat of captivity and bondage under the Christian Byzantines would not have been very compelling. Only if they were Muslims would their condition, already one of slavery, have been likely to be worsened by a Byzantine victory. Furthermore, the free Muslim minority would have been most reluctant, even in an emergency, to trust a more numerous group of Christian slaves with their freedom as equals. That the free Muslims offered their daughters in marriage might suggest that the slaves were not Christian, since Islam prohibits Muslim women from marrying non-Muslims. Godfrey Wettinger points out that had there been Christian survivors from before 870 who remained Christians, they would presumably have been relatively free *dhimmi* rather than slaves. He suggests a re-peopling of the island, however gradual, by Arabic speakers who might have come from North Africa or other areas to the east or west rather than from Sicily, and he notes that the Muslims are not known to have had Christian slaves on Sicily. Unless in 1053/4 there were *dhimmi* who were not mentioned by al-Qazwini or by al-Himyari, then there were only free men and slaves; and the latter were unlikely to have been Christian even in origin.[18] Had the free Muslims' wives and daughters been Christians according to the Sicilian practice reported by Ibn Hauqal, that would have allowed Christian slaves to marry them and might have explained why the Byzantines demanded the women; but that would be to pile hypothesis on hypothesis while leaving other problems unsolved. The reality may have been an untidy and fluctuating jumble of poorly defined personal conditions operating within a very small context.

Brincat writes of a 'total and abrupt change of language' and of the 'lack of a linguistic substratum' in the eleventh century. It could reasonably be supposed that such hypothetical developments would have been the result of some 180 years of total abandonment, if such an abandonment were proven. To assume such developments as facts which support an

18. This is merely to elaborate, in the light of al-Himyari's text, on what has been said by A. Mayr (1896), Brown (1975), 84-85, and Wettinger (1986), 91; *idem* (26 August 1990), 23; *idem* (30 September 1990), 16.

unproven hypothesis of a total abandonment would scarcely be logical. To say that a hypothetical immigration of Sicilians and Slavs in the eleventh century would solve the problem of those Maltese Semitic terms, including *knisja* for church and *qassis* for priest, which relate to the Christian religion, is to imply that the existence of the terms in modern Maltese strengthens the hypothesis that the slaves of 1053/4 were Christian and that they reached Malta from Sicily.[19] In reality there is no such problem, since the Semitic terms are totally undocumented in Maltese until much later and there is no way of demonstrating that they reached Malta as Christian terms in the eleventh century. They could have arrived in a variety of ways and at various times.[20]

The situation on Malta had changed by the time of Count Roger the Norman's attack on the island in 1091. The chief source for that event is the chronicle of Roger's French chaplain and biographer Geoffroi Malaterra, who was either with Roger or received a first-hand account of events. His chronicle included a passage describing how the Muslims' Christian captives, of whom a great number or *plurima multitudo* were held within the town, came in procession to greet the victorious count:

> Videntes autem captivos christianos, ab urve progredientes, prae gaudio suae insperatae liberationis ab imo quoque cordis lacrimis profundi, lingo vel calamis, prout quisque primo inveniebant, compositas cruces in dexteris ferentes, *Kyrie eleyson* proclamando, ad pedes comitis provolvi, nostri vero ad talem intuitum pietatis affectu lacrimoso rore perfunduntur. Comes ergo, taliter urbe sibi confoederata, captivos, asportet, per naves ordinans, reditum cum magno timore, prae nimio pondere captivorum, ut submersionem veritus, accelerat. Sed dextera Dei, ut credimus, ex eventu patuit: naves per undas sublevans, cubitu uno liberiores super mare ferebat, quam in aditu suo cum eas minus onus gravabat.

This means that by 1091 there were many Christian captives on Malta who went with joy to meet Roger, carrying crosses and crying *Kyrie Eleison*; Roger took them away, seriously overloading his ships, and devastating Gozo on his way. On reaching Sicily he freed the captives and offered to settle them in Sicily free of any 'servile exaction', but they preferred to return to their own 'fields and

19. Brincat, 7-9; Luttrell, 'Christianity' (1977), 420, provides the literature on these Semitic terms. Brincat has the merit of being the first of the 'philologists' to confront the earlier historical evidence and to seek to place the language in a more acceptable context: cf. J. Brincat, 'Language and Demography in Malta: the Social Foundations of the Symbiosis between Semitic and Romance in Standard Maltese', in *Malta: a Case Study ...* (1989). The article provides a more convincing account of the origins of the language.
20. Luttrell (1975), 24-25.

friends' and left for their various homelands, crossing the Straits of Messina.[21]

It might be argued that Malaterra was not present on Malta and was misinformed or inaccurate; certainly he was anxious to exaggerate Count Roger's achievements.[22]Yet his account of events on Malta appears detailed and circumstantial, so that it seems reasonable to accept the core of his story. Clearly the freed captives were not indigenous to Malta and were not, or mostly not, from Sicily, since they left for their homelands by crossing to mainland Italy. It might seem contradictory that the captives who were full of joy at their release should ask for mercy in Greek. If the captives were Greeks, or mainly Greeks, it might have been that they shouted various remarks and that Malaterra, who presumably knew no Greek but as priest would naturally have recognized the words *Kyrie Eleison* from the Latin mass and have known that they meant 'Lord have mercy'[23] thought that that was what he heard. Even if this were the case, it would be unlikely that after some forty years the numerous captives of 1091 were survivors from a Byzantine attack of 1053/4. It seems more probable that the 'captives' of 1091 had been taken more recently in battle or by pirates, or have been shipwrecked, or been imported as slaves. If these captives were mainly Latins, and quite possible Italians, they might have carried crosses and shouted 'Lord have mercy' in Greek, perhaps the only Greek words they knew, precisely to emphasize that they were Christians, their joy perhaps being tempered with the fear that the invaders were, as in 1053/4, Greek-speaking Byzantines whom they would have feared as recent and bitter enemies of the Latins.

Brincat claims that the supposedly Christian slaves of 1053/4, the Christian captives of 1091, and the Christians on Malta between 1130 and 1154 were 'markers of continuity'.[24] In the almost total absence of evidence it is difficult entirely to disprove even apparently unlikely suggestions, yet it is clear that even if the slaves of 1053/4 were Christian they would technically have been bound to have converted to Islam in order to become free men and marry the free Muslims' daughters; that would have broken the continuity. The Christian captives of 1091 did

21. Gaufredus Malaterra, *De Rebus gestis Rogerii ...*, ed. E. Pontieri, in *Refum Italicarum Scriptores*, n.s. v, part 1 (Bologna, 1927), 94-96: Cassar Pullicino, 100, points out that the story of the Christians carrying palms is a legend.
22. Cf. Pontieri's *prefazione*; Cassar Pullicino, 97.
23. Cf. P. Siffrin, 'Kyrie Eleison,' *Enciclopedia Cattolica*, xx (Rome, 1933), 767-768.
24. Brincat, 9.

not come from Malta and left the island in that year; they could have contributed little or nothing or any Christian continuity. What may be deduced about the Christians of 1127 to 1154, who are known to have been punished for killing a Muslim on Malta,[25] is that presumably they reached the island after 1091 when the Christian captives left; most probably they came after the renewed conquest of Malta by Roger I in 1127 and were few in number.[26] There was, therefore, little room for Christian continuities. The reality was probably confused and untidy with individual exceptions to general developments. If Geoffroi Malaterra was correct in reporting that Count Roger took away from Malta all, or perhaps most, of the Christian captives then on the island, it would follow that Malta was more Muslim after 1091 than before it.

25. Wettinger (1986), 98; Luttrell (1991), 37.
26. Luttrell (1975), 31. S. Fiorini, 'Malta in 1530', in *Hospitaller Malta: 1530-1798 - Studies on Early Modern Malta and the Order of St John*, ed. V. Mallia-Milanes (Malta, forthcoming), notes an Italo-Byzantine *familiaris* of Roger I who before about 1135 had been exiled to Malta where he spent fifteen years surrounded by Muslims.

# VI

# MDINA HOARD OF MUSLIM COINS: 1698

The discovery of a hoard of Arabic gold coins in 1698 was an outstanding event in the history of Maltese numismatics if only because the coins and their discovery were so fully recorded.[1] From the time of the earliest surviving written documents, that is in effect from the fifteenth century, there is evidence of coin hoards being sought and discovered in Malta, but they were treated as treasure and there is little indication of what kind of coins were found.[2] In addition to these hoards there must also have been occasional random discoveries of monies. In 1647 the historian Gian Francesco Abela had some pieces with Arabic lettering:

> *... facendo gl'Arabi scolpire lettere Arabiche nelle monete, delle quali fin hoggi se ne conservano tuttauia alcune presso di noi, nelle quali da vna parte si mostrano le sopraccenate note, e dell'altra la Croce, e nome di Christo Signor nostro, in significato, e dimostrattione del Dominio comune.*[3]

Given their Christian markings, these were probably Norman coins from twelfth-century Sicily.[4]

After the great earthquake of 1693 work was undertaken not only to rebuild the cathedral in the old capital of Mdina but also to enlarge the piazza to the front and side of it. On 12 April 1698 a small boy working on the site hit a metal pot from which gold coins spilled out.[5] The exact spot where the money was found is marked

[1] This study constitutes part of a joint investigation of coin collections in Malta and Gozo which resulted in Helen Brown's article "The Coins of Muslim Malta" (*supra*); Thomas Brown examined more than 800 Byzantine coins, but since only one or two have an assured provenance it seems unwise to base any conclusions on them.

[2] Details in G. Wettinger, "The Gold Hoard of 1538", *Melita Historica*, vii no. 1 (1976).

[3] G.-F. Abela, *Della Descrittione di Malta* (Malta, 1647), 256.

[4] Brown (*supra*), 15-16; Norman gold coins from the National Museum of Archaeology, Valletta, but without provenance are illustrated in G. Wettinger, "The Arabs in Malta" (2nd ed.), in *Malta: Studies of its Heritage and History*, ed. Mid-Med Bank (Malta, 1986).

[5] This article is largely based on the act of 13 April 1698 in Valletta, Notarial Archives, Acts of Giovanni Domenico Gatt R. 281, vol. 36, f. 521-523, and other texts in Mdina, Cathedral Archives, Misc. 10, 11, 63, 156, 174. C. Ciantar - G.-F. Abela, *Malta Illustrata*, 2 vols. (Malta, 1771-1780), i. 97-99, cited other acts of Giovanni Gatt and of Giambattista Dorbies dated 13 June and 13 and 15 July 1699 then said to be in the Atti Civili of the Inquisition; these cannot at present be traced in the Notarial or the Cathedral Archives; they are summarized in Misc. 174, f. 857-858, but are of little relevance. Wettinger (1986), 101 n. 30, also cites Valletta, Notarial Archives, R. 281, vol. 36, f. 34-35 et seq., and R. 282, vol. 38, f. 177-178; Valletta, National Library of Malta, Biblioteca, Ms. 21 (*Relazione del tesoro ...*); and Mdina, Cathedral Archives, Ms. 169, pp. 1227-1230, 1308-1309. Much gratitude goes to the Cathedral Archivist, Canon John Azzopardi, for his help in searching out and interpreting documents.

on an ancient map of Mdina *+luogo del tesoro rinvenuto* at a point immediately in front of the present front door of No. 1 Archbishop's Square.[6] The initial description of the event was given the next day in the act drawn up by Notary Giovanni Domenico Gatt. The discovery was made on the site of the house which had been purchased from Signora Eufrasia Tonna and had been demolished. At about 5 o'clock in the afternoon one of the workmen's boys struck the pot. Several canons of the cathedral at once ran to the spot and found at six or seven *palmi* below street level:

> *un Vaso, o sia Vrna di rame in forma più tosto Ovata, che tonda col suo Collo, alta in tutto da un palmo ed un quarto, e larga nel Ventre uerso due terzi di palmo, e nel Collo circa un quarto di palmo;*[7] *quale urna era situata col Collo in giù, e con un Colpo di Zappa datoui da un altro figliuolo pure degli operarij gli era stato leuato il fondo in guisa di Cranio, con essersi uersata in terra qualche poca quantità di Moneta di oro di cui era piena essa Vrna. Et allora raccolta da gli stessi deputati la moneta uersata in terra...*

The vase with the greater part of the money still in it was carefully locked away for inspection the next day, when it was described as an:

> *Vrna piena nella maggior parte di Moneta con altre monita sfusa tutta d'oro consistente in diuerse specie di Moneta d'oro di diuerse grandezze per lo più piccole come aspri torchischi, e forse minore con alcune assai poche quanto un ungaro tutte antiche credute arabe, hebraiche [etc.]*[8]

The coins weighed 35 *libbre* and 9 *uncie*, the gold being of varying *carata*; after 3 *uncie* had been deducted on account of the dirt and earth attached to the monies, the value was estimated at 8733 *scudi*.[9]

[6] This map is in private hands.

[7] Assuming a *palmo* of 26.2 cm, the pot was 32.75 cm high and nearly 17.5 cm across with a neck about 6.5 cm (high?); the broken copper urn preserved in the Cathedral Museum which is traditionally said to have contained the coins is now 17 cm high (but has lost its bottom which apparently projected downwards "in the shape of a skull") and 14.5 cm across with a neck 6.8 cm high and 11.5 cm wide. It has a bulbous body (*più tosto Ovata*) and a long straight neck. This pot has been described as "rather nondescript" but possibly parallel in shape to an eleventh-century Fatamid jug in the Ashmolean Museum, Oxford. The tradition might be correct. The presumed pot is illustrated in colour in G. Wettinger, "The Arabs in Malta" (1st ed.), in *Mid-Med Bank Limited: Report and Accounts, 1984* (Malta, 1984), 33.

[8] The "etc" is represented by a suspension sign.

[9] Act of 13 April 1698 cited in note 5.

The subsequent inquest showed that Gatt's account was incomplete. Domenico Mamo of Siggiewi testified that the boy Ignatio Pernis of Rabat gave a *colpo di zappone*, struck a *Vaso tondo* and let out a shout; Salvo Galea came and called the canons who had been by the church door and who carried the money to the sacristy; a great crowd, and "all the little boys" who worked there, searched and grubbed for coins but found no more. Domenico Mamo did not actually see the hoard or the vase, but Canon Mangion gave him a brief glimpse of some gold pieces the size of a *picciolo*. Domenico Xuereb of Rabat spoke of a *vaso di rame* which was *pieno di monete d'oro*; he said that the initial blow at the vase had scattered money around; that Salvo Galea had a hand full of money; Xuereb also had a handful, which he put under his *pettorale*, and so did Ignatio Pernis and another boy called Domenico. Xuereb and Galea and the two boys had surrendered their pieces, but the crowd picked up others; Xuereb admitted that two pieces had remained in his breeches and he had sold them to two clergy at four *tarì* each.[10] It is clear that some pieces escaped.

One account of the vase, described as *plena auro monete uetustissime, et numismatis omnino ignoti*, told how the crowd ascribed its discovery to the miraculous intervention of St. Paul who thus provided for the completion of his church: *audita est vox populi clamantis – Miraculum miraculum Diui Pauli Patroni pro fabrica complenda*. The Bishop hurried up from Valletta: the money was weighed, being $14^{1}/_{2}$ *rotoli*, or 35 *libbre* and 9 *uncie*; and a *Te Deum* was said in thanksgiving. The Grand Master thought differently and invoked his regalian rights so that the quarrel over the ownership of the coins went to be settled in Rome, with the Bishop and Chapter claiming them because they were found on Church land, and also arguing that they belonged to the Church *quia vox Populi vox Dei*.[11] Part of the evidence submitted to Rome stated that the vase was found at *da sette in otto pali di fondo* and described it as *un vaso sive urna di rame antichissima, plena di Moneta e Medaglie di St. Elena d'Oro al peso di R[otuli] 14 e mezzo*.[12] Eventually the coins were divided between the government and the Church. The Master gave away his half to the Monte di Pietà with instructions that it should be made into *zecchini*.[13] He kept one pear-shaped piece to put in his crown as his name was Perellos:

> *Si diceva che l'Illmo. Gran Maestro Fr. D. Raimondo Perellos aueua applicato la Somma tocata a lui al Monte della Pieta; ed essendosi oltre altre medaglie ritrouate tra detta moneta un Pero d'oro esso Illmo, G.*

[10] Mdina, Misc. 156, f. 3v-5v. Xuereb admitted: *ad ogni modo mi sono rimaste due dentro le Calzette, quali hier mattina hò vendute à persone esenti tarì quattro l'una.*

[11] Mdina, Misc. 11, f. 382-384=Misc. 174, f. 859-860.

[12] Mdina, Misc. 174, f. 856.

[13] Valletta, National Library of Malta, Archives of the Order of St. John, Cod. 264, f. 194v-195 (29 July 1699).

*Maestro l'aueua preso ed attaccatolo nella sua Corona trecatoria [?] uulgo Paternoster. ed io l'ho veduto piu volte.*[14]

The Church's share was finally worth 4743 *scudi* and 1 *tarì* and weighed 17 *libbre* and 11 *uncie*. Before it was melted down *due Sante Elene con altre medaglie* weighing $2^3/_4$ *uncie* and 1 *sedicino* were taken out to send to the Pope while a handful of pieces weighing 4 *uncie* and $1^1/_2$ *sedicini* was shared out among the Bishop, the Vicar, the Assessor, the Treasurer, the Prior of Venice, the Knight *di Noientes* and the Master of the Mint. What was left weighed, after refining, 14 *libbre*, 4 *uncie* and 2 *sedicini*, and it made 1319 *zecchini*.[15] According to a later writer, twelve of the largest and finest pieces went to the Pope.[16]

The most precise calculation of the coins' value, a part of the evidence sent to Rome, was as follows:

> *La quantità dell'Oro in moneta e Medaglie ritrovato, perche non era dell'istessa bontà intrinsica, ne dell'istessa perfezzione, è stato dal sudetto Orefice Rosselli valutato uno per altro confondendo il buono col megliore e più fino à ragione di scudi 20. di Malta l'Oncia, onde che quel tanto rimase conservato in Cassa, che ascende à libre 35. et Oncie sei nette, fatta la deduzione delle tare, importata scudi 8796. di rame, salvo più vero calculo alla ragione di sopra accennata.*
> *E ciò oltre l'Oro suolazzato nel colpo ò colpi dati con la Zappa dal ragazzo nell'atto che lo ritrovò, et anche nel mentre che il vaso ò urna di rame in che era rinserrato l'Oro del Tesoro con viva forza si svelse è distaccò da terra, e pietre, ovè era da molti Secoli fortemente attaccato, e quasi incorporato, come riferiscono quelle persone che sopra giunsero, e cooperor[o]no al detto distaccamento et alla ricuperazione dell'Oro disperso in tal contingenza; E si giudica che l'Oro mancante tolto, et usurpato da persone incognite eccede la somma di scudi mille, et il giudizio è fondato nella publica voce del popolo, et in considerazione della capacità del pezzo dell'urna rotta.*[17]

The revised value was a little higher than the original estimates and these figures imply that the total amount of gold originally in the vase weighed about 40

[14] Mdina, Misc. 63, f. 212-213.

[15] Mdina, Misc. 10, f. 412-416.

[16] According to Ciantar, ii. 99; these coins have not been traced in the Vatican collections.

[17] Mdina, Misc. Ms. 174, f. 857. The figures of 18 *libri* $1^1/_4$ *uncie* etc., in Ciantar, ii. 97, 99, are evidently incorrect.

*libbre*. It is clear that some of these coins, apparently about ten percent of them, were taken at the moment of discovery; perhaps twelve, including two pieces of *Sant' Elena*, were sent to Rome; the Master put a *Pero* in his crown; and a handful of coins was shared out before the Church's portion was melted down. Contemporaries were unsure if the monies were Islamic or Hebrew, while references to *Sant' Elena* suggest that there may have been some late Byzantine coins or possibly Arabic counterfeits of Byzantine types.[18] In the eighteenth century Gioacchino Navarro saw two well-preserved Islamic gold coins from the Mdina find in the collection of Carlo Antonio Barbaro,[19] who himself claimed that there were some Byzantine coins in this hoard.[20] Others were in some way known to Count Giovannantonio Ciantar whose account of them, published in 1771, stated that none of the coins remained, but he was able to describe them as being of six types. Some were the size of an Islamic *sceriffo*, a little smaller than a Venetian *picciola*, and others the size of a *mezzo grosso della moneta Romana*. The coins were inscribed in Arabic and Ciantar gave an Italian translation of these inscriptions which suggests that they dated between 1038 and 1087.[21]

One piece from the Mdina Hoard seems to have survived in Malta, but Maltese collections also contained coins from other sources many of them probably outside the island. The Maltese scarcely admitted to a Muslim past but there were a few references to Arabic coins. Gian Francesco Abela's collection was disastrously plundered and finally it passed from the Jesuits to the Knights of Malta and ultimately to the Public Library and the modern National Museum.[22] Gioacchino Navarro, Librarian of the Public Library, wrote of the *monete Arabe di bronzo, che quì sovente si trovano*,[23] and Carlo Antonio Barbaro had many Arabic coins,

[18] The *moneta di Sant' Elena* was commonly found in Malta: Wettinger (1976), 27-33. T. Bertelè, "Costantino il Grande e S. Elena su alcune monete bizantine," *Numismatica*, 4-6 (July-December 1948), shows that such coins were thought to be a cure against epilepsy in the middle ages. See especially *Michel Italikos, Lettres et Discours*, ed. P. Gautier (Paris, 1972), 208-210, and the references there given. This belief survived in Malta where a seventeenth-century Maltese doctor denounced it: Giovanni Francesco Buonamico, *Dissertatio de Graecis Numismatibus, quae Sanctae Helenae, magnoque Constantino vulgo tribuuntur, atque adversos Epilepticos insultus commendantur* (lost but cited in Valletta, Biblioteca, Ms. 2, f. 131-133).

[19] G. N[avarro], *Dissertazione sopra tre Bassi-rilievi di Marmo Bianco ...* (Palermo, 1778), 68.

[20] ... *alcune delle quali erano Bizzantine, e tutte le altre Saraceniche ...*: C. Barbaro, *Degli avanzi d'alcuni antichissimi edifizj, scoperti in Malta l'anno 1768* (Malta, 1794), 40-45, 76 n. 125.

[21] Ciantar, i. 692-693; Ciantar's text and the identifications based on it are given by Brown (*supra*), 7-12.

[22] I.S. Mifsud, *Biblioteca Maltese* (Malta, 1764), 249-254; R. Bonnici Calì, "Gian Francesco Abela: the Father of Maltese Historians and Antiquarians," *Scientia* (Malta), ix no. 2 (1953), 83-89; A. Bonanno, "Giovanni Francesco Abela's Legacy to the Jesuit College", *Proceedings of History Week 1983*, ed. M. Buhagiar (Malta, 1984).

[23] Navarro, 67.

including gold pieces: *Tanto più, che spesso in Malta si trovano monete Saraceniche ne' luoghi da que' barbari frequentati, anche del più prezioso metallo, molte delle quali si conservano nel mio medagliere.*[24] Though one small thin "brass" Arabic coin said to be datable roughly to the tenth century was found somewhere at Marsa at the head of the Grand Harbour,[25] no Muslim coin, and indeed no coin datable later than 829 at the latest, was recorded in the hoard found in the Marsa excavations of 1768;[26] this may suggest that this port area went out of use around the time of the earliest Arabic attacks on Malta possibly in 836 and well before the definitive Muslim conquest of 870.[27]

In 1883 the Librarian A.A. Caruana recorded that there were 5 gold and 15 silver Islamic coins in the Public Library, and probably there were others of bronze among the thousands of coins not then described; he also noted "wholesale pillage", empty cabinets and suchlike.[28] In 1899 Caruana mentioned that the Library had two gold Muslim coins, the fate of the other three being obscure, but he mentioned four gold pieces then in the collection of S.L. Pisani.[29] The published catalogue of Pisani's collection listed 5 gold, 1 silver and 2 bronze Islamic coins in 1896, saying that they were found in Malta: *trovate in paese.*[30] They may have included pieces which had migrated from the Library or been acquired elsewhere in Malta, but Pisani was a well-travelled medical man who could also have collected pieces outside Malta.

A new numismatic era began in Malta with the opening of the National Museum, but it is not known whether it received the 5 gold and 15 silver pieces listed in 1883. Among materials recorded by Themistocles Zammit as passing to it from the Public Library were "1 envelope with 79 Arabic and other coins",[31] and another list mentioned as item 945: "23 Arabic Coins in Case."[32] The Grenfell Collection of antiquities donated in 1904 included a "Collection of Arab Glass, found in the dust

[24] Barbaro, 41; L. de Boisgelin, *Ancient and Modern Malta*, i (London, 1805), 12, stated that Barbaro had two gold Arabic coins.

[25] *Report on the Working of the Museum Department 1955-56* (Malta, 1956), 8.

[26] Barbaro, 39-40, lists the finds.

[27] T.S. Brown, "Byzantine Malta: A Discussion of the Sources", in *Medieval Malta: Studies on Malta Before the Knights*, ed. A. Luttrell (London, 1975), 82.

[28] Valletta, Biblioteca, Ms. 1030 pt/1, pp. v, xix, xxv.

[29] A.A. Caruana, *Frammento Critico della Storia Fenicio-Cartaginese, Greco-Romano e Bisantina, Musulmana e Normanna-Aragonese delle Isole di Malta* (Malta, 1889) 25-26; cf. Brown (*supra*), 5-6.

[30] S.L. Pisani, *Medagliere di Malta e Gozo dall'Epoca Fenicia all'Attuale* (Malta, 1896), p. ix.

[31] Msida, University of Malta Library, Ms. 120.

[32] Valletta, National Museum of Archaeology: DAG 16.400 Ms. 49, p. 37 (written in Zammit's hand).

heaps of Cairo" but no mention was made of coins.[33] The Pisani collection was received in 1909 but its Islamic holdings were omitted from the published list;[34] presumably they included the 5 gold, 1 silver and 2 bronze pieces mentioned in his catalogue of 1896, since the catalogue said that one gold piece was illegible and the other four are now in the Museum.[35] Other accessions in 1908/9 included "16 Arabic coins found in Malta" which came from Mr. Abramo Gatt and "6 silver and 130 copper Arabic coins" from Dr. Alfredo Caruana Gatt, a naturalist and a member of the local nobility.[36]

Many of the Arabic coins in Maltese collections may have been imported. Very few, even of those in the museums, have a secure provenance and a considerable number are not available for study. These coins often date long after the Muslim period in Malta; thus three "Saracenic" coins whose discovery was recorded and which were drawn by Themistocles Zammit between 1921 and 1924 are Ottoman or Mamluk.[37] Nothing is known of the origins of the National Museum Hoard, except that the notes now accompanying the coins make it clear that they were in the National Museum by 1956; it seems likely that these are the coins presented to the Museum in 1908/9 and that they represent a hoard with a Maltese provenance. The Mdina coins have a unique importance in that their discovery is exceptionally well documented; five of the varieties were described in such detail that they can be identified, and apparently one coin still survives. A hoard of perhaps some 5000 or more gold coins hidden in the centre of Mdina in "the late 1080's" or possibly at the time of Roger the Norman's invasion of Malta in 1091 points to a considerable wealth in the hands of someone in the island's chief city. The small hoard of silver pieces deposited in the mid-twelfth century and now in the National Museum and another comparable hoard also probably concealed on Malta may have represented the takings of small tradesmen, and they suggest that at that point the Maltese economy was still very much part of the Sicilian commercial world.[38]

[33] Ms. inventory in Valletta, National Museum of Archaeology: DAG 16.450, Ms. 48.

[34] *The Annual Report of the Curator of the Museum for the Financial Year 1908/9* (Malta, 1909), p. E2.

[35] Brown (*supra*), 2.

[36] *Annual Report ... 1908/9*, p. E2.

[37] Valletta, National Museum of Archaeology: DAG. 16.400, Ms. 21, vol. 6, pp. 41, 53; vol. 8, p. 10.

[38] Cf. Brown (*supra*), 6-7, 12, 13. Brown, 7, notes that the survival of only four tenth-century coins might indicate that Malta's economy operated without coinage. It might also indicate depopulation: cf. A. Luttrell, "Steves and Captives on Malta: 1053/4 and 1091," Hyphen [Malta], vii no. 2 (1992).

# VII

# *L'effritement de l'islam*
## *1091-1282*

Le manque de connaissances à propos des îles Maltaises, durant le XII^e^ et la plus grande partie du XIII^e^ siècle, est bien le reflet du manque considérable de sources relatives à cette période. Il a fallu attendre le volume collectif *Medieval Malta*, publié en 1975, pour commencer à avoir un aperçu des recherches historiographiques. Cet ouvrage a rassemblé des études de chercheurs maltais et non-maltais utilisant une variété d'approches et de méthodes. Il donne également des informations d'ordre bibliographique et archivistique. Mais sa lacune principale est, sans aucun doute, qu'il n'est pas parvenu à donner une étude complète de la période musulmane à partir d'environ 780. On peut donc considérer comme complément essentiel à *Medieval Malta*, la mise au point par Godfrey Wettinger de "The Arabs in Malta", qu'on doit utiliser dans son édition révisée de 1986. A la suite de la publication de *Medieval Malta* en 1975, des efforts ont été faits pour sauvegarder l'idée d'une continuité chrétienne établie à Malte tout au long de la période musulmane. Cette idée de la continuité de la présence chrétienne s'était maintenue selon une ancienne tradition, supposée avoir survécu à travers les siècles. Cet argument a été contredit par la démonstration que cette tradition aurait été inventée au début des temps modernes (A. Luttrell, 1977b). Des développements importants sont intervenus depuis cette publication de 1975. De nouvelles interprétations ont été présentées dans une série d'études de Godfrey Wettinger se basant particulièrement sur les noms de lieux et de personnes. Des publications sur des thèmes artistiques, archéologiques et architecturaux ont été faites par Mario Buhagiar (dont la thèse de doctorat est sous presse). Par ailleurs, Henri Bresc a publié des études d'après des sources principalement siciliennes incluant une thèse sur la Sicile du bas Moyen Age et un volume d'études. On peut évoquer également bien d'autres publications dont un relevé annuel est établi dans le journal *Melita Historica.*

La difficulté fondamentale réside dans la grande insuffisance des sources écrites qui ont survécu. Avant 1400 on relève très peu de documentation, et encore moins avant 1282. De nouvelles sources d'informations se sont révélées décevantes : par exemple, Malte n'a apparemment jamais été mentionnée dans la grande collection de documents de la "Geniza" du Caire, étudiée d'une manière exhaustive par Salomon Goitein. Certes des découvertes inespérées ont été faites depuis 1975. Pour la période précédant 1091, on a attiré l'attention sur des passages non-exploités d'Ibn Hauqal (A. Luttrell, 1987b) et de Al-Himyarî (J. Brincat, 1991b). Une source byzantine pour le XII^e^ siècle a été relevée (A. Pertusi, 1977 : 289) ; un certain nombre de documents royaux siciliens relatifs à Malte ont été publiés (A Luttrell, 1976 ; C. Schroth-Köhler *et al.*, 1977) ; deux nouvelles études sur Henri, comte de Malte, ont vu le jour (J. Brincat, 1976 ; M.-L. Favreau, 1978) ; quant au rapport détaillé de Giliberto Abbate, datant approximativement de 1241, il a fait l'objet d'une nouvelle publication avec de nouvelles lectures et interprétations (A. Luttrell, sous presse). En ce qui concerne la fin du XIII^e^ siècle, la destruction des archives de la couronne de Naples en 1943 a constitué un désastre presque irréparable. Ce qui subsiste, en descendant jusqu'à 1282, a été recueilli dans les *Registri* reconstitués (R. Filangieri *et al.*, 1950-1979), mais la documentation pour cette période n'a, jusqu'à présent, pas été pleinement exploitée pour ce qui est relatif à l'histoire de Malte.

En ce qui concerne les sources non-écrites, la contribution de l'archéologie médiévale a été profondément décevante. Les résultats des principales campagnes de fouilles de la *missione* italienne concernant le Moyen Age, ont été résumés en 1975 (M. Cagiano, 1975), mais ces conclusions ont rencontré de sérieuses récusations (A. Luttrell, 1991c : n. 123 : 98 ; T. Blagg et A. Luttrell, 1991). Les rapports définitifs de ces fouilles n'ont jamais été publiés et l'essentiel des informations stratigraphiques concernant plusieurs sites importants semblent ou bien avoir été perdus ou bien être trop obscurs pour être utilisés. Les fouilles médiévales de Hal Millieri près de Zurrieq n'ont donné pratiquement aucune information pour la période allant de 1091 à 1282 (A. Luttrell, 1991c). L'archéologie médiévale à Malte rencontre de sérieux problèmes pratiques ; l'un d'entre eux réside dans la difficulté de dater les poteries, domaine dans lequel les progrès ont été négligeables. En dehors d'exceptions très isolées, aucune construction antérieure à 1282 ne subsiste à Malte ou à Gozo. Spéculer sur les développements architecturaux durant cette période demeure donc très hypotétique (ex. : L. Mahoney, 1988 : 45-79). La fouille du cimetière musulman à Rabat a donné quelques informations sûres (A. Luttrell, 1975 : 21-23, 26-27 ; G. Wettinger, 1986 : 88-89, 92, 99), et les inscriptions funéraires du XIIe siècle ont fait l'objet d'une nouvelle publication et d'études (V. Grassi, 1989). D'autre part, des doutes sérieux ont été émis concernant la provenance de la dalle tombale de 1174 de Maimuna qui se trouve maintenant au musée de Gozo (A. Luttrell, 1991b : 52-53). Quelques répertoires de pièces musulmanes ont été publiés (H. Brown, 1992), mais les provenances de la plupart des autres pièces musulmanes, byzantines et normandes des collections maltaises n'offrent pas de références dignes de foi qui permettraient de les utiliser en tant que preuve historique.

L'approche philologique présente aussi des difficultés. Les discussions concernant la période avant 1282 se fondent largement sur les noms de lieux ainsi que sur les micro-toponymes trouvés dans des documents qui, pour la plupart, ne sont pas antérieurs à la fin du XVe siècle. Ceux-ci supposent, non sans raison, un usage continu de certains noms arabisés. Même si les toponymes n'ont pas changé, leur signification a pu être modifiée. Notons que les sources écrites, en général des actes notariés, permettent rarement une localisation du toponyme sur la carte avec une précision topographique. Néanmoins, ceci devrait constituer une source sûre et importante d'information historique. La tentative de trouver des solutions aux problèmes médiévaux, grâce à une analyse de la langue moderne dont il existe peu de témoignages écrits avant le XVIIIe siècle, s'avère moins satisfaisante. C'est ainsi que quelques termes religieux très discutés, d'origine grecque, ont pu apparaître dans la langue maltaise relativement tardivement. Le terme *milqi* peut être une forme classique arabe mais il n'apparaît pas à Malte avant 1673 (A. Luttrell, 1977b, n. 125 : 97), tandis que l'existence, dans la langue maltaise du XXe siècle, de termes arabes relatifs à la construction n'est en rien significative de l'architecture du XIIIe siècle (*pace* L. Mahoney, 1988 : 54-55, 337-340). Une approche historique du langage semble essentielle pour la mise en évidence d'une période pour laquelle il n'y a pas de preuves écrites, et un pas dans cette direction a été fait par J. Brincat (1991a).

* * *

Les grands monuments préhistoriques de Malte et de Gozo étaient encore partiellement visibles durant la fin du Moyen Age et les habitants en avaient gardé conscience comme cela est démontré par l'usage en 1365 du nom de lieux *haiarkim* pour désigner le site du moderne Hagar Qim (A. Luttrell, 1982 : 158). Aux époques romaine et byzantine, les îles renferment un nombre important de temples. En réalité, le mode de vie de la population avait un ton provincial, bien qu'existait toujours la possibilité d'arrivées fortuites, la plus célèbre étant celle de saint Paul. La conquête musulmane de 870 est partie de Sicile ; elle a renforcé la dépendance de Malte envers la Sicile. Cela n'a pas pour autant donné à Malte une fonction stratégique ou commerciale, alors que les relations africaines des musulmans de Sicile se faisaient surtout avec la Tunisie. Un contact fréquent entre la Sicile et l'Egypte existait, mais il passait principalement le long des côtes d'Afrique du Nord ou par voie de terre vers Tunis, sans utiliser la route par Malte et c'est ainsi que cette île n'a pas pu ou n'a su entretenir des contacts étroits avec les deux continents (H. Bresc, 1993 : 320 *et passim*). La conquête de 870 fut accompagnée de violences, de destructions et de déportations de chrétiens (G. Wettinger, 1986 : 90-91). On ne sait pas dans quelle mesure le reste de la petite population antérieure à 870 a pu subsister ; quelques survivants furent peut-être obligés de se convertir ou même ont été éliminés. Quelques écrivains tardifs arabes ont dit de Malte qu'elle avait été entièrement dépeuplée (A. Luttrell, 1987b : 158-159 ; J. Brincat, 1991b : 2). Au milieu du XIe siècle, il y eut une attaque chrétienne, vraisemblablement byzantine, à l'encontre d'une population insulaire parmi laquelle les musulmans libres étaient en minorité ; ceux-ci persuadèrent la majorité servile – qui était certainement musulmane – de les aider à résister à l'invasion : ainsi la majorité serait devenue libre (A. Luttrell, 1992a : 97-102). A l'arrivée des Normands en 1091, on peut noter des signes de richesse de Mdina, si l'on en juge à la fois par la découverte de pièces d'or arabes enfouies probablement à cette époque (H. Brown, 1992 : 12), et par la présence de captifs chrétiens non-indigènes, libérés par les Normands (A. Luttrell, 1992a : 102-104).

En 1091, la reconquête chrétienne de la Sicile était virtuellement terminée. On a parlé d'une attaque normande sur Malte déjà en 1076. Le chef latin, le comte Roger, fit probablement voile vers Malte en 1091 dans le but de piller et de faire une démonstration de force sur sa frontière sud. Il est peu probable qu'il ait considéré que l'île était particulièrement prospère ou qu'il s'agissait d'une base commerciale stratégique qui nécessitait d'être reprise par force des mains ennemies. Les Normands débarquèrent sur l'île avec des forces restreintes et la ville se rendit. Il y eut des pillages et les chrétiens prirent *infinita peccunia*. Le chef musulman ou kaid promit un tribut annuel ; et après un bref séjour, le comte Roger fit voile à nouveau, emmenant avec lui les chrétiens captifs qu'il avait libérés sur l'île. Même procédé à Gozo sur le chemin du retour. En fait, il ne s'agissait point d'une réelle conquête et on ne sait pas pendant combien de temps le montant du tribut fut versé. La communauté insulaire demeura essentiellement musulmane avec ses propres règlements et institutions. Il n'y eut pas d'installation latine et il n'y eut pas de pression pour une conversion religieuse. La communauté entière devint "peuple du pacte", engagé à payer un tribut selon sa propre loi, *more legis suae*. Au cours des années suivantes, le contrôle normand sur les îles fut probablement faible et on peut penser que les insulaires se sont retrouvés sous la sphère d'influence africaine ou qu'ils ont refusé de payer leur tribut. En 1127, Malte fut prise au cours d'une nouvelle expédition, conduite par Roger II, à partir de la Sicile. Quelques écrivains arabes ont considéré, à juste titre, que cette expédition constituait la véritable conquête de Malte (A. Luttrell, 1975 : 29-31).

Durant la plus grande partie du XIIe siècle, Malte n'était évidemment pas une place importante. Pendant cette période, Roger II eut recours à la puissance normande en Méditérannée centrale pour établir une domination sur des parties de l'Afrique du Nord. En mai 1127, juste avant son expédition maltaise, Roger conclut un accord pour qu'un vaisseau de Savone effectuât un service régulier le long des côtes d'Afrique jusqu'à Tripoli. Puis en 1135, il s'empara de l'île de Djerba ; il prit Tripoli en 1146 et Mahdia en 1148. La piraterie fut réprimée et l'Afrique normande fut gouvernée avec justice et soumise à des taxes raisonnables, sous une administration de Grecs et de musulmans siciliens ; les Africains payèrent tribut mais leur autonomie religieuse fut respectée. Cette domination normande commença à s'effriter en 1158, quand Tripoli fut perdue, et aux environs de 1180, la Sicile fut en grande partie coupée de l'Afrique. A long terme, seules Malta et Pantelleria demeurèrent dans la sphère culturelle arabe. Les activités de Roger II étaient concentrées sur les ports d'Afrique, et Malte n'en profita que de façon marginale. Cependant l'expansion normande impliqua la participation de Pisans et de Génois dont certains fréquentèrent Malte, et au moment où la domination normande au sud de la Sicile disparut, les Génois restèrent à Malte afin d'utiliser cette île comme base (D. Abulafia, 1985 : 31-41 ; H. Bresc, 1991 : 48-49).

Les îles Maltaises restèrent à l'écart de la Sicile, ce qui retarda probablement leur développement ; pourtant elles tirèrent parti de l'expansion normande et les géographes arabes, tel le sicilien Idrisi, décrivirent leurs ports, leurs pâturages, leurs fruits, leur miel, tandis que certains Maltais, surtout parmi les plus cultivés, quittèrent l'île pour la capitale, Palerme. Les visiteurs latins considérèrent les îles comme totalement musulmanes ; mais on peut, toutefois, noter des contacts avec la Sicile et l'Italie : une quantité de coton provenant de Malte se trouvait à Gênes en 1164, et en 1184, un capitaine pisan s'empara d'un vaisseau tunisien à Malte et jeta l'équipage à la mer (A. Luttrell, 1975 : 28-35 ; G. Wettinger, 1986 : 96-98). Quelques-uns des habitants continuèrent à être enterrés juste en dehors des murs de Mdina avec des inscriptions koufiques sur leur pierre tombale (V. Grassi, 1989). Le processus de l'infiltration chrétienne semble avoir commencé après 1127 ; il semble probable que Roger II laissa à demeure une garnison latine et qu'il installa une petite administration composée de musulmans, Grecs, ou Arabes chrétiens ou melkites envoyés de Sicile. On cite le cas d'un Grec exilé de Sicile qui passa cinq ans à Malte dans la période comprise entre 1135 et 1151 et qui se plaint, dans un poème, de la population musulmane (A. Pertusi, 1977 : 289) ; et à une époque située entre 1127 et 1154, la Couronne sicilienne imposa un tribut aux chrétiens de Malte qui avaient tué un musulman. Un privilège royal de 1198 qui incluait une absolution pour ce crime fut adressé aux *homines* à la fois chrétiens et musulmans de Malte et de Gozo, et un appendice de neuf lignes écrit en caractères arabes y figure (C. Schroth-Köhler *et al.*, 1977 : 519-520).

Juste avant la fin de la dynastie normande, avec la mort du roi Tancrède en 1194, l'établissement de Génois à Malte conduisit à la nomination d'un certain nombre de comtes chrétiens. Le premier fut Margarito da Brindisi, un pirate devenu amiral du roi ; ses successeurs, Guglielmo Grasso et son beau-fils Enrico *Pescatore*, étaient génois. Ces comtes exploitèrent vraisemblablement les îles pour leurs revenus et introduisirent probablement des fonctionnaires, des garnisons et des marchands latins (A. Luttrell, 1975 : 35 ; D. Abulafia, 1975 : 107-110). La réaction des habitants envers Guglielmo Grasso, qui était devenu l'ennemi de Costanza de Sicile, eut pour conséquence l'établissement du privilège de 1198 par lequel la reine réincorporait les deux îles "à perpétuité" dans le *demanium* royal sicilien, comme elles l'avaient été, disait-elle, sous le règne de Guillaume II, entre 1166 et 1189 (C. Schroth-Köhler *et al.*, 1977 : 519-520).

Le nouveau privilège semble avoir eu peu d'effet tant que les comtes génois ont maintenu leur contrôle sur les îles. En fait, sous Enrico, comte dès 1203, Malte acquit provisoirement un rôle méditerranéen. Les pouvoirs de Enrico sur Malte ont été probablement considérables ; en 1212 il avait même reçu le droit de frapper la monnaie (*ibid.* : 521). En 1204, se servant de Malte, comme une base indépendante et vraisemblablement avec l'aide de Gênes, il fit rassembler quatre galères en vue d'une attaque à l'encontre des Pisans en Sicile. En 1205, il se trouvait à Tripoli en Syrie avec 300 *iuvenes Maltenses,* vraisemblablement marins maltais ; et en 1206, il établit une domination génoise en Crète. Il continua ainsi, jusqu'au moment où il fut nommé, en 1221, amiral de Sicile. Puis il tomba temporairement en disgrâce, à cause, apparemment, de l'échec de son expédition destinée à sauver les croisés à Damiette en Egypte. Lui-même et ses successeurs conservèrent leur titre de comte de Malte, mais le *castrum,* probablement celui de Birgu, retourna à l'administration de la Couronne (D. Abulafia, 1975 ; M.-L. Favreau, 1978). Dès lors, Malte fut administrée par un procureur ou un gouverneur royal. A partir de 1235 environ et jusqu'en 1240, ce fût Paolino de Malte qui envoya les revenus de la *curia* royale vers Naples, établit les garnisons, procéda à l'approvisionnement des châteaux et organisa la garde à vue des prisonniers en exil à Malte (A. Luttrell, 1976). Il aménagea aussi la ferme royale de chameaux et entretint les faucons maltais de Frédéric II (A. Luttrell, 1975 : 36).

Sous l'administration d'Enrico, les avantages stratégiques de Malte avaient été démontrés, comme base navale et pour ses possibilités de devenir une menace pour la Sicile. Après 1220, Frédéric II commenca à imposer une politique despotique et centralisatrice en Sicile qui conduisit non seulement à une attaque envers la population musulmane de Malte, mais aussi à l'intégration de cette île au sein de l'administration du royaume de Sicile. La politique de Frédéric à l'égard de Malte différait de celle à l'égard de Pantelleria qui bénéficiait d'une protection de la part du sultan tunisien. Pantelleria demeurait sous le contrôle de la couronne de Sicile qui avait nommé son gouverneur ; mais en 1221 un traité entre Frédéric et le sultan décida que l'administration reviendrait à un gouverneur et à ses subordonnés musulmans. La population et les institutions restèrent musulmanes, et ceci sans conversion, ni expulsion (H. Bresc, 1990 : IX 106-107). A Malte, il en fut autrement : les guerres contre les musulmans de Sicile commencèrent en 1220-1221 ; certains d'entre eux furent expulsés à Lucera dans les Pouilles en 1223 et en 1224 des rebelles italiens de Celano dans les Abruzzes furent envoyés en Sicile. Enrico, comte de Malte, fut impliqué dans ces événements durant les années 1223 et 1224 et on sait que des habitants de Celano furent déportés à Malte sur ordre de Frédéric. Vers 1241 la population de Malte et de Gozo se composait de 836 familles musulmanes et probablement de 1250 familles chrétiennes ; on relève aussi la présence de 33 familles juives. Combien de familles chrétiennes ont immigré de Sicile ou d'Italie et combien de musulmans indigènes furent convertis, on ne le sait pas. Mais la survivance générale de la langue arabe dans les îles Maltaises doit avoir résulté de conversions relativement massives. Frédéric II effectua d'autres expulsions de musulmans siciliens en 1245 et c'est à ce moment-là qu'a pu avoir lieu une nouvelle vague d'expulsions de Malte et de conversions de musulmans maltais. Des musulmans maltais se trouvaient à Lucera à la fin du XIIIe siècle, et on note au moins le cas d'un prisonnier de Celano qui avait été envoyé à Malte et qui y mourut. Ces musulmans, qui furent chassés de Malte par Frédéric II, perdirent leurs possessions.

Giliberto Abbate, gouverneur royal des îles Maltaises aux environs de 1241, appartenait à une grande famille sicilienne de Trapani qui possédait des offices royaux, ainsi que des réseaux d'intérêts familiaux en Sicile occidentale, dans les Egades, à Pantelleria et dans toutes les eaux autour de la Sicile. En 1240, Enrico Abbate, probablement frère de Giliberto, était consul royal à Tunis. Le rapport que Giliberto présenta au roi fait état des *quaternitiones*, ou registres, de son prédécesseur : son administration fonctionnait bien d'après des rapports écrits. Il était en charge de deux châteaux royaux à Mdina et Birgu sur l'île de Malte et d'un troisième sur l'île de Gozo. Leurs garnisons se composaient de 220 *servientes* ; 35 parmi ceux-ci étaient marins sur deux petits navires. On dénombre aussi bon nombre de *servi* et de *villani* qui travaillaient sur les domaines du *demanium* royal ; ils étaient aidés par 84 esclaves venus de l'île tunisienne de Djerba. Le comte de Malte semble ne pas avoir pris part à l'administration ; à cette époque, on ne note aucun signe d'inféodation ou de vassalité sur les îles. Un groupe de *homines* et de *fideles* donnait avis ou *consilium* au gouverneur. Celui-ci rapporta que les habitants de l'île appréciaient leurs propres coutumes, leurs *mores et constituciones*, différents de ceux de Sicile : le roi était prêt à accepter cette situation aussi longtemps qu'elle ne nuisait pas aux intêrets de la Couronne. Giliberto mentionne également un certain nombre d'usurpations des droits royaux.

Son rapport donne la liste des taxes royales provenant de la douane ou *dohana*, des jardins, des boutiques, des moulins, des taxes, etc. Celles-ci s'élevaient approximativement à 14 000 *tareni* : environ 10 900 provenaient de Malte et 3 400 de Gozo. Les dépenses sur les garnisons étaient d'environ 16 000 *tareni* : ainsi l'administration payait plus ou moins pour elle-même. La taxe incluait 3 100 *tareni* de *gisia* payée par les *villani* de la *curia* et les *villani* payaient également un quart de leur production en espèces. La *gisia* ou *jizya* était une taxe due par tous les musulmans en vertu de leur religion. Tous, ou certainement la plupart des musulmans, devaient être des *villani* et il pouvait y avoir quelques *villani* chrétiens. Les chrétiens, sicilens et italiens, possédaient vraisemblablement leurs terres, pour la plupart, en pleine propriété. En plus des paysans chrétiens, il devait y avoir des marchands, des chargés d'offices, des notaires et des membres du clergé. Le coton représentait probablement une exportation importante. Gozo payait ses taxes séparément. Son territoire et sa population représentaient chacun environ un tiers de ceux de l'île de Malte, à laquelle ils étaient reliés par un bac (A. Luttrell, sous presse).

Aprés la mort de Frédéric II en 1250 et de son fils Corrado en 1254, le contrôle de la Sicile fut disputé entre Corradino, le jeune fils de Corrado, et Manfred, le fils naturel de Frédéric II. Le royaume entra dans une nouvelle ère de troubles : à Malte on mit en œuvre une résistance contre Manfred, résistance conduite par un groupe de familles de Gênes qui tentèrent de rétablir des bases gênoises sur l'île. Ces Génois étaient apparemment alliés à Uberto Fallamonica, musulman converti qui avait pris un nom génois et avait exercé de plus hautes fonctions en Sicile. Ces Génois exploitèrent les revendications de Nicoloso, fils du comte Enrico, envers Malte. En 1257, Manfred, alors qu'il n'avait pas encore ceint la couronne, en termina avec ses opposants à Malte. Les Génois furent amnistiés et Nicoloso put de nouveau prendre possession de toutes les terres, les privilèges et les taxes que son père avait reçus à Malte. Manfred obtint le contrôle des châteaux des îles. Nicoloso pouvait, s'il le désirait échanger ses terres maltaises pour d'autres en Sicile, en Calabre ou dans les Pouilles. Cet accord est certes important ; il fut officiellement renouvelé en 1259 et à nouveau en 1261. Ce ne fut en aucun cas une révolte du peuple maltais organisée sur une grande échelle, mais plutôt une tentative renouvelée par les Génois de contrôler le port maltais ; en fait, ils s'en servirent comme base pour les 21 galères qui combattirent la flotte vénitienne en 1254. Manfred fut tué à Benevento en 1266 et Corradino retourna en Sicile l'année suivante. En juin 1268, Corradino était à Pise, où il conclut un traité qui garantissait différentes places, y compris Malte, aux Pisans en échange de l'usage de leur flotte. Mais en août il connut une défaite à Tagliacozzo et en octobre il fut exécuté. En 1270, Malte se trouvait aux mains du vainqueur, Charles d'Anjou (A. Luttrell, 1980).

Ainsi une dynastie française remplaçait une dynastie germanique en Méditerranée centrale et la bureaucratie royale sur Malte augmenta ses activités. Une administration sicilienne efficace continua à prélever les taxes, à commander une garnison de 150 Français et à maintenir un vaisseau armé. Il y avait des collecteurs de taxes et deux juges. La population prêta serment d'allégeance au roi auprès duquel elle présenta des pétitions. Tout d'abord les offices du capitaine et du châtelain à Birgu furent réunis en la même personne ; toutefois, en 1274, il y avait un châtelain distinct pour Mdina et un autre pour Gozo. Un *camerarius* prenait soin des domaines royaux ou *massarie* (A. Luttrell, 1975 : 40-41 ; S. Fiorini 1993 : 129). L'administration étrangère était centrée à Birgu au *castrum maris* où se trouvaient les officiers royaux qui devaient mettre en état le château, approvisionner la garnison, ramener des victuailles de Gozo, remplacer de vieux armements et traiter avec les pirates et les commerçants étrangers (G. Wettinger, 1993 : 34-36). Ce régime était probablement ressenti comme étant trop dur. A l'époque du massacre des Vêpres en 1282, la population maltaise semble avoir appuyé la rébellion avec quelque enthousiasme ; en vérité les meneurs de la révolte ont pu se rencontrer à Malte pour conspirer en vue de la défaite des Angevins (A. Luttrell, 1975 : 43). Les insulaires passèrent aux Aragonais, mais la garnison angevine tint bon dans le *castrum* à Birgu jusqu'en 1284, en dépit de la grande victoire aragonaise, par la flotte commandée par Ruggierio Loria, dans le grand port ; cet événement mettait une fois encore en évidence l'importance stratégique de l'île et de son port (J. Pryor, 1983 : 179-189).

Le problème des Gênois, qui utilisèrent Malte comme une base plutôt que comme un établissement ou une colonie, demeurait. En 1269, Charles d'Anjou avait concédé aux Génois le droit de commercer par delà Malte – *ultra Maltam versus Orientem* – ainsi qu'en Espagne et en Afrique (A. Luttrell, 1980 : 599). En 1271, la Couronne ordonna au châtelain de Malte de ne pas accueillir ces pirates qui molestaient les hommes de Tunis, avec le gouvernement desquels une convention avait été établie à ce sujet (Filangieri *et al.*, 1950-1979 : VII, 221). Cette année-là, on relève également le cas du sicilien Guido de Modica, qui avait fait naufrage dans les îles et qui ensuite libéra une femme chrétienne et ses trois filles de l'esclavage. En 1275, Raymondus, *civis* de Malte et marin ou *marenarius*, avait été capturé par des pirates génois tandis qu'il naviguait, en provenance d'Afrique, sur le bateau de Bonsignori de Gaudisana de Malte (A. Luttrell, 1987a). En 1272, les Génois de Malte connurent des litiges avec Charles d'Anjou qui avait procédé à des arrestations et bloqué leurs bâtiments dans le port de Malte. Deux années plus tard, les Génois saccagèrent Gozo pour se venger – *Gaudium depopulavit* (A. Luttrell, 1980 : 599). La vie sur les îles devait être souvent dangereuse.

La Couronne procédait à la culture des *massarie* au moins en partie avec les *servi* ou serfs. Quelquefois un surplus de ravitaillement était exporté de Malte ; d'autres fois il était nécessaire d'importer du grain de Sicile (A. Luttrell, 1975 :

41 ; G. Wettinger, 1993 : 36). Probablement, il y avait une population de *biduini* ou paysans qui détenaient quelques petites parcelles de terres en relative liberté ; on relève aussi la présence d'artisans et d'artistes, particulièrement à Mdina et dans la région portuaire à Birgu (Fiorini, 1993 : 143-145). La Couronne donna des instructions en 1271 pour que les terres non cultivées d'où les musulmans avaient été chassés soient louées à un *census* annuel aux *agricultores*, qui n'étaient probablement pas des serfs (R. Filangieri *et al.*, 1950-1979 : VI 213, 223-224). Le bois était toujours rare et la population, généralement groupée en petits villages ou *casali*, vivait dans des caves creusées dans le roc ou dans des cabanes de pierres au toit de paille. Il devait y avoir également des bâtiments citadins de dimensions plus grandes (M. Buhagiar, 1991 : 16-20 ; S. Fiorini, 1993 : 153-159).

Rien n'est sûr au sujet du processus de conversion à Malte et Gozo ; il était certainement possible de devenir chrétien tout en continuant à parler l'arabe. La conversion fut probablement complète vers 1250 ou peu après. Expulsions mises à part, les pressions fiscales et politiques encourageaient évidemment les Arabes à changer de religion. Il y avait un évêque à Malte depuis 1168, mais il semble avoir été toujours absent. Vers 1270, on note l'existence d'une organisation diocésaine qui employait un archidiacre et d'autres ecclésiastiques tenus de payer des dûs à l'évêque. Cependant, au XIIIe siècle, il semble qu'il n'y avait ni missionaire, ni ordre religieux, ni paroisse (A. Luttrell, 1975 : 33, 60-64 ; A. Luttrell, 1984a). Sans doute existait-il un problème de langage surtout pour les affaires liturgiques et confessionelles. Un certain nombre de personnes à Malte parlaient ou écrivaient le grec (A. Luttrell, 1991a : 37-38). En Sicile existait un groupe de musulmans antérieurement de rite grec et qui revinrent à leur rite initial. Il n'y avait pas de telles communautés à Malte, et il est improbable qu'il y en ait eu pratiquant réellement le rite grec à Malte, même s'il y avait des églises creusées dans le roc qui ont pu appartenir à des chrétiens grecs et à des moines basiliens de rite grec, peut-être venus de Sicile (M. Buhagiar, 1991 : 14). Il y avait probablement une cathédrale à Mdina et d'autres églises dans la ville de Gozo et quelques-unes ailleurs. Les premières églises étaient peut-être troglodites, décorées de fresques. En 1274, une église édifiée dans le *castrum maris* était dédiée à la Vierge, probablement celle qui fut connue plus tard comme Santa Anna, et une autre, celle de Sant' Angelo, fut construite à l'extérieur du *castrum.* Des inventaires de cette même année montrent que le clergé possédait des icônes, des objets liturgiques et des vêtements de type latin, vraisemblablement parce qu'il servait à la garnison (M. Buhagiar, 1991 : 459 ; S. Fiorini, 1993 : 136).

La particularité culturelle des îles Maltaises était devenue spécifique. De nombreux habitants avaient en effet renoncé à leur religion islamique pour conserver leur langage et leur culture arabe, et bien entendu leurs biens. Les peuples de ces îles avaient une certaine conscience d'une identité ethnique ayant des racines à la fois en Afrique et à Byzance (A. Luttrell, 1984b : 302-303).

L'influence grecque était probablement faible, mais le processus de latinisation et de sicilianisation continua durant la période angevine. En 1279, une liste des familles de Malte témoignait d'une considérable immigration sicilienne à côté de nombreux noms sémitiques et vraisemblablement indigènes (H. Bresc, 1991 : 53). Après 1282, les îles demeurèrent dans un isolement extrême, mais avec l'incorporation du royaume de Sicile dans la communauté de la Couronne aragonaise, les insulaires de Malte et de Gozo commençèrent à faire partie, quoique de façon distante, d'un groupement plus extensif.

## BIBLIOGRAPHIE

ABULAFIA (D), 1975, "Henry Count of Malta and his Mediterranean Activities: 1203-1230", in *Medieval Malta: Studies on Malta before the Knights*, éd. A. Luttrell, Londres, 104-125.

ABULAFIA (D.), 1985, "The Norman Kingdom of Africa and the Norman Expeditions to Majorca and the Muslim Mediterranean", in *Anglo-Norman Studies VII: Proceedings of the Battle Conference, 1984*, éd. R. Allen Brown, Woodbridge, 26-49.

BLAGG (T.) et LUTTRELL (A.), 1991, "Notes on San Pawl Milqi", in *Excavations at Hal Millieri, Malta*, éd. T. Blagg, A. Bonnano, A. Luttrell, Malte, 147-152.

BRESC (H.), 1986, *Un monde méditerranéen : économie et société en Sicile, 1300-1450*, 2 vols., Rome, 981 p.

BRESC (H.), 1990, *Politique et Société en Sicile : XII^e^-XV^e^ siècles*, Londres, 315 p.

BRESC (H.), 1991, "Sicile, Malte et le monde musulman", in *Malta: a Case Study in International Cross-Currents*, Malte, 47-79.

BRESC (H.), 1993, "Mercati e Mercanti nell'Alto Medioevo : l'Area euroasiatica e l'Area mediterranea", in *Settimane di Studio del Centro Italiano di Studi sull'Alto Medioevo*, 40, Spoleto, 285-321.

BRINCAT (J.), 1976, "Le Poesie 'Maltesi' di Peire Vidal", *Melita Historica*, 7 n° 1, 65-89.

BRINCAT (J.), 1991a, "Language and Demography in Malta", in *Malta: a Case Study in International Cross-Currents*, Malte, 91-110.

BRINCAT (J), 1991b, *Malta 870-1054: Al-Himyarî's Account*, Malte, 22 p.

BROWN (H.) 1992, "The Coins of Muslim Malta", *Melita Historica*, 9, n°1, 1-18.

BUHAGIAR (M.), 1991, "Post-Muslim Malta: a Case Study in Artistic and Architectural Cross-Currents", in *Malta: a Case Study in International Cross-Currents*, Malte, 13-31.

BUHAGIAR (M.), 1993, "The Artistic Heritage", in L. Bugeja, M. Buhagiar, S. Fiorini, ed., *Birgu: a Maltese Maritime City*, 2, Malte, 457-516.

CAGIANO DE AZEVEDO (M.), 1975, "Medieval Buildings Excavated at Tas-Silg and San Pawl Milqi in Malta", in *Medieval Malta: Studies on Malta before the Knights*, ed. A. Luttrell, Londres, 88-95.

FAVREAU (M.-L.), 1978, "Graf Heinrich von Malta, Genua und Boemond IV. von Antiochia", *Quellen und Forschungen aus italienischen Archiven und Bibliotheken*, 58, 181-215.

FILANGIERI (R.) *et al.*, 1950-1979, *I Registri della Cancelleria Angioina ricostruiti*, 1-26, Naples.

FIORINI (S.), 1993, "Malta in 1530", in *Hospitaller Malta 1530-1798: Studies on Early Modern Malta and the Order of St-John of Jerusalem*, ed. V. Mallia-Milanes, Malte, 111-198.

GRASSI (V.), 1989, "Materiali per lo studio della presenza araba nella regione italiana, i: L'epigrafia araba nelle isole maltesi", *Studi Magrebini*, 21.

LUTTRELL (A.), 1975, "Approaches to Medieval Malta", *in Medieval Malta: Studies on Malta before the Knights*, ed. A. Luttrell, Londres, 1-70.

LUTTRELL (A.), 1976, "Frederick II and Paolino de Malta: 1235", *Quellen und Forschungen aus italienischen Archiven und Bibliotheken*, 55-56, 405-409.

LUTTRELL (A.), 1977a, "The Christianization of Malta", in *The Malta Year Book 1977*, Malte, 415-421.

LUTTRELL (A), 1977b, "Girolamo Manduca and Gian Francesco Abela: Tradition and Invention in Maltese Historiography", *Melita Historica*, 7, n° 2, 105-132.

LUTTRELL (A.), 1980, "Malta e Gozo: 1222-1268", *Actas del X Congreso de Historia de la Corona de Aragon*, Zaragoza, 589-603.

LUTTRELL (A.), 1982, "The Benedictines and Malta: 1363-1371", *Papers of the British School at Rome*, 50, 146-165.

LUTTRELL (A.), 1984a, "Le origini della parrochia a Malta", in *Pievi e parrochie in Italia nel Basso Medioevo (secc. XIII-XV)*, 2, Rome, 1187-1198.

LUTTRELL (A.), 1984b, "Malta e Gozo: 1268-1282", in *XI Congresso di Storia della Corona d'Aragona*, 3, Palerme, 301-304.

LUTTRELL (A.), 1987a, "Christian Slaves at Malta: 1271", *Melita Historica*, 9, n° 4, 381-383.

LUTTRELL(A.), 1987b, "Ibn Hauqal and Tenth-Century Malta", *Hyphen* (Malte), 5, n° 4, 157-160.

LUTTRELL (A.), 1991a, "Medieval Malta: the Non-Written and the Written Sources", in *Malta: a Case Study in International Cross-Currents*, Malte, 33-45.

LUTTRELL (A.), 1991b, "The Roots of Medieval Gozo", *Al-Masaq: Studia Arabo-Islamica Mediterranea*, 4, 51-57.

LUTTRELL (A.), 1991c, "Historical and Archaeological Postscript", in *Excavations at Hal Millieri, Malta*, ed. T. Blagg, A. Bonanno, A. Luttrell, Malte, 103-131.

LUTTRELL (A.), 1992a, "Slaves and Captives on Malta: 1053/4 and 1091", *Hyphen* (Malte), 7, n° 2, 97-104.

LUTTRELL (A.), 1992b, "Mdina Hoard of Muslim Coins: 1698", *Melita Historica*, 9, n° 1, 19-25.

LUTTRELL (A.), sous presse, "Giliberto Abbate's Report on Malta: circa 1241".

MAHONEY (L.), 1988, *A History of Maltese Architecture from Ancient Times up to 1800*, Malte.

PERTUSI (A.), 1977, "Le Isole Maltesi dall'epoca bizantina al periodo normanno e svevo (secc. VI-XIII)", *Byzantinische Forschungen*, 5, 253-306.

PRYOR (J.), 1983, "The Naval Battles of Roger of Lauria", *Journal of Medieval History*, 9, 179-216.

SCHROTH-KÖHLER (C.), KÖLZER (T.), ZIELINSKI (H.), 1977, "Zwei staufische Diplome für Malta aus den Jahren 1198 und 1212", *Deutsches Archiv*, 33, 503-521.

WETTINGER (G.), 1986, "The Arabs in Malta", 2e ed., in *Malta: Studies of its History and Heritage,* Malte, 84-87.

WETTINGER (G.), 1993, "The *Castrum Maris* and its Suburb of Birgu during the Middle Ages", in *Birgu: a Maltese Maritime City,* ed. L. Bugeja, M. Buhagiar, S. Fiorini, Malte, 33-71.

# VIII

## FREDERICK II AND PAOLINO DE MALTA: 1235

In March 1235, from his castle at Orta (Nova) near Foggia in Apulia, the Emperor Frederick II granted the Sicilian *casale* of Stafenda to Paolino de Malta. Stafenda, nowadays described as a *contrata*, lies in South-east Sicily between Noto and the little town of Íspica, or Spaccafurno as it was called in the document of 1235[1]). In 1454 Nicholaus de Landolina of Noto, who had a claim to the *casale*, produced at court a version of the text of 1235, the original – he swore – being lost. The document he presented was described as an *extractum ex quodam Ins[trumen]to reddato In oficio nobilis prothonotarij*. This copy was then recopied into a viceregal document of 6 February 1454 which in turn was entered, in a very clear hand, in one of the registers for 1453/4. This act survives in Palermo, Archivio di Stato, Cancelleria, Registro 91, f. 544–545 v (olim 494–495 v), with Frederick II's grant included in it at f. 544 (olim 494); this grant is published below. The viceroy noted that Nicholaus de Landolina claimed descent from Paolino de Malta since half the *casale*, which had once been a *pheudum*, had passed into the hands of Bartholomeus de Landolina, the *avus* or ancestor of Nicholaus, and the viceroy's confirmation stated that, following researches in the archives, he accepted this claim.

In about 1510 the Sicilian official Gian Luca Barberi included in his Capibrevi a summary of the document of 1235, which he found in the Palermo register for 1453/4; he also noted that the same imperial grant was copied again in a document of 29 October 1457 by which Nicholaus de Landolina's son Johannes was invested with Stafenda[2]). A complete copy of the

---

[1]) Touring Club Italiano, Guida d'Italia: Sicilia (Milan, 1968), 676.

[2]) His Ms. was published only in modern times: I Capibrevi di Giovanni Luca Barberi, ed. G. Silvestri, 3 vols. (Palermo, 1879–1888), 1, pp. 343–345, where the form *feudum Stapheuda* (sic) is given. The text of 29 October 1457 was in the

grant, taken from the same chancery register for 1453/4, was sent to Malta in 1638. The copy of 1638 contained a few errors and variations with respect to that of 1454. The date was copied accurately in the body of the text itself, but it was incorrectly given at the head of the page as 5 March 1235, the *1235* later being changed to *1230*[3]). This version of 1638 was available to the Maltese historian Gian Francesco Abela[4]), who in fact published the greater part of the text in 1647, incorrectly dating it to 1230. Abela did not use this document in the historical part of his book, but inserted it in the genealogical section as evidence for the supposed existence of a family called *de Malta*[5]). That portion of Barberi's Capibrevi which covered Malta and Gozo was copied at Palermo in 1644 by the Sicilian notary Leonardo Biasini, along with many transcripts of documents from the Palermo registers; these were extensively used by Abela, but they did not include the 1235 text or any reference to it[6]).

A different version of the complete text of Frederick II's grant reached Malta in 1645, when it was included in the proofs of nobility presented to the Order of St. John by Fr. Agostino Ceva Grimaldi of Modica who was a Landolina on the maternal side. These proofs are now lost, but a manuscript copied at Malta in the eighteenth century contains a version of the 1235 document which was taken from them. This eighteenth-century copyist mentioned the texts of 1454 and 1457, but he made no reference to the

---

register for 1457 at f. 86. Cf. F. Liotta, Giov. Luca Barbieri, in: Diz. biogr. d. Italiani 6 (1964), pp. 158–161.

[3]) Two sheets bound into Valletta, Royal Malta Library, Ms. Università 7 (*olim* Biblioteca Ms. 858) [part II], f. 77–78v. At f. 77 was written *Ex Regia Cancell[er]ia Regni Sicilie ext[rac]ta est. Coll[atione] sal[va]*. On f. 78v, another hand noted *Mandatami dal S. D. Cesare ferro da Palermo l'anno 1638*. In this copy the word *prouenitari* ( ?) was crossed out and *promereri* written above it.

[4]) The cover of Ms. Università 7 carries a statement of contents signed by Abela as Vice-Chancellor of the Order of St. John.

[5]) G.-F. Abela, Della Descrittione di Malta Isola nel Mare Siciliano (Malta, 1647), 503. Abela published the section *Nos attendentes . . . pertinentiis suis*, copying the other variants it contained and giving the form *promereri*. He gave the date as *Dat. apud Ortam anno Dominicae Incarnationis 1230 quinto mensis Martii octavae ind.*, mistakenly taking *quinto* as being the day of the month. He referred, inaccurately, to the source in Palermo as *An. 1453, f. 455*.

[6]) Valletta, Royal Malta Library, Ms. Università 206 (*olim* Ms. Biblioteca 870); a receipt for his fee and expenses appears on f. 303, but with no indication as to who commissioned these transcripts, which were much recopied in Malta. Biasini did however copy the document of 1457, which included those of 1454 and 1235; this copy is in Valletta, Royal Malta Library, Ms. Biblioteca 657, f. 11–18.

Palermo registers. The copy of 1645 was possibly made at Modica from the originals of the documents registered at Palermo in 1454 and 1457, or from copies which derived from them. Again there were some errors and a number of words were omitted with respect to the 1454 version. The eighteenth-century copyist, incidentally, added a note correctly amending Abela's misdating of the 1235 text[7]). This burst of copying in Sicily and Malta throws interesting light on Maltese historical activity at that time. Abela's work was republished in revised form in 1780[8]), but the text of 1235 has generally escaped attention. Its existence at Malta in the copy of 1638 was briefly noted by the Italian scholar Roberto Valentini in 1935[9]), but it has apparently never been properly published and it is not given in the standard calendar, the Regesta Imperii.

Although the text of 1454 is, at best, a copy of a copy, it seems fundamentally reliable. The date can be accepted as Orta, March 1235, during which month Frederick was certainly at Foggia[10]). Paolino de Malta was mentioned as Frederick's proctor at Malta in four imperial documents issued between 21 November 1239 and 5 May 1240[11]); soon after, Paolino was dead and had been replaced by a certain Abbot Gilibertus, according to a document which most probably dates to 1241[12]). Paolino de Malta was probably a Sicilian or Italian whom Frederick sent as his agent to Malta; he was less

[7]) Mdina, Cathedral Archives, Ms. 27 f. 483 (*olim* part II, f. 292). This version gives *peruenire* and *Datum apud Ortum Anno Domi[nic]e In[carnacio]nis 1235 Me[nse] Martij, 8e Ind[iccion]is*. It appears at the end of a volume in which it follows many copies of the copies made by Leonardo Biasini in Palermo, but this particular copy is not in any way attributed to him. Instead f. 292v states: *In probationibus nobilitatis Fratris d. Augustini Grimaldi de Ciuitate Mohac de Anno 1645 reperitur dictum priuilegium Paulini de Malta extensum, ut supra in presentatione familiae Landolina, eius aui Materne*. Grimaldi's proofs of nobility are not now in the Archives of the Order of St. John at the Royal Malta Library; they were known to Abela, 503–505, in 1647, and they may survive in Sicily or elsewhere.

[8]) G. Abela, Malta Illustrata, revised G. Ciantar, 2 (Malta, 1780), 448, repeats the 1235 text as given in 1647 without change.

[9]) R. Valentini, Il Patrimonio della Corona in Malta fino alla venuta dell'Ordine, in: Archivio Storico di Malta, 5 (1934), 5 n. 3, using Ms. Università 7, and giving the date as 5 (sic) March 1235.

[10]) Details in J. Böhmer–J. Ficker–E. Winkelmann, Regesta Imperii, V in 5 parts (Innsbruck, 1881–1901), nos. 2079–2083.

[11]) J. Huillard-Bréholles, Historia Diplomatica Friderici Secundi, 6 vols. (Paris, 1852–1861), 5, pp. 525, 931–932, 969–971.

[12]) Text in E. Winkelmann, Acta Imperii Inedita seculi XIII. vol. 1 (Innsbruck, 1880), 713–715.

likely to have been a Latin who had settled on that island. The grant of the *casale* suggests that he was being rewarded for his Maltese service. It is also possible that Paolino acquired lands in Malta which later passed to the Landolina family since the will of Isolda de Landolina of Noto, drawn up in 1362, shows that she held a number of properties on the island[13]).

Very few acts recording the concession of a Sicilian *feudum* or *casale* by Frederick II survive[14]). The following document, of the type known as *licterae patentes*, constitutes a minor addition to the corpus of imperial acts, and it throws a little light on a still obscure period in Maltese history[15]). The dating by the Incarnation is somewhat unusual but not unknown in the acts of Frederick II. Since the surviving text is only a copy, contractions in the manuscript have been expanded and spelling, punctuation and capitals have been rationalized. The copy does contain a few obvious grammatical slips or corruptions, but they provide no reason to doubt its essential genuineness.

---

[13]) See D. La Ferlita, I possedimenti dei Benedettini di Catania a Malta, in: Archivio Storico di Malta, 7 (1936), 262–266. The fourteenth-century information concerning the Landolina available in Barberi, Capibrevi, 1, pp. 342–344, 340; 3, pp. 348–350, and V. Littara, De Rebus Netinis Liber (Palermo, 1593), 73, 84, 89–91, does not establish any connection with Paolino. However, the claim apparently passed through the heirs of Attardo la Barba who held both Stafenda and the Maltese fief of Tabria: text of ca. 1320/38 (misdated to ca. 1296) in R. Gregorio, Bibliotheca Scriptorum qui res in Sicilia gestas sub Aragonum Imperio, 2 (Palermo, 1792), 465. Tabria was granted to Attardo la Barba in 1316, and was confiscated from Simone la Barba in 1398 (texts in Valentini, 32–34, 43–46); it was recovered by Johannes de Landolina, who claimed descent from the la Barba, in 1441 (Capibrevi, 3, pp. 438–439); further details in Abela, 503–505.

[14]) Winkelmann, 1, p. 95, reproduces the text of the concession of the *casale* of *Milice* to the Hospitallers in March 1212. Huillard-Bréholles, 5, pp. 128–131, and 6, pp. 695–697, publishes those of Corleone in 1237 and Militello in 1249. The concession of the *feudum* of *Buchalca* in August 1229, when Frederick was at San Lorenzo in Apulia (as confirmed by Böhmer et al., no. 1762b), was known to Barberi (Capibrevi, 1, p. 244) but not to Böhmer; it may yet be traceable, through Barberi's references, in the registers at Palermo, but a preliminary search proved unsuccessful.

[15]) See A. Luttrell, Approaches to Medieval Malta, in: Medieval Malta. Studies on Malta before the Knights, ed. A. Luttrell (London 1975), 35–40.

*Orta, March 1235: the Emperor Frederick II grants the* casale *of Stafenda, near Noto in South-east Sicily, to Paolino de Malta.*

*Palermo, Archivio di Stato, Cancelleria Reg. 91 f. 544.*

Fridericus dei gratia Romanorum imperator semper augustus Ierusalem[16]) et Sicilie rex. Notum facimus universis[17]) fidelibus nostris tam presentibus quam futuris etc. Nos attendentes fidelia et grata servitia, que Paulinus de Malta fidelis noster dudum nobis exhibuit et que de bono in melius exhibere poterit in futurum, de gratia nostra, qua[18]) fideles et benemeritos nostros consuevimus prevenire[19]), concessimus ei[20]) et heredibus suis casale Stafende[21]) situm in pertinentiis Spaccafurni, cum omnibus iusticiis rationibus et pertinentiis suis tam in demanio quam in servitio in servitium[22]) salvo servitio quod inde curie nostre debetur, et salvo mandato et ordinatione nostra. Ad huius autem concessionis nostre memoriam et inviolabilem firmitatem presentem paginam sibi fecimus sigillo nostro muniri[23]). Dat. apud Ortam anno dominice incarnacionis millesimo CC°XXXV mensis marcii VIII[e] indictionis.

---

[16]) Ms: *Ierhlm.*

[17]) Ms: *vniuersibus.*

[18]) Word blobbed.

[19]) Ms: *p[er]venire* ( ?); the original possibly had *prevenire,* (cf. Huillard-Bréholles 4,2 pp. 800–801), while *promereri* was also given (*supra,* p. 417 notes 3,5).

[20]) Ms. omits *ei.*

[21]) Changed in the Ms. from *stafenda.*

[22]) The normal phrase was *de demanio nostro in demanium et que de servitio in servitium* (Huillard-Bréholles, 6, p. 697).

[23]) Ms. *munit[am].*

IX

# GILIBERTO ABBATE'S REPORT ON MALTA: CIRCA 1241

The official report on Malta and Gozo made in about 1241 survives only in the form of a letter from Frederick II to Giliberto Abbate, his governor in Malta, in which the emperor's chancery recapitulated information sent to him by Giliberto. Frederick was concerned primarily with the incomes of the Sicilian royal curia to which the Maltese islands belonged, and the result was a document now of fundamental importance in providing not only the earliest surviving written statistics for Maltese history but also an outline of the way in which the islands of Malta and Gozo fitted into the administrative pattern of the Sicilian kingdom. This study presents a revised and annotated edition of the text together with a discussion of the technical difficulties involved and an estimation of its implications for the history of Malta and Gozo and for the structure of their society at a key stage in their Latinization and Christianization. There are very few documents which illuminate the history of Malta in the time of Frederick II and it should be emphasized that interpretations of the period remain tentative and hypothetical, especially as evident corruptions in the surviving version of this text impose complicated considerations of the population and taxation details it includes.

The text printed below does not contain Giliberto's original report. Nor does Frederick II's chancery's summary of it survive in its original form or in the register in which it was originally recorded, but in the so-called *Excerpta Massiliensia.* That codex contains documents from the royal registers for the years 1230 to 1248 which were recopied in an Angevin milieu, presumably for the use of the royal curia, at the end of the thirteenth or the beginning of the fourteenth century. The extracts it contains were apparently taken from a whole range of materials rather than from a particular series of registers; there were numerous omissions and abbreviations, while often there was no date. Discrepancies in the taxation statistics in the surviving version of Giliberto's report, which do not add up correctly, mean that both the taxation and the population figures, which result from successive copying and recopying, should be used with considerable caution; furthermore, a number of words and figures are clearly corrupt while some incomes are given in round figures which suggest approximations or estimations rather than genuine statistics.

The document is in Marseilles, Archives départmentales des Bouches du Rhône, B 175, f. 14 verso - 15 recto (no. 78). It was published by E. Winkelmann in 1880,[1] and subsequently republished, without comment, first by A. Mifsud [2] and again, with a number of omissions and an occasionally unsatisfactory English translation, by C. Dessoulavy.[3] The problems of the *Excerpta*, and the relevant literature, are surveyed by W. Hagemann,[4] while E. Sthamer made a study of the documents in the register on the basis of the handwriting but added nothing with regard to this Maltese document.[5] The question of the document's date is especially difficult but, to judge merely from its place in the codex, it belonged either to about 1241 or to 1245/6 as it was placed between two groups of documents of those dates;[6] Frederick II died in 1250. 1241 is probably, but by no means conclusively, to be preferred on account of the reference to *quondam* Paolino de Malta who is known to have been Frederick's governor of Malta in 1239 and 1240, and possibly in 1235.[7] The report has been discussed by many

1. E. Winkelmann, *Acta Imperii Inedita Saeculi XIII.*, i (Innsbruck, 1880), 713-715 (no.938).
2. A. Mifsud, "Frammenti Storici", *La Diocesi* [Malta], i (1916), 17-19.
3. C. Dessoulavy, "Malta in the Middle Ages", *Journal of the Malta University Literary Society*, ii nos. 10-12 (1937).
4. W. Hagemann, "La nuova Edizione del Registro di Federico II", in *Atti del Convegno Internazionale di Studi Federiciani* (Palermo, 1952), 330-331.
5. E. Sthamer, "Studien über die sizilischen Register Friedrichs II.", *Sitzungsberichte der Preussischen Akademie der Wissenschaften*, xxxii (1920); see also J. Mazzoleni, *La Registrazione dei Documenti delle Cancellerie meridionali dall'Epoca sveva all'Epoca viceregnale*, i (Naples, 1971), 20-23, and tavole x-xii, and T. Kölzer, "Die sizilische Kanzlei von Kaiserin Konstanza bis König Manfred: 1195-1266," *Deutsches Archiv*, xl (1984).
6. Winkelmann (1880), i. 601, 715.
7. A. Luttrell, "Frederick II and Paolino de Malta: 1235," *Quellen und Forschungen aus italienischen Archiven und Bibliotheken*, lv-lvi (1976).

authors, including R. Valentini,[8] A. Luttrell,[9] H. Bresc,[10] A. Pertusi,[11] I. Peri[12] and G. Wettinger.[13]

The present edition contains a number of variations with respect to Winkelmann's text. Capital letters, but not punctuation or grammar, have been rationalized. The manuscript itself provides uncertainties and inconsistencies concerning the expansion of words such as *tar'* and in the case endings of numerals. The text at Marseilles sometimes gives these in the nominative and sometimes in the accusative, but contractions are here expanded in the accusative following the practice in a surviving fragment of the register of Frederick II for 1239/40. Where the Marseilles text gives the nominative it seems likely that the scribe would have copied what was a Roman numeral rather than a number which had been written as a word in the original version.[14]

* * * *

The Giliberto who governed Malta and Gozo has often been considered to have been an abbot, though it might seem unlikely that a religious would have been appointed to rule the islands. In reality, he came from an important and wealthy Sicilian family, the Abbate of Trapani. Giliberto was very probably the brother of Enrico Abbate, who was a leading functionary of Frederick II in 1239 and consul in Tunis in 1240, and who was *secreto* in Sicily from about 1253 to 1256.[15] Giliberto was dead by 1269, but his son Palmerio Abbate, who had been

8. R. Valentini, "Funzione storica e Dispersione del Patrimonio demaniale di Malta", *Archivio Storico di Malta*, xiii (1942), 3-6.

9. A. Luttrell, "Approaches to Medieval Malta", in *Medieval Malta: Studies on Malta before the Knights*, ed. A. Luttrell (London, 1975), 36-40.

10. H. Bresc, "The *Secrezia* and the Royal Patrimony in Malta: 1240-1450", *ibid.*, 129-131,134.

11. A. Pertusi, "Le Isole maltesi dall'Epoca bizantina al Periodo normanno e svevo (secc. VI-XIII) e Descrizioni di esse dal sec. XII al sec. XVI", *Byzantinische Forschungen*, v (1977), 282-286.

12. I. Peri, *Uomini, Città e Campagne in Sicilia dall'XI al XIII secolo* (Rome-Bari, 1978), 154-155.

13. G. Wettinger, "The Arabs in Malta," in *Malta: Studies of its Heritage and History*, ed. Mid-Med Bank (Malta, 1986), 98-99. On the historiographical background, S. Candido, "Contributi alla Storia di Malta dall'Età Araba in un Carteggio inedito di Michele Amari con Francesco Crispi: 1853-1854", *Atti della Accademia Nazionale dei Lincei: Memorie - Classe di Scienze morali, storiche e filologiche*, ser. VIII, xxxi fasc. 3 (1988).

14. Hans Martin Schaller of Munich most kindly checked the 1239/40 register on this point.

15. L. Sciascia, "I Cammelli e le Rose: gli Abbate di Trapani da Federico II a Martino il Vecchio", in *Mediterraneo Medievale: Scritti in onore di Francesco Giunta*, iii (Soveria Mannelli, 1989), 1174-1181.

governor of Pantelleria and of Favignana in the Egadi islands,[16] was a leading Sicilian who seems to have been one of the promoters of the Vespers uprising of 1282 when, according at least to *Lu Rebellamentu di Sichilia,* he was among those who moved to Malta to continue negotiations with Giovanni of Procida for the overthrow of the Angevin regime.[17] As governor of Malta, Giliberto Abbate fitted into a pattern of family predominance in Trapani, Erice, the Egadi isles and the waters between Sicily and Tunisia, a cultural and political zone which in his time extended to the Maltese islands.[18]

Any consideration of the structure of Maltese society in the thirteenth century must depend upon an interpretation of Giliberto's report and of the related problems of its population statistics, remembering that his letter to Frederick II mentioned the *quaternitiones* or registers kept by his predecessor as governor and that Giliberto himself presumably maintained administrative records; he thus had access to reliable written information.[19] Such bureaucratic procedures were in the tradition of Norman practice in Sicily where the government kept tax registers containing the names of the *villani*; originally these were written in Arabic but later they were in Latin as well.[20] There may have been such registers on Malta, possibly in Arabic, but virtually nothing is known of the island's administration in the twelfth century. The terminology of Giliberto's text was basically Sicilian but, as the document itself explicitly emphasized, Maltese customs and institutions differed fom those of Sicily. It seems probable that Malta, unlike Sicily, was almost exclusively Muslim during the twelfth century,[21] though the presence of at least a small group of Christians on Malta is documented

---

16. *Ibid.*, 1182-1185

17. Luttrell (1975), 43; but Sciascia, 1185-1188, shows that Palmerio's attitude was ambiguous.

18. H. Bresc, "Pantelleria entre l'Islam et la Chrétienté," *Cahiers de Tunisie*, xix (1971), 117.

19. The discussion in Luttrell (1975), 36-40, is far from exhaustive and requires amendment in the light of the new reading of the word *gisie* and of its implications.

20. J. Johns, "Entella nelle Fonti arabe: il Registro dei Confini (Jarida) di S. Maria di Monreale, 1182 D.C.," in *Alla Ricerca di Entella*, ed. G. Nenci (Pisa, 1993).

21. A. Luttrell, "The Christianization of Malta," *The Malta Year Book 1977* (Malta, 1977); *idem*, "Ibn Hauqal and Tenth-Century Malta," *Hyphen* [Malta], v no. 4 (1987); *idem*. "Slaves and Captives on Malta: 1053/4 and 1091," *ibid.*, vii no. 2 (1992); *idem*, "L'Effritement de l'Islam: 1091-1282", in *Le Carrefour Maltais = Reveue du Monde Musulman et de la Méditerranée*, lxxi (1994).

for the reign of Roger II who died in 1154.[22] Assuming that these Christians were not the descendants of indigenous islanders who had somehow survived Muslim rule, they may have been merchants and administrators who possibly settled only in the port or in urban areas, perhaps following the second Norman "conquest" of Malta by Roger II in 1127.

The situation on Malta may, in some ways at least, have been like that of Pantelleria where the tolerant arrangements introduced by the Normans continued into the fifteenth century. On Pantelleria the population paid tribute but remained Muslim; the island's Muslim governor, appointed by the Sicilian crown, governed according to Muslim laws; and in 1282 the king had to send an Arabic-speaking notary there from Palermo. There is some uncertain evidence that in 1115 the Normans restored an ancient Greek monastery on Pantelleria and that in the fifteenth century the Greek rite was in use there.[23] It is significant that Roger II imposed on the Christians of Malta and Gozo an annual fine paid in consequence of their having killed a Muslim,[24] and a Maltese legend of uncertain antiquity which concerns a massacre of Muslims by Christians may constitute a distorted reflection of some such event.[25]

It is uncertain to what extent Giliberto's report, essentially a bureaucratic and in no sense a "feudal" document, was concerned exclusively with royal matters such as curial incomes and possessions or the royal garrison and servants; it seems likely, though not certain, that the numbers of families given included all, or almost all, those on the islands rather than only those who were directly dependent on the crown and curia. In Sicily the distinction between what belonged to or was owed directly to the royal curia or *demanium* and what was let out by the curia, in fief or otherwise, was often unclear. In Malta the land must initially have remained in Muslim hands after 1091, and those Christians who arrived

22. G. Schroth-Köhler - T. Kölzer - H. Zielinski, "Zwei staufische Diplome für Malta aus den Jahren 1198 und 1212," *Deutsches Archiv,* xxxiii (1977), 519-520; this text of 1198 is also in T. Kölzer, *Constantiae Imperatricis et Reginae Siciliae Diplomata: 1195-1198* (Cologne, 1983), 238-240. The Latin text of 1198, now lost, was followed by nine lines in Arabic. S. Fiorini, "Malta in 1530," in *Hospitaller Malta 1530-1798: Studies on Early Modern Malta and the Order of St. John of Jerusalem,* ed. V. Mallia-Milanes (Malta, 1993), 112-113, emphasizes the presence of a few exiles, at least one of them Greek, on twelfth-century Malta.

23. Bresc (1971), 105-111; *idem, Un Monde méditerranéen: Économie et Société en Sicile, 1350-1450,* 2 vols. (Palermo-Rome, 1986), ii. 622-624.

24. Text in Schroth-Köhler *et al.*, 519-520.

25. J. Cassar Pullicino, "Norman Legends in Malta," in *Medieval Malta*, 99.

during the twelfth century may for a time have lived in the towns without occupying any land. In 1198 the men of Malta and Gozo received a royal charter incorporating their islands to the royal *demanium* in perpetuity,[26] yet from about 1192 to about 1222 Malta was a county under a series of counts, and in 1212 Enrico Count of Malta was granted permission to strike his own coinage.[27] These counts may well have taken over the royal position on the islands without seriously altering their taxation or land-holding systems. In 1222 Frederick II imprisoned Count Enrico and removed him from his countship, and though by 1223 he had been restored to royal favour, he was not given back the castle: *nulla restitutione facta de castro Malte.*[28] Enrico's son Nicoloso later called himself count and he retained claims to the islands but in 1243 he was not, apparently, using the title.[29] The crown had evidently taken back direct control of the islands. Paolino de Malta was royal proctor there by 1239 and in 1241 circa his successor Gilberto Abbate controlled the royal *demanium* and worked it with royal *villani* or *villani curie.* What lands were then held by the Christians, whether Latin immigrants or converted Muslims, is not known.

There was no sign in Giliberto's report of a count, of fiefs or of an ecclesiastical or monastic establishment. The document did mention the *homines* and *fideles* of the islands who had their own customs and who gave *consilium* to the governor; many of them had usurped curial rights. Some decades later, in 1270, the governor was to act *cum consilio sapientum.*[30] The islands' *homines* or *fideles* - the terms seem to have been interchangeable - certainly included Muslims when the royal privilege or incorporation was granted in 1198 to *universus populus totius insule Malte et Gaudisii tam Christiani quam Saraceni fideles nostri.*[31] Conceivably, some of these *homines* held lands and maybe some had

26. Text in Schroth-Köhler *et al.*, 519-520.

27. Text *ibid.*, 521.

28. Marchisio Scriba, *Annali Genovesi di Caffaro e de' suoi Continuatori*, ed. L. Belgrano, ii (Rome, 1901), 192-193.

29. In addition to Luttrell (1975), 34-40, see D. Abulafia, "Count Henry of Malta and his Mediterranean Activities: 1203-1230," in *Medieval Malta*; E. Mazzarese Fardella, *I Feudi comitali di Sicilia dai Normanni agli Aragonesi* (Milan, 1974); A. Luttrell, "Malta e Gozo: 1222-1268," in *Jaime I y su Época = X Congresso de Historia de la Corona de Aragón: Comunicaciones 1 y 2* (Zaragoza, 1980).

30. Text in V. Laurenza, "Malta nei Documenti angioini del R. Archivio di Napoli," *Archivio Storico di Malta*, v (1934), 7.

31. Text in Scroth-Köhler *et al.*, 519-520.

*villani* who were not royal *villani curie*. The surviving version of the text of Giliberto's report does contain one use of the phrase *feudales nostri Sicilie*, but it seems likely that *feudales* was a copying error for *fideles* and that the creation of a county had not led to enfeoffments or sub-enfeoffments within the Maltese islands. Nothing else is known of local laws and customs, except that a document of 1270 claimed that in the time of Frederick II certain *homines* of Malta and Gozo, whose status is not clear, had been obliged to watch over the swine on the royal *massarie* or estates.[32]

The most straightforward approach to the population question is to assume that, with certain statistically minor exceptions such as the garrison and slaves, the number of families reported did in fact represent all the settled inhabitants of the islands. It is curious that the population statistics in the text appear among the details concerning the *servientes* who depended on the curia, perhaps as a result of some rearrangement in the process of summarizing the original report, but the main difficulty is that the apparently unlikely figure of 47 Christian families for Malta does not seem to fit with the taxation statistics or with the proportion of Christians to Muslims on Gozo; it has usually been considered an error. It could in theory be that on Malta there were other Christians who were not listed for the reason that they paid no taxes to the curia, but that would seem unlikely and it would leave it unclear why so many Christian families were listed on Gozo. If the text is assumed to be corrupt, one answer would be to amend *quadraginta septem* to *quadr[ingentas] septem* or 407.[33] Palaeographically this would be quite likely, but it would give only 407 Christian families in Malta as against 203 in Gozo; it would leave the Christian families on Malta in a minority of 407 against 681 Muslim families there; it would give a hypothetical total population for the islands of only some 4500; and it would provide a set of ratios unlike the more regular series tabulated below as the result of the alternative assumption that 47 should be amended to 1047. It is certainly important to establish these ratios and proportions, but deductions from them may be suspect in so far as they are based on an assumption, which is not necessarily entirely justified, of close similarities between Malta and Gozo. It could be argued that, as has been the case in all recent centuries, there would have been a preponderance of administrators and immigrants on Malta rather than on Gozo in the thirteenth century; but in that case 407 Christian families for Malta would be too low.

32. Text in Laurenza, 8-9

33. Pertusi, 282-284; Peri (1978), 154, simply gives 407 without discussion.

Yet another possibility is that there were 747 Christian families on Malta, since that figure would produce very satisfactory ratios of 3.7 Christians on Malta to each Christian on Gozo, of 4 families on Malta to each family on Gozo, and of 1.1 Christians to each Muslim in Malta as against 1.3 Christians to each Muslim in Gozo; that would result in a total of 1453 families in Malta and a Christian majority in Malta, making a total of 1819 families or, hypothetically, around 7276 people for the two islands. In that case the situation would be as follows:

| FAMILIES | MALTA | GOZO | RATIO | TOTAL |
|---|---|---|---|---|
| Christian | [747] | 203 | 3.7 | [950] |
| Muslim | 681 | 155 | 4.4 | 836 |
| Jewish | 25 | 8 | 3.1 | 33 |
| Total | [1453] | 366 | 4.0 | [1819] |

Such an argument, derived strictly from a mathematical consideration of ratios, may well provide an acceptable solution,[34] but it is not explicable palaeographically. Though less statistically defensible, at least on the basis of the text in its surviving form, it seems easier to envisage the conflation of an *m* for *mille* with the abbreviation *m* of *christianorum* resulting, during a subsequent copying, in its complete disappearance; that is *christianorum mille* or *christianorum m* becoming *christianor' m,* then *christianor'm* and finally *christianor',* as in the surviving manuscript.[35] The resulting figure of 1047

34. Stanley Fiorini has kindly calculated that if those figures from Giliberto's text which are applicable to the whole of both Malta and Gozo - that is for the *dohana, tintoria, barbaria* and *baiulacio,* but excluding the *gisia* not paid by Christians - are utilized for a regression analysis, the Malta figures regressed to the Gozo data yield a gradient of 2.42 for the least-squares line; with 95 per cent confidence, the error in this gradient is plus or minus 1.48. With that level of confidence and on the assumption that the number of families on Gozo was 366, the total Malta population lies between 334 and 1428 families. It would follow that the Maltese Christian population was at most 722 (ie. 1428 minus 706), making the 1047 estimate rather unlikely and the 747 guess more acceptable. If a lower degree of confidence were accepted, then the 1047 hypothesis would become less unlikely.

35. As already proposed, but without the supporting arguments used here, in K. Beloch, *Bevolkerungsgeschichte Italiens*, i (Berlin, 1937), 164-165.

Christian families on Malta would produce a slightly higher proportion of Christians to Muslims on Malta, at 1.5 to one, than on Gozo, at 1.3 to one, as could indeed have been the case:

| FAMILIES | MALTA | GOZO | RATIO | TOTAL |
|---|---|---|---|---|
| Christian | [1047] | 203 | [5.2] | [1250] |
| Muslim | 681 | 155 | 4.4 | 836 |
| Jewish | 25 | 8 | 3.1 | 33 |
| Total | [1753] | 366 | [4.8] | [2119] |

A total of 1047 Christian families on Malta would imply a settled population on the two islands of nearly 8500 if a multiplier of 4 were used. Peri suggests a multiplier of 3.5 or 4 for thirteenth-century Sicily[36] but Bresc's multiplier of 5.3 for 1277 seems very high.[37] The fifteenth-century Maltese statistics might imply a multiplier of 5 or even 6, and a total population in 1419/20 of around 10,000.[38] A multiplier of 6 would give a remarkably high total population of around 12,700 for 2119 families in about 1241. Unfortunately, all such calculations ignore a number of complicating factors and are based partly on guesswork.

This discussion raises the question of the date or dates at which groups of Muslims were expelled from Malta. There had been a major Muslim revolt in Sicily in 1189, and from 1220/1 there was a series of Sicilian wars, mainly in the mountains; the final campaign there began in 1243 and ended in 1246.[39] There were certainly expulsions of Muslims from Sicily to Lucera in Apulia in 1223.[40] In 1224 there was also a transportation to Sicily of Italian rebels from Celano in

36. Peri (1978), 108-110, 246-247.

37. Bresc (1986), i. 60.

38. G. Wettinger, "The Militia List of 1419/20," *Melita Historica*, v. no. 2 (1969), 83. Figures from 1419 to the 1480s produce estimates varying between 8098 and 10,633: Fiorini, 122, 126. It is not known whether Muslim and Christian families were of the same average size.

39. F. Maurici, *L'Emirato sulle Montagne: Note per una Storia della Resistenza musulmana in Sicilia nell'età di Federico II di Svevia* (Palermo, 1987), 38-49.

40. E. Winkelmann, *Kaiser Friedrich II.*, i (Leipzig, 1889), 537-538; M. Amari, *Storia dei Musulmani di Sicilia*, ed. C. Nallino, iii (revised ed: Catania, 1937/8), 613-614.

the Abruzzi. The main evidence is provided by Riccardo di San Germano who wrote two versions of his reliable work, the first being essentially a monastic chronicle of Monte Cassino and the second a history of Sicily; he died in December 1243 or early in 1244.[41] The first version reported that in May 1224 Enrico de Morra, acting on the orders of the Emperor Frederick II, sent the rebels from Celano to Sicily with their wives and children, and that in 1227 Frederick II had them freed: *Celanenses omnes, qui captiui in Sicilia tenebantur, liberi dimittuntur, Imperatore mandante.* This version made no mention of Malta. The second version stated instead that, at the emperor's command, the Celanesi were in 1224, apparently in May, moved to Sicily by Enrico de Morra, and that Frederick II sent them to Malta: *Henricus de Morra iussu imperiali Celanenses reuocat ubique dispersos, ut ad propria redeant, et redeuntes capit et in Siciliam mittit, quos apud Maltam dirigit Imperator.* The second version was not continued beyond 1226 and so did not cover the liberation of 1227 mentioned in the first version.[42] Enrico Count of Malta may in some way have been involved; he lost control of Malta itself in about 1222, but in the following year he was active in the suppression of the Muslim revolt in Sicily; and, significantly perhaps, he was at Celano in April 1223 and at Catania during 1224.[43] There may have been people from Celano who went to Sicily but not to Malta and who were freed by Frederick II in 1227. That at least some Celanesi were at some point sent to Malta seems certain, since in 1252 Marino, son of Andreas Bacconensis of Celano, addressed a petition to the pope in which he claimed that his father had, on account of his devotion to the Roman Church, been captured by followers of Frederick II and imprisoned on Malta, where he died after much suffering.[44] There is, therefore, some evidence for the expulsion of Muslims from Sicily and for the transportation of Christians to Malta and Gozo in about 1224.

The so-called *Annales Siculi* recorded further expulsions of Sicilian Muslims to Lucera in 1245: *de mandato domini imperatoris comes Riccardus de Caserta*

41. *Riccardi de Sancto Germano notarii Chronica*, ed. C. Garufi, *Rerum Italicarum Scriptores*, ns. vii part 2 (Bologna, 1938), pp. xix-xxvi, xxxiii.

42. *Ibid.*, 112-113, 146. Peri (1978), 127, 154, writes of a Sicilian expedition which attacked Malta in 1224; it resulted, he claims, from Frederick II's desire to exterminate the Muslims on Malta, who were replaced with Latins from Celano. Peri is following Amari (1937/8), iii. 617, who deduces an expulsion of Muslims from Malta both from a passage in Ibn Khaldun and from the evidence for the immigration of Latins from Celano into Malta.

43. Abulafia, 121-122.

44. Text in *Registres d'Innocent IV*, ed. E. Berger, iii (Paris, 1897), 50: kindly communicated by Godfrey Wettinger.

*ejecit omnes Saracenos de Sicilia.*[45] Furthermore Ibn Khaldun, who was a great scholar but who was writing over a century later and was not well informed about Malta, stated that following the death of Abu Zakaraya Yahya, the Hafsid Sultan of Tunis who died on 2 October 1249, the Muslims of Palermo revolted and Frederick II besieged them and then sent them to Lucera: *When the news of the death of the Emir Abu Zakaraya reached Sicily, there were Muslims living in the city of Palermo. The sultan had negotiated on their behalf with the lord of the island [Frederick II] an agreement concerning the city and its environs. They lived side by side [with the Christians] until [the news of] the death of the sultan reached them. Then the Christians attacked them furiously, and they took to their strongholds and to the wilds. They gave command over themselves to a rebel from the Bani Abs. The tyrant of Sicily [Frederick II] surrounded them in their stronghold in the mountains and besieged them until he forced them to climb down. He carried them over the sea to the mainland and granted them Lucera as their dwelling. Then he crossed to the island of Malta and expelled the Muslims who were in it, and joined them with their brothers [in Lucera]. The tyrant of Sicily conquered Sicily and its islands, and he drove from them the word of Islam and replaced it with the word of his own infidelity. But God has triumphed over his power.*[46]

The elements of this account ring true, but its chronology seems confused. Frederick was not in Sicily in 1249 or the years before it and there is no record whatsoever that he went to Malta at any time; and in December 1250 he died. There were expulsions from Sicily in 1245 and probably in later years as well, and there were references, but in documents dated well after 1250, to expulsions of Muslims from Malta, to the confiscation of their Maltese properties and to Maltese Muslims at Lucera.[47] Giliberto's report shows that there was still a considerable number of Muslims on Malta in about 1242, and an expulsion from Malta in 1245, which possibly continued in later years, seems quite possible.[48]

45. *Annales Siculi*, ed. E. Pontieri, in *Rerum Italicarum Scriptores*, ns. v part 1 (Bologna, 1927), 119.

46. Text in M. Amari, *Biblioteca arabo-sicula: versione italiana*, ii (Turin-Rome, 1881), 212-213.

47. References in Luttrell (1975), 37; Wettinger (1986), 98-99, 103-104.

48. There is, however, no proof that any expulsions accompanied the obscure resistance on Malta in or before 1257 of certain Genoese who apparently had connections with the converted Sicilian Muslim Oberto Fallamonaca: Luttrell (1980), 592-597. A 1492 copy of Manfred's privilege of 1259 suggests that he was then on Malta: *ibid.*, 601. However, a 1284 copy gives *felfis* (Melfi) not *Malte*: Palermo, Archivio di Stato, Cancelleria 2, f. 53-55v (kindly communicated by Stanley Fiorini).

Ibn Khaldun was evidently wrong in placing such an expulsion in 1249 and in writing of an imperial visit to Malta made after October 1249, unless it was Frederick's son Manfred who was involved. Apparently, however, Ibn Khaldun confused Abu Zakaraya with Muhammed Ibn Abbad who led the Muslim revolt in Sicily which ended in 1225. It was presumably then that the "tyrant" Frederick II effected expulsions from Malta, though without going there himself. This was the one single reference Ibn Khaldun made to any Muslim revolt in Sicily. Unsure where to place various stories of such a revolt, but having perhaps some indication that Abu Zakaraya had helped the Sicilian Muslims, Ibn Khaldun may have decided to associate the incident with Abu Zakaraya's death. The sequence of a Tunisian ruler intervening on behalf of the Sicilian Muslims in and around Palermo, of a revolt following his death, of Christian repression and Muslim resistance, and of the defeat of the Muslims and their exile to Lucera is all acceptable. In Ibn Khaldun's text this sequence was followed by the mention of the Bani Abs; that is likely to have been a reference to Muhammed Ibn Abbad which probably involved a confusion, explicable in the Arabic, between the forms Abbad and Abs. The mention of the Bani Abs was followed by that of an attack on Malta and of expulsions and conquest there. The sequence of violences in Sicily did continue until 1246 or later, but the story of the Bani Abs and the attack on Malta probably belonged to an earlier period between about 1221 and 1225.[49]

If such an explanation is broadly correct, then it seems likely, though not certain, that there were expulsions from Malta and transportations there from Celano, perhaps in about 1224, with further expulsions in about 1245. Such expulsions, coming both before and after 1241, would have been consistent with roughly half the population of the two islands being Muslim in that year. The presumed 1250 Christian families on Malta and Gozo in about 1241 could have included Italians from Celano, other Latin immigrants and converted Maltese Muslims in proportions which cannot be established. The Latins transported from Celano could have been intended to replace Muslims who had been expelled, but that too is hypothetical. It seems that down to 1241 the king was prepared, perhaps because there were still insufficient Latins on the islands, to countenance

49. Ibn Khaldun's passage was kindly analysed in detail by Jeremy Johns. Amari correctly understood Ibn Khaldun's anachronism, but explained it in a way which Nallino showed to be incorrect: Amari (1937/8), iii. 609-610, 617-620. Various errors in this respect in A. Luttrell, "The Roots of Medieval Gozo," *Al-Masaq*, iv (1991), 55, are here corrected. Ibn Abbad probably died between 1222 and 1224: Maurici, 39-45; Johns (1993), 91. However Al-Himyari placed his death in 1219/1220: text and translation of excerpt, manuscripts and sources in *ibid.*, 83-88

a Muslim presence on them in 1241. Giliberto was, therefore, instructed to allow the islanders to live according to their own *mores* and *constituciones* as long as that appeared to be in the royal interest. Later, probably in coincidence with the Sicilian oppressions of 1243 to 1246, there were quite possibly renewed expulsions of Muslims from Malta, presumably accompanied by further conversions from Islam.

The governor's report of about 1241 was concerned with the royal or curial establishment. The records of Giliberto's predecessor Paolino de Malta showed that the garrison of the three royal castles had numbered 150 *servientes,* 25 of whom were the sailors of two small vessels; their pay had amounted to 11,000 *tareni* a year. The grammar is somewhat confused but, unless the report was somehow adding 70 wives to 150 *servientes* to make 220, the garrison appears to have risen to 220 by Giliberto's time; and he asked for another 20. The 220 men received a total of 35 *salme* of wheat per month, and seventy of the garrison had wives who were given a further 12 *salme* a month. In addition there were 5 granary men, 60 male and female *servi* and *ancille* who worked on walls, buildings and other services for the curia, and 4 *curatuli* or estate managers, who between them received 12 *salme* monthly; that made a total of 59 *salme,* to which were added cheese, butter, meat and other foodstuffs.[50] There were also 84 *servi* from the island of Gerba off the Tunisian coast who were presumably captives and who worked the curial lands of the *demanium*; these too must have been fed. The estates farmed directly by the curia consisted of 55 *paricole* or about 9 percent of the two islands' total surface; presumably these estates did not include the grazing lands of the curia, or common lands or fields cultivated either by the *villani* who owed their produce to the curia or by other landholders. The *jardena* or fields of the curia produced 19 percent of those curial incomes paid in money rather than kind. In addition there were 55 cowherds, 10 shepherds, 2 mule or horse keepers, 3 donkeymen and 12 other male and female *serui.* These servants, said to number 144 though the figures as given amount to 166, received a monthly total of 50 *salme* of barley; they received considerably less barley per person than the garrison and others who received wheat. The *serui* and *ancille* were presumably slaves.[51] Many slaves were taken in a raid on Gerba

50. If these figures were reliable and complete, they might indicate the diet of those involved; such calculations are not attempted here.

51. Cf. Amari (1937/8), iii. 240-244; I. Peri, *Il Villanaggio in Sicilia* (Palermo, 1965), 14/15 n. 9, 21 n. 6, 77n. 63, 101 n. 72.

in 1223.[52] Probably all or most of the *serui* were Muslims; the curia provided them with a food allowance in kind, and they were not listed as paying taxes in money or produce.

| AREA | MALTA | GOZO | RATIO | TOTAL |
|---|---|---|---|---|
| square kilometres | 243 | 69 | 3.5 | 312 |
| *paricole* of curia | 40 | 15 | 2.7 | 55 |
| | | | | |
| FAMILIES | | | | |
| Christian | [1047] | 203 | [5.2] | [1250] |
| Muslim | 681 | 155 | 4.4 | 836 |
| Jewish | 25 | 8 | 3.1 | 33 |
| Total | [1753] | 366 | [4.8] | [2119] |
| | | | | |
| INCOMES (in *tareni*) | | | | |
| *dohana* | 1900 | 500 | 3.8 | 2400 |
| *tintoria* | 800 | 260 | 3.1 | 1060 |
| *tube* | 800 | 170 | 4.7 | 970 |
| *barbaria* | 340 | 80 | 4.25 | 420 |
| *madia* | - | 300 | - | 300 |
| *baiulacio et uxorte* | 1390 | 600 | 2.3 | 1990 |
| *gisia villanorum curie* | 2516 | 584 | 4.3 | 3100 |
| *apothece curie* | 100 | - | - | 100 |
| *corbinorum* (?) | 150 | - | - | 150 |
| *centimulorum* | - | 890 | - | 890 |
| *jardena* | 2741 | - | - | 2741 |
| *orti* | 180 | - | - | 180 |
| Total as given | 10901 | 3781 | 2.9 | 14681 |
| [Total by addition] | [10917] | [3384] | [3.2] | [14301] |

52. Amari (1937/8), iii. 617-618.

Of the incomes listed, the *dohana* involved general customs dues, probably on both imports and exports; the *tintoria, tube, barbaria* and *apothece* taxed dyers, musicians, barbers and shopkeepers; the *uxorte* derived from petty fines; the *gisia* was paid by Muslims; *centimula, jardena* and *orti* were incomes from mills, gardens and orchards; the *madia* was the Gozo boat; and *corbinorum* remains obscure.[53] There was no mention of grain, of wine[54] or of cotton which later became vitally important;[55] all three may have paid taxes reported under the *dohana.* In 1283 the crown confirmed to the men of Malta and Gozo their existing permission to import 300 *salme* of grain from Licata in Sicily without paying tax.[56]

The curia did not necessarily manage or benefit from all taxes or gabelles, some of which might have been alienated or farmed out and thus have been omitted from Giliberto's list. In 1281, for example, there were the *decime sclavorum*, presumably tenths levied on the sale of slaves and captives.[57] The various taxes enumerated by Giliberto, most of which were Sicilian in origin, brought the curia nearly 15,00 *tareni;* the *villani sarraceni* also paid a fourth of their produce in kind. The garrison of 150 had cost 11,000 *tareni* just a little earlier when Paolino de Malta was governor, so a garrison of 220 may have cost some 16,000 *tareni*, while wheat, barley, cheese and so on were provided for men, wives and beasts; the types and numbers of animals were also reported. In the report the quantities provided for men and animals were added up, correctly, to 59 *salme* of wheat and 84 *salme* of barley a month. Malta and Gozo clearly had a money economy and they may have produced some wealth in the form of lucrative cotton exports; the report suggests that the islands may roughly have paid for their own defence and administration. A royal letter of 1277 claimed that in earlier reigns, which would have included that of Frederick II, Malta customarily brought to the crown an annual *proventus*, presumably income

53 Details, *infra*.

54. Fiorini, 130, incorrectly implies that Giliberto's report explicitly mentioned an *assisa vini* on wine and a *conciara* tax on tanning.

55. G. Wettinger, "Agriculture in Malta in the Late Middle Ages", *Proceedings of History Week 1981*, ed. M. Buhagiar (Malta, 1982), 15-21; L. Galoppini, "Notizie su Maltesi e il Cotone di Malta a Cagliari nella seconda metà del Trecento," *Melita Historica*, x no. 1 (1988).

56. Text in G. Silvestri, *De Rebus Regni Siciliae: 9 settembre 1282 - 26 agosto 1283* (Palermo, 1882), 316-317.

57. Texts in Laurenza, 51-56.

calculated before expenditures, of more than 30,000 *tareni.*[58] If the report of about 1241 was correct, this would seem to have been an exaggeration.[59]

The ruling group on the islands was composed of an essentially Sicilian administration consisting of a royal governor, who may also have held the military command, the officials of the curia and the garrison; probably there were a few Sicilian judges and notaries, a number of Genoese or other foreign merchants, and some clergy. At some point shortly before 1257 certain Genoese merchants on Malta were in revolt against the crown.[60] More permanently established were the *homines* or *fideles* of the Maltese islands, a number of them possibly converted indigenous Muslims and others presumably Christian immigrants and settlers; in about 1241 it may still have been the case that some of these *homines* were Muslims, as in 1198. The *homines* had their own customs and they gave *consilium* to the governor; presumably they held lands, though there was no indication of that in the report. Some of them had usurped unspecified royal *raciones* and *jura* which were not necessarily lands. A royal letter of 1272 claimed that the *fideles* had long held possessions, while another letter of 1270 showed that various inhabitants of Malta had asserted that Frederick II had despoiled them of their lands on that island.[61] Very little is known of this group, and much of what has been written about it should be treated with caution.[62]

---

58. Text *ibid.*, 42-43.

59. Another form of taxation, the *colletta*, involved variable sums imposed on all communities in the Sicilian kingdom, including those which did not belong to the royal curia. In 1277 Malta and Gozo were assessed to pay a *colletta* of 350 *uncie* or 10,500 *tareni* : Bresc (1986), i. 60-65. That figure may have been based on an earlier assessment and, at a debatable rate of 6 *fuochi* or hearths per *uncia*, it would imply 1750 *fuochi* for the two islands in 1277. That would mean a reduction in the number of families from the total of 2119 reported by Giliberto (assuming that 47 should be amended to 1047), a change which might be explained in part by the expulsion of Muslims after 1241. Note, however, that there never was a census and that the tax lists were affected by all sorts of exceptions and exemptions, while the number of hearths were arbitrarily changed to reflect local wealth and ability to pay: W. Percy, "The Earliest Revolution against the 'Modern State': Direct Taxation in Medieval Sicily and the Vespers", *Italian Quarterly*, xxii (1981). Furthermore, S. Epstein, *An Island for Itself: Economic Development and Social Change in Late Medieval Sicily* (Cambridge, 1992), 40, argues for a rate of 3 *tareni* per *fuocho*, which would give 3500 families for Malta and Gozo. These calculations all seem inconclusive.

60. Luttrell (1980), 591-597.

61. Texts in Laurenza, 9-10, 19.

62. Discussion in Luttrell (1980).

Possibly there were still a number of free Muslims on Malta in about 1241, but most of the Muslims there were *villani* who paid the *gisia* or *jizya* to the curia. The *gisia* was originally a Muslim tax imposed on non-Muslims, but in twelfth-century Sicily it was owed by all Muslims, whether *villani* or not, to their Christian rulers; in 1239 even the Muslims at Lucera in Apulia were paying the *gisia*.[63] The Normans also imposed it on the Muslims of Tunisia.[64] In Sicily the Normans normally made a Muslim-style pact or *aman* with subject groups who were assured certain freedoms as *ahl al-dhimma* or "people of the pact" and who were bound, probably by a written treaty, to pay a *tributum* or *censum*. Something similar evidently occurred on Malta in 1091 when the Muslims agreed to pay an annual *data* according to their own Islamic law: *more legis suae*.[65] In Sicily such a pact was the basis for the payment of the *gisia*, which was in part a religious penalty which could be avoided through conversion to Christianity; it set people apart by law as well as by religion. The tax could be assessed as a collective tribute payable by a community which raised it through its elders, but increasingly it became a personal tax collected with the help of a system of tax registers which listed the names of those who were due to pay it. In twelfth-century Sicily there was much diversity in the status of the *villani*, some of whom also paid part of their produce in kind as a form of the Islamic tax known as the *kharadj*. The standard *villani* on the royal estates were bound or "adscripted" to the land and their service was heritable. Other unattached *villani*, known as *muls*, commended themselves to a lord or to the church and owed *gisia* by virtue of the position or tenure they thus acquired. Another class which paid *gisia* was the *rijal al-mahallat* who were possibly Muslim *burgenses* from the villages.[66]

After 1091 Malta may have paid its *data* as a collective sum owed by all or most of the inhabitants. Then, as the island was Christianized, there would increasingly have been Christians who did not owe the *gisia* with the result that those who did, the non-Christians, paid as individual families of *villani curie* who were listed, or at least counted, according to Sicilian practice, as in Giliberto's

63. Amari (1937/8), iii. 255-264.

64. References in H. Idris, *La Berbérie Orientale sous les Zirides: Xe-XIIe siècles*, i (Paris, 1959), 360. Fiorini, 130, incorrectly implies that the *gisia* was "only a tax on the Jews".

65. Gaufredus Malaterra, *De Rebus Gestis Rogerii*, ed. E. Pontieri, in *Rerum Italicarum Scriptores*, ns. v part 1 (Bologna, 1927), 95.

66. J. Johns, *The Muslims of Norman Sicily: c. 1060-c. 1194* (unpublished D. Phil. thesis: Oxford, 1983); *idem*, *"Duana Regis": Arabic Administration and Norman Kingship in Sicily* (in press).

report. The fourth part of their produce which Giliberto reported that the Muslim *villani* of Malta and Gozo owed to the curia evidently corresponded to the *kharadj.*[67] Giliberto gave no figure for this income from produce, probably because it was paid in kind and consumed on the islands. There was again no indication that this *quarta* on produce was paid by non-Muslims or by any Muslims who were not *villani curie.* There seems, however, to have been some doubt in Sicily whether even notable Muslims were fully free.[68]

Given the ferocity of Frederick II's persecution of the Sicilian Muslims, it is possible that some of them fled to Malta. Conceivably there were also in Malta a few Muslims who had become Greek rather than Latin Christians, as did occur in Sicily.[69] The words *ego* and *martur*, for "I" and "witness", were written in Greek for a witness, who did not actually sign his name, at the bottom of a Maltese document of 1274, and in 1299 *arnaton pousale pete* witnessed an act in Gozo by writing his name in Greek characters.[70] There is little other explicit evidence for Sicilian or Maltese Greeks or for Greek-speaking or Greek rite converts from Islam on Malta at that time, presumably because all or most of the Greek Christians on Malta had, unlike those of Sicily, been eliminated long before the thirteenth century. Though Frederick II continued the Norman tradition

67. Peri (1965), 14 and n. 9, and C. Cahen, "Kharadj." *Encyclopaedia of Islam*, iv (revised ed: Leiden, 1978), 1030-1034.

68. Peri (1965), 14/15 n. 9. On Muslim lords and landholders in Norman and post-Norman Siciliy, see Amari (1937/8), iii. 267-276; V. von Falkenhausen, "I Ceti dirigenti prenormanni al Tempo della Costituzione degli Stati normanni dell'Italia Meridionale e in Sicilia," in *Forma di Potere e Struttura sociale in Italia nel Medioevo*, ed. G. Rossetti (Bologna, 1977), 347-351; H. Bresc, "Féodalité coloniale en Terre d'Islam: La Sicile (1070-1240)." in *Structures féodales et Féodalisme dans l'Occident Méditerranéen (Xe-XIIIe siècles); Bilan et Perspectives de Recherches* (Rome, 1980).

69. S. Caruso, "Una Pergamena greca del tempo di Frederico II: Nota su una Famiglia arabo-greca di Messina," *Byzantion*, xlvi (1976).

70. A. Luttrell, "Medieval Malta: the Non-Written and the Written Evidence," in *Malta: a Case Study in International Cross-Currents*, ed. S. Fiorini - V. Mallia-Milanes (Malta, 1991), 37-38. The conversion process and its chronology require further study. There is no clear proof for the existence of a Greek rite or of any Basilian monastery on Malta; the archaeological, topographical and toponymic evidence will be presented in Mario Buhagiar's doctoral thesis. On Muslim conversions to the Greek rite in Sicily, see Bresc (1986), ii. 587-594, 607, but his reference to Malta as "a point de resistance de la culture greque" rests on slender evidence; see also the articles in *idem*, *Politique et Société en Sicile: XIIe-XVe siècles* (London, 1991). Note that in 1336 circa a German traveller spoke of Christians in Sicily who were *ad ritum Sarracenorum:* Ludolfus de Suchem, *De Itinere Terrae Sanctae Liber*, ed. F. Deycks (Stuttgart, 1851), 20.

of favouring the Greeks in Sicily, Basilian monasticism declined after about 1270. The number of Greek rite Sicilians, many of them not connected to the Basilian monks, was apparently limited, while conversions from Islam were probably not numerous and may often have involved Greeks from families which had earlier converted to Islam and had retained their Greek speech; such Muslims of Greek origin were presumably not to be found on Malta.[71] That folk memories and scraps of vocabulary may nevertheless have preserved an awareness of a Greek past and a feeling that the islanders were neither Sicilians nor Africans is suggested by an extraordinary jumble of ancient mythology, Sicilian toponomy and garbled Byzantine history recounted by Bartolomeo de Neocastro of Messina.[72] According to this story, presented as an account given by an old Muslim on Gerba who was asked in 1284 to explain the origins of the inhabitants of Gerba, Kerkena, Pantelleria, Lipari and Malta, they were the children of the black Egyptian god Amman and a group of Byzantine women from Sicily who had been exiled in 1043 for their support of the rebellious Byzantine general Georgios Maniaces.[73] The islanders were said to have been their offspring who subsequently adopted Arabic speech and Muslim religion but retained some memory of their mothers' Greek tongue: *quaedam a graeco sermone memoriter teneamus.* Some Sicilian Muslims converted to the Greek, rather than the Latin, rite probably because they already knew some Greek and because Sicilian Greeks were familiar to them while the Latins were unknown conquerors and invaders. Maltese Muslims, having no Greeks to whom they could assimilate, were presumably converted to the Latin religion but they would have found the Italian language unfamiliar and so they retained their own Arabic speech.[74]

There were a few Jewish families on Malta and Gozo but their status is uncertain. In Sicily Jews paid the *gisia* from Muslim times until the fifteenth century, and Sicilian Jews were technically *servi* or slaves of the royal curia,

---

71. M. Scaduto, *Il Monachismo basiliano nella Sicilia medievale - Rinascita e Decadenza: sec. XI-XIV* (Rome, 1947), 228-232, 240-242; V. von Falkenhausen, "Il Monachesimo greco in Sicilia", in *La Sicilia rupestre nel Contesto delle Civiltà mediterranee*, ed. C. Fonseca (Galatina, 1986); J. Tohns, "The Greek Church and the Conversion of Muslims in Norman Sicily?," *Byzantinische Forschungen*, xxi (1995).

72.. Bartolomeo de Neocastro, *Historia Sicula*, ed. G. Paladino, in *Rerum Italicarum Scriptores*, ns. xiii part 3 (Bologna, 1921), 63-65.

73. Cf. V. von Falkenhausen, *La Dominazione bizantina nell'Italia Meridionale dal IX all'XI secolo* (Bari, 1978), 95-96.

74. "Arab" resistance is discussed in Bresc (1986), ii. 624-628.

though that was largely a point of jurisdictional significance.[75] In 1211 Frederick II granted the Palermitan Jews and their taxes, including the *gisia* they paid, to the Archbishop of Palermo, while in 1239 other Jews in Palermo who were known as *de Garbo* were paying the *gisia* to the crown.[76] Giliberto's report listed only 33 Jewish families in Malta and Gozo without making it clear to whom they belonged or whether or not they paid the *gisia;* probably they did belong to the curia and did pay the *gisia* in about 1241 just as they did in the fifteenth century.[77]

The rest of the analysis of Giliberto's report largely depends upon the interpretation of two ambiguous passages. The first, concerning Malta, reads in the surviving version: *Gisie quingentorum quadraginta villanorum curie tarenos duomilia quingentos sedecim.* The second, concerning Gozo, reads: *Gisie tarenos centum quadraginta quinque. Villanorum curie tarenos quingentos octoginta quatuor.* This is most likely to mean that on the island of Malta there were 540 *villani curie* who paid the *gisia* tax of 2516 *tareni*, while in Gozo 145 *villani curie* paid the *gisia* tax of 584 *tareni.*[78] Neither 2516 nor 584 *tareni* seems like a round figure fixed as a collective tribute, while both are divisible by four, which might suggest 629 and 146 households respectively paying four *tareni* each; on Gozo there were in fact said to be 145 *villani curie.* This would mean that in Malta each *gisia*-payer paid approximately 4.7 *tareni* while in Gozo each paid approximately 4 *tareni*; and that in Malta there were 540 Muslim and Jewish *villani curie* to 706 Muslim and Jewish families, and in Gozo 145 Muslim and Jewish *villani curie* to 163 Muslim and Jewish families, assuming that the Jews were *villani curie* and paid the *gisia.* In this case the ratio of *tareni* paid by *villani curie* in Malta to *tareni* paid by *villani curie* in Gozo, that is 2516 to 584 or 4.3, is precisely the same as the ratio of Muslim and Jewish families in Malta to that of Muslim and Jewish families in Gozo, that is 706 to 163 or 4.3; the result is very similar if the Jewish families are ignored. This again suggests that the figures for Muslim families are correct. Most of the Muslims counted in the report would, therefore, have been *villani curie* paying the *gisia* and also paying taxes in kind, since the report stated that the *villani sarraceni curie* paid an

75. Peri (1978), 87, 303 n. 3; Q. Senigaglia, "La Condizione giuridica degli Ebrei in Sicilia," *Rivista Italiana per le Scienze Giuridiche,* xli (1906), 77, 79-81, 87-88.

76. Texts in B. and G. Lagumina, *Codice Diplomatico dei Giudei di Sicilia,* i (Palermo, 1884), 12-15, 19-20.

77. G. Wettinger, *The Jews of Malta in the Late Middle Ages* (Malta, 1985), 17.

78. As assumed in Peri (1978), 154.

annual fourth part of their produce; the use of the term *villani sarraceni* might mean that Jews, probably town-dwellers, were *villani curie* but did not owe this annual fourth. This interpretation would involve a discrepancy - ignoring the Jews - in the region of 150 for the two islands between the number of Muslim families, given as 836, and the number of *gisia*-paying *villani*, which would have been 685. Conceivably there were some free Muslims, perhaps in the towns; or there were *villani* on those lands of the curia which Giliberto mentioned as having been usurped; or, as was common in Sicily, there were *villani* who did not belong to the curia but to ecclesiastical or other lords; or some Muslim slaves may have been counted as families. There may also have been widows, the blind, cripples or fugitives who did not pay the *gisia*, and that may have produced apparent statistical discrepancies. Maltese customs probably differed from those of Sicily and Sicilian practices varied greatly. As a general rule, all Sicilian Muslims paid the *gisia*, whether they were *villani* or not; if they were *villani curie* they could hold land and would pay the *kharadj* on it. Maybe there were Muslims on Malta who were *villani sarraceni curie* and who paid *gisia* and *kharadj* in cash and who also owed a *quarta* or *kharadj* in kind which was not included in Giliberto's accounts. All this would, at least, have been consistent with these two passages simply meaning that given numbers of *villani curie* paid given sums in cash as *gisia.*

This is in many ways the most satisfactory solution and it may well be the correct one. It would match the general ratios of inhabitants and payments in Malta to those in Gozo, as shown in the table above. The financial totals in the report are probably almost correct, since 10,901 plus 3781 amounts to 14,682 instead of 14,681 as given, a discrepancy of only one *tarenus*. The total for Malta is 10,901 while the figures reported actually add up to 10,917, again a small difference of only 16 *tareni*. For Gozo, however, one or more items have apparently been omitted or miscopied because the individual taxes given amount to 3384 *tareni* which is 397 less than the total recorded in the document. It also has to be assumed that for Gozo the word *tarenos* after *Gisie* and the full-stop, or more precisely two points, in the manuscript after *quinque* were inserted incorrectly; since the text survives only in a copy, this is quite possible. Furthermore, it supposes that most Muslims paid the *gisia* and were *villani curie;* that the considerable number of Christian families paid no direct tax, as is likely since no such tax was recorded in Giliberto's report; and that there were no Christian *villani curie*, which is also quite possible since there had been so few Christians on Malta in the twelfth century, since there were few, or almost no, Christian Greeks on Malta in the thirteenth century, and since Latin *villani* were by then almost unknown in Sicily.

The two passages might, however, be interpreted quite differently as meaning that in Malta the *gisia* produced 540 *tareni* and the *villani curie* paid 2516 *tareni* while in Gozo the *gisia* produced 145 *tareni* and the *villani curie* paid 584. In this case the various ratios and proportions between the two islands would be little changed, but it would have to be assumed that in the surviving version the word *quingentorum* was wrongly placed in the genitive and the word *tarenos* was dropped out after the *Gisie* for Malta; and whereas the totals in *tareni* reported in the surviving text are Malta 10,901, Gozo 3781 and the two together 14,681, the figures given would on this interpretation amount to 11,457 and 3529, making an overall total of 14,986. These discrepancies make this interpretation seem an unlikely one. It might be suggested that there were *villani curie* who, because they were Christians, paid a tax which was not the *gisia*; those might have been indigenous Muslims converted to Christianity. It is true that it was generally the case in Sicily that a Muslim *villanus curie* who converted to Christianity remained a *villanus curie* but paid the *gisia* at a lower rate or escaped it entirely; however, there is no evidence for the existence on Malta of a class of Christian *villani*, and the statistical discrepancies resulting from such an interpretation would remain without explanation. None the less, that there was eventually a considerable group of converts seems almost certain in view of the survival of the indigenous Arabic language in the islands, but nothing definite is known about this process of conversion. The apparent absence on Malta and Gozo of a class of Latin or Greek *villani* which might have absorbed converts from Islam presumably helped to ensure the survival of an Arabic speech.

Preliminary studies of land tenure and related matters show that, unlike Sicily, there was a considerable extension of peasant land ownership, of leaseholds and paid labourers in Malta during the fifteenth and the sixteenth centuries,[79] but that proves nothing conclusive in view of the profound changes which occurred on Malta between the thirteenth and fifteenth century.[80] As in Sicily, many free Christians on Malta and Gozo would have probably been Italian rather than Sicilian in origin, whether or not they came from Celano, and they would conceivably have held lands, following the Sicilian pattern, by non-feudal tenure, owing military service but not direct taxes.[81] Maltese society in about 1241 apparently included a group or groups of free Christians who paid no direct tax to the curia, an advantage which possibly attracted Muslims on Malta to convert

79. Wettinger (1982), 4-15, 43-48, and *idem*, "The Village of Hal Millieri: 1419-1530", in *Hal Millieri: a Maltese Casale, its Churches and Paintings*, ed. A. Luttrell (Malta, 1976).

80. Cf. Bresc (1975), 127-136.

81. Peri (1965), 45, 69-74; (1978), 96-99.

to Christianity; a class of Muslim *villani* belonging to the curia who paid the *gisia* and contributions in kind; and a few Jews. Hypotheses about these and other possible groups must largely be based on known situations outside the Maltese islands.[82] Particularly relevant are considerations concerning *villani* in Sicily. Unfortunately, variations in the status of the Sicilian *villani* were so considerable that it is impossible to be sure which of its elements might have been transferred to Malta. Christian *villani* were mostly indigenous Greeks or converted Muslims. Some Muslim *villani* had been landless, almost slaves, while others were relatively free and held lands which they farmed; some were *villani* by virtue of their tenure, others by personal status; some *villani* owed produce as well as money. By 1241 the Muslim *villani* of Sicily were disappearing as they converted, fled, or were deported or otherwise eliminated during the ruthless repressions of Frederick II, and by the second half of the thirteenth century Sicilian ecclesiastical lands had to be let out in emphyteusis as there were so few *villani* left.[83]

In the absence of further documentary evidence, there is not way of knowing how these Sicilian practices and developments were assimilated to the customs and situations of Malta. There had been a group of Christians who were foreign slaves or captives on eleventh-century Malta but Count Roger is said to have removed them all in 1091. In the twelfth century Malta was largely Muslim and presumably there were few, if any, indigenous Christians who could have become non-Muslim *villani*. The process of Latinization must have been furthered by the transportation of rebels from Celano in 1224. The Christian families listed on Malta and Gozo in 1241 circa were Latins, or converted Muslims or conceivably Greek immigrants from Sicily or Italy, or they were converted Muslim from Malta and Gozo. Indigenous Maltese and Gozitan Muslims, whether of town or country, may have gone into exile and some were expelled, though such expulsions may have taken place only after the time of Giliberto's report. On small flat islands it would not have been easy to flee from the curial estates and the temptation to convert would have been strong; many must have done so. The curia still possessed *serui*, possibly converted Muslims, in 1271, 1273 and 1281.[84] *Seruus* did not always means slave, and the *serui* who worked the royal

82 Eg. H.E. Mayer, "Latins, Muslims and Greeks in the Latin Kingdom of Jerusalem", *History,* lxiii (1978).

83. In addition to the works of Peri and Johns. see H. Bercher - A. Courteau - J. Mouton, "Une Abbaye latine dans la Société musulmane: Monreale au XIIe siècle," *Annales: Économies, Sociétés, Civilisations*, xxxiv (1979).

84. Texts in Laurenza, 17-18, 27-29, 51-52.

estates on Malta may well have been "serfs" or *villani* of the curia. A *seruus curie* was documented on Malta in 1372 and another on Gozo in 1373/4.[85] However, the ordinary tax-paying *villani* may have disappeared, or largely disappeared, in the late-thirteenth century. A text of 1271 referred to Muslims who had been expelled from the islands - it is not clear when - and whose possessions had passed to the royal curia, and in the same year the king ordered that uncultivated curial lands on Malta and Gozo were to be leased at an annual *census* to *agricultores* who were presumably not *villani.*[86]

Giliberto's report was a technical and statistical document concerned above all with taxation, and it classified people into categories which were probably not so clearly distinguished in real life as in the bureaucratic text in the form in which it survives. In Sicily, where there were Muslim revolts which received external support and where the complete Christianization and Latinization of the Muslim population proved impossible, Frederick II resorted to brutal repressions and expulsions. Something similar occurred on Malta, but there a section of the Muslims, unable to retreat to the mountains as did the Sicilian Muslims, preserved their language and to some extent their economic and social position by accepting conversion; in a sense they resisted Latinization by accepting Christianization. There must have been tensions between converted Muslims and Christian immigrants. Thirteenth-century Malta and Gozo evidently constituted a society in a state of political, religious, economic and social upheaval in which many men remained unsure of their status as the indigenous inhabitants changed their religion and condition or left the country, as Latin immigrants established themselves on the islands, and as the officials of the royal curia sought to squeeze the maximum profit from the land and people.

85. Bresc (1975), 130-131; Wettinger (1982), 11 n. 52.

86. Texts in Laurenza, 13-15, 18-19.

Fridericus etc, ad Gilibertum Abbatem[1] etc, Litteras et capitula que nostro culmini destinasti etc quod autem in ipsis capitulis vidimus contineri quod jura dohane Malte terre et maris tam vendencium quam emencium[2] ualent tarenos auri[3] mille annuatim et nongentos. Tintorie[4] tarenos octingentos. Tabule tubarum[5] tarenos octingentos. Barbarie[6] tarenos trecentos quadraginta. Cabelle Baiulacionis[7] et Sorte[8] tarenos mille trecentos nonaginta. Gisie[9] quingentorum quadraginta villanorum curie tarenos duomilia quingentos sedecim. Apothecarum[10] curie nostre tarenos centum. Cabella Corbinorum[11] tarenos centum

1. Giliberto Abbate.

2. *Dohana* : customs dues on buying and selling by land and sea.

3. Sicilian gold *tarì* varied considerably in weight, but the *tareni* of this text were evidently a standard unit of value; P. Grierson - W. Oddy, "Le Titre du Tari sicilien du milieu du XIe siècle à 1278", *Revue Numismatique*, VI ser., xvi (1974). The *tarì* may, in fact, have been used as a money of account.

4. A tax on cloth dyeing: *Acta Curie Felicis Urbis Panormi*, ed. F. Pollaci Nuccio - D. Gnoffo, i (reprint: Palermo, 1982), pp. cxi-cxiv, 338.

5. For *Tabule* read *cabelle; cabella* or *gabella* meant tax. At Palermo the *gabella tubarum* was a tax on musicians: *ibid.*, i, pp. xcv-xcvii, 323.

6. *Barbaria:* a tax on barbers. It survived in Malta in 1506, but was not known by that name elsewhere: J. Luca de Barberiis, *Liber de Secretiis*, ed. E. Mazzarese Fardella (Milan, 1966), 79 n. 77.

7. Bresc (1975), 134, gives the *baiulacio* as "petty fines and incomes". It apparently consisted of incomes from various rights: Luca de Barberiis, 78/9 n.76.

8. The *xurta* or *scorta* was the city guard or police patrol: Amari (1937/8), iii. 916-917. Bresc (1975), 134, gives *xorta* as "fines and taxes on games of chance".

9. *Gisia:* the *jizya*, a tax paid by Muslims and Jews. This term was identified in Peri (1978), 154-155. The surviving ms. clearly gives *quingentor'*. The reading *Gisie* is clear in both cases, but Winkelmann (1880), i. 713, incorrectly gave *cusie*. The interpretations of "*cusie*" in Dessoulavy, 539 (mintage), Valentini, 5 (*caxia*), and Bresc (1975), 134 (tax on tailors), may now be ignored.

10. *Apothece:* shops.

11. *Cabella Corbinorum:* Valentini, 5, suggested it might be a corruption of *centimulorum* (mills); this may be possible, since the curia had four such mills on Gozo while *centimula de cabelle* were not mentioned on Malta: *infra* n. 35. It would follow that mills produced 150 *tareni* on Malta and 890 *tareni* on Gozo. Dessoulavy, 539, proposes a tax on basketwork; possibly the tax was on some commodity contained in baskets. *Corbisierorum* referring to a tax on rope-making, is also a conceivable amendment.

quinquaginta. Cabelle decem jardenorum[12] curie nostre, tarenos duo milia septingentos quadraginta et unus. Cabella trium ortorum[13] centum octoginta. Quorum omnium prouentuum jura sunt in summa, tarenos decem milia nongentos et unus.[14]

Significasti etiam quod jura dohane maris et terre Gaudisij sunt annuatim tarenos quingentos. Tyntorie tarenos ducentos sexaginta. Barbarie tarenos octoginta. Cabella tubarum tarenos centum septuaginta. Cabelle madie[15] tarenos trecentos. Cabelle Baiulacionis et uxorte[16] tarenos sexcentos. Gisie tarenos centum quadraginta quinque. Villanorum curie tarenos quingentos octoginta quatuor. Centimulorum[17] curie nostre tarenos octingentos nonaginta. Quorum omnium tarenorum summa est triamilia septingentos octoginta unus.[18]

Et summa omnium prouentuum Insularum Malte et Gaudisij est tarenos quatuordecim milia sexcenti octoginta unus.[19]

Et continebant etiam ipsa capitula quod statute sunt in agricultura curie nostre Malte paricole quadraginta, et in Gaudisio paricole quindecim.[20]

Et quod villanj sarracenj curie nostre Insularum ipsarum soluunt annuatim curie nostre de omnibus victualibus eorum quartam partem.

---

12. *jardena:* possibly fields for trees and fruit with a wall to exclude animals and some form of irrigation.

13. *orti:* possibly enclosed vegetable gardens.

14. 10,901, but the figures given amount to 10,917.

15. The *madia* was the Gozo ferry boat: Bresc (1975), 133 n. 40, 134 n. 47. Apart from the names *Malta* and *Gaudisio* in place of the classical *Melita* and *Gaudos,* the Arabic terms *xorta* (*supra,* n.8), *marramata* (*infra,* n.28) and *madia* are in a sense probably the oldest surviving written Maltese words.

16. *uxorta,* given above as *Sorta: supra,* n. 8.

17. *Centimulum:* mill driven by animal power.

18. 3781, but the figures given amount to 3384.

19. 14,681: the two totals given amount to 14,682.

20. *Paricola,* a Sicilian field-measure documented as *paricla* in 1208 or 1209: Winkelmann (1880), i. 86, 89. A text of about 1247/8 read *quod feuda Sicilie statuta fuisse dicuntur in triginta periclatis de terris ad triginta salmatas per periclatam: ibid.*, i. 701-702. The Sicilian *salma* was 1.75 hectares: Bresc (1986), i. 55. So the curia cultivated about 29 square kilometres, or roughly 9 percent, of Malta and Gozo.

Et quod inuenisti per quaternitiones quondam Paulinj de Malta[21] quod dabantur annuatim pro solidis et uictu[22] centum quinquaginta seruientium, qui statuti sunt in custodia trium castrorum nostrorum insularum ipsarum, tarenos undecim milia, inter quos seruientes computati sunt marenarii vigintiquinque, qui deputati sunt etiam ut cum necesse fuerit armentur ex eis vackette[23] due pro seruicijs nostris.

Significasti insuper, in Insula Malte esse familias christianorum[24] quadraginta septem. familie Sarracenorum sexcentas octoginta unam. Iudeorum vigintj quinque.

Et in Gaudisio scripsisti esse familias christianorum ducentas tres. Sarracenorum centum quinquaginta quinque et familias Iudeorum viij.[25]

Et eadem capitula, continebant quod ducenti viginti seruientibus statutis in custodia castrorum nostrorum Insularum ipsarum dantur pro uidenda mense quolibet de frumento curie nostre salme[26] triginta quinque et septuaginta mulieres uxores, videlicet septuaginta seruientuum predictorum recipiunt pro uidanda de frumento quolibet mense salmas duodecim et quinque granecterijs et sexaginta seruis et ancillis[27] curie nostre deputatis ibidem ad marramata[28] curie nostre et alia seruicia nostra in castris ipsis.

Et quatuor curatulj agrorum nostrorum, dantur similiter pro uidanda de frumento curie mense quolibet salme duodecim.

---

21. Frederick II's governor of Malta in 1239 and 1240, and possibly in 1235.

22. Ms: *uit'* (?) or *uin'* (?).

23. *Vacketta* or *vacheta:* light ship.

24. 47: possible emendations are discussed *supra.*

25. The small island of Comino appears to have been uninhabited, or at least it paid no recorded taxes.

26. The Sicilian *salma* contained 2.75 hectolitres of grain: Bresc (1986), i. 55.

27. *Ancille:* female *serui.*

28. *Marramata:* wall or building work. This word, also used in Sicily, certainly derives from the Arabic: A. Varvaro, "Problematica dei Normannismi del Siciliano", *Atti del Congresso Internazionale di Studi sulla Sicilia Normanna* (Palermo, 1973), 364; G. Bautier-Bresc - H. Bresc, "*Maramma:* i Mestieri della Costruzione nella Sicilia Medievale", in *I Mestieri: Atti del II Congresso Internazionale di Studi Antropologici Siciliani* (Palermo, 1983); G. Wettinger - M. Fsadni, *L-G'anja ta' Pietru Caxaru: Poeżija bil-Malti Medjevali* (Malta, 1983), 52.

Cuius predicti frumentj summam scripsisti esse pro uidanda omnium personarum predictarum mense quolibet salme quinquaginta nouem.

Et quod significasti dari eis quolibet mense de caseo cantaros[29] nouem, de butiro, carnibus et alijs pro companagio[30] ad sufficienciam eorundem et quod octoginta quatuor serui Gerbinj[31] deputati in seruicijs paricolarum curie nostre quinquaginta quinque custodes boum et vaccarum decem pastores ouium et caprarum curie nostre, duo custodes jumentorum tres custodes asinorum duodecim seruj et ancille deputati in seruicijs curie nostre.

Que omnes persone sunt centum quadraginta quatuor,[32] recipiunt mense quolibet pro uidanda eorum de ordeo salmas quinquaginta.

Et quod dantur quinque mulis qui sunt in tribus centimulis castri maris Malte,[33] asinis quatuor et mulis duobus statutis in furno ipsius castri. duobus stallonis equinis et duobos stallonis asinis pro annona eorum singulis mensibus de ordeo salme tredecim. Et quod in castro ciuitatis Malte[34] sunt somerii duo et mulus unus in centimulo,[35] quibus datur de mense in mensem pro annona eorum de ordeo salma una.

Et in centimulo castri Gaudisij sunt asinj tres, roncinus unus et asinus unus stallonus.

Et in centimulis quatuor de cabelle muli sex, quibus datur per mensem pro annona ipsorum de ordeo salme tredicim.

Et sunt ibi asini triginta duo deferentes victualia curie nostre quibus statutj sunt per mensem de ordeo salme septem.

---

29. The Sicilian *cantaro* or *quintal* weighing 79.3 kilograms: Bresc (1986), i. 56.

30. *Companagium:* food provision.

31. 84 *serui* from the island of Gerba.

32. 144: but the figures given amount to 166.

33. *Castrum maris:* the earliest clear reference to a castle in the Grand Harbour.

34. The *castrum* of the *ciuitas Malte:* the modern Mdina.

35. *in centimulis quatuor de cabella:* the incomes given include nothing from mills in Malta but a *gabella* of 890 *tareni* from the *centimula curie* on Gozo, while there were three such mills in the *Castrum maris* and one in the *Ciuitas* on Malta and one in the *castrum* on Gozo. If the document is correct, four other *centimula de cabelle,* listed after the *centimulum* in the Gozo *castrum,* produced 890 *tareni* on Gozo.

Et quod tocius ordei quod datur pro nostris seruicijs supradictis. Summa est quolibet mense, salme octoginta quatuor.

Continebatur etiam in transmissis capitulis tuis te necessario statuisse in predictis tribus castris nostris[36] de consilio fidelium nostrorum Insularum ipsarum alios seruientes vigintj, quod placet nobis dum modo sint necessarij.

Continebant insuper ipsa capitula quod homines Insularum ipsarum uiuunt[37] alijs moribus et constitucionibus quam alij homines Regni nostri Sicilie, et consultasti Excellenciam nostram quid inde placeat culminj nostro, ad quod tibi taliter respondemus quod si uideris redundare ad maius[38] comodum curie eos uiuere, iuxta tenorem sacrarum constitucionum nostrarum[39] et secundum consuetudines quas habent alij feudales[40] nostri Sicilie, eos facias uiuere, secundum quod alij Siculj nostri uiuunt, quod si maiores[41] et constituciones eorum redundant ad maius[42] comodum curie nostre eos permictas, secundum soliti sunt uiuere hactenus in utroque tamen considera modum[43] curie nostre.

Consultasti etiam sunt[44] tibi delatum est, per fideles nostros multi de insula[45] ipsis detinent raciones et jura spectantia ad demanium nostrum et sine mandato nostro contra eos procedere noluisti. Cum igitur unicuique nostrorum fidelium sua jura illibata seruemus, pati minime uolumus nec debemus nostra ab alijs occupari. Quare uolumus ut inquisitis omnibus plene et cognitis racionibus et juribus nostris, a quibuscumque ipsa inueneris contra justitiam detineri, ad manus nostre curie sicut justum fuerit studeas reuocare.

---

36. The third castle is presumably that on Gozo, and not a third castle on Malta as Pertusi, 284, supposes.

37. Mss. *uiunt.*

38. Ms. *manus.*

39. Probably the Constitutions of Melfi promulgated in 1231: Pertusi, 285.

40. Possibly *fideles* since all other references are to *fideles,* while *feudales* might imply a group of feudatories which is otherwise totally undocumented on Malta in this period.

41. Read *mores?*

42. Ms. *manus.*

43. Read *consideras comodum?*

44. Read *quod sicut?*

45. Read *insulis?*

# X

## MALTA E GOZO: 1222-1268

Benchè i primi passi verso la *reconquista* di Malta e Gozo risalissero al 1090 con la breve spedizione dalla Sicilia del Conte Ruggero il Normanno, le isole maltesi rimasero in prevalenza musulmane almeno sino alla fine del dodicesimo secolo[1]. Soltanto allora il loro riassetto e la loro latinizzazione ebbero inizio sotto l'egida di una serie di Conti genovesi di Malta che erano legati in qualche modo alla corona della Sicilia. Importante fra questi Conti fu Enrico, detto "il Pescatore", un pirata genovese, che fece di Malta il centro delle sue ampie operazioni nel Mediterraneo, e che divenne anche Ammiraglio reale della Sicilia per conto dell'Imperatore Federico II di Hohenstaufen. Enrico, che apparteneva alla famiglia genovese dei Castello o De Castro, univa il talento amministrativo e diplomatico dell'uomo politico devoto alla sua città-stato all'opportunismo personale del pirata. A un certo momento sembrò si fosse affermato come il padrone quasi assoluto sia di Malta che di Creta. Poi intorno al 1222, il Pescatore cadde in disgrazia e la Contea di Malta gli venne confiscata da Federico II. Poco dopo gli vennero restituiti sia il titolo di Conte che, probabilmente, una parte degli introiti di Malta e di Gozo, ma non riuscì a riacquistare vero potere su Malta dove il controllo del *castrum* e l'amministrazione da allora in poi rimasero nelle mani degli ufficiali reali. Sembra che Enrico fosse morto già nel maggio del 1232, quando suo figlio Nicoloso deteneva il titolo di Conte di Malta[2].

---

[1] Questa tesi è stata studiata e approfondita da A. LUTTRELL, «Approaches to Medieval Malta», in *Studies on Malta before the Knights*, ed. A. LUTTRELL (Londra, 1975), 29-40.

[2] Particolari in D. ABULAFIA, «Henry Count of Malta and his Mediterranean Activities», *ibid.*; vedi anche J. POWELL, «Genoese Policy and the Kingdom of

La destituzione di Enrico e l'assunzione del diretto controllo reale su Malta e Gozo coincisero col raggiungimento della maggiore età da parte di Federico II e con la sua affermazione di potere sul suo regno. Questo fu anche il momento in cui la politica di Federico provocò una rivolta tra i Musulmani in Sicilia, e in cui una flotta imperiale attacò l'isola africana di Gerba nel 1223. L'espulsione o "conversione" dei Musulmani maltesi probabilmente ebbe luogo nel 1224 e, secondo il cronista Riccardo de San Germano, la popolazione della città abruzzese di Celano fu trasferita a Malta in quell'anno. Durante i decenni seguenti, fino alla morte di Federico II, Malta e Gozo furono parzialmente, ma soltanto parzialmente, latinizzati e ripopolati con Italiani e Siciliani. Vennero introdotte pratiche amministrative e istituzioni governative siciliane; molti dei Musulmani superstiti presumibilmente abbracciarono il cristianesimo; e la Chiesa di Roma venne stabilita sulle isole. I pochi documenti rimasti su questo periodo sono già stati studiati, benché lascino ancora molti problemi insoluti. Esistono dubbi e disaccordo circa la data e la natura della conversione delle isole; sull'entità e la composizione della popolazione; sui poteri conferiti al Conte di Malta; e sulla natura del singolare processo che vide la popolazione indigena delle isole sopravvivere in una terra di *reconquista* cristiana pur mantenendo la sua primitiva forma di espressione araba [3]. Questo processo probabilmente aveva qualche cosa in comune con la rioccupazione cristiana di Maiorca e di Valenza [4], e di altre

---

Sicily: 1220-1240,» *Mediaeval Studies*, XXVIII (1966), e D. ABULAFIA, *The Two Italies: Economic Relations between the Norman Kingdom of Sicily and the Northern Communes* (Cambridge, 1977). Nel 1243 *Nicolosus filius quondam comitis Enrici de Malta* era membro di una commissione a Genova, ma occorre sottolineare che in questo passo Nicoloso non portava il titolo di Conte: *Annali Genovesi di Caffaro e de' suoi continuatori*, III, ed. C. IMPERIALE DI SANT'ANGELO (Roma, 1923), 140-141.

[3] LUTTRELL, in *Medieval Malta*, 35-40, e IDEM, «Frederick II and Paolino de Malta: 1235», *Quellen und Forschungen aus italienischen Archiven und Bibliotheken*, LV-LVI (1976). Sull'aspetto amministrativo, vedi anche H. BRESC, «The *Secrezia* and the Royal Patrimony in Malta: 1240-1450», in *Medieval Malta*.

[4] Vedi il recentissimo R. BURNS, «The Language Barrier: the Problem of Bilingualism and Muslim-Christian Interchange in the Medieval Kingdom of Valencia», *Journal of the Faculty of Arts: Royal University of Malta*, VI, no. 4 (1977), e H. BRESC, «Mudejars des Pays de la Couronne d'Aragon et Sarrasins de la Sicile Normande: Le probleme de l'Acculturation», in *X Congreso de Historia de la Corona de Aragón, supra;* vedi pure A. LUTTRELL, «The Christianization of Malta», in *Malta Year Book 1977* (Malta, 1977).

isole minori del Mediterraneo come la vicina Pantelleria[5], ma la sopravvivenza della lingua araba in una terra cristianizzata era un fatto del tutto insolito. Questa relazione non vuole tuttavia riproporre ancora una volta alla discussione problemi relativi all'epoca di Federico II, ma approfondire gli ancora più oscuri anni che seguirono la sua morte avvenuta nel 1250.

Gli anni che terminarono con la morte dei successori di Federico, Manfredi e Corradino, nel 1266 e 1268, videro la disintegrazione e l'eclissi finale del potere Hohenstaufen in Italia e in Sicilia. Le notizie dirette su Malta durante questi anni sono scarsissime; ci sono soltanto varie redazioni di un accordo fra Manfredi e i Genovesi che risalgono agli anni 1257, 1259 e 1261; un accenno a un assalto genovese contro una flotta veneziana avvenuto nel 1264; e un trattato fra Corradino e i Pisani nel 1268. Questi documenti sono stati studiati da Roberto Valentini, e i risultati della sua ricerca sono poi stati pubblicati in un articolo del 1939[6]. Pare che non esistano altri documenti sul periodo in questione[7]. Ma è invece possibile riesaminare questo materiale approfondendo lo studio dei testi e dei dettagli che essi contengono, studiando le relazioni tra Sicilia, Genova e le altre potenze nel periodo dal 1250 al 1268, e interpretando i dati che ne risultano entro una più ampia prospettiva della storia medievale maltese.

* * *

L'ultimo documento dell'epoca di Federico II che riguardi direttamente Malta risale al 1241 circa[8]. Non si è in grado di dire

---

[5] H. Bresc, «Pantelleria entre l'Islam et la Chrétienté», *Cahiers de Tunisie,* XIX (1971).

[6] R. Valentini, «Il comune demaniale di Malta dall'origine alla crisi sveva», *Archivio Storico di Malta,* X (1939), 226-230; alcuni storici di Malta accettarono in gran parte i suggerimenti del Valentini, qualche volta aggiungendovi i propri errori.

[7] Un documento redatto da un notaio genovese in Agrigento il 13 ottobre 1252 fu sottoscritto da *Nicolaus de Malta,* ma non è possibile identificare quest'ultimo con Nicoloso figlio del «Pescatore» e neanche è certo che vi fosse coinvolto un «Maltese»; testo in P. Collura, *Le più antiche carte dell'Archivio Capitolare di Agrigento: 1092-1282* (Palermo, 1961), 151-152.

[8] Luttrell, in *Medieval Malta,* 36-40. Una ragazza schiava maltese fu venduta a Genova nel 1248, ma il venditore era fiorentino; così non si può dedurre nessun rapporto tra Malta e Genova da questo episodio: testo in R. Lopez, «La vendita d'una schiava di Malta a Genova nel 1248», *Archivio Storico di Malta,* VII (1935-6), 391.

cosa sia successo dopo la sua morte, avvenuta il 13 dicembre 1250. Corrado, figlio di Federico, morì el 21 maggio 1254 lasciando il figlio Corradino, che aveva appena due anni, in Germania mentre il potere effettivo sull'Italia meridionale e sulla Sicilia passò nelle mani di Manfredi, figlio illegittimo di Federico, nonostante l'opposizione del papa che cercava di porre sul trono della Sicilia un principe inglese. In un primo momento Manfredi esercitò il potere come reggente di Corradino. Verso il 1257 egli aveva il controllo sulla Sicilia, benchè si disinteressasse alquanto dell'isola e non ne fosse incoranato re fino all'agosto 1258 [9]. Tecnicamente egli era *baiulus generalis* di Corradino quando nel luglio 1257, vicino a Melfi, concluse un trattato con la repubblica di Genova, trattato che confermò in forma di privilegio reale il 22 marzo 1259, e che fu poi ratificato dai Genovesi a Genova il 17 settembre dello stesso anno. Con questo accordo i Genovesi cercavano di proteggere i loro vitali interessi economici in Sicilia con una serie di clausole riguardanti punti essenziali come la libertà di commercio, l'esenzione dalle tasse, e i consolati, mentre Manfredi costringeva i Genovesi a una politica di neutralità per la quale essi accettavano di non aiutare i suoi nemici. In una clausola del 1257 si parlava di alcuni Genovesi che, insieme a Nicoloso figlio di Enrico Conte di Malta, contrastavano in qualche modo l'autorità di Manfredi su Malta, dove avevano tenuto il *castrum* [10]; questi Genovesi erano Robertus Buccanigra e i suoi figli, Leone de Creta, Balduinus de Castello e i suoi figli, Bartolomeus de Monte e Vitale de Gaeta. Tutti costoro dovevano essere liberi sia di rimanere nel regno di Sicilia che di andarsene. Il trattato del 1257 conteneva anche un'amnistia per il siciliano Uberto Fallamonaca che, pur non essendo direttamente coinvolto nella questione maltese, presumibilmente era stato alleato dei Genovesi; tutti i suoi beni dovevano essergli restituiti ma i suoi figli avrebbero dovuto essere tenuti come ostaggi finchè egli

---

[9] I resoconti ufficiali danno poche notizie sugli avvenimenti della Sicilia: K. HAMPE, *Geschichte Konradins von Hohenstaufen* (Innsbruck, 1894), ristampata con una *Historische und Bibliographische Nachträge* da H. KAMPF (Leipzig, 1940); E. JORDAN, *Les Origines de la Domination Angevine en Italie*, 2 voll. (Parigi, 1909); G. CARO, *Genova e la Supremazia sul Mediterraneo: 1257-1311*, 2 voll. (ed. riv.: Genova, 1974-1975). Sembra che Siracusa non fosse coinvolta nella ribellione contro Manfredi, però i documenti relativi alla sua storia in questo periodo sono molto scarsi: G. FASOLI, «Incognite della storia cittadina di Siracusa tra l'età di Normanni e quella degli Aragonesi», *Archivio Storico Siracusano*, I (1955), 13.

[10] Presumibilmente si riferisce al *castrum maris*, ma possibilmente al *castrum* della città di Mdina: vedi LUTTRELL, in *Medieval Malta*, 58-59.

non avesse presentato il rendiconto della sua amministrazione nell' importante carica reale di *Secreto* di Sicilia. Fallamonaca era un saraceno convertito che aveva assunto un nome genovese, ed era anche stato *gaito* di Palermo[11]. Il trattato stabiliva anche che a Nicoloso dovessero essere restituiti i suoi privilegi, le giurisdizioni e gli introiti maltesi, benchè il controllo dei castelli maltesi dovesse essere nelle mani di Manfredi; come alternativa, Nicoloso avrebbe potuto scegliere terre e proventi di equivalente valore in Sicilia, Calabria o Puglia.

> super facto uero malte renouamus et confirmamus nicoloso priuilegia indulta patri suo. ob amorem comunis ianue concedentes sibi insulam malte cum omnibus pertinenciis iurisdictionibus et iuribus suis. uidelicet gaudii et comini. ita tamen quod custodia castrorum sit in manibus nostris quamdiu nobis placuerit. saluo quod si nicolosus eligeret magis et eligere inde uellet excambium in sicilia uel calabria uel apulia. concedemus eidem ipsum excambium sicut per inquisicionem inuentum fuerit et constiterit de ualore ipsarum insularum. omnibus etiam illis qui sunt cum nicoloso in malta remittimus omnem offensam et culpam recipientes eos in gratia nostra et restituentes eis possessiones eorum sique propter hoc ablate fuerunt. et si aliqui capti sunt liberamus eos siue sint de regno siue de extra regnum nisi ex alia causa fuerint proditores. promittentes quod pro eo quod fuerint cum nicoloso in castro et insula malte ipsos non grauabimus ulterius nec grauari ab aliquo paciemur et specialiter robertum buccanigram et filios eius. leonem de creta. balduinum de castello et filios eius bartholomeum de monte et uitalem de gaieta imo qui uoluerint in regno morari secure morentur et qui uolerint exire secure exeant. liberamus etiam ubertum falamonacam et familiam eius totam. restituentes eis domos et possessiones suas datis nobis duobus filiis suis obsidibus donec posuerit rationem de officiis que exercuit de quibus rationem nen posuit. nec habet ydoneam apodixiam[12].

[11] I documenti del 1257 e del 1259 forniscono gli unici riferimenti alla rivolta di Fallamonaca. Egli era *Secreto* dal 1240 ca. fino a qualche tempo intorno al 1245; fu mandato in missione in Morocco nel 1241; firmò un documento in arabo a Palermo nel 1266, ed era ancora vivo nel 1274: COLLURA, 120-128, 133-137; A. MONGITORE, *Bullae, Privilegia, et Instrumenta Panormitanae Metropolitanae Ecclesiae...* (Palermo, 1734), 128-137; M. AMARI, *Storia dei Musulmani di Sicilia,* III (ed. riv.: Catania, 1939), 627-628, 634. H. BRESC, «Società e politica in Sicilia nei secoli XIV e XV», *Archivio Storico per la Sicilia Orientale,* LXX (1974), 273, scrive, senza riferimenti, che Fallamonaca «conduce la Sicilia in un'avventura; con l'aiuto dei genovesi, suoi amici..., conduce la Sicilia in un rivolta immane che porterà alla distruzione di quei pochi musulmani che rimanevano in Sicilia i musulmani maltesi e all'espulsione dei musulmani a Malta». Tuttavia questo non risulta dai documenti del 1257 e 1259.

[12] Sui testi del 1257 e del 1259, e i relativi manoscritti, vedi appendice *infra,* ...—...

Questo trattato venne confermato ancora una volta ad Acerra nel luglio 1261, l'anno in cui i Genovesi riuscirono a imporre il proprio candidato come Imperatore di Costantinopoli. In questa nuova redazione il brano riguardante Malta così diceva:

> quod pro eo quod fuerunt cum nicoloso in castro et insula malte ipsos non grauabimus ulterius. nec grauari ab aliquo paciemur et specialiter robertum buccanigram et filios eius o leonem de creta. balduinum de castella et filios eius. bartholomeum de monte et uitalem de gaieta.

Il testo del 1261 ripeteva che chi avesse voluto lasciare il regno o rimanervi avrebbe potuto fare come voleva, ma non c'era cenno alcuno di Nicoloso o di Fallamonaca [13]. I testi del 1257 e del 1259 non parlavano di Nicoloso come *comes*, e non chiarivano quali diritti egli avrebbe potuto rivendicare su Malta. Presumibilmente egli, in teoria, avrebbe tenuto l'isola come feudo godendo di minori giurisdizioni e introiti, essendo in una posizione subordinata al castellano reale e senza il controllo dei castelli. Tale probabilmente era stata la posizione di suo padre dopo il 1222 [14].

Alla luce di questi documenti, Valentini ritiene che nell'isola ci fosse un partito "capeggiato dal clero e dai nobili" il quale, scontento delle estorsioni pecuniarie di Federico II e delle sue lotte contro il papa, si ribellò all'"indomani" della morte dell'Imperatore. Questo partito era appoggiato dai Genovesi che ancora una volta cercavano di assicurarsi la base di Malta, sostenendo in questa occasione le rivendicazioni del Conte Nicoloso; essi volevano anche rafforzare la loro posizione commerciale in Sicilia. Valentini suppone che nel nel 1257, anno in cui Manfredi aveva il pieno controllo sulla Sicilia, i presunti ribelli maltesi e i loro capi genovesi detenessero ancora il "castello a mare". Manfredi e i Genovesi avevano entrambi buoni motivi per raggiungere un accordo nel 1257 quando Manfredi perdonò i ribelli e riconobbe i diritti di Nicoloso. Valentini sostiene che il rinnovo dell'accordo nel 1261 rivela che Malta era ancora in rivolta contro Manfredi, e che c'era "un governo anarchico" nell' isola sostenuto da alcune città siciliane che a loro volta erano appoggiate da Genova o almeno da una fazione genovese alleata del papa e di Carlo d'Angiò, nemico di Manfredi. Valentini parla di "esilii e confische e tutte le esplosioni d'odio che accompagnano certe crisi di regime"; di un nuovo scoppio di disordini a Malta nel 1263 quando il papa Urbano IV si schierò decisamente contro

---

13 Testo in appendice *infra*, ...—...

14 Vedi LUTTRELL, in *Medieval Malta*, 36; ABULAFIA, *ibid.*, 121-124.

Manfredi; di una minoranza del clero maltese che si oppose a Manfredi; di "indipendenze municipali"; di esuli ansiosi di riavere i loro uffici e le loro proprietà maltesi; e di agitazioni che continuarono fino alla scomparsa di Manfredi nel 1266 [15].

L'interpretazione di Valentini, come egli stesso riconobbe, è largamente basata su ipotesi. Uberto Fallamonaca e alcuni individui genovesi che erano col Conte Nicoloso nel *castrum* o altrove nell' isola di Malta avevano certamente fatto qualcosa che richiedeva perdono. Tuttavia non c'è alcuna testimonianza esplicita che riguardi il clero, una nobiltà o un municipio durante questo periodo. Nè ci sono chiare indicazioni che ci fossero ribelli o esuli maltesi, nè che ci fosse un governo autarchico, nè un appoggio siciliano ad esso, nè agitazioni a Malta immediatamente dopo il 1250, o dopo il 1257 o più tardi. È vero che Manfredi aveva bisogno di un'alleanza con i Genovesi, durante e dopo il 1257 al fine di impedire che i candidati inglesi del papa al trono della Sicilia si assicurassero l'uso della flotta genovese, e più tardi per bloccare Carlo d'Angiò la cui base principale era in Provenza; d'altra parte, ai Genovesi occorreva l'aiuto di Manfredi per controbilanciare l'alleanza fra Pisa e Venezia e per proteggere il loro commercio in Sicilia [16]. La politica genovese era certamente molto condizionata dalle fazioni e dalle famiglie, e singoli individui e gruppi potevano perseguire interessi privati che, a un certo momento, potevano persino essere in contrasto con la politica ufficiale del comune, che del resto seguiva una linea politica così mutevole da non poter essere neppure conosciuta dai singoli cittadini in località così remote come Malta. Fino adesso non è stato dimostrato che alcuno dei Genovesi a Malta appartenesse ai Grimaldi o ai Fieschi o a qualsiasi altra fazione. Essi potevano pretendere l'appoggio ufficiale del goberno, e chiaramente lo ottenero dall'accordo del 1257; è anche possibile che le loro immediate motivazioni locali fossero più personali e piratesche che di ispirazione politica [17]. In prospettiva, Genova aveva certamente un costante interesse su Malta come utile centro per le sue attività commerciali e navali, per le sue operazioni nel Mediterraneo centrale, come tappa verso il Levante, e come base dalla quale sferrare gli attacchi contro i suoi rivali veneziani [18].

[15] VALENTINI, 226-228.

[16] JORDAN, I, 142, 183-185; II, 560-562 *et passim*.

[17] ABULAFIA, in *Medieval Malta*, approfondisce questi aspetti generici. Sulle famiglie genovesi, vedi J. HEERS, *Le Clan familial au Moyen Âge* (Parigi, 1974).

[18] Vedi A. LUTTRELL, «Venetians at Medieval Malta», *Melita Historica*, III, no. 1 (1960), 74-75.

Cogliendo l'occasione offerta dal crollo dell'autorità Hohenstaufen in Sicilia, i Genovesi cercarono ancora una volta di fare di Malta una base navale. Di quei Genovesi citati nel 1257 come presenti a Malta, Roberto Buccagnegra proveniva da una nota famiglia che aveva molti interessi nel Mediterraneo; un altro dei membri della famiglia, Guglielmo, era stato eletto *capitano del popolo* in una sommosa popolare del febbraio 1257 e fu responsabile del trattato con Manfredi [19]. Balduino de Castello dev'essere stato un membro della potente famiglia De Castro, a cui apparteneva anche Enrico "Pescatore" [20]. Alcuni dei Genovesi citati nel trattato erano accompagnati dai figli, un fatto che potrebbe suggerire che si sentivano sicuri a Malta. Il rinnovo delle rivendicazioni a favore di Nicoloso avrebbe potuto rafforzare la posizione dei Genovesi a Malta, benchè, di fatto, gli fosse anche concesso di scambiare i suoi introiti locali con altri altrove. È possibile che Nicoloso avesse già tentato di realizzare tali rivendicazioni perchè sembra che egli si fosse assicurato la conferma dei suoi poteri sull'isola di Malta e sui suoi possedimenti in Sicilia da Innocenzo IV, un genovese che è stato papa dal 1243 fino al dicembre 1254 [21]. Però il trattato non gli procurò vantaggi duraturi perchè lo stesso Nicoloso nel 1270 e nel 1271 rivendicava vigneti e case in Sicilia che gli erano stati tolti, a suo dire ingiustamente, da Manfredi [22]. La ripetizione delle clausole su Malta nel documento del 1259 e ancora, benchè solo in

---

[19] R. LOPEZ, «Guglielmo Boccanegra», *Dizionario biografico degli Italiani*, XI (Roma, 1969), 31-35.

[20] Sulla famiglia Castello, vedi ABULAFIA, in *Medieval Malta*, 111 *et passim*.

[21] Nel 1290 un certo Andriolo avanzò pretese sulla Contea di Malta e anche su alcuni possedimenti in Sicilia, compresa la *domus Guillelmi Crassi quam habuit in Messana, que fundicus dicebatur*, che una volta era appartenuta a Guglielmo Grasso, suocero di Enrico, padre di Nicoloso, con la motivazione che tutti questi possedimenti provenivano *ex collationibus et confirmationibus* dell'Imperatore Enrico VI, di sua moglie Costanza, di Federico II e di Innocenzo IV: testo in V. LAURENZA, «Malta nei documenti angioini del R. Archivio di Napoli», *Archivio Storico di Malta*, V (1934), 168-169. Sulla famiglia Grasso, vedi ABULAFIA, in *Medieval Malta*, 108-111; sul palazzo in Messina, vedi ABULAFIA, *Two Italies*, 207.

[22] I testi del 20 marzo 1270 e del 7 febbraio 1271 sono riportati in LAURENZA, 106, 1112-113 = *I Registri della Cancelleria Angioina ricostruiti*, ed. R. FILANGIERI, *et al.* (Napoli, 1950), III, 203; VI, 174. R. VALENTINI, in *Archivio Storico di Malta*, VI (1935), 14-15, interpretava il documento del 7 febbraio 1271 nel senso che Nicoloso non solo fosse andato a Malta ma avesse ricevuto la Contea e che fosse poi stato mandato in esilio («In questo tempo Malta sottostette a un feudatario-castellano in quanto non è presumibile che Manfredi cedesse a Nicoloso il comando militare dell'isola. Comunque, Nicoloso fue presto spogliato di tutto e di nuovo mandato in esilio»). Il documento però diceva che Manfredi si era impadronito dei possedimenti di Nicoloso in Sicilia, e non a Malta.

parte, in quello del 1261 può indicare, come suggerisce Valentini, che la resistenza dei Genovesi a Manfredi non fosse ancora cessata a Malta. Queste clausole potrebbero essere state conservate per difendere quei Genovesi da eventuali azioni legali. Molto probabilmente nessuno in Italia aveva nozione di quello che effettivamente stava accadendo a Malta[23].

L'importanza per Genova di una sua presenza a Malta fu ampiamente dimostrata nel 1264 quando ventun galere furono messe in mare al comando di Simone Grillo contro i Veneziani, che a loro volta ne armarono cinquanta. Grillo si diresse verso la Sicilia diffondendo poi la notizia che stava per andare verso la Siria. Invece egli andò a Malta dove probabilmente era sicuro di trovare buona accoglienza —*applicuerunt ad insulam Malte; ibique steterunt per plures dies*[24]; le galere veneziane inseguirono i Genovesi che credevano diretti verso est, e Grillo riuscì a piombare sulla indifesa flotta mercantile veneziana vicino a Durazzo nell'Adriatico catturando ventidue *taride* veneziane[25].

Nel frattempo il papato aveva contrastato il crescente predominio di Manfredi, rivolgendosi a Carlo d'Angiò e ai Francesi che sconfissero e uccisero Manfredi presso Benevento il 26 febbraio 1266. Le pretes degli Hohenstaufen furono allora riprese dal giovane Corradino che iniziò a preparare una spedizione in Italia dalla Germania. Il napoletano Corrado Capece, che era stato vicario di Manfredi in Sicilia, si recò a Pisa e poi a Tunisi dove si trovava riunito un gruppo di sostenitori, sia cristiani che musulmani, degli Hohenstaufen; poi nell'agosto 1267, toccando Pantelleria, egli sbarcò in Sicilia dove provocò una rivolta contro gli Angioini[26]. A Pisa il 14 giugno 1268, Corradino concluse un trattato con i suoi principali sostenitori italiani, i Pisani, secondo il quale essi avreb-

---

[23] Per quanto riguarda le discordanze nei testi superstiti, è difficile sapere se quelli del 1259 e del 1261 fossero semplicemente copiati da quello del 1257 o se invece le varianti avessero una motivazione politica.

[24] *Annali Genovesi*, IV (1926), 55.

[25] Oltre gli *Annali Genovesi*, IV, 55, vedi anche *Les Gestes des Chiprois*, ed. G. Raynaud (Ginevra, 1887), 169. Una versione veneziana della vicenda, che non fa cenno a Malta ma parla soltanto di *un port en la Sesile*, è riportata da Martin da Canal, *Les Estoires de Venise*, ed. A. Limentani (Firenze, 1973), 200-205. Le statistiche varianti delle cronache sono esaminate da Caro, I, 161-164. Valentini, 228, n. 108, localizza erroneamente questo attacco «nelle acque di Malta».

[26] P. Palumbo, «Corrado Capece e la Resistenza antiangioina in Sicilia», *Archivio Storico Pugliese*, X (1957); H. Kamp, «Corrado Capece», *Dizionario biografico degli Italiani*, XVIII (Roma, 1975), 411-415.

bero ricevuto, in cambio del loro aiuto, molte località nell'Italia meridionale e in Sicilia, Malta compresa [27]. Pisa aveva continuato ad opporre resistenza contro Carlo d'Angiò, però il trattato rimase lettera morta perchè Corradino fu sconfitto a Tagliacozzo nell' agosto 1268 e fu giustiziato poco dopo, il 29 ottobre. Quello che avvene a Malta dopo il febbraio 1266 è ancora una volta ignoto. Dopo la morte di Corradino, la Sicilia continuò, sotto il comando di Corrado Capece, ad opporre resistenza agli Angioini finchè Corrado non si arrese nell'aprile o nel maggio 1270. Le isole maltesi probabilmente caddero sotto il dominio angioino in quell'epoca, perchè i più antichi documenti angioini che riguardano Malta, risalenti al 3 e 5 agosto 1270, parlavano della sostituzione del castellano di Malta, Ugo de Brusone [28]. Le polemiche col papa sulla nomina del vescovo e sulla raccolta delle tasse ecclesiastiche riflettono presumibilmente una situazione politica instabile a Malta [29]. Il titolo di Conte di Malta fu riconosciuto a Nicoloso da Carlo d'Angiò, il quale ordinò ai suoi ufficiali di restituirgli i possedimenti siciliani sequestratigli da Manfredi [30].

Dopo un periodo di relativa anarchia durante il quale i Genovesi avevano tratto vantaggio da quell'assenza di potere, un forte governo Siciliano fu ristabilito a Malta sotto gli Angioini. Cosa sia successo dell'economia e del governo maltese in questo periodo di anarchia non si sa, nè si puo seguire il processo di insediamento e latinizzazione [31]. Malta era stata di nuovo usata come centro di resistenza contro il governo in Sicilia; questa situazione forse si sarebbe ripetuta alla vigilia dei Vespri Siciliani, quando l'isola di Malta —almeno secondo la testimonianza di un cronista— fu teatro dei complotti fra Giovanni da Procida e certi baroni siciliani dissidenti, complotti che preludevano all'avvento nel 1282 del potere catalano-aragonese in Sicilia con il re Pietro III, il marito di

---

[27] Testo in J. LAMI, *Deliciae Eruditorum seu Veterum 'Anektodon' Opusculorum Collectanea*, III (Firenze, 1737), 269-283 = F. DAL BORGO, *Raccolta di Scelti Diplomi Pisani* (Pisa, 1765), 201-210. VALENTINI, 229, erroneamente riporta la data del 1267.

[28] Testi in LAURENZA, 106-108 = *Registri Ricostruiti*, IV, 168-169.

[29] Informazioni più dettagliate in LUTTRELL, in *Medieval Malta*, 61.

[30] Testi citati *supra...*, n. 22. *Registri Ricostruiti*, IV, 110, riporta una breve nota tolta dal Registro Angioino «1269S, f. 158t» che leggeva *Nicolaus, Comes Maltensis*. Si può ritenere che Nicoloso fosse gia morto il 16 giugno 1290: testo in LAURENZA, 168-169.

[31] VALENTINI, 229-230, parla di un governo comunale, dell'uso del latino e dell'italiano, e di un «benessere economico» dovuto ai Genovesi, ma non c'è alcuna prova di tutto questo.

Costanza, figlia di Manfredi[32]. L'interesse di Genova per Malta risaliva al dodicesimo secolo[33], e continuò per tutto il periodo degli Angioini e degli Aragonesi. Un trattato del 12 agosto 1269 concedeva ai Genovesi un commercio senza limitazioni nei paesi al di là di Malta[34], ma nel 1272 Genova litigò con Carlo I che successivamente fece arrestare un certo numero di mercanti e bloccare delle navi genovesi a Malta; durante le ostilità susseguenti i Genovesi saccheggiarono Gozo —*Gaudium depopulavit*[35]. Dopo che Malta passò sotto il dominio aragonese, un certo Andriolo, apparentemente discendente di Guglielmo Grasso e di Enrico "Pescatore", venne riconosciuto Conte di Malta da Carlo II d'Angiò il 16 giugno 1291[36], ma l'anno seguente Andriolo si schierò con gli Aragonesi[37]. Ciò nonostante i Genovesi continuarono ad avanzare le loro pretese su Malta, alcune delle quali furono loro riconosciute dal re Federico di Sicilia nel 1300[38]. Non si può valutare con certezza quanto grande fosse l'influenza genovese su Malta durante il tredicesimo secolo[39].

---

[32] Su questo aspetto piuttosto oscuro, vedi LUTTRELL, in *Medieval Malta,* 43 n. 237.

[33] ABULAFIA, in *Medieval Malta,* 106-109.

[34] «...*quod Ianuenses possint ultra Maltam versus Orientem et in Yspaniam et Garbo atque Barbariam ... navigare libere in ligno Ianuensium uel Pisanorum vel aliis:* testo in *Annali Genovesi.* 115/122, n. 3. *Registri Ricostruiti,* IV, 270, riporta un frammento del 5 agosto 1270 ca. dal Registro Angioino 6, f. 98: *Francisco Malette de Janua, provisio quod liceat ei soluere unc. CXL Hugoni de Brusa, Castellano Malte.*

[35] Testi in *Annali Genovesi,* IV, 149-150. 168; LAURENZA, 119-124, 129-130 = *Registri Ricostruiti,* X, 12-14, 227-228; vedi *ibid.,* XIII, 109-110, e CARO, I, 201 e n. 23, 345 e n. 24.

[36] Testo in LAURENZA, 168-169.

[37] A. LUTTRELL, «The House of Aragon and Malta: 1282-1412», *Journal of the Faculty of Arts: Royal Malta University,* IV, stet no. 2 (1970), 159, però l'identificazione di Andriolo come il genovese Andreolo de Mari ivi segnalata è dubbia. C'erano parecchi Genovesi con questo nome, tra i quali Andreolus Ansaldi de Mari che era Ammiraglio di Federico II al quale potevano essere stati concessi diritti sull'isola di Malta, come già era avvenuto con altri ammiragli genovesi prima di lui; e un altro Andreolo de Mari che viveva nel 1322: GIORGIO STELLA, *Annales Genuenses,* ed. G. BALBI, in *Rerum Italicarum Scriptores,* XVII pt. 2 (ed. riv.: Bologna, 1975), 42, 61, 102-103. Il problema non è ancora risolto.

[38] *Item offerunt castrum malte dicto comuni ianue siue illis ianuensibus ad quos spectat ipsum castrum. ita quod comune ipsum siue illi ianuenses ad quos spectat castrum illud faciant ipsum custodiri per hominem fidedignum qui diligat partem et statum presentem. qui teneatur eidem domino regi sicut alii barones sibi tenentur in homagio et in fide. secundum consuetudinem regni sicilie.* Testo in *Liber Iurium Reipublicae Genuensis,* II (Torino, 1857), 415-418.

[39] Una presenza genovese a Malta potrebbe aver avuto influenza sulla toponomastica locale; ad esempio, i Conti Enrico e Nicoloso avrebbero potuto detenere

La politica genovese a Malta aveva imposto l'isola all'attenzione delle potenze del Mediterraneo. Il modo con cui i Genovesi hanno utilizzato l'isola piuttosto come base delle loro operazioni che come colonia nella quale insediarsi come dominatori, può in qualche strano modo aver aiutato la sopravvivenza di vari aspetti della vita indigena, fra essi compresa la lingua semitica maltese.

## APPENDICE

I trattati del 1257, 1259 e 1261 sono conservati nella collezione ufficiale, il *Liber Iurium*, da cui furono editi in *Liber Iurium Reipublicae Genuensis*, I (Torino, 1854); e questo è il testo a cui ci si riferisce sopra. Il manoscritto originale di questa collezione, il *Vetustior*, fu portato a Parigi nel 1808, così che i testi editi nel 1854 dovevano essere ricavati da esemplari posteriori che sono rimasti a Genova. Successivamente il *Vetustior* è ritornato a Genova, all'Archivio di Stato, però dei documenti studiati qui non è stata fatta ancora una nuova edizione. I testi editi nel 1854 spesso sono insoddisfacenti, specialmente per quanto riguarda le formule delle convalidazioni notarili. Vedi *Codice Diplomatico della Repubblica di Genova*, I, ed. C. IMPERIALE DI SANT'ANGELO (Roma, 1936), pp. vii-xxvi; N. CALVINI, "Il ritorno dei codici parigini, 2: Del presunto smarrimento dei *Libri Iurium* et de quibusdam aliis, "*Bolletino Ligustico*, V (1953). Altri testi con varianti si trovano a Palermo, Napoli e Cagliari; notizie preliminari in J. BÖHMER, *Regesta Imperii*, V pt. 1 (Innsbruck, 1881-1882), no. 4664, 4692, 4732, ed in G. LA MANTIA, *Codice Diplomatico dei Re Aragonesi di Sicilia*, I (Palermo, 1917), 139, 143, 145-147.

I. Il testo del luglio 1257 dato *in campis prope gualdum melfie:*

A: Inserito nel documento del 17 settembre 1259 (vedi *infra*, III); edito in *Liber Iurium*, I, 1293-1296 (da cui e tratto il passo di *supra*,...).

B: Gran Archivio di Napoli, "ex arca H, maz. 19, n. 12" (distrutto nel 1943); edito in B. CAPASSO, *Historia Diplomatica Regni Siciliae inde ab anno 1250 ad annum 1266* (Napoli, 1874), 130-133. Questo esemplare non è identico ad A (citato *supra*, ...) in quanto non menziona i nomi dei Genovesi a Malta o quello di Fallamonaca:

Rahal Arrig e Rahal *nicolosu*, documentati rispettivamente agli anni 1506 e 1365: G. WETTINGER, «The Lost Villages and Hamlets of Malta», in *Medieval Malta*, 203, 206, 210.

Super facto vero Malte renovat et confirmat Nicoloso privilegia indulta patri suo ac concedit insuper eidem insulam Malte cum omnibus pertinentiis suis, ita vero quod custodia castrorum sit in manibus suis quamdiu sibi placuerit; salvo quod si Nicolosus vellet potius excambium; omnibus vero illis qui cum Nicoloso in Malta erant et quibusdam aliis sive de regno sive non omnem offensam et culpam remittit[40].

II. Il testo del 22 marzo 1259 dato a Melfi:

A: Cagliari, Biblioteca Universitaria, Ms., forse della seconda metà del sec. XIV, intitolato "Pandetta delle gabelle e dei diritti della Curia della Città di Messina"; edito in Q. SELLA, *Pandetta delle Gabelle e dei Diritti della Curia di Messina* (Torino, 1870), 89-95. "Datum Melfis xxij° marcij ij$^{e}$ indic' nis". L'edizione segnala un numero di varianti dal testo del luglio 1257, come *Leonem de Aurea* (per *Creta*), e *Sillimona* (per *fallamonacam*). Una nota marginale precisava: *Facta est collatio de privilegio ipso cum registro pandecte archiui et concordat.*

B: Palermo, Biblioteca Comunale, Ms. Qq H 124, f. 145 sqq. (copia del 1492); edito in D. ORLANDO, *Un Codice di Leggi e Diplomi Siciliani del Medio Evo* (Palermo, 1857), 102-105. "Datum Malte [*sic*], XXII martii, II indictionis MCCLIV [*sic*]". Questo testo è molto diverso da IA e da IB, ed è molto più breve. Secondo LA MANTIA, I, 139, deriva da un breve sunto del 19 dicembre 1284, in Palermo, Archivio di Stato, Protonotaro del Regno 5, f. 227 sqq., e pure in Palermo, Archivio di Stato, Cancelleria 2, f. 37 sqq.

Super facto Malte, ad honorem comunis Janue, Renovamus, et Confirmamus Nicolosio privilegia indulta patri suo, Concedentes sibi insulam Malte cum omnibus juribus, pertinentiis, et jurisdictionibus suis, videlicet Gaudisii et Comini, ita quod custodia castrorum sit in manibus nostris, cum expensis nostris, quandiu nobis placuerit, et salvo quod si Nicolosius ipse eligeret excambium. Omnibus etiam illis qui sunt Nicolosio in Malta remittemus omnem offensam et culpam, recipientes eos in gratiam et cetera que sequuntur de lodandis et restituendis bonis eorum.

C: Palermo, Biblioteca Comunale, Ms. Qq E 28, intitolato "Quaternus continens gabellas et iura Curie felicis urbis Panor-

[40] Il testo di CAPASSO non è identico ad I A, anche se CAPASSO dice che lo è. Deriva, apparentemente, da «SARNO, *Esame di tre pergamene*, 31», lavoro che non è stato possibile controllare; sembra che il testo fosse datato il 7 agosto.

mi ad officia Secretiae et Procurationis spectantia", f. 80 sqq.: testo del sec xv che deriva dallo stesso sunto del 19 dicembre 1284, secondo LA MANTIA, I, 139.

D: Palermo, Archivio di Stato, Ms. intitolato "Liber Pandectarum ord. et const. Secretiae", f. 85-90: testo del 1594 che deriva dallo stesso sunto del 19 dicembre 1284, secondo LA MANTIA, I, 139.

III. Il testo del 17 settembre 1259 ["Indictione prima": *sic*], la ratifica del testo del 1257 fatta a Genova da Rufino Caballacio, podestà, e da Guglielmo Boccanegra, capitano del popolo:

A: Copiato a Genova l'8 novembre 1267 *de registro comunis ianue;* edito in *Liber Iurium,* I, 1293-1296. La datazione al 1258 data in BÖHMER, no. 4692, viene corretta in CARO, I, 100 n. 3.

IV. Il testo del giugno 1261, Acerra:

A: Genova, Archivio di Stato, B. 5/38, copia autenticata del 12 dicembre 1271 su pergamena; citata in P. LISCIANDRELLI, *Trattati e negoziazioni politiche della Repubblica di Genova (958-1797): Regesti* (Genova, 1960), 74-75.

B: Genova, Archivio di Stato, B. 5/38, copia autenticata del 10 febbraio 1562: citata *ibid.,* 74-75.

C: Genova, Archivio di Stato, B. 5/38, copia autenticata del 10 dicembre 1565 ricavata da altra copia autenticata del 16 gennaio 1562: citata *ibid.,* 74-75.

D: Altro esempio copiato nel *Liber Iurium* dalla copia A fatta a Genova *a registro comunis ianue* il 12 dicembre 1271; edito in *Liber Iurium,* I, 1346-1349.

E: Palermo, Biblioteca Comunale, Ms. QQ H 124, f. 145 sqq. (copia del 1492); edito in ORLANDO, 115-118. Il testo offre varianti minori rispetto a D, e riporta il mese di luglio come data; contiene passi mancanti in D; e, mentre riporta tutta la seconda parte delle clausole riguardanti Malta *Ceterum omnibus qui cum Nicoloso... secure exeant,* tralascia la prima parte *super facto uero... de ualore ipsarum insularum,* e anche la parte *liberamus etiam ubertum fala-*

*monacam... ydoneam apodixiam,* forse perche questi brani concernenti Nicoloso e Fallamonaca non avevano più nessuna importanza al tempo della copia, mentre il brano riguardante gli altri Genovesi a Malta fu incluso. Una variante di E, forse presa da Palermo, Biblioteca Comunale, Ms. Qq G 12, sembra che sia quella edita in R. GREGORIO, *Considerazioni sopra la storia di Sicilia,* II (nuova ed. Palermo, 1972), 120/2 n. 1.[41]

[41] Questo testo presumibilmente deriva dalle copie del 1284 e del 1285 citate *supra...* Altre copie derivanti da questi documenti sembra che siano in Palermo, Achivio di Stato, Cancelleria Reg. «1375», f. 383v sqq. (citato in CAPASSO, 166, n. 1) e Reg. «1392», f. 183 sqq. (citato in BÖHMER, no. 4372); per ragioni tecniche non è stato possibile controllare tutti i documenti palermitani.

XI

# CHRISTIAN SLAVES AT MALTA: 1271

Given the dearth of documents concerning Maltese history before the late fourteenth century, the chance survival of even a single text is of some importance, especially when it was drawn up on the island itself.[1] It is true that for a period following 1268 documents concerning Malta were entered in the registers of the Angevin kings of Sicily, and that some of these do survive, mostly in copies, and still await systematic study.[2] The manumission of 1271 published below was copied into a Pisan notarial formulary of which 24 paper folios survive, one document at folio 23 bearing the date 1306; the formulary inexplicably reached the archive of the Catalan Hospitallers now at Barcelona. The information contained seems reliable, though the formulae and phrases used at Malta in 1271 were, not unnaturally, unlike those found in a Pisan manumission of 1172 which are said to have come to constitute the standard Pisan form.[3] Why a Pisan formulary appartently compiled after 1306 should have made use of a Sicilianate text of 1271 from Malta in order to illustrate the correct form for freeing Christian slaves is unclear; the text could have been taken to Pisa by a notary, possibly the Angelo of the text, who had worked in Sicily. The fact is the more surprising as the manumission of 1271 follows immediately, and on the same folio, a brief and common form of manumission dated at Pisa and freeing another Christian girl apparently from Sardinia, Maria *de tali loco Judicatus arboree.*

The situation on Malta was doubtless unsettled following the Angevin occupation of 1268 and the continuing rivalries of Genoese and Pisans.[4] The new administration was working regularly by 1271,[5] though there were always dangers. In 1270 Guido De *Mohac* or Modica in southern Sicily complained that he and his sons, daughters and *familia* had been imprisoned after leaving Siracusa and being wrecked by a storm on the islet of Comino between Malta and Gozo, and on 18 December 1270 the King of Sicily ordered the Castellan of Malta and Gozo to release them.[6] In 1275 Raymundus, *civis* of Malta and sailor or *marenarius*, was captured by Genoese pirates while sailing from Africa on the *barca* of Bonsignori de Gaudisana of Malta.[7] It was on 4 March 1271 that Guido de *Moghio* freed a Christian woman named Margarita and her three daughters, Thomasina, Jacobina and Jannicta;

1. Summary of the sources in A. Luttrell, "Approaches to Medieval Malta," in *Medieval Malta: Studies on Malta before the Knights*, ed. A. Luttrell (London, 1975), 5-8. Charles Verlinden and Marco Tangherone most kindly supplied advice and information on particular points and problems.

2. *I Registri della Cancelleria Angioina ricostruiti*, ed. R. Filangieri *et al.* i - (Naples, 1950-).

3. Text and comment in C. Verlinden, *L'Esclavage dans l'Europe médiévale*, ii (Ghent, 1977), 396-397.

4. A. Luttrell, "Malta e Gozo: 1222-1268". *X Congreso de Historia de la Corona de Aragón: Comunicaciones 1 y 2* (Zaragosa, 1980); *idem*, "Malta e Gozo: 1268-1282". *XI Congresso di Storia della Corona d'Aragona*, iii (Palermo, 1984).

5. *Registri*, vi. 165-166, 193, 201, 213, 223-226.

6. *Ibid.*, vi. 187.

7. *Ibid.*, xiii. 109-110.

whether they had been imported from Africa, were baptized indigenous inhabitants of Malta, or came from elsewhere was not made clear. *Moghio* was not a name found in thirteenth-century Pisa[8] and was conceivably an error for Mohac, in which case Guido de Mohac had been freed by 4 March 1271 and was manumitting members of his *familia* who had been imprisoned with him; that is merely a hypothesis. The slaves involved were clearly in a different situation from that of the white girl from Malta, named Maimuna and presumably an indigenous islander, who was sold by a Florentine to a Genoese, presumably at Genoa, in 1246;[9] or from that of other Maltese slaves being sold by Sicilians or Florentines,[10] or from that of Catherina *Romannica slava* or *sclava Romanitica*, presumably a Greek girl, who had been freed on Malta in or just before 1324 by the late Basilio Limera, *civis* of Malta.[11]

The manumission was drawn up in proper legal form, using a Sicilian system of dating clauses, by Daniele de Danielis, public notary of Malta and Gozo, before Roberto de Ebulo or Eboli and Stefano de Matho judges of the *castrum* at Malta, and in the presence of witnesses whose names were not copied into the Pisan formulary. Daniele de Danielis is thus the earliest Latin notary recorded as acting on Malta. An Antonius de Cappillerio was a public notary there in 1274 and 1277,[12] while no less than four notaries appeared in an act drawn up on Gozo in 1299; one of them, Teninus de Daniele, may have been a kinsman of the Daniele de Danielis of 1271.[13] Thus in 1271, three years after an Angevin administration had been installed, the machinery of notary and *judices* was functioning on Malta.

Text from a Pisan notarial formulary in Barcelona, Arxiu de la Corona d'Aragó, Gran Priorato de Catalunya, Armari 24 Legajo 6, f. 2-2v (4 March 1271)

*Carta Liberationis Ancille, Angeli notarij camerari*[14]

In nomine domini Amen Anno dominice jncarnationis m̊cc̊lx̊ [15] quarta [16] die mensis marcij quartadecime jndictionis Regnante domino Serenissimo rege karolo dei gratia jnclito Rege Sicilie. ducatus apulee. Principatus Capue, Vrbis Senatorie,[17]

8. Information from Marco Tangherone.

9. Text in R. Lopez, "La vendita d'una schiava di Malta a Genova nel 1248". *Archivio Storico di Malta*, vii (1936), 391.

10. Indirect references in M. Balard, "Remarques sur les Esclaves à Gênes dans la seconde moitié du XIIIe siècles," *Mélanges d'Archéologie et d'Histoire*, lxxx (1968), 668-669. For Tuscan merchants dealing in girl slaves from Gozo, see R. Davidsohn, *Storia di Firenze*, vii (trans: Florence, 1977), 633-634.

11. Text in H. Bresc, "Malta dopo il Vespro Siciliano". *Melita Historica*, vi no. 3 (1974), 320-321.

12. A. Luttrell, "The Sale of Gumerin on Malta: 1318". *Estudios Históricos y Documentos de los Archivo de Protocolos*, vi (1978), 167.

13. Text in Bresc, 317-320.

14. MS: *camerini*?

15. Read *m̊cc̊lxx̊*, since Indiction XIV and regnal year six give 1270 of the Incarnation, ie. 1271.

16. The scribe wrote *iiij* and then crossed it out.

17. Sic.

Andegauie prouincie, et fulch[uerii] [18] comite Romani jmperij in tuscia per sanctam Romanam ecclesiam vicario generali. Anno vj sexto [19] Regni eius feliciter Amen. A primordio conditionis humane liberum hominem natura produxit, sed humana necessitate postmodum exigente, bellica inter gentes est orta calamitas. exqua de jure gentium introducta est seruitus. per quam quod natura contulit, jniquitas bellorum obduxit. Jdeoque necessaria fuit juris melioris origo. Per quod obductio facta detegitur et libertas obducta patet in publicum dum beneficio juris ciuilis manumissio celebratur. Hac igitur consideratione deducti, Nos Guido de moghio. Considerata fide deuotione et gratis seruitiis, que tu Margarita ancilla nostra, et filie tue Thomasia et Jacobina et Jannicta ancille nostre nobis diu et fideliter prestatis. Considerato etiam quod Xristiane estis et fideles nec debetis de jure laqueis seruitutis jnuolui. quam de seruitute xristi sanguis exiuit. Vt de tua et filiarum tuarum predictarum fide et fidelitate licteris [20] te et filias tuas predictas. Jn presentia Ruberti de Ebulo et Stephani de Natho judicum subscriptorum Castri malte [21] notarij danielis de danielis puplici jnsularum maltij et Guadicii [22] notari [23] et testium subscriptorum ad hoc specialiter vocatorum et rogatorum manumissionis beneficio tanquem bene meritas. adornamus dantes vobis predictis Margarite et Thomasie. Jacobine et Jannicte et heredibus uestris in perpetuum plenissimam libertatem. Vosque de manu et potestate nostra dimictimus. Vt sine aliquo servuitutis obstaculo ab omni jugo seruitutis extote absolute et libere. et vt in Ciuitate et libertate letemini et habeatis personam et potestatem emendi. vendendi. permutandi obligandi uos et in iudicio persistendi. perhibendi testimonium. testamentum et quamlibet uoluntatem ultimam faciendi. exercendi omnia que posset quelibet ingenua exercere. Nullo uobis super premissis uel similibus preterite condictionis obstaculo existente. Vnde ad huius Rerum certitudinem et Robur inperpetuum ualituram. presens scriptum puplicum factum est de premissis per manus mei predicti notarij danielis nostrum que supra jndictione subscriptionibus et testium subscriptorum testimonio ac sigillo pendente eiusdem domini Guidonis muninime roborate. Actum etc. M.cc. etc. Jndictione etc. tali die etc.

18. Ie. Count of Provence, Anjou and Forcalquier.

19. Sic.

20. A word or words seem to have been omitted.

21. MS: *Māt Mālt.*

22. Read *Gauditij*, ie. ot Gozo.

23. Sic.

# XII

## THE EARLIEST DOCUMENTS TRANSCRIBED IN THE CATHEDRAL ARCHIVES, MDINA: 1316-1372

The recent and invaluable organization of the Cathedral Archives at Mdina has enormously facilitated the consultation of documents there, while the publication of handlists and indices makes it easier for researchers to find materials; see J. Azzopardi, *Handlist of the Episcopal and Pro-Vicarial Archives (Curia Episcopalis Melitensis or CEM Archives) at the Malta Cathedral Museum=Handlist of the Ecclesiastical Archives of the Malta Cathedral Museum, Mdina,* 1 (Collegeville, Minnesota, 1975), which also explains why the Mdina archives now contain much material which was not originally part of the bishop's records. Fr. Azzopardi's work is now continued in this present volume. The documents here studied, the first fourteen in the eighteenth-century index to the archives which is published below, are arranged in the same order as that in which they appear in that index, which is not always a chronological order. Reference to each text is by Roman capitals in square brackets. The entry in the index is given verbatim in the original Italian, and is followed by a more correct summary of the document's contents derived from the most reliable text available. An asterisk indicates the modern reference to the Mdina transcript to which the index here published originally referred. No attempt has been made to provide a complete record of all transcripts or other references to the fourteen documents which might be found in the various Maltese archives concerned, while researches inevitably remain incomplete at Palermo where there are numerous *fondi* but where many of the royal registers have long been destroyed. Furthermore, the inaccessibility of documents in the possession of the Inguanez family continues to impede study of the decisive events of 1350 (*infra* Appendix II). One of the Inguanez documents [XII] was copied into a notarial register in 1511, but that volume has recently been lost; the document is republished below from an eighteenth-century transcript. The present author will also republish a further three of these documents [V-VII] and publish another three unpublished ones [VIII-X], together with a fourth of 1317 which is indexed below under "1397". Sincere thanks are due to Fr. John Azzopardi, Curator of the Cathedral Museum at Mdina, for his help and encouragement in the archive there, and to Dr. Godfrey Wettinger who saved the author from a number of errors. The following abbreviations are employed below:

| | |
|---|---|
| Abela | G.-F. Abela, *Della Descrittione di Malta Isola nel Mare Siciliano* (Malta, 1647) |
| ACM | Mdina, Archivum Cathedrale Melitense, Misc. [modern numerations and foliations] |
| ASC | Catania, Archivio di Stato, Fondo Benedettini, Ms. |

| | |
|---|---|
| ASP | Palermo, Archivio di Stato, Cancelleria, Registro |
| Barberi, iii | *I Capibrevi di Giovanni Luca Barberi,* ed. G. Silvestri, iii (Palermo, 1888) |
| Bresc (1973) | H. Bresc, "Documents on Frederick IV of Sicily's Intervention in Malta: 1372", *Papers of the British School at Rome*, xli (1973) |
| Bresc (1975) | H. Bresc, "The *Secrezia* and the Royal Patrimony in Malta: 1240-1450", in *Medieval Malta: Studies on Malta before the Knights,* ed. A. Luttrell (London, 1975) |
| *Memoirs* | Anon., *Memoirs of the Family of Inguanez* (Malta, 1888) |
| Mifsud | A. Mifsud, "Richiami alle Signorie del Passato di Malta...", *Archivum Melitense,* iii no.7 (1918). |
| Pirri | R. Pirri, *Sicilia Sacra,* iii (1st ed: Palermo, 1641) |
| RML | Valletta, Royal Malta Library, Biblioteca Ms. |
| RML Univ. | Valletta, Royal Malta Library, Università Ms. |
| *Secretiis* | J. Luca de Barberiis, *Liber de Secretiis,* ed. E Mazzarese Fardella (Milan, 1966) |
| Valentini, v-viii | R. Valentini, in *Archivio Storico di Malta,* v-viii (1934-1937) |

* * *

The present study concerns the fourteen earliest entries in the index from the Mdina archives which is published below. There are a considerable number of texts bearing on Maltese history in the thirteenth century while in the late-fourteenth century the documents become reasonably plentiful, but for most of the fourteenth century materials are comparatively scarce; for a survey of the sources, see *Medieval Malta: Studies on Malta before the Knights,* ed. A. Luttrell (London, 1975), 5-8 *et passim.* It is, therefore, worth treating the earliest items in some detail, even though most of them were known to such scholars as A. Mifsud and R. Valentini; in fact all but two or three were known, directly or indirectly, to Gian Francesco Abela whose *Descrittione di Malta* appeared in 1647. This study analyzes the texts down to 1372, which are sufficient to establish certain general patterns. The fourteen items include three papal bulls, two of them provisions to the Bishopric of Malta; eight royal privileges, of which one was granted to the islanders in general, two concern exemptions from customs dues, one is a royal collation to an ecclesiastical benefice, and four are grants or confirmations of grants of land; one episcopal act; and two notarial instruments, one a will and the other a formal act of possession. A comparatively rare type of act, a baronial letter of about 1397, is also given (*infra* Appendix III). This is a representative cross-section of the available documentation for the more formal political and religious side of fourteenth-century Maltese life. The earliest original document at Mdina is apparently that of 1404/5, the first in the collection entitled *Aragonensia* (ACM 33: text in Valentini,viii.73). Though the earliest materials survive at Mdina only in transcript, often indeed merely in copies of copies available in Valletta and elsewhere, it none the less seems important to study them; it should be emphasized, however, that only items mentioned in the index below are treated here and that others doubtless await discovery. In addition to saving time for those interested in the pre-1372 period, the present analysis serves to elucidate the early-modern process of copying and transcription and so to shed light on a formative period in Maltese historiography. In some cases the study of the transcripts leads to otherwise unknown originals or to early copies of important texts. It also indicates a method of approach for scholars studying the post-1372 records, particularly if they are concerned with the scientific edition of texts based on variant manuscripts.

Many of the documents and transcripts in the Mdina archives were indexed by Canon Gian Battista Borg between 1758 and 1772, as described above. The first volume of this index (ACM 32A) which goes down to 30 November 1529 is published in the present volume. Entries in the same hand occur in the first three volumes of the index, and this hand last appeared under March 1766 (ACM 32C, f.633); entries in a second hand continue until the year 1801 (ACM 32D). A collection of *Notizie* somewhat similar to this index and in Canon Borg's hand (ACM 274) contained fewer entries with differing descriptions of the texts concerned, as can be seen from the first few items down to 1372 which are reproduced below (Appendix I). Also in this same hand is ACM 18 which contains transcripts of many of the documents indexed, six of the first fourteen [III-IV, VIII-XI] appearing at f.1-9. The indices are often deficient or inaccurate, particularly as to dates, such errors sometimes deriving from the transcripts being indexed. Many fourteenth-century documents of which there are versions at Valletta are not found in transcript at Mdina; others which are at Mdina were not included in the index. Not mentioned, for example, is the late copy of what seems to be the earliest document in transcript there, an imperial grant of March 1235 to Paolino de Malta which was copied from the proofs of nobility of the Hospitaller Fr. Agostino Grimaldi which were presented in 1645. The transcript is in ACM 27, f.483;

the document is published in A. Luttrell, "Frederick II and Paolino de Malta: 1235," *Quellen und Forschungen aus italienischen Archiven und Bibliotheken,* lv-lvi (1976).

The early-modern transcripts of fourteenth-century documents in the Mdina archives are the product of much copying and recopying. The most scientifically valuable version of a document is normally the original act, which may itself exist in more than one copy or have been copied very soon after its initial date of issue. Sometimes the original was on parchment and often it had a seal, but no fourteenth-century originals survive at Mdina, and only in a few cases [II, VIII, XIV] can an original of the texts indexed be identified with certainty elsewhere; all but three of the fourteen texts [VIII-X] have been published. Often close to the original is the chancery copy registered in the archives of the office issuing the original at the moment of issue or soon after, for example bulls copied into the papal registers or acts in the royal chancery registers now at Palermo. Scholars often accord entries in the registers the same value in evidence as that of a genuine original, though in some cases the official copies may contain scribal errors or be so abbreviated and garbled as to be less reliable or complete; this was particularly the case with ASP 6 at Palermo, where chancery registers were sometimes very carelessly kept. A late but accurate copy of the original may on occasions be of greater value than a shortened, scribbled contemporary registration. This becomes clear when the text of the grant to Guglielmo Murina of 12 November 1372 [XII] as registered in the royal register is compared with an eighteenth-century transcript which was derived from the original at Malta. The transcript (RML 23, f.341v-342v) is given first:

Fridericus dei gratia Rex Siciliae, ac Athenarum et Neopatriae dux. Praesentis patentis scriptis serie notum fieri volumus Universis praesentibus et futuris; Quod ad humilem supplicationem Culmini nostro factam per Guillelmum Murinam de Meliveto fidelem nostrum; Considerantes puram fidem et devotionem sinceram quas idem Guillelmus erga Celsitudinem nostram semper gessit, et gerit, ac grata et accepta servitia per eum Majestati nostrae collata fidelitate ferventi, et viribus indefessis, quae confert ad praesens, et praestare poterit in futurum, concedente domino gratiora, eidem Guillelmo, et suis haeredibus de suo corpore legitime descendentibus in perpetuum, quoddam tenimentum terrarum nostrae Curiae vocatum Bucane situm et positum in Insula Meliveti prope tenimentum terrarum haeredum Michaelis de Bernardo, et secus terras fratris Benedicti Camenza viam publicam, et alios confines cum Iuribus limitibus redditibus, proventibus et pertinencijs suis omnibus. Sub servitio unius equi al forrati Curiae nostrae proinde praestandi, quod servitium idem Guillelmus in Curia nostra praesens, se, et dictos haeredes suos ipsi Curiae sponte obtulit praestituros, praestans proinde fidelitatis debitum Iuramentum, ac faciens manibus, et ore homagium iuxta Sacrarum constitutionum Imperialium Regni nostri continentiam et tenorem, de liberalitate mera, largitate munifica, speciali gratia, et ex certa nostra scientia duximus concedendum, fidelitate nostra, haeredum, et successorum nostrorum in eodem Regno nostro predicto servitio Curiae, et cuiuslibet alterius Iuribus semper salvis. Ad huius autem nostrae Concessionis futuram memoriam, et robur perpetuo valiturum presens patens scriptum proinde fieri et sigillo pendenti Maiestatis nostrae Iussimus communiri, datum In Insula Meliveti anno dominicae Incarnationis M$^{o}$ccc[c]$^{o}$lxxij. xij$^{o}$. Novembris xj$^{a}$ Indictionis.

Supplica    Regis[tratum] in Cancell[eria]
            Reg[istratum] poenes Prothonot[arium]

            Locus sigilli + pendentis in Capsula lignea per cordulam sericam crocei et rubei coloris.

La cordicella è una settaccia stretta lineata con due linee rosse e tre gialle.

This document was registered in chancery (ASP 6, f.190) as follows:

Eodem ibidem
Pro Guillelmo murina de miliveto et suis heredibus

Facte sunt:
Scriptum est per patentes licteras universis presentibus et futuris de concessione cuiusdam tenimenti terrarum dicte Curie vocatum bucana siti et positi in Insula Miliueti prope tenimentum terrarum heredum micahelis (*sic*) de lombardo et secus terras fratris benedictj camierza, viam publicam et alios confines, facta guillelmo murina de miliveto et suis heredibus de suo corpore legitime descendentibus in perpetuum sub seruicio unius equj alferratj dicte Curie per eum proinde prestando, quod servicium etc. in forma fidelitate nostra etc. Ad huius autem nostre concessionis futuram memoriam et robur perpetuo valiturum presens patens scriptum sibi proinde fieri et sigillo pendenti Maiestatis nostre Jussimus comuniri. Datum etc.

Sicilian chancery practice was slack. Rough drafts of royal mandates, sometimes marked *registrandum,* could wait for four years or more before they were copied into a register, and by that time there was probably a different scribe, the date or even the addressee might be forgotten, and scribbled corrections could be misread; some documents contained only the Indictional year, or just the day and month. Registers might be reused after many years while in some cases, such as ASP 7 and 8, fragments of different registers were bound together in relatively modern times, to the confusion of historians: R.-J. Loenertz, "Athènes et Néopatras. Regestes et notices pour servir à l'histoire des duchés catalans (1311-1394)," *Archivum Fratrum Praedicatorum,* xxv(1955),194-201. Sicilian royal acts could be presented and registered in the archives of the Protonotaro del Regno as well as in the chancery registers proper. The phrases *Registratum in Cancellaria* and *Registratum penes prothonotarium,* which were often added on the margin, the fold or the reverse of the document for greater authenticity, were generally copied across onto an eventual notarial *transumptum* or authenticated copy [eg.V-VIII,XII, XIV]; if the matter were an important one, the authentication by a notary public would take place before the local *judex* or *judices* as well as other witnesses. Evidence of registration *penes prothonotarium* first appears in 1319, and the second example known in Sicily is the royal act of 17 June 1320 concerning the Maltese fief of Gumerin, which is indexed below under the year "1397". Registration *penes Rationales* was becoming common after 1355, and the confirmation of the customs exemption granted to Lancea Gatto of Malta in 1372 was apparently "presented" in the offices of the royal *Dohana* and the *Secrezia* at Messina [XIV]. See G. La Mantia, "Su l'uso della registrazione nella Cancelleria del Regno di Sicilia dai Normanni a Federico III d'Aragona: 1130-1377," *Archivio Storico Siciliano,* ns.xxxi (1906), 208-209 *et passim.*

A number of fourteenth-century texts survive in nearly contemporary copies either in an original copy or in a confirmation, in chancery registers, or sometimes in notarial or other copies. Normally these copies are reasonably reliable, though there may be an element of suspicion that forgeries have been presented for confirmation or merely that scribal errors or alterations to proper names have occurred. Some grants were confirmed repeatedly, particularly as a result of political upheavals or changes in government such as occurred in Malta in 1350, in 1372 [V,XII-XIV] and in 1397/8 [V and index below *ad annum*]. On 22 June 1530 the Hospitaller Fr. Aurelio de Butigelli, who had just reached Malta as its new governor, commanded those concerned to present their diplomas and privileges, and as a result a number of persons holding properties or privileges sought to confirm or protect them by having them copied into the governor's *quaternus,* which is now bound into RML Univ.7. Such a process could create a separate tradition of copies, and this particular volume became well known; its cover bears the name of the seventeenth-century historian of Malta, Gian Francesco Abela. It preserves versions of documents which do not derive from copies entered by way of registration in the Palermo registers but which were taken from, or were derived from, the originals themselves. A more private tradition of originals and copies might also be created through a family archive such as that of the Inguanez at Mdina [V-VI,XII,XIV]. Monastic, municipal and episcopal archives also preserved documents, while transcripts were made by historians such as the eighteenth-century scholar I.S. Mifsud who worked on their own account.

While Butigelli's *quaternus* of 1530, which also had some original parchments and other documents bound into the back of it [eg.I,VI,XIV], came to constitute something approaching a *Libro d'Oro* for the Maltese nobility, a similar dossier had already been compiled, largely from the chancery registers at Palermo, for the whole Sicilian kingdom. The royal archives at Palermo were searched extensively during the first decade of the sixteenth century by the Sicilian bureaucrat Gian Luca Barberi, whose ultimate objective was a complete overhaul of the crown's rights and incomes with a view to the resumption of alienated or usurped fiefs and privileges. One result was the creation of two great reports, the *Capibrevi* and the *De Secretiis,* which were arranged topographically in such a way that the information concerning Malta and Gozo was collected together, often with extensive verbatim citations and with precise folio references to the chancery register used. These compilations have only recently been published, but they were available in manuscript at Palermo to guide those searching for materials; on Barberi's activities, see F. Liotta, "Barberi, Giovanni Luca," in *Dizionario biografico degli Italiani,* vi (Rome,1964), 158-161. The Maltese sections of both Barberi's works were copied at Palermo in 1644 by Leonardo Biasini into RML Univ. 206; there is also a late-seventeenth century copy of Biasini's work in RML 1226, while another copy of the *Capibrevi* and the *De Secretiis* made in the Palermo chancery by Notary Didacus Maiorana is in RML 1141 pt.2. These works were, in their turn, extensively recopied so that many transcripts deriving from the Palermo registers can be found at Mdina in versions which first reached Malta through Biasini [eg.I,V,XIII].

Barberi's successor Leonardo Biasini was *Primus Notarius* in the Sicilian royal chancery. His copy of Barberi's Maltese sections was done in his own hand and authenticated on 29 February 1644, while on the final folio he recorded his payment for the work but without stating who was paying for it (RML Univ.260, f.302,303). Probably this burst of copying was the result of quarrels provoked by the attempts made by the Knights of St. John in the years from 1643 to 1646 to enforce military service on the Inguanez and on other Maltese nobles who held fiefs (RML 670, f.195-204; RML Univ.7 pt.2, f.114-116; cf. Mifsud, 272-275); in one case (RML 670, f. 195) the noble party actually cited the royal grant of 1316 indexed below [I]. Biasini's work was particularly useful, because he did not merely limit himself to copying Barberi's summaries but went further and used Barberi's references to the registers to make verbatim transcripts of many of the Maltese documents which Barberi had merely summarized or noted. RML 1226 and ACM 27 pt.2, which are more or less identical, not only copied Biasini's RML Univ. 206 but also contained certain additions, notably the copy of the imperial grant to Paolino de Malta of 1235 and a copy of the notarized version made in 1511 of the concession of Bucana in 1372 [XII]. Gian Francesco Abela made considerable use of Biasini's materials in the history which he published in 1647; Abela may even have commissioned Biasini's work. Modern historians such as R. Valentini have also relied extensively on Biasini's transcripts.

It has, of course, become pointless and even misleading to cite the numerous manuscript copies of Barberi's *Capibrevi* and *De Secretiis* now that both are in print, especially if no reference is made to the published text. Biasini's copies of the chancery documents not given *in extenso* by Barberi do, however, constitute a special category of transcript and certain difficulties have arisen from their use, especially where references and dates are involved. Archivists delight in changing manuscript numbers and foliations, while dates and Indictions are all too easily miscopied or misunderstood, especially as the Indictional years do not commence on 1 January. Mistakes also arise when a document is said to be from the register for a certain year while it actually dates from an adjacent year. An extreme case of such confusions involves ASP 6, the chancery register brought to Malta with King Federigo in 1372. This register was originally begun in 1347, when its use was possibly interrupted by the plague. It is headed *4 INDS. 1347/FRIDERICVS/ 1370,* but it has often been cited as the register for "1347" so that, even though some historians realized that Federigo was not king in that year, many of his acts of 1372 have been misdated to 1347 or, occasionally, to 1370 [eg.XI].

In addition to the documents used by Barberi and Biasini, who concerned themselves largely with texts referring to fiefs and titles to property, the archives contain a wide variety of other copies or copies of copies: papal bulls, copies derived from the Hospitallers' archives, notarial acts, documents from a monastic archive in Catania, and transcripts from the Palermo registers done by others than Biasini. Some of the documents indexed below exist in forms derived from several of these categories. A scientific edition of their texts might need to take account of versions in many such categories, especially where the original is not available or is partly illegible. An analysis of the Mdina index, a study which should ideally be continued beyond 1372, not only serves to distinguish the significant from what can safely be ignored but it may also lead to useful discoveries; it shows how errors have arisen, and it helps to elucidate Maltese historiographical developments in the time of Abela and his successors. Finally, it should draw attention to the need for calendars and editions of late-medieval documents concerning Malta which survive in Maltese, Sicilian and other archives, and in private collections and religious houses in Malta itself.

* * *

**I 21.1.1313 Concessione del feudo Tabria ad Attardo de la barba eccetto i due giardini possessi da Arnaldo de Solimella Castellano e giustiziario di Malta. 26 139**

21 Jan. 1316 [not 1313], Messina: Federigo of Sicily grants the fief *(pheudum unum seu tenimentum terrarum Curie nostre)* of Tabrija *(Tabaria)* in return for the service of one *miles* to Actardus de Barba *miles*, excepting two *viridaria* belonging to Arnaldus de Solimella *miles*, Castellan and Justiciar of Malta.

Copied in an act of 18 July 1453, when Johannes de Landolina of Noto secured its confirmation (registered in ASP 93, f.416v-419v: *olim* 397v-400v) by the viceroy at Palermo. Having no original of his own, Johannes presented a notarial *transumptum* made at Noto on 3 Feb. 1405, when Muthius de Landolina presented *quoddam paruum Regale priuilegium tenoris subsequentis sigillatum cum cera Rubea In boxula lignea pendenti et cordula de serico collegate prout solitum*... The 1453 document was known to Barberi, iii.438-439 (and also in his *Secretiis*, 84), citing ASP "1453", f.388, with wrong folio and giving "1315". Transcripts by Biasini in RML Univ.206 [*olim* RML 870],f.145-149, and transcripts copied from Biasini in RML 1226, f.207-215, and in *ACM 27 pt.2, f.405v-409v, all giving the complete text of 1453 (as at f.387), the two latter with the date "1313". A version in an early-16th century hand on two paper sheets inserted in RML Univ. 7 [*olim* RML 858] pt.2, f.112-113 (with *Ferdinandus* in place of *Fridericus*), was possibly made in 1530 but gives no provenance; Valentini, v.32-34, published this version. The document was known to Abela, 87,464,530-531 (as "1315"), but is omitted from the list in Bresc (1975),153.

**II 10.VI.1316 Breve Pontificio che applica alcuni beni de Templari del Regno di Valenza alla Religione Gioannina. 27 589**

10 June 1317 [not 1316], Avignon: following negotiations with Jaime II of Aragon, Pope John XXII assigns properties in the Kingdom of Valencia which had once belonged to the Temple for the foundation of the Order of Montesa, which is also to have the Valencian properties of the Hospital of St. John, while the Templar properties in Aragon and Catalunya are to pass to the Hospitallers.

This long bull *(Ad fructus uberes)* survives in an original copy, eg. in the Archivo de la Corona de Aragón at Barcelona: F. Miquel Rosell, *Regesta de letras pontificias del Archivo de la Corona de Aragón* (Madrid, 1948), 204-205. It is registered in Archivio Vaticano, Reg.Vat.63, f.324v-326= Reg.Aven.2, f.242-245. This is not the bull of the same date *(Pia Matris Ecclesia)* founding the Order of Montesa. It is not among the bulls now surviving in the *bullaria* in the Hospitallers' archives at Valletta, nor was it in any of the several *bullaria* there which were lost in the 18th century: *Catalogue of the Records of the Order of St. John of Jerusalem in the Royal Malta Library,* ed. A. Zammit Gabarretta and J. Mizzi, vii (Malta, 1964); see also Valletta, Royal Malta Library, Archives of the Order of St. John, cod.1132 B, f.306-312. It has often been published, eg. in S. Pauli, *Codice Diplomatico del Sacro Militare Ordine Gerosolimitano, oggi di Malta*, ii (Lucca,1737),51-56, who took it from J. Lünig, *Codex Italiae Diplomaticus*,ii (Frankfurt — Leipzig, 1726), 1671-1676, and most recently (from Reg. Aven. 2) in S. Baluzius, *Vitae Paparum Avenionensium,* iii,ed. G. Mollat (Paris, 1921),255-263. It was transcribed from an "old register" in the episcopal curia in *ACM.28, f.296-303v *(Ex transumpto registrato in* *actis Curie Ep.lis Not.lis Cit.is in quodam Registro antiquo fol: 124).* This transcript, and the ones which follow it and which were taken from the same *registrum,* demonstrate an interest in the fundamental legal relationship between the Aragonese Crown, the Hospital and the Papacy, and possibly they were relevant to some dispute between the Maltese and the Hospitallers: cf. A. Luttrell, "The Aragonese Crown and the Knights Hospitallers of Rhodes: 1291-1350," *English Historical Review,* lxxvi(1961).

**III 10.1.1334 Bolle del vescovado di Malta a favore di errigo de cefaludo per morte del Vescovo Alduino. 18 1**

10 Jan.1334, Avignon; Pope John XXII provides Henricus de Cefalù, OFM, to the Bishopric of Malta, vacant through the death of Alduinus.

Registered in Archivio Vaticano, Reg.Vat.106, f.121v-122 = Reg.Aven.45, f.158v-159; published in L. Wadding, *Annales Minorum,* iii pt.2 (Lyons, 1635), 236, from which it was cited in Pirri, iii. 594, and Abela, 305, and from which it possibly reached Mdina in the transcripts in *ACM 2, f.3-3v; ACM 18, f.1; and ACM 165, f.32[*olim* 51]. Republished in Wadding, vii (rev.ed: Quaracchi, 1932), 544-545.

**IV 27.XI.1342 Bolle del vescovado di Malta a favore di Fr. Nicola Boneti de Minori, vacato per morte del vescovo errigo. 18 3**

27 Nov.1342, Avignon: Pope Clement VI provides Nicolaus Boneti, OFM, to the Bishopric of Malta, vacant through the death of Henricus [de Cefalù].

Registered in Archivio Vaticano, Reg. Vat.147, f.31v-32; published in Wadding, iii pt.2(1635),270, from which it was cited in Pirri, iii.594-595, and Abela, 305, and from which it possibly reached Mdina in the transcripts (with *omissis*) in *ACM,2, f.4-4v; ACM 18, f.3-3v; and ACM 165, f.33 [*olim* 53]. Republished in Wadding, vii (1932), 594-595.

**V 4.I.1350 Privilegio del giardino di Irbinet a favor di Chicco Gatto Castellano. Qual giardino lo teneva la Regia Corte per successione et estinzione della famiglia di Michele Bava. Qual privilegio fù di novo confirmato al Giudice Lancea Gatto figlio d'esso Chicco a 14 Febbraio 1397. 26 246.**

4 Jan. 1351 [not 1350], Messina: Lodovico of Sicily grants the *viridarium* of Dejr il-Bniet *(de Irbinet)* which had devolved to the royal *curia* on the death of Michele Bava, to Chicco Gatto, Castellan of Malta; the grant was confirmed by Martino of Sicily to Chicco's grandson Francesco [not to his son Lancea] on 14 Feb. 1398 [not 1397].

This document survives in two separate traditions. In the Palermitan tradition, the 1351 text and a confirmation of 12 Nov. 1372 were known, through the registration of a reconfirmation of 14 Feb. 1398, to Barberi, iii.442-443 (as ASP "1397", f.148, ie. ASP 32, f.173-174v: *olim* 148-149v), to Biasini who transcribed the whole 1398 text (from the same source) in RML Univ.206. f.251-253 (the latter was copied in both RML 1226, f.355-361, and *ACM 27 pt.2, f.460-462), and to Bresc (1975), 152; the 1398 confirmation was based on a single sealed *priuilegium* of 1372 which confirmed both the act of 1351 and that of 1372 which contained it. The registration of an act of 12 Nov. 1372 in ASP 6, f.209v [*olim* 190v], which is published in Bresc (1973), 195, summarized it very briefly: *Fridericus etc. presentis priuilegij serie etc. De confirmacione cuiusdam viridarij facta chicco gacto patri notarij lancee de gacto.* This *viridarium* was presumably Dejr il-Bniet; the whole entry in ASP 6 was subsequently crossed out, probably because the property was confiscated from Lancea Gatto in 1376: Bresc(1973),188-189. The Maltese tradition is that of the original. According to *Memoirs,* 18, the "original grant" was still in the possession of the Inguanez family, heirs of the Gatto, in 1888. The claim that there has been a Barony or "Noble fief" of Dejr il-Bniet since 1350/1 is based on this text, though it makes no mention of military service, of a *feudum* or of a title. Abela, 466-467, 485, stated that he saw the *priuilegio originale* then in the possession of Baron Inguanez; he also had a summary of it from Barberi's *Capibrevi* in a copy sent to him from Palermo. Abela, 485, knew of a royal *diploma* containing the 1372 confirmation; it is not completely clear whether this was his *originale* or whether he did in fact see an original text of 1351. I.S. Mifsud (born 1722) copied this version of the 1351 act (not the 1372 confirmation which contained it), apparently from Abela's papers, into RML 23, f.340-341, and this copy concluded:

*Supplica est* — *R[egistra]tum in Cancellar[ia]*
*R[egistra]tum penes Prothonot[arium]*
*Locus sigilli + pendentis in capsa lignea*

These were standard formulae in regular use when documents were presented for registration. They do not, however, appear in the confirmations of 1372 and 1398, and that does suggest that Mifsud was copying if not from an original of 1351 at least from a copy based directly upon a 1351 original. In Mifsud's transcript the dating clause begins on a new line, and he reproduces the dots between the words which spaced out its final line; he also stated that Abela found that the phrase beginning with the date was written in a different hand from the rest, all of which again suggests an original. Mifsud added that when Abela had the text in 1624 *il Sigillo che era impresso in cera rossa nella cassa di legno era quasi tutto guasto, seben nella circonferenza apparivano ancora alcune lettere antiche Gotiche all'intorno.* Mifsud gave the place-name as *uocatum de Ir Jelbinet*. This document was published, with minor inaccuracies, in 1888 in *Memoirs*, 19-20; it has not been possible to consult the "original" of 1351, or possibly 1372, from which this version was said to have been made. On the apparent authenticity of this text, see also *infra* Appendix II.

**VI 4.I.1350 Privilegio d'essenzione di Dogana. 22 745**

4 Jan. 1351 [not 1350], Messina: Lodovico of Sicily grants Chicco Gatto Castellan of Malta, and his son Notary Lancea Gatto, and their heirs in perpetuity, exemptions within the kingdom, and especially in Malta and Gozo, from customs dues *(a solucione Iuris dohane)*.

Known from a confirmation of 12 Nov. 1372 made for Lancea Gatto, an original of which, on parchment, is bound into RML Univ. 7 [*olim* RML 858], f.152, from which it is published in Valentini, v.34-36. Known to Abela, 485, who gave a brief extract from it. The 1351 text was included within a version of the 1372 confirmation copied, evidently from Abela's papers, by I.S. Mifsud (born 1722) in RML 23,f.338-340. Mifsud added: *Confirma del Sopradetto Priuilegio communicato al Comdr. Abela dal B. Inguanez nel Mese di Xbre 1624; copiata dall'Originale scritto in pergamena in lettere quasi gotiche.* Where RML Univ.7 gave *not[arius] Lancea*, Abela, 485, omitted the word *notarius;* Mifsud's transcript, apparently taken from Abela's notes, gave *Nobilis lancea*. Mifsud's version of the 1372 text ended with the phrase *Registratum in Cancella[ria].* It is impossible to be sure whether or not Abela's *Originale* was a document of 1351 or, as Mifsud's phrase suggests, an original of the 1372 confirmation; nor is it clear whether the parchment now in RML Univ. 7 was the one Abela saw in 1624. For doubts concerning the authenticity of the 1351 text, *infra* Appendix II. The brief extract from this document given in *Memoirs*,20-21, was apparently cited verbatim from Abela, 485 (as in the case of *infra*, XIV). The 1351 text, included in that of 1372, was reconfirmed for Francesco Gatto on 21 May 1406; then at Barcelona in 1432, at the request of Francesco's son-in-law and heir Antoni Desguanes, the privileges of 1351, 1372 (which repeated that of 1351 with minor variants) and 1406 were presented to Alfonso V — *ostensis in quadam Carta, siue publico pargameno Instrumento, duobus Priuilegijs per Serenissimos Reges Sicilie predecessores nostros memorie recolende Chicco gatto, et Francisco eius genero militi concessis*: these were then copied into a new confirmation of 29 Apr. 1432, of which the early-modern transcript in *ACM 10,f.745-749, apparently constitutes the only known version. This 1432 document speaks of "two privileges" granted to Chicco and Francesco Gatto (ie. those of 1351 and 1406), but of only one *Carta or* "instrument" which must have contained the three documents of 1351,1372 and 1406 which were copied into the 1432 confirmation; that of 1406 apparently had some lines omitted in the transcript, while that of 1432 mistakenly said that Francesco was *filius et heres dicti quondam Chicco gatt Patris sui*. The *Carta* presented in 1432 cannot possibly, therefore, have been the original of 1351. The transcript gives no statement of provenance but it follows, on the same sheet and in the same hand, a Viceregal text of 1531 concerning customs exemptions on grain imported from Sicily into Malta which was definitely taken from the Palermo archive. The 1432 document was apparently unknown to the Sicilian tradition of Barberi and Biasini; it might have been registered at Barcelona where it was issued, but it cannot be traced in the royal registers in the Archivo de la Corona de Aragón (information from Señorita Mercedes Costa who kindly searched the registers there).

**VII 7.X.1350 Privilegio del Rè Ludovico di Sicilia, nel quale l'Isole di Malta e Gozzo s'aggregano al Regio Demanio. 25 1**

7 Oct. 1350, Messina: Lodovico of Siciliy declares that Malta and Gozo will never again be alienated as a county, barony or fief, and reincorporates them in perpetuity into the royal *demanium*.

No original known; the text is preserved in a notarized parchment issued in Malta on 6 June 1440 when the *jurati* of the *ciuitas* and *insula* of Malta presented the *originalis priuilegium* of King Lodovico, complete with seal and cord, for copying; the 1440 parchment is now in RML Univ.3 [*olim* RML 854] no.3. In the 1440 *transumptum,* the 1350 text concludes *Registratum in Cancellaria Registratum penes Prothonotarium.* This document was known to Abela, 421. It was copied into the "Privilegi della Città Notabile" (Mdina), at f.16, whence it was recopied into the "Privilegij dell' Vniversita della Citta Valletta," according to the transcript in *ACM 27, f.4-4v. Other transcripts taken directly or indirectly from the Mdina "Privilegi" are in RML 494, f.3-3v; RML 737, f.1-2; RML 1119 [no.1]; RML 1120, f.1-3; ACM 30 [*olim* Ms.E], f.43-43v, and again at f.61-61v. A copy of 1759 in RML 2, f.586-586v, gives no indication of the source. There is another copy in Siracusa, Biblioteca Comunale, "Liber Privilegiorum et diplomatum nobilis et fidelissime Syracusarum urbis," ii, f.94-96[*olim* 67-69], a somewhat corrupt modern version derived from a notarial *transumptum* made in Malta on 29 Aug. 1420 before *Judex* Lemo de Falzono at the instance of the *universitas* of Malta which needed a copy to send abroad, presumably to protest against the virtual alienation of the island to Antonio Cardona. The text of 1420 described the seal as follows: ......*Sigillo Regio Magno de cera rubea infra quadam buxiulam ligeam Imprexo. sub scriptura, et Imagine cuiusdam hominis coronati sedentis in Solio, et tenentis Virgam in manu dextera, in cuius capite est quodam lilium, et in manu Sinistra Pomum pendere cum cordula de serico exercea et Rubea,...* Text published, from the Mdina "Privilegi", in P. de Jové y Hevia, *Indagaciones acerca de la dominación de España en Malta de 1285 a 1530* (Madrid, 1863),51-52, and by A. Mifsud, in *La Gazzetta di Malta,* no.3429

(10 Apr. 1895),3. Both published versions are notably inaccurate.

**VIII 17.VI.1362 Testamento di D. Isolda moglie di Lancea di Carobene a favore d'un erezzione di Convento di Benedittini in Malta. 18 5**

17 June 1363 [not 1362], Noto: Will of Isolda de Landolina, widow of Lancea de Carubeni, bequeathing properties in Malta to the Benedictines of San Niccolò d'Arena at Catania on condition that they found a convent in Malta.

Original parchment in Catania, Biblioteche Riunite Civica e A. Ursino Recupero, perg.543 [*olim* 1.59.E.51]. 16th-century and later transcripts in ASC 153, f.1-3; 155, f.63-63v [printed]; others in RML 360, f.333-337, and in *ACM 2, f.5-7 (both transcripts being copied ca.1708, apparently at Vittoriosa in Malta), and ACM 18, f.4-5v. Known confusedly, through a *memoria,* to Abela, 306,390 (and in his notebook: RML 140, f.38-38v), and to Pirri (1733 ed.), ii.1162. Cited, from the copy in ASC 153, in D. La Ferlita, "I Possedimenti dei Benedettini di Catania a Malta", *Archivio Storico di Malta,* vii (1936), 262-264. These documents [VIII-X] were much copied in connection with a lawsuit of 1708 concerning Isolda's Maltese possessions *(ibid.,* 272-276). The date is wrongly given in the original itself as 1362, but the regnal and Indictional year both indicate 1363.

**IX 11.X.1364 Il Vescovo di Malta Ilario commuta l'ultima volontà della fù D. Isolda, con assegnare le rendite di essa Signora al Monastero di S. Nicolò d'arena, et obligarlo a pregare continuamente per l'anima di essa Signora, senza mandar in Malta Frati del suo ordine a construire ivi il convento ordinato dalla testatrice sotto il 17 Giugno 1362. 18 10**

11 Oct. 1364, Catania: Ilarius, Bishop of Malta, allows the Benedictines of San Niccolò d'Arena at Catania to receive the incomes left by Isolda de Landolina for the foundation of a Benedictine house at Malta [VIII] without fulfilling the obligation at Malta, providing that they pray for her soul in Catania. It was claimed that the endowment was not large enough; that the journey to Malta was too dangerous; and that the Sicilian monks could not perform their tasks in Malta owing to difficulties of language.

Copied in an act of 17 Mar. 1365: original parchment in Catania, Biblioteche Riunite..., perg.557 [*olim* 2.27.Q.21]. Various early-modern transcripts in ASC 153, f.4-6; 155, f.63v-64 [printed]; 156, f.89-90; 159, f.115-116v. Other transcripts in RML 360, f.934-936 (derived from the Catania original: copy of ca.1708), and in *ACM 2,f.7v-8v (18th-century copy from Catania) and ACM 18,f.6-6v. Known, through a *memoria,* to Abela,390 (and in his notebook: RML 140, f.38v), and to Pirri (1733 ed.), ii.1162, and cited in La Ferlita, 264 and n.7 (with partial text), from ASC 153, f.4-6.

**X 7.V.1365 Possesso preso dai Procuratori del Monastero di S. Nicolò d'arena di Catania de' beni che godeva in vita la fù D. Isolda Carobene. 18 13**

7 May 1365, Malta: Notarial instrument recording the taking of possession by *fratres* Johannes and Maurus, proctors of the monasteries of Santa Maria de Licodia and San Niccolò d'Arena at Catania, of the Maltese properties bequeathed them in 1363 by the will of Isolda de Landolina [VIII].

16th-century copy in ASC 159, f.121v-123v; copy of 1678 in ASC 153, f.16-17v. Early-modern transcripts in ASC 153, f.16-17v; 155, f.66-67 [printed]; 156, f.91-92v; 159, f.121v-123v; also in RML 360, f.337-340, and *ACM 2, f.9-11, and ACM 18, f.7-8.

**XI 10.XII.1369 Provista Regia dell'ospedale di S. Francesco a Fr. Nicola Papalla, ed altro. 27 26**

4 [not 10] Dec. 1372 [not 1369], Messina: Federigo of Sicily collates his chaplain Niccolò Papalla, OFM, to the rectorship of the hospital of San Francesco [at Rabat] in Malta.

Registered in ASP 6, f.211 [*olim* 192], whence published in Bresc (1973), 200. Apparently unknown to Barberi, but copied at Palermo by Leonardo Biasini in 1619 for the Order of St. John, along with the two documents concerning Thomeo Axac noted below: Valletta, Royal Malta Library, Archives of the Order of St. John, cod 439, f.274-275. Known to Pirri iii.595,619 (as of 1370), and to Abela,391-392 (and in his notebook: RML 140, f.11,12), as being "in libro 1347" (ie. ASP 6), f.192. RML 140, f.11, contains an addition, possibly in Abela's own hand, stating *siue anno 1370 quia in anno 1347 non erat iste Rex federicus sed Ludouicus.* This document has been confused with another by which Federigo collated the benefice of *La Saccaya* on Gozo to his chaplain Thomeo Axac; the latter text was registered twice, once (without date) in the register for "1369-1373" (ie. ASP 12), f.164-164v [*olim* 144-144v] and again, in very abbreviated form (with the date 12 Nov. 1372 and the name as *Bartholomeus*), in ASP 6, f.190v [*olim 171v*], whence it is published in Bresc (1973),192. The version of the Axac collation in ASP 12 also mentions a *Nicolaus de panor. ordinis minorum,* which probably explains the confusion with the collation for Niccolò Papalla, OFM, and the incorrect date of 1369. The transcripts of the Papalla text in *ACM 28,f.16v-17, and ACM, 18, f.9, give it incorrectly as from ASP, "Ex libro Anni 1369, fol.144", and as of 3 Dec.; in ACM 28, f.17v-18, are summaries of the same text, with the correct reference to "libro 1347, fol.192". Published, from a copy, in B. Fiorini, "Il Convento di S. Francesco in Rabat (Malta) dei Frati Minori Conventuali," *Melita Historica*,iii no.3 (1962),32, with the incorrect date of 3 Dec. 1370 and with reference both to ASP, "Protonotaro del Regno, t.VI (1343-1373), p.192" (ie. ASP 6, f.211), and — incorrectly — as "ex libro anni 1369, fol.144" (ie. ASP 12, f.164-164v).

**XII 4.XI.1372 Concessione Regia di Bucana data in Malta dal Rè federico a Guglielmo Murina. 26 294**

12 [not 4] Nov. 1372, Malta: Federigo of Sicily grants the *tenimentum terrarum* of Bucana in perpetuity to Guglielmo Murina and his heirs *sub servitio unius equi alferrati.*

This document survives in two traditions. In the Palermitan tradition, it was registered, in abbreviated form, in ASP 6, f.190 [*olim* 171] (text *supra,* 33, date as 11 Nov.), cited in Barberi, iii.445 (as ASP "1347", f.171), transcribed by Biasini (RML Univ. 260, f.247, and copy in RML 1226, f.351), cited with the correct year (as at f.190) by Abela, 509, and published in Bresc(1973),191. The Maltese tradition derived from the original in the possession of the Inguanez family following a Gatto-Murina marriage and an Inguanez-Gatto marriage. This original was copied on 10 Jan. 1511, at the instance of Jacobus Angaraus de Inguanez, into the acts of Notary Gonsalvo Canchur: Valletta, Notarial Archives, R.140/5, f.20-20v, stating that the authorities inspected *quoddam priuilegium in carta membrana cum buxula de ligno et cordula de serico inpendenti coloris rubei et Jalni et signo consueto regio de cera rubea.* (This volume has been mislaid since 1974, but a transcript from it was kindly provided by Dr. Godfrey Wettinger). From the 1511 version it was transcribed in RML 1226, f.423-426, and in *ACM 27 pt.2, f.484-486. Abela, 422,509-510, stated that he saw the Inguanez original, and he published a version with omissions; he also knew the 1511 copy. I.S. Mifsud (born 1722) copied Abela's copy into RML 23, f.341v-342v (text *supra,* 32-33), misdated to 1472. Mifsud stated that Abela copied the original and checked it against the 1511 version, finding the latter to be accurate except that it guessed the date as 4 Nov., while the original could be read as "xij". The complete original is almost twice the length of the abbreviated registered version which contains errors concerning names, eg. *de lombardo* for *de Bernardo,* and *camierza* for *Camenza.* It has not been possible to consult the Inguanez original published, apparently inaccurately, in *Memoirs,* 29-31.

**XIII 12.XI.1372 Concessione del feudo Tabia e ariexem a enrico de Sosa per i servizii prestati nel ridurre il Castello di Malta al Regio Dominio. 26 113**

12 Nov. 1372, Malta: Federigo of Sicily grants the *tenimentum terrarum* of *Tabia et Garexumu* at an annual *census* of six *tumini* of grain to Henricus de Saso, a *seruiens* in the *castrum,* for his services *in Reduccione castri Insule Miliuetj.*

Registered in ASP 6, f.209 [*olim* 190], whence known to Barberi,iii.432 (as in ASP "1347", ie. ASP 6, f.190), whence transcribed by Biasini (RML Univ.206, f.91-91v) and published in Bresc (1973), 194. Transcripts deriving from Biasini's copy in RML 1226, f.149-150, and *ACM 27 pt.2, f.393v. Abela seems not to have used this document.

**XIV 12.XI.1372 Privilegio d'essenzione di Dogana. 22 746**

12 Nov. 1372, Malta: Federigo of Sicily confirms to *Judex* Lancea Gatto the exemptions from customs dues granted on 4 Jan. 1351 [VI].

Original on parchment in RML Univ.7 [*olim* RML 858], f.152, with the *datum* clause in a different hand on a separate line; published in Valentini, v.34-36. Transcript by I.S. Mifsud in RML 23, f.338-340, taken from Abela's copy, and another in *ACM 10 (details *supra*, VI); Mifsud's version ended with the sole phrase *Registratum in Cancell[ari]a*. Known to Abela, 485, who gave a brief extract from it, which was reproduced verbatim (clearly from Abela, as in the case of VI) in *Memoirs*, 21: Abela apparently saw a version, possibly that now in RML Univ.7, which in 1624 was in the possession of the Inguanez (*supra*, VI; *infra* Appendix II). Somewhat inexplicably, the document was not registered in the 1372 royal register (ASP 6) nor, it seems, in any other surviving register, and therefore it was not known to Barberi or Biasini, and not published in Bresc (1973), though on the back of the fold, written in various different hands with the date Jan. 1374, are the phrases:

*R[egistra]tum In Cancellar[ia]*

*Re[gistra]tum p[ene]s p[ro]th[onotariu]m*
*di la duana*

*Presentatum in Regia dohana mess[in]e et officie*
*secretie per dominum [judicem?] lanc[eam] gactum*
*octauodecimo Ianuarij xij Ind[ictionis]*
*xij nouembris xj Ind[ictionis]*

**Appendix I: THE 'NOTIZIE' IN ACM MISC. 274**

This appendix contains the first seven entries in the *Notizie* found in ACM 274 which is also in the hand of Canon Gian Battista Borg (*supra*, 7) but which does not give the codex and folio references; the eighth entry is for 1393. The first six entries are among the first eleven in ACM 32A, but the actual summaries of the documents concerned vary considerably from the summaries in the latter index; the six are, however, precisely the first six documents copied, in the same hand as that of the indices, into ACM 18,f.1-9, of which ACM 274 is in fact the index, though it also indexes documents which are not in ACM 18. The document of "1369", actually of 1372, is given with a slightly different date which is found in some of the copies of it (*supra* XI). The seventh entry concerns the supposed Genoese attack on Malta in 1372, given with the wrong date of "1371" which was taken by Abela, 421-422, from Foglietta's publication of 1585, and with the erroneous supposition, also taken from Abela, that the Genoese attacked Malta and provoked a royal riposte; the rest of the entry is accurate enough and the grant to Bartolomeo Axac is reasonably correct, though the original document described it as *la Saccaya* and not as *Nunciata;* details of Federigo's Malta expedition and the text of the Axac grant as registered in ASP 6 are given in Bresc (1973),192 *et passim.* In fact, Federigo went to Malta accompanied by ten Genoese galleys, apparently to suppress a revolt: ...*occasione felicis aduentus maiestatis nostre ad insolam prelibatam [meliueti] cum galeis decem januensium ipsam obsessam tenentibus spacio mensium duorum ad reducionis dicte insole ad dominium maiestatis nostre* (ASP 12, f.206v,207).

a 10 Gennaio 1334 da auignone furono spedite le bolle del uescouado di Malta da PP. Giovanni 22. a fauore di Fr. Errigo di Cefaludo dell'Ordini Minori. U. Giornale fol.

a 27 Novembre 1342. da auignone furono dal PP. Clemente 6. spedite le bolle del uescovato di Malta a fauore di Fr. Nicola Boneti Maestro di S. Teologia dell'Ordini Minori, e ciò per esser uacato per morte di Fr. Errigo Cefaludo.

In Noto di Sicilia i 17 Giugno 1362 fece il suo testamento D. Isolda vedova del fù Lancea di Carobene, in cui doppo diuersi Legati lascia erede universale il Monastero di S. Nicolò d'arena dell'ordine de Benedittini, con obligo di douer sei Frati dell'Ordine abitare in Malta nella Chiesa di S. Nicola esistente nell'istesse sue terre ereditarie. Uide Giornale fol.

Nel 1364. 11 Ottobre. Il Uescovo di Malta Ilario considerando che un Monastero de Benedittini non poteua erigersi in Malta con quelle poche rendite, e per esser i Maltesi anche di diverso linguaggio da Siciliani mutò la volontà della detta Testatrice D. Isolda, che, in uece d'erigersi in Malta altro monastero, i Frati di S. Nicolò d'arena esistenti in Catania s'appropriassero i beni, e pregassero continuamente per la testatrice e suoi parenti. Uid. Giornale fol.

Nel 1365. 7 Maggio. I Procuratori del Monastero di S. Nicolò d'arena prendono possesso de beni ereditarii esistenti in Malta lasciati dalla detta quondam D. Isolda. Uid. Giornale f.

Sotto i 3 Decembre 1369 Il Rè Federico prouede la Rettoria dell'Ospedale di S. Francesco dell'Isola di Malta in persona di Fr. Nicolò Papalla dell'Ordini Minori. Uid. Giornale fol.

Nel 1371. Essendo Capitano di Malta a Regio beneplacito Giovanni d'Aragona, dieci galere di Genova vengono in Malta e danno il guasto all'Isola, per la qual causa il Rè Federico 3° l'anno seguente 1372. viene in Malta per riparare li danni patiti per detta invasione, e sino al mese di nouembre ancor era in Malta, come si caua da più concessioni di terre a suoi Uassalli, e del Giuspatronato del Gozzo appellato della Nunciata conferito al Cantore Bartolomeo Axac sotto li 12 Novembre 1372.

## Appendix II: MALTA 1350-1351

The three documents of 1350/1 studied above [V-VII] provide the only direct evidence available concerning important developments in Malta. These occurred at a time of crisis and upheaval in Sicily, where the weak young King Lodovico was at the mercy of Papal-Angevin machinations, baronial intrigues and urban uprisings. Late in 1350 Lodovico was under the control of Matteo Palizzi, the Chancellor and joint Vicar-General of the kingdom who was the leader of the so-called "Sicilian" faction based on Messina, while the opposing "Catalan" barons established at Catania and elsewhere were led by Blasco de Alagona, who was guardian and tutor of Lodovico's young cousin Federigo of Randazzo, Duke of Athens and Neopatras: details in Michele da Piazza, *Historia Sicula*, in *Bibliotheca Scriptorum...*, ed. R. Gregorio, i (Palermo, 1791), 596-597 *et passim*. Federigo of Randazzo stood to inherit the claims to Malta of his father Giovanni of Randazzo, who made his will and died in April 1348: text in R. Starrabba, "Giovanni d'Aragona duca d'Atene e Neopatria," *Rivista Sicula di Scienze, Letteratura ed Arti*, i (1869), 454-459. Because he belonged to the "Catalan" opposition, Federigo may have lost possession of the County of Malta, while at the same time there may have been a royalist or pro-"Sicilian" movement on Malta, possibly reflecting the upheavals in Sicily. On 7 October 1350 a royal charter issued by Matteo Palizzi at Messina promised that the islands of Malta and Gozo would never again be alienated as a county, barony or fief, and it formally incorporated them in perpetuity into the royal *demanium* [VII]. The "Sicilian" party was anxious for general negotiations and on the next day, 8 October, Matteo Palizzi sent a mission to discuss a Sicilian peace with Blasco de Alagona at Catania, a settlement being reached in November: Michele da Piazza,i.597. This truce was followed by a major uprising in Palermo which lasted from 13 December 1350 until 25 January 1351: dates established in S. Bozzi, "Un errore di data e la Cronica di Fra Michele da Piazza," *Archivio Storico Siciliano,* ns.i (1876). It was on 4 January 1351, in the midst of these difficulties, that Chicco Gatto, who had become royal Castellan of Malta and may have led a royalist movement there, was granted both the *viridarium* of Dejr il-Bniet on Malta to be held without any obligation of military service, and also — assuming that the text was not a later forgery — an important exemption from the payment of customs dues [V-VI].

These two documents of January 1351 mark the first known appearance in Malta of a family which steadily rose to prominence there. Whether the Gatto came from Sicily, or from Pisa, Genoa or elsewhere in Italy, is still uncertain. They again chose the winning side during the troubles of 1372 when Chicco's son, Judge Lancea Gatto, secured the confirmation of the privileges of 1351 by King Federigo when he was in Malta in November 1372 [V-VI,XIV]; but then Lancea went into revolt and lost his lands in 1376: Bresc (1973), 189. Later Lancea's son Francesco Gatto chose to support the crown, and he was rewarded in 1398 [cf.V]. By that time Francesco had married the daughter of Guglielmo Murina and had thus acquired possession of Bucana [cf.XII]. Francesco died without a male heir, but his daughter Imperia married Antoni Isguanes, Desguanes or Inguanez, from the Catalan Dez-Guanechs, who succeeded to the Gatto's Maltese privileges, possessions and predominance [cf.VI]; Tabrija [1] and Garexim [XIII] also passed to the Desguanes in the fifteenth century: Bresc (1975),152-155 *et passim*. During the fifteenth century the Gatto and the Desguanes had some difficulty in establishing their extensive claims, as they could not always produce proper written privileges and sometimes the claims themselves were not technically valid: references and texts in Barberi,iii.442-446; *Secretiis*,80,84-85,87; RML Univ.206, f.223-240v. Francesco Gatto's possession of Timisia was confirmed to him by King Martino of Sicily on 14 February 1398 despite the fact that no text was available; Gatto claimed that he had lost his predecessors' deeds *(casualiter ammiserit priuilegia)* when Artale de Alagona threw his goods into the *castrum maris* at Malta: text, from ASP 30,f.30-31v, transcribed in RML Univ.206, f.227-229v. On the general question of administrative inefficiency and the widespread tendency to ignore the rules of succession, see H. Bresc, "Società e politica in Sicilia nei secoli XIV e XV," *Archivio Storico per la Sicilia Orientale,* lxx(1974).

Given this background of opportunism, chicanery and "lost" documents, it might be suspected that the two privileges of 1351 were forgeries which King Federigo was persuaded to confirm in 1372. The royal registers for the year 1350/1 are lost, but the few surviving fragments of Lodovico's registers had at least five false documents inserted in them, while in another text the original name was scratched out and another inserted: G. La Mantia, "Su i frammenti di due registri originali degli anni 1353-1355 di Ludovico d'Aragona re di Sicilia," *Archivio Storico Siciliano,* ns. xxx (1905), 505. On the other hand, the loss of *certa registra* was mentioned in 1352, while *omnia registra Cancellariarum* were burnt at Messina in 1356: on losses and survivals in the Sicilian chancery, see G. La Mantia, *Codice Diplomatico dei re aragonesi di Sicilia: 1282-1355,* i (Palermo, 1917), xl-xliii *et passim.* In 1372 Federigo would already have found it difficult to check Lancea Gatto's claims, quite apart from the fact that the king was in Malta where he would have been unable to consult such registers as might have survived in the various royal offices in Sicily.

The title *Ludovicus Dei gratia rex Sicilie,* the dating clauses for 7 October 1350 and 4 January 1351 in the IV Indiction when the king was at Messina, and the name of the Vicar and Chancellor Matteo Palizzi, all fit satisfactorily with what is known of contemporary events and chancery practice. Yet the oldest surviving version of the royal charter of 1350 is the notarial copy made, for some unspecified reason, in 1440 [VII]. Meanwhile the archives of the Inguanez family remain closed, and it is impossible to be sure whether anyone has ever seen both acts of 1351, let alone inspected their authenticity. The author of the anonymous *Memoirs* of 1888 relied on Abela. Abela, 485-486, knew that Francesco Gatto had claimed in 1398 that his family deeds had been thrown into the *castrum maris,* though he could have argued that they might have been recovered later. The 1432 confirmation of the customs exemptions of 1351,1372 and 1406 was also based on a single *Instrumentum,* which cannot, logically, have been that of 1351 [VI,XIV]. The eighteenth-century scholar G. Agius de Soldanis made some notes under the title *Memorie della Nob. Casa Inguanez estratte dal MSS. sciolto che tiene il Sig. Barone Inguanez* (RML 142E, f.320-321), which contained a reference to "Il privilegio di Alfonso Re per l'esenzione delle Dogane fol.329", but included nothing which points explicitly to the existence of any fourteenth-century documents. The authenticity of the 1372 acts is beyond reasonable doubt since originals and registrations survive, though it is strange that an original of the 1372 confirmation of the customs exemption survives in Valletta. The question remains as to whether Abela actually saw the 1351 privileges or whether he saw and copied the "originals" of 1372.

It should be remembered that these documents have long been important because they have been held to demonstrate that the Inguanez titles of nobility went back to 1350/1. It was probably Abela, or possibly Mifsud, who changed the *not*[*arius*] Lancea of the 1351 customs exemption into *Nobilis,* and there may have been motives either for obscuring the 1351 originals, if they still existed, or for disguising their non-existence. The author of the Inguanez *Memoirs,19,* even presented the phrase *rationabiliter devolutum* in the Dejr il-Bniet grant of 1351 as *ratio nobiliter devolutum*! Abela must have believed in a pre-1530 Maltese nobility but in the light of the documents, from which he gave excerpts, he wrote with some scholarly restraint and the caution natural to a Vice-Chancellor of the Order which found itself in conflict with the nobility in his time. He described the Gatto family as "nobilissima", but he knew that Francesco Gatto was a *miles* in 1404. Tabrija was definitely a fief owing military service in 1316 [1], but Abela,449,464,466,485-486,492, incorrectly wrote of Dejr il-Bniet, which was described as a *viridarium,* as being a "feudo" by 1351; he gave the Gatto fiefs as "Baronie" in 1398, and he described the *miles* Antoni Desguanes as a "Barone". Dejr il-Bniet was granted *sub militari seruicio* in 1372 and 1398, but there was no clause concerning military service in the 1351 act, as was noted in *Correspondence and Report of the Commission appointed to inquire into the claims of the Maltese Nobility* (London,1878),21, where, incidentally, the commissioners referred vaguely to "authentic documents" but did not state that they had seen the originals.

In the absence of the originals of 1351 no definite pronouncement can be made. Both texts fit into the known events of 1350/1 and both were confirmed in 1372; on diplomatic grounds there is little to suggest any falsification. Mifsud's transcript of the Dejr il-Bniet grant and his version of Abela's description of it do suggest that Abela really saw an original of 1351, though it could conceivably have been a forgery [cf.V]. In the case of the customs grant, a very different kind of concession, there is more room for doubt, and the phrasing of Abela's remarks in his *Descrittione* and the copy of Abela's copy made by Mifsud all imply that the *Originale* which Abela had from the Baron Inguanez in 1624 was in fact the *confirma* of 1372; where Mifsud copied the 1351 text of the Dejr il-Bniet grant as such, he did not do so for the customs exemption, nor did he give details of registration, seals and so forth for the 1351 customs exemption [cf.VI]. An exemption from customs duties would have been an extremely valuable privilege for anyone on Malta, and it is again conceivable that a forged text purportedly of 1351 was presented for confirmation in 1372. There is no compelling reason for rejecting the authenticity of either of the two 1351 texts, even supposing that the originals were lost at an early date, but until the "original" can be consulted, an element of doubt must continue to surround these key documents concerning what was apparently the most significant event in Maltese politics in the ninety years between 1282 and 1372, the incorporation of the islands into the royal *demanium* in 1350.

## Appendix III: A BARONIAL LETTER

6 April 139[7], Agrigento: Raimondo Guglielmo Moncada, Marquis of Malta, sends his proctors Benedictu Calvinu and Johanni Panpina to receive fealty and homage from the Maltese authorities.

The original letter survives on paper in RML Univ.4, f.81 [*olim* RML 855, doc.41]; published in Mifsud, 289. Where there is a hole in the manuscript, Mifsud supplied the year "1396" from the transcript in *ACM 28, f.11 [*olim* 27, p.15], which gives *4e. In'is 1396;* Valentini, vii.63, also gave 1396. Moncada was apparently created Marquis on 13 Dec. 1396 and destituted on 16 Nov. 1397; these facts, together with what is known of the confused political situation at the time, suggest that the date should be early in 1397: details in A. Luttrell, "The House of Aragon and Malta: 1282-1412," *Journal of the Faculty of Arts: The Royal University of Malta,*iv no.2(1970), 164-166.

Fideles ac patres fratres et filij carissimi, Nuj mandamu Illocu nostri procuraturj et nuncij speciali cum plenaria potestate li nobilj et Egregij miss. benedictu caluinu et miss. Johanni panpina Informati plenissime de nostra Intencionj, aliqualj et eorum Relatibus dijatj darj Indubia et plenaria fidi Comu ala nostra propria persuna fachendulj fidi et homagiu pro parte nostra, Comu si nuj fussimu illocu presente, Scripta agrigent[o] vj° aprilis [......] *M'chio Mlt'*

Guill[er]mus Raymundus de Montecathino m'

*Reverse*: Nobilibus et Egregijs Capitaneo Judicibus Juratis
et Uniuersitatj Ciuitatis et Insule Meliuetj fidelibus
ac patribus fratribus et filiis nostris carissimis

Marchio meliuetj, [at]que Regni Sicilie magister
Iustitiarius et conestabilis etc.

# XIII

## The sale of Gumerin on Malta: 1318

During the thirteenth century the islands of Malta and Gozo were colonized from Sicily and Sicilian institutions were introduced. These included the notaries who drew up acts in the presence of *judices* and witnesses.[1] Scarcely any documents survive from the Hohenstaufen period, but an Antonius de Cappillerio, *publicus insularum Malta et Gaudisii notarius,* was acting at Malta on 29 July 1274 and again on 2 April 1277.[2] The will of Guillelmus de Malta was drawn up in Gozo on 8 February 1299 by Leone de Puntetremulo, *regius publicus insularum Malte et Gaudisii notarius,* and it was witnessed by Henricus de Montemurro *notarius* while two other notaries, Nicolaus de Lentini *publicus insularum Malte et Gaudisii notarius* and Teninus de Daniele *regius publicus insularum Malte et Gaudisii notarius,* both signed for witnesses who could not write; thus four notaries were gathered together simultaneously on the tiny island of Gozo.[3] On 23 January 1324 an act manumitting a slave at Malta was drawn up by Rogerius de Alammano, *regius publicus notarius Insularum Malte et Gaudisii.*[4] On 8 May 1318 at Malta this same Rogerius de Alammano drew up an act recording

1. Though earlier individual acts survive in original or copy, the earliest notarial register in the Notarial Archives, Valletta, dates to 1467; on these archives see G. Wettinger, «Our Medieval Historical Archives and their Care», in *Maltese History: What Future?*, ed. A. Williams and R. Vella Bonavita (Malta, 1974), 96-98.

2. Texts in V. Laurenza, «Malta nei documenti Angioini del R. Archivio di Napoli», *Archivio Storico di Malta*, v (1934), 132-136 (1274), and R. Moscati, «Fonti per la Storia di Malta nel R. Archivio di Stato di Napoli», *ibid.*, vii (1935-1936), 504-506 (1277).

3. Original parchment published in H. Bresc, «Malta dopo il Vestro Siciliano», *Melita Historica*, vi no. 3 (1974), 317-320. Cf. A. Luttrell, «The Administration of Gozo: 1335», *ibid.*, vii no. 2 (1977).

4. Original parchment published in Bresc, 320-321.

the sale of Gumerin on Malta, which well illustrates the Maltese judicial bureaucracy at work and the part the notary played in it, again with the witnesses including two other notaries, Petrus Marranchi and Symon de Carlo who was notary to the royal *castellanus* of Malta; the document survives in a copy of 1398.

In February 1398 Martino, King of Sicily, was carrying out a general reorganization of fiefs and other royal concessions, confirming old privileges and rewarding his supporters with confiscated lands, arrangements which included a number of new grants and confirmations on Malta and Gozo.[5] On 9 February from Catania he instructed the *secreto* of Malta to restore to Anonio or Antonello de Santa Sofia the Maltese *viridarium* of Gumerin which had once belonged to Antonello's father, the late Guglielmo de Santa Sofia, but which had subsequently passed to the royal *curia;* Antonello had produced a privilege of King Federico III and other notarial documents *puplica documenta.*[6] On the same day Martino, who was also acting in the name of his father King Martin of Aragon and of his wife Maria of Sicily, confirmed and granted *de novo* to Antonello, who was described as a *civis* of Malta, a royal privilege of 1320 which had confirmed the purchase of Gumerin by Guglielmo de Ragusia; the 1320 privilege itself contained two other acts of 1317 and 1318. Antonello claimed to be a direct descendant of Guglielmo de Ragusia. Following the evidence of «sifficient» witnesses and the presentation of a document drawn up in Malta by Rogerio *de laturrj,* another public notary of Malta, the Crown accepted that Thomasio de Santa Sofia had married Ylagia, daughter of Guglielmo de Ragusia, and that their son Antonio had a son Guglielmo who was Antonello's father. This privilege of 9 February 1398 was copied into the register of the Chancery [7] and into that of the Protonotaro.[8]

5. See H. Bresc, «The *Secrezia* and the Royal Patrimony in Malta: 1240-1450», in *Medieval Malta: Studies on Malta before the Knights,* ed. A. Luttrell (London, 1975), 152-155; see also R. Valentini, «Il Patrimonio della Corona in Malta fino alla venuta dell'Ordine», *Archivio Storico di Malta,* v (1934), who published and discussed a number of the 1398 texts.

6. Palermo, Archivio di Stato, Cancelleria, Reg. 32, f. 162v.

7. Palermo, Archivio di Stato, Cancelleria, Reg. 32, f. 181-184v [*olim* 156-159v]: text published below.

8. Palermo, Archivio di Stato, Protonotaro del Regno, Reg. 11, f. 18-20v.

In 1316 Guglielmo de Ragusia, along with Symon de Carlo of Messina, were both notaries who were serving the king as *procuratores iurium, redituum et proventuum gabellarum, jurium et bonorum Curie nostre dicte insole Malte.*[9] On 17 June 1320 at Messina King Federico III confirmed to Guglielmo de Ragusia, who was described as a *ciuis* of Malta but not as a notary, an earlier act of 8 May 1318 which recorded his purchase of Gumerin from Guglielmo de Surdu. Guglielmo de Ragusia and his heirs were to hold the *viridarium* or *jardinum* in perpetuity, owing to the Crown the same obligations owed by Guglielmo de Surdu, that is they had, at least in theory, to reside in the Kingdom of Sicily or the island of Malta; they had to hold Gumerin from the royal *curia* and to perform the services due, which were not explicitly listed in the document; and they were to hold the property *iure francorum*, that is the eldest son was to inherit and males were to take precedence over females.

The document of 8 May 1318 was witnessed in Malta by two *Iudices*, Johannes de Lavagna and Ansaldus Dragone; by Rogerio de Alamanno, the royal public notary of Malta and Gozo, who drew up and validated the instrument; by Arnaldo de Solimella, the royal castellan, justiciar and procurator for the island and *castrum* of Malta; and by seven other witnesses. They declared that Gumerin had previously been granted to Skius de Solimella who had died intestate and without legitimate heirs, so that it had devolved to the Crown. The document testified that Guglielmo de Surdu, a royal *familiaris*, had produced both a document issued at Messina on 17 June 1317 by which the king had granted him Gumerin and also a royal licence given at Mazzara on 3 February 1318, the text of which was repeated in the instrument of 8 May 1318; this licence empowered him to sell or otherwise alienate the property on certain conditions preserving the Crown's rights there. Guglielmo de Surdu received 58 gold *uncie;* he formally invested Guglielmo de Ragusia

9. Text in Valentini, 32-34.

*per lapidem*,[10] that is with a symbolic stone, and he handed over to the purchaser his royal licence to alienate.

These documents were known at the beginning of the sixteenth century to the Sicilian archivist and bureaucrat Gian Luca Barberi, who summarized them in his *Capibrevi*.[11] A copy of those parts of the *Capibrevi* which concerned Malta and Gozo was made in 1644 at Palermo to be sent to Malta; this transcript was made by Leonardo Biasini, who also copied the complete text of 1398 which included the earlier documents of 1317, 1318 and 1320.[12] The details given by Barberi concerning the families of Santa Sofia, Solimella and Surdu were used by the Maltese historian Gianfrancesco Abela in the history he published in 1647.[13] This information has subsequently been repeated, sometimes inaccurately,[14] but the text has never been published, despite its interest. Previous to the grant of Dejr il-Bniet to Francesco Gatto, who was himself a notary, in 1351,[15] only one other royal grant or confirmation of property on Malta is known; that is the grant of Tabrija to Actardus de Barba in 1316.[16] The texts concerning Gumerin show the Crown's theoretical rights over lands of the royal *curia* on Malta, with the king granting properties or licences and seeking to maintain the conditions of service. They illustrate the local machinery of royal castellan, notary and judges at work. They also provide an early toponym in *Gumerin*, the modern Ghemieri lying some three kilometres north-west of Rabat; they give details concerning Latin settlers on Malta; and they show the Santa Sofia family maintaining the Maltese claims it had established

10. On investiture *per vexillum*, see E. Mazzarese Fardella, *I feudi comitali di Sicilia dai Normanni agli Aragonesi* (Milan, 1974), 82-84.

11. *I Capibrevi di Giovanni Luca Barberi*, ed. G. Silvestri, iii (Palermo, 1888), 440-441.

12. Valletta, Royal Malta Library, Ms. Università 206 [*olim* Biblioteca 870], f. 205-214; modern copies in Royal Malta Library, Ms. Biblioteca 1226, f. 293-309, and Mdina, Cathedral Archives, Ms. 27, f. 437-444.

13. G.-F. Abela, *Della Descrittione di Malta* (Malta, 1647), 530-531.

14. One paragraph derived from Barberi and Biasini contained at least eleven errors, some of them gross (eg. wrong king, dates incorrect by ten years, husband as father, etc.).

15. Text (with minor inaccuracies) in Anon., *Memoirs of the Family of Inguanez* (Malta, 1888), 19-20.

16. Text in Valentini, 32-34.

by marriage. In addition, the text of 1320 was noted by G. La Mantia as the second earliest known example of a royal document being registered in the office of the Protonotary as well as in the Chancery.[17] The text is here given from the Chancery register, with a few words supplied or expanded from the Protonotary version which seems to have been copied with less care and which contains numerous variations in word order, spelling, contractions and above all in punctuation; only in a few significant cases are these noted. As far as possible, the text is generally given as found, without alterations to capitals, spelling or punctuation.

17. G. La Mantia, «Su l'uso della registrazione nella Cancelleria del Regno di Sicilia...», *Archivio Storico Siciliano*, ns. xxxi (1906), 208-209.

## DOCUMENT *

Martinus dei gratia Rex Aragonum, Et Martinus eadem gratia Rex Sicilie [18] etc. Presentis priuilegij serie notum fieri volumus Vniuersis tam presentibus quam futuris, quod Antonius de sancta sophia filius quondam guillelmi de sancta sophia ciuis Ciuitatis meliuetj coram maiestatis nostre conspectu nuperrime constitutus obtulit culmini nostro et presentauit quoddam priuilegium serenissimi principis dominj domini friderici Regis Sicilie proaui nostri memorie recolende sigillo pendentj dicti Illustrissimi principis commonitum, confirmationis videlicet cuiusdam venditionis vnius viridarij vocati de Gumerin positi in Insola meliveti facte olim guillelmo de ragusia ab auo ipsius Antonellj per quondam guillelmum surdu dominum et patronum ipsius viridarij sive Iardinj cui guillelmo Surdo concessum extitit viridarium predictum per serenissimos principes predecessores nostros diue memorie, quod priuilegium nos Inspici fecimus diligenter et viderj cuius quidem priuilegij tenor per omnia talis est, Fridericus dei gratia Rex sicilie per presens privilegium notum fierj volumus universis tam presentibus quam futuris quod pro parte guillelmi de ragusia Ciuis malte fidelis nostri ostensum et presentatum fuit nostro culminj quoddam Instrumentum publicum de quadam venditione cuiusdam viridarij dicti de gumerin positi In Insola malte facta per guillelmum Surdu familiarem et fidelem nostrum dicto guillelmo de ragusia, et heredibus suis continentie talis. In nomine domini nostri Ihesu Christi Amen Anno eiusdem ab Incarnatione m°ccc°octauodecimo, mense madij octauo eiusdem prime Indictionis Regnante serenissimo domino domino nostro Rege friderico dei gratia Inclito Rege Sicilie, felicis dominij regni eius, anno xxiij° feliciter Amen, Nos Iohannes de lauagna et Ansaldus draconus Iudices malte rogerius de alamanno regius puplicus Insolarum malte et gaudisij notarius et testes subscripti ad hoc uocati specialiter et rogatj, presenti scripto puplico notum facimus et testamur, quod guillelmus surdus familiaris domini nostri regis, dominus et patronus cuiusdam Iardinj dicti de gumerin positj In Insola malte cum terris Iuribus, et pertinentijs suis ex concessione sibj facta per regiam maiestatem prout in priuilegio concessionis ipsius sub pendenti sigillo eiusdem maiestatis regie datum messane per nobilem dominum fridericum de Incisa de Sacca militem Regni Sicilie cancellarium Anno dominice Incarnationis m°ccc°decimoseptimo mense Iunij xvj° eiusdem xv° Indictionis plenius continetur, Auctoritate sibi traddita ab eadem regia maiestate Infrascripta omnia faciendj in patentibus litteris

* Hemos mantenido la transcripción enviada por el autor, respetando su original.
18. Reg. 32 omits *sicilie*.

Regijs subscriptj tenoris videlicet. fridericus dei gratia Rex Sicilie, notum fierj volumus vniuersijs presentes litteras Inspecturis Quod nos ad supplicationem guillelmi Surdu familiaris et fidelis nostrj culmini nostro pro Inde humiliter factam, eidem guillelmo pignorandj vendendj dandj distrahendj permutandj pro anima Indicandj et quicquid Infe voluerit tamquam de re propria faciendj Iardinum dictum de gumerin positum In Insola malte cum omnibus Iuribus rationibus et pertinentijs suis quod ex concessione sibi et heredibus suis sub certis forma et modo per celsitudinem nostram facta a curia nostra sub debito et consueto seruitio per eum pro Inde et heredes suos curie nostre prestando tenet et possidet sicut in quodam priuilegio Sub pendenti maiestatis nostre sigillo sibi pro Inde facto plenius continetur, Sub forma modo et seruitio quibus Sibi per nostram excellentiam est concessum licentiam et liberam facultatem gratiose duximus concedendum lege seu constitutione aliqua huiusmodj concessionj nostre contraria non obstante, fidelitate nostra nec non constitutionibus serenissimi domini Jacobi Aragonum et olim Sicilie regis Illustris Reuerendj et carissimi fratris nostrj dum regno sicilie prefuit editis atque nostris nec non seruitio quod pro Inde curie nostre debetur ac curie et cuiuslibet alterius Iuribus semper saluis In cuius rei testimonium certitudinem et cautelam presentes sibi ex Inde fierj Iussimus maiestatis nostre sigillo munitas, datum mazarie tercio februarij prime Indictionis Iure concessionis predicte et sub forma modo et seruitio in predicto priuilegio contentis consentiens prius in nos predictos Iudices et notarium tamquam in suos cum sciret sx certa nostra scientia nos suos Iudices et notarium non esse per se et heredes suos uendidit et ex ipsa causa venditionis presentialiter assignauit et tradidit guillelmo de ragusia ciui malte et suis heredibus inperpetuum predictum Iardinum de gumerin cum terris mandris criptis spacijs misiratis aquis Ingressibus et egressibus accessibus Iusticijs et pertinencijs suis et omnibus alijs Iuribus ipsi Iardino pertinentibus et adiacentibus, quod quidem Iardinum cum predictis terris Iuribus et pertinencijs suis quondam skio de solimella et heredibus suis de suo corpore legitime descendentibus regia celsitudo dudum concesserat ipsumque dum vixit idem quondam skius tenuit, et possedit, et pro eo dictus quondam skius ab intestato mortuus extitit liberis legitimis non relictis ad manus regie curie rationabiliter et Iuste deuenit pro pretio Inter eos conuento unciarum auri quinquaginta octo ponderis generalis quas uncias quinquagentaocto eiusdem ponderis predictus guillelmus venditor ibi presentialiter recepit et habuit et fuit confessus recepisse et habuisse a predicto guillelmo emptore ex predicta causa, renunciat ... exceptioni non numerate et non recepte dicte pecunie spei future numerationis et receptionis et dicti aurj non bonj non Iusti et non recti ponderati exceptionj doli malj metus causa actionj in factum conditioni siue causa et exceptioni deceptionis in dimidia seu vltra dimidiam Iusti precij beneficio restitutionis et omni legum auxilio omnique probationj et defensioni in contrarium, quod quidem priuilegium concesionis facte per dictum dominum regem predicto guillelmo surdo et predictas patentes regales literas ibi presentialiter, dictus venditor dedit et assignauit predicto emptorj, conseruandas penes eum ad cautelam et defensionem dicti Iardinj terrarum eius et Iurium predictorum, Quare predictus guillelmus venditor ex predicta causa venditionis cessit dedit atque mandauit predicto guillelmo emptorj omnes acciones utiles et directas reales et personales et omnia Iura quocumque modo et Iure competentes et competentia in predicto et pro predicto Iardino et eius terris et Iuribus superius venditis et eorum occasione transferens predictus guillelmus venditor in predictum guillelmum emptorem plenum dominium et plenam possessionem uel quasi predicti Iardinj terrarum Iurium et pertinenciarum suarum, cui dominio et possessionj illico renuntiauit et se absentem ex Inde fecit uolens eum facere suo ministerio possessorem uel quasi, Insuper predictus guillelmus uenditor Inducens predictum guillelmum emptorem per lapidem [19] in corporalem vacuam et expeditam possessionem predicti Iardinj terrarum et Iurium predictorum ad habendum tenendum et possidendum dandum vendendum et alienandum et quicquid sibi suisque heredibus de Inceps placuerit perpetuo faciendum tamquam de re sua propria, sibi Iusto emptionis titulo acquisita promisit et conuenit sub obligatione omnium bonorum suorum mobilium et inmobilium presentium et futurum predicto guillelmo emptorj stipulanti pro se et suis heredibus quod defendet guarentabit et excalumpniabit eidem emptorj et suis heredibus et sui dederit predictum Iardinum cum predictis terris Iuribus pertinentijs et adiacentijs suis ab omnibus et singulis personis puplicis et priuatis omni tempore siue de facto siue de Iure de predicto Iardino et eius terris et predictis Iuribus litem seu questionem Inferentibus dicto emptorj et quod restituet eidem emptorj omnes expensas dampna et Interesse quas et que pro Inde faceret et sustineret in Iudicio et extra Iudicium et credatur de omnibus supradictis et de omnibus expensis faciendis in curia uel extra occasione dicti Iardinj terrarum eius et predictorum Iurium simplici et nudo uerbo ipsius emptoris et quod non teneatur dictus emptor se defendere et post latam sententiam appellare nec eidem uenditorj aliquatenus denunciare si occasione dicti Iardinj terrarum et Iurium predictorum dictus emptor siue de facto siue de Iure in curia uel extra aliquatenus molestetur ab aliquibus personis puplicis uel priuatis dans et concedens eidem emptorj dictus uenditor quod propria auctoritate siue magistratus decreto possit Intrare capere et vendere tantum de bonis ipsius venditoris quod sibi satisfiat de precio dampnis et Interesse factis In curia uel extra de quibus omnibus statur simplici et nudo uerbo ipsius emptoris, Quam quidem uenditionem

19. For a transfer of a *fedum* at Scicli in Siciliy made *pro quadam lapide*, see a text of 1346 in E. Sipione, «Tre documenti trecenteschi», *Archivio Storico per la Sicilia Orientale*, lxiv (1968), 246-248.

et omnia et singula supradicta predictus uenditor promisit attendere obseruare et adimplere rata et firma habere et tenere et contra non facere nec venire nec pro Inde litem seu controuersiam mouere nec mouerj facere aliqua ratione uel occasione sub pena solemni stipulatione promissa dublj predicti precij per ipsum uenditorem Si contrafaceret regie curie persoluenda et a me predicto notario tamquam puplica persona per eandam curiam stipulata, qua pena soluta uel non soluta semper nihilominus presens contractus et omnia supradicta in suo robore perseuerent, Et ad maiorem cautelam prenominatus uenditor renunciauit expresse in premissis omnibus beneficio restitutionis et appellationis priuilegio et beneficio curialibus Indultis exceptioni delj malj conditioni siue causa et in fact.. priuilegio forj quod nullum forum dictus uenditor possit eligere sed in quolibet foro a predicto emptore electo possit et debeat conuenirj ferijs literis Impetratis uel impetrandis et omnibus generaliter Iuribus legibus canonicis et ciuilibus constitutionibus consuetis exceptionibus et allegationibus scriptis et non scriptis hic expressis et non expressis de predictis uel aliquo predictorum in contrarium facientibus mentionem omnique alij probationj auxilio et defensionj Iuris et facti quibus se tuerj uel contrauenire posset, quod autem abrasum est supra in xva linea ubi legitur atque nostris necnon pro autentico habeatur, quia per me predictum notarium abrasum et emendatum est non vitio sed errore, unde ad futuram memoriam et predicti guillelmi emptoris cautelam suorumque heredum presens puplicum Instrumentum sibi ex Inde factum est per manus mei predicti notarij signo et subscriptionibus tam nostrum qui supra Iudicum et notarij quam testium subscriptorum subscriptionibus et testimonio roboratum. Actum malte anno die mense et Indictione premissis, + Ego Johannes dela vagna [20] qui supra Iudex malte + Ego Ansaldus dragone quj supra Iudex malte. + nos arnaldus de solinella miles regius castellanus Iust[itiarius] et procurator Insole et castri malte scribere nescientes per manus notarij Symonis de carlo notarij nostri nos scribi fecimus et testamur. + Ego benedictus de friderico testis sum + Ego notarius petrus marranchi testor + Ego homodeus de salerno testor + Ego nicolus de asmundo testor sum + Ego Symon de carlo testor + Ego nicolosus de trapano testor + Ego benedictus de scuto testor + Ego Rogerius de alamano qui supra regius puplicus Insolarum et malte et gaudisij notarius predictis omnibus Interfuj rogatus scripsi et solito signo meo proprio signaui. Et nostro culmini fuit humiliter supplicatum ut predictam vendicionem predicti Iardinj cum omnibus Iuribus rationibus et pertinentijs suis factam per dictum guillelmum surdum dicto guillelmo de ragusia et suis heredibus In perpetuum ratificare acceptare et confirmare de benignitate regia dignaremur, Nos huiusmodj supplicatione benigne admissa predictam venditionem dictj Iardinj Iurium rationum et pertinenciarum suarum per dictum guillel-

20. Protonotaro gives *de alauagna.*

mum Surdu dicto guillelmo de ragusia et dictis heredibus suis inperpetuum ut predicitur factam quatenus Iuste rite et rationabiliter factam extitit eidem guillelmo et dictis suis heredibus sub illis tamen forma modo et seruitio sub quibus predicto guillelmo Surdo et suis heredibus predictum Iardinum cum Iuribus rationibus et pertinencijs suis per nostram excellentiam fuit concessum ratificamus acceptamus et pleno fauore regio confirmamus. Ita tamen quod dicti guillelmus de ragusia et eius heredes sint Incole regni nostrj sicilie uel dicte Insole malte et in eodem regno uel dicta Insola sub nostro et heredum nostrorum dominio habitent et morentur, et quod dictum Iardinum cum omnibus Iuribus rationibus et pertinencijs suis a nostra curia teneant et cognoscant et ex Inde seruire dicto seruitio eidem nostre curie teneantur et vivant Inde Iure francorum videlicet quod maior natu minoribus fratribus et coheredibus suis et masculus feminis preferentur, fidelitate nostra nec non constitutionibus serenissimi dominj Iacobj aragonum et olim sicilie regis Illustris reuerendj et carissimi fratris nostrj dum regno sicilie prefuit editis atque nostris predicto seruitio ac curie nostre et cuiuslibet alterius Iuribus semper saluis. In cuius rei testimonium certitudinem et cautelam presens priuilegium sibj ex Inde fierj et sigillo maiestatis nostre pendentj Iussimus communirj. datum messane per nobilem fridericum de Incisa de Sacca militem Regnj sicilie cancellarium Anno dominice Incarnationis millesimo ccc° xx° mense Junij xvij° eiusdem tercie Indictionis Registratum In cancelleria Registratum penes Prothonotarium. Et Maiestatibus nostris idem Antonellus humiliter supplicauit vt cum ipse Antonellus exponens sit heres legitimus per rectam lineam descendens eiusdem quondam guillelmj de ragusia per modum Infrascriptum Videlicet quod dictus guillelmus de ragusia primus emptor dicti viridarij fuit pater legitimus et naturalis quondam ylagie ex qua ylagia et quondam [margherita] [21] thomasio de sancta sophia eius viro fuit natus quondam Antonius de sancta sophia auus dicti exponentis et ex eodem Antonio et quondam eius vxore natus fuit quondam guillelmus de sancta sophia pater legitimus ipsius Antonellj exponentis cui quondam guillelmo patri suo idem antonellus tamquam filius et heres legitimus successit, et succedere debet in bonis dicti quondam guillelmi patris suj et potissime in viridario predicto eidem Antonello et suis heredibus de suo corpore legitime descendentibus In perpetuum prefatum viridarium ac privilegium predictum et omnia et singula contenta in eodem acceptare approbare ratificare et de nouo ipsum viridarium sibi et suis heredibus supradictis concedere et donare benigniter dignaremur, Nos autem ipsius antonellj Supplicationem benigne admictentes consideratione presertim seruitiorum per dictum quondam guillelmum patrem ipsius Antonellj nostris

21. Reg. 32 and Protonotaro both give *mag*ª; Barberi, iii. 441, Abela, 530, and others give *magna*.

predecessoribus gratissime prestitorum pro quorum nomine et seruitijs fuit ut percepimus Interfectus, habita informatione plenaria per testes ydoneos in numero competentj et Instrumento testimonialj omnibus solemnitatibus roborato confecto In Insola meliuetj manu notarij rogerij de laturrj puplici notarij dicte Insole, quod propterea Inspici fecimus et viderj ac in archivo dilecti nostrj prothonotarij propterea conservarj de genologia supradicta et qualiter dictus Antonellus exponens per rectam lineam est successor dicti guillelmi de ragusia primj dominj emptoris dicti viridarij, ac etiam actendentes seruitia que idem Antonellus nostris conatur continue prestare maiestatibus et que prestare poterit In futurum dante domino gratiora eidem Antonello et suis heredibus Inperpetuum predictum viridarium de certa nostra scientia, ac gratia specialj approbamus confirmamus acceptamus ratificamus et de nouo concedimus et donamus sub debito tamen et consueto seruitio per eundem Antonellum et heredes suos predictos nostre curie prestando prout in priuilegio superius Inserto continetur, nostre curie et aliorum Iuribus semper saluis. Ad huius autem nostre confirmationis ac noue donationis et gratie futuram memoriam et robur perpetuo valiturum presens priuilegium ex Inde fierj Iussimus nostri magni sigillj pendentis munimine roboratum, Renunciatisque prius sponte per eundem Antonellum in manibus nostre curie omnibus et singulis Iuribus sibi forsitan competentibus ex gratia seu gratijs sibi uel antecessoribus suis super Iuribus cuiusuis secretie regni nostrj aut super Iuribus tractarum portuum et maritimarum dicti regni nostrj per maiestates nostras seu diue memorie gloriosos principes predecessores nostros factis uel concessis, p[rimus] cancellarius primogeniti aragonum Rex Martinus.[22]

datum cathanie per nobilem bartholomeum de Iuuenio militem regni sicilie cancellarium consiliarium etc [23] Anno dominice Incarnationis m°ccc°x°c septimo die nono februarij sexte Indictionis. Regnique nostrj dicti regis Aragonum anno secundo dicti regis sicilie sexto et dicte Regine[24] xx primo:

dominus rex mandauit michi
I. de aricio In consilio -
p.

22. Reg. 32 gives *p' canc.' p' mog.' arag' Rex Mart.'*.
23. Protonotaro gives *consiliarum familiarem et fidelem nostrum.*
24. Queen Maria's name was not, in fact, mentioned at the head of the document.

# XIV

# THE ADMINISTRATION OF GOZO: 1335

Owing to the loss of the royal registers in Sicily, the materials available for the internal history of Malta from 1282 to about 1355 are extremely scanty, while documents concerning Gozo are even more rare. The text of 1335, which survives in a seventeenth-century copy at Siracusa (1), was known through the brief excerpt published by Rosario Gregorio (2) and, through Gregorio, to Alfredo Mifsud (3). It is presented here in the form found in the transcript, which contains some apparent corruptions. A will of 1299 shows that Gozo then had three judges or *judices Gaudisii* though it is not clear who appointed them, and that Gozo shared with Malta at least three royal notaries, the *regii publici insularum Malte et Gaudisii notarii;* the Count of Malta and Gozo had his agent or agents, his *procuratores bonorum,* to manage his personal possessions or *bona* in both islands, and it was the Count or his representative who nominated a castellan for the Gozo castle, the *castellanus in castro Gaudisii,* as well as a *capitanius* or two *capitanii* to govern for him in Malta (4). The document of 1335 mentions a number of officers conducting the administration of Gozo separately from that of Malta, and it provides evidence of Sicilian trade on Gozo as well as in Malta. The relative powers and precise jurisdictions of the royal *curia* and the Count, and of the Maltese and Gozitan officials mentioned in 1299 and 1335 are still far from clear, and the text of 1335 raises a number of problems which require detailed discussion not attempted here. There was considerable confusion on many such matters in fourteenth-century Sicily,

1. Siracusa, Biblioteca Comunale, *Liber Privilegiorum,* I, f.92v-94 [*olim* 79v-81]; a marginal note in a later hand states *Collatum cum originale,* and a few corrections can be seen. Further details in S.L. Agnello, "Il 'Liber privilegiorum et diplomatum nobilis et fidelissimae Syracusarum urbis'," *Archivio Storico Siracusano,* v-vi (1959 1960).
2. R. Gregorio, *Considerazioni sopra la Storia di Sicilia,* iv (1st ed: Palermo, 1807 prove 38 n.55), and in subsequent editions, eg. *Opere rare edite ed inedite riguardanti la Sicilia* (2nd ed: Palermo, 1873), 329 n.2.
3. A. Mifsud, "Richiami alle signorie del passato di Malta," *Archivum Melitense,* iii no.7 (1918), 277 n.1, and subsequently A. Luttrell, "The House of Aragon and Malta: 1282-1412," *Journal of the Faculty of Arts: The Royal University of Malta,* iv no.2 (1970), 161 n.23.
4. Text in H. Bresc, "Malta dopo il Vespro Siciliano," *Melita Historica,* vi no.3 (1974), 317-320. On late-medieval Muslims as royal captains and Jews as *secreti* on the island of Pantelleria, see H. Bresc, "Pantelleria entre l'Islam et la Chrétienté," *Cahiers de Tunisie,* xix (1971), 106-107, 117.

and Maltese institutions should not be inserted into supposely permanent, rigid "feudal" or bureaucratic systems and hierarchies which, in practice, did not function regularly in Sicily, let alone in the lesser islands.

In 1316 Arnaldus de Solimella *miles* was *Castellanus castri et Iustitiarius eiusdem insole Malte,* while two *notarii,* Simone de Carolo of Messina and Guglielmus de Ragusia, were *procuratores iurium, reddituum et proventuum gabellarum, jurium et bonorum Curie nostre dicte insole Malte* for the king (5). In 1318 the same Arnaldus was *regius castellanus Iustitiarius et procurator Insole et castri Malte* (6), and he was still the *iusticiarius* and *castellanus* in 1320 (7). Arnaldus de Solimel'a was a royal official, and probably there was no Count at that point; indeed it is not clear when Guglielmo Federico d'Aragona, Duke of Athens, actually became Count of Ma'ta and Gozo. It must have been before 18 November 1330 when he ceded the County to his natural brother Alfonso Federico d'Aragona and his heirs; they were to hold it *in capite* from Guglielmo's *curia* to which they were to owe the military service of three *milites,* and they were to enjoy the criminal jurisdiction and the *merum et mixtum imperium,* though Guglielmo reserved rights of appeal to his *curia.* A'fonso Federico's father, King Federico of Sicily, confirmed the act of cession two days later. To what extent the Count of Malta had powers to appoint officia's and raise taxes is not altogether clear, but the grant of 1330 expressly excluded the royal rights to the *exite,* the *tercius dohane,* the *collecte* and the *subvenciones,* all these incomes being reserved to the Crown (8). At about this time the Count of Gerace in Sicily was administering his castles and estates through a *curia* with an archive and a scribe, with a *magister procurator,* a *magister racionalis* and a wide variety of *castellani, cabelloti* and other estate managers and *officiales* (9).

Some time before 1330 the Kings of Sicily had exempted the men of Siracusa and Messina from payment of certain taxes, the *iura dohanarum.* and of other dues owing to the royal *secrezia* throughout the royal

5. Text in R. Valentini, "Il Patrimonio della Corona in Malta fino allo venuta dell' Ordine," *Archivio Storico di Malta,* v (1934), 32-34.
6. Copy of 1398 in Palermo, Archivio di Stato, Cancelleria, Reg. 32, f.181-184v.
7. Text in *Acta Siculo-Aragonensia,* ii: *Corrispondenza tra Federico III di Sicilia e Giacomo II d'Aragona,* ed. F. Giunta — A. Giuffrida (Palermo, 1972), 181-182.
8. Text in A. Rubió i Lluch, *Diplomatari de l'Orient català*: 1301-1409 (Barcelona, 1947), 482-485.
9. Text of 1307 or 1322 in E. Mazzarese Fardella, *I feudi comitali di Sicilia dai Normanni agli Aragonesi* (Milan, 1974), 109-116 (discussed *ibid.,* 74-77); the document refers to a *ritus dohane,* to *gabelle* and so forth, but it is not clear whether the royal *iura dohane* or other incomes were involved. This important work throws much light on some obscure questions but leaves many documents to discuss and problems to solve.

*demanium* (10). In 1335, however, the councils or *universitates* of the two cities complained that the officials on Gozo were proceeding against their merchants trading there on the grounds that the island had become part of a county, the implication being that it was no longer part of the royal *demanium* and that the royal exemptions had therefore lost their validity in Gozo. On 28 April 1335 Pietro II, who acted as king during his father's lifetime, sent instructions both to the *Iustitiariis, vel capitaneis, ac Procuratoribus Insule Gaudisii,* and a'so to the financial officials on Gozo, the *dohaneriis, credenceriis, seu gabellotis dohane* (11). Pietro affirmed the validity of the exemptions enjoyed by Messina and Siracusa which, his letter stated, had been explicitly safeguarded in the cession of 1330 and were being recognized in Malta, if not on Gozo. He instructed the *Iustitiarii*, the *Capitanei* and the *Procuratores* to ensure that the *dohanerii,* the *credencerii* and the *gabelloti* should repay whatever they had taken by way of the *iura dohane* since the previous September. It is not, however, clear either from the text (12) or from general Sicilian practice which, if any, of these officers were royal officials, whether all of them were appointed by the Count, or who controlled the office of the *secrezia.*

DE NON SOLVENDO IVRE DOHANAE in Insulis Gaudisij, & Melitae

PETRVS II, Dei gratia Rex Sicilie Serenissimi Domini Domini Friderici Reuerendissimi Patris sui Regis eiusdem Regni in ipsius administratione generaliter Locumtenens Iustitiariis, vel captaneis, ac Procuratoribus Insule Gaudisii pro parte Curie seu (13) Alfonsi Friderici Comitis ipsius Insule, ac Insule Meliueti Fratris sui, nec non dohaneriis, credenceriis, seu gabellotis dohane eiusdem Insule Gaudisii tam presentibus, quam futuris fidelibus suis gratiam suam, & bonam voluntatem. Pro parte Vniuersitatum hominum Ciuitatum Messane, & Syracusarum nostrorum fidelium fuit nuper cum querela coram nostra expositum Maiestate. Quod cum singuli Messanenses, & Syracusani ex priuilegiis eis ab olim per Dominos predecessores nostros Clare Memoriae dictum Dominum Regem Patrem nostrum, & nos indultis, atque concessis sint, & esse

10. It is not clear to which of numerous royal exemptions the document of 1335 referred: cf. Agnello and C. Trasselli, *I privilegi di Messina e di Trapani*: 1160-1355 (Palermo, 1949), with numerous references.
11. On the gabelles of Gozo, including the *dohana,* in 1372/3, see H. Bresc, "The *Secrezia* and the Royal Patrimony in Malta: 1240-1450," in *Medieval Malta: Studies on Malta before the Knights,* ed. A. Luttrell (London, 1975), 130, 134 *et passim.*
12. See especially *infra,* n.13.
13. Gregorio, *Opere,* 329 n.2, published the first few lines with a number of changes and errors, omitting the *seu* which is in the Siracusa copy although it reads clumsily and increases doubts as to whether the *Iustitiarii, vel capitanei, ac Procuratores* were all comital rather than royal officials; possibly the original had *atque* (cf. *infra,* n.15).

debeant in singulis ciuitatibus, terris, & locis nostri demanij a solutionibus iurium quorumcunque dohanarum, & aliorum directuum spectantium ad officium secretie liberi, & immunes, ac huiusmodi immunitate, & libertate ante scilicet concessionem factam dicto Comiti de Insulis supradictis in eis tanquam in terris nostri demanii, & post concessionem eandem in dicta Insula Meleueti usi fuerint, & gauisi, (14) ac gaudeant, & utantur Vos presentes Dohanerij, seu gabelloti dicte dohane tenoribus priuilegiorum dictorum penitus obauditis dicentes dictam Insulam Gaudisii in Comitatu esse, et propterea, & Syracusanos prefatos ac Messanenses in ea predictis libertate, & immunitate gaudere non posse, nonnullos Syracusanos, ac Messanenses accedentes ad dictam Insulam cum diuersis eorum rebus, & mercibus, ac negociantes ibidem ad soluendum vobis proinde iura dicte dohane, ac aliorum directuum spectantium ad dictum officium secretie, tanquam rendabiles compulistis, compellitis, & etiam molestatis ipsos propterea pignorando, tam contra tenorem dictorum priuilegiorum, quam in eorum damnum preiudicium, & grauamen; & nostro Culmini humiliter supplicatum super hoc eis per nostram Curiam opportuno Iusticie remedio prouideri, huiusmodi itaque supplicatione utpote iusta per nos benigne admissa quia de tenoribus priuilegiorum predictorum; quodque dicti Messanenses, & Syracusani in dictis Insulis a solutionibus dictorum Iurium, & directuum liberi, et exempti tractandi sint itaque libertate n dicta Insula Meleueti gaudeant Curie nostre constat, Volentes in obseruantia predictorum priuilegiorum eisdem Messanensibus, & Syracusanis predictam libertatem per uos in predicta Insula gaudisii tenaciter, & inuiolabiliter obseruari quatenus in illa dicta Insula Meleueti utuntur, & gaudent, & maxime quia sub ipsa conditione, & onere dictus Comitatus predicto Comiti fuit concessus, & de iis in priuilegio sibi comitatu ipso facto expressa mentio facta est fidelitati Vestre sub obtentu nostre gratie firmiter, et expresse mandamus quatenus vos predicti dohanerii credencerii, seu gabelloti dicte dohane predictos Messanenses, & Syracusanos a solutionibus quorumcunque Iurium do hanamur, & aliorum dirittuum prescriptorum pro quibuscunque rebus, & mercibus eorum per eos in dictam Insulam immissis, & de cetero immittendis 'ab inde extractis, & extrahendi immunes, & exemptos trattare, Vosque predicti Iustitiarii, atque (15) Capitanei ac Procuratores eosdem dohanerios, credencerios, seu gabellotos ad premissa inuiolabiliter obseruanda ad restituendum cum integritate qualibet dictis Messanensibus, & Syracusanis, si quid contra tenores immunitatum, & libertatum ipsarum a proxime praeteriti mensis Septembris huius III. Inditionis usque nunc per dictos presentes dohanerios, seu gabellotos perceptum fertur fuisse eosdem praesentes dohanerios, seu gabellotos dicte dohane stricte prout expediens fuerit compellere debeatis in exequtione presentium taliter uos gerendo, quod hiusmodi immunitates dictis Messanensibus, & Syracusanis quatenus in dictis eorum Priuilegis sunt expresse sine difficultate qualibet in dicta Inula obseruentur, & ad vos proptereo iterari alias nostras literas non sit opus sicut nostram gratiam caram habetis. Datum Cathaniae Anno Dominice Incarnationis M.CCC XXXV. XXVIII. Aprilis III. Inditionis.

---

14. Read *gaudisi*.
15. *seu* is written above *atque* in the same hand

# XV

## THE BENEDICTINES AND MALTA: 1363–1371

In the later middle ages the small islands of Malta and Gozo were politically and economically dependent upon the Kingdom of Sicily and its Aragonese rulers. During the thirteenth and fourteenth centuries both islands underwent a process of Christianization and Latinization in which many of the inhabitants were converted from Islam but retained their Arabic speech. Sicilians and Italians established themselves either as settlers or as absentee lay landlords and ecclesiastical benefice-holders, but the religious orders were slow to participate in this gradual process. The attempt by a Sicilian widow to implant the Benedictines of Catania on her Maltese estates was therefore of some historical significance, and the controversy it provoked generated a small collection of documents which have survived in the archives of the monks at Catania. Given the scarcity of sources for the fourteenth-century history of Malta, these documents provide precious information concerning Sicilian influences and the general development of the island.

On 17 June 1363 Ysolda de Landolina of Noto made a will leaving various properties on the island of Malta to the Benedictines of San Nicolò d'Arena at Catania on the condition that they were to found a house on Malta. Following her death the Sicilian monks succeeded in securing her considerable Maltese estates without having to establish any brethren on the island, but first they had to take the legal actions necessary to persuade the Bishop of Malta to commute the provisions of Ysolda's will in 1364 and then, in 1371, to prevent that Bishop's successor from claiming part of their new Maltese endowment. The original document of 1363 and two other parchments of 1364 and 1371 were preserved in the monks' archives at Catania where they are now in the Biblioteche Riunite Civica e A. Ursino Recupero: Tabulario dei Monasteri di San Nicolò L'Arena di Catania e di Santa Maria di Licodia, Pergamene 543, 557, 581.[1] Other documents on paper, some in the original but most in early-modern copies which are often notably inaccurate, survive in the Fondo Benedettini in the Archivio di Stato at Catania, where they have been bound into Mss. 153–156 and 159. The earliest though not necessarily the most reliable series of copies, datable to the sixteenth century, seems to be that in Ms. 159, and where this codex is damaged it is apparently best supplemented from Ms. 153.[2] These five codices concern the monks' Maltese properties, and they contain a number of fifteenth-century donations as well as later materials documenting the management and incomes of the Benedictines' estates on Malta down to the eighteenth century; Ms. 153 is especially rich in fifteenth-century documents, both originals and copies.[3]

Something was known of Ysolda's will when the Apostolic Visitor Pietro

[1]Cited here as Perg.; calendared, with notable inaccuracies, in C. Ardizzone, *I Diplomi esistenti nella Biblioteca Comunale ai Benedettini: Regesto* (Catania, 1927), 255, 261, 270.

[2]Cited here as Ms. Some of these Mss., but unfortunately not Ms. 159, were used in D. La Ferlita, 'I Possedimenti dei Benedettini di Catania a Malta', *Archivio Storico di Malta*, vii (1935/6); this work, which did not use the parchments from the Biblioteca Comunale, contains a number of errors.

[3]Cf. S. Leone, 'Una ricerca in corso: il patrimonio rurale dei Benedettini di S. Nicolò l'Arena di Catania dalla metà del secolo XVII alla liquidazione dei beni ecclesiastici: Consistenza ed amministrazione', *Archivio Storico per la Sicilia Orientale*, lxvii (1970), 41 n. 14, 50–1 *et passim.*

Dusina was on Malta in 1575, though at that point its provisions were thoroughly confused with those of the will of Paulus de Peregrino made in 1436.[4] In an unpublished work written at the beginning of the seventeenth century the Maltese Jesuit Girolamo Manduca advanced the incorrect claim that the Benedictines had held lands in Malta before Ysolda's donation.[5] The materials concerning Ysolda's bequest effectively entered the Maltese historiographical tradition through the historian Gian Francesco Abela who took up points already made by Manduca and who copied into his notebook a note concerning the bequest which had been sent to him from the Benedictine archives at Catania.[6] When he reproduced this note in the history of Malta he published in 1647, Abela described it as *vna nota dataci da vn Religioso, (che parimente ci affermò essere stata estratta in sostanza alcuni anni sono da' libri del monastero di Catania)*.[7] He employed the information in this note, together with some of the other details he had received from Catania, in various parts of his history.[8] Unfortunately Abela misinterpreted a document concerning the Dalmatian island of Meleda in an erroneous attempt to demonstrate the supposed foundation of a Benedictine monastery on Malta in 1130, and he buttressed his theory with an unlikely popular interpretation of the Maltese place-name Abbatija Tad-Dejr, and with a reference to a papal letter of 598 which did instruct that the Bishop of Malta be imprisoned in a monastery but which did not say that the monastery was in Malta. Abela stated clearly, and indeed correctly, that the lands held by the Benedictines of Catania were those bequeathed in 1363 by Ysolda and by other later donors, and he rejected the theory that they were the possessions of a twelfth-century foundation which had somehow passed to the monks of Catania on the extinction of this earlier monastery; he offered no explanation for the presumed disappearance of this hypothetical earlier house.[9]

These controversial issues were revived in 1707 in the course of an extraordinary incident in which the Bishop's decision of 1364 was challenged, after well over three hundred years, by the procurator in Malta of the Fabbrica di San Pietro at Rome who had certain powers in connection with pious legacies and who attempted to secure several centuries of incomes amounting to 300,000 Sicilian *scudi* by claiming that Ysolda's intentions had never been fulfilled. It was alleged that the monks had cunningly kept the documents hidden in their archives at Catania so that the Bishop and the Fabbrica could not see them, while they allowed people on Malta to think that they held the estate as the result of a much earlier and very ancient

[4] *Infra*, 159.

[5] Valletta, National Library of Malta, Biblioteca Ms. 25, f. 31.

[6] Valletta, Ms. 140, f. 38–9.

[7] Text, with minor variations and description of the *nota*, in G.-F. Abela, *Della Descrittione di Malta* (Malta, 1647), 390.

[8] Ibid., 305–6, 389–91.

[9] Ibid., 387–90; cf. A. Luttrell, 'Malta nel Periodo Normanno', *Atti del Congresso Internazionale di Studi sulla Sicilia Normanna* (Palermo, 1973), 474–5, and *idem*, 'Approaches to Medieval Malta', in *Medieval Malta: Malta before the Knights*, ed. A. Luttrell (London, 1975), 1–3, 33–4; cf. A. Luttrell, 'Girolamo Manduca and Gian Francesco Abela: Tradition and Invention in Maltese Historiography', *Melita Historica*, vii no. 2 (1977). On place-names in *dejr*, which did not necessarily mean 'convent', see G. Wettinger, 'Some Maltese Medieval Place-Names of Archaeological Interest', in *Atti del Colloquio Internazionale di Archeologia Medievale*, ii (Palermo, 1976), 344–6.

Benedictine foundation supposedly documented by Abela. Then in 1707 the monks tried to sell or otherwise alienate the estate and were therefore compelled to produce their title deeds. The Fabbrica's procurator at once instituted what proved to be an extremely lengthy legal action which generated much inaccurate copying of documents and false argumentations, with the monks of Catania claiming that many of their documents had been destroyed or damaged in the great earthquake of 1693. Much of the legal debate was based anachronistically on legislation and authorities which dated well after 1364. The Benedictines eventually retained their Maltese estates after an appeal to the Roman *curia*, though the Fabbrica reopened the case through a new appeal in 1721. The legal arguments went against the monks but they were eventually allowed to keep Ysolda's Maltese bequest through the prescription of time, simply because they had held it for so long.[10]

During these lawsuits the monastic party advanced in evidence Abela's claims for an ancient Benedictine foundation which were founded in part on the contents of his *nota* on Ysolda's legacy, but their opponents pointed out that Abela's book of 1647 was 'modern'; that he had not seen the original documents; that his *nota* was suspect in that it had been supplied by a Benedictine; that it was not an original document and could not be accepted as a proof; and that Abela had himself admitted that the notion of an early Benedictine foundation was merely a hypothesis based on the toponym Abbatija Tad-Dejr. In the course of the case Abela's printed text was checked against a manuscript copy of the original *nota* in Malta.[11] Copies of various documents made in connection with these litigations still exist on Malta in Valletta, National Library of Malta, Biblioteca Ms. 360, f. 333–340, 896–950, and in Mdina, Archivum Cathedrale Melitense, Ms. 2, f. 2–11, and Ms. 18, f. 4–8. The Valletta Ms. contains copies or summaries of many of the relevant late-medieval documents, along with lists of the monks' properties in 1591, 1597, 1682 and

[10]Mss. 154 and 155 *passim*. This voluminous documentation cannot be detailed here. The affair is partly summarised in La Ferlita, 272–6. G. P. Cardillo, '*Melevitana Praetensa Devolutio*' (unpublished thesis: Faculty of Jurisprudence, University of Catania, 1967/8), is a purely juridical study based only on Mss. 154 and 155, and largely on the seriously corrupted printed materials therein. Cardillo ignored even La Ferlita's work, and the medieval details he gives are partly misleading. This thesis induced A. Vella, 'I Normanni a Malta', *Atti del Congresso* . . . (1973), 505–6, and *idem*, *Storja ta' Malta*, i (Malta, 1974), 164–5, to speak of Ysolda as a Maltese 'sinjura', to give an anachronistic reference to the 'feudo di Lancillotto', to suppose that the Benedictines were already established on Malta and that in 1363 six monks were already in residence there, and to describe the attacks of Muslim pirates who sacked the convent and slaughtered the monks causing Ysolda to flee to Sicily; none of this results from the contemporary documents, nor does the phrase commencing *monachi quoque* . . . Furthermore Vella states that Ysolda left in Malta *and* Gozo 'le terre di Garmieli e del Habit di Seffuda, quelle di Casal Chidieri, Iddaura tal-Himieri ed il ricchissimo feudo di Lancillotto', quoting this phrase as if it were part of her will, yet these places are not mentioned either in the will or in the text of 1365 (Docs. I, III *infra*); some of them seem to have been part of the legacy of Paulus de Peregrino made in his will of 1436 in Ms. 153, f. 69–76v (copy of 1439), while the confused reference to *Benarratu* comes from Doc. IV *infra*. Vella, in *Atti*, 505–6, also connected Ysolda's church with Abela's supposed Benedictine foundation of 1130, but that supposition must now be rejected, as Vella (*Storja*, i. 73–95) implicitly recognises.

[11]Ms. 154, f. 92v–93, 98–98v, 108; 155, f. 95–99v, 123–5.

thereafter, and later materials connected with the Benedictine estates and the lawsuits of 1707–1723.[12]

Apart from a will of 1299,[13] Ysolda's bequest constitutes the earliest known documented example of a pious endowment in Malta. After about 1400 the documentation still available for the history of Malta is comparatively rich, so that only the fourteenth-century texts at Catania are studied in any detail here.[14] The Benedictines' post-1400 documents do, however, provide a continuous picture of the development and management of a major Maltese estate across more than four centuries, and they certainly merit detailed investigation. In particular, these later documents provide indications of the whereabouts and extent of Ysolda's properties.[15] The texts published or discussed below contain precious early information concerning Malta's place-names and inhabitants. Many of the toponyms receive their earliest known mention in these texts, even if their form may be distorted because they were written by Sicilians in Sicily, so that it is important to seek their precise date and form. The transcription of originals and copies is, as far as possible, faithful to the manuscripts, no consistent attempt being made to improve spellings or grammar, even though these are often illegible or evidently erratic; however, proper names have been capitalised and in Documents I–III punctuation, which is almost totally lacking, has been arbitrarily supplied.

* * *

When Ysolda de Landolina of Noto, widow of Lancia de Carubeni also of Noto, made a will at Noto on 17 June 1363, she chose to be buried in the cemetery of the church of San Nicolò at Noto in the Diocese of Siracusa, and she left certain sums of money and incomes to various relatives and to others, including a number of persons on Malta where she had close connections. Apparently she had no living children. She bequeathed a *viridarium* on Malta to Francia, wife of Avanella de Landolina, and another piece of land at Mtarfa near Mdina to the priest who already held it, with the provision that on his death her executors should choose a new priest who would hold the same land and celebrate masses for the souls of her husband and her relations.[16] The rest of her goods in the city and island of Malta were to pass to the Benedictines of San Nicolò d'Arena at Catania with the condition that they were to maintain a house for six monks who were to live in

[12]Cf. A. Luttrell, 'The Earliest Documents Transcribed in the Cathedral Archives, Mdina: 1316–1372', in J. Azzopardi, *Archives of the Cathedral of Malta Misc. 32 A: 1313–1519* (Malta, 1977), 42–3. The Maltese archives of the Fabbrica di San Pietro are now in the Cathedral Museum at Mdina, where their reorganisation is being completed.

[13]Text in H. Bresc, 'Malta dopo il Vespro Siciliano', *Melita Historica*, vi n. 3 (1974), 317–20.

[14]Note that Ardizzone, 299, wrongly refers to a Conradus *Episcopus Melitensis* in 1402. He was actually Bishop of *Militen* or Mileto: Perg. 650.

[15]Leone and La Ferlita provide preliminary details, but unfortunately the latter's lists do not give either dates or exact word-forms for the toponyms. Ms. 159, f. 33–33v, 43–6 *et passim*, provides lists of properties in 1591 and 1628; see also Valletta, Ms. 360, f. 910–50.

[16]A list of clerical incomes of 1436 mentioned *lo Animagio di Solda* paying one *uncia*: early-modern copy in Valletta, Ms. 255, f. 224–226v. This might suggest that this clause in Ysolda's will was satisfactorily executed.

Malta at the church of San Nicolò, which already existed on her lands there, and to pray for herself, her husband and her kin.[17] How Ysolda had acquired these properties was not stated; conceivably some or all of them were inherited from an ancestor named Paolino de Malta,[18] or possibly some or all of them were part of the lands granted by the king to the Landolina family after being confiscated from the traitors Muchio, Paolo and Pietro de Barba in 1358.[19] In any case they constituted an estate which may have been typical of the possessions which a Sicilian family could accumulate on Malta. There was no declaration that Ysolda had herself constructed the church which she presumably held under some form of private patronage or *juspatronatus*.[20]

Ysolda lived long enough to add codicils to her will[21] but by July 1364, if not earlier, she was dead.[22] Her executors would have paid for her burial at Noto, probably using monies available to them there, and there is no hint of any controversy in Noto. The Benedictines were, however, reluctant to establish a house on Malta, and they probably benefitted from the age-old situation in which the

[17]Perg. 543 (Doc. I *infra*, where the date of 1363 is established).

[18]Ysolda's will stated that she was *consobrina* of Renaldus and Safira de Landolina; La Ferlita, 262, mistakenly assumes Ysolda was their sister. In 1454 the Viceroy in Sicily accepted claims that the Landolina descended from Paolino de Malta to whom Frederick II granted the *casale* of Stafenda in 1235 and who was Frederick's proctor on Malta in 1239 and 1240: A. Luttrell, 'Frederick II and Paolino de Malta: 1235', *Quellen und Forschungen aus den italienischen Archiven und Bibliotheken*, lv–lvi (1976). This seems quite probable. In 1371 Renaldus sold the Sicilian *pheudum* of *Gisira* which bounded that of Stafenda: A. Giuffrida, *Il Cartulario della Famiglia Alagona di Sicilia: 1337–1386* (Palermo, 1978), 79. Conceivably Paolino acquired properties on Malta which later passed to the Landolina family and thus to Ysolda. Ysolda also bequeathed to various persons in Malta certain incomes from *bona* which had once belonged to Lorenzo de Abello, but her will did not state that those *bona* were in Malta and it seems that they were not, since they were not mentioned as being exempted from her legacy to the monks. *Laurentius de Apello* was at Scicli on 21 January 1335: copy in Siracusa, Biblioteca Comunale, Liber Privilegiorum, ii. f. 47–49v. Abela, 306, 390, inaccurately described Ysolda as *Maltese* and *una donna Maltese*; according to the act of 11 October 1364 (Doc. II *infra*), she was *habitatrix terre Nothj*.

[19]On 31 July 1358 the king consulted Artale de Alagona, governor of Noto, concerning a request from the sons of the late Johannes de Landolina for the goods in Noto, Malta and Gozo which had once been held feudally and in *burgensatica* by the traitors Muchio, Paolo and Pietro da Barba of Noto and which had already been assigned to their late father: Palermo, Archivio di Stato, Protonotaro 2, f. 349 [*olim* 337]. On 28 July 1358 property in Noto of Muchio de Bono of Noto, an assassin of Johannes de Landolina, Captain of Noto, had been assigned to Thumeus and Vassallus, sons of Johannes: Protonotaro 2, f. 347–347v [*olim* 333–335v]. The Landolina did secure the Maltese *pheudum* of Tabrija which had been granted to Actardus de Barba in 1316: Luttrell (1977), 36–7.

[20]The question of the private church in medieval Malta is discussed in A. Luttrell, 'Historical and Architectural Postscript', in *Excavations at Ħal Millieri, Malta*, ed. T. Blagg, A. Bonanno, A. Luttrell (Malta, forthcoming).

[21]Some of those who eventually received legacies, for example Nicolaus de Stabili and Sibilia wife of Renaldus de Landolina (*infra*, 153 and n. 34), were not named in the original will, while the text of 8 July 1370 explicitly mentioned codicils (*In eisdem testamento et codicillis*): copy in Ms. 159, f. 127v–128.

[22]The Benedictines appointed proctors to advance claims to her estate on 30 July 1364: Doc. II *infra*. If by 11 October 1364 the Bishop was arguing, as he may have been (Doc. II *infra*), that a year had passed during which the executors had failed to execute Ysolda's will, then she was dead by 11 October 1363.

Bishop and some or many of the canons of the Maltese diocese were usually Sicilians resident in Sicily, and in which the Bishop was sometimes favourable to or influenced by the monks of Catania. In January 1357 the king had instructed that a Canon of Siracusa, whose goods and incomes at Lentini in Sicily had been usurped by Iohannes de Regio, Canon and *archidiaconus* of Malta cathedral, was in recompense to have the rights and incomes of Iohannes' canonry and *archidiaconatus* in Malta. On 5 March 1357 the king wrote that since the newly-elected Bishop of Malta *frater* Ilarius was occupied in negotiations at Avignon, the new Bishop had named Raynerius de Philippono, Canon of Palermo, Mazzara and Malta, as his vicar-general to go to Malta to take possession of the see; the Notary Lancea Gatto had already published the papal provision and the episcopal procuration in Malta.[23] On 7 August 1358 the king ordered his officials in Malta and Gozo to assist the Bishop's proctors in recovering various goods usurped by the priests and canons in Malta and to collect tenths and other dues.[24] In October 1360 the clergy in Malta were in rebellion against Ilarius, who was a royal chaplain and councillor as well as a *frater*;[25] he had been Bishop of Bethlehem when on 15 June 1356 he was provided to the Bishopric of Malta by the pope acting at the king's recommendation.[26]

A notarial act drawn up at Catania on 11 October 1364 recorded that Bishop Ilarius had, at the monks' request made to him in Catania, agreed to alter the terms of Ysolda's will. It was apparently accepted that she had the right to dispose of her estates and to alienate her church and its *juspatronatus* to a monastery; it was the general rule that the Bishop's permission was not needed provided that his interests were not harmed but he did have various rights in matters involving wills and legacies, and with regard to the foundation of monasteries the Bishop had powers to intervene if the executors did not fulfil their duties within one year. Bartolo da Sassoferrato, the famous lawyer who died in 1357, held that no delay should for any reason be allowed to injure a charitable bequest; that if a convent for which provision was made in a will could not be built within a year, another house should be purchased or rented in order to carry out in the meantime the testator's intention; and that a legacy for a charitable purpose could be converted into another use if it were not possible to carry out the original intention.[27] The monks probably argued in detail along such lines.

The Bishop's apparently somewhat confused assertion of jurisdiction may have been based in part on local custom. The claim *quod Illud quod Relictum est ad pias*

[23]Texts in G. Cosentino, *Codice Diplomatico di Federico III di Aragona Re di Sicilia: 1355–1377*, i (Palermo, 1885/1907), 322–3, 338–40.

[24]Palermo, Protonotaro 1, f. 207.

[25]The royal document commenced *pro parte Reverendi In Christo patris, fratris Ylarij Melivetanj episcopi, cappellani, consiliaris, familiarj et devoti nostrj* . . .: text in Cosentino, i. 525–6.

[26]Archivio Vaticano, Reg. Aven. 132, f. 60–60v, 67v–68; he was not a Benedictine as supposed by Abela, 306, 390, and it is not clear why C. Eubel, *Hierarchia Catholica Medii Aevi*, i (2nd ed: Munster, 1913), 135, gives his name as Conradus and describes him as a Dominican.

[27]*Corpus Iuris Canonici*, pars 2, ed. E. Richter (2nd ed: Leipzig, 1851), 539, 540, 612–13, 1055–6 = Decret. III 26 iii, vi, 38 viii, xi, and Sect. III 19 i. Cf. Bartolus de Sassoferrato, *Omnia, quae exstant, Opera* . . ., 10 vols. (Venice, 1590–1602), iii, f. 136; iv, f. 66v; x, f. 65 (references kindly provided by Professor Julius Kirshner of the University of Chicago). These matters were much debated by the legal commentators.

*causas per Ips*[*um*] *tanquam diocisanum episcopum debet exequtionj mandarj*, that is that the Bishop had control over part of Ysolda's inheritance which she had left *ad pias causas*, was a technical one since all Ysolda's properties in Malta had been bequeathed, with certain specified exceptions, to the Benedictines, and she made no generic gift *ad pias causas* in which the Bishop could claim an interest; *ad pias causas* was here being used in a very broad sense to justify the Bishop's claims to have powers to intervene. The Bishop seems to have claimed, again rather curiously and obscurely in a passage which scarcely makes sense, that although he lacked jurisdiction to act outside his own diocese, he had no need of such jurisdiction in this case since the matter was not, he asserted, a contentious one and therefore he had powers to act as if he were a private person; he was presumably arguing that there was no contested case requiring his jurisdiction and that he was merely making a declaration. Somewhat facilely perhaps, Bishop Ilarius accepted the monks' contentions that the bequest was too meagre to support a house on Malta with the proper complement of priests, deacons, subdeacons, *lectores* and *cantores* required by the monastic constitutions;[28] that there were no buildings in which the brethren could conduct the monastic life of prayer, meditation, reading and teaching;[29] that the journey to Malta by land and by sea was dangerous and difficult; and that the monks could not speak the Maltese language.[30] For these and various other reasons which the Bishop stated that he had considered but which his document did not record, including the alleged negligence of the executors which, according to the monks, gave the Bishop powers to execute the will himself, the Bishop commuted the original terms of Ysolda's testament so as to allow the Benedictines to accept her Maltese inheritance while fulfilling its conditions merely by offering their prayers from Catania where, as he pointed out, there were more than fifty monks available to intercede for the souls of Ysolda and her kin.[31] Exactly why the Bishop neglected his own rights in the matter and why he favoured the monks at the expense of Ysolda's intentions cannot be known.

On 17 March 1365 the Benedictine proctors were at Noto where the text of the Bishop's commutation of 11 October 1364 was read to Ysolda's surviving executors, Renaldus de Landolina and Petrus Camagninus, who were still said to be responsible for the execution of her will; Avanella de Landolina had apparently died without being replaced. Following this reading Petrus Camagninus resigned and refused to take any further part in the execution of the will, presumably in protest against the Bishop's action which he did not, however, formally oppose.

[28]The Benedictines of Catania probably had such a regulation in their constitutions, but no text can be found. They did have a Sicilian translation of the Rule: G. Palma, 'Le Costituzioni Benedettine: Testo Siciliano del Sec. XIV', *Archivio Storico Siciliano*, xxxvii (1912). F. and G. La Mantia, *Consuetudini di S. Maria di Licodia* (Palermo, 1898), contains statutes for the monks' agricultural dependents.

[29]. . . *nec quod sit Ibj locus aptus monachis ad agendum penitentiam Iuxta santiones sanctorum patrum nec quod sint Ibi aliqua officina monachalia* . . .

[30]On the language problem and non-Maltese clergy in the fifteenth century, see G. Wettinger—M. Fsadni, *Peter Caxaro's Cantilena: A Poem in Medieval Maltese* (Malta, 1968), 25–6.

[31]Text of 11 October 1364 (Doc. II *infra*) in a notarial transcript of 17 March 1365; witnesses to the latter included Notary Nicolaus de Carubeni and Notary Gullielmus de Landolina: Perg. 557.

Yet another notarial instrument was written out which included the text of the commutation and recorded its acceptance by the sole remaining executor Renaldus de Landolina, who agreed that the monks were to receive Ysolda's goods, empowered them to collect various debts still owing to Ysolda, and repeated that they were to pay the legacies detailed in her will. In effect, the Benedictines of San Nicolò d'Arena became Ysolda's executors.[32] The monks' proctors then sailed to Malta and took possession of Ysolda's Maltese estates by an act of 7 May 1365 which listed the properties involved.[33]

The Benedictines sought to squeeze the maximum advantage from Ysolda's will. On 5 January 1366 Renaldus de Landolina had to intervene against the monks. He was still acting as Ysolda's executor and also on behalf of his own daughters Safira and Blanca, who were jointly owed 40 *uncie*, and of his sister Safira, who was the wife of Bernardus de Milocca and who was owed 40 *uncie*; Renaldus was furthermore executor of the will of the late Avanella de Landolina, himself one of Ysolda's executors. Renaldus secured testimony to prove that although these sums were to be found out of Ysolda's Maltese properties or incomes, they were to be paid in Sicilian coin and not, as the monks pretended, in the seven times less valuable *pecunia Insule Meliueti*; Bartolomeus de Guasto who had drawn up her will swore that Ysolda had explicitly stated that the legacies were to be paid in money of Sicily.[34] In 1369 and 1370 the Benedictines received receipts from Renaldus de Landolina, who had been paid 50 *uncie* on behalf of his daughters Blanca and Safira and of his wife Sibilia;[35] from Nicolaus de Stabili, the son of Notary Prudentio Stabili of Noto, for one *uncia* and 15 *tarini*;[36] from Francia, widow of Avanella de Landolina, for one *uncia* and 15 *tarini*;[37] and twice from Safira de Landolina, widow of Johannes de Berlinni, once for 4 *uncie*[38] and again for 10 gold florins.[39] The monks' Maltese accounts for the years 1365 to 1371 showed an income of 56 gold *uncie* almost all of which, 49 *uncie*, was spent on the payment of these legacies, though there were also expenses on *apothece* or shops which Ysolda had owned in Mdina; other legacies were paid at Paternò in Sicily.[40] A final note suggested that the total expended on Ysolda's legacies was 94 gold *uncie*.[41]

A few years later a different issue arose to threaten the monks' exploitation of

[32]Perg. 557. Avanella was certainly dead by 5 January 1366: Ms. 159, f. 123v–125v.

[33]Copy in Ms. 159, f. 121v–123v (Doc. III *infra*).

[34]Copy in Ms. 159, f. 123v–125v (damaged and supplemented from another copy in Ms. 153, f. 20–21v); on the mysterious *moneta Malte*, see Luttrell, in *Medieval Malta*, 10 n. 66.

[35]3 February 1369: copy in Ms. 159, f. 125v–127.

[36]8 July 1370: copy in Ms. 159, f. 127v–128; another copy in Ms. 153, f. 26–26v, shows that the document came *Ex actis meis Tomasij de Benintende Melitensis*. This legacy was not mentioned in the original will and must have been instituted by a codicil.

[37]19 July 1370: original inserted in Ms. 159 at f. 114, *ex actis Raynaldj lu Murellu In Malta*.

[38]19 August 1370: copy in Ms. 159, f. 128–128v (giving *de beolione*); another copy in Ms. 153, f. 31, states *Ex actis meis Not. Rogolini de Andrea Melitensis*.

[39]15 December 1370: copy in Ms. 159, f. 128v; another copy in Ms. 153, f. 30, mentions the same Notary Rogolinus.

[40]Original in Ms. 159, f. 114. This account was not complete; it showed Renaldus de Landolina receiving 40 *uncie* whereas ultimately he received 50.

[41]Original in Ms. 159, f. 114.

Ysolda's inheritance. She had made no legacy to the Bishop and in 1364 he had not reserved or assured his rights to a quarter or canonical portion of Ysolda's Maltese legacy. However, in 1371 a new Bishop of Malta, Antonius de Musto, who was a Franciscan,[42] claimed this *quarte canonice portio* and when the monks failed to pay it he sequestered their newly acquired Maltese incomes. The Bishop could have advanced some weighty arguments, but his position had in effect been surrendered in 1364 when Bishop Ilarius commuted Ysolda's will without attempting to protect his own rights. Ysolda's parish was not on Malta nor was she buried there, but there was a considerable body of legislation, much of it controversial, designed to prevent bishops' rights being eroded through gifts to monks or friars who often in fact encouraged people to make legacies in such a way as to avoid having to give the bishop a *portio*. The nature of this *portio* was normally determined by local custom or constitution, and since the Benedictines must have been among the earliest, if not the first, of the religious orders to receive endowments in the Maltese islands, this was perhaps the first occasion on which such an issue had arisen there precisely in this form. It was in any case a tricky point much debated by canon lawyers. The Bishop could claim rights over legacies *ad pias causas* and over wills made, as Ysolda's was, *pro anima*, and he had general rights against executors and heirs where there was any attempt to defraud or deprive him of his due; and such rights could be asserted even against the express will of the testator. The quarrel went to arbitration and was decided by three laymen, two judges and an *advocatus* of the *Magna Regia Curia*, one of the judges being a *professor* of Civil Law; they gave their sentence at the Franciscan house in Catania on 1 July 1371. The Bishop argued that the execution of the will devolved on him since the executors had been negligent, a point already advanced in 1364, and he gave other arguments not recorded, while the monks maintained that it was impossible both in law and in practice to carry out the will in its original form. The Bishop's commutation of 11 October 1364 was invoked and in part rehearsed while the monks stated, correctly, that they had paid the legacies detailed in Ysolda's will. They also claimed to have built at Catania a *cappella* or *oratorium* of San Nicolò in which six or more of them would pray for Ysolda and her kin.[43] The documents did not repeat all the arguments, and the case may have been decided on some technicality. The arbitrators reversed Bishop Antonius' decision to sequester the monks' Maltese incomes, declaring that the monks did not owe the payment which he claimed: *Idem dominus Episcopus nullum Ius quarte seu canonice portionis habeat nec habere debeat ex legato* . . . They annulled the Bishop's sequestrations and they also ruled that as a result of the executors'

[42]Ilarius was alive at *Levinium* (Lentini?) on 2 June 1370: text in P. Sella, *Rationes Decimarum Italiae nei secoli XIII e XIV: Sicilia* (Vatican, 1944), 146. Following Ilarius' death, Bishop Antonius was translated from the see of Thessalonika on 19 August 1370: Archivio Vaticano, Reg. Aven. 171, f. 96–96v, partially published in C. Eubel, *Bullarum Francescanum*, vi (Rome, 1902), 446–7. On 22 August 1370 the pope was sending Antonius with 25 Franciscan missionaries to Georgia: text ibid., vi. 447. Antonius seems, however, to have been litigating in person (*Episcopus asserebat*) at Catania on 1 July 1371: Perg. 581.

[43]La Ferlita, 265 n. 8, wrongly states that the new chapel was in Malta.

negligence the execution of the will devolved not on the Bishop but on the monks.[44] The Benedictine proctors travelled to Malta with this sentence, and there on 5 December 1371 the Vicar, Thomeus Axak, and the chapter of the Maltese church, acting while the bishopric was vacant owing to the Bishop's death, formally accepted the sentence that they were not to molest or interfere with the monks' Maltese incomes.[45]

* * *

The Benedictines did well out of the whole affair. They received Ysolda's estates on Malta while escaping any obligation to found a house or support monks there. Bishop Ilarius had done no more than instruct in very general terms that they should pray for Ysolda's soul in Catania. Ysolda had wanted six monks who would intercede for herself, her husband and her kin, and she had also planned arrangements which would have furthered the cause of religion on Malta itself. The Bishop's commutation entirely defeated this second implicit intention and, although the monks claimed to have built an oratory in Catania in which six or more brethren would pray for Ysolda, nothing more was ever heard of any such chapel. Whether the commutation of 1364 was legal was never really clear and it is doubtful how the matter could have been decided in law. It was not ratified by the pope, and though it was accepted by one of the two surviving executors and by the chapter at Malta, their recognitions would not have legalised the original commutation if it were not in itself legitimate. Furthermore, the priest of Ysolda's Maltese church of San Nicolò does not seem to have given his assent while one executor resigned apparently in protest and Bishop Antonius challenged the arrangement in 1371. The opportunities for dispute over a topic governed by local custom and by the conflicting and shifting corpus of canon law with its numerous interpreters and interpretations were probably endless. In such cases arbitration offered the only hope of any settlement.

The Bishop's powers were uncertain, especially as he was more or less permanently established *extra diocesim*, and when he acted at Catania to alter a will made at Noto in the Diocese of Siracusa concerning lands in Malta granted to the monks at Catania there was room for debate. The Bishop did have certain powers to alter wills and he was probably correct in claiming that as a result of the executors' failure to carry out the will its execution devolved on him. On the other hand he did not summon or consult Ysolda's executors or the rector of her Maltese church

[44]Perg. 581; cf. *Corpus Iuris Canonici*, pars 2, 542 = Decret. III 26 xiv. For general discussions of relevant though not identical questions, see R. Trexler, 'Death and Testament in the Episcopal Constitutions of Florence: 1327', in *Renaissance Studies in Honor of Hans Baron*, ed. A. Molho—J. Tedeschi (Dekalb, Illinois, 1971); *idem*, 'The Bishop's Portion: Generic Pious Legacies in the Late Middle Ages in Italy', *Traditio*, xxviii (1972).

[45]Ms. 159, f. 132–137v (sixteenth-century copy); this act was made by Notary *Lanceas Gacti* before witnesses *Bachu de Bochi* who was *Iudex Malte* and *Jacobus de Peregrino miles . . . Lucas de Sillato . . . Bartucius de Mileto . . . Iohannes de Sancta Sophia . . . presbiter Simon de Cassano . . . Literius de Barba.* On 27 April 1379 the Benedictines at Catania secured a new *transumptum* of this act: copy in Ms. 153, f. 44–51. Bishop Antonius died before 3 September 1371: Archivio Vaticano, Reg. Aven. 173, f. 173v–174.

or the parish priest of the parish in which it was situated before making his commutation, perhaps because he could not cite them outside their own dioceses. It was apparently true that the endowment was insufficient; that the construction of a house on Malta would have meant an initial investment of capital by the monks;[46] that monastic buildings would have been necessary; and that the statutory minimum number of monks required for the foundation of a community was more than six. Why the difficulties of the Maltese language should have prevented Benedictines from living on Malta was not made clear; monks were supposed to live apart, and they could have recruited Maltese brethren or found Sicilians to learn Maltese. The Benedictines were accustomed to carrying out pastoral and quasi-parochial duties at Catania[47] but by Ysolda's time Malta apparently had its own parochial system,[48] and so the monks would not have needed to speak Maltese in order to conduct confessions and the care of souls. It was true that these were years of upheaval and great political uncertainty in Malta with piracy of all sorts and Muslim razzias being frequent hazards,[49] and that the other orders which were to come to Malta soon after established themselves in the city or its *borgo* rather than in an isolated spot such as that where Ysolda's church was situated; the Carmelites at Lunzjata were outside the urban area but only a short distance from it. Whether all these considerations justified the commutation of Ysolda's testament would presumably have been difficult to decide.

Ysolda de Landolina's will was somewhat ingenuous. She was behaving in an entirely conventional way when she selected the oldest of monastic orders rather than the more fashionable mendicant friars to safeguard her own soul and those of her family. She left no house but only a small rural chapel with an endowment which was probably insufficient, and for the monks of Catania Malta was distant, dangerous and strange while Ysolda's estates were in an exposed part of the island. The large Benedictine house at Catania was rich, urban and grasping; it was unlikely to be interested in so inconvenient a foundation. The Bishop, like the monks, lived in Sicily and he too probably regarded the Maltese islands as a source

[46]It is difficult in the fifteenth-century and later documents to sort out which incomes came from which endowment, and in any case by then circumstances had already changed. The 56 gold *uncie* received in 1365/1371 (Ms. 159, f. 114) might suggest an income of about 10 *uncie* a year, but may not give a reliable picture.

[47]Cf. A. Longhitano, *La Parrocchia nella Diocesi di Catania prima e dopo il Concilio di Trento* (Rome, 1977), 21–40.

[48]Cf. A. Luttrell, 'Le Origini della Parrocchia a Malta', in *Pievi e Parrocchie in Italia nel Basso Medioevo* (*Secoli XIII–XV*) (Rome, forthcoming); amend Luttrell, in *Medieval Malta*, 63, where the passage given *supra*, 152 n. 29, is wrongly interpreted as a reference to pastoral work.

[49]Details in H. Bresc, 'Documents on Frederick IV of Sicily's Intervention in Malta: 1372', *Papers of the British School at Rome*, xli (1973); the text of an appeal of 1393(?) from Gozitan captives in Tunis is in F. Casula, *Carte Reali Diplomatiche di Giovanni I il Cacciatore, re d'Aragona, riguardanti l'Italia* (Padua, 1977), 134–55. For an example of the insuperable difficulties encountered by a Benedictine community on a small Mediterranean island, see S. Scalfati, *Les Relations entre la Gorgona et la Corse du XIIIe au XVe siècle = Cahiers Corsica*, 84–85 (Bastia, 1980).

of income but not as a place in which to reside.[50] His successor, Bishop Antonius de Musto, did attempt to oppose the monks but he lost his case at arbitration and died very soon after. The affair represented a triumph of absentee Sicilian attitudes and mentalities over the real interests of the Maltese islanders. The Benedictine monks never did set up a house on Malta, having acquired estates on the island without the trouble of founding a community there. The other orders were surprisingly late to implant themselves within a community which was under Latin domination and which was still being converted to Christianity in the thirteenth century: the Franciscans were possibly established in Malta by 1372; the Augustinians by 1413 or a little earlier; the Carmelites by 1441; the Dominicans in about 1450, after they too had rejected an opportunity to establish themselves there in 1431; and the Benedictine sisters at some moment before 1479.[51]

Though the Benedictines did not found a Maltese house, the acquisition of Ysolda's estates was followed by a series of donations to San Nicolò d'Arena. On 24 November 1381 Philippus de Novello *habitator ciuitatis Meliuetane*, acting at Paternò in Sicily, bequeathed to the monks of San Nicolò the goods which he had inherited in Malta when his *consobrinus* Thomeus, son of Johannucius de Santa Sofia and an inhabitant of Mdina, had died intestate, but the monks had to recover the lands which had fallen into the hands of the *curia* of Manfredo Chiaramonte, Admiral of Sicily and Count of Malta.[52] On 15 November 1414 two brethren of San Nicolò were in Malta where they secured notarial recognition of earlier royal tax exemptions granted to their house.[53] During the fifteenth century the monks continued to receive lands in Malta and to lease out their properties there, the most notable acquisitions resulting from the will of Paulus de Peregrino drawn up

[50]Thus on 19 October 1375 the Benedictine Antonius, *archidiaconus* of Catania, was provided to the Bishopric of Malta: Archivio Vaticano, Reg. Aven. 198, f. 55v–56. This Benedictine, Antonio de Vulponno, continued for many years to reside at Catania: S. Fodale, *Scisma Ecclesiastica e Potere Regio in Sicilia*, i: *Il Duca di Montblanc e l'Episcopato tra Roma e Avignone, 1392–1396* (Palermo, 1979), 63.

[51]A. Luttrell, 'The Augustinians at Malta: 1413', *Analecta Augustiniana*, xxxviii (1975); the text of 1441 (ibid., 391), when taken with the evidence in S. Abela, *L'Ewwel Karmelitani f'Malta u l'Ewwel Knisja u Kunvent Taghom 'Il-Lunzjata l'-Qadimi': 1418–1659* (Malta, 1976), 6–8, confirms that the Carmelites had a Maltese convent by 1441. The will made by Margarita d'Aragona on 5 June 1418 suggested the difficulties involved in such foundations; it did not leave her Maltese church and properties to the Carmelites but instructed that her executors should, after her death, find an order which would accept them: modern copy in Mdina, Cathedral Archives, Ms. 28, f. 1–10v.

[52]Ms. 159, f. 137v–139v: ... *quod bona prefati Thomei possidebantur per curiam magnifici et potentis domini domini Manfridi de Clara[monte] nomine regni Scicilie admerati et sua cum socijs vicarij generalis, et Comitis Insole Meliueti*, ... In the anarchy which followed the death of Federico IV of Sicily in 1377, Malta fell into the hands of the Chiaramonte: A. Luttrell, 'The House of Aragon and Malta: 1282–1412', *Journal of the Faculty of Arts: Royal University of Malta*, iv no. 2 (1970), 163.

[53]Perg. 674, drawn up in Malta by Notary *Nicolaus de Insula* before *Michael de Bernardo* who was *Iudex Malte ... notarius Laurentius de Miglorino* (or *Buxmeruta*?) ... *Notarius Rogerius de Turrj ... notarius Antonius de Azupparda ... dompnus Michel de Fabro ... Petrus Meylac ... Pinus de Santoro.*

in 1436.[54] The Benedictines of Catania carefully preserved these distant properties, with occasional difficulties, until 1834, drawing wealth from the island while offering little more than competent estate management and three masses a week in return.

## A NOTE ON THE TOPOGRAPHY

Without attempting a detailed study of the place-names, it may be noted that the 1365 text spoke of Ysolda's lands as situated in various parts of Malta, some being in *Rachalkybir*, some in *Rahalnicolosu* and others elsewhere. Raħal Nicolosu, presumably derived from San Nicolò,[55] is the modern Ta' San Niklau just under 2 km. due west of Qrendi at approximately 496660;[56] it was described in 1365 as being in the place known as *haiarkim*, that is the modern Ħaġar Qim with its prehistoric monument at 496652 just under 1 km. south of Ta' San Niklau.[57] Raħal Kbir was in the same area; sheet 127 of the 1: 2500 map of 1907 places 'Il Kasam il Cbir' just south of 'San Niclau tal-Merhla' at approximately 497658, while local tradition associates it with the neighbourhood of the church of Tal-Providenza, south of Siġġiewi but north-west of Ta' San Niklau at approximately 491667;[58] possibly the name has shifted its position, or maybe the estate was a large one, since *Kbir* means 'big'.[59]

The passage of 1365 may also throw some light on the problems of *raħal* and *casale*, terms which were often interchangeable but which varied their meanings as many Maltese settlements were abandoned. The document of 1365, which was originally written in Malta, stated:

> . . . Quequidem Bona sua sita sunt In eadem Insola Malte In contrata dicti casalis vocati Rahalkibir. Item quoddam tenimentum terrarum, dictum pheudum de Rahalnjcolosu, situm In eadem Insola In contrata ejusdem casalis In loco dicto Haiarkim . . .[60]

This was paraphrased a little later as follows:

> Tenuta altra di terrj uocata lu fegu di Rachalnjculosu in lu casalj di Rachalbibir alu locu dictu Haiar Kym, . . .[61]

It seems that there was a *tenimentum terrarum* (or *tenuta*) known as the *pheudum* (or *fegu*) of *Rahalnicolosu* situated in the *contrata* of the *casale* of Raħal Kbir at the place known as Ħaġar Qim. The *casale* of Raħal Kbir, therefore, still survived as a *casale*, which did in fact provide 24 militiamen in 1419,

[54]Preliminary details of legacies and leasings in La Ferlita, 266–8, 271. Note the will of Fridericus de Burdino *civis Melite* (10 August 1414) in Ms. 159, f. 140–3 (sixteenth-century copy) and the original *informationes* secured by the monks when his son Bartolus died without issue in 1428 in Ms. 156, f. 101–3 (original); the will of Lemmus de Firrario *habitator ciuitatis Melite* (25 December 1432) in Ms. 156, f. 105-105v (fifteenth-century copy from acts of Notary Luca de Sillato); and the will of Paulus de Peregrino *Ciuis Ciuitatis Malte* (5 September 1436) in Ms. 153, f. 69–76v (*transumptum* of 1439). The estate was not described in the fourteenth-century documents as the *feudo* or *fegho* of Lancilotto; nor was it ever a 'fief' in the normal 'feudal' sense.

[55]Nicoloso Count of Malta (floruit 1232–71), the son of Henry Count of Malta, is another possibility.

[56]G. Wettinger, 'The Lost Villages and Hamlets of Malta', in *Medieval Malta* (1975), 210; the six-figure reference system is there explained.

[57]For Ħaġar Qim, see Wettinger (1976), 332, 355. For *Haiarkim*, Abela, 390, incorrectly has 'Har el Bin, (emendisi, Ghar el Bir)'; in his notebook Abela had *haraelbin* (Valletta, Ms. 140, f. 38). A text of 1597 mentioned *un'altro pezzo di terreno detto il chasam dentro il quale ui sonno li pedamenti di una torregia disruppata nominata Chagiar Chim* . . .: Ms. 153, f. 526.

[58]Wettinger (1975), 209.

[59]The *Raħal* of the 'Big One' (a nickname) is also possible.

[60]Doc. III *infra*.

[61]Doc. IV *infra*.

while Rahal Nicolosu did not appear on the militia list of that or later years.[62] *Rahalnicolosu* had become merely a place-name given to a *tenimentum* or holding, and this could well mean that it had been abandoned as a settlement by 1365. By 1647 it was known as *el Chereb*, that is 'the ruined buildings', traces of which were still visible together with many cisterns.[63] The same eventually happened to Rahal Kbir, which by 1907 was a *Kasam* or *Qasam*, that is an estate. The original Rahal Nicolosu had become a *tenimentum terrarum* but it was still known as a *pheudum*; the confusion of terminologies was already complete. It was not technically a fief owing service, and Ysolda could apparently alienate it without difficulty.[64]

Ysolda's will mentioned a church of San Nicolò which already existed on her lands in 1363: *quadam ecclesia vocata sub uocabula beatj Nicholai existente*.[65] Many churches around Siġġiewi, including the parish church, were dedicated to this saint who was extremely popular in Malta.[66] Ysolda's church was presumably that at San Niclau tal-Merhla which was rebuilt, probably around the end of the seventeenth century,[67] and where 'poche vestige' of the original church were still visible in 1866[68] though there is nothing to be seen now. In 1575 the Apostolic Visitor Pietro Dusina visited five churches dedicated to San Nicolò within the single parish of Siġġiewi, and two others in the *casale* of Hal Kbir. The Benedictines' church was said to be *in territorio alchibir seu anniclus*, that is at Hal Kbir or Hal Nicolosu, but Dusina was confused by hearsay reports about the circumstances of its endowment:

> dicitur quod quidam Paulus Pellegrinus, et Zolta coniuges melitenses uigore testamenti et legati cuius copia penes R. Decanum modernum dicitur existere legauerunt magnas quantitates terrarum, et clusarum circumcirca dictam Ecclesiam existentium monacis Ecclesie Sancti Nicolai de Larena . . .

The report stated that the monks were obliged to celebrate mass thrice weekly and also to reside there:

> ac etiam habitare in dicta Ecclesia et ibi fratrum habitationem habere quibus oneribus in presentiarum satisfaciunt, et Donnus Gregorius Mamus est Capellanus ad dictas missas celebrandas.[69]

Paulus de Peregrino did leave lands and properties on Malta to the monks on condition that they celebrated three masses a week in the church of San Nicolò—*in ecclesia dictj sanctj Nicholaj*—by which he presumably meant the San Nicolò which the Benedictines had received from Ysolda rather than San Nicolò at Catania, though he did not specify precisely which church was intended; but that was in 1436 and Paulus' wife was named Garita.[70] His was possibly the will of which a copy was said to survive in Malta, and *Zolta* was evidently not his wife but Ysolda de Landolina. The alleged obligation of residence, which was not mentioned in the will of Paulus de Peregrino, perhaps derived from that of Ysolda, and in 1575 it was being satisfied by a secular chaplain rather than by resident monks. According to Abela, the monks enlarged the church some time before 1647.[71] In about 1723

[62] Wettinger (1975), 186.

[63] Abela, 99.

[64] On *fegho*, *qasam* etc., in addition to Wettinger (1975), see Luttrell, in *Medieval Malta*, 55–7; cf. E. Sipione, 'La smobilitazione dal servizio militare della feudalità siciliana: 1342', *Archivio Storico Siracusano*, ns. i (1971).

[65] Doc. I *infra*.

[66] On the late-medieval parish church of San Nicolò at Siġġiewi, see M. Buhagiar, 'Medieval Churches in Malta', in *Medieval Malta*, 172–3 and Plate 12a.

[67] The date is proposed on stylistic grounds; the church was *nuova* in 1723: Valletta, Ms. 360, f. 943.

[68] A. Ferris, *Descrizione storica delle chiese di Malta e Gozo* (Malta, 1886), 409.

[69] Valletta, Archiepiscopal Curia, Visitation Dusina C, f. 52v, 56v, 57v, 61v, 151–2; the description of the San Nicolò d'Arena church, at f. 151–2, was partially reproduced in Abela, 369–70. Later visitation records show that the Bishop visited the church from time to time, e.g. in 1618 (f. 191v–192), 1708 (f. 92v–93), 1859 (f. 216v).

[70] Ms. 153, f. 69–76v (copy of 1439); Abela, 390, wrongly has Paolo *di Ferregnino*.

[71] Abela, 99.

there was a *nuova Chiesa* and three weekly masses were still being celebrated in *San Nicolo detta tal Merhla.*[72] Probably—but not quite certainly in view of the number of local dedications to San Nicolò and the confusions in their history—this was the church which still stands at San Niclau tal-Merhla on land which once belonged to Ysolda de Landolina.[73]

## DOCUMENT I: 17 JUNE 1363[74]

IN Nomine dominj Amen Anno dominice Incarnationis millesimo Tricentesimo sexagesimo Secundo mense Iunij decimo septimo die ejusdem mensis prime Indictionis, Regnante Serenissimo et Illustrissimo domino domino nostro Rege Friderico dej gratia Inclito Rege Sicilie ac ducatuum Athenarum et Noupatrie[75] ducce Regnj ejus anno octauo feliciter Amen. Coram Nobis Notario Petro de Notho Guidone Iudice terre Nothj Bartholomeo de Guasto Regio puplico Totius Vallis Nothj Notario et testibus subscriptis ad hoc vocatis specialiter et Rogatis, domina Ysolda vxor quondam Lancie de Carumbenj licet egra Corpore sana tamen mente et Intellectu existens in sua bona memoria suum sollemne condidit testamentum seu suam vltimam voluntatem in hunc modum videlicet, Inprimis annichilauit et annichilat ac annullauit et annullat omnia testamenta et omnes vltimas voluntates per eam hactenus condita temporibus Retrohactis volens et Iubens suum presens testamentum obtinere seu habere Robur et firmitatem, Item elegit sibj sepulturam suam in Cimiterio ecclesie sanctj Nicholai dicte terre Nothj, Item legauit pro anima sua subscriptis personis subscriptas peccuniarum et Rerum quantitates videlicet, Blance et Safire filiabus Nobilis Renaldj de Landolina consobrinj suj vncias aurj quatraginta ponderis generalis, Item Nobilj Safire de Landolina sororj dicti Renaldj alias vncias aurj quatraginta ponderis supradictj, Item Safire vxorj quondam Petri Monacj florenos aurj viginti ponderis generalis, Item Francie vxorj Auanelle de Landolina quoddam viridarium suum cum terris contiguis situm et positum in Insola Meliuete in contrata dicta de Gemeueluburiu[76] Infra hos fines quod ab vno latere possidet dominus Iacobus de Pilligrino[77] ab alio possidet presbiter Petrus de Chipullata ab alio possidet Notarius Bartholomeus de Milito et domina Francia vxor quondam Vthonj de Muta,[78] Item legauit eidem Francie vncias aurj decem ponderis supradictj, Item legauit quandam petiam terre vocatam la Mitarfa[79] sitam in dicta Insola suis terris finibus limitatam Cuidam presbitero quj tenet eam post cujus mortem voluit eam darj alicuj alij[80] presbitero ad arbitrium fidecomissariorum suorum quj celebret diuinum officium pro anima ejus dicti quondam virj suj et quondam parentum suorum, Item voluit et mandauit quod dicta legata soluantur et satisfient dictis legatarijs de primis Redditibus omnium bonorum dicte testatricis existentibus in dicta ciuitate Meliuete et ejus Insola preter dictum viridarium legatum dicte Francie et dictam petiam terre legatam dicto presbitero quos voluit sibj darj statim post mortem dicte testatricis, Item voluit et mandauit quod solutis dictis legatis de primis Redditibus dictorum bonorum dicte testatricis ut predicitur ex nunc prout ex tunc legauit omnia bona sua

[72] Valletta, Ms. 360, f. 933, 943.

[73] The church was near *Merhila* in 1597: Valletta, Ms. 360, f. 925.

[74] Original parchment in Catania, Biblioteche Riunite Civica e A. Ursino Recupero: Tabulario dei Monasteri di San Nicolo L'Arena di Catania et di Santa Maria di Licodia, Perg. 543, incorrectly dated to 17 January 1362 in Ardizzone, 255, and to 17 July 1362 in La Ferlita, 262. The document itself, all contemporary and later copies of it, and all published references to it have always dated the will to 1362, but the regnal and Indictional years give 1363, which is the more likely, as the machinations following Ysolda's death did not begin until mid-1364.

[75] *Sic* for *Neopatrie.*

[76] *Gemeueluburiu*: unidentified, possibly Ġnien el *Wuriu.*

[77] Giacomo de Pelligrino was the royal captain on Malta from 1361 to 1372, when he was exiled: Bresc (1973), 183–7.

[78] This Francia, apparently the owner with Bartholomeus de Milito of adjacent lands (in which case read *possident*), is apparently the Franzuna, widow of Symonis de Muta, granted two *tareni* later in this will, and not the *eidem Francie* who was to receive 10 *uncie.*

[79] Mtarfa just north of Mdina.

[80] *Sic.*

stabilia existentia in dicta ciuitate et Insola preter dictum viridarium et dictam petiam terre Monasterio Sanctj Nicholai de Rena Ita tamen quod fratres sex dicti Monasterij Inperpetuum habitent in quadam ecclesia vocata sub uocabulo beatj Nicholai existente in dicta Insola in terris testatricis Ipsius quj celebrent diuinum officium pro anima ejus dicti quondam maritj suj et dictorum quondam parentum suorum, Item legauit dicto Monasterio totum Id quicquid et quantum dicta testatrix asserit habere Recipere super bonis hered[itarijs] que fuerunt quondam Laurentj de Abello, Item legauit et Reliquit Iure Institutionis et hered[itatis][81] personis subscriptis Istas particulares peccuniarum quantitates, Videlicet presbitero Friderico de Friderico habitatori dicte ciuitatis tarenos duos in quibus tarenis Instituit Ipsum heredem, Item Benedicto de Friderico tarenos duos, Item domino Iacobo de Vaccario tarenos duos, Item Franzune vxorj Symonis de Muta tarenos duos in quibus tarenis quemlibet Ipsorum Instituit heredes suos volens et mandans quod per predictas peccuniarum quantitates teneant se contentos de tota hereditate et bonis ipsius testatricis adhymendo eis et cuilibet Ipsorum omne Ius falcidie et tribellianice, Item legauit cuicumque persone quod de Iure veniret ad hereditatem suam tarenos duos volens et Mandans quod pro predictis tarenis teneant se contentos de tota hereditate et bonis testatricis eidem adymendo eis omne Ius falcidie et tribellianice et cujus libet alterius generis detrahactionis, Item legauit Yrinj grece[82] sue prout plenam et Meram libertatem Ita quod ex nunc in antea sit et esse debeat libera ab omnj Iugo et vinculo seruitutis dans sibi licentiam etc. Item legauit dicte Yrinj augustales aurj duos, Item constituit ordinauit et fecit suos fidecommissarios et exequtores suj presentis testamenti dictum Nobilem Renaldum de Landolina dictum Auanellam de Landolina et Petrum Camagninum quibus et quilibet Ipsorum In solidum dedit plenam licentiam et auctoritatem liberam predicta omnia et singula libere faciendi et exercendi Intrandi Incontinenti et capiendi bona omnia dicte testatricis absque licentia Curie seu heredum omnia contenta in presenti testamento adimplendi absque aliqua heredum contradictione seu cujuscumque alterius contradicentis, et si forte dicti fidecommissarij decederent antequam exequeretur presens testamentum quod [vtrius] eorum posset substituere alium seu alios fidecommissarios ut predictum testamentum exiquiri posset cum eadem licentia et auctoritate quam presentes fidecommissarij habent in presenti testamento, et hanc asseruit esse suam vltimam voluntatem quam valere voluit Iure testamenti, et si Iure testamenti non valeret saltim valeat Iure codicillorum seu cujuscumque alterius vltime voluntatis melius valere posset, Vnde ad futuram memoriam et ut de premissis omnibus et quolibet premissorum fiat et plene constet aput omnes et singulos Inposterius plenam fidem presens puplicum Instrumentum exinde factum est per Manus mej notarij puplicj supradictj ad cautelam dictorum fidecommissariorum nostrum quj supra Iudicis et Notarij ac subscriptorum testium subscriptionibus et testimonio Roboratum. Actum Nothj anno mense die et Indictione premissis:

+ Ego notarius Petrus de Notho Guidone qui supra Iudex Nothj testor

+ Ego notarius Petrus de Guasto Testor:—

+ Ego Trankedus de Melj—testor

+ Ego Nicolaus Rotius—Testor

+ Ego Petrus Camagninus testor

+[83] Ego Bartholomeus de Guasto quj supra Regius puplicus Totius Vallis Nothj Notarius predictis omnibus Rogatis Interfuj premissa subscripsi et testor:—

*Testes Notarius Petrus de Guasto Trankedus de Melj Nicolaus Rotius Petro Camagninus Nicolaus de Baldo Guillelmus de Landolina Iacobus de Aliotta Petro Vaccaru et Auanella de Landolina*

[81]The reference is apparently to the *institutio heredis* of Roman Law.
[82]*greca*: slave.
[83]Notarial signum.

## DOCUMENT II: 11 OCTOBER 1364[84]

In nomine dominj Amen Anno dominice Incarnationis millesimo Tricentesimo sexagesimo quarto mense octubris vndecimo die ejusdem mensis tertie Indictionis, Regnante serenissimo domino domino nostro Rege Friderico dej gratia excellentissimo Rege Sicilie ac duce Athenarum et Neupatrie Regni ejus anno nono feliciter Amen, nos Matheus de Anichito Iudex Ciuitatis Cathanie, Iohannes de Thocaristo puplicus ejusdem Ciuitatis Notarius, et testes subscriptj ad hoc vocatj specialiter et Rogatj, presentj scripto puplico Notum facimus et testamur quod Venerabilis et Religiosus vir Frater Garsias Monachus monasterij Sancte Marie de Lichodia ordinis sanctj Benedictj Cathaniensis diocisis ac procurator abatis et conuentus dictj monasterij ut constitit que quidam procuratio scripta est manu notarij Nicolaj Biczonj penultimo die mensis Julij secunde Indictionis de anno predicto, constitutus personaliter dictus frater Garsias Coram Reuerendo domino patre Ylario Mel[i]uitano episcopo proposuit et dixit quod cum quondam domina Ysolda uxor quondam Lancie de Carumbenj habitatrix terre Nothj olim in suis ultimis constituta quibus decessit suum sollemne condiderit testamentum scriptum manu notarij Bartolomej de Guasto publicj Totius Vallis Nothj Regij Notarij et subsignatum subscriptum manu Notarij Petri de Notho Iudicis terre ipsius ac testium quampluri-mum Rogatorum et Vocatorum decimo septimo die mensis Iunij prime Indictionis de anno Incarna-tionis dominj Millesimo trecentesimo sexagesimo secundo,[85] dimississet omnia bona sua stabilia existentia in Ciuitate et Insola Malte prout in dicto testamento continetur monasterio sanctj Nicholaj de Arenis dicte Cathaniensis diocesis dum tamen sex fratres de dicto monasterio in dicta Insola vbj continue pro anima dicte testatricis et quondam Maritj suj ac parentum suorum dicti fratres Intercederent preces ad deum, dicto domino episcopo supplicauit nomine proprio et procuratorio nomine quo supra tamquam exequtorj vltimarum voluntatum legitimo ad quem predicti testamenti executio legitime est deuoluta ut asserit ut voluntatem dicte testatricis in melius commutaret ut fructus Redditus et prouentus dictorum bonorum conuerterent[ur] in vsus et vtilitatem dicti Monasterij sanctj Nicholaj, Cum Monachj monasterij sanctj Nicholaj sint paratj continue et Inper-petuum pro anima dicte testatricis et quondam virj suj atque parentum suorum fundere preces ad deum, dictus Reuerendus pater Respondidit ad premissa et dixit quod licet de Iure voluntas testatoris pro lege servanda sit tamen ex causa talis uoluntas potest mutarj, considerans Ipse paucitatem Reddituum pro sustentatione monasterij et mon[a]chorum per dictam testatricem assignatorum et dotem non consistere in tanta quantitate unde fabrica monasterij possit fundarj et monachi congrue possint sustentarj, Actendens ectiam diuersitatem linguarum in dicta Insola nec quod sit Ibj locus aptus monachis ad agendum penitentiam Iuxta santiones sanctorum patrum nec quod sint Ibi aliqua officina monachalia, considerans ectiam discrimina viarum maris et terre, Actendens ectiam quod monasteria de Iure fundarj non debet nisi tanta sit dos constituta quod non est ut asserit per dictam testatricem quod possint Ibj esse presbiterj diaconj et subdiaconj cantores et lectores, considerans quod Illud quod Relictum est ad pias causas per Ipsam[86] tanquam diocisanum episcopum debet exequtionj mandarj maxime cum facultates et bona dicte testatricis sint in sua dyocesi et ut asserit dominus episcopus Ipse sit exequtor dicti testamenti in nigligentia exequtorum et licet sit extra suam dyocesim exequtio testamenti cause cognitionem non desiderat cum non sit Ibj forus contentiosus cum per quamcumque personam priuatam et extra Iudicium exercerj potest et ea que cause cognitionem non desiderant extra diocesim per quemcumque episcopum expedirj possu[n]t, ex predictis causis dictus dominus episcopus, uolens prouidere animabus monachorum et dicte testatricis, mutauit voluntatem dicte testatricis sub forma que sequitur, et voluit quod in dicto monasterio sanctj Nicholaj ubj veget numerus monachorum quinquaginta et vltra orent continue pro [anima][87] ejusdem testatricis, et quod omnia bona dicte testatricis sint et conuertantur in vtilitatem dicti monasterij, Vnde ad futuram memoriam et dicti fratris Garsie procuratoris dicti

[84]Notarial copy in a parchment of 17 March 1365: Catania, Biblioteche Riunite Civica e A. Ursino Recupero: Tabulario dei Monasteri di San Nicolò L'Arena di Catania et di Santa Maria di Licodia, Perg. 557 (copy in Ms. 159, f. 115–116v). Ardizzone, 261, wrongly dates the text of 17 March 1365 to 1364.

[85]An error for 1363: *supra*, 160 n. 74.

[86]*Sic.*

[87]Omitted in original.

monasterii et procuratorio nomine quo supra et successorum eorum cautelam presens publicum Instrumentum factum est exinde per Manus mej predictj notarij publicj nostrum quj supra Iudicis Notarij signo et testium subscriptorum subscriptionibus et testimonio Roboratum, actum Cathanie anno mense die et Indictione premissis, Ego Matheus de Anichito quj Supra Iudex ciuitatis Cathanie, Ego Guillermus Pisis testor, Ego Berardus de Panormo testor, Ego Thomasius de Veg[a] testor, Ego Thomasius de Benintende testor, Ego Notarius Iohannes de Thocaristo quj supra puplicus Ciuitatis Cathanie notarius Notarius[88] presens publicum Instrumentum scripsi et meo signo signauj.

## DOCUMENT III: 7 MAY 1365[89]

In Nomine Domini Amen Anno Incarnacionis Ejusdem Millesimo Trecentesimo Sexagesimo quinto mense maij Septimo die Ejusdem tercie Indictionis, Regnante Excellentissimo principe domino domino Rege Friderico dej gratia Illustrissimo Rege Sicilie. Ac ducatuum Athenarum et Neopatrie duce dicti dominij Anno nono feliciter Amen. Nos Bertolus de Burdino Iudex Insole Malte, Lanceas Gacti Regius publicus Insolarum Malte et Gaudisij notarius, et Testes Subscripti ad hoc vocati specialiter et rogati, presenti Scripto publico Notum facimus et testamur quod constituti In presentia nostra frater Johannes et frater Maurus monachi abbates conuentus monasteriorum sancte Marie de Lichodia et sancti Nicolai de Arenis ordinis sancti Benedicti Catheniensis diocesis ut constitit per quendam publicum Instrumentum confectum per manus Nicolai de Bulzono regij publici terre Paternionis notarij Actum In eadem terra Anno dominice Incarnacionis millesimo trecentesimo sexagesimo quarto mense martij terciodecimo die mensis Ipsius Tercie Indictionis Subscriptum per Guillelmum Spulpa ejusdem terre Iudicem et alios In competenti numero testes procuratorjo nomine Conuentuum et monasteriorum predictorum Ad hec et alia per eos tenore dicti Instrumenti constitutos ut constitit,[90] Exposuerunt quod cum quondam nobilis domina Isolda uxor quondam Lancee de Carubenj habitatrix terre Nothi olim In suis vltimis constituta quibus decessit Suum Sollempne Condiderit Testamentum Scriptum manu notarij Bartholomej de Guasto publici tocius Vallis Nothj regij notarij Subscriptum manu notarij Petri de Notho Iudicis terre Paternionis Ipsius et testium quamplurium Rogatorum et Vocatorum decimo septimo die mensis Iunij prime Indictionis De anno Incarnacionis dominj millesimo trecentesimo sexagesimo Secundo, et Inter alia in dicto testamento contenta dimisisse omnia bona stabilia In ciuitate et Insola Malte sistencia eiusdem testatricis, prout tenore ejusdem testamenti manifestatur, monasterio sancti Nicolai de Arenis dicte Cathaniensis diocesis. Et dicta domina Isolda fuerit et sit viam vniuerse carnis Ingressa, dicti fratres Maurus et Johannes, actendentur et considerantur[91] quod bona relicta per dictam testatricem per mortem Ipsius habeant roboris firmitatem, presentibus nobis notarjo Iudice et testibus Infrascriptis corporalem possessionem bonorum stabilium Infrascriptorum que fuerunt dicte quondam domine Isolde In Insola et Ciuitate Malte Sistencium per eam dicto monasterjo ut asserunt relictorum Infrascriptis eorum confinibus limitatorum Intrauerunt et adepti fuerunt, que quidem bona Sunt hec Videlicet In primis quoddam hospitium cum domibus tribus adminaduertentibus[92] deputatis pro apotecis Situm In eadem ciuitate Malte In platea Ipsius ciuitatis, quod confinatur ex parte orientjs cum hospicio magnifici dominj Iacobi de Peregrino militis ex partibus Meridiei et occidentis cum eadem platea ex parte septentrionis, cum domibus Bertucij[93] Piche, et heredum quondam Guctonj de Fichi, Item quoddam tenimentum terrarum

[88]*Sic.*

[89]Sixteenth-century copy in Catania, Archivio di Stato, Fondo Benedettini, Ms. 159, f. 121v–123v; this text is partly destroyed and gaps or difficult readings are supplied from a copy of 1678 in Ms. 153, f. 16–17v, and (for the passage *Videlicet In primis quoddam . . . Prini et alijs confinibus*) from the quotation from the original in the parchment of 1 July 1371 (Perg. 581) which differs considerably from the copy and seems in some ways much more accurate, except that it omits the passage *cum terris Bertini . . . dicti Pricii Murrua.* Elements of doubt inevitably remain.

[90]Ms. 153: *constitit, et constat.*

[91]Ms. 153: *actendentes et considerantes.*

[92]Perg. 581: *circumadiacentibus.*

[93]Perg. 581: *Bar'thi.* or *Bar'chi.*

aratorjarum diuisum In tres partes quas[94] vna pars vocatur casalj,[95] alia Bayadat et alia Biranis[96] collaterales et Insimul se tenentur[97] cum quodam spatio terre Incalce[98] adiacentur dictis terris vocatis Biranis ex parte meridiej quodquidem tenimentum terrarum confinatur ex parte orientis cum via publica ex parte meridiej cum quadam peccia terrarum ex dicta parte vocata Beranis[99] via publica diuidentur, et demum[100] cum via publica ab occidente cum rupeo et spacijs comunibus et ex parte septentrionis cum dicto milite[101] In parte cum heredibus quondam signorj Barru In parte cum Manfrido cum Manfrido[102] de Viculo[103] cum Bartholo Meylat, cum heredibus quondam Bartholj Para,[104] cum Aloysio de Augusta, et cum Nardo Bugea, Item dicta peccia terrarum collateralis dictis terris vocatis Biranis ex parte meridiei, Item quedam quedam[105] pecciuncula terre muro circumdata deputata pro Includendis animalibus, sita In quodam spacio comuni casalis uocati Rahalkybet[106] quod spacium nuncupatur de Ysabella,[107] que tangitur cum domibus Iohannis Surdi et cum domibus heredum quondam Bartholi Bundalj et alijs confinibus, Quequidem Bona sua sita[108] sunt In eadem Insola Malte In contrata dicti casalis vocati Rachalkbiex.[109] Item quoddam tenimentum terrarum, dictum pheudum de Rahalnjcolosu, situm In eadem Insola In contrata ejusdem casalis In loco dicto Haiarkim[110] consistens In diuersis pecijs terrarum cum spacijs domibus et mandris Ibidem Sistentibus, Quodquidem pheudum confin[atur ab oriente][111] cum terris Nardi Bugea, In parte cum quadam flomarja vocata Guedmihyra[112] cum terris heredum Lucij Basalis[113] cum terris Pini de Bonanno cum terris Pricij Murrua,[114] cum terris Bertinj et Frankinj Xara[115] cum terris Iohannis Spiterj et Philippi Tunne a meridie cum terris Benedicti de Friderico In parte, et In parte est litus maris ab occidente cum terris dicti Pricij Murrua,[116] In Parte cum terris heredum quondam presbiterj Thomasij Appay, cum terris heredum quondam Paulinj Bunichi cum terris heredum quondam Nicholachij de Friderico a septentrione cum via publica In parte et In parte cum terris dicti Pricij[117] et alijs confinibus, In cujus rei testimonium, Et ut de premissis omnibus et singulis apud omnes et singulos fides et vera probatio habeatur et constet ad requisicionem dictorum fratrum et cauthelam dicti monasterij: Presens publicum Instrumentum exinde factum est per manus mej predictj notarij, nostrum qui supra Iudicis notarij et subscriptorum testium signo subscriptionibus et testimonio Roboratum. Actum Malte Anno die mense et Indictione premissis.

[94]Perg. 581: *quarum.*

[95]Ms. 153: a later hand deleted *casalj* and inserted *Ibulet il gham.*

[96]Perg. 581: *Biranis,* but Ms. 153 adds in a later hand *seu Branes.*

[97]Perg. 581: *detenentes.*

[98]Perg. 581: *Inculte.*

[99]Perg. 581: *Biranis via.*

[100]Perg. 581: *deinde.*

[101]Perg. 581: . . . *milite et in parte* . . .

[102]*Sic.*

[103]Perg. 581: *Vetulo.*

[104]Perg. 581: *Xara.*

[105]*Sic.*

[106]There is some confusion between 'ly' and 'ki' (e.g. 'lym' for 'kjm' in Doc. IV *infra*), while the same passage in Perg. 581 (written in 1371) has *Rahalkibir.* In other copies it often appears as *Sijbiex* (cf. also *supra,* 158).

[107]Ms. 153: added in later hand *id est Isolda.*

[108]*sita* omitted but Perg. 581 has *stit'.*

[109]Perg. 581 (of 1371) has *Rahalkibir.*

[110]or *Haiarlym*: Perg. 581 has *Haiarkim.*

[111]Perg. 581: *confinatur ab oriente.*

[112]Ms. 153 deletes and inserts in a later hand *Viedbihim.*

[113]Perg. 581: *Busalis.*

[114]Perg. 581: *Prinj Murua.*

[115]Ms. 153: *et Francisce Nixara.*

[116]Perg. 581 omits one line in the ms. from *cum terris Bertini* to *Pricij Murrua.*

[117]Perg. 581: *Prinj.*

\+ Ego Bertolus de Bundius qui supra Iudex Malte
\+ Ego presbiter Alafunctus de Bonanno
\+ Ego Ponczu de Mullica[118] Testor.
\+ Ego presbiter Antonius de Spacio Testor
\+ Ego clericus Antonius de Beninato de Janer testor
\+ Ego presbiter Pinus de Lauagna testor

+[119] Lanceas Gacti Regius publicus Insolarum Malte et Gaudisij notarius predictorum bonorum possessionem corporalem Ingressionem Interfuj eamque rogatus scripsi et publicauj meoque Signo Signauj.

## DOCUMENT IV: BETWEEN 1372 AND 1429[120]

ihs

MALTA

Tinimentu .j. di casi ala plaza di Malta[121] et confina cum li potigi dilu mon[asteru], et cum li casi di miss[er] Loysi de Pluzasca[122] et la uia puplica.

Potigj trj ala plaza di Malta et confinanu cum li dicti casi di lu mon[asteru] et la uia puplica.

Tenuta .j. di terrj alu casalj di Rachalbibir[123] diuisa in pezi .iij. collateralj dili qualj luna si clama casalj, laltra Bayadat, e laltra Biranis, Insembla cum certu spaciu di terra Inculta coniunta ali dicti terrj clamati Biranis dila parte di mezu Iornu la qualj tinuta di terrj confina a parte orientis cum la uia puplica, a parte occidentis cum lu dirrupu et cum li spacij comuni et cum altri confinj diuersi.

Peza altra di terrj collateralj dala parte di mezu Iornu ala dicta peza uocata Biranis.

Pizecta .j. di terra muratu atornu per mandra alu casalj di Rachalbibir in lu locu dictu di Ysabella.

Tenuta altra di terrj uocata lu fegu di Rachalnjculosu in lu casalj di Rachalbibir alu locu dictu Haiar Kym,[124] diuisa in diuersi pezi cum spacij, cum casi et cum mandrj siti in lu dictu fegu, la qualj tinuta confina a parte orientis cum li terrj di Nardu Bugea et altrj diuersi, a parte meridiei confina cum li terrj di Benedictu di Fridiricu et cum lu litu di lu marj, a parte occidentis confina cum li terrj di Prinu Murua, et altrj diuersi, a parte septentrioniscum la uia puplica et altrj diuersj confinj.

Tenuta altra di terrj consistentj in .j. bella peza alu portu di Benarratu, et estj chi unu puzu ala parte di punentj et un altru a tramuntana.[125]

[118]Ms. 153: *Pontius de Mollica.*

[119]Notarial signum.

[120]A single undated sheet of paper now bound into Catania, Archivio di Stato, Fondo Benedettini, Ms. 153, f. 505–505v, published, with some inaccuracies, in La Ferlita, 262/3 n. 5, who dates it to the early fifteenth century. It is a close paraphrase of the relevant section in Doc. III *supra*, but is interesting for the vernacular Sicilian forms and for certain extra details. The same sheet, possibly torn out of a general estate book, also contains (at f. 505v) a list of properties at Siracusa, but the names it contains do not enable the sheet to be more precisely dated. Giacomo de Pelligrino was exiled in 1372 (*supra*, 160 n. 77) and the house he had held at Mdina (Doc. III) passed to Lodovicus de Plozasco, but the latter cannot be documented at Malta before 26 February 1398 when he was already married: Palermo, Archivio di Stato, Reg. 30, f. 62–62v: (this reference was kindly provided by Dr. Godfrey Wettinger). Lodovicus married Giacomo's daughter Francia, according to the will of 5 June 1418 by which Francia's mother, Margarita d'Aragona, bequeathed them parts of houses in Mdina which do not seem to have been in the piazza: modern copy in Mdina, Cathedral Archives, Ms. 28, f. 1–10v. Lodovicus was dead by 20 May 1429 when Francia remarried: modern summary in Valletta, Ms. Biblioteca 1365, f. 1, 255. Words such as *alaplaza* are here transcribed as *ala plaza*.

[121]Presumably the main square at Mdina.

[122]Ludovicus de Plozasco held the *pheudum* of *Maccalabim* on Malta in 1408: text in B. Muscia, *Sicilia Nobilis* (Rome, 1692), 114–15.

[123]i.e. Raħal Kbir.

[124]i.e. Ħaġar Qim.

[125]The *tenuta* at *lu portu di Benarratu* (now Salina Bay) does not appear in the 1365 text (Doc. III *supra*).

# XVI

## THE AUGUSTINIANS AT MALTA: 1413

The religious orders established themselves at a remarkably late date on an island which was being converted from Islam at least as early as the beginning of the thirteenth century.[1] An endowment made in 1362 for the foundation of a house on Malta was evaded by the Benedictines of Catania on the grounds that the island was too distant, that travel to it was dangerous and that Sicilian monks could not understand its language; the Benedictine brethren thus acquired property on Malta though they never had a community there.[2] A hospital and a church at Rabat, the suburb of Malta's main fortified town of Mdina, had both been dedicated to St. Francis by 1372 when a Franciscan was appointed by the king to be rector of the hospital.[3] The Augustinians had a convent in Malta by 1413;[4] the Carmelites were probably on the island by 1441;[5] the Dominicans seem to have rejected a legacy of 1431

---

1 General survey in A. Luttrell, "Approaches to Medieval Malta," in *Medieval Malta: Studies on Malta before the Knights*, ed. A. Luttrell (London, 1975), 33-34, 63-64, which itself requires revision in the light of what appears below. There is an extensive and confused literature, much of it 'tradition' and post-medieval invention, and much of it deriving from errors propagated in G.-F. Abela, *Della Descrittione di Malta* (Malta, 1647); even the most recent general histories still require a complete revision, which should be based on contemporary documents or on reasonably reliable copies or summaries of them, and should distinguish between the presence of one or more religious and the formal establishment of a convent. Dr. Godfrey Wettinger most kindly provided advice on a number of particular points.

2 D. la Ferlita, "I possedimenti dei Benedettini di Catania a Malta," *Archivio Storico di Malta*, vii (1935/6), using documents in Catania; the present author will publish these with various corrections.

3 Text in H. Bresc, "Documents on Frederick IV of Sicily's Intervention in Malta: 1372," *Papers of the British School at Rome*, xli (1973), 200; correct B. Fiorini, "Il Convento di S. Francesco in Rabat (Malta) dei frati minori conventuali," *Melita Historica*, iii no. 3 (1962), 3-5, 16-17, 32, who follows Abela, 391, in misdating the document to 1370.

4 Text *infra*, 300-301.

5 Text *infra*, 301, and n. 17. Margarita de Aragona's will of 5 June 1418 spoke of an *ecclesia*, not a convent, and of *fratres* not Carmelites (... *subsidia fratrum vel canentium seu psallentium et celebrantium et dicentium in eadem ecclesia* ...); though the term *fratrum* is somewhat puzzling, the fact that the Carmelites later possessed the Annunciation church which Margarita had rebuilt at San Leonardo outside Rabat does not prove their presence there in 1418, as Abela, 393-394 (with extracts from the text), and many others since, have proposed. The best copy of Margarita's will is that in Valletta, Notarial Archives, Notary Andrea Allegritto, R. 16/28, f. 823v-824: partial text in G. Wet-

which would have endowed them with the church of St. Mark at Rabat if they would establish a community there,[6] but they were in Rabat from about 1450 onwards;[7] and a bequest of 1492 provided for the building of what became the convent of the Observant Franciscans at Rabat.[8] Some time before 1479, when their convent of San Pietro in Mdina was in ruins, Benedictine nuns were also established in Malta.[9]

Some of the above dates are by no means fixed or final. The controversies concerning the uncertain timing and order of arrival of the monks and friars in Malta have grown into a scarcely penetrable jungle of myth and invention, much of which goes back to Abela's history of 1647. Controversy and confusion culminated in two works by L. Muscat, *Antichità e priorità del Convento di S. Agostino della Notabile: Dissertazioni storico-apologetiche* (Malta, 1913), which consisted of 202 pages, and *Replica al Molto Rev. P. Alberto M. Grech S. Th. Lect. de' Predicatori* (Malta, 1914), of 128 pages. This dispute was mercifully smothered with ridicule by *Il Magno Responso dato dalla Commissione neutro-mista presieduta da Fr. Rustico Seriocomico nella vertenza teologico-canonico-filosofico-storico-letteraria tra il P. M. L. Muscat O.E.S.A. ed il P. L. A. Grech O.P.* (Malta, 1915). A. Mifsud had meanwhile explained that there was no serious evidence for the continuous presence of the Augustinians

---

tinger, "Artistic Patronage in Malta: 1418-1538," in *Hal Millieri: a Maltese Casale, its Churches and Paintings*, ed. A. Luttrell (Malta, 1976), 116 n. 30.

6 Modern copy of the will of Michele de Fabro dated 17 May 1431 (from the lost acts of Notary Luca de Sillato) in Valletta, Royal Malta Library, Biblioteca Ms. 635, f. 224v-227: partial text in Abela, 398.

7 There were several Dominicans at Rabat in about 1450, but the formal establishment of a convent apparently came in 1462: M. Fsadni, *Il-Miġja u l-Hidma ta' L-Ewwel Dumnikani f'Malta: 1450-1512* (Malta, 1965), 19-32, 79-84; Abela, 403, gave 1466.

8 The will of Giacbu Hakim of Mdina dated 6 April 1492 (from the lost acts of Notary Ingomez de Brancato) exists in an 18-century copy in Valletta, Ms. 1122, f. 2-2bisv; Abela, 409-410, gave part of the text. Other references in G. Xerri, *Erbgha mitt sena ta Apostolat tal Patrijet Minuri Osservanti Geuua Malta* ... (Malta, 1927), 8.

9 ... *super facto abbacie monialium ipsius civitatis urgentis ad ruinam*: text in Valletta, Royal Malta Library, Università Ms. 11, f. 407v, published in E. Leopardi, "*Bandi* of the XV Century," *Melita Historica*, ii no. 4 (1959), 258; the date 1479, which Leopardi did not explain, is presumably correct since a document of Fernando II (1479-1516) which is also dated to the XIII Indiction appears at f. 415v-416. This must have been San Pietro, since the Benedictine nunnery of Santa Scolastica at Mdina was not founded until several decades later (Abela, 356). It has been argued (eg. by Abela, 355) from a passage in Margarita de Aragona's will of 1418 (... *apothecam unam quam habeo intus Ciuitatem Melitueti prope hospitale Sancti Petri* ...: for text, *supra* note 5) that there was a hospital of San Pietro which later became the Benedictine nunnery.

in Malta since the time of St. Augustine nor for their establishment there in 1386, a proposition which had been deduced merely from the existence in Sicily at that date of a Franciscan named Francesco da Malta. Mifsud mentioned a text recording a donation to the Augustinian convent in 1440.[10] This record survives in an early-modern summary of a lost will:

> Testamento di Pino Bertolo est in actis Notarij Luce Sillato de anno 1440 in quo legauit Ecclesie Ste. Caterine Conuentus Sti. Augustini unam apothecam in Rabbato.[11]

References to this notice, and to others showing donations made to the *ecclesia* of St. Augustine between 1440 and 1483, were given in 1957.[12] It is now certain that the Augustinians had a convent in Malta by 1413 at the latest,[13] and possibly they were the second order to be established on the island. The document of 1413 shows that the Augustinians held an *apotheca* or shop, but it does not suggest where the convent or the *apotheca* were then situated; probably the convent was in Rabat,[14] just outside the walls of Mdina in the area known as Saqqajja, since a later proclamation instructed that vegetables should not be sold outside the gate of Mdina — *extra portam ciuitatis videlicet In planicie santi agustinj.*[15] This point, however, awaits firmer documentation. Mazullo

---

10 A. Mifsud, reviewing Muscat (1913), in *Archivum Melitense*, ii (1912-1913), 104-105; Abela, 397, gave 1460.

11 Mdina, Cathedral Archives Ms. 280, f. 219 = Valletta, Ms. 695, f. 334v.

12 J. Galea, *Storia tal-Knisja ta' San Mark u tal-Kunvent tal-Agostinjani tar-Rabat* (Malta, 1956), 17-18: wills of Agostino and Fiorenza Cassar, 6 October 1447, and Francesco Vassallo, 24 January 1455 (calendared in Mdina, Ms. 280, f. 2, 78 = Valletta, Ms. 695, f. 2, 116).

13 The Augustinians were also mentioned in the will of Federigo de Bordino made in Malta on 10 August 1414: *Item lego fratri[bus] sancti augustinj unam quartaram vinj* (16th-century copy in Catania, Archivio di Stato, Fondo Benedettini Ms. 159, f. 140-143).

14 Galea, 9-17, who states that Ingerau Desguanes exchanged lands in Saqqajja just outside Mdina for Augustinian properties at Mellieha known as Ġnien Ingraw, supposes that the Augustinians, or alternatively individual Augustinian hermits, were established at Mellieha before 1442; he also maintains that the Augustinians were in Mdina by 1427 and in Rabat by 1449. All this, however, is based on non-contemporary evidence, while the text of 25 October 1442 which he cites concerns Antoni Desguanes and a property in Saqqajja but it makes no mention of Ingerau Desguanes, of Mellieha or of the Augustinians: early-modern copy of a *vidimus* of 2 August 1443 of the document of 1442 in Valletta, Università Ms. 7 part ii, f. 73-73v.

15 Valletta, Università Ms. 11, f. 254: text in E. Leopardi, "*Bandi* of the XV Century," *Melita Historica*, ii no. 2 (1957), 127, with the date of 8 July 1472; July of the VI Indiction actually gives 1473 (cf. f. 225v, where the Incarnation year is given).

and Capano, the Augustinians mentioned in the texts of 1413 and 1441, do not seem to have had Maltese names, which suggests they were foreigners.

## I

*Viceregal act concerning the Prior of the Augustinian Convent at Malta: Palermo, 9 November 1413* (Palermo, Archivio di Stato, Cancelleria Reg. 48, f. 165 [*olim* 125], with evident corruptions in the text and various uncertain abbreviations).

Ferrandus etc. Judicis capitane[o] ciuitatis meliuetj, thomeo de a[u]lerj et Johanne de chillino ciuibus et Juratis ciuitatis eiusdem fidelibus nostris, gratiam et bonam uoluntatem, querula nuper supplicatio mazullj prioris conuentus sancti augustini de meliueto benignitate nostrj culminis supplicitur Inplorauit, cum eodem querulante In conuentu prefato quiete per momente et ad ministrante officium prioratus sub dei obedientia et tenore et assecuratione sibi facta, per uicem capitaneum eiusdem ciuitatis, Ipsique certi homines noctis tempore conquassatis et dirutis muris et parietibus dicti conuentus cameram ubi prior antefactus morabat violenter Intrauerunt eundemque priorem uerberibus affixum vulnibus grauiter percussum, qui semimortuum relinqerunt, quj pro huiusmodi Insultu sibi facto ad uicecapitaneum occurens, nullum potuit Juris consequj remedium ut asseruit, de super cum uniuersitas ciuitatis eiusdem, loerij nouem quandam, ab eodem conuentu teneat apothecam de qua conuentus Idem nullum Jus loerj huiusque potuit habere super hijs et quolibet premissorum de Iuris oportuno remedio sibi et eidem conuentuj prouidere dignaremur, cuius supplicatione benignius Inclinati uolentes similes excessus debita punicione corrigere, de vestris namque fide sufficiencia et legalitate plenius confidentes uobis causam utraque predicta duximus commictendam, Itaque presentium uigore citatis uocatis et requisitis presentibus que tanguntur Iusticiam super hijs et horum quolibet plenarie ministratis, et si constiterit dictam uniuersitatem ratione loerj dicte apothece dicto conuentui fore obligatam ipsam ad solutionem dicti loherij compellatis omnia et singula prenotata cum omnibus dependentibus emergentibus et conexis sententialiter fingatis sentenciam uestram super utroque premisso debito exequcionj mandando, ratum gratum et firmum habiturj quod quid preduxeritis per tractandum, mandantes quo circa vniuersis et singulis officialibus predicte ciuitatis meliuetj presentibus et futuris uobis In premissis et quolibet premissorum assustant et obediant auxilium consilium atque fauorem, quotiens requisiueritis Inpendant oportune, datum In nostra felici urbe panormj die nono mensis presentis nouembris vij$^{e}$ Indictionis sub anno domini Incarnacionis m$^{o}$cccc$^{o}$xiij$^{o}$, vidit Magister ferrando de vega vidit ferrandus cancelarius, vidit martinus.

d[ominus] Vice[rex] mandauit
mihi n. de moletis prothonot[ario]

## II

*Fragment of a document dated 24 January 1441*[16] *contained in a document of 26 March 1446 and copied "from a parchment" into the notebook of Gian Francesco Abela during the seventeenth century; the text is given here, without expanding the contractions, in the form there found* (Valletta, Royal Malta Library, Biblioteca Ms. 140, f. 39$^{v}$ [*olim* 37$^{v}$]).

*Ex quodam Pergameno:—*

In nomine D'ni Amen. Anno Dominice Incarnationis millesimo quadring.mo quadrages.mo sexto. mense martij uigesimo sexto die mensis eiusdem nona Ind'e Regnante Alphonso etc. nobis asseruit et dixit quod olim quondam Magr. Senator de Meli Episcopus Melitensis concessit etc. concessionis, et confirmationis contractus talis est Pro R.mo D'no Senatore Episcopo meliuetano etc. 24$^{o}$ Januarij quarte Ind.s Nos Judex et testes Infrascripti etc. fr. Guillelmus Cassar Prior Conuentus Sancte marie Nuntiate.[17] fr. Jacobus de Capano Prior Conuentus S.ti Augustini Bernardus Saliba, Magr. filius Mulinella, Jacobus manduca, fr. Periconus Ord.s Carmelitan' uocibus Cleri confirmati. uz. Donni Henrici de bordino Vicarius et Cantoris d.e Ecclesie meliuetane Donni Bernardi Gener Decani Donni lancie de Inguanes Archdiaconi, Donni Guiglelmi Richulce Thesaurarij, Donni Nicolai lombardo, Donni Nicolai de Budno[18] Donni Nicolai falzone Donni michaelis Calleya Donni Andre etc.:—[19]

---

16 Since Senatore de Mello was bishop from 1432 to 1445, the IV Indiction can only have fallen in 1440/1.

17 The text mentions a *fr. Periconus Ord.s Carmelitan'*, which increases the likelihood that the *Conuentus Sancte marie Nuntiate* was that at San Leonardo outside Rabat which eventually passed to the Carmelites; therefore, the Carmelites were probably, though not certainly, established there as early as 1441.

18 *Sic*: presumably the *Domnus Nicolaus de Burdino* who witnessed an act in Malta on 28 April 1439: modern copy in Valletta, Ms. 360, f. 908-910.

19 The transcript ends here.

# XVII

# THE CAPPELLA OF BIRKIRKARA: 1402

After 1378 the Roman Church was divided by the schism between two papal obediences, the Roman and the Avignonese, and in the Kingdom of Sicily this complication was further confused by the political situation resulting both from internal quarrels and from Aragonese intervention in that island. (1) Such difficulties increased the opportunities available to those in search of benefices, since there were more popes and bishops who could confer appointments. Competing popes were encouraged to augment their incomes by making provisions, because those to whom they granted benefices had to make payments to the papal *camera*. Popes could take advantage of legal clauses and constitutions which gave them rights to interfere in appointments according to considerations which were carefully set out in their lengthy bulls of provision.

On 13 November 1402 the Roman pope, Boniface IX, instructed the Dean of Negroponte and Petrus de Vetulo, a Canon of Malta, to install the *presbiter* Bernardus de Janer as *decanus* or Dean of the Maltese Chapter. The previous Dean, Simone de Sciacca, was dead but that was not the reason given for the vacancy. Instead it was decreed that Simone had held his Deanship with a Maltese *cappella*, a benefice with cure of souls; that although he had been canonically collated or appointed to the *cappella* — which suggests that he held it before he became Dean — and had held the *cappella* and its incomes for a number of years without challenge, it was technically uncanonical, according to Pope John XXII's bull *Execrabilis*, to hold simultaneously, and without any special dispensation, two benefices one or both of which was with care of souls; and Simone's position as Dean had therefore been illegal, a point it was important to establish since it gave the Pope, rather than the Bishop or the Chapter, the right to fill the vacancy. (2) In nominating Bernardus de Janer, Boniface IX also dispensed him from the prohibitions which would

1. S. Fodale, *Scisma Ecclesiastico e Potere Regio in Sicilia*, i: *Il Duca di Montblanc e l'Episcopato tra Roma e Avignone*, 1392-1396 (Palermo, 1979), 63-65, 91-92 *et passim*, gives various details concerning Malta; see also S. Fodale, "Le Parrocchie in Sicilia: il Cumulo di Benefici curati nella Diocesi di Siracusa tra la fine del XIV e l'inizio del XV secolo," in *Pievi e Parrocchie in Italia nel Basso Medioevo: secoli XIII-XV* (Rome, forthcoming). Technically nominations to offices in the Maltese church, including that of Dean, belonged to the Sicilian crown, though in 1396 both the Roman and Avignonese popes claimed jurisdiction: texts in Fodale (1979), 214-216, 220-221.
2. Text in *Corpus Juris Canonici*, pars ii, ed. E. Richter (2nd ed: Leipzig, 1879), 1207-1209. The language of the bull published here should not be regarded as proof that the Dean of Malta's benefice was an office with *cura animarum*.

otherwise have resulted from his illegitimate birth, perhaps because Bernardus had become a priest without such a dispensation or maybe because he wished to reinforce the legality of his position. Bernardus certainly became Dean; he resided on Malta where in 1421 he was one of two *vicarii* of the *maior ecclesia*, and he was still Dean when he made his will on 4 January 1442. (3)

Boniface's bull, grammatically somewhat obscure, illustrates one way in which Sicilian clerics could secure leading positions in the Maltese Church, and it also provides the earliest known reference to a Maltese *cappella* with cure of souls, that is to a Maltese parish. Simone de Sciacca must have secured the *cappella* of Birkirkara some years before 1402. Birkirkara is documented as a *casale* in 1419/20 when it was a large village providing 89 men for militia service; its population may then have been around 500. (4) In the thirteenth century pastoral work, including the provision of the sacraments, had probably been centred on the Cathedral at Mdina, being conducted by the Canons or by other *cappellani* of the Cathedral who came, as the Christian population grew, to exercize the cure of souls outside Mdina in local centres or *cappelle* where they also enjoyed incomes; such *cappelle* were not necessarily situated in the larger villages but may, as at Bir Miftuħ, have been placed in rural positions between several settlements which they served jointly. (5)

The bull of 1402 reflects some ambiguity as to whether the *cappella* of *Birkarkam*, evidently an error for Birkirkara, was dedicated to Elena or Maria. Apparently there was once a parish church of Sant'Elena at Tal-Għargħar some 1.5 km north-east of Birkirkara, where the apostolic visitation of 1575 recorded the *ecclesia ruralis* at *Arar* then rumoured to be a former parish church: *que alias dicitur fuisse parochialis ecclesia*. (6) The so-called episcopal

3. Texts in R. Valentini, "Gli ultimi Re Aragonesi ed i primi Castigliani in Malta," *Archivio Storico di Malta*, viii (1936/7), 84-85; G. Wettinger, "Artistic Patronage in Malta: 1418-1538," in *Hal Millieri: A Maltese Casale, its Churches and Paintings*, ed. A. Luttrell (Malta, 1976), 117 n. 31. Janer's name suggests a possible Catalan origin.
4. G. Wettinger, "The Militia List of 1419-20," *Melita Historica*, v no. 2 (1969), 82, 92-93.
5. A. Luttrell, "Le Origini della Parrocchia a Malta," in *Pievi e Parrocchie in Italia...*
6. Valletta, Archiepiscopal Curia, Visitatio Dusina (Copy C), f. 155. This is the earliest reference to the church at Tal-Għargħar having been a parish church. The tower named Ta' Ċieda at L'Imsieraħ stood in a field which was named after Sant'Elena and was traditionally associated with her cult. Excavations showed the tower to have been occupied in Imperial Roman times, to have had a Roman cistern and to have had within it "a great number of Saracenic burials, some outlined in stones": *Report on the Working of the Museum Department for the Year* 1960 (Malta, 1962), 6 and Fig. 3. It seems unlikely that a Christian church would have been built directly on a Muslim cemetery but the church may well have been close to the remains of the tower.

"rollo" of 1436 listed *La Capella di Birkarkara cum terris suis* which was then held by *Don'us* Mattheus Galia, probably a Cathedral Canon, and was worth 20 *uncie.* (7) As late as 1544 the parish church of Birkirkara was still being described ambiguously as dedicated to Santa Maria or Sant'Elena. (8) The centre of the parish seems to have been moved at some point before 1402 from the outlying Sant'Elena at Tal-Għargħar to Santa Maria in populous Birkirkara, (9) with the Birkirkara church retaining its dedication but the parish continuing to regard Sant'Elena as its patron saint. (10) Presumably, therefore, the dedication to Santa Maria had been established some time before 1402. This new parish church was apparently the church at Mrieħel which had a curved apse (11) and which was therefore probably medieval; it too presumably dated before 1402.

A parish system involving a *cappella* with care of souls was clearly functioning in Malta in the second half of the fourteenth century. By 1402 at the latest the centre of one *cappella* had, apparently, already been transfered from the church of Sant'Elena at Tal-Għargħar to the village of Birkirkara where a church dedicated to Santa Maria had already been constructed.

Archivio Vaticano, Reg. Lat. 107, f. 71v-72v (12)

Bonifacius etc. Dilectis filiis decano Nigroponten[sis] et Cantori ac Petro de Vetulo Canonico Meleuitane ecclesiarum Salutem etc. Vite ac morum honestas aliaque laudabilia probitatis et uirtutum merita super quibus apud nos dilectus filius Bernardus Janer Canonicus ecclesie Meleuitane fidedigno commendatur testimonio nos inducunt ut sibi reddamur ad gratiam liberales Cum itaque sicut accepimus decanatus dicte ecclesie exeo uacauerit et uacet ad presens quod

7. Copy in Valletta, National Library of Malta, Ms. Biblioteca 255, f. 224-226v.
8. *parrochialj ecclesia sancte Marie seu Helene de Birch*[*ir*]*kara*: Valletta, Notarial Archives, Reg. R. 376/9 (Notary Giuliano Muscat), f. 710v-711v; reference kindly provided by Dr. Godfrey Wettinger.
9. M. Buhagiar, "Medieval Churches in Malta," in *Medieval Malta: Studies on Malta before the Knights*, ed. A. Luttrell (London, 1975), 172, anticipates such an interpretation which the bull of 1402 tends to confirm.
10. In the seventeenth and eighteenth centuries Sant'Elena remained the parish patron while the church at Għargħar was considered to have been the original parish church: G. Bugeja, *Storia Critica sulla Vita di Elena Imperatrice* (Malta, 1875), 82-88, and E.B. Vella, *Storja ta' Birkirkara bil-Kolleġġjata Tagħna* (Malta, 1934), 36-38, 47-49 *et passim.*
11. V. Borg, "Tagħrif Ġdid dwar il-Bini tal-Knisja l-Qadima ta' Birkirkara", in *Birkirkara tqim lill-Patruna tagħha Sant'Elena* 1976 (Malta, 1976). Mgr. Vincent Borg most kindly provided considerable help and advice.
12. Proper names are capitalized but no corrections or modernizations are introduced.

quondam Symon de Sacka olim eiusdem ecclesie decanus, decanatum ipsum tunc obtinens Capellam sancte Helene alias sancte Marie de Birkarkam meleuitane diocesis que curata existit tunc uacantem canonice sibi collatam pacifice assecutus illam vnacum decanatu prefato post et contra Constitutionem pie memorie Johannis pape xxij predecessoris nostri que incipit execrabilis nulla super hoc canonica dispensatione obtenta pluribus annis detinu[i]t fructus percipiens ex eisdem Nos attendentes quod si est ita nullus preter Romanum pontificem hac uice decanatu predicto disponere potuit siue potest pro eo quod idem predecessor omnes dignitates personatus et officia ceteraque beneficia ecclesiastica cum cura et sine cura per Constitutionem huiusmodi uacatura collationi et dispositioni sue et sedis apostolice reseruans decreuit ex tunc irritum et inane si secus super hijs aquoquam quauis auctoritate scienter uel ignoranter contingerit attemptari, ac uolentes dicto Bernardo qui presbiter est et cum quo alias ut non obstante defectu natalium quem patitur de clerico in minoribus dumtaxat ordinibus constituto genitus et soluta ad eos etiam sacros ordines promoueri et duo beneficia ecclesiastica etiam si alterum ipsorum curatum foret recipere et retinere posset fuit auctoritate apostolica dispensatum Postquamquidem dispensationem prefatus Bernardus ad huiusmodi ordines rite promotus in Canonicam dicte ecclesie canonice receptus fuit premissorum intuitu gratiam facere specialem discretioni uestre per apostolica scripta mandamus quatenus uos uel duo aut vnus vestrum per uos vel alium seu alios decanatum predictum qui dignitas non tamen maior post pontificalem in dicta ecclesia existit et cuius fructus redditus et prouentus Septuaginta florenorum auri secundum comunem extimatonem ualorem annuum ut ipse Bernardus asserit non excedunt si ut premictitur uacat etiam si tanto tempore uacauerit quod eius collatio iuxta Lateranensis statuta Concilij ad sedem predictam legitime deuoluta uel etiam si decanatus ipse dispositioni apostolice specialiter reseruatus existant et curam habeat animarum et ad eum consueuerit quis per electionem assumi dummodo tempore dat[um] presencium non sit in eo alicui specialiter ius quesitum cum omnibus iuribus et pertinencijs suis prefato Bernardo auctoritate nostra conferre et assignare curetis Inducentes eum uel procuratorem suum eius nomine in corporalem possessionem decanatus iuriumque et pertinentiarum predictorum et defendentes inductum amoto exinde quolibet illicito detentore ac facientes eundem Bernardum uel dictum procuratorem pro eo ad dictum decanatum ut est moris admicti sibique de ipsius decanatus fructibus redditibus prouentibus iuribus et obuentionibus vniuersis integre responderi Contradictores auctoritate nostra etc. Non obstantibus tam felicis recordationis Bonifatij pape viij etiam predecessoris nostri quam alijs constitutionibus apostolicis necnon statutis et consuetudinibus ipsius ecclesie contrarijs iuramento confirmatione apostolica uel quacumque firmitate alia roboratis Seu si aliqui super prouisionibus sibi faciendis de dignitatibus personatibus uel officijs ipsius ecclesie speciales uel alijs beneficijs ecclesiasticis in illis partibus generales dicte sedis uel legatorum eius litteras impetrarint etiam si per eas ad inhibicionem reseruationem et decretum uel alias quomodolibet sit processum quibus omnibus predictum Bernardum in assecutione dicti decanatus uolumus anteferri sed nullum per hoc eis quo ad assecutionem dignitatum personatuum uel officiorum aut beneficiorum aliorum preiudicium generari Aut si venerabili fratri nostro Episcopo et dilectis filijs Capitulo Meleuitanis uel quibusuis alijs comuniter uel diuisim ab eadem sancte sede indultum quod ad receptionem uel prouisionem alicuius minime teneantur et ad id compelli aut quod interdici suspendi uel excomunicari non possint quodque de dignitatibus personatibus uel officijs ipsius ecclesie aut alijs beneficijs ecclesiasticis ad eorum collationem prouisionem presentacionem electionem seu quamuis aliam disposicionem coniunctim uel separatim spectantibus nulli ualeat prouideri per litteras apostolicas non facientes plenam et expressam ac de uerbo ad uerbum de indulto huiusmodi mentionem et qualibet alia dicte sedis indulgentia generali uel speciali cuiuscumque tenoris existat per quam presentibus non expressam uel totaliter non insertam effectus huiusmodi gratie impediri ualeat quomodolibet uel differri et de qua cuiusque toto tenore habenda sit in nostris litteris mentio specialis Seu si dictus Bernardus presens non fuerit ad prestandum de obseruandis statutis et consuetudinibus ipsius ecclesie ratione dicti decanatus solitum iuramentum dummodo in absentia sua per procuratorem ydoneum et cum ad ecclesiam ipsam accesserit corporaliter illud prestet Aut quod idem Bernardus Canonicatum predictum cuius fructus redditus et prouentus Trium florenorum auri secundum extimacionem predictam ualorem annuum non excedunt canonice noscitur obtinere Nos enim cum dicto Bernardo ut decanatum predictum si ei presentium uigore conferatur recipere et retinere libere et licite ualeat defectu predicto ac Pictauensis Concilij necnon quibuscumque alijs constitutionibus apostolicis ac statutis et consuetudinibus supradictis contrarijs nequaquem obstantibus auctoritate apostolica tenore presentium de uberioris dono gratie dispensamus Et insuper prout est irritum decernimus et inane si secus super hijs aquoquam quauis auctoritate scienter uel ignoranter actemptatum forsan est hactenus uel imposterum contigerit actemptari datum Rome apud Sanctum Petrum Idus Nouembris Anno Quartodecimo. *Jac. xxviij de Eberam'*

# XVIII

## *Le origini della parrocchia a Malta*

Lo sviluppo della parrocchia maltese fino al 1436, a differenza di quella italiana e anche di quella siciliana, fu condizionato dal fatto che Malta, piccola isola, fu un paese musulmano convertito alla fede cristiana soltanto nel Duecento. Le origini della parrocchia maltese sono state quasi totalmente ignorate per la mancanza di qualsiasi documentazione prima del Quattrocento, e questa assenza di fonti ha contribuito alla propagazione di una serie di errori sull'argomento. La presente sintesi è di carattere introduttivo e sfrutta solo una parte della documentazione disponibile; inizia con una ricognizione storiografica prima di proporre alcune interpretazioni nuove, le quali sono estremamente ipotetiche e saranno certamente modificate alla luce di ulteriori ricerche di archivio[1].

Le fonti per la storia della Chiesa in Malta fra la riconquista iniziale del 1090 e l'anno 1372 circa sono scarsissime, e anche prima del 1436 sono esigue. Lo studio del testo del cosidetto « Rollo » del 1436, il quale sarà pubblicato in forma completa come contributo supplementare al presente lavoro, richiede l'elaborazione di molti dettagli prosopografici e topografici. È difficile, per di più, capire lo sviluppo della parrocchia maltese quando tutta la storia della Chiesa medievale a Malta aspetta ancora uno studio sistematico. Esistono i materiali pubblicati nel 1647 da Gianfrancesco Abela e più recentemente da Alfredo Mifsud; i lineamenti poco attendibili della *History of the Church in Malta* di Arthur Bonnici; e tutta una raccolta di monografie e di articoli, incluse alcune

[1] Questa sintesi deve molto al gentile aiuto di Mgr. Vincenzo Borg e del Dott. Godfrey Wettinger.

pubblicazioni di grande valore. Ma tutto questo non fornisce un quadro generale soddisfacente. Il clero della cattedrale, la chiesa privata, i benefizi e le decime, la cura pastorale e la devozione popolare esigono una ricerca da condurre negli archivi della cattedrale, dell'*universitas*, dei notai maltesi e della corona siciliana [2].

Una informazione limitata può essere fornita dall'approccio « archeologico », dallo scavo, dallo studio di chiese, cimiteri e pitture. Sono interessanti anche le numerose chiese minori, le quali avevano una importanza nell'ambito della parrocchia [3]. Purtroppo le molte pubblicazioni sulle parrocchie e chiese individuali portano poca informazione per il periodo anteriore al 1450. Per questi secoli bisogna effettuare una serie di comparazioni, un processo rischioso ma inevitabile. I primi raffronti devono essere derivati dalla storia della stessa parrocchia maltese in età successiva, ma anche questo argomento manca di ricerche approfondite per tutto il periodo anteriore all'importante rapporto, ancora inedito, della visita apostolica di Pietro Dusina nel 1575 [4]. Soltanto dopo lo studio di tutta la documentazione sulla Chiesa isolana, si procederà a diversi confronti con la situazione in Sicilia e in Italia [5].

[2] Per le fonti, vedi *Maltese History: What Future?*, a cura di R. VELLA BONAVITA e A. WILLIAMS, Malta 1974, e *Medieval Malta: Studies on Malta before the Knights*, a cura di A. LUTTRELL, Londra 1975; cf. J. AZZOPARDI, *Handlist of the Episcopal and Pro-Vicarial Archives (Curia Episcopalis Melitensis or CEM Archives) at the Malta Cathedral Museum*, Collegeville, Minnesota 1975, e A. LUTTRELL, *The Earliest Documents Transcribed in the Cathedral Archives, Mdina: 1316-1372*, in J. AZZOPARDI, *Archives of the Cathedral of Malta, Misc. 32 A: 1313-1529*, Malta 1977.

[3] Vedi gli studi raccolti in *Hal Millieri: a Maltese Casale, its Churches and Paintings*, a cura di A. LUTTRELL, Malta 1976, e in *Excavations at Hal Millieri, Malta*, a cura di T. BLAGG, A. BONANNO, A. LUTTRELL, Malta: in corso di stampa; cf. anche M. BUHAGIAR, *St. Catherine of Alexandria: her Churches, Paintings and Statues in the Maltese Islands*, Malta 1979.

[4] Per la visita di Dusina, vedi LUTTRELL in *Medieval Malta*, p. 8, e in *Hal Millieri*, pp. 138-139; cf. A. J. BORG, *The Reform of the Council of Trent in Malta and Gozo*, Malta 1975, pp. 34-41. Nel 1575 c'erano quattro parrocchie greche a Malta.

[5] Mancano, purtroppo, anche fra gli atti di questo convegno, uno studio sulle origini della parrocchia in Sicilia. Lo studio di A. LONGHITANO, *La Parroc-*

Non si conosce quasi niente sulla parrocchia in Malta prima del 1436, quando il vescovo di Malta, Senatore di Mello, ordinava una inchiesta con il motivo di terminare una lunga causa fra il clero di Malta e quello della vicina isola di Gozo sulla porzione delle *taxe* ecclesiastiche che ciascuno doveva pagare [6]. Il risultato fu il « Rollo », un elenco delle rendite della Chiesa maltese comprendente i nomi di dodici *cappelle;* non disponiamo di un analogo « Rollo » gozitano. Questo elenco è stato mal interpretato come l'atto di fondazione delle dodici parrocchie, le quali evidentemente esistevano già prima del 1436 [7]; questo errore si ripete ancora in molte pubblicazioni, nonostante tutti gli argomenti in contrario. Per di più, il 1436 è spesso considerato come l'anno della costruzione di queste chiese parrocchiali, oppure come la data della loro dedica; è stato anche preteso che le dodici parrocchie menzionate nel « Rollo » furono istituite dal papa Eugenio IV [8].

Il « Rollo » o *quinterniolus pro concordia taxarum* del 1436, il quale elencava dodici *cappelle* e più di cento fra *beneficii, animagii* e *prebende*, iniziava:

Inprimis

| | | |
|---|---|---|
| Donnus Archidiaconus cum suo officio et introitu | Vnc. | lxxxv. |
| Donnus Decanus cum terris di Sta. Dominica | | l. |
| Lo Animagio di Rahal ain Hupulli | | iij. |
| Lo Animagio di la mugliera di Notario Paulu | | ij. |
| Lo Animagio di Antonio Santa Sophia | | vij. |

*chia nella Diocesi di Catania prima e dopo il Concilio di Trento*, Roma 1977, pp. 21-40, è importante; però Malta dipendeva da Palermo, mentre la situazione fu molto diversa a Catania dove tutto stava nelle mani dei monaci benedettini, dove i « cappellani » furono soltanto *cappellani quasi parochi* (*ibid.*, p. 23, nota 9), e dove c'erano chiese sacramentali ma non parrocchie nel senso pieno dalla parola.

[6] Copia della lettera vescovile del 1° luglio 1436 in Mdina, Cathedral Archives, Ms. 28, f. 128*v*-130.

[7] Per esempio, A. Bonnici, *History of the Church in Malta*, I, Malta 1967, pp. 70, 88. L'affermazione che sono state fondate delle parrocchie a Malta dall'undicesimo al quattordicesimo secolo (*ibid.*, I, p. 87) è senza fondamento.

[8] Cf. Luttrell, in *Medieval Malta*, p. 63 n. 345.

1190

| | |
|---|---|
| Donnus Cantor pro prebenda Scte. Catharina | xv. |
| La petia di lu Ciantrato | xiij |
| Lo Animagio di Presti Nardu Xeberras | tt xv |
| Lo beneficio di S. Nicolao di la Mellecha | tt x |
| Lo beneficio di la Monica | vij |
| Lo beneficio di Mitalfas | viij |
| Don' us Thesaurarius la Thesauraria | iiij |
| lo beneficio di Sansuni | vij |
| lo Animagio di lu Xara | iij |
| la Puttiga di Don'a Margarita | iij |

Un altro tratto elencava:

| | |
|---|---|
| La Cappella di lu Zurrico cum terris suis | xij |
| lu beneficio dila Gebie | i |
| Don'us Albanus de Franco prebenda Bir Tauil | xxiiij |
| La Capella di San Paulu di fora | xxv |
| lo beneficio di San Georgi | i. tt xv. |

L'originale è perduto, ma il documento può essere ricostruito da varie copie moderne; e una nuova edizione è in preparazione. La versione pubblicata da Gianfrancesco Abela nel 1647 tralasciava tutti i particolari finanziarii, e sembra che sia stato Abela diffondere l'erronea idea che tutte le *cappelle* fossero state fondate nel 1436 [9]. Per una più sicura interpretazione del « Rollo » sarà necessario l'identificazione di tutte le persone e i toponimi nominati, e la spiegazione del significato delle disposizioni finanziarie; sembra che i valori indicati fossero quelli degli introiti dei benefizi.

* * *

Dalla conquista dell'870 fino all'« espulsione » dei musulmani nel primo Duecento le isole maltesi furono in predominanza musulmane. Non ci sono prove convincenti per la sopravvivenza di una comunità cristiana, e tanto meno per una coerente organizzazione ecclesiastica. Probabilmente la « ricon-

[9] G.-F. Abela, *Della Descrittione di Malta*, Malta 1647, pp. 312-316.

quista » siciliana del 1090 aveva avuto poco rilievo, ma a un certo punto, fra il 1127 e il 1154, un gruppo di cristiani fu insediato nelle due isole, forse una guarnigione nel *castrum maris* più qualche mercante, i quali avevano bisogno di uno o più preti. I latini stabili a Malta all'inizio del Duecento furono dei Genovesi, ed è possibile che impiantassero una chiesa assicurando ad essa un prete o *presbiter capellanus* come facevano in Sardegna, Corsica, Siria, Cipro e in altri luoghi d'Oltremare [10]. Il numero di coloni cristiani pertanto aumentava e, probabilmente verso il 1224, un certo numero di musulmani fu espulso; altri si convertirono, pur mantenendo la propria lingua semitica. Intorno al 1240 le isole avevano forse 10,000 abitanti, dei quali forse 1500 in Gozo; sembra che in quel momento un terzo di questa popolazione fosse ancora di fede musulmana. A questo punto il lavoro di conversione fu, evidentemente, in pieno svolgimento, e necessitava certamente dei preti; probabilmente questi lavoravano nei casali alle dirette dipendenze della chiesa maggiore, la cattedrale nella *civitas* di Mdina [11]. Si compiva anche lo sforzo di costruire chiese, alcune delle quali sono ricordate dalla metà del Duecento in poi [12]. Si fondavano molte chiesette rurali costruite da un individuo o da una piccola comunità; molte di esse furono tenute in *iuspatronatus*. Gli ordini religiosi arrivarono a Malta con un ritardo sorprendente: gli agostiniani sono menzionati per la prima volta nel 1413, i carmelitani nel 1441, e i domenicani intorno al 1450 [13].

[10] Cf. la relazione di G. PISTARINO su *Diocesi, pievi e parrocchie nella Liguria medievale*, presentata nelle relazioni regionali di questo convegno.

[11] LUTTRELL, in *Medieval Malta*, pp. 25-40; IDEM, *The Christianization of Malta*, in *Malta Year Book: 1977*, Malta 1977. La presenza di un gruppo cristiano prima del 1154 è indicata da un documento pubblicato in G. SCHROTH-KÖHLER, T. KÖLZER, H. ZIELINKSI, *Zwei staufische Diplome für Malta aus den Jahren 1198 und 1212*, « Deutsches Archiv », 38 (1977), pp. 519-520.

[12] M. BUHAGIAR, *Medieval Churches in Malta*, in *Medieval Malta*, pp. 163-164. La cattedrale è menzionata per la prima volta nel 1299: testo in H. BRESC, *Malta dopo il Vespro Siciliano*, « Melita Historica », 6 n. 3 (1974), pp. 317-320.

[13] A. LUTTRELL, *The Augustinians at Malta: 1413*, « Analecta Augustiniana », 38 (1975); cf. IDEM, in *Medieval Malta*, pp. 63-64, e in *Malta Year*

1192

Il vescovo di Malta, suffraganeo di Palermo [14] e menzionato la prima volta nel 1168, fu normalmente un siciliano residente in Sicilia [15]. La cattedrale aveva il suo clero: un *Maltensis canonicus* nel 1244 [16]; un *archidiaconus civitatis* e un *vicarius capituli* nel 1270 [17]; un *Malte Ecclesie cantor* nel 1274 [18]. Il « Rollo » del 1436 elencava un arcidiacono, un cantore, un tesoriere e altri dodici canonici con il titolo di *donnus*. Di un clero parrocchiale non c'è alcun cenno, e non è chiaro come la *cura animarum* fosse effettuata. La frase *cappella* certamente significava parrocchia [19], ma non si trova prima del 1402 quando la *cappella* di Birkarkara — la *Capella Sancte Helene alias Sancte Marie de Birkarkam* — con cura d'anime fu benefizio del decano della Chiesa maltese [20]. Nel 1419/20 si menzionava la *capella Sancta Dominica Tartarni et Dinkili* come circoscrizione per il servizio di milizia [21]. Sullo sviluppo di un sistema parrocchiale non si sa niente, ma sembra possibile che nella seconda metà dell'undicesimo secolo, nel Duecento e forse nel Trecento, Malta fu una « diocesi-parrocchia » di tipo calabrese, come Bellocastro che nel 1276

*Book*: *1977*, p. 418. La data del 1372 per i francescani non è sicura. La prima parrocchia affidata a un ordine religioso fu quella di Porto Salvo della Valletta, affidata ai Domenicani nel 1571.

[14] Eg. testi del 1272 in R. Moscati, *Fonti per la Storia di Malta nel R. Archivio di Stato di Napoli*, « Archivio Storico di Malta », 7 (1935/6), p. 480; del 1308/10 in P. Sella, *Rationes Decimarum Italiae nei secoli XIII e XIV*: *Sicilia*, Città del Vaticano, 1944, p. 26; e del 1528 in A. Mifsud, in « La Diocesi: Bollettino Ufficiale Ecclesiastico di Malta », 2 (1917), pp. 23-24.

[15] Luttrell, in *Medieval Malta*, pp. 33, 61-62.

[16] *Ibid*., p. 61, n. 332.

[17] Testo in V. Laurenza, *Malta nei documenti angioini del R. Archivio di Napoli*, « Archivio Storico di Malta », 5 (1934), p. 108.

[18] Testo *ibid*., pp. 132-136.

[19] Luttrell, in *Medieval Malta*, p. 63, n. 345.

[20] Archivio Vaticano, Reg. Lat. 107, ff. 71*v*-72*v*: testo indicato da S. Fodale, *Le parrocchie in Sicilia*: *il cumulo di benefici curati nella diocesi di Siracusa tra la fine del XIV e l'inizio del XV secolo*, in *Pievi e parrocchie in Italia nel basso medioevo* (*secc. XII-XV*). *Relazioni regionali*, Bologna 1981, p. 276.

[21] Testo in G. Wettinger, *The Militia List of 1419-20*, « Melita Historica », 5 n. 2 (1969), p. 9.

fu una diocesi latina di 6000 anime, retta, con un solo fonte battesimale, dal vescovo e dal capitolo [22].

Indubbiamente la parrocchia maltese fu creata secondo le tradizioni italiane, tradizioni difficili da definire a causa della loro grande diversità. Nel Mezzogiorno e in Sicilia la cura pastorale fu spesso esercitata direttamente dalla cattedrale o da un monastero, sia latino sia greco. Poi, con la crescita demografica, non conveniva più che i sacramenti si amministrassero soltanto in un solo posto, e spesso la diocesi fu divisa in pievi o matrici, ciascuna con una sua *ecclesia baptismalis* o *plebs cum capellis*, cioè un centro per i varii sacramenti con fonte battesimale e cimitero, e talvolta con un gruppo di chierici i quali abitavano insieme, ricevevano le decime, confessavano, e così via. Questi preti parrocchiali servivano anche le capelle minori, le fondazioni private dove si celebravano, occasionalmente, le messe. Sovente il prete maggiore, il *plebanus* o *archipresbiter*, apparteneva al clero della cattedrale. Poi, per un processo di suddivisione, le chiese minori tendevano a divenire parrocchie e i loro *rectores* a divenire parroci. Questo ultimo sviluppo poteva essere l'effetto di un sentimento di orgoglio, o dell'iniziativa di una confraternita, o dal culto di un santo locale. Talvolta i parroci furono eletti dai parrocchiani. In molti casi il capitolo della cattedrale assumeva *collegialiter* una responsabilità per la cura d'anime e per la nomina dei parroci. Spesso i canonici tenevano le parrocchie come benefizi, esercitando essi stessi la cura d'anime; forse questo fu un modo di sfuggire alla vita comune del capitolo o del collegio [23].

La parrocchia in Malta seguiva, grosso modo, una tale tipologia. Nel Duecento c'era, evidentemente, il lavoro della

[22] P. de Leo, *Per la storia delle parrocchie nella Calabria dal XIII al XV secolo*, in *Pievi e parrocchie in Italia*, pp. 257-259.

[23] A parte gli atti di questo congresso, vedi *Le Istituzioni ecclesiastiche della « Societas Christiana » dei secoli XI-XII: Diocesi, Pievi e Parrocchie = Atti della VI Settimana Internazionale di Studio*, Milano 1977; cf. R. Brentano, *Two Churches: England and Italy in the Thirteenth Century*, Princeton 1968, pp. 67-76, e D. Hay, *The Church in Italy in the Fifteenth Century*, Cambridge 1977, pp. 20-25.

conversione dall'Islam e dell'istruzione nella fede cristiana, lavoro che richiedeva l'uso della lingua maltese; questa operazione fu, presumibilmente, diretta dalla *civitas* ma doveva svolgersi nei casali. Prima della seconda metà del Trecento non c'era alcun monastero o convento che potesse fornire un aiuto. Inoltre, nessuna confraternita è conosciuta a Malta prima del 1445 all'incirca [24]. Ciononostante, un gruppo di *ecclesie baptismales* emergeva nei nuclei urbani e nella campagna maltese. Nel 1436 c'erano almeno dodici *cappelle* o *parrochie*, una delle quali in Rabat, il borgo della *civitas* di Mdina, un'altra in Birgu, il borgo del *castrum maris;* probabilmente c'era una tredicesima parrocchia, servita dalla cattedrale, nella *civitas* stessa [25]. Le date di fondazione di queste *cappelle* — se mai ci sono state delle fondazioni formali — non sono conosciute, ma nel 1436 alcune *cappelle* avevano introiti minimi e si trovavano con pochi abitanti [26]; sembra quindi probabile che queste *cappelle* avessero una considerevole antichità già in quell'anno. Il « Rollo » del 1436 elencava, apparentemente, sedici canonici o *donni*, e nove di questi, compresi l'arcidiacono, il decano, il precentore e il tesoriere, non tenevano alcuna *cappella.* Sette *canonici* tenevano *cappelle* il cui valore, con una

[24] La confraternita della Vergine a Birgu: copia del testo del 1445 in Mdina, Ms. 18, f. 20-20*v*. Il documento accennò a *la cappella di Santo Lorentio* a Birgu.

[25] Un documento del 1474 diceva *per cappellas Rabatum et Ciuitatem*: testo in Mifsud, in « La Diocesi », 2 (1971), p. 305. Nel 1539 c'era una parrocchia della cattedrale curata da un *Cappellano Maggiore Curato della Chiesa Cattedrale*: Abela, pp. 337, 359-360. *Lu mastro Capellano* fu menzionato in documenti del 1481 (testo citato in nota 35), del 1492 (copia in Valletta, National Library of Malta, Ms. Biblioteca 670, f. 20-21*v*), e del 1507 (copia in Mdina, Ms. 171, f. 21*v*-22). Nel 1507 il *castrum maris* aveva un *cappellano* nominato dalla corona siciliana e con una propria giurisdizione: copia in Mdina, Ms. 28, f. 113-114. Una regia nomina della *cappella* del *castrum maris* fu fatta nel 1410 al *Presbiter* Rogerius de Sauna, *canonicus* di Malta, con un salario di 8 *uncie*: Palermo, Archivio di Stato, Reg. 47, ff. 121, 123*v* (gentilmente communicato dalla Professoressa Marina Scarlatta).

[26] Cf. G. Wettinger, *The Lost Villages and Hamlets of Malta*, in *Medieval Malta*, p. 212, n. 73. Mellieha e Dingli-Tartarni, *cappelle* nel 1436, non furono più *cappelle* nel 1472 e nel 1474: Valletta, Ms. Università 11, f. 229*v*-230, 302.

eccezione [27], andava fra le 11 e le 25 *uncie*. Il « Rollo » nominava anche tredici *presbiteri*, forse dipendenti dalla cattedrale, dei quali cinque tenevano delle *cappelle* valutate fra le 2 e le 14 *uncie* [28].

L'isola di Gozo è assai più piccola di Malta. Su Gozo c'erano case contadine ma non veri insediamenti, non casali, e la vita gozitana fu concentrata nel *castrum* [29]. Analogamente, l'attività religiosa si svolgeva nel *castrum* e nel suo borgo di Rabat; non c'erano *cappelle*, e di fatto il termine *cappella* non fu adoperato in Gozo, anche se si usava il vocabolo *cappellanus*. Le parrocchie di Gozo furono troppo lontane da Mdina perché il clero della cattedrale potesse sfruttarle come proprie *cappelle*. La chiesa maggiore, situata nel *castrum*, fu conosciuta come *matrice*; ciò è documentato per la prima volta nel 1435, quando aveva un *cappellanus* come capo: *Item cappellano Sanctae Mariae matricis ecclesie*. Nel Quattrocento c'erano tre altre parrocchie, tutte situate in Rabat: San Giacomo, documentata per la prima volta nel 1449; Santa Maria ta' Sabina, nel 1479; e San Giorgio, nel 1506. Fuori città, c'erano le chiesette minori sparse per l'isola. In origine c'era in Gozo, presumibilmente, una sola chiesa, la *matrice;* poi la *matrice*, conosciuta anche come *maior ecclesia terrae et insulae*, diventava la chiesa madre di altre chiese, che a loro volta diventavano più tardi chiese parrocchiali [30]. Poteva acca-

[27] Non è chiaro perché la *cappella* di Birgu avesse un valore di solo 2 *uncie* nel 1436; forse si tratta di un errore di trascrizione.

[28] La condizione di questi *presbiteri* non è chiaro; non è del tutto sicuro che furono canonici solo quelli con il titolo di *donnus*.

[29] G. WETTINGER, *The Place Names and the Personal Nomenclature of Gozo: 1372-1600*, in *Oriental Studies presented to Benedikt S. Isserlin*, a cura di R. EBIED e M. YOUNG, Leiden 1980, pp. 187-188 (*lapsus* in nota 52: per « fourteenth » leggi « fifteenth »).

[30] G. WETTINGER, *Il Grajja Bikrija tal-Knisja Matrici t'Ghawdex: 1435-1551*, Malta 1975. Non è certo se San Jacobo è indicato come parrocchia per la prima volta nel 1421 o nel 1449. È dubbio se il termine *matrice* prova l'esistenza di più di una parrocchia. Un testo del 1517 *contra cappellanum et clerum Terrae Gaudisii* è pubblicato in MIFSUD, in « La Diocesi », 1 (1916), p. 238. Vedi anche A. BONNICI, *Il-Matrici Kolleggjata ta' l'Assunta u l-Ewwel Parocci ta' Ghawdex*, Gozo 1975.

dere che il termine *matrice* fosse impiegato a Malta nel Quattrocento, quando, per esempio, la *cappella* di Bir Miftuh fu chiesa madre della chiesa del casale di Gudia; ma in questo caso la chiesa di Gudia non fu parrocchiale [31].

La distribuzione geografica delle parrocchie maltesi rifletteva, più o meno, quella della popolazione [32]. Nel 1419/20 la *cappella* di Santa Domenica includeva due casali, Dingli e Tartarni. Dragu, che fu un casale, venne menzionato come *parrochia seu cappella* intorno al 1495, ma in quel momento era quasi abbandonato. La chiesa parrocchiale a Bir Miftuh fu situata nella campagna aperta, fra varii casali [33]. La *cappella* fu utilizzata come circoscrizione civile per il servizio di milizia e per l'esazione delle tasse; doveva inviare i suoi rappresentanti al consiglio della *universitas* [34]. Non c'è traccia di elezione di parroci, salvo il caso particolare del *cappellano* della cattedrale; quando nel 1481 il vescovo nominò un prete che non parlava la lingua maltese, l'*universitas* protestò *maxime ki antiquitus tali cappellanu si solea eligirj per consigliu dicte civitatis* [35]. Il « Rollo » elencava quattro *cappelle ... cum terris suis*, terreni presumibilmente comportanti un reddito. Le decime si pagavano direttamente al *decanus* della cattedrale, ma nel 1531 *lo Reverendo Vicario Generali di la Diocesi di Malta come uno delli Cappellani insieme cum tutti li altri Cappellani di li parrochij di li Casali di ditta Insula di Malta* riscuotevano le *iura primitia* pagate in frumento e cotone. I *cappellani* godevano anche di benefizi come quelli nominati

[31] ... *ad opus ecclesie sancti Nicolai casalis Gudie necnon et matricis ecclesie sub vocabulo sancte Marie cappelle Bir Mifituch*: citato in WETTINGER, *Matrici t'Ghawdex*, p. 3.

[32] Carte in *Medieval Malta*, pp. 142, 185.

[33] WETTINGER, in *Medieval Malta*, pp. 187, 207, 211, 212, n. 73. La unica comparsa della *parrochia seu capella de casali dragu* è curiosa. Forse fu brevemente *cappella* dopo l'abbandono del vicino e più esposto casale di Mellieha (cf. nota 26).

[34] MIFSUD, in « La Diocesi », 2 (1917), pp. 42, 305 (ma il documento del 28 luglio XIII Indizione in Valletta, Ms. Università 11, f. 431-434*v*, non accenna ai « sindachi dalli parrochi trenta »).

[35] Testo in MIFSUD, in « La Diocesi », 3 (1918), pp. 203-205.

nel « Rollo » del 1436. La stessa *cappella* fu considerata come un benefizio, e ci furono delle proteste contro le estorsioni dei cappellani [36]. Anche la vita morale dei parroci fu materia di scandalo [37].

L'impiego a Malta della parola *cappella* per quello che in Italia fu chiamato *matrice, archipresbiterus* o *plebs cum cappellis* dà luogo a confusioni; ma il processo attraverso il quale la *cura animarum* passava dal clero della cattedrale ad altri preti residenti fuori del centro della diocesi, seguiva un modello italiano. Il termine *cappellanus* includeva una molteplicità di significati, incluso quello di « parroco » [38]. A Malta, il clero della cattedrale [39], cioè i « cappellani » della cattedrale, conservavano i benefizi delle parrocchie, le loro *cappelle*; e protestavano quando il loro monopolio era minacciato dalla nomina di stranieri, asserendo che questi non erano capaci di esercitare la cura pastorale a causa della loro ignoranza della lingua maltese [40]. Nel 1436 sette delle dodici *cappelle* erano nelle mani di canonici della cattedrale, i quali ricevevano le primizie e i redditi, anche se, forse, pagavano dei *rectores* per esercitare la cura pastorale; nessuno, tuttavia, te-

[36] Testi in A. MIFSUD, *Sulle nostre decime*, « La Diocesi », 1 (1916), pp. 168-175.

[37] G. WETTINGER, *Concubinage among the Clergy of Malta and Gozo: ca. 1420-1550*, « Journal of the Faculty of Arts: University of Malta », 6 n. 4 (1977).

[38] Una bolla papale del 1219 nominava *cappellanus* un parroco di Cefalù in Sicilia: testo in C. GARUFI, *Cataolgo illustrato del Tabulario di S. Maria Nuova in Monreale*, Palermo 1902, pp. 171-172 (testo indicato dal Dott. G. Wettinger).

[39] Nel 1357 il *canonicus et archidiaconus maioris melivetane ecclesie* fu, apparentemente, stabilito a Lentini in Sicilia: testo in G. COSENTINO, *Codice diplomatico di Federigo III di Aragona Re di Sicilia*: 1355-1357, I, Palermo 1885-1907, pp. 322-323.

[40] Valletta, Ms. Biblioteca 643, f. 27-28, 630-631. Il termine *cappellano* fu utilizzato in altro senso in un documento, scritto però in lingua castigliana a Madrid il 15 maggio 1514, il quale diceva che Malta aveva soltanto trenta *cappellanos*, la maggior parte impiegata nella cattedrale, sicché la *cura animarum* nei casali fu compromessa: copia in Mdina, Ms. 28, f. 253-254*v*. WETTINGER in *Medieval Malta*, p. 184, utilizzando una copia difettosa, parla di trenta parroci residenti nelle parrocchie.

1198

neva più di una *cappella*[41]. Nel 1512 la maggioranza dei *cappellani* di Malta era ancora impiegata nella cattedrale, e non è possibile stabilire quando i *cappellani* hanno cominciato a risiedere nelle loro parrocchie. In ogni caso, i parroci mantenevano il titolo di *cappellano*. Nel 1575 dovevano ancora trascurare le loro funzioni nelle parrocchie per adempiere, nella cattedrale, un servizio corale dovuto *ex antiqua consuetudine*[42].

[41] Nella diocesi di Siracusa c'era egualmente una concentrazione notevole dei benefizi parrocchiali da parte dei canonici della cattedrale: S. Fodale, *Le parrocchie in Sicilia*, pp. 276-277.

[42] V. Borg, *Important Canonical Enactments on the Ecclesiastical Benefices of the Maltese Islands* (D. Theol. tesi inedita: Università di Malta, 1960), pp. 9-20.

# XIX

## THE ROOTS OF MEDIEVAL GOZO

The appearance in 1990 of *Gozo: the Roots of an Island* [1] marks a significant advance in Gozitan historical studies, replacing the older work of Anthony Gauci which, however, retains some value.[2] This large de luxe publication, which displays many of the characteristics of a coffee-table book, is produced on fine paper and is profusely illustrated in colour. Its expense may unfortunately limit its circulation, though it is also available in a cheaper soft-back version. The brief introductions by the editor and, curiously, by the Italian prime minister hint at some dilution of academic purpose, and various slips and confusions in the footnotes suggest a hasty production. Maurizio Urso's photographs include a number of fine plates which are frankly artistic in character and do not seek directly to illustrate the texts, with which in fact they are not always satisfactorily matched. Though one might be glad to exchange some of these photographs for plans or diagrams, they go far to invalidate the general rule that good black- and- white is preferable to misleading colour and they should be accepted as an aesthetic contribution in their own right. Their captions sometimes fail to provide complete information and the precise whereabouts of their subject and the relevant references are not always indicated. The printing of such beautiful plates across two facing pages so that the illustrations are broken in half and partially obscured is most unfortunate. The practice, increasingly common in Malta, of putting together materials from a variety of authors has undeniable advantages, but its success depends on firm editorial judgement and control over themes, contributors and the integration of texts and illustrations. The tendency to a certain fragmentation of the subject is partly offset by the excellent analytical index compiled by George Mifsud-Chircop.

The fact that this work is lavishly produced and dependent in part on a visual impact should not detract or distract from its academic achievement. In so far as it approaches a single subject from multiple viewpoints, this book does for medieval Gozo what the earlier work on *Medieval Malta*, a volume containing little Gozitan material, did for the companion island.[3] This Gozo volume covers a smaller subject over a much longer time span, and as a result the essays, though still providing significant details and insights, are inevitably flatter. Whereas the Malta volume involved both foreigners from different countries and Maltese of differing backgrounds, the Gozo volume is the work of five "foreigners", all Maltese, with only the editor being a Gozitan; the five authors represent a new generation of scholars all from the University of Malta. The coverage is comparatively thin on the modern side, while there is little systematic analysis of the sources and of the historiographical problems involved, though such matters are touched on throughout. The "father" of Gozitan historical study, Gozo's counterpart to Malta's Gian Francesco Abela, was the eighteenth-century cleric Giovanni Pietro Francesco Agius de Soldanis, whose work remained in manuscript until the mid-nineteenth century and has not had a historiographical influence comparable to that of Abela.

In Gozo the middle ages may be considered to have commenced at the end of the Romano-Byzantine period, that is with the Muslim conquest of *ca.* 870 , and to have concluded with the Turkish devastations of 1551. The predominantly archaeo-logical study by Anthony Bonanno provides the essential background on the island's geology, pre-history and early history, briefly covering the Byzantine and Muslim periods. The municipal autonomy of Roman Gozo, which even had its own coins, is striking; a plan of the Roman villa on Ramla Bay seems a notable omission. The lead seal of a Byzantine *archon* named Theophlact was found on Gozo (p.42), but its inscription did not actually mention the island.[4]

The medieval section of Mario Buhagiar's chapter on painting is unavoidably brief. This chapter complements Buhagiar's survey of painting on Malta, and a com-parison with that work suggests how much has been destroyed on Gozo.[5] Some evidence is assembled for works of art which are lost, partly perhaps as a result of Turkish destructions in 1551, but which were once in Gozitan churches. There were some 49 churches on Gozo in 1575, and Buhagiar shows that they contained frescoes, altarpieces, crosses, burial monuments and so forth, but nothing datable before 1551 survives. That a part of the *retable* from the *matrice* church on Gozo can be attributed to a master who painted at Bir Miftuħ on Malta late in the sixteeenth century emphasizes that there were strong similarities between the art of the two islands (pp.84-87; plates 3,6). Buhagiar discusses the Gozitan limestone relief of two saints which is apparently medieval, but strangely it is not illustrated.[6] Three of the inexplicable "ancient carved stones" bearing ecclesiastical and heraldic motifs are excellently illustrated (p.69) towards the end of the historical chapter but merely with the description "of obscure age and provenance"; yet, according to the index, they are nowhere mentioned in the book's text. Buhagiar, discussing these stones elsewhere, considers them to be tombstones of late fifteenth- or early sixteenth century date.[7] The artily illustrated chapter on folklore by Marlene Mifsud-Chirop has little direct bearing on the medieval period, though folk memories do go back at least to the great Turkish razzia of 1551. The story that Gozo's main church was restored by Roger the Norman in *ca.* 1090 (p.167) is now accepted as an early-modern invention.

The core of the volume's approach to medieval Gozo is contained in the historical chapter by Godfrey Wettinger, much of it based on his own archival discoveries and publications. There is a clear statement of the language question (pp.48, 51) but other problems remain. Muslim Gozo was presumably very much like Muslim Malta, but the latter's history is still most obscure, though recent discussions of the texts of Al-Ḥimyarī provide another step forward.[8] The Majmuna tomb slab of 1174 (p.47 fig.1) once constituted an uncontested monument of the Muslim presence on Gozo but its provenance has lately been questioned, since it was not known to Agius de Soldanis and is, in fact, first documented in Valletta.[9] Bonanno (p.44) and Wettinger (p.50) accept it as a Gozitan piece since a Gozitan locality known as *Mejmuna* is documented as early as 1398. However, that may have been a common name;

for example, a Maltese Majmuna was sold as a slave in 1248.[10] A "tomb slab in Kufic characters" seems to have been uncovered in or near Santa Sabina church in the town of Gozo on 19 June 1901 and been taken to the Valletta Museum.[11]

The Gozo taxation figures in the surviving copy of Giliberto Abbate's report of *ca.*1241 add up correctly, unlike those for Malta, and may be accepted as accurate; they imply a Gozitan population of 366 families, with Christians outnumbering Muslims by 4 to 3. It would follow that a complete expulsion or conversion come after about 1241. There is some evidence for expulsions in about 1224, though the transfer of Italians from Celano to Malta does not necessarily imply expulsions from Malta and Gozo.[12] Wettinger (pp.50-51) speaks of an expulsion which he places in 1249. That seems an unlikely date. It depends on a passage in Ibn Khaldūn, a great scholar who was not however a contemporary and who was not well informed about Malta. Ibn Khaldūn treated Frederick II's expulsions from Malta and Sicily only in one passage. He stated, correctly, that Sicilian and Maltese Muslims were exiled to Lucera, something which could have taken place at some time or times between about 1221 and about 1246; it is known that there were Maltese at Lucera, but they are documented there only at a much later date.[13] Ibn Khaldūn must have been wrong in placing the expulsions in 1249 and in writing of a visit to Malta some time after 2 October 1249 by Frederick II who died in 1250, if indeed he did intend to imply such dates. No such imperial visit is known, though one could have taken place at some earlier time, but a visit could not have been made after October 1249, unless it was Frederick's son Manfred who was involved. It is in fact impossible that Ibn Khaldūn made a confusion, palaeographically explicable in the Arabic, between Abū Zakariyā, the Ḥafṣid ruler of Tunis whom Ibn Khaldūn mentioned and who died on 2 October 1249, and an earlier Muḥammad Ibn ᶜAbbād who led a Muslim revolt in Sicily which ended in 1225. Ibn Khaldūn said that on Abū Zakariyā's death, the Muslims of Palermo revolted under an exile of the house of Banū ᶜAbs and were defeated and sent to Palermo, after which the "tyrant" went to Malta. The presumption is that there was a confusion between Ibn ᶜAbs and Ibn ᶜAbbād.[14] All that can clear is that Maltese, and presumably also Gozitan, Muslims were exiled to Lucera at some time after about 1220, possibly even after 1250; that in about 1241 nearly half the population of Gozo was still Muslim; and that many of those on Malta and Gozo must have remained on their islands, converting to Christianity and retaining their Arabic speech.

Wettinger notes the general destruction of Gozo's medieval archives and the fact that rather few documents concerning Gozo survive for the period before about 1400. Considerable use of Sicilian materials relating to Gozo is made in a number of works by Henri Bresc, some of them cited in Wettinger's chapter. Wettinger presents an excellent and quite detailed analysis of Gozitan medieval society and is especially interesting on its relations with Malta. A chance survival of 1335 at Siracusa exemplifies the ways in which Gozo had its own separate administration.[15] By contrast with the larger island, Gozo's life was concentrated in the *castello* and the suburb below it; outside that centre there were no villages and parishes as became common in Malta, no place names in *raħal* and *bir*. An Augustinian friar was granted a pension from Gozo in 1375/6 (p.61), but there is no evidence that any religious order established a house there before the fifteenth century. Curiously, this section is illustrated (pp.56-61) with photographs of post-medieval houses, churches and statues, while the most significant complex of late-medieval houses in the Maltese islands, that in the Gozo citadel, receives only one partial illustration (p.136 fig 14). This chapter undoubtedly includes what is now the best existing introduction to the history of medieval Gozo.[16]

Dennis De Lucca's essay on the "built environment" opens with a treatment of the prehistoric and pre-medieval periods which partly covers the same ground as Bonanno's chapter. It notes the shrinkage of life into the *castello*, maybe in Byzantine times, and the virtual absence of Muslim remains. De Lucca implies (p.136) that the winding street pattern in the citadel derives from Muslim times, a hypothesis which excavation might confirm, though irregular winding streets are found in many parts of the world which were never Muslim. It should be noted that the passage way with pointed arches has been very heavily restored;[17] it is undeniably constructed on the "bent entrance principle", yet it is not placed near the entrance to the citadel. Wettinger states (p.61) that while everyone on Gozo was supposed to pass the night in the *castello* or in the *rabat* below it, there were "several farm buildings dotting the countryside round about". De Lucca speaks (pp.134-135 and fig 13) of scattered medieval settlements in fields such as the abandoned post-medieval houses just below the plateau at Għar Ilma near Santa Luċija. No evidence for this is given in the book, but the existence of such dispersed settlement is presumably indicated by various references to "rustic" houses published by Wettinger elsewhere.[18]

The book makes no mention of the most medieval-looking church to survive on Gozo, that is to Santa Ċeċilja with its stone slabs carried on transverse arches;[19] that building, however, is not documented before 1615.[20] De Lucca (pp. 136-137) discusses the date of the comparatively well preserved group of early houses in Milite Bernardo Street within the citadel which have hitherto attracted remarkably little scholarly comment. He remarks that this group is unique in the Maltese islands, and he describes their small rooms and the absence of regularity in their internal layout; the provision of some plans and more illustration would have been useful here. De Lucca suggests that the master masons may have been of Sicilian extraction, and he advances an interesting distinction between two different late-medieval Sicilian styles, the "Gothic Chiaramonte" type found in Mdina on Malta and the later "Gothic Catalan" type preserved in Milite Bernardo Street and implying, De Lucca says, that the first-floor facades of these Gozitan buildings were built or modified in the first part of the fifteenth century on ground floors which could be of the fourteenth century. Arcading similar to that on one of these houses in Gozo (p.136 fig 14) is also found in Vittoriosa on Malta.[21] Such points all deserve more detailed discussion, and it is to be hoped that careful records of these buildings and of any changes made to them will be kept and made available.[22] Meanwhile the plate provided shows the chocolate and white window shutters which have been inserted behind the late-medieval stone frame.

Gozo's development has always been conditioned by its size, for it is considerably smaller than Malta and so tiny that it was difficult to defend; hence the greater insecurity resulting from what Wettinger (p.48) aptly calls its "greater smallness". Fernand Braudel and other Mediterraneanists have distinguished large cosmopolitan "miniature continents", such as Cyprus or Sicily which had mountains, rivers, cities and relatively complex economies, from small islands, such as Malta, which lacked so many amenities and possibilities. There was in addition an even smaller class of island so minute and isolated that it was scarcely defensible and was easily depopulated, offering few resources or elements of civilization so that its dimensions affected the whole quality of life upon it.[23] Gozo was perhaps not quite in this last category and its close proximity to Malta prevented the most extreme isolation. The relative populations of Malta and Gozo during the later middle ages were roughly in proportion to their relative sizes at 3.5 to 1. The situation altered only after the arrival of the Knights in 1530 when Malta's population began to rise rapidly while Gozo was depopulated in 1551. Profound change arguably reached Gozo only after 1798 or, in some ways, after 1964.

The notion that problems in Gozitan history might be solved by excavation appears in several places in this multi-author volume. The existence of quite extensive areas within the citadel which were ruined in 1551 and have not subsequently been rebuilt may well have created archaeologically sealed deposits in which excavation now offers attractive possibilities, though it might prove disappointing for the medievalist. The archaeological problems of Gozo's citadel are closely bound up with those of the conservation of the standing monuments, of the encouragement of tourism, of the development of the whole walled complex and of the landscape outside it, and indeed of the economy of the entire island. These questions pose a series of difficult technical obstacles, matters which have been considered in detail in an unpublished report.[24] Charles Cini's introduction to the Gozo volume alludes to the dangers and erosions threatened by change and contamination on the island, and it implies that an attractive and convincing presentation of the community's historical "roots" should heighten an awareness of such problems and develop opinion on the very genuine dilemmas involved. This is surely correct, but unfortunately experience elsewhere in the world suggest that the salutary effects may be only very marginal. A small and backward island can be especially vulnerable to devastation by development, and effective resistance depends on the vigilance and sensitivity of an informed public. This book should prove an important contribution to the educational process its editor evidently envisages.

## NOTES

1 *Gozo: The Roots of an Island* , ed. C. Cini (Malta: Said International, 1990).

2 A. Gauci, *Gozo: A Historical and Tourist Guide to the Island* (Malta: St. Joseph's Home Printing Press, 1966).

3 *Medieval Malta: Studies on Malta before the Knights* , ed. A. Luttrell (London: British School at Rome, 1975).

4 Published by T. Brown, *ibid* ., 87.

5 M. Buhagiar, *The Iconography of the Maltese Islands 1400-1900: Painting* (Malta: Said International,1988).

6 Illustrated in *Excavations at Ħal Millieri, Malta* , ed. T. Blagg - A. Bonanno- A. Luttrell (Malta: Malta University Press, 1990), Plate 43.

7 M. Buhagiar, "Post-Muslim Malta: A case study in artistic and architectural cross-currents", *Malta: A Case Study in International Cross-Currents* , ed. S. Fiorini and V. Mallia-Milanes (Malta: Malta University Publications, 1991), 21/23 and Fig. 4a-b.

8 Cf. J. Brincat, "Language and demography in Malta: The social foundations of the symbiosis between Semitic and Romance in Standard Maltese", *Malta: A Case Study in International Cross-Currents* , ed. S. Fiorini and V. Mallia-Milanes (Malta: Malta University Publications, 1991), 95 n.23.

9 Buhagiar, *ibid.* , 15 n.11.

10 A. Luttrell, in *Medieval Malta* , 37.

11 Gauci, 42; Buhagiar (1991), 14/15 n. 8.

12 A. Luttrell, "Giliberto Abbate's Report on Malta: ca. 1241" [forthcoming].

13 G. Wettinger, "The Arabs in Malta", *Malta: Studies of its Heritage and History* (Malta: Mid-Med Bank, 1986; revised 2nd ed.), pp.98, 103-4.

14 Jeremy Johns most kindly discussed the passage in Ibn Khaldūn, explaining in detail how it could have come to contain such errors; in fact, it may have been that Ibn Khaldūn did not intend to associate his remarks about the expulsion with the immediately preceding passage which apparently implies the date of 1249. Ibn Khaldūn's anachronism was understood by Amari, but he explained it in a way which was subsequently shown by his editor Nallino to be incorrect: M. Amari, *Storia dei Musulmani di Sicilia* , rev. ed. C. Nallino, Volume III (Catania: Romeo Prampolini, 1939), 609-610. Amari's view has therefore been rejected, but it seems after all to have been correct even if his explanation of it was not.

15 A. Luttrell, "The Administration of Gozo: 1335", *Melita Historica* , 7, i (1976): 61-64.

16 Further Gozitan detail in G. Wettinger, "Aspects of daily life in late-medieval Malta and Gozo", and H. Bresc, "Sicile, Malte et Monde Musulman", both in *Malta: a Case Study in International Cross-Currents* , ed

S. Fiorini and V. Mallia-Milanes (Malta: Malta University Publications, 1991), pp.81-90, and 47-79.

[17] Pp. 51 fig. 5, 132-135 fig. 10, 136; cf. the less restored pre-1966 view in Gauci, 48/9, where the gate is described as "pointed-Saracenic", though at p. 36 it is also said to be "siculo-norman".

[18] G. Wettinger, "Agriculture in Malta in the Late Middle Ages", *Proceedings of History Week 1981* , ed. M. Buhagiar (Malta: Historical Society, 1982), p. 35.

[19] View of interior showing construction method in Q. Hughes, *Fortress: Architecture and Military History in Malta* (London: Lund Humphries, 1969), p. 168.

[20] Mdina, Cathedral Archives, Ms. 180, f. 439-440.

[21] J. Ward-Perkins, in *Medieval Malta* , 220 and Plate 21b.

[22] The call number of note 17 on p. 132 is misplaced and should refer to p. 57 of the work cited in note 18; the text of 1442 mentioned on p. 134 is cited by H. Bresc, in *Medieval Malta* , p. 136 n. 62.

[23] A. Luttrell, "The Latins and the smaller Aegean Islands: 1204-1453", *Mediterranean Historical Review* , 4, i (1989): 146-157.

[24] A. Luttrell, *Gozo Citadel, Malta: Report submitted to the Division of Cultural Heritage, UNESCO* (unpublished: Malta, 1981); it includes R. Vella Bonavita, "The fortifications: Evolution and recommendations" Though technically a reserved document, this manuscript has become generally available, and is, correctly, cited in *Gozo : The Roots* , which makes some use of it; its historical and architectural portions languish in a form of limbo and their publication might prove useful.

# XX

# AN INTRODUCTION TO ĦAL MILLIERI*

Ħal Millieri is situated in very gently rolling country at the centre of Malta's largest plain, a zone of globerigina limestone lying in the south-eastern part of the island. Within an open area between the villages of Żurrieq, Qrendi, Mqabba and Kirkop, it stands 2.3 kilometres from the sea and some 100 metres above it on a relatively high point with considerable views towards the neighbouring villages in every direction. This rather flat and fertile farming district was always well inhabited in prehistoric and historic times. There are no prehistoric find-spots in the immediate vicinity,[1] but there is a Punic tomb in a field called Tal Ġonna.[2] The nearest ancient remains of importance are the Late-Roman catacombs some 500 metres away at Tal Mentna.[3] However, the presence of what is apparently a Roman olive-crusher and of a number of ancient worked stones suggests that there was possibly a Roman farm as well as a quantity of olive trees at Ħal Millieri,[4] and such an establishment might have continued to function until the Muslim conquest in 870.[5] Although the campaigns of Count Roger in 1090 and of Roger II in 1127 brought Malta under the somewhat distant dominion of Norman Sicily, the population remained fundamentally Muslim in culture until the early thirteenth century; there was little Christian penetration before about 1200.[6] The antiquity of the settlement at Ħal Millieri is unknown.[7] The term *Raħal* or *Ħal*, which derived from the Arabic, and its Sicilianate equivalent *casale*, indicated some sort of settlement or village.[8] Ħal Millieri is first documented in 1419/20 when it was a *casale* with 14 men liable for militia service out of a population which perhaps amounted to 50 or 60.[9] The Annunciation church had been built by about 1450,[10] and the small fields, lanes and cisterns which are still visible

*This brief introduction is intended mainly to provide a comprehensible framework for the succeeding chapters. It naturally leans heavily on the researches published below, but cross-references and references to figures and plates have been kept to a minimum. The emphasis in the appendices is on possible means of constructing a pre-fifteenth-century picture of a Maltese *casale* from non-written sources.

may have changed little since late-medieval times; some fields still have the same name.[11]

In the decades after 1200 Malta underwent a steady process of Christianisation, in which the Latins actively converted and imported men, built churches and created an ecclesiastical organisation. By 1436 the island was divided into twelve districts known as *cappelle* which apparently functioned somewhat in the manner of an Italian rural *pieve*, each being served by a priest, later known as the archpriest or *kappillan*, and having a central church for baptisms and the other sacraments. Scattered around the *cappelle* were village churches and country chapels, often grouped together in clusters. The pious foundations, and the chapels and *ex voto* paintings inside them, expressed the devotion of a people which, while retaining its Semitic language, adopted the Christian faith. Often these churches were supported by benefices or by *animagii*, that is endowments in *juspatronatus* which remained in the gift of the founding family.[12] The church of St. John existed by 1481 when it had already been endowed by a member of one of the leading families of Ħal Millieri, Giovanni Zammit.[13] In 1575 there were four churches or chapels there, those of the Annunciation and the Visitation which abutted one another, and St. John and St. Michael which also abutted one another; none of these churches was a *cappella* in 1436[14] or a parish church in 1575.[15] The Visitation chapel was very similar to that of the Annunciation to which it was connected by a doorway through the north wall of the Annunciation church. The earliest written references to the Annunciation church are apparently those from 1495 and the decades following when it was known as Santa Maria and possessed fields of its own within the *casale*, while in 1508 the village cemetery was attached to it; by 1575 the church had, however, lost its fields.[16] The Visitation church and that of St. Michael were first mentioned in 1575 when they may only recently have been built. Perhaps founded in the fourteenth century, the Annunciation church was a small, single-aisled rectangular building with a rounded apse at the east end. Four slightly-pointed arches supported a flat roof of stone slabs; inside were an altar, wall benches and frescoes painted between the arches. It was a typical rural Maltese church.

The wall-paintings were executed in fresco by a single artist working in the contemporary Sicilian manner, probably around the middle of the fifteenth century. The colours, red and yellow ochre, a dark blue-grey, a green and an occasional patch of light blue, were painted on in flat tones. Apparently the apse was never painted, but the arch which frames the apse still contains parts of the *sinopia* or preparatory sketch of a figure, possibly of the Angel Gabriel, which could have been part of an Annunciation scene. On either side of the west door are two large paintings of St. George, the dragon and a maiden; this repetition is an unusual feature. Nine of the ten side bays contain pictures of standing saints every one of whom, somewhat strangely, carries a book. This out-dated iconographical scheme suggests that the fifteenth-century artist may have copied an existing programme taken from earlier frescoes in some other church, just as in 1496 a painter was commissioned to paint in a church at Attard a copy of a Madonna at Mosta. The saints' names, written in a Sicilianate Latin near their heads, indicate twelve of the standard Maltese saints many of whom appear in the dedications of pre-1500 churches and also in the Christian names of the contemporary inhabitants at Ħal Millieri. In one panel, written in pinkish red on the *sinopia* in a flowing late-medieval court-hand, is the unexplained name *Garinu*, possibly a Sicilian form of the Norman-French Garin; perhaps he was the artist or the assistant to whom the fresco-painting was allotted.[17] Whether the artist was a visiting Sicilian or had Maltese origins and connections is not known; but he produced a series of fine paintings of no mean quality which was presumably financed by a lay patron of some wealth, since confraternities were scarcely known in Malta and there is no indication that there was one at Ħal Millieri.

Though Ħal Millieri was situated in a relatively populous area, its cluster of churches was not supported by a large population. In addition to Żurrieq, Qrendi, Mqabba and Kirkop, which survived, there were two other nearby settlements, Ħal Lew and Ħal Armanin, which disappeared, perhaps in the same way that Ħal Millieri itself was abandoned around 1700. The *casale* at Ħal Millieri produced 14 men for militia service in 1419, but it did not appear in the *angara* or *corvée* list of the 1480's. Some of the land was held by notables from Mdina or by the cathedral and was farmed by tenants, not all of whom lived within the *casale*. There was some share-cropping according to *mezzadria* arrangements, but the normal practice was for fields and houses to be held by peasant freeholders who formed a comparatively small, isolated and close-knit rural settlement. Apparently there were no fiefs, and no crown lands or lands belonging to the *università* at Mdina; and there was no serfdom or servile tenure in the *casale*. There was no local fief-holder, no notary, priest or doctor in the community. The families were apparently of local stock, probably the descendants of those who had inhabited the area in Muslim times. The population was relatively static. There was little emigration towards the towns, but in so small a settlement most marriages had, for reasons of consanguinity, to be made with partners from nearby villages. Money was scarce; land was the fundamental source of wealth and object of investment, and marriages, dowries and wills were concerned above all with its ownership.[18] The Maltese *casale* apparently had no clearly defined geographical limits, but it could on occasion be represented, however informally, by a local council or *universitati* which gave the *casale* something of a corporate juridical existence.[19] In the sixteenth century the two small *casali* of Ħal Millieri and Ħal Armanin shared a *comestabulis* who acted as a local official and occasionally represented them in the council of the *università* at Mdina.[20] The outstanding local family was that of Zammit, patrons of the church of St. John in 1481 and still procurators of the village churches in the seventeenth and eighteenth centuries; in 1635 Leonardo Zammit of Ħal Millieri was sufficiently prosperous to own a negro slave.[21]

The *casale* was grouped around a piazza and its churches. A map of Malta painted by Matteo Perez d'Aleccio in the Grand Master's palace at Valletta in about 1576 (plate 1) gives a good impression of the way in which Ħal Millieri was linked by a network of tracks to the villages surrounding it.[22] There is no sign of a tower or any defensive building. The *casale* had churches, and cemeteries attached to them, but its houses spread out among the fields and lanes. At the beginning of the sixteenth century, one or two wealthier villagers possibly occupied single-storey houses built of stone with a roof supported on timber beams. There was often a yard for the animals, a small enclosure or kitchen garden, and the all-important cisterns. Other farmers probably lived in caves and crude stone huts, or possibly in houses built of mud-bricks. At Ħal Millieri any evidence of such habitation has disappeared almost completely, leaving only the cisterns and wells, a road and a field pattern, the ancient field-names, some squared stone blocks built into the fieldwalls, some field-huts and the churches.[23]

Malta's wealth and manpower rose steadily after the installation of the Knights of Saint John in 1530. The *casale* at Ħal Millieri did not decline. It consisted of 15 houses in 1575[24] and in 1647 it still had 15 houses and a population of 66; at that time its militiamen were subject to the captain at Żurrieq.[25] Some inhabitants did move away. In 1554 the *comestabulis* of Ħal Millieri, Gregorio Schembri, had gone to Sicily, while Andrea Zammit had moved to Senglea by 1598.[26] In 1585 Joannes Schembri, who was once an inhabitant of Casale Millieri but who had moved to Qrendi, was permitted to found a church in Qrendi in place of the altar he had promised, during the siege of 1565, to erect in the parish church of Żurrieq if the island were saved from the Turks.[27] A joint total of 172 deaths was reported for Żurrieq, Qrendi and Ħal Millieri during the great plague of 1593,[28] but it was only after about 1685 that the population began, dramatically, to dwindle. The decade 1600/09 saw the *casale* at its height with no less than 25 child-bearing couples; between 1650 and 1680 there were roughly ten child-bearing couples; but after 1686 only five children were born there, the last birth being in 1711.[29] Changes in the economics of cotton cultivation may possibly have forced some farmers off the land;[30] more generally, perhaps, people simply moved away to larger, expanding villages which offered a broader range of services and a richer social life.[31]

The fields, unlike the houses, were never abandoned and probably many of the same farmers continued to till the land. Their houses were used as huts for animals and agricultural utensils, until finally some of them collapsed or were pulled down for their stones, some of which seem to have been built into the fieldwalls. Certain fields presumably remained in the hands of the families which had traditionally worked them. Some properties passed to larger land-holders or foundations, who apparently leased them out, or to other proprietors who were established some distance away. An act of 1735, for example, concerned a field or *clausura* which had been purchased by the Monte di Redenzione degli Schiavi; the surrounding land was held by the heirs of Baron Stanislao Xara, by an *aromatario* or chemist of Żebbuġ, and by a towncrier or *bandoliere* from Luqa, while the site of some ruined houses which had once belonged to Pasquale Zammit had been purchased by another ecclesiastical institution, the Fabrica di San Pietro di Roma.[32] Some of the other fields formed part of the endowments of the parish church of Żurrieq, being leased out to local farmers. For example the episcopal visitation of 1759 mentioned a *locus domorum situs in Casali Milleri*, and a *clausura* situated *in regione Casalis Milleri* which was called 'ta Garruba' and had been leased in emphiteusis for three generations.[33]

The village stood aloof from the cosmopolitan life and commercial activity of Valletta and its port. Agriculture apart, the chief focus of interest in the quiet, open countryside at Ħal Millieri lay in its chapels, which remained a centre of activity after the *casale* had become deserted. Even when Ħal Millieri was inhabited, there was no parish priest and there were no regular services; the villagers had to go to Żurrieq for their weekly Sunday mass, for baptisms and for the other sacraments. The churches in the *casale* must usually have been shut, though there were provisions for lighting the lamps on Saturdays and Sundays. The church of St. John had a window with a grille in its façade to allow a view of the interior, while the Annunciation church had its wooden screen with gates which could be closed but which still left the altar fully visible. The churches, however, were a permanent centre of devotion and piety, with their altars and altar-lamps, with their annual titular feasts and the gatherings which accompanied them, and with the burial places which stood next to them. The chapels and altars were endowed either with land granted to the church outright, or with 'pious burdens' in the form of obligations attached to particular fields, or with capital which could be invested. The procurators of each church or altar were responsible for the administration of these endowments, for financing the feasts and for maintaining the furnishings, which included altars, altar-paintings, doors, locks, screens, altar-cloths, candlesticks and sanctuary lamps. From the late-sixteenth century onwards the bishop or his representative periodically inspected the churches, in the spirit of the reforms of the Council of Trent, to ensure that all was in decent order and to repair or deconsecrate neglected churches.

The Visitation church, which stood beside the Annunciation church, was almost identical to it in structure and was connected to it by a doorway; it had a fixed endowment in 1575, but in 1667 it was deconsecrated and condemned to demolition. The Annunciation chapel underwent a few changes, notably the construction of a new altar on a new altar platform. Both churches had a small paved burial area or *zuntier* in front of their west door, and there was a cemetery with tombstones to the south. After the abandonment of the *casale* the Annunciation church was poorly looked after and it in turn was deconsecrated in 1787. The chapel of St. John, some seventy metres to the north, was deconsecrated for a brief period as early as 1575, but it was rebuilt in the Baroque style, perhaps as the result of local munificence, shortly before 1646; it still stands with its *zuntier* and a pillar in the piazza in front of it. Abutting St. John's church was that of St. Michael; it too was reconstructed just before 1608 at the expense of Andrea Zammit of Senglea, only to be deconsecrated in 1667 and demolished.

One reason why the Annunciation church survived relatively untouched was the absence of funds to improve it; another was the wall around it which was mentioned, together with the *introytus longus*, in 1636. On the other hand, the small endowment the Annunciation chapel did enjoy after 1632 probably prevented its complete disappearance, as did its use and veneration as a burial ground. It must have been in a state of abandon in 1754 when a fugitive seeking asylum was living there and it was the subject of a curious incident of rural *dolce vita* involving talk of abortions and aphrodisiacs. Shortly after that the burial area was being leased for farming. The church was deconsecrated in 1787, but was reopened in 1809, thanks to the initiative of Giuseppe Magro of Żurrieq. A liturgical life and the celebration of the annual titular feasts lasted fitfully through the nineteenth century, and the episcopal visitations continued at least until 1927, though the furnishings were in an increasingly poor state.[34] Ħal Millieri achieved notoriety once again in 1856 when a baby girl was found dead in a seven-foot-deep field tank, and the mother Giuseppa Buttigieg was condemned for a crime which was never explained.[35] The devotional tradition persisted into the twentieth century, and in 1931 Michelangelo Coleiro of Żurrieq provided the church of St. John with a new altar, restored the titular painting and supported an altar-lamp and the celebration of masses.[36] The 'pious burdens' dwindled into insignificance and, without being deconsecrated, the Annunciation chapel was effectively abandoned early in the twentieth century. In 1946 Hugh Braun drew attention to it and its frescoes: it 'is very ancient and contains a remarkable series of mediaeval wall-paintings, which need careful restoration and preservation.'[37] Luret Cutajar launched a determined campaign for its protection in 1956,[38] and this bore fruit after 1968 in the intervention of Din l-Art Ħelwa and the creation of a trust which has safeguarded and restored the church.[39]

# *Appendix*: TOPOGRAPHICAL SURVEY*

The results of this survey are essentially contained in the map in fig. 2, which should be studied in conjunction with the aerial photographs in plates 2 and 3. This map, which is derived from Sheet 129 of the 1 : 2,500 map compiled by the Office of Public Works in 1908, covers part of the north-west quarter of that sheet; for the historian, it is important not to use the later, revised versions of the 1908 map. The tracks and fieldwalls, some of which have been altered to divide existing fields since the map was first made, are those shown in 1908. The master map of archaeological finds kept in the National Museum at Valletta shows only one find, a Punic tomb, in the whole area. The Ħal Millieri district appears to contain no major archaeological feature, the Roman catacombs at Tal Mentna being a few metres outside the extreme north-west corner of the survey area.

This survey does not lack significance simply because its findings are largely negative; such controlled information is valuable. The possibilities of topographical investigation were in fact limited by certain factors. The soil is shallow and has been intensively farmed for centuries, with the resulting obliteration of almost all traces of early occupation. Furthermore, a preliminary inspection showed that soil-shifting and the widespread use of urban rubbish or 'sludge' have covered the fields with so many intrusive pieces of broken pottery that the collection of sherds, such as the piece of Roman *terra sigillata* found in front of St. John's church, was very unlikely to produce any archaeologically reliable evidence.[40]

A number of houses and other stone buildings survive in the area, but it seems impossible to establish any date for their construction. Little is known of the modern cemetery in the field 'ta San Gwann' to the very north of the survey area or of the much older cemetery with an adjacent cluster of cisterns in the extreme south-west corner of the area. The most important features are undoubtedly the cisterns. Within the 710 by 445 metre area covered by the survey 67 wells or cisterns were marked (W) on the 1908 map; a further 20 were plotted on the present map (M) during the survey, but it cannot be said how many of those 20 were built before 1908. In the vicinity of the churches there are many large or shaped stones built into the fieldwalls; column bases and other decorative elements are also scattered on the ground. The soil contains numerous sherds of indeterminate age and provenance, many of them pinky-red and possibly early-modern. All this seems natural in an area where churches and houses have been dismantled.

*This appendix has been written by the editor, but it is based on work carried out by the five members of the Żurrieq Youth Section of Din l-Art Ħelwa who properly appear as its authors.

In addition to finds within the precincts of the Annunciation church, listed *infra*, 75–79, other significant items noted were:

A Presumed Roman olive-crusher, carved in stone and approx. 148 cm. in diameter and 58 cm. high, now in front of St. John's church (plate 8A). Mr. Tancred Gouder of the National Museum, Valletta, has tried in vain to establish the provenance of this stone.

B Rows of regular squared stone laid in a straight line at the foot of fieldwalls immediately to the left as one leaves the Annunciation precincts, and to the south of the piazza in front of St. John's church.

C Relief carving in stone with the arms of the Monte di Redenzione, 58 cm. wide by 55 cm. high, inserted in the north-west wall of a field-hut (plate 10D); the courses of this hut are very regular at a height of 27 cm.; the roof is supported by metal girders. This hut and the carving were severely damaged with a gelignite bomb on 7 September 1975: photo and report in *Times of Malta* (9 Sept. 1975).

D Oval rock-cut storage silo or cistern, approx. 3.50 m. high and 2.50 m. in length, unlined and with a massive stone arch and evidence of other arches across its top; a square entrance is built in at one end (plate 8B).

E Rows of extremely large stones of ancient, perhaps pre-medieval, appearance up to 1.50 m. in length (plate 23) on the south side of the track leading east from the piazza in front of St. John's church. Some of these stones are definitely worked and shaped, and some could be *in situ*. They may have been associated with the same site as the olive-crusher.

F Field-hut with corbelled roof (plate 9) and six wells nearby.

G Built into the walls of a farmhouse in the south-west corner of the survey area are a number of roundels showing leaf or abstract patterns carved in light relief in the stone (plate 11); this house also has an old carved stone window-frame (plate 10C). There is another roundel on a house on the road from Żurrieq to Ħal Millieri as well as many others in different parts of Malta. The roundel carvings cannot be dated, but the designs are undoubtedly ancient in origin. Something similar was scratched on a wall of the Annunciation church at Ħal Millieri (fig. 7A, B, C); similar designs were carved on Muslim tombstones at Rabat; they are found in Sicily and Catalunya; and they are still extremely common on Tunisian houses and survive on the façade of the Great Mosque at Kairouan. They are also found in Tunisia on Latin funerary inscriptions and Neo-Punic votary stele dating from the first century B.C. onwards; there are examples in the Bardo Museum at Tunis. The Rabat tombstones are illustrated in E. Rossi, "Le lapidi sepolcrali arabo-musulmane di Malta," *Rivista degli Studi Orientali*, xii (1929/30), tavole IX–X. The collection and study of further Maltese motifs of this type would be of interest.

Within the survey area the 1908 map recorded the names Ta' Ħamillieri, Tal-Hida, Ta' Dusa and Tal Gonna; the names Il-Menka and Il-Marsa were marked just outside the area. The lists originally compiled in 1944 and now preserved at the Government Farm, Għammieri, provided a further sixteen names: Bunixeff, Hlantun, Tal Bajjada, Tal Bandieri, Ta Betta, Tal Brill Marsa, Tal Gnien, Ta Harruba, Tal Korbin, Tal Kortin, Tal Kumpass, Tal Mejtin, Tal Mentna, Tal Nazzarenu, Ta San Gwann and Tat Torba.[41] In 1944 many fields were simply called 'Hal Millieri', and most of the names cover a group of several modern fields, as shown in fig. 2; presumably these names originally applied to large areas or to fields which have subsequently been divided. A number of these names appear in the notarial records for the period 1470–1530 which are discussed in chapter II. The field named 'ta Garruba', which was mentioned in the episcopal visitation of 1759,[42] can in this way be placed with some precision where 'Ta Harruba' appears on the modern map. In the absence of any official land register or *catasto*, the importance of these modern records for Maltese topography, toponomy and history, as also for the study of the Maltese language itself, is evident. They make it possible not only to rescue but also to locate numerous micro-toponyms across the whole island, an exercise apparently never before attempted even for a limited area.

The survey confirmed the existing impression that the area contains very few immediately recognisable surface traces of medieval or earlier occupation. The many cisterns grouped around Ħal Millieri and the way in which the ancient tracks converge on the area show that such features, taken in conjunction, should normally attest the presence of an abandoned settlement. The existence of the *casale* at Ħal Millieri was already known from other evidence, but this modest example of survey technique should be useful in identifying lost sites elsewhere in Malta.

MARY ANN AQUILINA AND OTHERS

## *Appendix:* HOUSES AND CISTERNS

At present the task of creating a picture of the pre-1400 Maltese *casale* from non-written sources can scarcely proceed beyond a few preliminary suggestions and hypotheses. Progress depends not only on meticulous archaeological and survey work, but on a range of interdisciplinary collaboration involving scientists equipped to analyse soils, ceramics, mortars and so forth. Buildings and stonework can almost never be dated, though the possibilities of analysing stone and other materials, or arguing from the size, shape and arrangement of individual stones and courses, and of studying other aspects of building techniques have yet to be explored. Documentary evidence is extremely scarce, while the information provided by a superficial preliminary survey such as that at Ħal Millieri is limited. Many modern Maltese country houses and courtyard plans, and their arrangement within village complexes, seem to be Roman or Sicilian, rather than Muslim or African, in pattern. Crudely speaking, most older Maltese houses are entered directly through a hall or entrance which faces onto the street and leads into a courtyard behind, whereas the Muslim house is more protected and private, often being approached from a side street which leads into an entrance which zig-zags indirectly into a courtyard, behind which are the living quarters.[43] In any case, in the absence of datable medieval examples on Malta or Gozo, little or nothing can at present be deduced from house plans or stylistic details. As an alternative, arguments based upon analogies with other lands provide tempting, but uncontrollable and possibly unsound, hypotheses.

Within the immediate vicinity of the Ħal Millieri churches are a number of small houses and huts with solid regular stone walls and roofs of long stone slabs supported at each end on corbels projecting from the side walls (plate 9); only a few such houses have an upper storey, and many of them are in ruins. Close to the Annunciation chapel are a number of footings to fieldwalls which consist of stretches of regular well-laid, squared-stone courses which probably were once part of a building. Numerous squared stones are also built in an irregular way into the nearby fieldwalls. Documentary references to stone-built country houses are very rare before 1545,[44] but in 1516 a house at Ħal Millieri needed ten wooden beams to support its roof[45] which may mean that it had reasonably strong walls. Timber was scarce and expensive in Malta. There is some pre-1530 evidence for caves and for roofs built of thatch or reeds,[46] and there may have been huts built of branches or of mud-bricks which could dissolve without trace. Mud-brick buildings are still found in many Mediterranean lands. Cave dwellings seem to have been common throughout much of the Mediterranean during medieval times, especially where the rock was easily worked, not only in places as distant as Anatolia and Spain[47] but in regions nearer Malta such as Apulia,[48] south-eastern Sicily[49] and Tunisia.

From 870 until about 1200 Malta had close links with Tunisia as well as with Sicily. Conditions in Tunisia were somewhat different, owing to the availability of wood and the prevalence of nomadic forms of life which encouraged tent-dwelling. Modern Tunisia still provides a wide variety of rural housing. There are many shades of variation from the truly nomadic tent to the semi-permanent tent with a brushwood or palm-leaf corral or courtyard in front of it; the tent built back into earth or soft rock; the wooden *capanna* or hut; the low dry-stone building with walls reinforced with earthern mortar and with a reed or thatched straw roof, or a roof made with a mixture of mud and straw or some type of concrete; and the small stone hut, sometimes corbelled like the Maltese *girna*, sometimes with a vaulted brick roof.[50] These arrangements have one feature in common, which is that they can all disappear without trace; it is difficult, therefore, to establish that they existed in Malta. A more permanent type of residence is the cave. In particular the large and deep cylinder-shape hollows or 'bear-pits' cut down into the ground with cool and commodious rooms excavated horizontally sideways into the rock are common at Matmata and elsewhere in the dry, rocky lands of Southern Tunisia.[51] Something very similar existed in Malta, both in prehistoric and historic times, notably at Għar il-Kbir near Dingli, which is documented as early as 1544 and had 117 inhabitants in 1647.[52]

The most striking topographical feature at Ħal Millieri are the 87 wells or cisterns found within the survey area (fig. 2). Groups of cisterns, sometimes as many as seven in a single small field, suggest probable dwelling sites. The distribution of such groupings, taken together with the tracks which converge on the churches, clearly indicates the centre of settlement. There may have been underground springs, or possibly channels were cut into the rock beneath the soil to drain the ground and lead water into the cisterns. More probably many cisterns were clustered around buildings so that rainwater could be collected from their roofs. A field with at least four cisterns is documented at Ħal Millieri in 1523, and the notarial documents reflect a natural concern with water. 'Dry farming' may have been the rule, despite the preoccupation with cisterns, but a quarrel between two brothers in 1517 over rights to storm-water running from the house of one brother to that of the other brought three jurats from Mdina to settle so important a matter on the spot.[53] Many of the wells or cisterns at Ħal Millieri appear to be flask-shaped, but investigation is naturally difficult and dangerous, and the shape, width, height, capacity and style of these cisterns have not been ascertained; it is also important to establish whether they are constructed or rock-cut, whether lined or unlined, what lining may have been used, and how the water was collected into them. A detailed study of the cisterns and their typology is most desirable, particularly in so far as they could be dated.

It has been suggested, without evidence, that the Muslims improved the irrigation systems on Malta and that they possibly introduced the animal-powered wheel for raising well-water,[54] but nothing is known about medieval water-pumping and little attempt has been made to study the pre-modern water supplies on which agriculture, and indeed country life itself, depended.[55] In certain cases, since many Maltese soils are relatively modern in formation, an analysis of the soil itself should provide an element of dating, for example in places where new terraces have been constructed. Modern statistics on geology and hydrology are available,[56] but rainfall varies from one part of the island to another. Few firm conclusions have been reached, either from the documents or by the scientists, on possible changes which might, during the last two thousand years, have had significant effects on water tables, sea levels, tree coverage, soil erosion or the building up of alluvium in the valleys. General historical variations in the Mediterranean climate are, in fact, still a subject of unresolved debate,[57] and a comparison of the map of abandoned Maltese villages with that for the annual modern rainfall distribution does not suggest any direct correlation between rainfall and desertions.[58]

Malta is well endowed with natural underground water resources, and the declaration in 1473 that lack of rain would force the population to emigrate certainly suggests inefficient conservation methods, even if the threat was perhaps somewhat exaggerated. There is no demonstrably medieval or pre-medieval evidence for dams, reservoirs or aqueducts, and the medieval population apparently relied on springs and cisterns, as suggested by late-medieval place-names in *bir* or well and in *għain* or spring. Some of the cisterns provided brackish drinking-water, sometimes collected off roofs, as reported by the Hospitaller commissioners of 1524 and by Jean Quintin in his description of Malta in 1533.[59] Abela, writing in 1647, gave many names in *bir* and *għain*, and mentioned cisterns, wells, canals and aqueducts. He described cisterns found near the sea with built bottoms and lead linings: *di cui dicesi esser il fondo lastricato, e ricoperto con lamine di piombo.* He also spoke of built rainwater cisterns lined to keep the water from penetrating the rock; they had *grosse lapide sostentate da pilastri di pietra, et incrostate poi nel fondo, e per ogni parte da' lati di bittume, perche l'acqua non venghi succhiata dal sasso.* He mentioned one place where there were at least fifteen of these cisterns known as *latmie* or *gebie*.[60]

One method of compensating for the lack of written documents is suggested by the researches of M. Solignac in Tunisia, where he has shown that the Aghlabids, who ruled there from 800 to 909 and who conquered Malta in 870, not only used the existing Roman waterworks but inaugurated a great new hydraulic programme using altogether new techniques. Their chief concern was to capture stream-water before it soaked into the ground; to lead it by aqueducts to great basins or reservoirs; and to prevent its evaporation. Solignac worked with literary sources, aerial photographs, surveys and measurements, and he studied mechanisms and construction methods. He identified different types of construction and applied chemical and other analyses to the mortar, plaster and other coating materials used, establishing their constituents, the proportions of the lime, sand and other materials used, and measuring their capacity for hardening under water, all with such success that he could confidently distinguish three different construction periods within a century of Aghlabid rule; furthermore he could check his results against dated monuments.[61] Subsequently he has also suggested applying radiocarbon-dating techniques to organic materials, especially to the wood charcoal in the mortar used in the cisterns;[62] other modern dating procedures could doubtless be employed as well.[63] Irrigation systems based on small reservoirs and on the channelling of spring water through stone-cut troughs still survive in the Maltese countryside; such systems, which may in some cases be ancient, should be mapped and compared to practices elsewhere.[64]

Solignac did not study smaller wells and cisterns. In Malta there are at least 10,000 rock-cut cisterns marked, as 'wells', on the 1 : 2,500 map-sheets.[65] Many, though not all, of these are not only rock-cut but unlined, and therefore not susceptible to scientific analysis. None the less, it remains important to survey and measure the cisterns, to collect fragments of pottery, wood, plaster, mortar and other analysable materials. A comprehensive study of Roman and pre-Roman cisterns in Malta is desirable. Some Maltese cisterns may originally have been tombs or grain-pits. One water-logged Maltese pit produced materials datable to around 1000 B.C.; many cisterns are demonstrably Roman; another is dated to 1541.[66] Maltese information could then be compared with studies made in Africa, where small Roman cisterns, circular, rectangular or square and measuring between 0.50 and 1.50 m. in diameter, have been recorded.[67] Some Roman and some sixteenth-century cisterns in Malta are large and complex, being built with supporting arches or columns, and with slabbed or vaulted roofs. For the medieval period there is an almost total lack of information, but it may be that, churches apart, cisterns are the most important of the datable material remains of the medieval Maltese settlement. They should constitute precious evidence concerning rural settlement and agrarian development.

## *Appendix:* SELECT DOCUMENTS

*Valletta, Royal Malta Library, Università Ms. 13, f.330 (discovered by Mr. Anthony Vassallo)*

xvij maij xij Ind. 1554

gauchj quia In casali millerj [et] casali manj ex parrochia delo zurrico erat comestabulis gregorius scembrj qui diu est quod discessit ab Insula ad regnum Sicilie Ideo propter eius absentiam fuit creatus comestabulis petrus gauchj unde ad futuram rej memoriam facta est presens nota unde [etc]

*Valletta, Royal Malta Library, Archives of the Order of St. John, Treasury B 309 = Cabreo de Beni Del Venerando Monte della Redentione de Schiavi . . . 1735, f.116–116v; for the accompanying plan at f.115, see plate 4.*

CLAUSURA TA DUSA

La sudetta Clausura si troua situata nella contrada di S. Michele di Casal Millieri consiste in diuerse lenze, et in canne quadre tremila duecento sessanta cinque, e palmi cinque, che compongono tummula tredici, mondella quattro, e mezzo di terreno di buona qualità con tre cisterne, due de quali nella testa Superiore di detta Clausura; confina da leuante con adito, et in parte con li beni degl'eredi del Barone Stanislao Xara, da mezzodi con li beni delli sudetti eredi, et in parte con li beni di Giuseppe Azzuppard Aromatario di Casal Zebbug, da ponente con li beni di Maruzzo. . . . e di Vincenzo. . . . Bandoliere di Casal Luca, e da tramontana con strada, ed adito.

Il Dr. Gio: Antonio Balsamo e Denapoli per gl'atti del Not° Pasquale Debono sotto li 12 luglio 1672 diede insolutum al V$^{do}$ Priore d'Ingilterra Lomellino come Presidente del Monte della Redentione l'accenata Clausura franca d'ogni peso per la somma di scudi mille, che trà loro hanno compensato, in quanto a scudi trecento per altri tanti, che detto Denapoli douea à detta Monte in atti di detto Not° li 5: Giugno 1672: e li restanti scudi settecento a conto delli scudi 5000; che detto Sig$^{e}$ Denapoli vanto à nome suo, quanto à nome del Sig$^{e}$ Gio: Antonio Francesco Balsamo, e Denapoli suo figlio erede della fù Paulina Denapoli in atti del sudetto Not° Debono sotto li 30: Luglio 1663 s'obbligò di pagare a detto Monte come Successore nei beni di Don Gio: Domenico Felice fratello di detta Paulina.

La retroscritta Clausura in atti del Not° Baldasare Demodica sotto li . . .

Alla detta Clausura s'incorporo un luogo di case, ch'era diuiso dalla medesima con uicolo, il quale per esser diruto è stato uenduto nell'officio della Reuerenda fabrica di San Pietro di Roma come beni che erano del fù Pasquale Zammit, e liberato sotto li 10: Aprile 1725 al Not° Pietro Antonio Buhajiar pro persona nominanda per scudi 22 il quale sotto li 12 Giugno susseguente nominò per compratore detto Monte in piede del Bando promulgato all'instanze del Sig$^{r}$ Procuratore Fiscale di detta Fabrica.

Il Not° Gaspare Domenico Chercop come esattore di detto Monte sotto li 12: Giugno 1725 depositò detti scudi 22 in uigor di cedula presentata in dett'ufficio.

*Mdina, Cathedral Archives, Archivum Inquisitionis Melitensis, Processi CXXIII no. 101 (discovered by Miss Mary Zammit of Żurrieq)*

Die xij ms. Sept'is 1754

Coram Ill'mo. et Rmo. Dno. Genl'i. Inq'te Mel. Assiste. D. Assessore

Maria Vxor Salvatoris Attard de Casale Zurrico

Etatis suae annorum triginta trium filia quondam Pascalis cui fuit delatum Iuramentum de veritate dicenda prout juravit tactis SS. Dei Evangelijs, et pro exoneratione suae conscientiae denunciavit infra Videlicet:

Otto giorni in circa sono un tal Germano di Cas. Curmi oggi perseguitato dalla curia laicale fugitivo per la campagna venne a trovarci a me, e mio marito nella chiesa rurale della nonciata in Cas. Millieri ove, detto mio marito trovasi rifugiato, e ci disse, non essendovi persona alcuna presente che lui avea il modo, e maniera di far abortire una donna gravida, Piu di saper anche il modo, e maniera di far istupidire i cani per non bajar pigliando un pezzo di carne d'altro cane morto, ed un puo di sua pelle facendo con essa diversi nodi e finalmente che sapeva un sortileggo mediante il quale forzava una donna ad amare un uomo, e farla impazzire per esso, ed all'incontro, a fine che l'abbandonasse, e non lo cercasse più, come in effetti Esso lui mi disse d'averlo sperimentato, e dopo che una donna s'era impazzita per esso portandola una mane in una spiaggia di mare nel spuntar del sole, presente la medesima proferì alcune parole che non mi ha specificate, e poi detta donna non lo cercò più.

ANTHONY LUTTRELL

## NOTES

1 Distribution map in J. Evans, *The Prehistoric Antiquities of the Maltese Islands: a Survey* (London, 1971), fig.1.

2 Two-chambered Punic tomb just east of the survey area in fig. 2; inspected on 24 February 1971 and marked on master mapsheet 129 at the National Museum, Valletta, where Mr. Tancred Gouder has a plan of the tomb.

3 E. Becker, *Malta Sotterranea: Studien zur altchristlichen und jüdischen Sepulkralkunst* (Strassburg, 1913), 59–60, and in more detail, with plans, P. Bellanti, *Studies in Maltese History* (Malta, 1924), 60–67.

4 These heavy stones (described *supra*, 26) are unlikely to have been moved far; on Roman

oil-mills in Malta and elsewhere, see Ma. P. Rossignani, "Note sui Pressoi," *Missione Archeologica Italiana a Malta: Rapporto preliminare della Campagna 1965* (Rome, 1966), 101–107, with detailed bibliography.

5 For examples of such continuity, see A. Luttrell, "Approaches to Medieval Malta," in *Medieval Malta: Studies on Malta before the Knights*, ed. A. Luttrell (London, 1975), 21–23.

6 This thesis is sustained by Luttrell, in *Medieval Malta*, 29–34.

7 The possibility that the name of *Raћal Milleri* derived from a family name Milleri is discussed *infra*, 36–37. G. Bautier Bresc suggests (*infra*, 99–100) that there may have been an early 'Norman-Byzantine' iconography for the Ħal Millieri frescoes, but this hypothetical early programme need not have been at Ħal Millieri itself; the suggestion constitutes no more than a vague indication of a possible thirteenth-century date for the settlement. Following the unlikely conviction that the church and its architectural features are 'Norman', L. Cutajar, in *Il-Berqa* (29,30,31 May 1956), argues that *Milleri*, the ancient form of the name, derived from *mille rei*, that is from a 'thousand criminals' whom he identifies with a thousand inhabitants of Celano exiled to Malta ca. 1223, and that the *Martinus* of the frescoes was a Pope *Martinus* or *Marinus* who came from Celano. Apart from the fact that no post-Muslim Maltese church can be documented so early (Luttrell, in *Medieval Malta*, 62), and that the architectural style is probably, though perhaps not demonstrably, later (*infra*, 81–88), the inhabitants of Celano sent to Malta, if they did arrive, were not exactly criminals; furthermore, it is unlikely that the local inhabitants would have referred to them with a Latin expression such as *rei* (which is not apparently documented in medieval Italian, let alone Maltese), or that there would have been a thousand of them clustered around a small *casale*, had it then existed. The theory seems untenable. The evidence for a St. Martinus or Marinus connected with Celano is not given, and in any case there is no Martinus or Marinus in the frescoes (*infra*, 98–99).

8 On the uncertainties surrounding the meanings of *raћal* and *casale*, see G. Wettinger, "The Lost Villages and Hamlets of Malta," in *Medieval Malta*, 182–183 *et passim*. The prefix *Ħal* does not necessarily imply that a *casale* was founded in Muslim times before ca. 1200. On the placename, *infra*, 36–37.

9 *Infra*, 38–39.

10 This dating is deduced from the style of the painting (*infra*, 102).

11 See aerial photos (plates 2, 3), survey map (fig. 2), *supra*, 26, and *infra* cap. II.

12 These matters are largely unexplored; introductory observations in Luttrell, in *Medieval Malta*, 60–66.

13 Modern summary from the lost acts of Notary Luca de Sillato, in Mdina, Cathedral Archives, Ms. 280, f. 95: *1481. Tes'to di Gio'e Zammit est in actis Not'ij Luce de Sillato, in quo instituit heredem Zacchariam Zammit eius filium cum obligat'ne cuiusdam pij legati in fauorem Eccl'e Sti' Jo'is Cas. Milleri*. For another summary, see *infra*, 67 n. 195.

14 Ħal Millieri was not mentioned in any recognizable way in the *rollo* listing *cappelle* and ecclesiastical benefices drawn up in 1436: text in G. F. Abela, *Della Descrittione di Malta* (Malta, 1647), 313–316. Abela's text is badly garbled, and a new edition of this important document is in preparation.

15 Text *infra*, 139–140.

16 The references to a single church of Santa Maria and to a village cemetery appear in notarial deeds concerning properties discussed *infra*, 50–51, 57–58.

17 On the paintings and patronage, *infra*, cap. IV; on the inhabitants' names, *infra*, cap. II. The identification of certain saints is doubtful.

18 Details *infra*, cap. II; background in Luttrell and Wettinger, in *Medieval Malta*, 53–55, 181–204; comparative modern materials in J. Boissevain, *Saints and Fireworks: Religion and Politics in Rural Malta* (London, 1965).

19 See A. Luttrell, "A Maltese Casale: 1436," *Melita Historica*, vi no. 3(1974).

20 Text *supra*, 31.

21 Details *infra*, caps. II, V.

22 Reproduced in part in plate 1, and in I. Lockhead and T. Barling, *The Siege of Malta 1565* (London, 1970), 33. This painting gives a good general impression of the *casali*, their distribution and communications, but it cannot safely be used as evidence for particular topographical detail. Note that the engraving made after this painting differs from it considerably, and is clearly much less realistic; it is reproduced in *The True Depiction of*

*the Investment ... by Matteo Perez d'Aleccio*, ed. D. Calnan and G. Testaferrata Abela (Malta, 1965), foglio III.

23 On the topography, houses and cisterns, *supra*, 25–31.

24 Text *infra*, 139–140.

25 *CASAL MILLERI, Contiene questo picciol luogo quindeci case con sessanta sei anime, sogette nella militia al Capitano del Zorrico* (Abela, 101).

26 Texts of 1554, 1575 and 1598, *supra*, 31; *infra*, 139–140.

27 Copy in Valletta, Royal Malta Library, Biblioteca, Ms. 1019 unfoliated.

28 P. Parisi, *Breve Discorso sopra il Medicamento di vino, et oglio, per guarire ogni sorte di ferita* (Palermo, 1603), 56.

29 Statistics from the baptismal records, *infra*, 120–121, 136–137.

30 The fluctuations and effects of cotton-growing await study, and only detailed researches in the notarial and other records can establish how and why the pattern of land tenure may have changed; see *infra*, cap. II.

31 In this respect, Ħal Millieri fits conveniently into the hypothesis in B. Blouet, *The Story of Malta* (London, 1967), 95–97.

32 Text *supra*, 31–32; again, the hypothetical intrusion of the greater landlords awaits firm documentation.

33 1759 visitation (cited *infra*, 138), f.395, 398v.

34 Texts *supra*, 32; *infra*, 141–142; other details on the churches, *infra*, cap. V.

35 This case is written up from the court records in the series "Ġurijiet Kbar f'Malta", in *Il Mument* (16, 23 Dec. 1973): Mario Buhagiar kindly drew attention to the 1856 incident.

36 According to M. Spiteri ['Kilin'], *Wayside Chapels of Malta* (Malta, nd.), 31–33, with illustration.

37 H. Braun, *Works of Art in Malta: Losses and Survivals in the War* (London, 1946), 46.

38 L. Cutajar, "Il-Knisja Normanna ta' Ħan-Millieri," *Il-Berqa* (29, 30, 31 May 1956), and "Il-Knisja Ta' Ħal Millieri," *L-Orizzont* (28, 29 Oct. 1968).

39 On the creation of the Trust, *supra*, 16–17; see also M. Buhagiar and G. Serracino Inglott, *Teenagers Din l-Art Ħelwa: the Annunciation Sicolo Norman Church Ħall Millieri Żurrieq* (Malta, 1968).

40 Cf. Luttrell, in *Medieval Malta*, 12–13.

41 The editor is most grateful to Mr. Anthony Scicluna Spiteri of the Government Farm, who kindly facilitated his indirect access to this information.

42 Eg. *supra*, 23.

43 Another subject awaiting research; on the differences between 'Roman' and 'Muslim' plans, see the interesting observations in A. Lézine, *Deux villes d'Ifriqiya: Sousse, Tunis* (Paris, 1971).

44 Godfrey Wettinger has found only one or two clear references to the actual process of building stone village houses in the pre-1545 notarial records.

45 *Infra*, 48.

46 Preliminary details and bibliography in Luttrell, in *Medieval Malta*, 53–55; *idem*, "L'abitato medievale a Malta: un approccio archeologico," *Colloquio Internazionale di Archeologia Medievale: Palermo, 1974*, 2 vols. (Palermo, 1976). This last publication also contains important Sicilian material; on caves, wood and straw in Sicily, see H. Bresc, F. d'Angelo and C. Trasselli, in *Gruppo Richerche Archeologia Medievale: Palermo* (20 May and 20 Aug. 1971).

47 Eg. M. Riu, "Cuevas-eremitorios y centros cenobiticos rupestres en Andalucia Oriental," *Actas del VIII Congreso Internacional de Arqueologia Cristiana* (Barcelona, 1972).

48 Eg. C. Fonseca, *Civiltà rupestre in Terra Jonica* (Milan-Rome, 1970).

49 See most recently A. Messina, "Paolo Orsi e la *Civiltà Rupestre* medievale della Sicilia," *Archivio Storico Siracusano*, ns. ii (1972–1973); G. Uggeri, "Gli insediamenti rupestri medievali: problemi di metodo e prospettive di ricerca," *Archeologia Medievale*, i(1974).

50 A. Bernard, *Enquête sur l'habitation rurale des indigènes de la Tunisie* (Tunis, 1924), and *L'habitat rural en Maroc, en Algérie et en Tunisie = Cahiers des arts et techniques d'Afrique du Nord*, v(1959).

51 O. Crawford, *Archaeology in the Field* (London, 1953), 151–164, compares the Tunisian and Maltese caves, giving the older bibliography; see also G. Prost, "Habitat et habitation

chez les Ouderna et les Matmata", *Cahiers de Tunisie*, vii–viii(1954); A. Louis, "L'habitation troglodyte dans un village des Matmata," *Cahiers des arts et traditions populaires*, i part 2 (Tunis, 1968). There are, of course, problems involving the chronology and prehistoric origins of such caves and pits.

52 Wettinger, in *Medieval Malta*, 188 n.1, and Abela, 79–80; cf. also A. Luttrell, "Case rupestri a Malta," *Notiziario di archeologia medievale* (Dec. 1974), 2–3.

53 Details *infra*, 46, 48, 55, 57; see also the three wells in the plan of 1735 in plate 4.

54 Blouet, 41.

55 The best historical approach is T. Zammit, *The Water Supply of the Maltese Islands* (Malta, 1931); but it deals only with the post-1530 period. For early-modern details of cisterns and capacities, but in Valletta and the Three Cities only, see Valletta, Royal Malta Library, Archives of the Order of St. John, cod. 6651 (Romano Carapecchia: 1708), f. 78–83v; cod. 6554 (17th-century), f. 236–242; Biblioteca Ms. 195 (Romano Carapecchia: 1723). Many *cabrei* in the Maltese archives contain field-plans showing cisterns.

56 Tables and statistics in H. Bowen-Jones *et al.*, *Malta: Background for Development* (Durham, 1961), the standard manual; especially important, because concerned with historical changes, is D. Lang, *Soils of Malta and Gozo* (London, 1960).

57 Various hypotheses involving major physical changes which have been advanced (e.g. *infra*, 46) are quite plausible; see C. Vita-Finzi, *The Mediterranean Valleys: Geological Changes in Historical Times* (London, 1969); F. Braudel, *The Mediterranean and the Mediterranean World in the Age of Philip II*, i (revised ed: London, 1972), 267–275.

58 Maps in Wettinger, in *Medieval Malta*, 185, and Bowen-Jones *et al.*, 75.

59 References of 1473, 1524, 1533 in Luttrell, in *Medieval Malta*, 18–19, 54 *et passim*; Zammit, 5–7.

60 Abela, 82–83, 99 *et passim*.

61 M. Solignac, "Recherches sur les installations hydrauliques de Kairouan et des steppes tunisiennes du VIIe au XIe siècles J.C.," *Annales de l'Institut d'Études Orientales: Faculté des Lettres de l'Université d'Alger*, x–xi (1952–1953).

62 M. Solignac, "Remarques de Méthode sur l'Étude des Installations Hydrauliques Ifriquiyennes au Haut Moyen Âge," *Cahiers de Tunisie*, xlvii–xlviii(1964).

63 R. Berger *et al.*, *Scientific Methods in Medieval Archaeology* (Berkeley, Cal., 1970); see also *Science in Archaeology: a Survey of Progress and Research*, ed. D. Brothwell and E. Higgs (revised ed: London, 1969).

64 Eg. T. Glick, *Irrigation and Society in Medieval Valencia* (Cambridge, Mass., 1969); H. Bresc, "Les jardins de Palerme: 1290–1460," *Mélanges de l'École française de Rome: Moyen Âge – Temps Modernes*, lxxxiv(1972).

65 As calculated in Bowen-Jones *et al.*, 45.

66 References in Luttrell, in *Medieval Malta*, 12 n.83, 19; see also T. Ashby, "Roman Malta", *Journal of Roman Studies*, v (1915). Much information is scattered in archaeological reports and other printed sources.

67 J. Birebent, *Aquae Romanae: recherches d'hydraulique romaine dans l'Est algérien* (Algiers, 1962), 494. For an introduction to the extensive bibliography, in addition to Vita-Finzi, see P. Romanelli, *Topografia e archeologia dell'Africa Romana = Enciclopedia classica*, sez. III, vol. x, tomo vii (Turin, 1970), 259–263. The cisterns apart, the smallness and irregularity of the fields in the immediate vicinity of Ħal Millieri also suggest that the present walls might represent the original limits of the houses once there; away from this centre, a pattern of larger and squarer fields can be discerned (fig. 2).

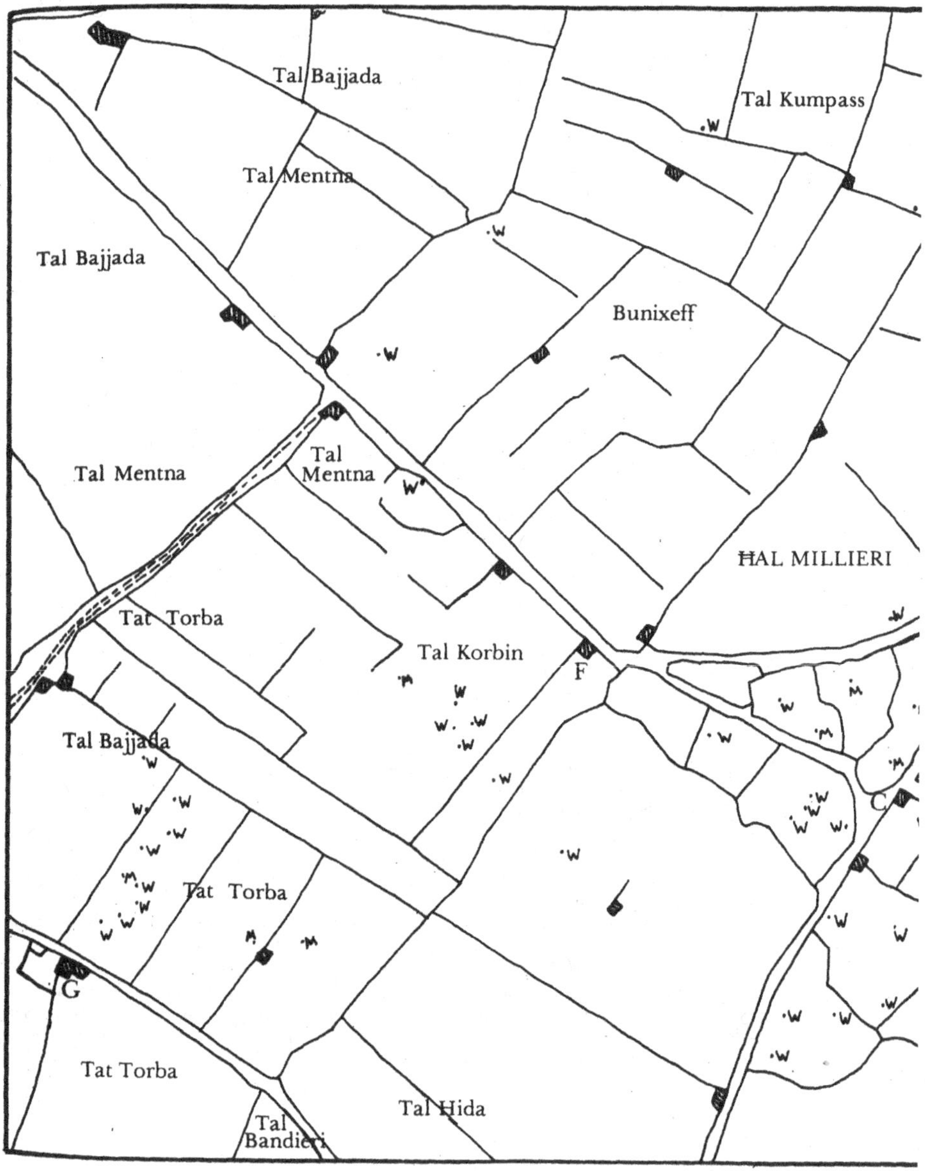


Fig. 2. The Ħal Millieri Survey Area as shown on the Map of 1908 at the same Scale of 1 : 2500, with some Cisterns and Field-Names added: Key and References, *supra*, 25–26.

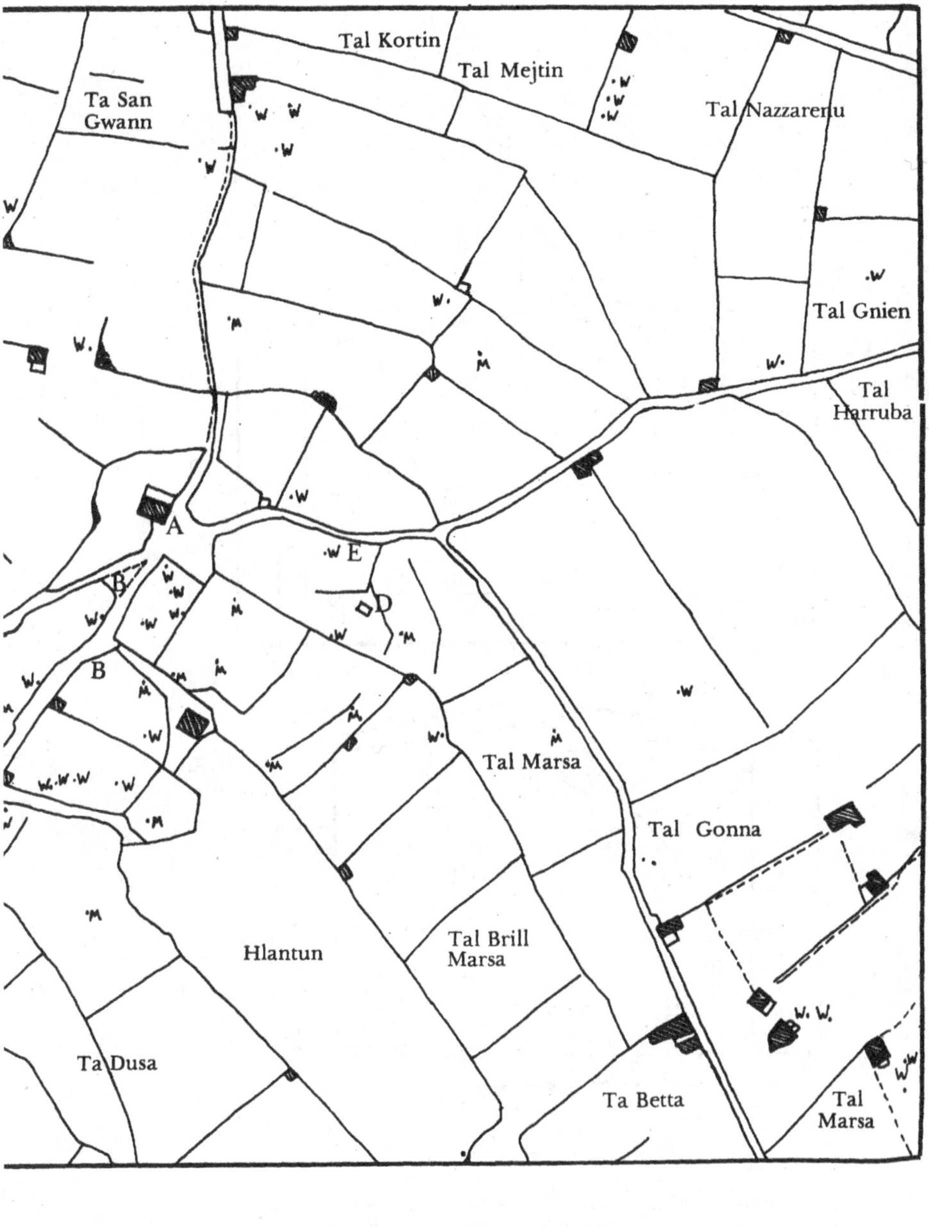
Tal Kortin
Tal Mejtin
Ta San
Gwann
Tal Nazzarenu
Tal Gnien
Tal
Harruba
A
E
B
D
B
Tal Marsa
Tal Gonna
Hlantun
Tal Brill
Marsa
Ta Dusa
Ta Betta
Tal
Marsa

XX

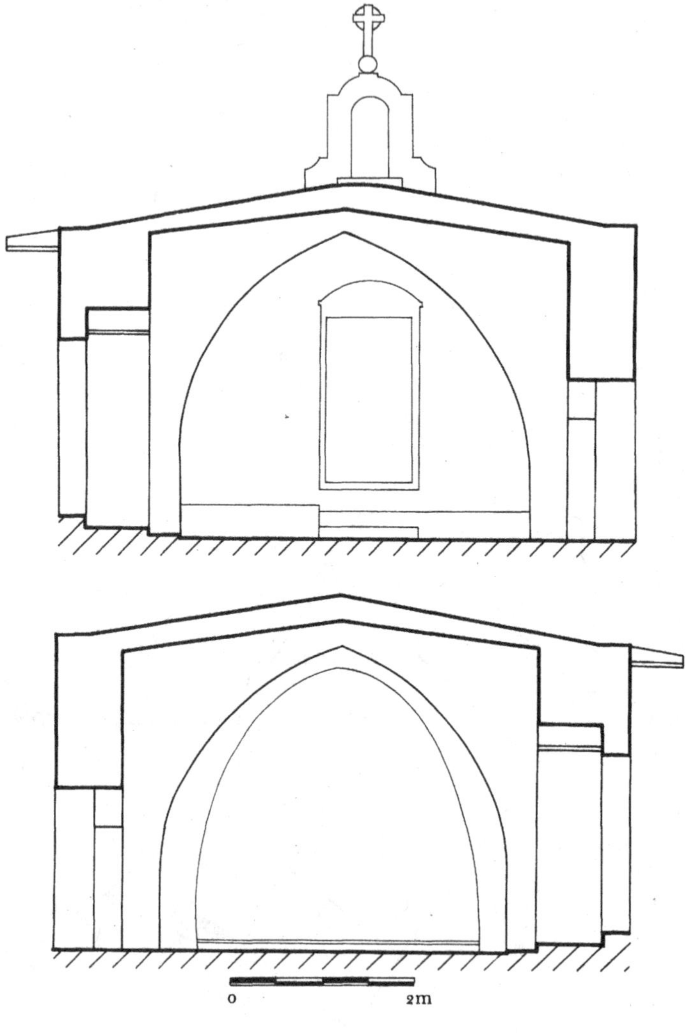

Fig. 3. Annunciation Church: Above S–N section looking West
Below N–S section looking East and showing Apse

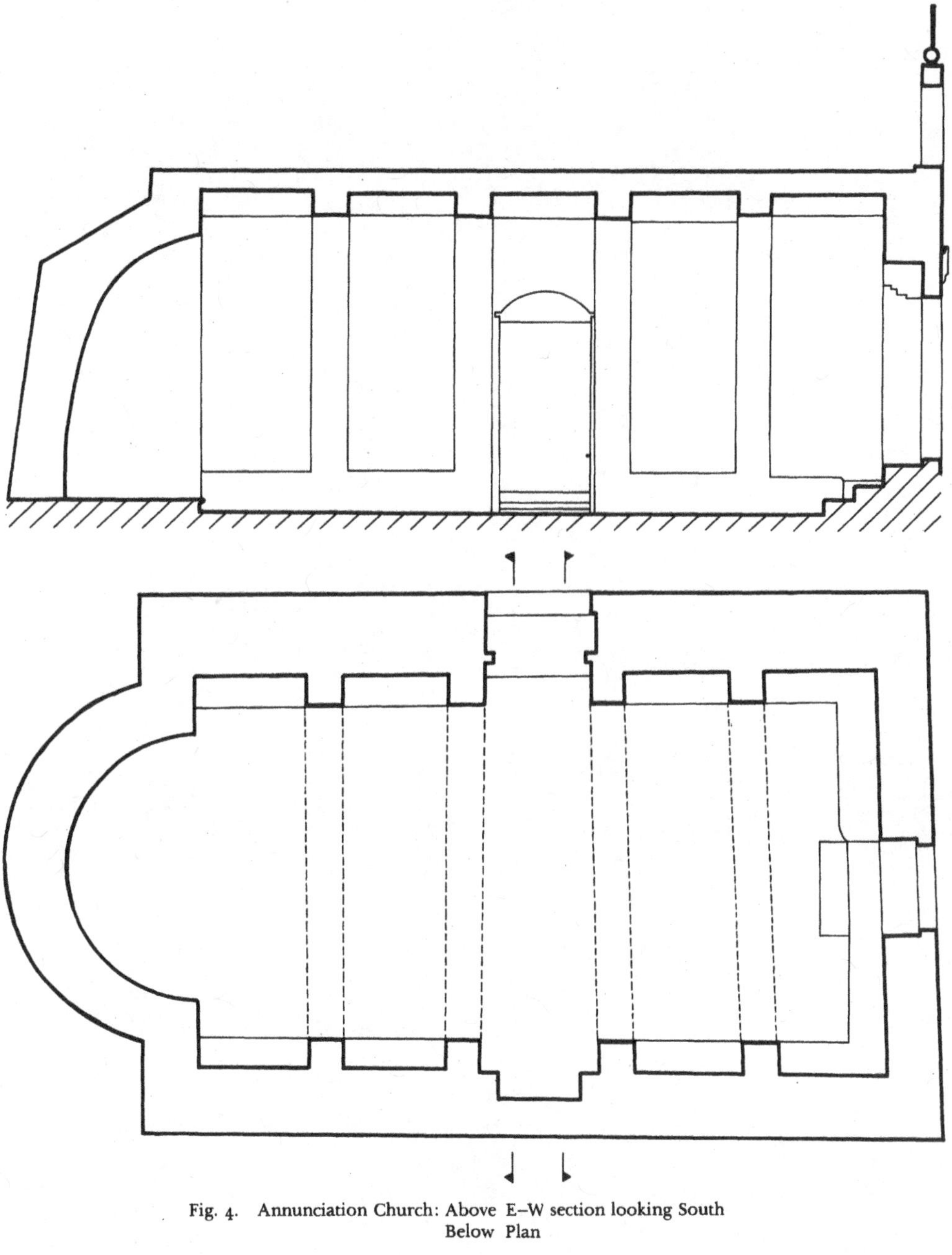

Fig. 4. Annunciation Church: Above E–W section looking South
Below Plan

# XXI

## Ħal Millieri: Historical and Architectural Postscript

The excavations conducted at Ħal Millieri in 1977 may acquire a significance for Maltese historiography extending beyond the archaeological objectives proposed and the limited historical information gained. It had become clear that the study of the available documentation, of the surviving monuments and paintings, and of the surrounding topography could not advance the medieval history of the *casale* beyond a certain point, if only because the scarcity of written materials imposes the strictest limitations on what can be discovered anywhere on the island concerning the history of Malta before about 1400.[1] Some solution to this general problem evidently lay in archaeological activities, in the inauguration of a serious and sustained study of the pottery, and in a determined campaign to protect all sites suitable for excavation.[2] Some aspects of such a programme have been initiated by the various investigations at Ħal Millieri which are, therefore, notable as including the first purely medieval excavation carried out in Malta where they also introduced the scientific consideration of the post-classical pottery, a difficult but essential aspect of such attempts to elucidate the obscure history of medieval Malta.[3] It is, moreover, still the case that no reliably stratified pottery of the Roman period is available for comparative study on Malta, with the consequence that it is difficult on a site such as Ħal Millieri to distinguish Roman from medieval finds.[4] The quantity of glazed or other identifiable post-Roman materials found at Ħal Millieri is disappointingly small but the beginning of a systematic classification of Maltese medieval pottery, the results of which can eventually be applied to other post-classical sites, may in the long run prove to be the most valuable consequence of the 1977 campaign.[5]

1. A. Luttrell, in *Ħal Millieri: a Maltese Casale, its Churches and Paintings*, ed. A. Luttrell (Malta, 1976), 11–13. The quite lengthy review of this work by F. Toker, in *Speculum*, liv (1979), 398–400, contains pertinent comments, but its author was naturally unaware of various local problems. The review by A. Messina, in *Archivio Storico Siracusano*, ns. iv (1975–1976), 237–240, contains interesting suggestions.

2. A. Luttrell and G. Wettinger, in *Medieval Malta: Studies on Malta before the Knights*, ed. A. Luttrell (London, 1975), 11–13, and 204; cf. A. Luttrell, "L'Abitato medievale a Malta: un approccio archeologico," and G. Wettinger, "Some Maltese Medieval Pace-names of Archaeological Interest," both in *Atti del Colloquio Internazionale di Archeologia Medievale*, 2 vols. (Palermo, 1976). For some recent developments in Sicilian medieval archaeology, see G. and H. Bresc "Ségestes médiévales: Calathamet, Calatabarbaro, Calatafimi," *Mélanges de l'École Française de Rome: Moyen Age – Temps Modernes*, lxxxix (1977); J.-M. Pesez, "Recherches sur l'Habitat médiéval: Fouilles de Calathamet," *Sicilia Archeologica*, xiii no. 44 (1981).

3. The published study of medieval pottery found in Malta began with F. d'Andria, "Note sulla ceramica invetriata: catalogo," in *Missione archeologica italiana a Malta: Rapporto preliminare della Campagna 1968* (Rome, 1969), and F. Mallia, "Una ceramica dipinta in rosso su bianco," in *Atti del Colloquio*, i. 281–283 and plate; for further references, see *Medieval Malta*, 13, 22, and *Atti del Colloquio*, i. 276–279.

4. The publication of the final reports of the Italian *Missione* would offer the best prospect of progress, though at Tas-Silġ the stratification was much disturbed. For numerous relevant studies and surveys, especially from North Africa, see *La Céramique médiévale en Méditerranée Occidentale, Xe–XVe siècles: Valbonne 11–14 septembre 1978* (Paris, 1980).

5. Brief preliminary accounts appeared in T. Blagg, A. Bonanno, A. Luttrell, "Ħal Millieri, Malta", *Notiziario di Archeologia Medievale*, xxi (dicembre 1977), 44–45, and in A. Bonanno, "Ħal Millieri Explored," *Vigilo* [Malta], ns. i (1978); both accounts are entirely superseded by the present work. The plans of the Annunciation church in *Ġrajjet Malta*, i (Malta, 1976), 24, are not quite accurate and the disposition of the paving stones is altogether imaginary.

The excavations have thrown more light on the general history of the Ħal Millieri area, and tend to confirm the hypothesis of ancient settlement somewhere near the churches. The discovery of an earlier, possibly thirteenth- or fourteenth-century, church beneath the surviving late-medieval church suggests that the *casale* dated back well beyond its earliest written documentation in 1419/20. The earlier church beneath the present Annunciation church was certainly frescoed, and this discovery supports the intuitions of Geneviève Bautier Bresc who had already suggested that an earlier fresco cycle, not necessarily in the Annunciation church itself, would explain the archaic, possibly thirteenth-century, iconography of the surviving fifteenth-century paintings.[6] The excavations also permit a new study of the construction methods in all three churches studied. It is now clear, for example, that the arches which supported the slabbed roofs of such churches were built separately from the side walls and were not bonded into them. It is possible, therefore, to revise the original accounts of the architecture of the Annunciation church and of the general development of Maltese medieval ecclesiastical architecture. In other cases, such as that of the data provided by the skeletal remains, the findings add rather little at this stage, but once further bones become available the Ħal Millieri information may be most valuable;[7] eventually such materials may also provide data which can be used ethnologically.[8] Finally, the variety of ancient materials already recorded on the site[9] has been broadened.

6. G. Bautier Bresc, in *Ħal Millieri*, 100; coloured photographs, with unreliable colours, were subsequently published in A. Luttrell, "Ħal Millieri," *Heritage* [Malta], no. 1 (1977), 9–12.

7. Note that the recently studied bones from Żejtun are not necessarily medieval: *infra*, 143.

8. To the considerations and references in *Medieval Malta*, 16–17, add R. Gayre of Gayre, "Malta in the Ethnological Context of Europe," *St. Luke's Hospital Gazette* [Malta], vi (1971).

9. Luttrell, in *Ħal Millieri*, 19, 26; the piece of Roman *terra sigillata* recorded on the surface (*ibid.* 25) has no safe provenance and is probably best ignored. Some of the "wells" or "cisterns" clustered in certain spots nearby (*ibid.*, Fig. 2) may have been grain-pits; cf. H. Bresc, "Fosses à grains en Sicile: XIIème – XVème siècle," and other contributions to *Les Techniques de conservation des grains à long terme: leur rôle dans la dynamique des systèmes de culture et des sociétés* (Paris, 1979). The cultivation of cotton also led to the construction of wells and cisterns: details in J. Debono, *Aspects of the Cotton Trade in Malta: 1750–1800* (unpublished thesis: University of Malta, 1976), 4–8 [information kindly provided by its author]. Several ancient cisterns are studied in A. Bonanno, "Two Archaeological Sites recently discovered at L-Iklin," *Hyphen* [Malta], ii no. 5 (1981), 215–220.

# 1. Early Settlement at Ħal Millieri

To the ancient stones, the olive-crusher and the other scraps of evidence for early settlement around Ħal Millieri, there can now be added a few prehistoric sherds which could all have come from one or two pots; some large, presumably Roman, worked stone blocks re-used in the Annunciation church foundations; and a considerable quantity of late Roman pottery. There is no identifiable Punic or Roman pottery datable before the first century BC, though there is one Punic coin, a *Melitaion* piece datable to the second or first century BC, and one, or possibly two, Byzantine coins. The coins, stray survivals in the later excavation layers, are insufficient in number to constitute evidence for occupation on or near the site at the date they were issued. The datable pottery, none of it notably luxury or burial ware, may point to a late Roman farm which may have continued to function until the Muslim conquest in the ninth century.[10] This would be consistent with a broad picture of continuity elsewhere in the island,[11] but since there is almost no pottery which can be dated with confidence between about 650 at the latest[12] and the date of the Muslim conquest in 870 this last question remains uncertain; it may be that pottery of that period or of the succeeding period was in fact present, but unidentifiable, in some of the layers excavated.

There is still no clear evidence for any occupation in the area of the *casale* during the Muslim period between 870 and about 1200.[13] If it were demonstrable in Malta, as it seems to be in parts of England, that chapels which had burial rights but which were not parish churches were often associated with the establishment of communities in lands newly brought under cultivation,[14] it might follow that Ħal Millieri was a late-medieval foundation or re-foundation; but, given the lack of early datable evidence in Malta and the scantiness of space available for expansion and settlement, it is doubtful if that theory can be applied to the island.[15] The placename provides little help. If, as seems most probable, it derives from someone with the Sicilian or Italian name *Milleri*,[16] that might, though it does not necessarily, imply a post-

10. Cf. A. Bonanno, "L'habitat maltese in età romana," *Kokalos*, xxii–xxiii tomo 1 (1976–1977); *idem*, "Distribution of Villas and Some Aspects of the Maltese Economy in the Roman Period," *Journal of the Faculty of Arts: University of Malta*, vi no. 4 (1977); *idem*, "Malta in the Third Century," in *The Roman West in the Third Century: Contributions from Archaeology and History*, ed. A. King and M. Henig (Oxford, 1981).

11. Cf. Luttrell, in *Medieval Malta*, 21–23.

12. J. Hayes, *Late Roman Pottery: a Catalogue of Roman Fine Wares* (London, 1972).

13. The dating "around 1200" is here maintained but it should now be noted that a royal document of 1198 makes it clear that there was a Christian community of some sort on the island in the time of King Roger II who died in 1154: text in C. Schroth-Köhler, T. Kölzer, H. Zielinski, "Zwei staufische Diplome für Malta aus den Jahren 1198 und 1212," *Deutsches Archiv*, xxxiii (1977).

14. Cf. D. Owen, "Chapelries and Rural Settlement: an Examination of some of the Kesteven Evidence," in *Medieval Settlement: Continuity and Change*, ed. P. Sawyer (London, 1976).

15. B. Blouet, *The Story of Malta* (revised ed: Malta, 1981), 39–43, correlates parishes and settlements, but only after 1436. There seems to be no clear correlation between the ten rural *cappelle* or "parishes" of 1436 and the use of the prefix *Raħal or Ħal*: data collected in Wettinger, in *Medieval Malta*, 205–213.

16. Wettinger, in *Ħal Millieri*, 36–37.

reconquest foundation after about 1200. An alternative and less likely suggestion is that the village was on a local route and that *millieri* derives from the Latin *millarium* or mile in the same way as the Sicilian toponyms at *Casale Tremilie* three miles from Siracusa and at *Casale Millarini* near Lentini mentioned in 1169.[17] In either case *millieri* would be a Latin term, which might suggest a post-conquest foundation.[18] The excavations unfortunately provide no clear evidence relating to the origins of the *casale*. The earliest published written reference to Ħal Millieri is still that contained in the militia list of 1419/20, though seven of those mentioned in that list also appeared in the guard list of 1417 doing watch duty, some at Ras Juliana far away at Birżebbuġa and others at Meneq near Kalafrana.[19]

The layers immediately above the natural rock surface and below the earlier Annunciation church, which are dated by their pottery to late Roman or later times, might perhaps be interpreted as the remains of an artificially terraced field. It is conceivable that they represent an attempt to build up new fields, *campi artificiali*, on the sloping, exposed rock edge of the slight escarpment on which the church now stands, forming relatively narrow terraces by cutting a back wall and using the rock fragments cut out to build up the front of a terrace which is kept in place with a front retaining wall.[20] It has generally been presumed that the Muslims improved the agriculture of Malta,[21] but this presumption perhaps ignores the prosperity of pre-Muslim Malta which may at times have been considerable. It is based on the very general and somewhat debatable Arabic descriptions of the prosperity of the Maltese islands.[22] Furthermore the assumption that Muslim irrigation techniques were original is now disputed, as many of them demonstrably derived from Roman or other earlier practice.[23] There is just one slender and inconclusive piece of archaeological evidence which was found in a section of a terrace at Baħrija where a sloping rock surface had been levelled to provide a flat soil surface; at one end was a depth of 25 cm of plough soil while 20 m away, sustained by a terrace wall, was 2.20 m of deposit. The soil trapped behind this sustaining wall contained pottery and other items dating from prehistoric periods down to the "green-glazed Arab ware" which give a somewhat wide range of possibilities for the date of the terracing; in this case at Baħrija the level was not made up with rock placed beneath the soil.[24] At Ħal Millieri these layers may indicate a late Roman or later phase of activity.

17. Messina (1976–1977), 238.

18. On the early history of the Sicilian *rahal* or *casale* and its buildings, see I. Peri, *Uomini, Città e Campagne in Sicilia dall'IX al XIII secolo* (Bari, 1978), 33–36, 295–296 *et passim*; on the material aspects, see H. Bresc, "La Casa Rurale nella Sicilia Medievale: Massaria, Casale e Terra," *Archeologia Medievale*, vii (1980). The situation in Malta differed considerably from that in Sicily.

19. G. Wettinger, "The Militia Roster of Watch Duties of 1417," *The Armed Forces of Malta Journal*, xxxii (1979), 29.

20. *Supra*, 16–17; cf. D. Lang, *Soils of Malta and Gozo* (London, 1960), 20; Fig. 6.

21. Blouet (1981), 36, 125.

22. References in *Medieval Malta*, 26 n. 155, 82–85.

23. T. Glick, *Irrigation and Society in Medieval Valencia* (Cambridge, Mass., 1970), 149–197 *et passim*. It is true that the Muslims did much to spread these techniques, just as they spread the cultivation of citrus fruits, though the orange, for example, was established in Italy in the first century AD: S. Tolkowsky, *Hesperides: a History of the Culture of Citrus Fruits* (London, 1938), 122–128.

24. D. Trump, "The Later Prehistory of Malta," *Proceedings of the Prehistoric Society*, xxvii (1961), 258; Fig. 3.

# 2. Church Patronage And Burial Practice in Malta

Founded on these layers of earth and rubble was a church with an apse, altar, wall piers, burials, and a floor composed of compacted plaster. It is a reasonable, though unprovable, guess that this lower church which was beneath the present Annunciation church had the same dedication. A piece of ostrich egg found in the fill beneath the pavement of the upper church[25] possibly came from the lower church though it is true that much of the pottery in that fill was brought in from outside the church. Ostrich eggs were commonly hung in medieval churches, where they were connected with fertility and the Virgin; and they were especially associated with the Annunciation.[26]

Information concerning the social and economic life of the medieval community was not necessarily to be expected from excavations within its churches, but the burials provide a number of points of interest. The burials in the lower church must be prior to about 1480, the latest date for the upper church suggested by the archaeological evidence and by the study of the paintings; the burials in the upper church cannot be earlier than about 1480 and some were mentioned in 1636;[27] most of those excavated in the east part of the church date before 1636 when the wooden screen which was fitted into them is first mentioned; but others were probably later.[28] The burials in the south-west corner of the church, in what may have been an ossuary, were not excavated; they could be late, though after the 1598 episcopal visitation, which said that many sought burial there, the reports all spoke of burials as having been in the past rather than the present.[29] Some of the tombstones are incised with a modicum of decoration, sometimes merely a cross or a patterned border, but none has any name or inscription. In no case was there any sign of a tomb built or lined with brick or stone; the bodies were simply placed one on top of another in the earth, the earlier burials, and especially the skulls, often being disturbed by later bodies being deposited on top of them. This practice was still common in 1575 when the Apostolic Visitor Pietro Dusina denounced it at many places, including Żurrieq.[30] In both the Annunciation church and that below it the graves all seem to have been dug through the respective floor levels; at least, there is no positive evidence that they were planned as part of the original construction. The burial in the centre of the Visitation church was not dug through its pavement floor and probably dates from the time of that church's foundation, but that on the north

25. *Supra*, 24.

26. M. Meiss, "*Ovum Struthionis*: Symbol and Allusion in Piero della Francesca's Montefeltro Altarpiece," in his *The Painter's Choice* (New York, 1976), 112–113 *et passim*; cf. G. Galavaris, "Some Aspects of Symbolic Use of Lights in the Eastern Church: Candles, Lamps and Ostrich Eggs," *Byzantine and Modern Greek Studies*, iv (1978).

27. Text in *Ħal Millieri*, 141.

28. Discussion *supra*, 29–30.

29. *Ħal Millieri*, 123, 140.

30. *Infra*, 132, n. 1.

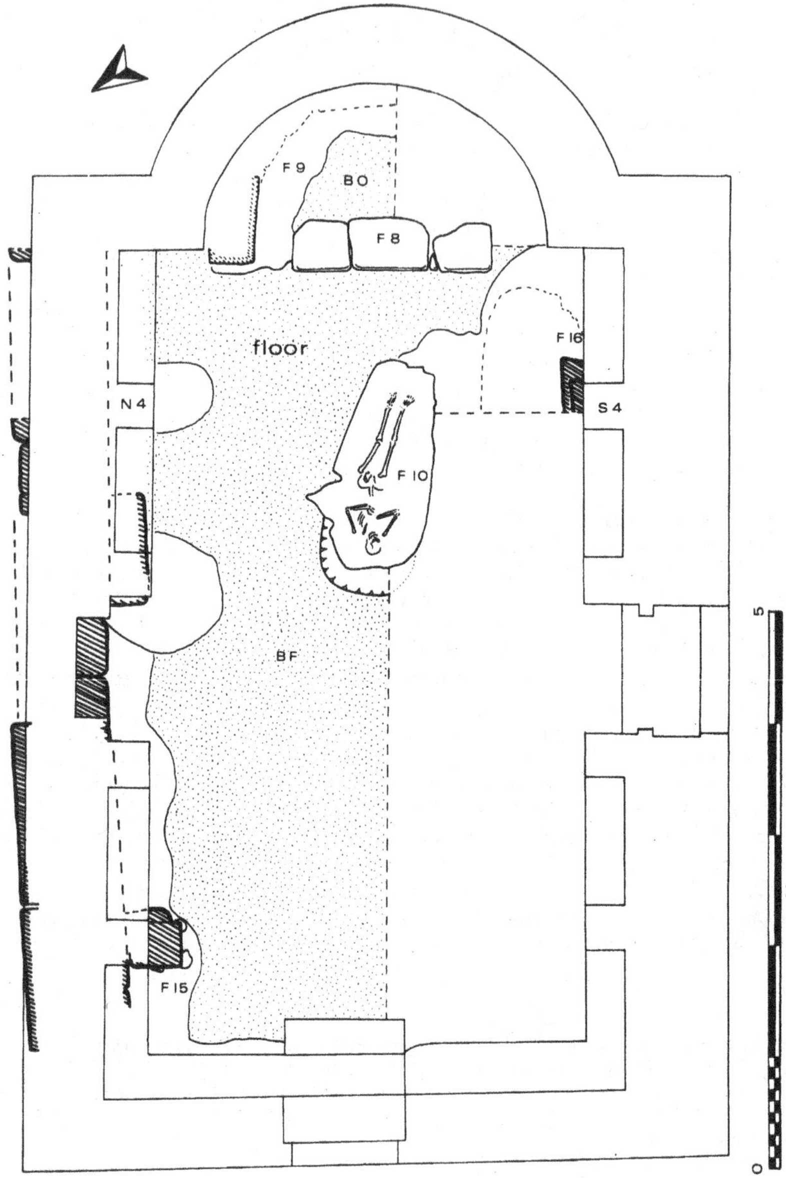


5. Church of the Annunciation: features associated with the Lower Church, phases (b) and (c).

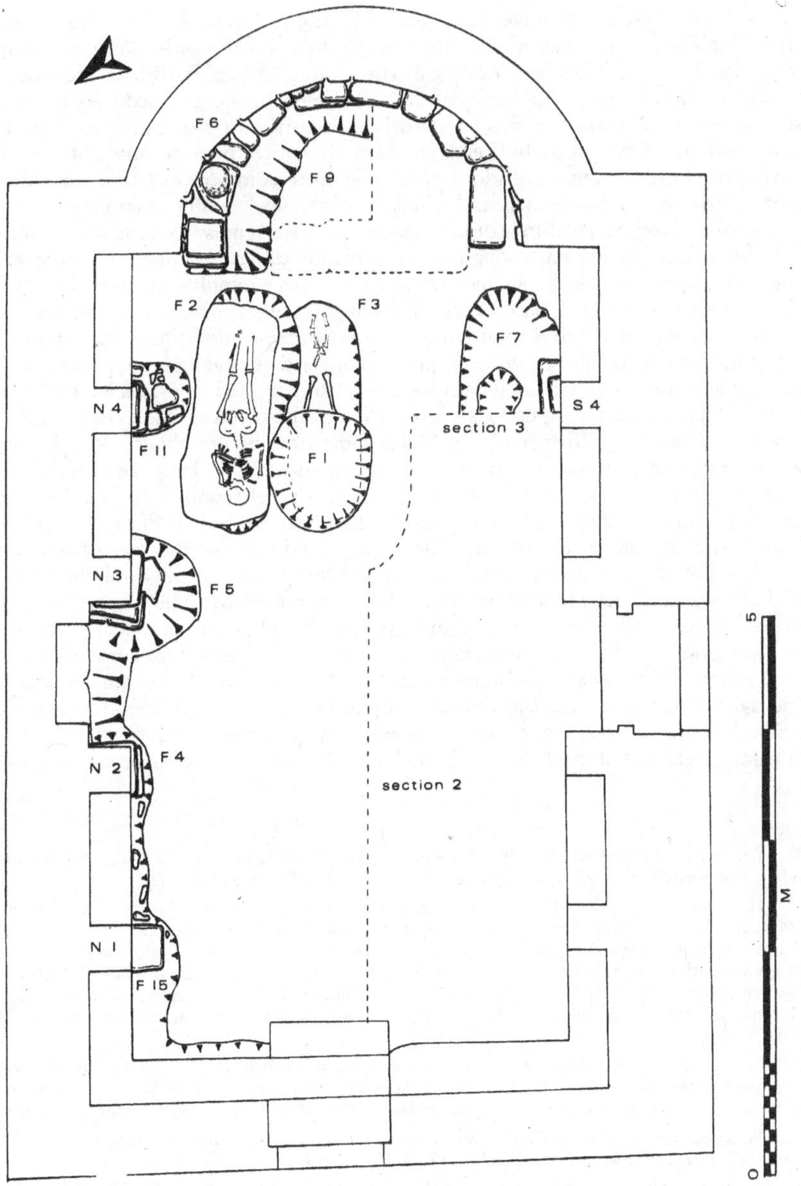


8. Church of the Annunciation: features excavated in the Upper Church phases (d) and (e).

side of that church may have been related to the position of a side altar such as that which was mentioned in the visitation records of 1575 and 1598,[31] or the side altar which can still be seen nearby in the church of San Bażilju at Mqabba.

The rosaries held in the hands of some of those who were buried were a normal sign of piety. The custom was apparently established in the Latin West by the thirteenth century[32] and the beads do not, therefore, provide any criterion for dating the burials. Representations of rosaries were common in late-medieval art, particularly in the fourteenth and fifteenth centuries,[33] while funerary sculptures and slabs showed the dead in attitudes which may have represented the way in which they were actually buried, though it was probably difficult to inter a corpse with the hands joined in prayer. To give just two Northern examples: on an incised grave slab at Villiers-le-Temple, dated 1274, the Templar Gérars, who in this case however seems to be walking rather than lying in an attitude of burial, held a rosary in his left hand across his chest, while in another incised slab at Épernay, dated 1351, Abbess Marguerite de Chastelvilain held her hands joined in prayer with a rosary over her right wrist.[34] The earliest burial at Ħal Millieri attests the existence of the practice of burying with rosaries in Malta some time before about 1480. In 1600 a rosary made of six beads and an ebony medallion showing St. James and St. Dominic attached to a green silk cord was dug up in the chapel founded by Pietro Caxaro in the Dominican church of Santa Maria della Grotta at Rabat; Pietro Caxaro was buried in that chapel in 1485 and the rosary could just possibly have been his.[35]

The burials raise questions concerning the foundation of the rural churches at Ħal Millieri and the identity of those who were buried in them. Apart from the major churches at Mdina or Rabat and the "parish" churches or *capelle*, each with its "archpriest" or *kappillan*, numerous country churches were spread across the island by the fifteenth century. Some were private foundations in which the founder retained the right of patronage, the *iuspatronatus*, and in Malta these were known as *animagii*. From the earliest times legislation had attempted to restrain the general urge of the faithful to seek burial inside a church; such burials were made dependent on a special

31. Eg. text in *Ħal Millieri*, 139–140. The text is somewhat ambiguous, and any altar on the north side of the Visitation church remains hypothetical: cf. *supra*, 38, 48 and Fig. 12.

32. H. Thurston, "Chapelet," *Dictionnaire d'Archéologie Chrétienne et de Liturgie*, iii (Paris, 1948), 399–406; *500 Jahre Rosenkranz: 1475 Köln 1975* (Cologne, 1975). E. Wilkins, *The Rose-Garden Game: the Symbolic Background to the European Prayer Beads* (London, 1969), 30 n. 7, provides a twelfth-century example of a burial with rosary at Palermo, but it depends on the story of the discovery in 1624 of the body of Santa Rosalia who died ca. 1160 and was found holding prayer beads: G. Cascini, *Di S. Rosalia Vergine Palermitana* (Palermo, 1651), 253–254. There is no necessary connection with the Dominicans or any other movement.

33. See G. Kaftal, *Iconography of the Saints in Tuscan Painting* (Florence, 1952), index s.v. "Beads"; *idem*, *Iconography of the Saints in Central and South Italian Schools of Painting* (Florence, 1965), index s.v. "Beads"; *idem.*, *Iconography of the Saints in the Painting of North East Italy* (Florence, 1978), index s.v. "Beads".

34. W. Greeny, *Illustrations of Incised Slabs on the Continent of Europe* (London, 1981), nos. 20, 43; F. Greenhill, *Incised Effigial Slabs*, ii (London, 1976), Plate 121A.

35. M. Fsadni, *Il-Miġja u l-Ħidma ta' l-Ewwel Dumnikani: 1450–1512* (Malta, 1965), 53–54; the rosary was acquired by the historian G.F. Abela, but is now lost. [Fr. Fsadni most kindly communicated additional details concerning this rosary].

permission. One response to these limitations was to secure burial as close as possible to a sacred place, to be buried in holy ground just outside the church, *in atrio*, or *in porticu* or at least in an adjoining cemetery. Another was to found one's own church and to maintain family control of it through the *iuspatronatus*. Canon law laid down general conditions for various types of *iuspatronatus* but the interpretation of these rules was much disputed by the commentators, and their application was determined by local custom and, in some cases, by local diocesan legislation. Usually the *iuspatronatus* was founded and endowed by a free individual acting, in theory at least, with the bishop's consent and according to a notarial act. Sometimes there was no written act of foundation but exercise of the right from time immemorial constituted a *praesumptio juris*. In the case of a church, the founder of the *iuspatronatus* would generally have been the person who built it. Normally, the founder and his or her successors were bound to maintain, repair or even rebuild the church; they named the priest or rector and often had the *ius sepulturae*, the right to be buried in the church. The right of patronage normally passed to the patron's heirs within the family but, again with the bishop's consent, it could be alienated.[36]

The earliest known Maltese example of the alienation of a *iuspatronatus* dates to 1363 when Ysolda de Landolina of Noto in Sicily granted the church of San Niccolò near Siġġiewi to the Benedictines of Catania, an arrangement which was subsequently modified by the bishop.[37] In 1431 Michele Fabro made a will instructing that he was to be buried in a church which he had built and endowed, and which he hoped to bequeath to the Dominicans.[38] Other churches did not pertain to a particular individual or family but were in a sense communal, being administered by a procurator who came under the bishop's jurisdiction and who managed the church's incomes which often derived from certain fields allotted for that purpose. There is no documented Maltese example of the actual foundation of this type of church before the sixteenth century, and there seems to be no way of elucidating the earlier development of this system. By the sixteenth century the practice was for the local community to create a small church on its own initiative and, in theory, with the bishop's permission; quite often the motive would be one of collective thanksgiving or devotion to a particular saint, such as St. Roque or St. Leonard, who was held to have been responsible for protecting the community from some disaster.

There was no known wealthy Sicilian lady or grand landholder in the *casale* of Ħal Millieri, and presumably all four churches there were foundations of this second

36. There is no study of such matters in Sicily. For general summaries, G. Pacelli, "Patronato, Diritto di," *Enciclopedia Cattolica*, ix (Vatican, 1952), 978–982, and E. Marantonio Sguerzo, *Evoluzione storico-giuridica dell'Istituto della Sepoltura ecclesiastica* (Milan, 1976); for the commentators, P. Thomas, *Droit de Propriété des Laïques sur les Églises* (Paris, 1906). There are numerous wills briefly calendared in modern times in Mdina, Cathedral Archives, Ms. 280, and Valletta, National Library of Malta, Ms. 695, but unfortunately none of them dates before 1400.

37. Cf. A. Luttrell, "The Benedictines and Malta: 1363–1371," *Papers of the British School at Rome*, 50 (1982). In 1418 Margherita de Aragona bequeathed the Lunziata church near Rabat which she had built: references in A. Luttrell, "The Augustinians at Malta: 1413," *Analecta Augustiniana*, xxxviii (1975), 297/8 n. 5.

38. *Infra*, 133.

type, the church of St. John receiving a "pious obligation" from Johannes Zammit some time before 1481, and the church of *Santa Maria*, presumably that of the Annunciation, having lands by 1495.[39] Exactly how such churches were originally founded and by whom does not seem to be recorded at Ħal Millieri or anywhere else in Malta; possibly no material act was involved. It may be, however, that individuals did build churches and then endow them without actually creating a *iuspatronatus*;[40] such churches may then have passed to the community in general. None of the Ħal Millieri churches is known to have had a procurator before 1575,[41] though the system of procurators existed considerably earlier.[42] Such churches served the community; they were visited by the bishop, while their festivities were conducted by a priest from the local parish. In some cases there may have been a council or *universitas* of the *casale* which could take initiatives and responsibilities.[43] Alternatively, certain individuals may have intervened either by granting lands and incomes to be administered by a procurator, as Johannes Zammit may have done before 1481, or by paying for buildings, repairs, altars or paintings.[44] In such cases the minor rural churches, often abutting one another as at Ħal Millieri, were fulfilling the functions of a chapel in a "parish" or conventual church or in the cathedral. They permitted an individual to safeguard his soul while at the same time earning social prestige through a measure of locally conspicuous expenditure.

The small rural churches of Malta may also have provided a burial place for a local family, or even perhaps for some part of the community. That might explain why such small churches were often clustered in groups of two or more in a way that might be comparable to the foundation of altars or chapels within the larger churches. Unfortunately the first *Liber Mortuorum* of Żurrieq is lost and the second volume begins as late as 1609. At that time a dead person was normally taken from his house to the parish church at Żurrieq where a funeral service was held; the body was then buried in the nave of the parish church from which bones were periodically moved to an ossuary pit within the same church; only those who died of plague or other contagious diseases were buried in the country chapels.[45] What happened

39. Wettinger, in *Ħal Millieri*, 50–51, 58, 67/8 n. 195.

40. This might explain cases where a *pium legatum* was made by the founder to a church he himself founded. Manfredo Xeberras in his will of 20 Jan. 1449 made his son his heir universal, but he also "fecit quoddam pium legatum in favorem ecclesie ssme. Annunciationis per eum constructe in Casale Bircarcara:" Mdina, Cathedral Archives, Ms. 280, f. 179 (text in *Medieval Malta*, 62). In 1490/99 Pietro Azzupardo's will instituted his sons as his heirs "cum onere pij legati pro Ecclesia S. Marie Assumptionis in Cas: Siggeui per ipsum edificata"; *ibid.*, f. 220. Tantio Mangione's will of 10 July 1463 bequeathed a "pium legatum" to the church of San Leonardo "per ipsum construende": *ibid.*, f. 65. Each of these cases differs somewhat from the others, but there is no reference to foundations or to burials in these brief modern summaries of the original texts.

41. T. Mangion, in *Ħal Millieri*, 131–132, 135.

42. Eg. the procurators and their burial rights in 1502 and 1538: *infra*, 134, 137.

43. For an *universitas hominum* in a Maltese *casale* with a juridical existence independent of the *università* at Mdina, see A. Luttrell, "A Maltese Casale: 1436," *Melita Historica*, vi no. 3 (1974).

44. Cf. Wettinger, in *Ħal Millieri*, 108–113.

45. Information, derived from the *Libri Mortuorum* in the Żurrieq Parish Archives, kindly provided by Tony Mangion.

before 1609 is not clear. At Ħal Millieri, there were burials in the lower Annunciation church well before about 1480 and a cemetery was recorded in the *casale* in 1505; subsequently each of the four churches had a *żuntier*, that is an enclosed area in front of the church which was used for burials, and both pairs of abutting churches had a *cemeterium*. In 1598 the churches of St. John and St. Michael were described as being constructed "in the same cemetery", and there are examples elsewhere of small churches actually built within a cemetery.[46] The 1598 visitation report also mentioned that people were being buried in front of the Visitation church.[47] The existence of burials within the Annunciation church and in the *żuntier* in front of it, and of other cemeteries within the *casale*, all show that some, if not all, of the inhabitants of Ħal Millieri were buried in their own settlement. Canon law laid down that a payment had to be made so that the priest was not defrauded of his dues if burial took place away from the parish church,[48] but whether a priest came from Żurrieq to conduct a service at Ħal Millieri or whether bodies were carried to Żurrieq and then back again for burial is not clear.

The remains of at least fifteen bodies were found inside the Annunciation church, and there were almost certainly more since the bones in the grave in the south-east corner of the church had been disturbed before excavation. There were also the burials in the *żuntier* and others beside the church, while it is possible that long slabs in the south-west corner of the church covered an ossuary pit, especially as two of the slabs had sockets to enable them to be lifted easily; though not excavated in 1977, the slabs are known to have had bones beneath them.[49] There is no way, therefore, of discovering how many bodies were buried in or near the church or of estimating what percentage of the population of Ħal Millieri was buried in or around its four churches. Whatever the initial motive for their foundation, these churches did to some extent act as burial chapels, the Annunciation church having a south doorway which led directly into the cemetery to the south of the church. This practice may have been ancient in origin, since the Byzantine village at Kaukana on the south coast of Sicily apparently had a "burial" church with a floor mosaic, two side

46. Details in Wettinger and Mangion, in *Ħal Millieri*, 67 n. 194, 123–126, 135, 140; plague burials were apparently recorded as early as 1592 and burials were taking place in the Annunciation cemetery in 1598 – *perplures Ibidem . . . humantur*. The place-name Tat-Torba is now found near another cemetery near Ħal Millieri: *ibid.*, Fig. 2. Wettinger, in *Atti del Colloquio*, ii. 329–344, suggests that this toponym may indicate a Muslim or Christian cemetery. On churches or chapels in cemeteries, see Mdina, Cathedral Archives, Ms. 280, f. 3 ("Iurispatronatus di S. Michele nel cemeterio del Gozzo": founder's will of 1441), 206 (will of founder of "Iuspatronato di S. Paulo nel cemeterio del Gozo": 1435); 219 (will providing for the building of a *cappella* "in Cemeterio Sti. Pauli de Rabbato": 1444).

47. According to the visitation report of 1646 (text *infra*, 120), there was a considerable cemetery in front of the two churches, Annunciation and Visitation. This might have included a *żuntier* immediately in front of the Visitation church alongside that of the Annunciation church. However, only a few much disturbed and very worn bones, with no clear indication of any burials, were found in front of the Visitation church. As the post-excavation clearance of the north end of the area immediately west of the Visitation church revealed a very large stone apparently *in situ* with its top at about 20 cm above the level of the church floor, it would have been very difficult to make burials in this section of the *żuntier*, if there was a *żuntier* there.

48. *Corpus Iuris Canonici*, ii, ed. E. Richter (2nd ed: Leipzig, 1879), 548–553, 1045–1047.

49. This area was disturbed before the excavations proper began.

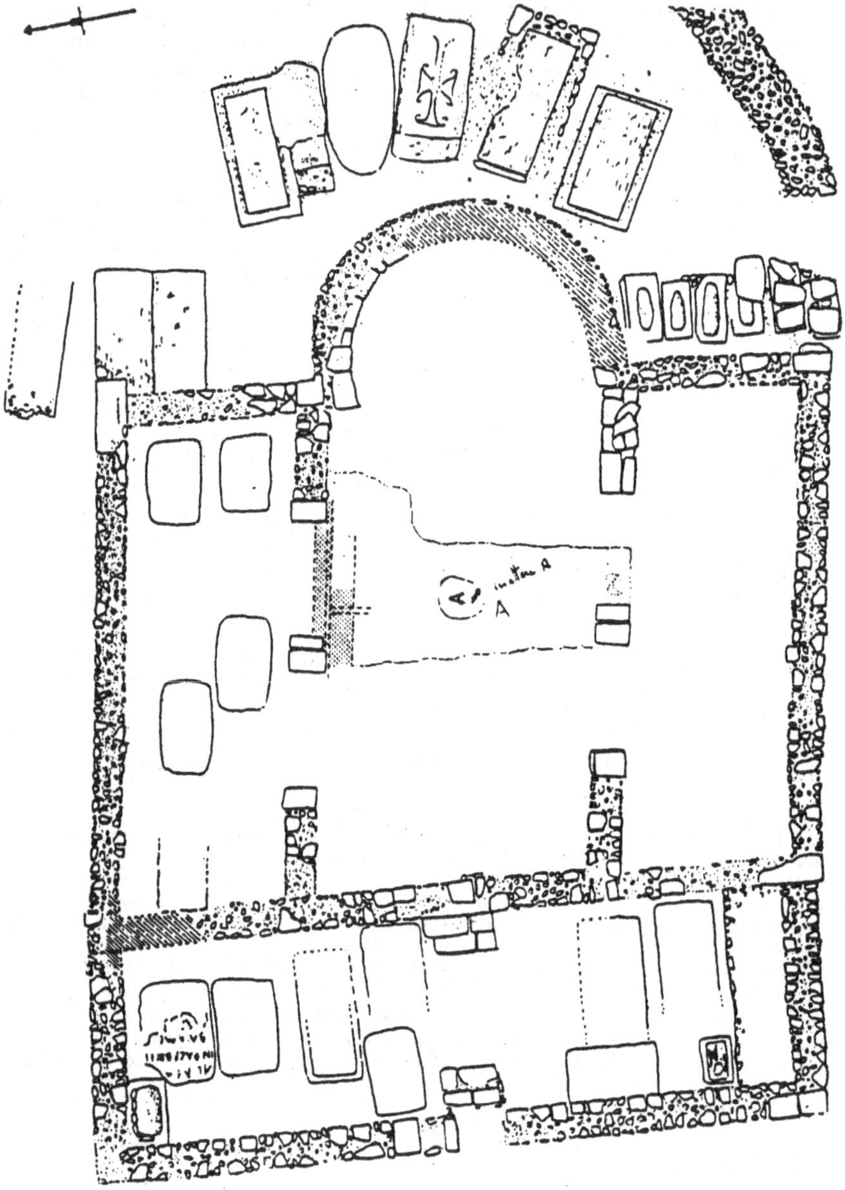

22. The 'Burial' Church at Kaukana, Sicily (after P. Pelagatti).

aisles, a narthex with graves, and other burials outside the church (Fig. 22).[50] The Maltese *zuntier* may in fact have been an atrophied form of narthex, either because this arrangement of "burial church" and narthex with burials was a survival from Byzantine times[51] or, perhaps more likely, because it was imported from south-east Sicily after about 1200.[52]

The evidence concerning the main burial in the Visitation church, where the central trench was in a disturbed area and excavation was limited, permits of varying interpretations. Possibly the area was used for burials before the church was built.[53] In any case the ground was already bare rock or was cleared to bare rock when the church was built, since there was no construction trench for the one pier which was excavated. The area was then filled with rubble into which was dug a trench for a grave which contained a burial, probably a female, at a point centrally in front of the altar and carefully oriented in line with the church (Fig. 10). The grave was cut 20 cm down into the rock, presumably in order to allow room for further burials in the earth on top of the first corpse buried there. The grave was then filled with earth, exactly in the way so often described by Dusina in his report of 1575. The female found in the grave may have been a patron of the church; apparently she was between 40 and 50 years of age, and the church may have been built on her death or soon after. The original floor of the church was then laid above the burial which must have taken place at the time the church was built, and the foot incised on a paving stone at the east end of the tomb may have marked its position, though in fact the grave never was reopened.[54]

Some of those laid to rest inside the churches presumably had some special claim to such preferment as against those buried outside them. The arrangement of the roughly but not directly central burials in the lower and upper Annunciation churches (Figs. 5, 8), and also in the Visitation church, suggests that they may have received the founders, patrons or possibly the procurators of the churches, or members of their families. The cost of building or painting a new church may not have been beyond the richest families in the *casale*, and the reconstruction, paving and frescoing of the Annunciation church, all probably undertaken at roughly the same moment, require some explanation, especially as there is no sign that the earlier church

50. P. Pelagatti, "Kaukana: un ancoraggio bizantino sulla costa meridionale," *Sicilia Archeologica*, v nos. 18–20 (1972), 96–99; on the evidence provided, there is nothing to show that this church had a roofed narthex rather than a *zuntier*. On Kaukana, see *idem*, "Scavi e ricerche archeologiche nella Provincia di Ragusa: 1961–1966," *Archivio Storico Siracusano*, xii (1966), 23–29. The structure of this church was quite different from any of those at Ħal Millieri.

51. On narthex burials in Byzantine churches, see G. Babić, *Les Chapelles annexes des Églises byzantines: Fonction liturgique et programmes iconographiques* (Paris, 1969); such burials are also found in Western, Latin Europe.

52. *Zuntier* or *Zintier* is of Romance origin from the Sicilian *Zimmiteri*, cemetery: J. Micallef, *The Sicilian Element in Maltese* (unpublished MA Thesis: University of London, 1959), 705. [Reference kindly provided by Joseph Cassar Pullicino].

53. In this case there might have been a north doorway in the Annunciation church to give access to the cemetery area before the Visitation church was built, but the balance of the archaeological evidence tells against that: *supra*, 41–42.

54. Details *supra*, 34–35,87; Figs. 10, 12.

collapsed. There is no indication that the graves in the Annunciation church were planned as an integral part of the church at the moment of construction, though such planning may have been unnecessary when a simple inhumation in earth required no more than the lifting of the pavement and, in some cases, the preparation of special covering slabs. There is no evidence for the existence of guilds or corporations in Maltese *casali* in the late-medieval period, and the patron could well have been a prosperous local resident such as the Johannes Zammit who endowed the Ħal Millieri church of St. John some time before 1481.[55] There are many examples of arrangements by which individuals secured burial, *sepultura* or *monumentum*, within the cathedral or a *cappella*, that is a "parish" church, by endowing chapels, paying for repairs, financing masses and lamps, and so on; normally the burial was to be "perpetual" and the tomb chamber was to be for the use of the individuals' children and their heirs in perpetuity, which presumably meant that their bones were not to be disturbed and removed after their burial to a common ossuary. Some of these arrangements refer to the parish of Żurrieq.[56] There is just one known rural example, however, in which the burial was to take place in a church which was not either the parish church, the church of a religious order or a church held in *iuspatronatus*. This occurred at Żejtun in 1502 when Antonius Randuni arranged with the deputy parish priest and with the procurators of the church of St. Mary at Ħal Bisqallin to secure a perpetual burial place in the church in return for a field which was sold to pay for building work on the church's walls and structure.[57] That is what could have happened at Ħal Millieri in order to build churches, to rebuild them, to found altars or to pay for frescoes. These were local manifestations of a widespread religiosity which flourished strongly among people who may, consciously or perhaps through established traditional forms, have been compensating, by such overt expressions of Christian zeal, for their Muslim past and their continuing use of an Arabic speech.[58]

55. Text in *Ħal Millieri*, 33 n. 13, 67 n. 195; this Joannes and his son Zaccaria do not appear in the Zammit family tree given *ibid.*, 61. Endowments were given to an existing church, possibly being rebuilt or enlarged, by Bartolomeo de Bordino whose family arms were carved in relief on the floor suggesting a grave there, though his family did not hold the church in *juspatronatus*: M. Buhagiar, "The Crypt and Church of S. Marija tal-Virtù at Rabat," *Melita Historica*, vii no. 4 (1979), 329–330. Note however that as early as 1414 Fridericus de Burdino *civis Melitae* made a legacy to Santa Marija tal-Virtù: copy in Catania, Archivio di Stato, Fondo Benedettini, Ms. 159, f. 140–143.

56. Texts and extracts in G. Wettinger, *infra*, 132–137, and *idem*, *Il-Ġrajja Bikrija tal-Knisja Matriċi t'Għawdex: 1435–1551* (Malta, 1975), 3 n. 10, 7 n. 19, 8 n. 20, 12 nn. 31–32, 13 n. 33.

57. *Infra*, 134.

58. Cf. A. Luttrell, "The Christianization of Malta," *Malta Year Book* (Malta, 1977).

# 3. The Structure of the Ħal Millieri Churches

The excavation of the three churches at Ħal Millieri has clarified the process by which the medieval Maltese rural church was constructed, from its foundations, which at Ħal Millieri were dug down so that even the upper church rested firmly on the solid rock, to its wall piers, its compacted plaster floor, its burials, its frescoes, its benches, doorways and screens; none of the churches had any windows.[59] Much of this information was already available and has merely received confirmation, but certain new points have emerged.[60] For example, and contrary to what was previously thought to be the case,[61] it appears that the parallel arches supporting the slightly-pitched roof were not bonded into the main side walls; the arches, incidentally, do not have a normal keystone. It is still not clear whether the arches at the side walls were built first. In the church of Santa Ċeċilja at Xewkija on Gozo the arches were bonded into the walls, but that is probably a very late example.[62] In the surviving wall of the old parish church of San Niccolò at Siġġiewi the points at which the arches met the side walls are clearly indicated by the absence of plaster, and it is evident that the arches were not bonded in.[63] At Ħal Millieri, the lower Annunciation church lacked the side benches found in the upper church, while the

59. The standard accounts are those of M. Buhagiar, in *Medieval Malta* and in *Ħal Millieri*. What follows is intended to supplement and refine but not to replace Buhagiar's accounts; it should preferably be read along with them. *Malta's Heritage in Stone*, ed. Din l-Art Ħelwa (Malta 1976), contains useful photographs. Clear details concerning the system of building with slabs on arched ribs, the components of *torba* and *deffun*, the double walls with a rubble fill, and the making of floors, are given in H. Jones, "Memoranda and Details of the Mode of Buildings, etc, in the Island of Malta," *Papers on Subjects Connected with the Duties of the Corps of Royal Engineers*, v (London, 1842). The medieval floor of the lower Annunciation church at Ħal Millieri was, however, composed in a different way from that described in Jones: see the analysis *supra*, 15, 18; Fig. 7.

60. The altar slab now in the church measures 164 × 57 × 11 cm and the altar step 160 × 80 × ca. 11–12 cm: amend *Ħal Millieri*, 72. The waterspouts are on the east, west and south walls: amend *ibid.*, 73. The other portion of the strange fragment of carving found in the precincts of the Annunciation church and illustrated *ibid.*, 75–76 and Plate 10B, has been identified at the house of the Missionary Society of St. Paul at St. Agatha's, Rabat. No date for it has yet been proposed; nor can the strange divorce of the two pieces be explained. It seems unlike the numerous late-medieval carved stones at St. Agatha's, which deserve further study; it does not necessarily have any bearing on the medieval history of that church, as suggested in J. Felice Pace, "St. Agatha Sacred Complex," *Heritage* [Malta], 22 (1979), 435.

61. Eg. Buhagiar, in *Ħal Millieri*, 82.

62. Illustrated in Q. Hughes, *Fortress: Architecture and Military History in Malta* (London, 1969), 168; it is not documented before 1615 (*infra*, 122, n. 103).

63. *Medieval Malta*, Plate 12a. Buhagiar, *ibid.*, 172–173, maintains that the original roof at Siġġiewi was supported on timber beams and that the non-bonded wall piers were a later addition, precisely because they were not bonded in. This is apparently to be amended, since (1) the piers were not bonded in at the Annunciation and Visitation churches at Ħal Millieri; (2) the width of the church at ca. 8.70 m was probably too great to be spanned by timbers; (3) the supposed putt-log holes for the alleged timbers are somewhat dubious and are at different levels; (4) it seems unlikely that a timber roof would be replaced by a stone one since the general pattern in Maltese roofing was for timber to replace stone.

Visitation church had some such benches which may or may not have run the whole length of the building. Even in the Annunciation church the benches had no firm foundations, but they did contribute something to the solidity of the structure by creating a firm framework of arches, piers, slabs and benches, all of which gave one another some support, with the benches acting as a brace at the foot of the piers. There is no evidence that these benches had any liturgical function, and the pattern painted on the wall immediately above them, portions of which still survive, suggests that the bays which contain the benches were not used as rudimentary side-chapels such as those found nearby in the church of San Bażilju at Mqabba.[64] A system of slightly-pointed arches, a gently-sloping roof, side walls with two skins and a rubble infill and a rounded apse with a slightly-pointed arch, all much like the Annunciation church, could once be seen in the now destroyed church of San Ċir at Bubaqra, also near Żurrieq (Plate 42).[65] The interior plastering which was used to cover much of the stonework at Ħal Millieri at the time when the frescoes were restored in 1974 somewhat impedes investigations of the stonework and building technique. The ashlars of the arches were carefully cut, and very little mortar was used between the stones. Irregularities of build in the arches which have no proper keystone, in the benches and elsewhere give the impression that the materials were adapted to fit the construction and to use the particular sizes of stones which were to hand as the building progressed. The floor slabs of soft limestone, many as much as 15 or even 18 cm thick, appear surprisingly unworn. These and other points might eventually be elaborated by excavations in churches such as those at Bir Miftuħ and Siġġiewi.

The pavement floor dates from about 1480[66] and the eastern and central tomb-slabs covered burials which had been cut through the pavement and which therefore date after about 1480.[67] The sockets for the screen, which was probably the one described in 1636 as newly made,[68] were sunk into these slabs, so that the graves were very probably there before 1636. The sockets also show that before that date the central slab had been lifted, presumably for an extra burial, broken and replaced with its western end at the east.[69] The visitations of 1636, 1646, 1658 and 1667,

64. Similarly, there is no evidence that the seventeenth-century screen in the upper Annunciation church (*Ħal Millieri*, 71, 77, 126) had any liturgical function. It seems to have been a late innovation, and probably it allowed the church to be kept open so that people could enter it and see the altar and its painting while anything of value around the altar was protected.

65. The church has been destroyed but something of its construction can be seen in Plate 42, first published in L. Zammit, "Remains of St. Cyrus Church dated back to 10th Century," *Sunday Times of Malta*, no. 2,379 (11 Dec. 1966), 10; this title is misleading. No documentation survives concerning this church, on which see *Medieval Malta*, 177 and Plate 9a; it may eventually be identified with a church of some other name.

66. *Supra*, 26, 46–47, for the archaeological evidence; Bautier Bresc, in *Ħal Millieri*, for the dating derived from the style of the paintings and their inscriptions. Note that the word *Garinu* painted behind the frescoes (*ibid.*, Plate 30) could not, on palaeographical grounds, be much earlier.

67. The detailed description of the tomb-slabs, screen and altar platform in *Ħal Millieri*, 71–72, 76–79, and Fig. 6, now requires revision; the following account also makes use of notes taken by Mario Buhagiar in 1968.

68. Text *ibid.*, 141.

69. Cf. *ibid.*, Fig. 6.

but not that of 1747, reported that the altar was approached up two steps;[70] these must have been between the screen and the altar, but nothing more is known of them. At some point a platform was built which stretched westwards some 2.10 m from the east wall; this platform was demolished in 1968 but the position of its front step is still shown by a line of concrete on the floor.[71] The platform covered the three tomb-slabs almost completely; the southern slab was broken into three, and two of its pieces were used to build part of the platform in the apse; they were replaced in 1968. The platform itself had new sockets for a screen; a screen was mentioned in the visitations of 1747 and 1759, and there was a screen in the church within living memory; possibly this was the screen of about 1636 cut down so that it fitted onto the raised level of the platform. The front edge of that platform consisted of stones now employed in the front edge of the raised floor in the apse as rebuilt in 1968; the altar did not sit directly on the platform but on a raised podium which could have been considered as a "step".[72] This platform apparently dates to after about 1740 because a coin of 1736–1741 was found between the platform and the original pavement.[73] It may have been associated with the wooden doors and the whitewashing mentioned in the visitation of 1747.

Further study of the outer walls of the Annunciation church leads to the conclusion that, on its exterior, only the north wall and probably the much mutilated arched west doorway are original. The outer skins of the west and south walls are built with neat courses of ashlars (Plates 2,4), unlike the north wall where the outer stonework is notably irregular (Plate 3). It seems likely that the south wall had an extra skin added to it, possibly during the time that the Visitation church was standing; this would account for the whole south wall being thicker by the width of the extra skin of stones added to it than the north wall which served also as the south wall of the Visitation church and would not, therefore, have been thickened, as clearly it could not have been; the arches in the two churches roughly coincided with each other on either side of their common wall, and thus they supported one another (Fig. 2). The south doorway was not mentioned in any visitation record until 1634,[74] but there was apparently an original south doorway since its inner section is still built in a way very similar to that of the west doorway where the stones are covered by the frescoes and must, therefore, be dated as part of the original church. Furthermore, there seems to be no positive evidence that there was a bench or a fresco in the area where there is now a doorway; the existing pattern of paving stones suggests that there was never a bench there as the pavement projects, admittedly in a somewhat inexplicably confused manner, into the area where there would otherwise have been a bench. Presumably, therefore, there was never a fresco

70. References *ibid.*, 137–138.

71. *Medieval Malta*, Plate 13b, shows the platform.

72. The altar now on the podium is a modern construction using the slab mentioned *supra*, 114 n. 60.

73. *Supra*, 83 no. 39.

74. *Ħal Millieri*, 72, 125; Plate 14A; cf. text of 1636 *ibid.*, 141. Buhagiar, *ibid.*, 72, thought that the south doorway was a seventeenth-century innovation the opening of which destroyed a fresco.

in that space. The outer part of the existing south doorway is definitely of the same build as the outer skin of the south wall and must have been reconstructed at the time the outer skin was added. The coursing of the side walls of the doorway follows, for a stretch of one stone, that of its outer jamb, which means there must have been considerable rebuilding of the whole doorway. The doorway itself was not mentioned in the reports of 1747, 1754 and 1759,[75] and it was blocked up long before 1968. The south wall has very regular courses 26–29 cm high. Its stones are well cut and closely jointed, and many have vertical axe-marks possibly intended to key in a covering of plaster; apart from a decorative band of projecting stones above the doorway, the whole wall was covered with several thin skins of plaster rendering. The two waterspouts seem also to be of one construction with the outer part of this wall. If this outer skin of ashlars was added before the destruction of the Visitation church it dates before 1667, a dating which might well fit with its simple squareness. It is unlikely to be much latei, given that the *casale* was abandoned by about 1700.

The west wall is at present approximately 64 cm thick when measured through the doorway. On the inside is a course of stones some 42–45 cm thick which evidently constitute the original inner section of the doorway, since they are covered both to the north and south by the original frescoes. Outside this original stonework is a skin some 20–22 cm in thickness, which is detached from the inner stonework and the courses of which in no way match the courses of the inner wall; at present there is in places a space of some 2 cm between these inner and outer sections. This outer skin contains a doorway which was once an arched doorway with a simple hood-moulding, with rosettes and chamfered door-jambs, the mutilated traces of which can still be seen. This doorway was later heightened and cut square (Plate 2). Similar arched doorways were cut square in this same way at Bir Miftuħ, at Ħal Xluq and at Ta' Qali.[76] The coursing on the west facade is less regular than that on the south, and evidently had to be adapted to various changes. However the stones are also square-cut and very neatly fitted with a minimum of mortar; this facade also was covered with plaster. On top of the slightly-pitched gable is a bell-cot. Bell-cots were an early-seventeenth century innovation, to judge by the visitation reports,[77] and the simple one at Ħal Millieri could well be of that period, especially as the visitation reports mentioned a small bell in 1598 and 1608, and a bell on the roof in 1634.[78]

It seems likely that the west facade was reconstructed, and that raises the question whether the mutilated arched doorway is the original one. The doorway could date to about 1480 from a stylistic point of view, judging by similar probably fifteenth-century features at Bir Miftuħ, Ħal Xluq and Tal-Virtù,[79] though it could also be much later; a similar doorway at St. Catherine tax-Xwejki near Għargħur was built

75. Text of 1759 *ibid.*, 142.

76. Buhagiar, in *Medieval Malta*, Plate 10b, 10d, 11a.

77. Personal communication from Mario Buhagiar. Q. Hughes, The Building of Malta: 1530–1795 (revised ed: London, 1967), 123, dates the bell-cot on the church of St. Anne, Castel Sant'Angelo, to about 1534, but he is assuming that it was not a later addition.

78. Buhagiar, in *Ħal Millieri*, 73

79. *Medieval Malta*, Plates 11b, 11c, 12b.

as late as 1611.[80] The builders of the present facade had some difficulty in adjusting the alignment of their courses, neatly built as they were. The corner-stones at the south-west corner are an integral part of the added south facade, and could not have been part of the original west facade which would not have stretched so far west before the south wall was thickened. Yet as the west wall is continued northwards its courses follow the heights determined by the south-west corner-stones; that part of the facade must therefore be contemporary with or later than the outer skin to the south, and might be seventeenth-century. As the coursing approached the doorway, however, it had to be adjusted so as to fit the courses around the doorway. This is probably because the original arched doorway was being left in place, in which case the west wall was always as thick as it is now and the original facade was replaced; the arched doorway may have been cut square at the same time.[81] The existing facade is unlikely to be a skin added on outside an existing wall, as occurred on the south, because there is no sign of an outer doorway in the stonework of the inner section of the wall, and little or no room for one either; if there had been, the west wall would have been only 42–45 cm thick, a very thin wall compared to the ca. 75 cm of the north wall, and that is most unlikely to have been the case.[82]

The north wall is of a notably clumsy build, with courses ranging between 21 and 34 cm and several very large stone blocks; some awkward gaps have been filled in with flakes of stone. The stones show oblique axe-marks, and at one point the wall was plastered. The north wall was never rebuilt with neat ashlars, probably because the rebuilding on the south and west walls took place before the destruction of the Visitation church. It may have been a desire to keep the west front of the Annunciation church flush with that of the church next to it, as in fact it was, which led to the reconstruction of the west facade rather than the addition to it of a skin which would have protruded forward. The rebuilding of the north-west corner of the Annunciation church also caused trouble with the alignment of the courses as they approached the west doorway, as occured also to the south of that doorway and indeed above it where the addition of the bell-cot seems further to have complicated the alignment of the courses. At the foot of the north-west corner are two very large corner-stones which were never squared up and still jut forward westwards; they may have been part of the original facade which was left untrimmed perhaps because the ground level obscured them or for some other reason. Why the northern face of the corner-stones above these two was neatly and smoothly squared is not clear; it may have been to accommodate the south-west corner of the Visitation church which may itself have been neatly squared, or it may have been a tidying operation carried out after the Visitation church had been demolished.

The varieties of stone used in the church and the quarries from which they came have yet to be identified, and the way in which Maltese limestone blocks act in

80. Buhagiar, *ibid.*, 180; Plate 11d.

81. The plastering over of the west doorway during the restoration of the frescoes partly obscured the evidence. Six old stones surrounding the west doorway were replaced in 1980, making its study much more difficult.

82. Various disturbances have obscured the analysis in this area.

compression and tension when employed in arches of the traditional type awaits theoretical investigation.[83] The need to support stone rather than timber meant that the arches had to be spaced rather closely together, since the stone slabs could not be longer than between 1.80 and 2.10 m without breaking. The north wall of the Annunciation church, which was not rebuilt and thickened, was until 1667 given extra support by the counterthrusts from the Visitation church. The extra course along the top of the north wall may be a late addition designed to increase its resistance to sideways thrusts from the roof and arches of the Annunciation church. The apse appears from the outside to have been built in two styles which do not join neatly, and the coursing of the masonry on the inside is also irregular (Plate 11).

The structure of the Annunciation church has been analyzed in a separate technical study published below.[84] Though it seems that no other medieval Maltese church of this type has survived without additional buttressing,[85] the weight of the stone roofing rests essentially on the internal arches which would have been strong enough to support this weight without the extra skin added to the south wall of the Annunciation church; in fact, the carefully built arches tend to survive even when the rest of the church collapses, as occurred at San Ċir, Bubaqra (Plate 42). There, however, the stones in the spandrels were laid in much more regular courses than at Ħal Millieri. There was no serious indication in the Annunciation church that the voussoirs of the arches were moving or opening or that the plaster between them was cracking, in so far as could be seen before they were repointed and plastered during the restoration of 1974;[86] nor have any significant cracks in that plastering developed between 1974 and 1980. The arches are not bonded into the side walls but these walls do to some extent act as buttresses. They counter an outward thrust at the foot of the arches, the upper parts of the wall adding a weight which increases the walls' resistance to this outward thrust. The side walls carry no direct weight from the roof, but their upper sections do receive a minor thrust from the rubble walling placed on top of the arches, especially because this walling is not bonded into the arches themselves; this last point was clearly evident at San Ċir, Bubaqra. If such a church were to collapse it would not do so on account of the structure of arch and roof but for other reasons. It might be that there would be some settling of the foundations, that roof slabs break, or that there were imperfections in the stones of the voussoirs of the arches. It could be that roots grow into the walls themselves, as clearly occurred in the Annunciation church;[87] or that the roots of trees outside the structure unsettle it, as happened with the palm tree at the north-west corner of that church which caused cracks clearly visible in the frescoes on the interior.[88] Finally, if water penetrates through the roof it will erode the earth

83. Cf. A. Valentino, "Stone Beams," *Sunday Times of Malta*, no. 2989 (20 Aug. 1978), 18.

84. *Infra*, 138–142.

85. Buttressing at San Mikiel is-Sinċir and at San Ċir, Bubaqra, is shown in *Medieval Malta*, Fig. 10; Plates 9a, 10c.

86. *Ħal Millieri*, Plate 17A, and other photographs taken at the time of the restoration.

87. *Ibid.*, Plate 26.

88. *Ibid.*, Plate 13A.

of the rubble fill between the inner and outer skins of the walls, or possibly cause the earth to expand; such developments would weaken the resistance of the wall. Something of this sort may have caused the slight outward bulge visible in the upper part of the centre of the north wall of the Annunciation church which was not built in carefully squared ashlars.

The system employed was almost unique to Malta, and was presumably imposed by the need to build without wood. The proposition that "this dogged conservative application of an imported technique to such an inappropriate context demonstrates how dependent monumental Maltese architecture was on foreign sources"[89] is not altogether acceptable. There may be quasi-parallels for the system outside Malta,[90] but it cannot be demonstrated that the technique was imported. The paucity of datable examples precludes the construction of a chronology of the diaphragm arch in Malta, but datable churches survive from the fifteenth century and at least one of these does in fact show an evolution away from the system of the simple slightly-pointed arch with horizontal slabs found at Ħal Millieri. In St. Catherine at Żejtun, rebuilt in 1492, the ribs and roofing slabs followed the curve of the supporting arches, thus hiding the upper part of the arches themselves; this more sophisticated innovation was adopted in later churches.[91]

The Visitation church presents different problems. It cannot be dated in any way at all before the apostolic visitation of 1575, though references to a single church of *Santa Maria* may mean that it was not yet built in 1508.[92] It seems, however, to have been a typical medieval Maltese church both as revealed by excavation and as described in the visitation report of 1646, which commenced:

> Subsequenter uisitauerunt Ecclesiam Visitationis B.M.V. positam in dicto Cas: milleri Cuius tectum est constructum ad modum lamiae supra quatuor arcatas, ad cuius Ecclesiae pauimentum descenditur per tres gradus lapideos, et ad altare ascenditur per duos, quod est firmum, et decens, et habet pallium telae depictae et mappas candidas necessarias, et omnia necessaria, Icona in tabulis est depicta referens in medio B.V. uisitantem Sanctae Elisabeth, Sancti Josephi a dexeris, et Sancti Zachariae a sinistris, ante altare est lampas, Janua Ecclesiae respicit occidentem[93] uersus antequam est cemeterium spatiosum nimis deseruiens dictae Ecclesiae, et alteri secum coniunctae inter quas est aperta Janua ita ut ab una ad aliam ingredi possit, in dicto Cemeterio adsunt uestigia plurium sepulcrorum in quo cadauera defunctorum tempore pestis humata fuisse perhibentur, habet Introytum per longum, et latum ac foris muris septum.[94]

The church described in 1646 had four transverse arches carrying slabs *ad modum lamiae*. Three stone steps led down to a floor which was evidently a stone one,

89. Toker, in *Speculum* (1979), 400.

90. For a possible similar church in Sicily and for much earlier examples from Syria, *infra*, 123–124.

91. Buhagiar, in *Medieval Malta*, 174; Plate 13d.

92. Wettinger, in *Ħal Millieri*, 67 n. 192, and text *ibid.*, 139.

93. The phrase *respicientem ad Orientem* in a similar document of 1636 (text in *Ħal Millieri*, 141) clearly referred to a west door, as did this text.

94. Floriana, Archiepiscopal Curia, Visitatio Balaguer da Camarasa (1646), f. 129v–130.

and from which two steps led up to the altar with its saints, furnishings and lamp[95]. The doorway which connected the church to the Annunciation church next to it was probably not an original feature of the Annunciation church. Outside the west door was a large cemetery serving the two churches and containing the remains of a number of burials.[96] Beyond that was the "entrance which was long and large, and shut off from the outside with a wall". There was no mention of any burials in the church probably because, while there were tombstones in the Annunciation church and in its *zuntier*, there was nothing to indicate the presence of the grave in the centre of the Visitation church, which must in fact have been there since the church was built. The grave on the north side of the church was, however, marked by a variation in the stones of the pavement there which indicates that it was inserted after the building of the church and its floor.

95. Correct *Hal Millieri*, 125, which states that the *pauimentum* was mentioned only in 1575. The episcopal visitations contain further minor but unpublished details concerning this church.

96. The ditch immediately outside the west facade was left unfilled after excavations in order that the position of the west wall could clearly be apparent from its footings; the wall to the west of that ditch and the steps at its south end are later additions which unfortunately confuse the visitor's appreciation of the site.

## 4. Medieval Maltese Rural Church Architecture

On the basis of these excavations and of other minor researches it is now possible to revise the corpus of plans of medieval Maltese apsed churches published in 1976; this corpus documented the churches at Tal-Baqqari, Maqluba, Luqa and the upper Annunciation church at Ħal Millieri as having some sort of rounded apse.[97] Two other churches, those at Tas-Silġ[98] and San Pawl Milqi, may be omitted as doubtful; there was a late-medieval church at San Pawl Milqi, but its plan does not survive and there seems to be no clear evidence that it had an apse.[99] The lower Annunciation church at Ħal Millieri possibly had a square apse,[100] while the Visitation church at Ħal Millieri had a rounded apse but probably it was constructed after 1500. Santa Marija tal-Virtù had an apse but its shape is unknown.[101] San Mikiel is-Sinċir outside Rabat apparently had no apse;[102] nor did Santa Ċeċilja on Gozo[103] or the church at Ta' Qali.[104] Santa Maria at Birkirkara, datable before 1402, apparently had a curved apse.[105] Santa Domenica, Żabbar, had a rectangular apse; San Ċir, Bubaqra, apparently had a curved apse which has been destroyed; while two other churches with squared apses, the lower church of St. Agatha and the church

97. *Ħal Millieri*, Fig. 8.

98. At Tas-Silġ the evidence for a post-Muslim church and for its plan appears to consist only of one large stone mortared into place at an angle to a line of stones at a comparatively late date, and of a spread of glazed "Norman" pottery: *Medieval Malta*, 92; Fig. 3a; Plates 7b, 8a,b. The "Norman" pottery may date to the pre-1200 Muslim period in Malta; one non-aligned stone, though difficult to explain, scarcely creates an apse; such a church would, peculiarly, have an apse with a diameter as wide as the church; the church would be 11 m wide and extremely difficult to roof; and the walls would seem somewhat thin. It seems best to suspend judgement on this hypothetical church pending publication of the final excavation report and the dating of the pottery.

99. This results from a close inspection of the excavated remains: *infra*, 144–149.

100. *Supra*, 19.

101. Buhagiar (1979), 330.

102. Cf. C. Cassar, "Restoration Work at Medieval Chapel of Sancir;" J. Azzopardi, "Rehabilitation of a Medieval Monument at Rabat;" D. Cutajar, "The Medieval Chapel of Sancir, Rabat," *The Times* [Malta], nos. 1046, 1052, 1064, 1069, 1075 (1, 8, 22, 27 March, 3 April 1982). The church has received excellent treatment, but the assertion that the church was "an estate's chapel, erected to serve the original community of *villani*" on a royal estate seems unlikely, because the church's date is unknown; the *viridarium di lu Re* is not documented as a royal estate before 1361 (*Medieval Malta*, 152); it was not a parish church providing sacraments; no *raħal* or community is documented there, while the agricultural workers are more likely to have lived in nearby Mdina or Rabat; and all *villani* on Malta were probably Muslims, as suggested by the evidence discussed in A. Luttrell, "Gilibertus Abbate's Report: Malta ca. 1241" [forthcoming].

103. A church of S. *Cecilia in contrata ta* S. *Cilia* existed in 1615: Mdina, Cathedral Archives, Ms. 180, f. 439–440.

104. Hughes (1967), 43–44; Plate 127.

105. A. Luttrell, "The *Cappella* of Birkirkara: 1402," *Melita Historica*, viii no. 3 (1982).

known as Tal-Abbatija, both at Rabat, were rock-cut churches.[106] The Tal-Baqqari church provides an interesting variation in that the roofing arches were not built of carefully cut ashlars but rested on reused monoliths.[107]

It is still the case that there is almost no exact parallel for the Ħal Millieri type church in Sicily. A few Sicilian churches have some of its features but the roof, though it is in certain cases constructed entirely of stone slabs, is never flat. One problem is that the rural churches of Sicily are relatively unstudied, and those which have survived are frequently difficult to interpret because much restored; publication often involves a ground plan but no clear indication of the roofing system. Sant'Ippolito at Erice in Western Sicily has five transverse arches which are, however, modern; these are supported on projecting piers and carry semi-circular arches at intervals of one metre. The arches now "sustain rows of stone slabs resting one on another and rising from one side and the other to meet at the point of a tapering roof *a carena*"; on top of the slabs is a layer of cement combined with pounded sherds to form *cocciopesto*. There may originally have been one central transverse arch, but the nature of the original roofing system is not clear. The interior is frescoed with saints and the church probably originated in the twelfth century.[108] Other churches in the Trapanese are deceptively similar to that at Ħal Millieri in their apsed ground plans but totally different in their vaulted roofing systems. The much rebuilt Santa Maria della Guimare or the Madonna dell'Alto, which is 29 m long and 5.50 m wide and is divided by three transverse arches, is apparently rather similar to that at Ħal Millieri; its transverse arches have somewhat the same shape but the space between each arch and the next is vaulted.[109] The Greek Basilian churches and monasteries concentrated in North-east Sicily had an entirely different architectural tradition.[110]

The only other really close parallels to the typical medieval Maltese church are still the early Christian churches of another treeless area, in Syria, where stone is also the only one available building material. In the Syrian churches, which are mostly datable between the fourth and sixth century, the stone roofs slabs were carried from arch to arch but the arch itself was somewhat different, with the pier protruding

106. Buhagiar, in *Medieval Malta*, 177; Fig. 9; Plate 14a; in *Ħal Millieri*, 84; and in M. Buhagiar, *St. Catherine of Alexandria: Her Churches, Paintings and Statues in the Maltese Islands* (Malta, 1979), 155–158.

107. *Ħal Millieri*, 93; Plates 20–21.

108. V. Scuderi, "Contributo alla Storia dell'Architettura Normanna in Val di Mazara," *Atti del Convegno Internazionale di Studi Ruggeriani*, i (Palermo, 1955), 317–320; *idem*, "Architetture medievali del Trapanese inedite o poco note," *Sicilia Archeologica*, i no. 3 (1968), 17–18; Figs. 10–13; *idem*, *Arte Medievale nel Trapanese* (Trapani, 1978), 25–34; Figs. 29–49.

109. Scuderi (1955), 318–325; *idem*, in *Sicilia Archeologica*, i no. 4 (1968), 38–41; *idem* (1978), 16–17; Figs. 9–13. This church can probably be dated ca. 1130/50: B. Patera, "Affreschi bizantini inediti a Mazara del Vallo," *Bizantino-Sicula*, ii (Palermo, 1975), 396.

110. *Monasteri Basiliani di Sicilia*, ed. C. Filangieri (Messina, 1979).

much further from the wall.[111] Something similar in the way of freestanding pointed arches was used in the Cyrenaican countryside probably somewhere between the fourth and seventh centuries, but the system of roofing with slabs was not, apparently, found there.[112] Even closer to Maltese practice, and probably roughly contemporaneous with the earliest of the late-medieval Maltese churches, is certain crusader work of the twelfth or thirteenth century from Caesarea in Syria in which, though they cover a street rather than a church, the slabs of the flat stone roof rest on arches with piers which protrude from the sidewalls and are not bonded into them; the result seems to have been almost exactly similar to the construction of the Annunciation church at Ħal Millieri though the arches appear to be further apart. As in Malta, the arches are slightly pointed and built without keystones, with courses of ashlar masonry filling the spandrels to the height of the top of the arch where they must have supported not a vault, such as the pierced groin vault of the triple bazaar at Jerusalem, but a flat or very slightly pitched roof. The arches at Caesarea are spaced at intervals of about 3.50 m and probably carried a roofing of timber or canvas rather than of stone, yet in other respects they offer a striking parallel to Maltese arch construction whether in churches as at Ħal Millieri or in a covered street such as that in the Gozo citadel where pointed arches and regularly-coursed spandrels carry a roof of stone slabs, though the arches spring directly from the side walls.[113] In Malta this style of building did not necessarily originate in ecclesiastical buildings and it may well have predated the revival of Christianity in the thirteenth century.

111. Hughes (1967), 43–44; Fig. 20, based upon G. Milani, *L'Ossatura murale*, iii: *La Costruzione* (Turin, 1920), Plate 16. J. Strzygowski, *Origin of Christian Church Art: New Facts and Principles of Research* (trans: Oxford, 1923), 67, considers, without explaining why, that the slab-type roof originated in Arabia. Similar techniques were common in Syria, another country short of wood, at least from the first century BC; they were used in secular Christian and Muslim buildings: eg. H. Butler, *Early Churches in Syria*, i (Princeton, 1929), 13–17 *et passim*; A. Negev, *Encyclopaedia of Archaeological Excavations in the Holy Land*, 4 vols. (Jerusalem, 1975–1978), ii. 345–355; iii. 722–735; iv. 1116–1124. Syrian houses used slabs, often with a system of corbels: R. Thoumin, *La Maison syrienne dans la Plaine hauranaise, le Bassin du Baradà et sur les Plateaux du Qalamūn* (Paris, 1932), 21–24. A. Ovadiah, *Corpus of the Byzantine Churches in the Holy Land* (Bonn, 1970), 202, notes some examples in Palestine of slabs laid to form cylindrical roofs, as at Żejtun parish church in Malta. Denys Pringle of the British School of Archaeology in Jerusalem most kindly supplied information; the subject awaits fuller exploration.

112. S. Stucchi, *Architettura Cirenaica* (Rome, 1975), Figs. 522–523.

113. Plates in M. Avi-Yohna, *A History of the Holy Land* (London, 1969), 251; M. Benvenisti, *The Crusaders in the Holy Land* (Jerusalem, 1970), 29, 144, 146; R. Smail, *The Crusaders in Syria and the Holy Land* (London, 1973), Plate 1; for the Jerusalem vault, see Benvenisti, 29–30. A. Gauci, *Gozo: a Historical and Tourist Guide to the Island* (Malta, 1966), 48/49, shows the pre-restoration citadel arch.

# 5. The Wall Paintings of Ħal Millieri

The influences behind the paintings cannot be identified with precision. Parallels in style and programme could be adduced from Byzantinesque or Romanesque art in various provinces and periods, but the paintings can be dated with reasonable confidence and it is more reasonable to look to such nearby regions as Sicily or Apulia than to distant origins, even if the latter cannot, strictly speaking, be excluded entirely.[114] The discovery that there was an earlier church at Ħal Millieri and that it contained frescoes reinforces the hypothesis that there was an earlier and iconographically similar cycle of paintings from which the apparently anachronistic programme of the surviving fifteenth-century frescoes in the upper church may directly have been derived. A fair quantity of painted plaster was recovered during the excavations and distinctions can be made between plaster from the different churches, but such distinctions do not lead to any useful conclusions about the paintings themselves. The question of whether the inner curved section of the apse was ever painted remains unsettled; the stones were left in a rough state as if in preparation for painting, and the apse was frescoed in some similar churches such as San Ċir at Bubaqra, but no sign of plaster or fresco was found during the restoration work at Ħal Millieri. There are indications that the sections of east wall which frame the apse carried Annunciation scenes with the angel to the north and the Virgin to the south. The same two scenes framed the much smaller frescoed apse behind the altar in the Tad-Dejr rock-cut chapel at Rabat which consisted of a Crucifixion scene.[115]

In some ways the Ħal Millieri saints in the main body of the church seem to descend from the Byzantinesque frescoes of South-east Sicily which are certainly in a local Byzantine tradition. The hieratic, frontally-presented figures imparting a blessing and contained within painted rectangular frames are probably a development from Byzantine models such as those in the catacomb of Santa Lucia at Siracusa.[116] Later but broadly similar examples from the same Sicilian catacomb which have Latin rather than Greek inscriptions beside the saints' heads may date to the thirteenth century; among this group are two saints, James and Nicholas, who are at Ħal Millieri and also a saint on horseback who is somewhat reminiscent of the mounted saints at Ħal Millieri but who is apparently Hippolytus.[117] The paintings once in the lower church at Ħal Millieri might perhaps have been similar to some of the frescoes in the crypt of San Marziano at Siracusa which are datable between the twelfth and fourteenth century.[118] The rock-cut crypt of Santa Lucia

114. For Apulian parallels see, for example, C. Fonseca, *Civiltà rupestre in Terra Jonica* (Milan–Rome, 1970), Plates 3, 14 *et passim*. For Western Sicily, where Catalan influence was less strong than at Siracusa, see the detailed analyses in G. Bautier Bresc, *Artistes, Patriciens et Confréries: Production et Consommation de l'Oeuvre d'Art à Palerme et en Sicile Occidentale, 1348–1460* (Rome, 1979).

115. Buhagiar, in *Medieval Malta*, 166–168, and Plate 142; this painting was restored in 1981.

116. G. Agnello, *Le arti figurative nella Sicilia bizantina* (Palermo, 1962), 159–169; Figs. 175–179.

117. *Ibid.*, 170–178; Figs. 181–185.

118. *Ibid.*, 181–216; Figs. 191–208.

at Lentini, between Siracusa and Catania, has deeply-recessed blind arches along its side walls which create a framework for wall paintings as, but in a different way, do the transversal arches at Ħal Millieri, and in each of the panels so formed were one or more saints on a blue background with a red-painted frame and an internal margin made, again as at Ħal Millieri, with a thin white strip.[119] The paintings in the rock-cut Grotta del Crocifisso at Lentini, probably datable to the fourteenth or fifteenth century, also have the rectangular painted frame, the front-facing saints and the angular Gothic letters of the inscriptions found at Ħal Millieri.[120] The Bishop of Malta and his canons were often in the area around Catania, and they had property at Lentini in the fourteenth century; the bishop was at Lentini in 1320 for example.[121] In 1357 the Archdeacon of the Maltese cathedral was also at Lentini.[122]

The Ħal Millieri paintings seem altogether more stylish and sophisticated than much of this somewhat provincial Sicilian work.[123] Aldo Messina suggests that the Ħal Millieri saints derive not so much from the circle of leading masters such as Tommaso de Vigilia or the *Maestro del Polittico di Trapani* as from a Sicilian peasant milieu, an "ambiente contadino"; he accepts the comparisons with the paintings at Castelbuono[124] and proposes other comparisons with rather dissimilar frescoes in the church of San Biagio near Cefalù.[125] Another example of frontally-facing, blessing saints with haloes, apparently Peter and Paul, who once had their names beside their heads, is provided by a stone block with relief carvings with no known date or findspot; it is now in the Gozo Folklore Museum (Plate 43). It is presumably Gozitan in origin but it too fits into this same tradition, "peasant" or "provincial" maybe but Byzantine or Byzantinesque in distant origin and Sicilian in its more immediate provenance. The existence of close artistic links between Malta and Sicily is abundantly clear and they were by no means all at an artisan level. At the turn of the fifteenth century there were contacts with the circle of the followers of the great Antonello da Messina, whose sister married a Maltese named Saliba and had

119. A. Messina, "La cripta di *Santa Lania* (Lentini) e il problema delle arcate cieche nell'architettura altomedievale," *Byzantino-Sicula*, ii (Palermo, 1975), 387 n. 12.

120. Agnello, 229–235; Figs. 215–216, as late-fourteenth or early-fifteenth century; A. Messina, *Le Chiese Rupestri del Siracusano* (Palermo, 1979), 36–48, as fifteenth and late-fifteenth century. See also a fifteenth-century saint in S. Domenico, Trapani: Scuderi (1978), Fig. 146.

121. Texts and references in R. Pirri, *Sicilia Sacra*, ii (3rd ed: Palermo, 1733), 906–909.

122. Text in G. Cosentino, *Codice Diplomatico di Federico III di Aragona Re di Sicilia: 1355–1377*, i (Palermo, 1885–1907), 322–323.

123. Messina (1975–1976), 239–240, suggests that the painting in Agnello, Fig. 219, is by the hand of the Ħal Millieri painter; this seems, from the illustration, to be rather unlikely. Notes on a triptych of St. Leonard and the Annunciation in the Minsija church at San Ġwann which is in some ways comparable to the Ħal Millieri paintings will be published by Mario Buhagiar.

124. *Ħal Millieri*, 116 n. 18 and Plate 32; A. Mogavero Fina, "Gli affreschi trecenteschi di Castelbuono," *Sicilia*, lxxv (1974), with a date which is too early.

125. G. De Simone, "Un Tesoro nascosto in Sicilia," *Sicilia*, lvi (1967), where these paintings are incorrectly dated to the ninth or tenth century.

a son called Pietro.[126] A *mastru Petru de Missina pingituri* was in Malta and receiving commissions between 1477 and 1481,[127] possibly the very moment at which the Ħal Millieri frescoes were executed. There is still no clear indication that Malta possessed an indigenous artistic school or tradition.[128] The Ħal Millieri artist could have been Maltese or part-Maltese rather than a complete foreigner, but it seems that local pride or wealth produced decorations for the Annunciation church which went some way beyond mere rural peasant art in their style, even if the programme appealed to popular taste and sentiment.

126. Luttrell, in *Medieval Malta*, 64–66; Bautier Bresc, in *Ħal Millieri*, 103–104; A. Luttrell, "The Madonna del Soccorso at Mdina," *Heritage* [Malta], 47 (1983); see also *Antonello da Messina*, ed. Regione Siciliana – Assessorato dei Beni Culturali e Ambientali e della Pubblica Istruzione (Rome, [1981]). Another painting, possibly a copy, which may somehow be connected to the workshops of the followers of Antonello da Messina has now been identified at Żejtun: Buhagiar (1979), 97–99. The report of the recent restoration of the Bir Miftuħ frescoes has yet to appear; before their restoration, both Buhagiar, in *Medieval Malta*, 173 n. 63, and Bautier Bresc, in *Ħal Millieri*, 99, dated them, tentatively, to the sixteenth century.

127. Wettinger, in *Ħal Millieri*, 111.

128. The "roundels" found near Ħal Millieri and elsewhere in Malta, notably at St. Agatha's, Rabat (*Ħal Millieri*, 26 and Plate 11), are an extensive phenomenon datable across many centuries and found in many places between Armenia and England: M. Schmitt, "Random Reliefs and Primitive Friezes: Reused Sources of Romanesque Sculpture," *Viator*, xi (1980).

# 6. The Abandonment of the "Casale"

The excavations have done nothing to increase any understanding of the decline and abandonment of Ħal Millieri late in the seventeenth century, and they could scarcely have been expected to do so. The medical information acquired provides no evidence for any major physical catastrophe,[129] though there was no excavation in the cemeteries outside the churches in which plague burials, which are known to have occurred at Ħal Millieri,[130] would probably be found. The process of abandonment still awaits more precise investigation in the notarial and other archives, as well as a study of the way in which the cotton industry may have impinged on the villages by altering patterns of farming and land-holding.[131] Abela, writing in about 1647, mentioned that the principal activity of the people of Żurrieq was in the sale and working of cotton thread and the weaving of woollen stuffs.[132] There is no evidence of a general shift away from the area. The population of Żurrieq parish and its district was estimated at 2120 in 1670 and at 2042 in 1680.[133] In general the bigger villages and the new towns around the Grand Harbour attracted men away from the *casali* to centres of greater social, economic and religious activity. This process occurred elsewhere, in Southern France for example, and was doubtless affected in a complex way by a number of factors which varied from one individual case to another.[134] There is evidence that some inhabitants of Ħal Millieri moved to the urban area around Valletta and the Grand Harbour,[135] and in a village of fifteen households it required only a few deaths by plague, such as those of three males at Ħal Millieri in 1676,[136] a number of childless households, some emigration and the marriage out of the *casale* of several young men or women for the younger part of the community to be much reduced. At that point the survivors might well

129. On diet and disease in medieval Sicily, see H. Bresc, "Prima dello Scavo antropologico: Cibo e salute dalle fonti archivistiche," *Archeologia Medievale*, viii (1981).

130. *Ħal Millieri*, 123.

131. Background in J. Debono, "The Cotton Trade of Malta: 1750–1800," *Archivum: Journal of Maltese Historical Research*, i (1981); cf. A. Luttrell, "Eighteenth-Century Malta: Prosperity and Problems," *Hyphen* [Malta], iii no. 2 (1982).

132. G.-F. Abela, *Della Descrittione di Malta* (Malta, 1647), 102.

133. Valletta, National Library of Malta, Università, Ms. 2, f. 213, 246.

134. Cf. B. Blouet, *The Changing Landscape of Malta during the Rule of the Order of St. John of Jerusalem: 1530–1798* (Ph.D. thesis: University of Hull, 1964), 153–156: [Professor Blouet most kindly permitted the consultation of his thesis]. The availability of further information has not led to any major change in interpretation: B. Blouet, "The Impact of Armed Conflict on the Rural Settlement Pattern of Malta: A.D. 1400–1800," *Institute of British Geographers: Transactions*, ns. iii no. 3 (1978), 375–378.

135. A few confirmations of children from Ħal Millieri in 1575 are given in Mdina, Cathedral Archives, CEM, Reg. Confirmatorum et Defunctorum (cum comunia): 1560–1615 (quaderni): [information kindly provided by Fr. John Azzopardi]. Population estimates based on records of baptisms at Żurrieq should be qualified by the possibility that some new-born children were taken to Valletta for baptism. Some baptisms and marriages of people from Ħal Millieri in the period 1630–1650 are recorded in the records of St. Dominic's at Valletta: [information kindly provided by Mr. C. Testa of Floriana].

136. These three males were buried at Ħal Armanin: Valletta, National Library of Malta, Archives of the Order of St. John, cod. 6402, f. 291v–292: [information kindly provided by Miss Jessie McLeman].

have moved away from the *casale*, while continuing to hold and farm lands at Ħal Millieri.

At Ħal Millieri, as elsewhere, the drift away from the *casale* to the growing larger villages was doubtless accompanied by the aggrandisement of the parish church of the *casale* at Żurrieq and by a tendency for altars, dedications and incomes to be transferred from the smaller country churches to the parish church. It has been suggested that as "people began to feel the need for larger churches" they tended to move to larger villages.[137] It is true that the Council of Trent was followed by a centralizing movement within the Maltese diocese and that Pietro Dusina, the Apostolic Visitor of 1575, closed and deconsecrated some forty-six churches on Malta because they were in ruins or because their revenue had dwindled.[138] But this cannot be connected directly with a move away from the *casale*. At least two of the Ħal Millieri churches were in decay in 1575, but the village was not abandoned until more than a century later. Dusina did order the church of St. John to be deconsecrated, but instead it survived to be threatened with abolition once again in 1634, and it was only in 1667 that the Visitation church and that of St. Michael were deconsecrated and destroyed. The population of the *casale* stood at around fifty between 1650 and 1680, but dropped rapidly thereafter.[139] One of the last recorded survivors was Filippo Farrugia of Ħal Millieri who was baptized on 1 May 1644. There were Farrugias in the *casale* as far back as 1419/20.[140] Filippo Farrugia's children were Vincenzo baptized on 3 April 1680, Angelica baptized on 19 December 1682, Salvo baptized on 27 May 1690 and another daughter Apollonia baptized on 9 February 1695. After Salvo and Apollonia only two other baptisms from Ħal Millieri were recorded at Żurrieq.[141] On 23 September 1699 Filippo Farrugia *de Casali Milleri* leased a field at Ħal Millieri called Ta Zacca in *censo perpetuo* from the Hospital of Santo Spirito at Rabat, and he was still alive on 15 September 1700.[142]

There is, therefore, no obvious correlation between population change and the physical decay of the churches, and it is doubtful whether people left the *casale* merely in order to seek larger churches. In fact a striking aspect of the liturgical life of Ħal Millieri was precisely the way in which the former inhabitants and their heirs continued to make efforts to maintain the two surviving churches after the community itself was extinct, which suggests that people left the *casale* despite their attachment to its churches. It was probably because these former inhabitants retained and continued to cultivate their fields around Ħal Millieri that the religious life of the churches, the payment of dues and the maintenance of the churches and their festas continued after the population had disappeared. There was, however, a limit to such

137. J. Cassar Pullicino, "Malta in 1575: Social Aspects of an Apostolic Visit," *Melita Historica*, ii no. 1 (1956), 26–28.

138. *Ibid.*, 23.

139. Details in Mangion, in *Ħal Millieri*, 120–121, 136–137.

140. Text *ibid.*, 39.

141. Żurrieq Parish Archives, *Liber Baptismi Terrae Zurrici 1567–1758*: [information kindly provided by Mr. Tony Mangion].

142. Valletta, National Library of Malta, Università, Ms. 23 (16–23 Sep. 1699; 15 Sep. 1700): [information kindly provided by Mr. Anton Mallia].

phantom survivals, and even before the population declined the Bishop had, in 1667, found the Visitation church to be derelict and ordered it to be pulled down. These events left little archaeological trace. A coin of Grand Master Despuig dating to 1736–1741 was found below the new altar platform in the south-east corner of the Annunciation church, and the construction of this platform did reflect a continuing urge to embellish the church. A third of a farthing dated 1827 and a farthing of 1913 were in the soil above the floor of the Visitation church, but they prove little; the effective life of the church was over,[143] even if the remembrance of its past has recently been revived.[144]

143. The maps of De Palmens of 1752 and of De Behrend of 1821 indicate an altogether different system of tracks at Ħal Millieri to that shown on the survey map of 1908 reproduced in *Ħal Millieri*, Fig. 2; these maps, which seem to show that there were still buildings standing there, are reproduced in Mary Zammit, *Żurrieq: 1750–1801* (unpublished BA thesis: University of Malta, 1976), Maps 1–2. This thesis contains useful information on population, agriculture and so forth, but the period covered is a late one.

144. An indirect achievement of the excavations has been a reshaping of the precinct garden and the presentation of the remains of the Visitation church to the visitor, who can see the outlines of its floor, benches, walls, facade and apse, while its cypress tree has been neatly bordered with local stones. To inaugurate the opening of the churches to the public Din l-Art Ħelwa organized a literary evening in the full moon of 18 August 1978 at which a *Ballata* in Maltese, written by Tony Mangion to celebrate the Annunciation church and its frescoes, received its first performance.

# INDEX

This selective index is largely confined to medieval places and persons, who may be under a first or a second name; churches are listed under 'church'.